Voices of
SOCIAL
EDUCATION
1937–1987

Voices of
SOCIAL
EDUCATION
1937–1987

National Council for the Social Studies

Edited by
DANIEL ROSELLE

MACMILLAN PUBLISHING COMPANY
NEW YORK

Collier Macmillan Publishers
LONDON

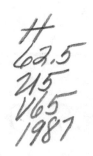

Macmillan Publishing Company
866 Third Avenue, New York, NY 10022

Collier Macmillan Canada, Inc.

Library of Congress Catalog Card No.: 87-12260

Printed in the United States of America

printing number
1 2 3 4 5 6 7 8 9 10

Library of Congress Cataloging-in-Publication Data

Voices of social education, 1937–1987.

  Includes index.
  1. Social sciences—Study and teaching—United States.
I. Roselle, Daniel, 1920–   II. National Council
for the Social Studies.
H62.5.U5V65   1987   300'.7'1073   87-12260
ISBN 0-02-922380-6

We gratefully acknowledge permission to reprint many articles in this book.
A credit line appears on the opening page of each article for which
it was necessary to obtain permission.

To the Memory of
Erling M. Hunt,
First Editor of SOCIAL EDUCATION

Contents

Preface

Any anniversary worthy of celebration reminds us that, even as we cut the anniversary cake, there have been days in the past when there was only bread upon the table. An anniversary deals with simple beginnings as well as mature endings, and it is the process of development that becomes the principal source of satisfaction and pride.

The journal *Social Education* is a case in point. From its first issue in January 1937 (simple cover, no photographs, no illustrations) to its November/December 1986 issue (four-color cover, photographs, illustrations), its development has been extraordinary. Indeed, no journal has had a greater cumulative impact on social studies education. Thus, *Social Education* has good reason to celebrate its fiftieth anniversary with a special anthology.

This book presents some of the finest writing that has appeared in *Social Education* from 1937 to 1987. Its purposes are to preserve a record of landmark ideas, innovations, and interpretations in the social studies; to acquaint readers with the multiplicity of stimulating educational ideas that are still available for use; and to present a solid foundation of experience and thought to assist educators in their tasks of developing new curricular patterns for our times.

It is a book designed for teachers of social studies and social sciences at the elementary, secondary, college, and university levels; for curriculum developers; for educators in supervisory and other administrative positions; and for anyone interested in sharing the thoughts of sixty-five stimulating authors. Its cornucopia of material should be of value to a variety of readers.

What is in store for the reader? Provocative ideas—heated exchanges—candid confessions—imaginative views—original proposals—yes, all of these. And one thing more: the conviction that the fifty years were just a beginning. Robert Browning was not the only one to believe that "the best is yet to be."

DANIEL ROSELLE

Acknowledgments

I am grateful to a number of individuals for their cooperation and assistance: Lloyd Chilton, executive editor, and Elly Dickason, editing supervisor, Professional Books Division, Macmillan Publishing Company; Fran Haley, executive director of the National Council for the Social Studies (NCSS); Charles Rivera, director of publications, NCSS; Wilbur Murra, first executive secretary of NCSS; Louis Vanaria, Department of History, State University of New York at Cortland; Margaret Cromartie, NCSS publications assistant; and Thelma Ferges for her continued encouragement and support. As always, my wife, Lois Mitchell Roselle, worked side by side with me. Her assistance was invaluable.

Introduction

Fifty years have passed since the founding of the journal *Social Education*, a half-century of change from the New Deal of FDR to the New Beginnings of Ronald Reagan; from the opening of the Golden Gate Bridge to the hundredth birthday of the Statue of Liberty; from the America that was to the America that is.

Fifty years! In retrospect, they seem less like time moving to the beat of a metronome than time flowing without restraint—like a liquid watch by Dali—uninterrupted time which, for the sake of convenience, we have divided into days, months, and years. Nevertheless, for the specific purposes of this book, it is time that must be delineated. Call it 1937 to 1987.

This is an appropriate moment, then, to review the past of *Social Education*, and to do so with a mixture of realism and nostalgia that permits both understanding and feeling. Thus, if the pictures conjured up merge past, present, and future, it is a union that is as desirable as it is inevitable. We begin with the birth of the National Council for the Social Studies (NCSS).

The National Council for the Social Studies was born in a hotel room in Atlantic City, New Jersey, on March 3, 1921. Wilbur Murra, who became the first executive secretary of the Council in 1940, attests to this fact, and adds the provocative information that the paternity was multiple. Figuring prominently in the birth were J. Montgomery Gambrill, Daniel C. Knowlton, Harold O. Rugg, Earle U. Rugg, and Roy W. Hatch.

Even then, the voice of the new arrival could be heard nationally. From 1921 to 1933, the journal *The Historical Outlook* served as a channel of communication for members of the National Council for the Social Studies. Albert E. McKinley was the publisher and managing editor of *The Historical Outlook*, which could trace its beginning back to 1909. (Its original name was *The History Teachers Magazine;* in 1918 its title was changed to *The Historical Outlook.*) The NCSS was able to use this journal of the McKinley Publishing Company as "a continuing outlet for announcements, plans, programs, resolutions, and transactions of interest to social studies teachers." Dues for membership in the NCSS were $1.00 (annually, not monthly, in those pre-inflationary days), and dues of $2.50 included a regular subscription to the journal. Albert E. McKinley also served as the first president of the NCSS, and Edgar

Dawson played an important role in the formative years of the organization.

In 1933 the American Historical Association (AHA) reported that its Commission on the Social Studies, which was engaged in the publication of a series of volumes on the social sciences, the social studies, and education, had an unexpected balance of about $45,000 left from the funds granted to it for its work. With reasonable expectations and equally logical foresight, the AHA decided to use this sum for the support of a journal that would explore the educational implications of the commission's work and study developments related to teaching.

With the concurrence of Albert E. McKinley, representatives of the American Historical Association therefore arranged to take over the editorial functions and editorial expenses of *The Historical Outlook*, which was not self-supporting. The McKinley Publishing Company continued to hold title to the journal. In 1934 the name was changed to *The Social Studies*, and William G. Kimmel became the managing editor. NCSS members now expressed their views in this publication, which was in the hands of the association of historians.

The desire for a new journal remained strong, however, and in 1936 the dream was realized. An arrangement was worked out with the American Book Company under which this company graciously consented to publish a new journal that would be the official publication of the National Council for the Social Studies. It was to be edited under the joint direction of the NCSS and the AHA. (In 1941 publishing responsibilities were relinquished by the American Book Company.) *The Social Studies* continued to exist as a privately published journal, and it is still published today; but beginning in January 1937 the new journal began an independent life of its own. In the beginning, both the AHA and the NCSS had responsibilities for its development.

What was the new journal to be called? Possibilities were as numerous as improbabilities. Indeed, the names suggested reflected a wide spectrum of beliefs about the proper approach to be used in education: *Teaching the Social Sciences, The Social Science Teacher, Social Education, The Social Educator, Society Past and Present, Society Today and Yesterday, The History and Social Science Teacher, The History and Social Studies Teacher, The Social and Historical Review, The Social and Historical Journal, The Social Review, The Magazine of Social Science, The Journal of Social Change, The Social Outlook, The Social Scene, The World We Live In, Past and Present in the Schools, Journal of Social Education, Society in Education, The Study of Society, Society in Review, Society, Society: Its Study in Education,* and *Society: Its Study in the Schools.*

Finally, *Social Education* was selected for the name. Through the years, it has proven to be a popular choice. One editor later did declare, however, that "names can be confusing. There probably always have been some individuals who persisted in erroneously thinking of the

National Council for the Social Studies as some type of government agency, aligned, perhaps, with the Department of Labor." And Wilbur Murra, one of the leaders of the Council, recalls: "The title *Social Education* was interpreted by some people as indicating that the magazine dealt with etiquette, the education of debutantes, etc.!"

Such was obviously not the case. The National Council for the Social Studies was, and is, a professional association of educators at all levels—elementary, secondary, college, and university—concerned with the teaching of social studies. Social studies are those instructional courses, programs, and projects that are designed to assist students to understand, analyze, react to, and act upon three relationships: the relationships of human beings to the world in which they live; the relationships of human beings to other human beings; and the relationships of human beings to themselves. Quite a job!

What is more, *Social Education* was never designed to indoctrinate any one point of view. Thus, although it was sometimes difficult for the editors of the journal to obtain manuscripts representative of every position (and, as in many journals, some readers claimed that they detected what they considered either a too liberal or a too conservative bias), efforts were made to publish articles that reflected the full spectrum of opinion on educational issues. A note preceding one "Letters to the Editor" column was indicative of the overall philosophy of the journal:

> *Social Education* believes in the right to dissent and the right to assent. It rejects with conviction the anti-Voltairean dictum: "I will defend with my breath your right to speak, provided you agree with me." It opens its pages to all. [This column] is designed to be a forum for every point of view: for the serious scholar of note and footnote, for the youthful St. George in search of a dragon, for the relativist certain there are no certainties, for the teacher too busy teaching to lament the decline of the best, for the wise and the foolish and those who see no distinction between the two [*Social Education* 33 (1969), p. 501].

In addition, the readers of *Social Education* were so diverse (including classroom teachers, curriculum developers, research scholars, department heads, subject-matter specialists, and others) and their educational needs were so varied (including the need for materials, methods, curricula, evaluation procedures, and numerous teaching aids) that it was a major task to provide something of interest and value in every issue for every reader of the journal. Obviously, not all readers would be constantly satisfied by the journal's multihued content, anymore than individuals with monochromatic preferences would be satisfied with a rainbow that appeared periodically. Nevertheless, although they did not always succeed in their protean efforts, the editors sought the spice of life that came with variety.

Erling M. Hunt, professor and head of the Department of Social Studies at Teachers College, Columbia University, served as the first editor of the new journal and provided leadership during the first decade of its existence, including the difficult period of World War II. Novelist James Michener, who was an active member of the NCSS in its early years and who contributed to several of its publications, described Hunt in this way:

> the man who gave me the most important personal help was Erling Hunt of Columbia, a shy, taciturn gentleman whom it was never easy to know.
>
> Hunt happened to be editor of this journal in the years when I was beginning, and also chairman of the editorial board for which I worked. He was an excellent editor with a dry sense of propriety and a lean style. He taught me much about writing, not in personal sessions, for he was an aloof man, but through his total manner. His comment on what I wrote, his precept in what he wrote, his unemotional professionalism all had a deep impact. From him I learned how to put an article together, how to express ideas succinctly, how to keep copy reasonably cleaned up. My professional debt to him was then and is now considerable, for throughout my adult life I have continued to write social studies [James M. Michener, "The Mature Social Studies Teacher," *Social Education* 34 (1970), p. 761].

Hunt expressed his philosophy concerning the editorship of *Social Education* in the "Editorial Announcement" for the first issue (January 1937, volume 1, number 1):

> In the *Charter for the Social Sciences in the Schools* Dr. Beard points out that "instruction in the social studies in the schools is conditioned by the spirit and letter of scholarship, by the realities and ideas of the society in which it is carried on, and by the nature and limitations of the teaching and learning process." With all three of these factors *Social Education* is concerned. The major findings, interpretations, and reinterpretations of scholars must from time to time be reported in book reviews, articles, or comments on new courses of study or curriculum experiments. The realities and ideas of our troubled and restless times must be described, analyzed, constantly re-examined and reinterpreted. Certainly the science of education and the art of teaching must receive due attention.

Hunt was more than a disseminator of the ideas of others. He was also a vigorous spokesman for the NCSS and for the social studies profession. Under his editorship, the complicated issues involving nationalism, censorship, internationalism, and war and peace that were raised by World War II were handled in the journal with a high degree of common sense.

Erling Hunt completed his ten-year editorship of *Social Education* in May 1947, and Ralph Adams Brown served as acting editor from May to December 1947. When in December the editorial functions were turned over to the new editor, Lewis Paul Todd, the transition involved a geographic change. The editorial headquarters of the journal now moved from the bustling urban environment of Teachers College, Columbia

University, in New York City to Lewis Paul Todd's home in Truro, Massachusetts, a small New England village on Cape Cod where, in Todd's words, "the ocean is on one side, the bay on the other, and the great dome of the heavens arches overhead from horizon to horizon." Here the journal would remain for twenty-one years.

Lewis Paul Todd had taught at Queens College, New York, Western Connecticut State College, and New York University. Later he would coauthor with Merle Curti *Rise of the American Nation*, one of the most widely used textbooks ever published in this country. During his long term of dedicated service as editor of *Social Education*, Todd carried out plans to strengthen the publication still further. A new format for the journal, broader coverage of developments in social studies, special issues on culture areas, dialogues on controversial approaches to teaching, and increased services to readers—all these were accomplished with limited funds, limited time, and limited staff. In addition, after more than two decades of financial cooperation with the American Historical Association, the National Council for the Social Studies took over full responsibility for its journal in 1955.

The years from 1948 to 1969—the period of the Cold War, the dramatic change of power in China, the Vietnam War, the conflict in the Middle East, and mounting international tensions—were also marked by ferment in the social studies. There arose constant and vigorous demands that *something* be done to prepare youth to think clearly in a world teetering on darkness.

So, aided by federal funding, educators gave serious attention to developing innovative ways of moving away from traditional methods of teaching, mechanical memorization of unrelated facts, and heavy reliance on textbooks. *Social Education* played its part by publishing articles on the importance of decision making, reflective thinking, and democratic school environments. Equally important, it disseminated information about projects and programs of the New Social Studies that encouraged critical thought. Students were to be taught to think effectively, and social studies educators explored a variety of ways to achieve this goal.

In 1969 I succeeded Lewis Paul Todd as editor and served until 1982. As the first full-time editor of *Social Education*, I operated out of the NCSS's permanent headquarters in Washington, D.C. In the January 1969 issue, three policies of the new staff were announced:

1. We shall *explore*, not merely a narrowly conceived and artificially delimited area of social studies, but the related fields of art, music, literature, science, philosophy—any activity that will add to our knowledge and understanding of man. In addition to a solid fare of scholarly articles, *Social Education* will print poetry, art, dialogues, interviews, and other forms of highly personal expres-

sion. Our subject is *social* education; we will not be boxed in by pedantic boundary lines.

2. We shall *analyze* in depth, in the feature article or articles, subjects of significance to social studies education. . . .

3. We shall *feel* a sense of compassion for people everywhere. . . . We have always preferred the Human Being to the Naked Ape.

Merrill Hartshorn, NCSS Executive Director, supported innovation. A new format was designed for the journal; photographs were added; and, under the direction of the first full-time production editor, Willadene Price, *Social Education* maintained a modern and attractive appearance.

New features—the "Classroom Teachers' 'Idea' Notebook," to provide classroom teachers with concrete and practical methods; the "Research Supplement," to report the latest research findings in social studies education; and columns written by parents and students, to obtain a wider spectrum of opinion—were introduced. As the country heatedly debated issues raised by the war in Vietnam, the civil rights movement, the treatment of minorities, and other vital matters, *Social Education* responded by publishing articles on contemporary problems involving war and peace, global education, racism, sexism, world hunger, civil rights, urban tensions, ethnicity, and environmental pollution.

In the 1970s, lamentations were heard in educational circles about the rise of a "Now" generation that preferred instant gratification to academic scholarship; and in the early 1980s, there were admonitions that youth was more concerned with personal careers than with community service. *Social Education* did not despair because of such jeremiads. Instead, the journal continued to express its conviction that, with proper education, today's generation could be as sound as its predecessors—or sounder.

Howard J. Langer became editor in August 1982. His in-depth interviews with leading interpreters of contemporary affairs were effective in stimulating discussion of ideas among readers. Langer was succeeded as editor by Charles R. Rivera, whose first issue appeared in April 1984.

Charles Rivera came to *Social Education* with extensive experience as editor of publications dealing with international education, civil rights, and minorities. Using strong organizational skills, he expanded the staff, added a full-time art director, and arranged for the redesigning of *Social Education*, which attracted favorable attention for the modernity of its new look. Striking covers; four-color reproductions of photographs, maps, charts, and paintings; and the positioning of type to highlight content all contributed to the attractiveness of the journal.

Content, too, continued to be substantive. New or neglected areas of study were examined in depth. Special sections, such as "The Children of Yesterday," were poignant reminders that the past is prologue to the present; others, such as "Australia Through Australian Eyes," provided evidence that the present is epilogue to the past.

As for the future, even now it is being probed by Charles Rivera and his staff as they make plans for the development of the journal. The next fifty years are off to an exciting start.

The United States had changed greatly in the last fifty years, "from here to there to everywhere," as Dr. Seuss might say. Scholars continued to speak of change and continuity as being two powerful factors in history, but change was often the more dominant. Throughout these years the journal kept up with events by focusing on major changes in social studies education. If "the times they were a-changin'," so was *Social Education*, and the journal built a reputation for the soundness of its innovations.

Social Education was probably the first journal to introduce the idea of using science fiction in the teaching of social studies; the first journal to reproduce on a regular basis original documents from the National Archives in Washington, D.C., for use by social studies teachers; one of the first journals to encourage extensive use of Landsat maps in the teaching of geography; and one of the most ardent supporters of integrating Asian art, Asian literature, and Asian history for classroom instruction. It became known as "the most prestigious journal in the field of social studies education."

It is not surprising that the journal attracted many authors. June R. Chapin and Richard E. Gross analyzed a sample of approximately 600 articles published in *Social Education* during four periods, 1937–38, 1947–48, 1957–58, 1967–68 (Chapin and Gross, "A Barometer of the Social Studies: Three Decades of *Social Education*," *Social Education* 34 [1970], pp. 788–795) and showed that higher education institutions supplied the highest proportion of the authors, and that authors in colleges and universities were more likely to come from departments of education than from other academic departments. Nevertheless, every editor of *Social Education* tried constantly to obtain and publish manuscripts written by secondary school teachers, elementary school teachers, and other educators.

Leaders in other fields were also invited to contribute pieces to the journal, and a number of them did. Features such as "*Social Education* Asks," in which individuals in various professions were asked to respond to provocative questions, proved to be particularly productive. Scientists, artists, novelists, and others shared their viewpoints with the readers of *Social Education*.

This book is an attempt to recapture the voices of the many contributors to *Social Education* from 1937 to 1987. Facing a richness of material, the individuals preparing this anthology had problems of abundance rather than of scarcity in focusing on the authors whose writings were most stimulating, most provocative, or simply most enjoyable. The criteria used in the selection of the pieces were: impact on the social studies profession; importance of ideas; persistence of viewpoints through the years; value to social studies educators today; historical interest; originality; and attractiveness of style.

The NCSS Board of Directors, NCSS Publications Board, past presidents of NCSS, the *Social Education* Editorial Committee, and the general NCSS membership were all invited to submit recommendations of memorable pieces that had appeared in the journal. They were generous with their time and energy in providing suggestions to the central editorial committee (Daniel Roselle, editor of the Anthology; Fran Haley, executive director of NCSS; and Charles Rivera, editor of *Social Education*). Where there was consensus, their advice was closely followed.

Finally, there are several things that this book is *not*. This anthology is not designed to focus on the history of the National Council for the Social Studies (Louis Vanaria's excellent doctoral dissertation has already covered this topic up to a recent period). It does not intend to present a chronological survey of all major developments in the teaching of the social studies. And it does not attempt to provide a comprehensive view of all the types of writing that have appeared in *Social Education*.

What its planners *did* say, in essence, was this: "A cornucopia of stimulating material has appeared in *Social Education* in the last fifty years. Let us choose the most interesting and significant pieces and present them to readers for their sheer pleasure. What better time to do it than now—the 50th anniversary of the journal."

So, here it is. A book to conjure up the wisdom of the past, the challenge of the present, the promise of the future. A book with which to discover the new in the old and the old in the new. A book to be instructive because it does not deliberately instruct. Above all, a book to be enjoyed!

DANIEL ROSELLE

I.

The Past in Perspective

MEMORY INVOLVES THE ABILITY—and often the courage—to move backward and forward in time. Some memories, of course, are wispy, ephemeral, transient, and our fascination with capturing them stems from our knowledge that they must always remain free. Others are branded permanently into our conscience and can never be obliterated. With them, we remember what it is in our power to remember, and have limited choice in deciding what we will forget. Thus, there is a variety of style, mood, and tone in the four selections that appear in this section, "The Past in Perspective."

Edgar B. Wesley and Howard E. Wilson were two of the leaders of the social studies profession during the formative years of the National Council for the Social Studies, and they played major roles in the establishment of a permanent headquarters for the organization in Washington, D.C. Wesley, a professor of education and a highly effective teacher, was described by Wilbur Murra, the first executive secretary of NCSS, as a man whose "imagination and foresight were happily combined with diplomatic savvy and political clout." Most persons who knew him agreed with James Michener, who wrote that Wesley had a "salty and sane approach to life."

Howard E. Wilson of the University of Chicago and Harvard University was dynamic and mercurial, and a person of "enormous optimism." He was a charismatic leader who insisted on high standards of scholarship and teaching, and it was not surprising that he was greatly concerned

1

when his investigation of schools in 1936 disclosed that many students thought that *habeas corpus* was a disease and that poverty was best defined as "the boyhood of great men."

Wesley and Wilson became lifelong friends and colleagues and, in their efforts on behalf of the social studies, shared numerous experiences. In 1966 Wesley's *Too Short the Days*, a delightful book of reminiscences that the author declared was "about 92 percent factual and true," was published. Wesley sent a copy of the book to Wilson, and their exchange of letters presented in this section reveals much about the spirit of these two extraordinary men.

As a member of the National Council for the Social Studies during its early years, novelist James A. Michener played a significant part in its development and contributed to its publications. Thus, when in 1970 he was invited to write an article for the special issue of *Social Education* commemorating the 50th anniversary of the founding of NCSS, Michener responded:

> Your invitation . . . could not possibly have come at a worse time. I am absolutely jammed to the hilt with obligations which I am finding it difficult to discharge, and normally I would have to say no. . . .
>
> [Nevertheless] I think of myself still as a teacher, and as a teacher of social studies, so that in a very real sense I am one of you and could not possibly say no to your invitation. . . . . I will do what I can.

James Michener did what he could, and came up with a candid article that conjured up soft memories and hard facts concerning "Why Did I Quit Teaching?," "How I Work," and "The Shameful Period." Of added interest in the article are the fortuitous references to both Wesley and Wilson, whose comments appear in the first selection.

The silences produced by the writings of Nobel Prize Laureate Elie Wiesel are as meaningful as the sounds, and the unanswered questions are as significant as the unquestionable facts. Deported to Auschwitz and then to Buchenwald, Wiesel carries with him tragic memories that he dares not try to erase lest he succeeds in doing so. In "Then and Now: The Experiences of a Teacher," he shares with us his thoughts, his dreams, his images of a past that, he feels, should always remain a part of the present. Memories must be kept alive, he insists, and whoever engages in teaching about the Holocaust becomes "a missionary, a messenger."

The final selection is an interview with political reporter Theodore H. White, author of such works as *The Making of the President 1960* and *America in Search of Itself: The Making of the President 1956-1980*. It is entitled "Confessions of a Second-Look Liberal," which White defines in this way: "A 'second-look liberal' like me is a guy who looks back over the past 20 or 30 years and says, 'God, we've done some wonderful things, we've achieved stupendous triumphs. We've also made some awful mistakes. So let's look back and figure out what we did right and what we did wrong.' " In the interview, White does so, as he comments on past elections, primaries, television, the "pencil press," reporting election results, and related topics. Nor does he hesitate to play the "lion and fox" game in classifying American presidents (Franklin D. Roosevelt, he observes, was a lion; Richard M. Nixon was a fox), or to stress that young people need heroes and villains. The interview provides additional evidence that one way to perk up the present is to let the past percolate through it.

Wilson to Wesley to Wilson:
An Exchange of Letters

Dear Edgar:

We have been friends and colleagues now for more than 40 years, so it was altogether appropriate for you to send me your latest book, *Too Short the Days*. I did resent a little, however, your telephoning me a few hours later to find out if I had already read the volume. I had detected at once that the book was a series of essays about your boyhood. I could even see a resemblance to you in the excellent pen-and-ink drawings which your daughter Elaine drew for the book. So I put aside all the other duties I had, and settled down to read the volume. "At last," I thought, "I will find out what made Edgar Wesley the vigorous, creative, obstreperous man I have known for 40 years."

Well, the book is beautifully written and beautifully printed. There is a calmness in its prose which matches the quality of its printing and is thoroughly at odds with the Wesley I know. The book is a real collector's item for a book-lover—especially for a book-lover who also loves the Kentucky mountain area. Through all its pages appears the scenery of rural Kentucky. In a sense the book is like a painting or a group of paintings, giving to the Kentucky-Ohio hills an aura as distinctive as the Hudson Valley received early in the last century from the school of landscape artists who found inspiration there. But was your purpose in writing that of being a Grandmother Moses for Kentucky? I enjoy the hillsides and trees, the shafts of sunlight you describe, the pastures and farm houses immensely; they bring back to me vividly scenes of my own Illinois boyhood. But was it for this that you wrote the book? Or titled it *Too Short the Days?*

NOTE: This exchange of letters appeared in *Social Education*, October 1966, pp. 427–428.

As I read through the chapters my mind kept looking, not for Kentucky or for an almost vanished American rurality, but for young Wesley. I know that in the book's preface you warn the reader that its chapters are separate reminiscences. You even illustrate the blunt, belligerent individualism I have known in the adult Wesley by suggesting that the reader read the chapters in an order different from that of the book. This is one of the few instances through all the years I have known you in which you did not make up your mind and try to make up other people's minds for them. Of course, what I am writing about is not just the order of the chapters, but the focus and framework of the whole series of them. Your readers are looking for that boy Wesley—they want to see how he grew—and you rather keep your eyes on Kentucky, and the bundle of memories floods out without an adequate framework.

The main point I am driving at—and I might as well be blunt about it—is that this beautiful little book lacks the fire and directness and obstinacy and general cussedness that I long ago came to love in its author. I simply cannot believe that Edgar Wesley was as mild a child as this book describes. Why, you have made yourself a barefooted, suntanned Lord Fauntleroy, when I am sure you were an exaggerated version of Tom Sawyer. Even the fights the book describes were carried on according to rules which the older Wesley would have "despised and ignored," to use one of your favorite phrases. I began to chuckle a bit in the chapter on the Wesley boys' explorations on "Scientific Magic"—thought for a moment that the old Wesley spirit was at last on hand—but the pages passed and what should have been fireworks (if I know Wesley) actually turned out to be whimsicality. The chuckles never exploded into a roar!

I still want to know what made you the character you are, old friend. There is little in this book, for example, that explains what a perverse and successful politician you are. Do you remember the policy fights we used to have in the Board of Directors of the National Council? The time—I think at a session in Pittsburgh—when the Board seemed to us about to do something foolish. We moved for a brief recess, "caucused," and agreed on what action ought to be taken, came back into session and launched a bitter fight between the two of us, each arguing on untenable ground until our colleagues finally negotiated us into a compromise action by the Board which was exactly what we had first agreed upon. You master-minded that strategy. Did you learn it as a boy?

Or the time the two of us went into a bar at the annual meeting in Atlantic City. As we went into a little place where we were the only customers, you mumbled to me to follow your lead. You then indicated to the bartender that we were two teachers at our first convention, that we had never had a drink before, and you wanted him to advise us. After due cogitation, he recommended old fashioneds, and we had them as if they were a new taste sensation. Continuing our talk about our newness in these sinful paths, and praising the bar's bourbon, we maneuvered the bartender into offering us second drinks on the house; he joined us in them, and then refused to take pay even for the first round. Now where did you learn behavior like that in Kentucky? It is not shown in your book.

I treasure such little vignettes of you as these two just described. I treasure even more the occasions when you sallied forth to blaze new trails in social studies teaching or to destroy some professional tradition no longer valid. You were an "innovator" before the present generation even knew about the popular word. You could be—and often were—as sarcastic in argument as Darrow was in dealing with William Jennings Bryan. You have stirred graduate students in to intellectual ferment, made staid professional committees move from pontification to action, fought bitter battles for the National Council for the Social Studies—or just for the fun of fighting for a good cause.

So you see, I left *Too Short The Days* unenlightened as to how the belligerent, blunt, creative drive of your adult years was affected by your boyhood days. I have a hunch that there are more reminiscences sparkling in your mind than you put down on paper. I still crave to know more about what made Wesley! What I want to know is, what made you, as an adult, so pugnacious, so reform-bent, so thoroughly critical as to be constructive, so original as to be worth knowing, so direct and upsetting and steadying to your friends that they have loved you all these years?

Howard

Howard E. Wilson, Dean
College of Education
University of California
Los Angeles

Dear Wilson:

I am pained but not surprised by your confused and confusing letter about my latest book, *Too Short The Days*. Often in the 40 years of our cooperative togetherness I have had to point out that the pigmies that you saw were not giants, that the chaos that swirled before your eyes was not order, and that the change that you perceived was not progress. All these hasty impulses testify to your goodness and generosity, but they do not exactly exemplify percipient perspicacity.

One of your very successful techniques—one that I have often admired—is overdrawing your account. Years ago you pushed the National Council into employing a full-time secretary when it could scarcely pay the printer. With gleeful finesse, you drew up a $40,000 budget on the basis of an $8,000 income. You planned a convention for two thousand teachers when four hundred were actually coming. Enlarging the future is often a marvelous technique, but it can be overworked. For example, you glanced at my new book and dashed off a letter to me without ever actually reading the book. This was a mistake.

Let me see if I can reduce your double-barreled indictment to elemental simplicity. First, you accuse me of being a hammer-swinging iconoclast; an imperious, impatient reformer; a cussed, obstinate, arrogant, even though creative, leader. Second, you accuse me of painting a picture of my boyhood self that is at a variance with your image of me as an adult.

That is it. How shall I, how can I answer?

I plead not guilty to any responsibility for the image of me that you have built up over the years. Whether it resembles or does not resemble me is not my problem. I uphold your right to be wrong; it is your personal privilege to exemplify the vitality of error. Therefore I shall pass no judgment upon your image of the adult Wesley.

Now turn to the book, *Too Short the Days*, and behold the normal, honest boy depicted therein. Concerning him I am an authority. I have long liked him and at times admired some of his traits; I have even imitated him now and then. I cannot allow you to malign him by stirring up the dust of irrelevancy that inevitably rises when you mention Little Lord Fauntleroy.

The boy in *Too Short the Days* has imagination. He preaches to the chickens; he invents a telephone; he imagines himself a baseball player. He is resourceful and independent. He does not ask his parents if he might go away to school at Middleburg and Barbourville; he decided and he went. He did not ask Pa if he might order groceries from drummers; he ordered them. He did not ask if he should collect accounts; he collected them. He was not overly modest. He memorized the poems in McGuffey's *Fourth Reader*, and he computed problems alongside Fonder, who was the best in the class. He planned to kiss Lorna, and with a little help from her, he did. He finally made the baseball team even though it was a team that he himself had organized. And so on and on for 182 pages.

Amid the whirling dust of irrelevancy raised by your mentioning Fauntleroy, allow me to observe that that dainty adolescent would scarcely have eaten fried snake off a tin lid; he would not have squeezed a dog's paw for experimental or any other reasons; he would have been afraid of even the butt end of a shotgun; he would not have even tried to make the baseball team; he would not have had the courage to gaze into Lorna's eyes for even one minute; he would never have rolled a cannon ball toward an unseen monitor's shins. In brief, there is no similarity between the boy in *Too Short The Days* and the polite little fellow you bring into the picture. And apparently it never occurred to you that because of modesty and restraint I might have shown my hero as a follower, a participant, a member of the group, whereas he may at times have been the radical innovator, the bold leader.

With some hesitation I mention a characteristic of the book that I had assumed a social studies teacher might be expected to perceive and appreciate; namely, its cohesive unity—a unity of family, of neighborhood, of playmates, of the county, of the state, of fellow students. This depicted unity may be partly responsible for your failure to individualize the boy. But shouldn't an appreciative reader perceive both the social unity and the individual boy?

It is too bad that you probably overpraise the one part of the book that you might have read; namely, the first two chapters that provide the geographical setting. While this setting is clearly described, it does not, as you erroneously argue, dominate the book. Time and place met over Bethelridge and produced, not a unique, but a universal boy.

Even though you scold and nag, I was delighted to hear from you. In fact, I become a bit sentimental and nostalgic when I recall our long, unbroken alliance to reform the social studies, uplift mankind, and redirect civilization. You rescued the National Council from years of aimless desert wanderings and set it firmly on the road as a national organization of teachers—not just for social scientists and humanists. As President in 1934 and as Secretary in the years that followed you were in a position to inspire, stimulate, and lead—and you did. You heartily supported me in establishing the independent meetings of the Council when I was President in 1935. And, of course, everyone benefited from the help of Hughes, Ellis, Kelty, Murra, Hunt, Anderson, and other vigorous leaders. So we belong among the ancients, but I am somewhat reconciled because today's leaders are more numerous, imaginative, and informed than we were. Such is my comfort.

Edgar

Edgar B. Wesley
Hacienda Carmel
Carmel, California

The Mature Social Studies Teacher

JAMES A. MICHENER

One of the best things I ever wrote was an article in the Social Studies Yearbook for 1939 in which I explored a subject with which I had had personal experience, the beginning social studies teacher. The article was well received; some of the good things about it suggested to me that perhaps I could one day write professionally.

Today I think of myself as a somewhat older social studies teacher, still preoccupied with the same problems that faced me thirty years ago. The only change that I am aware of is that my audience has changed; the subject matter remains the same.

I tried, in my early days, to be a good social studies teacher but I was never so good as the excellent associates with whom I had a chance to work. Howard E. Wilson of Harvard was as fine a man as I was ever to know, and my debt to him so considerable that it could never be repaid. Edgar B. Wesley of Minnesota was the most effective teacher I worked with and whenever I watched his salty, sane approach to life I realized that he possessed a secret and a skill that I would never match. Augustus C. Krey, also of Minnesota, was the most penetrating scholar in our field and it was a privilege to work with him. But the man who gave me the most important personal help was Erling Hunt of Columbia, a shy, taciturn gentleman whom it was never easy to know.

Hunt happened to be the editor of this journal in the years when I was beginning, and also chairman of the editorial board for which I worked. He was an excellent editor with a dry sense of propriety and a lean style. He taught me much about writing, not in personal sessions,

NOTE: This article appeared in *Social Education*, November 1970, pp. 760–767. Reprinted by permission of James A. Michener.

for he was an aloof man, but through his total manner. His comment on what I wrote, his precept in what he wrote, his unemotional professionalism all had a deep impact. From him I learned how to put an article together, how to express ideas succinctly, how to keep copy reasonably well cleaned up. My professional debt to him was then and is now considerable, for throughout my adult life I have continued to write social studies.

Any young man who knew both Wilson and Hunt—the former so mercurial and charismatic, the latter so acerb and deflating—realized that he was in the presence of two first-class minds. I learned from each and would have been deprived had I been denied either. Wilson's enormous optimism has colored much of my work; Hunt's hard insistence on clarity has accounted for its type of structure. I could wish beginning teachers no better luck than to encounter in their education two contrasting men like these two, or two great teachers like the gentlemen from Minnesota. As a beginning teacher I was lucky, for I met these men early, worked with them intimately, and profited from almost every experience I had with them. Without such preceptors I wonder how I would have learned my trade.

Permanent Values

When I started my professional career, the new field of social studies was just coming into being, and when I received my training in the subjects which comprised it I could not have known that I was absorbing material which would have relevance for the rest of my life, but that was the case. I believe that one of the lasting values of social education is that if well organized it does prepare one to grapple with the wild fluctuations of his time.

Any young person well grounded in the scholarship of the various fields, who has learned to explore developing problems, and identify likely sore points, and commit himself to their solution, comes away with an insight into our society that prepares him to face recurrent crisis. Practically everything I learned in my days of exploration from men like Arthur M. Schlesinger, Sr., Kurt Lewin and Louis B. Wirth has been relevant to the large questions which I have had to confront. Time has confirmed the significance of what they foresaw.

Thus, I began to worry about the race problem thirty years ago and nothing that has developed in the interim has surprised me except that fact that the nexus of the problem was to be faced in the north rather than in the south, and even this I should have foreseen had I paid more attention to population shifts. All else has been anticipated.

Similarly, I was informed about the impending crisis of the cities from the first day I started my studies; later I wrote about it and always

I have returned to it with fascination. No recent developments in this area have surprised me very much except, as I indicated above, the reluctance of northern cities to act upon the race question.

Wars, depressions, political shifts and the rapid modifications of our moral postures should not have surprised anyone trained in the work of men like Harry Elmer Barnes and Lewis Mumford, and even the hippie movement ought not to startle those familiar with The Children's Crusade or the roving bands that circulated during the Hundred Years' War. I was, however, unprepared for the sudden emergence of drugs as a major problem and I have spent much time recently speculating on what data I ignored which might have warned me of this development.

Because of this background and this continuing interest, I have always thought of myself as a social studies teacher and continue to do so. Not long ago I had the opportunity of serving as secretary to the convention which revised Pennsylvania's constitution; we became the only major state in recent years able to bring forth and adopt a new document, all of our neighbors failed, and I was impressed with the permanence of problems that confront us in government. Each of the difficult areas identified in classrooms forty years ago continues to perplex us, plus new ones that develop with each decade. I found that those delegates who had been well trained in government or law were prepared to grapple with whatever new problems arose, while having at their command the solid groundwork from which they could analyze the recurring problems. Delegates with no philosophical footing were apt to be immobilized by either the new or the old.

Similarly, when I served as president of our Electoral College I found that each of the problems identified by our Founding Fathers as they struggled with the question of how to elect a President continued to have relevance. The dangers they foresaw are more alive today than when they discussed them, and in those dangerous days of early November 1968, when it looked as if the Nixon-Humphrey contest might wind up in a deadlock, with election being thrown into the House of Representatives, I often referred to the debates of the Constitutional Convention of 1787 and found them strikingly pertinent.

So, as a more mature social studies teacher I find that the field I committed myself to many decades ago is more vital now than it was when I started, more rewarding to those who work in it, more exciting in the challenges it faces, more essential in the help it can provide. I can think of no field that I could have elected which would have been more productive, and every value that I uncovered then is doubly viable now.

Why Did I Quit Teaching?

I was a diligent teacher and with some of my students I found success, for I could get them interested in fields which they had not previously considered. I enjoyed teaching, worked hard to perfect myself, and looked forward to a lifetime of service, which in the normal course of events would now be drawing to its close.

Suddenly, however, I quit the profession. It was not, as some suspected, because the new salary was higher; and it was certainly not because my interest or commitment had in any way diminished. It was with a pang of regret that I left and I have never lost a sense of disappointment in not having stayed with a field I liked so much.

What happened was this. As I was finishing my graduate work at Harvard precisely the kind of position for which I had been preparing myself fell open, almost providentially. I was a little young for the post and could have been rejected on that score, and I knew that at least two of the other professors under consideration were better scholars than I, so I was not foolish enough to think that I either had the inside track or the right to it.

The job went to another man and I was neither hurt nor surprised, but some months later one of the men on the selection committee told me inadvertently that I had never been seriously considered. "Not because of your age. We really wanted a man your age. And not because of your scholarship, because we thought that you might in the years ahead become the best scholar of the bunch. It was because you didn't have a doctor's degree. We had to have that above all else."

Now my education had been irregular, the crucial years having been spent in European universities, and whereas I had degrees that in some ways exceeded the doctorate and an education that certainly did, I lacked the degree itself and was thus ineligible for serious consideration when the top jobs were being filled.

I concluded that if my profession enforced such criteria, I had no future in it and no further interest. When, a few months later, an enticing position was offered me by a large publishing company I accepted automatically and thus left a profession in which I had prospered and which I loved. It was my work in the publishing company that introduced me to the world of books and convinced me that I could find a place in that world.

I wish I could say, as the storyteller ought to, that the man chosen to fill the position I had wanted had turned out to be a much better professor of the teaching of social studies than I would have been. Unfortunately that was not so. Through the succeeding decades I followed his accomplishments with much interest and felt that he wasted the splendid opportunities provided him. His university became no beacon light to illuminate the way of others, no magnet to attract the best young men and women, no proving ground for the preparation of excellent instructors.

Had the attainment of the doctor's degree automatically insured that the recipient would be a superior professor, I think a case could be made in favor of it. In the succeeding decades I have picked up more than a dozen doctor's degrees and I never receive one without a most wry recollection of how poorly this system operated at a crucial period in my life.

I could, I suppose, adopt a sour-grape attitude and claim that my failing to have the degree at a crossroads in my life projected me into a much happier and more productive experience, but that would not be true. I have never ceased to regret my departure from teaching; I have never erased a sense of guilt; I have never felt that what I was doing was other than an extension of my early interest in the social studies and I remain convinced that the writing of books is in no way a better form of life than constructive teaching.

I have always supposed that when I retired I would look around for some small college that could use my background and that I would end my working life as a teacher. In fact, I think of my books as an extension of my early commitments; creative teaching expressed in a different way. Certainly my concern with the social studies—geography, politics, economics, cultural history, current social problems—has never diminished and I have tried in general to keep abreast of new developments in these fields.

One might say that I was dismissed as a professor but retained as a teacher.

How I Work

I approach each new field as if I were an advanced college senior, or perhaps a graduate student, entering a tough seminar where the competition was to be keen. I stress this because when I write my term paper it is going to be judged by some of the toughest intellects operating, many of whom know more about my subject than I do. Thus, for me education has become always a more exacting process, the requirements more demanding, the final examination even more demanding.

I start my self-imposed seminar by background reading of as profound a type as I can find and handle. I do much more library work now than when I was in college and with a much greater intensity. But the major difference is that since my goals are self-determined and since they can be rigorously delimited—for I work at only one idea at a time—I no longer take notes. I can carry in my head the relevant contents of about five hundred master books and in any one of them I can locate a passage I might want to recover within a few moments, because I can visualize where on the page the sought-for passage occurred and about how far through the book.

I have given so many demonstrations of this capacity that I no longer doubt its accuracy. What I have said, however, applies only if I knew when I read the book that I was going to be interested in such-and-such a topic; if I flagged the topic when I read it, I simply never forget. But if I did not know at the time I read the book that I might later want to refer to an idea which matured later, I am quite powerless to recall where precisely it was that I came upon it. I know that the data resides somewhere among the five hundred books, but I am powerless to find it and only the most lucky kind of reconstruction enables me to recover it. Usually I don't even try, for I have learned that to do so is a waste of time. Of course, when the seminar ends, and the book is written, I cannot recall even the names of the principal sources, so complete does the slate of my mind wipe itself clean.

As one grows older, and his mind better balanced, the book one cherishes is the book which provides generalizations, insights, fresh approaches or oblique and unexpected illuminations. Of the five hundred basic books I refer to in any subject with which I am concerned, I am lucky if I find two or three with this kind of fortuitous insight. Sometimes they are books that the general public holds in little regard; more often they are books which scholars have known favorably for many years and whose reputation has seeped out to the general public. The specific gravity of such works is unbelievably high, sometimes an idea to a page, and much of my intellectual life has been built around them.

When I was writing about Hawaii I found such a book, in which the writer honestly speculated upon what Polynesian life must have been like; a great part of his work was mere guessing, but it was based upon a wide accumulation of fact, and this produced a body of philosophical insight which proved invaluable. The same thing happened when I was working in Israel; among the thousands upon thousands of books written on the subjects I was interested in there was a small book which endeavored to spell out what exactly happened when Greek civilization met Judaism face to face, and the author developed so many brilliant speculations that reading his conclusions was like tossing a bundle of lighted firecrackers from hand to hand.

I do not give the names of these books because to the next reader, without my interest and years of preparatory work, they might prove to be ordinary or even dull. With the developing intellect it is so often a case of coming upon the right book at the right time; if one misses the fortunate moment it cannot be reconstructed and that particular part of one's brain remains undeveloped.

I spend about two years thinking about a book, two years doing background work, two years writing, and whenever I have abbreviated this schedule it has been to my detriment. Since I have published a book every two years, obviously there is an overlap in preparatory work, but I have not been able to do actual writing upon more than one book at a time. I have occasionally halted work on the writing of a major book to complete some lesser job, but this has usually been to my disadvantage and now I try to avoid such interruptions.

I write everything on a typewriter, two fingers at a time and on the slow side. I edit heavily with pen, then retype, then re-edit and retype. People often ask me what the major problem of the writer is and although I rarely tell them, I know the answer: "Saving your eyes." Practically everything I do—original research, drafting the first run-through; editing, retyping, reading galleys—requires eyesight and mine has never been very good. I therefore have to discipline myself strictly; as a result I do not very often read for mere pleasure, a loss which at times seems quite terrible, nor do I look at television as much as most.

It has often occurred to me that if my high school or college had had a perfect counseling system the expert in charge would have told me, "With eyes as poor as yours, Michener, you should not think of research and writing as a career," which would have been sound advice, physiologically speaking, and rather wide of the mark philosophically. I often rewrite up to seven times, never less than three. I have never thought of myself as a good writer, but I am one of the world's great rewriters. I never send out even an important letter in first draft.

Every working hour I am conscious of the fact that I am a trained social-studies scholar. Even the art books which I have published in Asia have stressed the social backgrounds of the artists and I am as deeply involved in the field today as I was when I first started. My reading is in this field; my research is usually upon topics wholly social in origin or largely so. Today the field seems richer than when I started, more rewarding, and certainly more necessary to the good functioning of our society.

Geography: The Queenly Science

The more I work in the social-studies field the more convinced I become that geography is the foundation of all. When I call it the queenly science I do not visualize a bright-eyed young woman recently a princess but rather an elderly, somewhat beat-up dowager, knowing in the ways of power.

When I begin work on a new area—something I have been called upon to do rather frequently in my adult life—I invariably start with the best geography I can find. This takes precedence over everything else, even history, because I need to ground myself in the fundamentals which have governed and in a sense limited human development. (The second book I read is a cultural history, something like Parrington if I can find it, but such books have not yet been written about many parts of the earth, so that frequently I have to do without; in such cases I try the best available history of literature, sometimes with good results.) Most geography books, like most geography courses, are drab affairs and a waste of time. I have dissipated many hours looking at geographies that were not worth the reading, but when you come upon something like Preston James' speculative works on South America the philosophical returns are apt to be high. However, even the poorest regional geography is better than none at all; it at least delimits the field, fixes certain relationships, and drives the reader to a contemplation of his own.

The virtue of the geographical approach is that it forces the reader to relate man to his environment. It forestalls loose generalization founded mainly on good intentions or hope. It gives a solid footing to speculation and it reminds the reader that he is dealing with real human beings who are just as circumscribed as he. Finally, studying the geography of a region like East Africa compels the reader to draw comparisons with Eastern North America.

With the growing emphasis on ecology and related problems of the environment, geography will undoubtedly grow in importance and relevance. I wish that the teaching of it were going to improve commensurately; most of the geography courses I have known were rather poorly taught and repelled the general student like me.

I could make the same wish about geographical writing. It really ought to be much better than it is, with more emphasis upon generalization and philosophical meaning. Television has done much to awaken the general viewer to geographical matters, and many of my neighbors schedule their evenings so that they can watch one or another of the fine color programs featuring the highlights of foreign lands, but this is not what I have in mind when I call for an increase in geographic study. This is merely a pleasant tourism, sightseeing. What is required is the perceptive analysis of the land and man's relation to it. If one has this solid footing, then the television travelogue can be of enormous additional value. Without it, the television program is harmless entertainment and provides little evidence for reaching conclusions on major problems.

I suppose that my books on Hawaii, Israel and Spain have won a rather wide readership primarily because my extended work in the geography of those areas—really minute field work carried on over periods of many years—has provided a solid tactile base for what I had to say. My characters were not drifting in space; they were rooted in the ground. The Hawaiians were in Hawaii and not in some other place, and they were on an island of special construction and not some generalized mainland. Similarly, I could not have written as I did of Israel had it not been for my sustained study, through many decades, of the principle of the Fertile Crescent—purely a geographical concept—and even though I could not accept the thesis that it was this crescent that called forth much of the history of the area, the thesis and its antithesis were constantly in my mind.

Similarly, one cannot understand Spain without repeated reference to its geographical footing; its peninsula is quite different from Italy's or Scandinavia's and no European nation has been more influenced by its geographical setting than Spain. I was astonished by the reception accorded my book on Spain. I wrote it not for the general public but rather as a kind of reflection by a social-studies teacher who had been pondering certain ideas for a long time. The fact that so many general readers showed themselves to be hungry for such a book, and willing to spend long hours reading it and then writing letters about it, proves I think that there is a need for men trained in geography to explain the significance of other large portions of the world.

I have been asked a hundred times why I do not do the same kind of writing about South America or Africa. The answer is simple. I would love to do such books but I don't know enough. When I write about Asia I have behind me thirty years of reading and travel and speculation. If trouble were to break out in Tibet tomorrow I would be qualified to say something about it for I have been on each of its borders; I know the history of all the nations that surround it; I have read biographies of perhaps a score of men whose lives touched it in the last two hundred years; I understand its religion, its economy, and above all its cultural geography. After a year's intense concentration, I could write fairly intelligently about Tibet, for I would have a large cognitive base on which to draw.

But if the same kind of trouble were to erupt in Paraguay what could I do? I am not familiar with the history of its neighbors, do not know the biographies of famous Brazilians or Argentinians whose lives might have touched Paraguay. I know little of the wars between Paraguay and Bolivia; above all, I know nothing of the cultural geography or the intellectual history of the region. It would take me a good eight or ten years of reading to make myself proficient in this area, and when a man is in his sixties he cannot devote so much time to any project, no matter how much he might wish to do so. When I started to write about Israel, I had behind me a decade of living in Muslim countries, two decades of study of comparative religions, and a lifetime of familiarity with the Bible. Knowledge does not come quickly; competence requires years of investment.

If I were a young man with any talent for expressing myself, and if I wanted to make myself indispensable to my society, I would devote eight or ten years to the real mastery of one of the earth's major regions. I would learn languages, the religions, the customs, the value systems, the history, the nationalisms, and above all the geography, and when that was completed I would be in a position to write about that region, and I would be invaluable to my nation, for I would be the bridge of understanding to the alien culture. We have seen how crucial such bridges can be.

What area would I specialize in? I personally would choose the Arab lands, for we are more in need of understanding there than anywhere else in the world. If I were someone else, I would probably choose

Africa, just north and south of the equator, for this region will have enormous impact on American life during the foreseeable future. If I were of a philosophical or religious bent, and especially if I had just written on Spain, I would choose South America, the most misunderstood of our neighbors, the area most deserving of a sympathetic depiction in American letters.

Believe me, if I were well schooled in one of these vital areas and if I had even a modest gift for writing I would have an insurance policy for the rest of my life, because we need perceptive books about these cultures.

The Shameful Period

If my days in the social studies produced great satisfactions, they were responsible also for one of the regrettable segments of my life, one which even now I look back upon with a sense of shame.

In the period of witch hunts sponsored by Senator Joseph McCarthy the axe of suspicion fell heavily upon social studies teachers, or those with similar interests. Because I have throughout my life been constitutionally opposed to joining I luckily entered this era without my name appearing on anyone's blacklist, even though I was more liberal in thought than many of those thus trapped. Also, my last three employers had been *The Reader's Digest*, the *New York Herald Tribune* and the *Saturday Evening Post*, three journals of stable reputation. I was therefore a popular witness for those accused, for my name was known and my record was impeccable, and I was called to give testimony on behalf of numerous friends. In two instances I knew the claimants to have been revolutionaries urging the overthrow of our government and I despised their attempts to weasel out of their former beliefs and to ask my assistance in denying what they had clearly proposed; I refused to testify for them.

For all the others, men and women whose records were sounder than mine except for their having joined this or that group or having made this or that intemperate statement within the hearing of informers, I testified, sometimes repeatedly and before frightening tribunals. Often my testimony was of no use; prosecutors pointed out that while it was true that I was a writer now, I had been a professor not long previously, and of social studies to boot. But on many occasions what I said helped the innocent to clear themselves, even though, in one instance, we had to fight clear to the Supreme Court, where one of the most damaging character assassins was demonstrated to have been a liar and an inventor out of whole cloth.

How wretched that period was! I could weep when I look back on the wrongs that were done, the foolishness that was enshrined in tribunals.

I remember testifying before one such group for two days, going over the same testimony again and again. When a guilty verdict was brought in I was told, "You were one of the most damaging witnesses against your friend." When I asked why, I was told, "Again and again we brought the discussion around to the point where any logical man would have volunteered information about the affair in Alabama, but since you said nothing we could only conclude that you were trying to hide the facts because you too were a participant in them." I had never heard of any Alabama incident, could have said nothing had I wanted to; you see, these trials were held without the accused's ever being told what he was charged with. If I didn't mention Alabama it was not interpreted as proof that I knew nothing of it; it was proof that I was implicated. But no one was allowed to tell me that Alabama was the root problem.

No case of this kind was more disgusting than the charges brought in the state of California against my revered teacher Howard E. Wilson. Because he had spent a spell working for the United Nations, McCarthyite-types waged a strong campaign against him and sought to have him fired from his job at a California university. His defenders were reduced to the ignominy of soliciting from his former students testimonials as to his loyalty. I have found in Twentieth Century history that whenever young people are required to testify as to the legitimacy of older people, something has gone terribly wrong (Indonesia, Hitler's Germany, pre-war Japan, Stalin's Russia), but when students are asked to give evidence either against or for their professors the whole damned system is rotten and falling apart.

I gave testimony, at Dr. Wilson's urgent personal request. I was told later that it helped him hold onto his job, but I have remained so ashamed of this incident that it scars my memory as if a rusty sword had been drawn across my heart. That was a disgraceful age and to have participated in it in any respect was a lasting shame.

I recall these distasteful matters because the social studies is an area which attracts irresponsible attack, and it will do so in the future. I am much struck these days by the fact that certain powerful critics call both for the abandonment of social studies as a discipline and the solution of those social problems which only the social studies can analyze and solve. The more precarious our position becomes, the more we are needed.

I am particularly impatient with critics from the physical sciences who castigate the social sciences for being less subject to mathematical proof than the physical sciences. The fact that proof is more difficult in the social sciences does not mean that the subject matter being dealt with is less significant; the reasoning should be just the opposite: because the subject matter of the social sciences is so inescapably crucial and so fraught with emotion, systems of attack and proof must be more tentative.

I have said what course I would pursue if I were a young man with writing talent eager to work in the kinds of fields I have worked in. If I were a young man with a political talent—to be used in government, or the management of business, or the law, or the ministry, for example—I would specialize in the humanities, with a strong helping of the social studies, in the sure knowledge that whereas I might have a most difficult time finding a job at age 22, at age 42 I would be among the pool from which this society would be picking its leaders. Government, business, the church, the communicative professions, education will continue to be run by men and women with broad philosophical backgrounds. Scientists will be eligible if after graduation they give themselves the kinds of education I am talking about; if they fail they will continue to man the laboratories while men of broad vision run the nation.

The field grows bigger, not smaller. The need for good teachers is greater, not less. My association with it was one of the principal factors of my life and my debt a lasting one.

Then and Now:
The Experiences of a Teacher

ELIE WIESEL

It is with a sentiment of gratitude more than anything else that I speak to you tonight. I know what it is to be a teacher and to teach a subject that brings one into close contact with anger, despair, and madness. I myself cannot teach the subject of the Holocaust. I do so very rarely. I believe, therefore, that we should all thank you who are teaching it for the risks you take and the dangers you face.

April, 1945. All I remember of that event, of that month, is that there was no joy. There was no joy in those who opened their eyes at the end of a nightmare. They were alive but something of them had remained on the other side. In a way they were dead but did not know it. No dancing marked the occasion, no festivities, no exuberance, no speeches, no solemn declarations, nothing. Only emptiness, nothing else. Fatigue, perhaps. For months and months, for eternities and eternities, they had waited for this moment. And now it was here, but so many friends were not here. So many comrades, so many faces and eyes vanished as they flickered in the middle of darkness. Darkness triumphed; not the glory of the flame, but its ashes.

The question of questions that we faced then and shall face forever is: What does one do with such knowledge? There were children who were my friends: some were eight years old, one was six, others were ten, twelve; the oldest—and I belonged to that group—were 15 or 16. Those children were the real teachers of their generation and of all

NOTE: This selection, a transcript of an address, appeared in *Social Education*, April 1978, pp. 266–271. Reprinted by permission of Elie Wiesel.

generations. Somehow they knew more than the oldest of their old teachers about life and death, about the poetic aspect of immortality. How did Paul Valery put it? "Now, civilization, we know that you are mortal." We knew that everything was mortal. Perhaps not the executioner, who in his own weird way had achieved immortality by producing so much death.

There was such knowledge in those children, in those people whom we today call survivors, and perhaps they were crushed by it. They possessed all the questions and they knew there were no answers. There never will be, there never should be. And the more they knew, the more they accumulated, the less they knew. The more they read, the less they understood. The more they came to absorb, the more they felt that the words that served as vehicles were the wrong words. What, then, should they have done, what should we have done with our knowledge?

As teachers, surely you will agree that this is the problem man has faced since he was supposed to be human. We could then have asked for the impossible for we had lived the impossible. We could have imposed our will, our vision, on mankind. We could have asked (do not laugh) for the ultimate redemption. We had an authority unmatched in history, the authority of cumulative suffering, and, again forgive me for the arrogance, the authority of remaining human. We spoke on behalf of a kingdom inhabited by martyrs and victims numbering six million. We had the power, the moral strength, to speak up and demand and compel mankind to change, to give up intolerance and hate, bigotry and fanaticism. We had the right then to say we are your teachers. And we had the power, the metaphysical power to say that we shall teach mankind how to survive without linking survival to betrayal.

But we did not know how to go about it. We were hesitant to speak. Had we started then, we would have found it impossible to stop speaking. Having shed one tear, we would have drowned the human heart. As invincible as we had been in the face of death and the enemy, we felt helpless then. When man is in pain, said Goethe, when he becomes mute because of that pain, God gives him the strength to think of his trial. But how is he to make use of that pain? And what if he decides to remain mute? And what if he chooses to carry his secret with him into his grave?

Such questions could not but haunt all those teachers that we became. The witnesses felt remorse, they were mad with disbelief. People refused to listen, to understand, to share. There was a division between us and them, between those who had endured and those who read about it or refused to read about it.

Many survivors will tell you today that they are tired. They really are. After the liberation, all illusions were hopes. We were convinced that on the ruins of Europe a new world would be built, a new society would be formed. There would be no more wars, no more hatred, no more bloodshed. We thought people would remember our experience, our testimony, and how we managed to suppress our violent impulses to kill or to hate.

Well, look at the world today. People know little or nothing today, and therefore I believe that there is no subject more urgent, more burning, than the one you and I are teaching. There is no subject that is more linked to justice than ours. Today the greatest injustice is being accomplished; that is, the obliteration of those memories, the erasing of those events. Let me give you a few examples. I received at Boston University a post card addressed to me by a certain Jew. "I recently completed reading the book by Arthur Butz called *The Hoax of the Twentieth Century*," he wrote, "and the professor who wrote the book claims that the six million are a total fiction and that no Jews were gassed or toasted in the ovens in German concentration camps. This appears to be consistent with the professor's argument that there was nothing in German records to substantiate the Jewish claims. The confessions that were obtained were obtained under duress. I guess Hitler was right when he said the Jew is the master of the big lie." In a letter I received from a professor at the Sorbonne, he says, "Yes, there were ovens in the camps but only for the sick people. There never were any gas chambers." There seems to be a real movement which has one sole aim: Not only to rewrite history but to destroy it and in so doing to humble and humiliate those teachers, some of whom are in this very room, who still not only remember but also carry their wounds secretly. If we are to believe those morally deranged, perverted, so-called historians, the Holocaust never took place, the victims did not perish. Auschwitz, they say, is a fraud, Treblinka a lie, Belsen a convalescent home.

That is what dozens and dozens of pamphlets being produced today state in a variety of languages, warning their readers against Jewish propaganda on the subject. A former associate professor of English at LaSalle in Philadelphia has said that the six million swindled, blackmailing the German people for hard marks and with fabricated corpses. As if that is not enough, a former SS judge says openly in his book that, yes, there were crematoria in Auschwitz; there were ovens, he remembers them, but they were bakeries.

What does one say to such witnesses? What does one say to those Nazi leaders in California today who on national television proclaim that they are the new Nazis and are bringing their children up in the Nazi theology—poor children with swastikas celebrating Hitler's birthday. And when the reporter (on "Sixty Minutes") asked the Nazi leader, "Don't you feel embarrassed about Treblinka, Auschwitz?", he replied: "Oh, those were lies." Then, after a moment of suspense, he said, "I wish they were true." Millions of people saw that program and nobody spoke up, the silent majority remained silent. In Germany today, wine bottles are being sold with labels that read "in celebration of the 89th birthday of Adolph Hitler."

What does one say to all this, and why have more people not protested? Some of the survivors and many of the executioners are still in our midst, and now we understand why during the Auschwitz trials the defendants, whenever they came into the court, were laughing. All of them were laughing. The fighters from Warsaw and Bialystock, they were told, you have not witnessed the death of your families. Survivors of Birkenau, you have not lost your parents to the flames. Lodz, Babi Yar, Sobibor are not places where entire communities were reduced to ashes. The Nuremberg trials, the Eindorf commando trials, the Frankfurt trials were never held. Himmler was just another officer and Eichmann a bureaucrat. There was no uprising in Treblinka, no selection at Maidaneck. And Raul Hilberg's book was apparently not even written.

But then we may ask: Where have the people disappeared? Where are the three million Polish Jews? What happened to the Jews of Germany? What happened to the Jews of my town and the other towns in Hungary, Estonia, Lithuania, Greece, Holland, and the Ukraine? Where are the more than a million Jewish children hiding? If there was no Holocaust, where have they vanished?

Think about these questions, teachers. For you are the ones who must answer them. I believe this attempt to deprive the victims of their past is obscene, an outrage. But it is not new. *The Diary of Anne Frank* was only recently termed a forgery by an ambassador to the United Nations. And there was no one at the UN, to my shame as a human being, to go and spit in his face. A prominent European playwright wrote a drama about the Auschwitz trial and managed not to mention the word Jew once during the three acts. There is no monument for Jewish victims in Auschwitz. And I just read a story that six Jews were arrested in Moscow because they were about to go to Babi Yar for a commemoration. Jews are not even allowed to observe their days of remembrance. In the Talmud we find a very characteristic passage. As you know, when the Romans destroyed the Temple, Jews were expelled from Jerusalem and had no right to live in the Holy City. They did not even have the right to come close, except for one day of the year, on Tisha Ba'av, when we remember the destruction of the Temple. The Romans wanted the Jews to come near Jerusalem then so that they should see the ruins and weep more.

Our Jews today are not even allowed to weep. I confess, I do not know how to handle this situation. Are we really to debate these charges? Is it not beneath our dignity and the dignity of the dead to refute these lies? But then is silence the answer? Since silence never has been an answer, the survivors chose to teach; and what is their writing, their testimony, if not teaching? To tell the tale and to bear testimony. But apparently their words have not been accepted. But what then are they to do with their memories? They would much rather speak of other things. But who then would protest against the indecent attempts to kill the victims again? Where are the humanists today? What about the human rights of the survivors, the most tragic minority of all, and where are those who usually fight for such rights? And why are the professors of history all over America not speaking out in one voice of outrage? And what about the American soldiers who liberated the camps? I saw them, I remember them. Why don't they speak up? Why don't they become witnesses?

There was no Treblinka, there was no Buchenwald. And we were never there. I do not know how you react to all this. But I can tell you that, more than sadness, I feel despair; and even more than despair I feel disgust. But we go on teaching because we believe that our life is grace. No one in the world is as capable of gratitude as we are because we know what it means to live one extra moment, one extra day, and we know what it means to meet a smile and not a fist. Every word of friendship touches us. So we go on teaching. But we despair.

In my class of Holocaust studies at Boston University, some eighty students, both graduate and undergradute, were asked to identify names, places, concepts related to that period. Only one out of twenty knew who Eichmann was. One answer was that he was an important Nazi living in the U.S.A. Even though they read, and I begin whatever I teach with Raul Hilberg's book, *The Destruction of the European Jews*, somehow it eludes them. In a high school in Seattle, Washington, only five out of one hundred students correctly explained the meaning of the word "Holocaust," but five others thought it was a Jewish holiday. This is a dangerous situation.

If we are to forget the spirit, I can foresee now, though in the past I could not, not a new Holocaust—that cannot happen; that is to say, not a systematic undertaking with ghettos, camps, barbed wire—but, given the proper circumstances, the political situation in the Middle East, the economic situation here, [there could be] an upsurge of anti-Semitism that would bring fear to this country. Certain right-wing groups, more precisely Fascist groups, plan to organize a public rally in Munich under the overall slogan "Eternal Penitence for Hitler." At the same time ten young German officers, after a joyous party at their military university in Munich, staged a burning-of-Jews comedy sketch while exchanging Nazi salutes and singing Nazi hymns. In Skokie, Illinois, the place where 5,000 survivors live, the Nazis wanted to stage a rally and again—to my shame as a liberal, a Jew, and a human being—I do not understand why the American Civil Liberties Union found it necessary to defend not the survivors, those people who would be exposed to obscenities and threats, but the Nazis. Of course I understand the argument: the First Amendment.

There are so many signals that show a pattern that frightens me. A movie made in Germany shows the good side of Hitler, how he really meant well, that he did not know. It tries to rehabilitate the poor man, especially with regard to the Holocaust. This seems to be part of a Hitler wave in Germany. Books about him and his lieutenants are best-sellers. Goebbels' diaries are being read now as much as were his editorials when he was alive. The killers were not killers since there were no victims. In Oregon, a young professor, Reverend Douglas Hunecke, a righteous Gentile, was asked by one of his best students: "Tell me, professor, whom should we believe, Elie Wiesel or Arthur Butz?" Again, I do not know what to do.

I can only tell you that should the teachers fail, and I include myself among them, should these desecrators succeed in erasing the memories of their victims, only then will we feel and experience something worse than what we experienced then. We shall feel shame because we will have betrayed the victims for the last time, we will have completed the killers' work. Their task was to destroy the living Jews and burn dead Jews, and only now will they have succeeded.

In all earnestness, anyone who does not engage actively today in keeping these memories alive is an accomplice of the killers. Surely you teachers, you have read the history books and you know that the killers' final step was to burn, to kill the killed, in order to erase their memory. Should it happen now, we would have to hide ourselves, we would be afraid to face anyone in the street because then people would accuse us of having invented this tragedy.

So we teach. But how can I, a teacher, explain to my students so many things related to the Holocaust? How can I explain to them the indifference of so many nations and so many leaders to so many Jews? I always start at the beginning, I go back to the roots. And when we read about the Evian Conference, we remember that the *New York Herald Tribune* published a report under the headline, "650,000 Exiled Jews Refused at Evian." Refused by the world, rejected by the world. As for the German papers, one headline read: "Jews for Sale . . . Who Wants Them?" No one. Another editorial stated that "Other nations pity German Jews, but nobody is ready to take them in." Nor is that all. When Winston Churchill was asked by one of the Nazi leaders in July, 1938 whether Hitler's anti-Jewish measures would create obstacles to a German-British pact, the British leader answered, "No, not at all." How explain that to your students? How explain that it was Switzerland, humanitarian Switzerland, that suggested that Germany stamp Jewish passports with the distinctive "J" so that they could be refused visas everywhere, not only to Switzerland? How explain that the French government told Hitler's government that no nation has the right to interfere in Germany's inner affairs with regard to its anti-Semitic laws? How explain the St. Louis affair in which everybody followed the journey of the ship filled with refugees, which was not allowed to land in the United States? In *Mein Kampf* we read as follows: "The Jew is void of idealism. He is a parasite who contaminates his surroundings. Where the Jew settles, other people disappear, and that is his aim, to eliminate all non-Jews." This was the ideology of Hitler, a deranged mixture of political expediency, religious bigotry, social intolerance, and even sexual perversion. He said that the world does not want the Jews, and there was something in what he said that should make us think.

What shall we as teachers say to our students when they learn that all the Jewish children were not admitted into the United States even though quotas were still available, and when they learn that while the ghetto fighters were fighting in Warsaw there was silence here. No wonder that gradually Hitler, Himmler, Heinrich, and their associates came to the conclusion that Jews were unwanted everywhere, that all nations would be glad to be rid of them, that what was taking place in Germany was but an example to be followed. This meant that one day—the Nazi leaders were convinced of that—one day all nations would be grateful to them for doing their work for them. Goebbels mentions this frequently in his diaries. The extermination of Jews, he was convinced, was a service to humanity. What other conclusion was possible? The world was silent.

I confess I do not know how to teach these matters, especially the later periods, when we speak of that extraordinary confrontation between the killer and his victim; something happened there, something theological, metaphysical, something transhistorical and historical. I cannot comprehend them. How do you teach events that defy knowledge, experiences that go beyond imagination? How do you tell children, big and small, that society could lose its mind and start murdering its own soul and its own future? How do you unveil horrors without offering at the same time some measure of hope? Hope in what? In whom? In progress, in science and literature and God? In the viability of human endeavors? And what if man were but a spasm of history, a smile, a snear, a rejection by fate? The Holocaust was preceded not by the Middle Ages but by emancipation and enlightenment, by generations of humanists and liberal revolutionaries who preached their gospels, advocated their faith in universal brotherhood and ultimate justice.

Something that haunts me is the nocturnal processions, in the thousands, in the hundreds of thousands, those silent processions in which very few victims cried, very few shouted—as we know from their documents—as they were led to the grave, to be shot by the Einsatz-commandos. Something in that silence breaks you. One generation after the event, we find it difficult to absorb its anguish and fervor. The child in me, where is he? Did he dream or live his dreams of fear and fire? Did he really witness the agony of mankind through the death of his community? Did he really see the trial for brutality? Did he really hear or did he imagine the laughter of the executioners? Did he really see the killers throwing children, Jewish children, into the flames, alive?

For a long while I resisted telling the story. I refused to accept it as mine. For years and years I clung to the belief that it was all a dream, a bad dream, mine or God's. No, I did not see the children; I did not see their world consumed by flames. But it was no dream, it was true. How do you teach the cries of those children?

You must encounter difficulties in teaching and so do I. It was easier for a camp inmate then to imagine himself or herself free than for a free man or a free woman to imagine himself or herself today in the victim's predicament. Imagination fails us. Usually in literature imagination precedes reality, but this time reality preceded imagination. And one of the worst disasters that could happen to us was that the killer had more imagination than the victim. And that is probably one of the reasons why so many victims were victims.

But you do not know and you will never know what it was. That was the *leitmotif* in all testimonies of all survivors. Let me give you a small example. Teachers in the ghetto were my heroes, but they had problems in explaining simple words to their young pupils. How do you describe to a child in the ghetto who had no bread what it is to have a cake? Or fruit? Or sugar? "What does an apple look like?" a child asks a father. "And what about white bread?" Another wants to know, "What does happiness mean?" "Are there happy Jews in the world?" a Jewish child wants to know. "Have there ever been?" And a third child inquires, "You told us that people are good at heart. Are they?" And a five-year-old girl asks, "Am I going to die? Have I lived enough?" A friend whose name is Shimon told me that in Lodz there was once an *action*, an operation against children. Families were allowed to save only two children. Since he and his wife had three, they had to decide which one to give up. They discussed what to do and decided that the older child had a chance to survive. So too the second one, who did not look Jewish. Their youngest girl, only five years old, had to be the one to go. Somehow the operation ended before the selection, and all three survived. But after that, the little girl refused to look at her father.

We read stories by and about teachers in the ghettos and are filled with admiration for their devotion, sacrifice, and courage. We can never know what they endured, what they knew. We will never know what their teaching meant to them and to their pupils, what it meant to teach children history, literature, fairy tales, geography, and Bible and Talmud, and morality, knowing all the while that one month later, one week later, one day later, one hour later, they would be gone. That was part of the uniqueness of the experience. One hour before being led to the altar, children learned about the immortality of the Jewish spirit and about the invincibility of the human mind.

After the event, we tried to teach, we felt we had to do something with our knowledge. We had to communicate, to share, but it was not easy. Behind every word we said, a hundred remained unsaid. For every tear, a thousand remained unshed. For every Jewish child we saw, a hundred remained unseen.

When we think of the past, we are faced with two options: We can despise the living or we can try to help them. We can either spread misfortune or curtail it. We can either join the madness, the criminal madness, or fight it with another madness, a humane madness. We possess a strange truth that can either destroy or prevent destruction. How do we do it? As Albert Camus used to say, for modern man there are two options: One can be either a smiling pessimist or a weeping optimist. We study and we are both.

Our problem was and remains what to do with our words, with our tears. Because we did not know how to say certain things, we went back to our sources, to the past. That was the only link we had. Let me give you an example. I love the prophet Jeremiah because he is the one who had lived the catastrophe before, during, and after, and knew how to speak about it. There is a beautiful legend in the Talmud in which God says to Jeremiah: "Go and call forth Abraham, Isaac, and Jacob." And Jeremiah asks, "What for?" And God says, "They have to prevent a new catastrophe." "What can they do?" Jeremiah asks. And God says, "They can weep." Jeremiah did not know how to weep, but Isaac and Jacob did.

In Jeremiah, I found two expressions which baffled me. One expression was "a shaky ground," which he used to describe Jerusalem. He did not use "earthquake," for which Hebrew has a perfectly good word. I did not understand what he meant until one day I was in Kiev and learned from eyewitnesses that 30,000, 40,000, or 50,000 Jews had been buried there in ten days, some while still alive, and for days and weeks the ground was shaky. And then I understood Jeremiah. The prophet uses another beautiful, baffling expression when he speaks about a deserted air space over Jerusalem. I understood what that meant only when I learned that somehow there were no birds to be seen above the streets of Treblinka or Buchenwald. There was a deserted space over those places.

We go back to our sources, hoping to find some links—not consolation. There can be no consolation.

When I teach these matters, I teach of children. When one thinks of children or reads of them, one usually sees images of innocence, sunshine, happiness, play, laughter, teasing, dreaming, simple chants, so much promise. But not for us because to us childhood meant something else. It meant death, the death of childhood.

Children for me evoke war, thunder and hate, shouts, screams, dogs howling, children in the street hunted, beaten, humiliated. I see them walking and running like the old men and women who surround them, as though to protest, as though to protect them without protecting them. There is no protection for Jewish children. Thirsty children, and all one wants is to offer them a glass of water. Hungry children, and all one wants is to give them a crust of bread. Frightened children, and all one wants is to comfort them. You watch them marching, marching, and you know they will never come back; and yet you go on seeing them, but they no longer see you.

So what do you do? I will tell you what I do. I teach. I teach about the children because those children became philosophers, they became theologians, they became historians, they became poets. And, in a strange way, whenever I need to be uplifted I read their poetry, and it breaks my heart at the same time that it lifts my spirit.

What can I tell you as a teacher who teaches? It is more than a matter of communicating knowledge. Whoever engages in the field of teaching the Holocaust becomes a missionary, a messenger.

Confessions of a
Second-Look Liberal

An Interview with Theodore H. White

Theodore H. (Teddy) White is disarmingly friendly, gracious, and hospitable. He greets you at the door of his townhouse in New York himself, with a warm smile, an invitation to take off your jacket and have a drink. Who are you, exactly? What is *Social Education*? It is just much easier to talk to someone you know something about than a blank face.

During the interview, the words will flow as easily as words flashing by on the typewritten page. White will quote the statistics, cite the sources, and even play the part of the aggrieved blue-collar worker, the humiliated black woman beaten up by the Mississippi police for daring to vote, or the defiant Winston Churchill vowing to fight on.

When he talks of his great moral dilemma—whether or not to reveal that the election is over many hours before the polls are due to close—he is genuinely concerned at what the ethical answer is. And he wants *you* to tell him what he should do.

The interview took place early this summer in New York, conducted by then editor-designate of *Social Education*, Howard J. Langer. It was shortly after White's book, *America in Search of Itself*, had been published. Of all of White's books on American politics, this is undoubtedly the most controversial. White does more than report—he takes positions and expresses strong opinions about where America has been and where it is going.

NOTE: This interview appeared in *Social Education*, November/December 1982, pp. 516–524. Reprinted by permission of Howard J. Langer.

Born in Boston in 1915, White attended the Boston Latin School and Harvard, majoring in Chinese history and languages. He started a trip around the world after graduation, but stopped in China—where he would remain throughout World War II. He was *Time* magazine's first correspondent in the Orient, witnessing the air war in Asia, the ground fighting in China, and the Japanese surrender aboard the *Missouri*.

Returning to America in the fall of 1945, White collaborated with Annalee Jacoby on *Thunder Out of China*. He worked for *The New Republic*, *The Reporter*, and *Collier's*.

In the late 1950s, White began covering American politics in depth. Though the traditional wisdom among newspaper people had been that nothing is deader than last year's political campaign, White decided to do a book about the campaign of 1960.

The Making of the President 1960 not only became a best seller—but won a Pulitzer Prize. It also spawned a whole genre of imitators. White has since produced a series on the various campaigns, culminating in the new book which covers a quarter century of change in American life and politics.

America in Search of Itself: The Making of the President 1956–80 is published by Harper & Row.

Q. *You say in your book that since World War II, there have been five great landslides, but only one "repudiation."*

What do you mean by that? Why was the election of 1980 a repudiation?

A. *If you ask me, I think Jimmy Carter gave the American people no sense whatsoever of where he was going.*

He promised them the gospel and human rights and equal rights for everybody. He was going to take care of the sick, the old, the women, the minorities, the students, and the teachers. He was full of goodwill, but he had no sense of where the country was going or of all these vast events going on from the outside.

You had the sense of humiliation over the hostages in Iran. You had the sense of an uncontrollable inflation. All Jimmy Carter was promising were visions—but the visions were more of the same. They were the same visions that had been promised to the American people since at least the time of John F. Kennedy, perhaps since the time of Franklin D. Roosevelt.

Finally, the American people had it. They could not see where these visions, where the Democratic party, if such exists, was going. In that sense, it was a repudiation of a sitting President—and that hasn't taken place since Herbert Hoover.

[EDITOR'S NOTE: President Ford was, of course, defeated in 1976. But he was a special case, never having been originally elected to either the Presidency or Vice Presidency.]

Q. *We'll get back to the issue of one-term Presidents later on.*

I want to ask you this. Years ago, political scientists used to say that Americans voted on the basis of the head, the heart, and the pocketbook. You put it into sharper focus.

You categorize the basic voting issues as bread and butter, war and peace, black and white.

A. *I think if you take any period of American history and tap on it, and the magnetic filings line up around the magnetic poles, the elections revolve around one or another of these issues. 1932 was a bread and butter election; 1940 was a war and peace election; 1916 was "Wilson, he kept us out of war." Lincoln's election was black and white. How will our black citizens live?*

As I say, bread and butter, black and white, war and peace. Of these, I can't say which is the most important. All three of them have torn America apart since at least 1800, with the Alien and Sedition Acts.

Q. *You write in your book, "In trying to eradicate racism, the politics of the sixties and seventies had institutionalized it." What do you mean?*

A. *We have now categories of people who are entitled to special protection or special privileges because of their birth, their race, their ethnic heritage or their sex. So you have a situation where a policeman seeking a promotion in Miami has to prove that his name, which sounds German, conceals the fact that his grandfather was Cuban, so he can qualify as a Hispanic minority.*

I have documents this thick on all the laws and federal interpretations of the laws of just who is a minority. An Asian American is an officially classified minority. As an Asian American, he is entitled to certain privileges, legally and statutorily. So is an American Indian. So are Blacks. But then you have to define with laws almost like Nuremburg—who is a Black? If you have one-half black blood in you . . . these are horrible words, these words have never occurred in American history before. But you find them now in Supreme Court decisions, the famous Stevens and Stewart dissents in Fullilove versus Klutznick, bloodlines, what percentage of black blood makes you entitled to a protection or a privilege as a member of that minority? In Hitler's Germany, you were defined as Jewish if you had one Jewish great-grandmother, you were tainted. Here, we haven't got Nuremburg laws, but in this country, if you had a black grandmother or a great-grandmother of minority heritage, you can be classified as entitled—the legal phrase is "a member of the protected classes."

Now these things amount in the end, I believe, to a reverse discrimination that could tear America apart.

Q. *Let me take another quote from your book where you say: "The liberals had set out to free everyone, and had created a nation of dependents instead."*

A. *I think after that I follow with the phrase, "and dependency does not go with liberty."*

I define myself as a "second-look liberal." No one can take the badge away from me. You don't hand out badges called "liberal," it's a self-defined category. A "second-look liberal" like me is a guy who looks back over the past 20 or 30 years and says, "God, we've done some wonderful things, we've achieved stupendous triumphs. We've also made some awful mistakes. So let's look back and figure out what we did right and what we did wrong."

Now almost everything we liberals did in the past 30 years was colored with virtue. It's what I call the "tyranny of virtue." You can't vote against aid to the handicapped, you can't vote against rat control programs in the big city, you can't vote against the enormous development of medical services. Your conscience won't let you. You can't vote against Medicare or Medicaid. You can't vote against free school lunches.

When you add all of these things up, and put them all together in a package—when you set down the old package of privileges, like veterans' bonuses or veterans' pensions, or the farmers' protected prices, and the banks get their bit of it and the big aircraft companies get their bit of it—you have a society which is more dependent on the largesse of the federal government than we liberals ever conceived of in the beginning.

There are 36 million people on Social Security, or there were back in 1980 when I wrote this book—36 million people on Social Security, 26 million on Medicare, 22 million on Medicaid, 18 million on food stamps, 27 million on school lunch programs. You have 3½ million college students on federal loans or grants, plus the kids who are going to state universities, which also are publicly subsidized for funds. You've got the peanut farmers with their protection. All in all, probably between one-third or one-half of all the American people in some way or another are supported, subsidized or protected by the American government.

When you've got a government that large, you have, in effect, a bureaucratic tyranny.

Here in New York City, at 63rd Street, we are building the most magnificent subway station in the USA. In one of the clauses, I think, of the Rehabilitation Act, it says that no federal funds will go to a mass transit project unless it provides ramps, lifts, and elevators for the handicapped.

The subway stations over here at the corner of 63rd and Lexington will be a dream of ramps, lifts, elevators. That's lovely—except for the fact that the poor handicapped, once they get down safely into that subway, will have no place to go. Because they can't get out at 34th Street, they can't get out at Chambers Street, they can't get out at Far Rockaway, they can't get out in the Bronx. Because it would take untold millions to equip all the hundreds of subway stations in New York with ramps and elevators.

So here we have this enormous expenditure for building this magnificent subway station, and then all that it'll do is ride around the circuit and come out at the same place.

Is there a politician in New York who would dare to say that's a waste of money? But it would be cheaper to take the handicapped by cab or by bus to their jobs in the morning than put in the installation over there. It will be one of the most expensive in the USA. This subway system—this stretch of subway over here between Central Park and the East River will probably cost us as much as one of these spectacular aircraft carriers.

We've created a nation of dependents. How to unravel that, no one knows. How to pay for it, no one knows. That gets us to a social, cultural, economic crisis the like of which we haven't seen since 1932.

Q. *The next quote I pulled out from your book dealt with the election of 1956, but it might have implications for today. You're talking about the Suez crisis—and the election of 1956—which had "befuddled America's ability to discriminate between its moralities and its interests." Is that still true today?*

A. *I think it's the malignancy of American foreign policy—it's still true today.*

Q. *Now let's go on very specifically to the 1980 election. Carter blamed his defeat on Ted Kennedy, inflation, and Iran. Based on the election results, do you agree with him?*

A. *Here you get into the realm of ifs. I think it was the combination of those three things that torpedoed Carter. I really doubt whether Carter would have won even if Kennedy stayed out of it. I doubt whether Carter could have won if Iran had not taken place. But the combination of those three things sunk him.*

We had lost our power to control events, either at home or abroad.

Q. *Let me ask you this. Here I'm pulling a name out of the past—Governor George Wallace. Do you think he possibly had more to do with the Reagan sweep than we gave him credit for?*

A. *No.*

Q. *No, I mean, even in terms of finding the blue-collar voter?*

A. *If you were a sociologist and you wanted to describe the trends and movements, there'd certainly be a paragraph.*

I would go to the Wallace rallies, and these were the kind of people I knew in the war. Although World War II was commanded and directed by intellectuals from Marshall to Oppenheimer to Stimson, the guys who fought the war were blue-collar workers. The truck drivers drove tanks, the construction workers went into the Engineer Corps, and the farmers became infantrymen. These blue-collar kids—and we used them well—were really the guts and the core of the U.S. Army and the U.S. infantry.

Now, these guys had always felt aggrieved. The other guys went to college under the GI Bill of Rights, but they went back to their jobs in the factories. They always felt aggrieved. Infantrymen always do, and they have every reason to feel that way.

Certainly, the blue-collar workers had voted for Roosevelt. He was their President more than anybody else's President. There was that thrust of the blue-collar worker. The blue-collar worker was behind Harry Truman. He spoke their language.

Wallace was the first guy to try to take the blue-collar worker away from the Democratic party. And that's where he had his success. There was also in Wallace, of course, a radical streak of racism, and that made it a hell of a lot easier for him to get his message over in the blue-collar areas.

But Reagan did something else. Reagan really addressed himself to the ethnic background of the blue-collar workers. To a very large extent, at least here in the East, our ethnics are very socially conservative. An Italian American family looks forward to buying its own little house in the suburbs, with a little bit of land around it. They have a fig tree or a grapevine, and that's their house they love. They love their house. They don't want to be pushed around by the local taxpayer. They are also family oriented—that goes for the Slavs, the Italians, many other ethnics.

Reagan tapped that one—he tapped that one easily. Wallace may have made more visible in politics the presence of the blue-collar worker as an alienated group, but he himself was a passing phenomenon.

One of the things I tried to do with this book is try to pinpoint where the groundswell, an underswell, a movement in American history—comes to a peak or finds its spokesman in characters who are now probably long since forgotten.

Why do I give Estes Kefauver so much space in this book? Estes Kefauver invented the modern primary system. He was the first guy who really took advantage of it to make this nonsensical marathon across the country back in 1952. He deserved some space. Fannie Lou Hamer—and I'm sure you've forgotten her name—Fannie Lou Hamer was a black woman from Mississippi who got beat up for trying to vote. But boy, when she came to the Atlantic City Democratic convention in 1964, she told her story, sobbing. They had beat her in a cell in Mississippi. They had pulled her dress up and they had humiliated her.

You couldn't not gulp with shame and agony that people would do this in the USA. So I put Fannie Lou Hamer in the book because I think her one day of glory there did much more to change the rules of the Democratic party, and thus bring about the Voting Rights Act, than any other episode.

So in a parade of characters like this, the last 25 years of American history—I find George Wallace a hell of a lot less significant than the other characters I've tried to describe.

Q. *You point out in you book that 90% of the Blacks voted for Carter and 56% of the whites voted for Reagan, and only 35% of the whites voted for Carter. Now isn't this a very dangerous trend in American politics—I mean really dangerous?*

A. *That's why I printed the figures. There it is, the stark and glaring fact. That's something we have to pay attention to—because with all the talk of building bridges, there's a* cleavage *going on, and I find the cleavage not only in the voting statistics, but in the big cities. In the Northeast, the Whites are abandoning the big cities. They are fleeing from the big cities for whatever reasons—but they are. The big cities are becoming ever inceasingly populated by minorities. So instead of building, as we should, instead of building bridges between the races, we're digging a gulf—we're digging a moat around the big cities.*

The very rich and the very underprivileged can live in the big cities. The rest of America lives in the suburbs. That's not a healthy phenomenon. Nor are the voting statistics a healthy thing.

Q. *You spoke before about the primaries. In your book, you talk about primaries being "a triumph of goodwill over common sense."*

When I went to school, we were taught that the primary was the democratic thing. You say whom you favor for your party's candidate. How has that changed over the last 25 years?

A. *The largest factor in changing the primary system has been television. It incubates an artificial interest—it's like the National Football League. It goes on for four months, from February in New Hampshire to June in California. There are more different primaries, and more different rules. Even people like myself, who are supposed to report these things, cannot keep up with all the changes in the rules.*

You thus develop a corps of professionals who know the rules and know the ethnic breakdown of every state, and on top of that corps comes the "T-corps" of the people who know how to use it—television. They put on a series of vaudeville acts in each primary state, partly to reach the locals—but more to reach the national audience.

It's become not so much a reasoned choice of local citizens voting by local journals. It's become a kind of mass dance where you all dance to the tune of television. ABC and NBC and CBS descend upon a state, and they drench it, when they decide on whom to report and on whom not to report. The people in the state say, "Oh, you must be important because you're getting all that time."

And if ABC, NBC and CBS decide not to report somebody like a Terry Sanford or a John Anderson, then the person doesn't exist. Then the local people say, "Well, we didn't see him on the air."

The primaries were an idea of goodwill—take the choice of a candidate out of the hands of the bosses, and put the choice of a candidate in the hands of the people. Now, it's into the hands of a new breed of professionals. Professional analysts, professional television manipulators—people who can pare your message into a 30-second message or a 60-second message or a five-minute message—they spend so much time sandpapering these messages, it's going into the hands of a new breed of people—they don't smoke cigars; they know how to work computers.

If you talk of the back room boys right now, it's the back room guys punching the keys of computers. It's not the back room boys smoking cigars that are handing out the spoils.

Q. *We'll get back to television in a little bit, but I want to ask you this. Right now, we have the Democrats and Republicans, of course. But we also have the "boll weevils" and we have the "gypsy moths," and now I think there's something called the "yellow jackets," a whole other group. What is happening to party discipline? What is happening to the party responsibility?*

A. *I could give you the same answer there. They're no longer dependent upon the party machinery to get elected—either to Congress or to the Presidency. They get elected by mobilizing—very frequently by ignoring totally the party structure. They organize their own meetings, their own television, their own appearances. They're divorced. They're not dependent. They don't come up from being a city councilman or a sheriff or a member of the local school committee. They raise a bit of dough and off they are.*

Most of the younger Congressmen are of a quality higher, better, intellectually more preceptive, more honest than the Congressmen I knew 25 years ago. The trouble is, they're all so damned bright that each one of them has his pet issue, his pet project, and will do anything to move his pet project to the fore.

They cannot be controlled by the old Dick Daley, who used to send 11 Congressmen from Chicago to Washington. When Franklin D. Roosevelt or Harry Truman or Lyndon Johnson needed those 11 or 12 votes, they would call up the Cook County machine, whether it was Jake Arvey or Dick Daley, and they'd say, "Hey, we need those votes." And he would call the Congressmen and tell them how to vote.

There are very few Congressmen left who are controlled by the party machinery back home. They act out of conviction. They act under the pressure of special interests.

Party control is eroding year by year.

Q. *In* The Making of the President 1960, *you had this wonderful story about Senator Humphrey paying a bill of $750 for televsion time in the West Virginia primary.*

A. *Yes.*

Q. *In 1980, you estimated that $400 million was spent to elect the President.*

A. *The costs have gone up immensely. Look, do you know what it costs now? In the 1970s, the prime spot people would buy—if you'd try to buy it—was one minute at the Olympics. I forget what it cost—$200,000 or $300,000 for a minute.*

By 1984, to buy a minute on the Olympics, a full minute on the Olympics—will cost $700,000 or $800,000. Not even the richest candidate can afford that. What's going up also is the professionalism of politics, and maybe that's good.

In the old days, the party would be staffed by local party people, who *would expect a little patronage, a slice of the pie, after everything was won. Most of the guys who are staffing campaigns right now won't do it for a cheap job or a cheap favor. They don't want a parking ticket fixed, or you know, an overdue library card fixed. Most of the guys now are professionals who expect to be paid professional fees. The wonderful young kids of the McCarthy movement in 1968 are now, generally speaking, approaching 40. You want to hire them for a campaign, they want $50,000 a year! You have to have them. Rich amateurs can work without money. The old days—when you could get a horde of student volunteers to work for peanut butter sandwiches and bus fare—are over. Those people all want to be paid now, all across the board.*

The cost of television time has gone up so enormously that it's the largest expenditure.

Q. *Speaking of television, you quote TV news producer Don Hewitt: "We may be in for a series of one-term Presidents. Presidents are overexposed, become targets, they get taken apart. They're like a TV series—four years, and the public gets bored, they tune out. They want a new show every four years."*

A. *The reason I quoted him was very simple. I happen to agree with him. This is a typical week in American life. Ten days ago we saw Ronald Reagan in Versailles. Then we saw Ronald Reagan the next day in London. Then we saw Ronald Reagan—it was like the Rover Boys adventures.*

Then we see Ronald Reagan in Bonn; then he comes home and we see Ronald Reagan announcing the resignation of Al Haig—and tomorrow night he's going to give a press conference.

Five nights out of the week you see something more or less about Ronald Reagan. Charming as he is, the charm will wear thin—and it's beginning to wear thin. You can't take all that in your home every evening. You begin to know his quips, you begin to know his reactions. I think people do get bored.

Q. *Ronald Reagan is the first President we have ever had who was a trained actor. Is that the direction we're moving in? Looking for candidates who have had, literally, acting experience?*

A. *No, no, no. I think you're only about five degrees off true course. We vote for a brand name, we look for recognizable names. The recognizable names can come to us in a star basketball player like Bill Bradley of New Jersey. They can come to us via the astronaut thing, like Harrison Schmidt or John Glenn. They can come to us by heredity—recognizable brand names, like a Kennedy or a Taft or a Roosevelt. Actors are only one of the recognizable types in American life.*

A village actor would get nowhere; Ronald Reagan was a minor national actor. Most of the great Presidents have been good actors.

Churchill was a tremendous actor, you know. Those phrases of his and then the way he used his hands: "Some chicken . . . some neck!"

A politician has to know how to hold a crowd.

Q. *You've been on* Time *magazine and* The New Republic, *and* Reporter *and* Collier's. *What has been happening to the "pencil press," as you call it? What's happening to the newspapers and the magazines?*

A. *You're talking about a vast universe of things when you speak of the "pencil press," which is a phrase I admit I use. The daily newspapers are going through a kind of trauma of their own. The afternoon newspaper in the big cities of the USA is dying. Good God, the* Cleveland Press *is gone, the* Washington Star, *the* Philadelphia Bulletin, *all of those within the past year or so.*

The average American now gets all the news he thinks he needs on the half-hour television show. Furthermore, they don't much ride home on the subways now—they drive home. The great papers of the country are flourishing, they're making money—The New York Times is, the Boston Globe is, the Los Angeles Times is, the Washington Post is. But the great national papers of the country become more and more the domain of the American thinking elite.

Your average guy doesn't read The New York Times *on the subway—I bet you do!*

Q. *Of course.*

A. *Which one of us can get along without* The New York Times? *In Chicago you read the* Trib *or the* Sun-Times.

I'll try to avoid the word "elitist," but I think we're going to have to recognize that the full-bodied national newspaper that we used to take for granted is now becoming something that, in terms of marketing, delivers an upscale audience. The newspapers below that are competing with television—and they can't compete with television, either for violence or action. "You are there at the scene of the crime," says the guy on TV, and you are there at the scene of the crime. You see the woman crying, or you see the dead body covered in canvas. You are there at the horrors. So TV is undermining any newspaper, any afternoon newspaper that tries to compete with television. In this universe of Gutenberg, the magazines are not doing badly. The mass magazines that try to address everybody were killed off by television—Collier's, the Saturday Evening Post, all of them are gone. Television took our audience away from us.

The specialized magazines are doing fairly well. Time magazine has never done better, business magazines have never done better, the art magazines as well. Magazines now shoot for the specialized audiences, and magazines are prosperous these days. Not the old fashioned mass magazine. There'll be no Collier's or Saturday Evening Post any more. They're through. That audience has gone to television. But specialized magazines are doing better than ever. Books—take books—the book business is in very serious trouble. There is a price resistance now to the high price of books. I hope my book is not going to be too highly priced for the average reader, it still costs less than a bouquet of flowers. But the great explosion in reading has come in the paperback book, the mass market paperback book. You take a trip on an airplane and you walk down that aisle, and you'll find one-fifth of the people pulling a paper-back out of their bags.

Though it doesn't look so good in the dollar statistics, the paperback book is holding and gaining a tremendous share of the American audience.

All in all, as I say, you can't wrap up this universe of the Gutenberg world as one thing. Some are prospering and some are dying.

Q. There's a great deal of controversy over the networks using polls on Election Day to declare a winner before the polls are closed.

Art Buchwald really had the greatest column on this about two days after the election. Buchwald calls his friend in California and his friend says, "Please don't bother me, I'm going out to vote." Buchwald says to his friend, "What are you going to bother for? CBS just interviewed two guys in Harlem and one guy in Chicago, and somebody else in Atlanta—and Reagan has won. Everybody knows it—you're wasting your time."

Of course, Buchwald was kidding—but not really. There was an element of truth in what he was saying—and there is talk about passing a law so you can't do that, you can't have your poll results declared while the voting is still going on, at least in the continental United States.

A. I've been in this trade, if you want to call it that, 28 years. In those 28 years, scientific polling has become an instrument of such sophistication that you can't imagine.

When I began back then, the rule of thumb was if either party gains one seat in Connecticut, it'll gain 10 seats across the country. If they gain two seats in Connecticut, they'll gain 20 seats across the country—old veteran reporters' folklore. The town you'd wait for would be Bridgeport, Connecticut. Bridgeport, Connecticut had a heavy working-class blue-collar population. They also had voting machines so that they got the results very quickly.

If the Democrats didn't carry Bridgeport, Connecticut by 65 to 70%—they were dead across the country. It was a bellwether city. You waited for that one. The 1956 election was the first one I covered. In Bridgeport, Eisenhower was running neck and neck with Stevenson. We knew then that Stevenson didn't have a chance. It was true. Eisenhower was going to sweep.

Today, you don't judge by such a rule of thumb. You have poll takers out there, in hundreds and hundreds of carefully selected precincts across the country—blue-collar, white-collar, black, white, rural, urban, subur-ban. NBC interviewed 38,000 people on Election Day. You do that by two slices. There's a morning slice and an afternoon slice. You interview key precincts—very scientifically. You interview one out of seven voters. You ask them a few questions about their background, who they've voted for, things like that. By 11 o'clock in the morning, you have a pretty good idea of how the country is going. By three o'clock in the afternoon when you do the second slice, you almost hit it exactly on the nose as to what it's going to be.

I worked for NBC this last election, and I knew how the results were running in our straw poll. Before I got to the studio at five o'clock in the afternoon, I made a call to the White House to see how their polls were running.

The White House people said, "It's all over. We're 10 points behind. We've lost it." They say "We lost it and we're 10 points behind." That's a fact. I go in to NBC, and say, "Hey fellows, you know what I just learned?" And they said, "We got it, too." And you knew at that point, if they've got it, then CBS has got it, ABC has got it, and Ronnie Reagan's camp has it, also. It's a fact, now, that at five o'clock in the afternoon, every network knows, both headquarters know, that Reagan is going to win by more or less, 10 points. What do you do?

Can you conceal that fact from the public? I had to go on the first half hour of the show, and I asked the producers, "Now what the hell do I say?" And they said, "Well, talk as if the thing were undecided. Talk as to what may be in the offing tonight. Make believe you don't know, and talk about the potential for a landslide tonight that we must watch during the evening." Some of these reviews, which are very critical, tell that story from the book and say, "He admitted he lied on election night." Okay.

Was I lying when I said we must wait and see what the results of the evening show us? Who was I kidding? Should I have responded to my critics by saying, "At five o'clock, you know, the polls in California are still open. It's two in the afternoon"?

This is a moral question. I know when the moral question first came up, when all this scientific stuff began to develop, in 1964. Johnson was a landslide winner, and he knew it at two o'clock in the afternoon. With the apparatus we had, we knew who was going to win in 1964.

Most of the Democrats, most working-class people, vote in the evening, after they come home from work. They come home, they get supper with their wives and then they go out to the polls. The blue collar vote comes in basically between five and eight everywhere. School teachers, older people—vote in the morning. Pierre Salinger was running against George Murphy for the U.S. Senate. Pierre Salinger believes to this day that the fact that the networks announced that the race was all over, that there was no point in California voting, because Johnson was elected by a landslide—kept hundreds of thousands of workingclass people home. They would have voted for Pierre, who was the Democrat, against Murphy, the Republican, had they gone to the polls.

But since the Presidency was decided, what the hell? They decided not to go to the polls. Sure, the early prediction has an effect on the entire West Coast voting.

What am I supposed to do? You suggest that the votes should not be counted in the continental USA until a given hour all across the country? That doesn't take care of the pollsters. You can't forbid CBS or NBC or

ABC from putting their pretty girls outside the polling places, precincts, and asking questions. And then what do we do—conceal? So you see, I don't know. I described the situation as it appears to us. I ask your readers to give me their opinion. Do we conceal what we know?

Q. *Okay, we're going to ask our readers, and when the results come in, I'll let you know. I promise.*

I want to go into the methods that you use in doing your book. First of all, there's the subtitle of the new book, The Making of the President, 1956–1980. *Now what I thought was interesting about that, your first book was really 1960—obviously you started before that, but why did you start with '56 in this particular book?*

A. *There's a two-part answer to your question. What we had in 1956 was America at perihelion. You know those historical maps, "Rome at the greatest extent of its power." America's greatest extent to its power and the greatest period of its prosperity was 1956. It was an election in a tranquil, happy, contented country, with all the old-fashioned machinery of politics still in place.*

[Editor's NOTE: 1956 was a year of virtual tranquility until the very last weeks before the election, when the Russians invaded Hungary and the Israelis, British, and French invaded Suez. In his book, White makes extensive reference to these events.]

Eisenhower was chosen by the bosses, make no mistake about it. Stevenson was chosen by the bosses. Make no mistake about it. This is 1956 I'm talking about. All the old mechanics and machinery were there. Television played almost no role in it. That was what I call the Old Country. That's one reason why I started there.

The second is because—it's highly personal—I'd been a foreign correspondent for 15 years, I got back from all those years overseas in 1954, and it was only then that I began to cover American politics. In 1954, I began to cover the campaign of '56.

So, for two reasons—America at apogee. America prosperous and content. America, with the suburbs growing like mad, America with oil coming out of its ears. America with the highways crisscrossing it. America with television just invading the mind. So you begin there in the Old Country, and then you try to show how the country changed and what changed it.

Q. *In your book, you drew on two basic documents, which I found absolutely fascinating. One was Pat Caddell's memo to Jimmy Carter and the other was Richard Wirthlin's memo to Reagan, in effect setting forth what they felt was the way to go to win. How do you get access to documents like that?*

A. *I'll tell you a story. When I was a youngster, trying to work my way through college—I tried my hand at selling magazines from door to door. But an old-timer in the business said, "Don't get discouraged. If you*

*knock on 100 doors a day and you say, 'Lady, you want to buy a magazine?',
you'll find one lady who says yes."*

I have found that the best way of getting things is by being direct and
forthright and asking for it. I won't put on any false humility. I'm a
known quantity. I think I am recognized as one of the major political
writers in the country . . .
Q. *If not the major political writer . . .*
A. . . . and if when I go to Dick Wirthlin and say, "Look, the election is
over now, Dick. I'd like to see the planning documents, and I won't use
them until 9 months from now or a year from now." And I go to Pat
Caddell and I say the same thing—these are now historical documents.
The election is won and lost. Working with Pat Caddell for 10 years and
Dick Wirthlin for a year and a half, and talking to them all the time—you
say, "Please, please." They like to be recognized for their influence on a
campaign, and you'd be surprised at how much they give you.
Q. *James MacGregor Burns once wrote about Roosevelt. He titled his
book,* The Lion and the Fox, *quoting Machiavelli. Which recent Presi-
dents would you classify as lions and which ones as foxes?*
Let's start with Franklin Roosevelt.
A. *A lion.*
Q. *Harry Truman?*
A. He became a lion. He was the most miserable and unfortunate Presi-
dent of the USA for the first full year of his Presidency. After he learned
how to handle foreign affairs, he became a superb President. It takes a
year to learn the job. They all make their mistakes in the first year.
Q. *Eisenhower?*
A. *Neither a lion nor a fox.*
Q. *Kennedy?*
A. *Lion.*
Q. *Johnson?*
A. *Fox.*
Q. *Nixon?*
A. *Fox.*
Q. *Ford?*
A. *He doesn't fall into either one of those two things. Caretaker.*
Q. *Carter?*
A. *He can't fit the mold.*
Q. *I guess it's too early to ask about Ronald Reagan?*
A. Again, too early to ask about Ronald Reagan. The Machiavelli thing,
the lion and the fox, was written in an age of princelings, dukedoms,
hereditary autocrats, where wars and affairs were managed by legitimate
rulers. They fell generally into a lion category or a fox category: the sly
ones like Louis XI, the lion characters like Frederick the Great. But we
live in an age of democracy right now, of popular will. The forum has
changed, the elements have changed. The complexities have grown so

overwhelmingly that you cannot divide rulers. You can take the dictators, easy. Stalin was the fox. Mao Tse-tung was the lion. That's where the personality of the autocrat determines the policy of the state.

In our kind of country, I think Eisenhower was the most placid President we had in 50 years, and that was exactly what the American people wanted. They wanted the perimeters of America at perihelion. They wanted the perimeters preserved, they wanted no fooling around with any future war, they wanted him to shake a finger at Lebanon and Lebanon would collapse. He was a very placid President. The country prospered, and that's exactly what the country wanted. They didn't want any sly tricks—no more conquests, no more wars, no more grandeur.

Q. This will be the last question. You're talking now to about 18,000 social studies teachers around the country. What should they be teaching young people about American history and American politics?

A. Young people need heroes and villains. They can't and they shouldn't be loaded down with statistics. They should be taught, "Here are the men who changed things, heroes and villains alike." But then you go on to say, "You can't understand how these people followed one another unless you know the dates."

I believe that you can't understand history unless you know the dates. You know the Missouri Compromise, the Dred Scott decision, the Civil War. You've got to know the relationship between those things. You've got to know the simmering of the dates of the Black revolt in the South: the episodes of 1960, and the arrest of Martin Luther King, Jr.; 1961, the sit-ins; 1962, Old Miss; 1963, Birmingham; the growing indignation, until you get to 1964 and the Civil Rights Act.

So, first of all, heroes and villains. Next, that these people don't float airy-fairy unattached to their period. I think you need to know 50 key dates in American history and 50 key dates in world history to have some outline of the skeleton of history. But those they've got to know. They taught us that in 1492 Columbus discovered America; it was damned important. It was also important to know that William the Conqueror landed in England in 1066. And by 1099, only 30 years later, the Norman Crusaders are storming and capturing Jerusalem. What a surge of energy must have been latent in the Normans! That's a period of only 30 years—what happened?

You've got to say that these things are locked together in a certain time frame. The most difficult thing of all is to teach the youngsters that these men and these dates represent only the swelling of the forces. They have to know what the forces were which led up to these episodes, these heroes, and these villains. It's a most difficult thing to teach kids. It's a most difficult thing for you and me to grasp.

How do I describe the women's revolt? Or the gay revolt? Or any one of the other things in the USA? But these episodes are happening. There's a microcomputer revolution going on and the kids would be bored stiff.

But maybe they wouldn't be bored stiff if you talked about Henry Ford and the automobile. I don't know how you'd write a textbook to do that.

But dates are the nails that nail down history. Heroes and villains make it come alive. But the forces: the automobile, James Watt and the steam engine, education, the GI Bill of Rights—all these things have changed the contours of life. They force new groups to the front and lead to the development of these movements.

Q. *Thank you very much, Theodore White.*

II.

―――――

The Many Faces of Social Studies

IT MAY BE TRUE FOR POETS that a good poem "should not *mean* but *be*." Yet, for social studies educators, meaning can lead to being in the crucible of the schools. As a result, the search for a comprehensive and meaningful definition of the social studies has gone on for decades. It still continues today.

It has been pointed out that there are at least three major approaches to the social studies: social studies as a means of transmitting knowledge for effective citizenship; social studies as a modified form of the social sciences; and social studies as a process to develop reflective thinking. However, many teachers combine all of these and other approaches into a variety of personal patterns. Thus, there is not one but many faces of social studies and many ways of describing educational purposes, methods, and goals. The second section of this anthology is devoted to an examination of the various ways in which individuals writing in *Social Education* have viewed the social studies.

Although history is an important part of the social studies, tensions between those who advocate that education focus on either history or social studies have existed for years. In "A Memorandum from an Old Worker in the Vineyard," Charles A. Beard, whose *An Economic Interpretation of the Constitution* (1913) was a major contribution to historical scholarship, presents his position on the issue. "I do not propose 'either or'," he writes. "The social studies should be the crown of history, not a substitute for history." At the time of the publication of the article, Beard was a member of the Executive Board of *Social Education*.

In June 1942 a report published in the *New York Times* purported to show that colleges neglected the study of the United States. Then, in the *New York Times* of Sunday, April 4, 1943, another report, sponsored by the newspaper, concluded from a test of college freshmen's knowledge of American history that high school graduates had a deplorable lack of knowledge about the United States' past. A major point at issue was the relationship between the social studies and history.

Erling M. Hunt, the first editor of *Social Education*, responded to the first report by writing: "The joker in that report was the assumption that the students can learn about the United States only in courses labelled 'American History.' Courses in 'contemporary civilization,' 'social science,' government, economics, sociology, American literature, and modern history were coolly ignored, both in the statistics and in the demand for compulsory college courses in American history." As for the *New York Times* "test" on American history, Hunt continues, it was of questionable validity, amateurishly graded, poorly administered, and concerned exclusively with the ability to remember information.

No, Hunt insists, "social studies do not replace, or reduce, American history. They ought to make it more intelligible." It was never advisable to make Erling Hunt angry!

In 1959 *Social Education* asked the question: "How can authors and publishers add to the public's understanding of the structure and function of the American Government? Specifically, what areas of American Government should be given more thorough treatment in books that are published in the future?" Seven senators responded to the query, and their answers were published in the March 1959 issue of the journal. At the time, there was no way of knowing that two of the respondents would become president of the United States.

As in all professions, there are certain terms that have become a part of the basic vocabulary of social studies educators. One of these terms is "decision making," and few individuals have had the influence of Shirley H. Engle, then associate director for graduate development at Indiana University, in gaining support for it. As author of the selection "Decision Making: The Heart of Social Studies Instruction," Engle states his position clearly:

> My theme is a very simple one. It is that, in teaching the social studies, we should emphasize decision making as against mere remembering. We should emphasize decision making at two levels: at the level of deciding what a group of descriptive data means, how these data may be summarized or generalized, what principles they suggest; and also decision

making at the level of policy determination, which requires a synthesis of facts, principles, and values usually not found on one side of any question.

In 1955 Maurice P. Hunt and Lawrence E. Metcalf coauthored a social studies methods textbook, *Teaching High School Social Studies*, in which they stated: "The foremost aim of instruction in high school social studies is to help students examine reflectively issues in closed areas of American culture." By closed areas the authors meant "areas of belief and thought which are largely closed to rational thought." Irrational responses, they felt, often occur in such areas as economics, race and minority-group relations, and nationalism and patriotism. For their position the authors acknowledged the influence of the thinking of John Dewey, Boyd H. Bode, H. Gordon Hullfish, Alan Griffin, and Ernest E. Bayles. The article "Some Guidelines for Changing Social Studies Education" explores significant aspects of social studies education from this point of view.

Edwin Fenton, professor of history at Carnegie-Mellon University, provided leadership for the New Social Studies movement, and was one of its dominant figures. Of particular interest to him was the training of students in the process of inquiry, although Fenton's thinking also encompassed a variety of other ideas concerning ways to improve teaching. Thus, he developed stimulating approaches to teaching of social studies, directed the preparation of innovative materials for students and teachers, and wrote extensively in order to discuss viewpoints with colleagues. Fenton's article, "History in the New Social Studies," brings together several of his key ideas on objectives, teaching strategies, materials, and evaluation.

At the beginning of the 1960s Harvard psychologist Jerome Bruner came out strongly for what was called the "structure" of a discipline. In *The Process of Education*, he wrote: "the curriculum of a subject should be determined by the most fundamental understanding that can be achieved of the underlying principles that give structure to that subject." Discussion of the term "structure" and of its implications, not only in physics and mathematics but in the social studies, became widespread—and often heated—among educators. In the article "Bruner's New Social Studies: A Critique," Mark M. Krug of the University of Chicago sets down his reactions to Bruner's idea of structure, as well as to Bruner's views on objectives, methodology, and the role of history.

In the article "Social Studies: The Need for Redefinition," James P. Shaver, professor and associate dean for research at Utah State University in Logan, claims that the point of view in which the social studies are defined as the social sciences adapted and simplified for pedagogical purposes "has perhaps done more to stifle creative curriculum work in the social studies than any other factor." Shaver urges that attention be given to a more viable definition: social studies as that part of the school's general education program that is concerned with the preparation of citizens for participation in a democratic society. Shaver was writing in 1967. Two decades later, the debate about finding a workable definition of the social studies persists.

The writings of C. Benjamin Cox, professor of education at the University of Illinois at Urbana-Champaign, consistently demonstrate that he has the ability to combine scholarship with common sense. Cox's sense of balance is illustrated by his article, "Behavior as Objective in Education," presented here in abridged form. Recognizing that the popularity of the idea of behavioral objectives is both "warranted on solid grounds and mindlessly promoted," he judiciously examines the major aspects of the idea as he assesses the nature, uses, and kinds of behavioral objectives.

As William F. Russell Professor in the Foundations of Education at Teachers College, Columbia University, R. Freeman Butts worked closely with a variety of leaders of American education: Edward H. Reisner, R. Bruce Raup, Kenneth D. Benne, Donald G. Tewksbury, George S. Counts, John L. Childs, William H. Kilpatrick, Harold Rugg, I. L. Kandel, and Merle Curti. As a result, he is able to examine educational and societal developments from a broad viewpoint. His article, "The Revival of Civic Learning," which was originally delivered as an address at the 1978 National Conference on Civic Education in Los Angeles, is a strong statement urging us to "give a new sense of meaning to the ideas and values which have been dislocated from our traditional civic community." Like the American poet Edgar Lee Masters, Butts makes clear that the time has come to approach America not with the circumscribed two-step but with the grand stride; not with the quibbling footnote but with the master themes.

A Memorandum from an Old Worker in the Vineyard

CHARLES A. BEARD

There seems to be a decided tendency among teachers of the humanistic subjects to discard history as a kind of old almanac and to concentrate upon events of the day or, perhaps it would be more correct to say, events of the last few days. A more than casual glance at recent textbooks and articles in teachers' magazines discloses some warrant for that conclusion. Where the long past is not entirely discarded, it is likely to be employed merely in furnishing illustrations of current conceptions and practices or, perhaps, the processes by which they came into being.

This tendency is, in my opinion, wholesome in many respects. It reveals a growing interest in public affairs and a desire to come to grips with pressing issues of our own time. It also represents a healthy revolt against the political and military history that almost monopolized for many years the thought of historians, especially those who wrote for the schools. If history is being shot out to the rubbish heap, no small part of the responsibility rests upon historians themselves.

Yet the tendency to throw history away or treat it as a kind of convenient nuisance raises doubts in my mind. Does it represent a widening and enriching of knowledge and thought? Do the substitutes offered give pupils a more realistic understanding of the world in which they are to live and work? If the prime end of education is to enrich personalities and help to prepare them for life and labor in their times and circumstances, can this be done best by instruction essentially con-

NOTE: This article appeared in *Social Education*, September 1938, pp. 383–385.

cerned with current systems of thought and current events? And, finally, is this the best methodology, the best way of giving pupils an insight into great issues of life and society and into the manner of considering them?

For many reasons I have arrived at negative answers to these questions. What I have to say, of course, may be discounted on the ground that I am a maker of old almanacs myself and am defending my own craft. There may be something in that response. Yet I have been all along deeply interested in current affairs, in present day systems at work, in the issues of the hour. Surely the most critical reader will concede as much. Nevertheless in the lengthening shadows of a long and busy life, I am more convinced than ever that social studies which discard or minimize history are superficial in the worst sense of that word, dilute rather than enrich thought, and give pupils a false perspective of life itself and even the very subjects taught.

My reasons? In the first place it must be conceded that economics, sociology, politics, civics, and all the other subjects which deal with the surface of our time are enclosed in a larger context of time which we call history. Some economists are fond of saying, for instance, that their system would work all right if it were not for politicians and wars. They may be correct in this verdict, but there are politicians and wars—in history. Pure reason may do little with them, but historical backgrounds can help to account for them and their doings. As Croce has said, men make their little systems, and the movement of history as actuality destroys them. Any treatment of a current system of thought which does not deal with its development or dynamics and with the forces outside that impinge upon it is as unreal as the old drum and trumpet history once taught in the schools. And how are we to get an idea of its dynamics, if we know little or nothing of the time trend in which the system appeared? How indeed?

Hence in my opinion books and courses on current systems or current "problems" lack the substance of life, which is dynamic. And only out of history can come knowledge of dynamics, for it is not given to us to trace the far trajectory of the future. Social studies are necessarily superficial in that they treat of matters within a shallow time depth—the alleged present which does not exist—or two, three, or more little years. They are wanting in the time sense. They belong with the movies and sports rather than with education as preparation for dealing with the world and its works, its tough heritage which is ever with us, and its grand and universal conceptions. Nobody is so unpractical as the practical person who knows only his little corner and his narrow today.

Now I come to methodology. Much is made in the social studies of so-called current problems. Of course they are not problems at all in the correct sense of that term. We can solve problems in arithmetic, test the answers, and call them settled. In large human affairs there are no neat little problems. There are issues, contested issues, with which we can and do grapple. History does not repeat itself, but in times past nearly every one of the issues that are so hot today has appeared in one form or another, and men and women have grappled with them, and have disposed of them in some fashion—for their time, or passed them on.

Now everybody knows that we all have a lot of roaring prejudices on current questions of labor and capital, for example, and that it is a frightful strain on our common sense to look at such matters calmly. Yet it is the business of education to train our minds for considering such issues. If we are to fight them out with our fists in the streets, then we might as well shut up the schools. To my way of thinking it is bad pedagogy, that is, likely to defeat the ends sought, to jump right into the middle of current disputes without having any knowledge of their history, of the complicated circumstances in which they arose. A knowledge of the rise of the industrial system and the labor movement is, as I see things, a far better equipment for dealing with the Committee for Industrial Organization than any textbook on contemporary economic theory or civics.

And the acquisition of such knowledge through the study of history is not accompanied by the heats and distempers that accompany the reading of current news stories about strikes and riots. If the marks of an educated person are moderation, judicial qualities, acquaintance with origins and developments, then the study of matters that do not arouse immediate passions is especially conducive to bringing up a generation of educated persons. It is possible to find in distant debates on the tariff question, for example, arguments and conclusions of minds superior to the average run today and at the same time pertinent and informing in respect of a matter as current as the discussion of reciprocal trade treaties.

A final point is even more conclusive for me. No person can be called truly educated unless he has come into intimate and immediate contact with first rate minds. With all due respect for the makers of textbooks, of whom I am one, few among them can claim the strength, insight, mastery, and dignity of style to be found in the great writings of history—Aristotle, Plato, Adam Smith, or Alexander Hamilton, for instance. In my opinion the wishy-washy, slovenly, third-rate style of modern books, betraying poverty of thought and lack of energy, is largely due to the fact that the authors have made no long and assiduous study of works truly classic, that is, historical, in wisdom and expression. And power of style is power of mind. If history is thrown out and we concentrate on contemporary newspapers and textbooks, we are bound to be at best second rate. Even if the maker of a text is a distinguished stylist, he is certainly not likely to be a distinguished maker of history in the manner of Jefferson or Hamilton.

In closing I do not propose an "either or," but a considerate adjustment, for a balanced emphasis. The social studies should be the crown of history, not a substitute for history. Obligations rest upon those who are too hotly pursuing the morning newspaper to stop their light-hearted running and give more thought to the place of history in social instruction. Historians also have an obligation—to make their written history touch human life on all sides, the life of the great and the humble. Then that which should never have been put asunder may be wisely joined again.

The *New York Times* "Test"
on American History

ERLING M. HUNT

Twice within a year the *New York Times* has made the teaching of American history the subject, not to say the victim, of an excursion into sensational journalism. Last June an elaborate report, complete with statistics, purported to show that colleges neglect the study of the United States. The joker in that report was the assumption that students can learn about the United States only in courses labelled "American History." Courses in "contemporary civilization," "social science," government, economics, sociology, American literature, and modern history were coolly ignored, both in the statistics and in the demand for compulsory college courses in American history. So was the fact that most pupils in elementary and secondary schools are required to survey American history three times, and that such study of the United States is supplemented by required study of geography, civics, and often of modern problems and European or world history.

The *Times* may have had a sincere interest in advancing the study of American history. But if its campaign has the effect of decreasing attention to economics, government, sociology, current issues and problems, and the history of the rest of the world, it is likely best to serve the interests of extreme nationalists and those reactionaries who prefer not to have present social and economic issues and our world relationships considered.

No one questions the value, or the indispensability, of American history. But certainly it has no monopoly on the study of the United States.

NOTE: This article appeared in *Social Education*, May 1943, pp. 195–200, 240.

American history need not be jingoistic. Nor need it neglect current issues and problems. But the kind of history which the *Times'* second venture into misleading statistics seems to advocate certainly has little connection with the living present.

Is the *Times* Test Valid?

The test of freshman knowledge of American history sponsored by the *New York Times*, and reported in the issue of Sunday, April 4, is an incredibly casual instrument of measurement. Ignoring the fact that testing is a highly technical field, requiring experts such as those employed by the College Entrance Examination Board, the Cooperative Test Service, the Regents in the State of New York, and many leading universities, the *Times* used a test put together by a graduate-school professor of history, inexperienced in such testing, and a journalist with no educational experience other than some recent publicity work for the U. S. Office of Education. Some questions seem to have been taken from a Regents' test, though correlations with the results in New York State are not reported. The test is concerned exclusively with ability to remember information. Items on which students did badly included:

1. Name the thirteen original states—Only 6 per cent answered without error. The percentage with only one or two errors (as including Maine or Vermont) is not reported.

6. "Put in their proper sequence" questions, including (1) The Boy Scout Movement, (2) First Social Settlement Houses, (3) Transcendentalism, and (4) The First Women's Colleges.—A single error throws out the entire answer in each of four such series, though dates for (3) and (4) are arbitrary, as is the *Times* "correct answer."

10. Who was President during the War of 1812?—during the Mexican War? . . .

14. What has been the traditional American policy toward China? The only "correct answer" calls for a parrot's response; "Open Door" is mere verbalism, and we have policies toward China that antedate John Hay.

15. When was the Homestead Act passed? Before the passage of the Homestead Act what was the minimum price per acre of Federal public lands sold at auction?—The answers, 1862 and $1.25, must be precise to be allowed. Is this information characteristic of the history that is to be drilled into the heads of young Americans? Does this take precedence over history—or "social studies"— concerned with vital aspects of, say, the agricultural problem in America?

21. Which was the first United States census in which railway mileage could have been reported?—The answer, given as 1840, ignores roads built before 1830.

22. Beginning with Massachusetts, name the eleven States in their geographical order from north to south.—The question does not make sense. The "correct answer," which omits Pennsylvania, reveals that the word "coastal" was left out. The question was tricky in the first place, became unintelligible when incorrectly put, and the "correct answer" is simply wrong.

Similarly wrong is the "correct answer" to the question on the location of Portland, Oregon, which is on the Willamette, not the Columbia River. The Editor of the *Times*, in defending the "correct answer" against a Brooklyn College freshman's protests, declares it to be right since the Willamette is a tributary of the Columbia—which would seem to put Cincinnati on the Mississippi!

Other items call for naming the home States of Thomas Hart Benton, James K. Polk, and Mark Hanna, and for indicating what Jay Cooke, Carl Schurz, James J. Hill, Nicholas Biddle, and Alexander H. Stephens were "principally famous as." No doubt these names belong in the textbooks, and young Americans should hear of them. But is effective teaching to be judged by the ability even of college freshmen to identify them? Are they more important than study of the history and present status of agriculture, industry, labor, the role of government in modern life, programs of social security, and our changing relations to the rest of the world?

The chronological distribution of the questions calls for attention. Excluding seventeen geography items and eight men currently conspicuous in American affairs, a total of 101 answers is called for.[1] Of these, one relates to the colonial period (Roger Williams). Sixty-three relate to the period from 1787 through 1865. Thirty relate to the period 1866 through 1900 (ten persons lived on into the twentieth century). But *only five items* are specifically concerned with the period since 1900, though six others might be answered in terms of this later period if the students so chose. Two items, on areas purchased, can be answered within any of the three periods.

Is this extraordinary lack of balance further evidence of the haste and carelessness with which the test was constructed, or does it reflect a conviction that recent history is unimportant, or should not be taught? Why include such items as have been cited but neglect the past forty years except for an item on McKinley's assassination, two items on Theodore Roosevelt, one on the Boy Scouts, and one on Woodrow Wilson—and the eight current figures?

Was the grading more carefully done than was the construction of the test? The test and system of scoring are so set up that mere clerical grading, implied by the sharpness of the "correct answers," yields the worst possible results. It appears, further, that only thirty minutes was allowed for the test, though as given to freshmen it called for some 139 responses and a great deal of writing.

A further example of the amateurish nature of the test is found in its irresponsible administration. The sampling of colleges may be good, though it is interesting that Harvard, Yale, Princeton, Cornell, Wisconsin, Minnesota, Stanford, and California are among the institutions not included. How were the 7000 students selected? What controls were set up over the administration of the test? Why should students take it seriously, or put effort into so meaningless an exercise? The *Times* itself observes that "it is obvious that some of the students were not serious in answering the questions." How many were not? And what are the facts on the *Harvard Crimson's* contention that the answers are a hoax and a farce, and the comment of Dean Henry W. Holmes of Harvard, quoted in the *Times*, "that there 'was poor motivation for serious taking of a test. In fact, no one would take it seriously unless he took everything seriously.'"

Experts in testing do not open themselves to such questions and charges. The instructions read:

> The object of the examination is to determine in a general way the class's knowledge of American history. No effort will be made to identify individual papers. Your academic standing will not be in the slightest affected by the results of this quiz.

Is this adequate motivation? If the *New York Times* was seriously interested in finding out what information about American history college freshmen retain, and seriously interested in a constructive effort to improve American history teaching, it needed the services of experts. Amateurish questions, dubious grading, and irresponsible administration certainly contributed much to the sensational nature of the findings.

The Implications of the Findings

The *Times* finds that "college freshmen throughout the country reveal a striking ignorance of even the most elementary aspects of United States history, and know almost nothing about many important phases of this country's growth and development." Ignorance of facts is not news to those familiar with the dozens of testing programs that have been carried on in recent years. That ignorance has been repeatedly demonstrated not only for American history but for every other field tested. (See, for example, the 1938 Bulletin of the Carnegie Endowment for the Advancement of Teaching, prepared by William S. Learned and Ben D. Wood, on *The Student and His Knowledge*, in Pennsylvania. The Bulletin indicates how a competent study should be made, and includes some constructive suggestions as well as carefully substantiated findings.)

It may also be true that freshmen "know almost nothing about many important phases of their country's growth and development," though the *Times* test can not establish that conclusion; it tests only recall of miscellaneous items of information, not knowledge of American growth and development. The findings of reliable tests, administered at all grade levels, have, however, repeatedly and consistently demonstrated the need for better teaching of movements, institutions, and related understandings, as well as of individual facts.

Is, then, American history neglected in the schools? By no means. It dominates, as has been said, the social studies program in the elementary, the junior high (or grammar) grades, and it is universally required for graduation from public high schools.[2] Moreover the content is history—"chronological" history, to be redundant—covering just the sort of data the *Times* has tested, studied from texts written by many of our best known historians. Then why the poor results?

1. The courses are overcrowded with detail. Trying to teach too much results in teaching very little.

2. The courses at successive levels are repetitious, though they need not be. The history becomes dull, unstimulating, and the quality of learning suffers.

3. There is too much textbook teaching—reading, reciting, testing. The interest which promotes good learning is killed. Too many pupils acquire a hearty, and a most disturbing, dislike of history, of the names, dates, places, which are often all that they encounter in their courses.

4. Teachers of history, many of whom have been prepared for other fields, lack sufficient command of the subject to make it vital and stimulating. Teachers who are overworked and underpaid, even if well prepared, fail to keep up with the field and become "textbook teachers."

5. The school population now includes many pupils of low academic ability. Many read badly, and some can not be taught to read well. They need materials—including pictures and motion pictures—and teaching methods adapted to their abilities. Failure to recognize and adjust to individual differences results in failure to learn. High-ability pupils are left to drift, unstimulated. Low-ability pupils are left untaught. And the needs of "average" students are often neglected as teachers try to "cover the ground" and "get through the text" before the end of the year.

The Social Studies Movement

The *Times* has failed to point out that the improvement of history teaching has been a major concern of historians and educators for more than half a century. Through a long series of reports by distinguished committees, the American Historical Association has, since 1896, helped to establish three cycles of American history in the schools, and has helped to adapt the school program to changing needs and changing scholarship. More than thirty years ago the National Education Association appointed a committee which, while reinforcing the dominant position of American history in the civic-education program of junior and senior high schools, supplemented that history with courses in community and vocational civics, in problems of American democracy, and in world history, giving to the entire group of subjects the name "social studies." Fifteen years ago the Carnegie Corporation granted a quarter of a million dollars to the American Historical Association for an Investigation of the Social Studies in the Schools. The Commission on the Social Studies included:

> Frank W. Ballou, Superintendent of Schools, Washington, D.C.; Charles A. Beard, historian and political scientist; Isaiah Bowman, then of the American Geographical Society; Ada Comstock, President of Radcliffe College; George S. Counts, Professor of Education, Teachers College, Columbia University; Avery Craven, Professor of History, University of Chicago; Edmund E. Day, then of the Rockefeller Foundation; Guy Stanton Ford, then Dean and Professor of History in the University of Minnesota; Carlton J. H. Hayes, Professor of History, Columbia University; Ernest Horn, Professor of Education, University of Iowa; Henry Johnson, Professor of History, Teachers College, Columbia University; A. C. Krey, Professor of History, University of Minnesota; L. C. Marshall, economist and sociologist, formerly of the University of Chicago; Charles E. Merriam, Professor of Political Science, University of Chicago; Jesse H. Newlon, Professor of Education and Director of the Lincoln School, Teachers College, Columbia University; and Jesse F. Steiner, Professor of Sociology, University of Washington.

This Commission analyzed the purposes and responsibilities of social studies instruction in American schools, with attention to the requirements of scholarship, the changing needs of our democratic society, and the nature and limitations of the teaching and learning process.

Its Report, published in seventeen volumes, makes clear that the study of American society is the dominant concern of social studies teaching, with American history necessarily playing its important role, though supplemented by the other social studies—geography, civics, economics, current affairs, European backgrounds, and modern world relationships. The philosophy and general recommendations of the Commission have been generally accepted by leaders in the social studies field and by other educators.

This Report, together with parallel efforts of the National Council for the Social Studies and other professional organizations, has tried to meet changing needs. The high school population has increased since 1900 from about 700,000 to over 6,000,000. High schools, once mainly concerned with the preparation of able students for college, have now become schools for all youth—including those who learn from the printed page only with great difficulty, including those from underprivileged homes and who need personal guidance as well as knowledge, and including those who need "practical" vocational and "practical" citizenship experience as well as information. Meanwhile society has changed. Industrialization and resulting economic and social problems; the changing role of government and the menace of fascism; the changing relation of the United States to the rest of the world; new problems of youth as employment and adult responsibilities have been postponed, as home discipline has been relaxed, and as the automobile, the movies, and the radio have changed habits and attitudes—all these have called for changes in education.

These changes, and the effort to face them, have complicated the teaching of history, but have by no means lessened attention to it. On the contrary, a second and third cycle of American history have been experienced by literally millions of boys and girls who, thirty or more years ago, would have dropped out of school with not more than a first cycle. And, again, the history has been supplemented with more attention to the "other social studies"—civics, Problems of American Democracy, current events, and often some European history. *These social studies do not replace, or reduce, American history.* They ought to make it more intelligible.

Professional historians have taken the lead, in school textbooks as well as in committee reports, in modifying the kind of history taught. The authors of texts used throughout the country include Charles A. and Mary R. Beard, and James Truslow Adams; David S. Muzzey, Harry J. Carman, and Henry S. Commager of Columbia; Harold U. Faulkner of Smith; Ralph H. Gabriel of Yale; Nelson P. Mead of the College of the City of New York; Roy F. Nichols of the University of Pennsylvania; Ralph V. Harlow of Syracuse; Eugene C. Barker and Walter P. Webb of Texas; Ellis M. Coulter of Georgia; Henry E. Bourne and the late E. J. Benton of Western Reserve; Frederic L. Paxson of California; Marcus W. Jernegan and the late William E. Dodd of Chicago; and the late John H. Latané of Johns Hopkins, Charles R. Lingley of Dartmouth, Willis M. West of Minnesota, and Carl R. Fish of Wisconsin.

The texts written by these authorities, and many others, are "straight American history." They give less attention to the colonial period than was once customary. They include much social, economic, and cultural history. Some of them are developed, in part, around topics. But they include names, places, dates, and events, and they are chronologically organized. They represent increasingly competent efforts to make children and youth aware of what America has been and has come to be. They, and their continued sale and use, refute charges, if refutation is needed, that American history has disappeared from the schools, or that the schools are neglecting American history.

Who Is Fraser?

Why, then, the charges, advanced by Allan Nevins and currently by Hugh Russell Fraser, and repeatedly played up in the *New York Times* during the past year, that nowadays "a little American history is inter-jected into a course in 'social studies,' confusedly and half-heartedly" (Nevins), and that "'social studies extremists' [are] responsible for the present appalling neglect of American history in the high schools and elementary schools of the nation" (Fraser). Professor Nevins' lack of knowledge of school offerings and requirements, and his inaccurate and incomplete use of readily available statistics and other data, were dealt with in this journal last October and December.[3] The *Times*, in its articles on its recent test and in its editorial of April 4, has abandoned Nevins' claim that American history is not taught, and swung to the view, presented in *Social Education* last fall, that, to quote the *Times*, "our high schools need better teaching in that subject."

But who is Fraser? The *Times* identified him on April 5 as "an official of the Office of Education," and on April 11 as an "information officer" in the Office of Education. He has been a newspaper man, not an educator; recently he has been employed to prepare newspaper releases for the Office of Education. He attended a private preparatory school before entering newspaper work at the age of eighteen. He is author of a book on the political history of the 1830's and 1840's. He has never taught or made a firsthand study of schools or history teaching. Nevins, according to *PM*, describes Fraser as "a crusader with a grim deter-mination." According to statements quoted from Fraser by *PM* on April 7, Fraser organized his "Committee on American History" after the *Times* published its survey of college requirements and enrollments last June. "'I can only say that for 16 years before the *Times* came out with its story, I was boiling about the way the teaching of history was being neglected in the colleges. I was boiling because I felt the situation was hopeless.'" At Nevins' suggestion, according to *PM*, Fraser approached Mrs. Sulzberger, daughter of the late Adolph Ochs, publisher of the *Times*, and wife of the present publisher; she, "though interested in the work of the Committee, is not a member."

Who *are* the members of the Committee? Fraser is chairman. Says *PM*: "Fraser says he is the 'mouthpiece' for the Committee on American History. He 'estimates' the membership at about 45 people in various walks of life. Most of the members, he said, live in Washington." The letterhead of the Committee, which uses only Fraser's home address, gives no names. Nevins first told *PM* that he was not a member; then informed that Fraser had said he was a member, he is reported as saying: "Well, if he says I am, I am." On April 11 the *Times* described the Committee as "an organization composed of prominent historians"—but named none. Fraser told *PM* that he finances the Committee: "It cost me about $1000 of my own money." *PM* reports Fraser's claim that he prepared the resolution presented to the Senate by Senator Guffey, and conferred with other Senators prior to the publication of the *Times* report. He described some of his activities last December in a letter protesting because, among other things, he thought the Editor of *Social Education* had referred to him as a reactionary. He wrote, on his Committee letterhead:

> Usually I am considered a wild-eyed radical. I wrote the first series of nationally syndicated articles on the plight of the Southern sharecropper. I write a column for the Progressive. One of the largest newspapers in Washington considered running a column by me but finally decided I was too much of a damned Socialist, to the left of the New Deal! Assuredly, my friends Claude Pepper, Bob La Follette and Bill Lemke will be delighted by your reference! . . .

Fraser identifies "social studies" with efforts to correlate, fuse, or integrate history with other fields. There have been some such efforts, but they have affected very few schools. They have not reduced attention to American history in junior or senior high schools; the Rugg texts, for junior high school, include three volumes on American history, each chronologically organized. Junior high school civics and senior high school problems of American democracy, which do draw on several fields and which are usually not chronologically organized, supplement but do not displace American history. The overwhelming majority of elementary schools retain "straight history"; in those others where "new themes" such as the story of food, clothing, housing, transportation, and the migrations of peoples are studied, sometimes prior to fifth- and sixth-grade American history, the content certainly includes much history.

Fraser has consistently ignored the fact that "social studies," as generally used since 1916, is the name for a group of subjects, the chief of which, at three levels, is American history, chronologically presented. He has now specifically charged neglect of American history in the Milne School, Albany, New York; the Wisconsin High School, University of Wisconsin; the Eugene, Oregon, Public Schools; and the Denver Public Schools. Responsible authorities in the first three demonstrated the inaccuracy and irresponsibility of his charges in statements published in

Social Education last December. The Superintendent of Public Schools in Denver, in a statement published in the *Times* on April 6, called Fraser's charge "completely erroneous," adding: "It is difficult to believe that Mr. Fraser is so uninformed as not to know that the term 'social studies' is used to designate an area of subject matter, chief of which are history and geography, just as mathematics includes algebra, geometry, and so forth. . . . [At Denver] history, geography, civics, and other branches of 'social science' have, during all these years, remained basic. . . ." Fraser, though apparently possessing no firsthand knowledge, has reiterated his irresponsible charges in all four cases.

The *Washington Times-Herald* of April 5 reports an attack by Fraser on the American Historical Association for failing to fight the social studies movement. In his letter of resignation from his position in the Office of Education, published in the *Times* on April 11, he attacks the Office on similar grounds and denounces the National Council for the Social Studies. In all truth, "a crusader with a grim determination"!

Why does the *New York Times* take the educational views of Fraser, *alias* the Committee on American History, seriously? Why sponsor and finance a preposterous test, the results of which can only reflect his narrow view of history, his incompetence in devising a test, and the refusal of an unknown proportion of the freshmen victims to take the absurdity seriously? Why does the *Times* play up and keep republishing the uninformed charges of both Nevins and Fraser, neither of whom have had experience in the schools or made even perfunctory studies of actual textbooks and courses of study or of actual classroom materials and practice? Why does the *Times* thus support efforts to persuade the public that American history is neglected, or that American history is something different from social studies, or that social studies have abolished chronology in history? Why does the *Times* allow its two self-constituted authorities on the school program in history and social studies to attribute the progress that has been made in increasing attention to recent American history, to economic, social, and cultural development in America, and to civics and problems of American democracy to be branded as the work of "extremists" rather than of our most responsible educators, including such historians and social scientists as constituted the Commission on the Social Studies? Does the *Times* accept the Nevins-Fraser implication that leaders in American education—including superintendents, principals, teachers, textbook authors and publishers, and the professors of history and social science in colleges, universities, and schools of education—have joined in a great nation-wide plot against American history, or been hoodwinked by a few "extremists" who for some unexplained reason want to subvert American history teaching? Hasn't it occurred to the *Times* that its two crusaders for return to drill on political details may be "extremists?"—that the responsible officials who have denounced Fraser's charges may know better than he what goes on in their schools?—and that those educators who actually know and work in the schools or who, like the Commission on the Social Studies, have spent years in studying the purposes, possibilities, and responsibilities of education, may have a better idea of what social studies should be taught than the two *Times* authorities have picked up in a few months of spare-time campaigning? Does the *Times* feel no responsibility for seeing to it that the impressions of American history teaching that it is persistently etching into the mind of the American public bear some relation to actuality? Does the *Times* believe that its test and report and frequent republication of the Nevins-Fraser charges can do no harm?

Dangers in the Test and Report

Many commentators, who have taken, at face value, the *Times* test and report, and thus been understandably horrified at the ignorance—if not the flippancy!—of freshmen, have assured the *Times* that it has rendered a public service. If the test reflects both the purposes of history teaching and the knowledge of high school graduates—neither of which is likely—such may be the case. But there are other possibilities. America can no longer be understood by studying America alone. Young Americans need to study, in school and college, the history of other countries. America can not be understood by learning and drilling on the names, places, dates, and events of our history from 1787 to 1900. Such study is futile if the information lacks meaning and if it is not kept fresh through use—as several commentators, including President MacCracken of Vassar, have been prompt to point out, and we can not afford to cut young citizens off from a study of contemporary times and issues. There are dangers that some groups will seize upon the report to prevent study of other countries and peoples, and that reactionaries will seize upon it to prevent study of issues that are controversial and considered "dangerous."

The report is calculated to reduce confidence in the schools and in responsible school authorities. Relying on amateurs and "crusaders," and ignoring educational specialists, the *Times* purports to show that the school authorities have not known what they were about, have been negligent in laying the foundations for informed and patriotic citizenship. The *Times* invites, wittingly or not, the kind of legislative interference that characterized the years during, and after, the First World War, and against which the *Times* then threw the weight of its influence.

American schools during the past generation have had to adjust to a new school population, to new responsibilities, to new techniques as the science of education has steadily developed, and to a new world as the domestic and international scenes have changed rapidly. Experiments and adaptations have been necessary. Those made have been incomplete and imperfect. But in the social studies, as in some other fields, the schools have had leadership and financial support from such sources as the Carnegie Corporation, the Rockefeller Foundation, the General Education Board, and the College Entrance Examination Board, to name but a few. It has leadership from college and university professors and learned societies as well as from professors of education and professional educational associations. It has had increasingly earnest and well-prepared, and less increasingly well-paid, teachers. The armed forces have been paying tribute to the educational advances made during the past twenty-five years, and the response of young Americans to the war emergency would seem to speak well for the program of citizenship education that has been carried on—and to speak fully as loudly, one might think, as the results of the kind of test to which the *Times* has lent its name.

Yet the *Times*, at a critical moment, casually adopts a highly imperfect test, whose results can only be misleading, in a field on which wartime emotions can play swiftly and powerfully, and it permits private, personal, and irresponsible interests to exploit what is presented as a national educational scandal. The *Times* could have had in advance, for the asking, the advice that it has since received, that tests limited to information always yield low scores, that the situation in American history is no worse than on other subjects, and that its test had little relation to a vital and defensible program of civic education.

What Needs to Be Done?

We need effective teaching of American history. As already indicated, that involves decisions as to what knowledge is basic to an understanding and appreciation of America. It involves articulation of the three cycles of American history now generally taught in the schools, so that learning is effective, and so that the second and third cycles are fresh and vital rather than repetitious and deadening. We need teaching materials for groups, like poor readers, that present special problems. We need social studies teachers with the means and the leisure to buy books and magazines, to read, to travel, to keep professionally alert. And we need the sympathy and support of the public—including the press—as we try to achieve what everybody wants: a body of young citizens informed about our past, conscious and informed about problems and issues in the present, devoted to our democratic traditions and ideals, and capable of participating in the advancement of those traditions and ideals now and in the future.

Notes

[1] Thirteen items, including two entire questions, were left out of the test as printed in the *Times*. The following figures are based on the latter version.

[2] See the statement reporting the responses to Commissioner J. W. Studebaker's inquiry addressed to the State departments of education, reprinted on page 240 of this issue.

[3] Nevins' charge of neglect of American history is repeated in an article in the *New York Times Magazine* for April 18, 1943. He again misinterprets Office of Education figures and neglects other reliable data to which attention has been called in this journal.

Social Education Asks: How Can Books on American Government Be Improved?

UNITED STATES SENATORS REPLY

NOTE: The two feature reviews in this issue evaluate books in the fields of education and philosophy. To supplement these evaluations, Social Education *addressed the following question to a small and carefully selected group of United States Senators:*

"How can authors and publishers add to the public's understanding of the structure and function of the American Government? Specifically, what areas of American Government should be given more thorough treatment in the books that are published in the future?"

Seven Senators responded to our inquiry. Their answers are printed below.

Hubert H. Humphrey (D—Minnesota)

Luckily, in the last few years, a number of fine books have been written by people with experience in government at many levels. The great improvement, in my mind, has been that they deal with government as a *process* rather than merely as a *structure*. Students now are able to get a much more realistic view of government and an appreciation of its dynamic, human component. Specifically, some of the concepts that are now put across are the tremendous role of group action in politics, without the connotation that somehow such activity is evil; the influence of the background and associations of government personnel in their

NOTE: These responses appeared in *Social Education*, March 1959, pp. 140–141.

making of decisions; the contribution made by Congress in the modification of policies and the adjustment of interests, as opposed to the popular view a few years ago that executive agencies were the font of all wisdom and ability.

What worries me in education is not the lack of sound writing, but the lag in getting these new understandings to the students. Busy teachers, often without the opportunity to refresh themselves with modern instruction, are likely merely to pass on the concepts of their own professors, perhaps formed many years ago when the social sciences were far less developed than today.

Books, therefore, are the only hope for reaching the student of today. I hope they will be written by people of large enough grasp to convey economic conflict, the sociology of group behavior, and the actions of political men in their true, intimate relationship.

Irving M. Ives (R—Formerly Senator from New York)

I would suggest two areas of American Government which might be given more treatment in future books:

1. The functioning of the Committee System in the legislative branch of the government. So many people appear to feel that the work of the House or the Senate is done on the Floor of either House, whereas the great bulk of the task of shaping legislation—the preliminary investigations and the actual drafting of bills—occurs in committees.

2. The self-perpetuating bureaucracy in the Executive branch which continues regardless of the decision made by the voters in a presidential election. While I do not quarrel with the need for a career civil service, and in fact consider it essential to the smooth functioning of the government, the Executive branch has become so vast that in many respects it functions independently of the will of the people as expressed in the outcome of a presidential election. A thoughtful study of this subject might contribute considerably to public understanding.

Jacob K. Javits (R—New York)

In response to your inquiry, I believe that authors and publishers can add to the public's understanding of the structure and functioning of the American Government by making clear how the individual can most effectively function as a citizen. We deeply admire the patriotism of one who would die for his country, but we must also strive to teach how best to live for it. The Romans said, *"vox populi vox dei"* ("the voice of the people is the voice of God"); our people must effectively sound this voice. The areas I think best adapted for consideration are:

1. The system of protection for the individual rights and dignity of the individual and how it works.

2. The self-imposed disciplines on those in the three branches of Government required to make the system of checks and balances work.

Lyndon B. Johnson (D—Texas)

I suppose that every man always feels that the things which are closest to him are the most misunderstood by the outside world. In response to your question, I would reply that the United States Senate as an institution has had the least thorough and understanding treatment of any of our basic institutions.

I do not have the time and space to elaborate on my point. But I have served in the House, the Senate, and in the Executive branch of the Government. In addition, I have many close friends in the Judiciary.

I believe that a real service would be performed by a basic examination of the Senate, devoted not merely to form but to function. In many respects, the Senate is unique, and I am not certain that this point has been clarified in the academic literature I have read.

Estes Kefauver (D—Tennessee)

Very briefly, it seems to me that among the subjects which authors and publishers might well be exploring at present are these:

1. While a vast amount of material has been written on the Supreme Court, its functions and its limitations are not well understood even sometimes by educated people.

2. It seems obvious, also, that the place of the quasi-judicial agencies of the government are not fully understood, even by the agencies themselves on occasion. Some attention ought to be paid these statutory agencies, their history, powers, methods, and so forth.

3. It might be useful as well to have more material on how the Congress works, written in popular form, and available at a low price, perhaps in paper covers.

John F. Kennedy (D—Massachusetts)

In my judgment, public understanding of American government could be stimulated by greater attention—especially in the writing of biography—to politicians "below the summit." There are very few good books on Senators, party leaders, and municipal officials, who help to shape our history and heritage but who are forgotten in the welter of material on Presidents and Generals. In general, there has perhaps been a disinclination to appreciate more fully the role of the politician—of his frequent stand against certain groups and masses and trends that might otherwise be shaping our history.

There has been very little careful study of the legislative process either in historical or contemporary perspective. I have found in my own work no really outstanding study of the Senate and very little first-rate work on the passage of important bills or the work of committees. I think that in recent times there has been somewhat greater interest in such matters, but it seems to me that much effective work remains to be done.

Leverett Saltonstall (R—Massachusetts)

I certainly believe as you do that it is most important to promote the fullest possible public understanding of the functions of the various departments of our government for only when people fully understand the functions of their government can they in turn fully appreciate the institutions which we as a democracy so treasure. I do not have any specific thoughts as to particular areas of the government which have been inadequately treated by authors and publishers. I do think, however, that a continuing examination of the means by which our democratic government preserves and protects our civil liberties is vital. A complete public understanding of this aspect of government is very important. At times we become so preoccupied with the immense structure of government that we overlook some of the basic principles that the entire structure serves.

Decision Making: The Heart of Social Studies Instruction

SHIRLEY H. ENGLE

My theme is a very simple one. It is that, in teaching the social studies, we should emphasize decision making as against mere remembering. We should emphasize decision making at two levels: at the level of deciding what a group of descriptive data means, how these data may be summarized or generalized, what principles they suggest; and also decision making at the level of policy determination, which requires a synthesis of facts, principles, and values usually not all found on one side of any question.

In order to make my case, it is useful to draw certain distinctions between the social sciences and the social studies. The social sciences include all of the scholarly, investigative work of historians, political scientists, economists, anthropologists, psychologists, and sociologists, together with such parts of the work of biologists and geographers as relate primarily to human behavior. Closely related fields include philosophy, literature, linguistics, logistics, and statistics. The social studies, including the content of the textbooks, courses of study, and whatever passes in the school for instruction in civic and social affairs, are based on the social sciences but they clearly involve always a selection of and distillation from the social sciences—they encompass only a minor portion of the social sciences.

Selectivity, therefore, is one of the features which distinguishes the social sciences from the social studies. To social science, knowledge is

NOTE: This article appeared in *Social Education*, November 1960, pp. 301–304, 306. Reprinted by permission of Shirley Engle.

useful for its own sake; all knowledge is of equal worth; there is no concern for immediate usefulness. To the social studies, a central consideration must always be that of determining what knowledge is of most worth. If all of the knowledge of a field of study is to be boiled down into one textbook, what is to be emphasized? If all of the knowledge of the area is to be boiled down into one course of study, what is most important?

There is a more basic distinction to be drawn between the social sciences and the social studies than merely that of selectivity. The impelling purpose of the two is quite different. The orientation of the social scientist is that of research. The more scientific the social scientist, the more specialized becomes his interest, the more consuming becomes his desire to know more and more about less and less, the less concern he shows for broad social problems. He is far more inclined to analyze, dissect, and proliferate than to unite, synthesize, and apply. His absorbing interest is to push back the frontier of dependable knowledge in some limited sector of the social scene.

In marked contrast to the meticulous research orientation of the social sciences, the social studies are centrally concerned with the education of citizens. The mark of the good citizen is the quality of decisions which he reaches on public and private matters of social concern. The social sciences contribute to the process of decision making by supplying reliable facts and principles upon which to base decisions—they do not supply the decisions ready made. The facts are there for all to see but they do not tell us what to do. Decision making requires more than mere knowledge of facts and principles; it requires a weighing in the balance, a synthesizing of all available information and values. The problems about which citizens must reach decisions are never confronted piecemeal, the facts are seldom clearly all on one side, and values, too, must be taken into consideration. A social problem requires that the citizen put together, from many sources, information and values which the social sciences treat in relative isolation. Thus in the social studies the prevailing motive is synthesis rather than analysis. The social studies begin where the social sciences end. Facts and principles which are the ends in view in the social sciences are merely a means to a further end in the social studies. The goal of the social studies lies not merely in information but in the character of people. The goal is the good citizen.

A good citizen has many facts at his command, but more, he has arrived at some tenable conclusions about public and social affairs. He has achieved a store of sound and socially responsible beliefs and convictions. His beliefs and convictions are sound and responsible because he has had the opportunity to test them against facts and values. In the process of testing his ideas he has greatly increased his fund of factual information and he has become increasingly skillful at intelligent deci-

sion making. The development in the mind of students of such a synthesis of facts and values, together with the development of skill in
making decisions in the light of numerous and sometimes contrary facts
and values, is the special forte of the social studies.

If the purpose of the social studies is to be education for citizenship,
if its primary concern is to be the quality of the beliefs and convictions
which students come to hold on public questions, and if we are to be
concerned with the development of skill at decision making, then there
are some things which it becomes imperative that we do in teaching the
social studies. I would like to develop briefly some of these imperatives.

We must abandon our use of what I shall call the ground-covering
technique, and with it the wholly mistaken notion that to commit information to memory is the same as to gain knowledge. By ground covering I mean the all too familiar technique of learning and holding in
memory, enforced by drill, large amounts of more or less isolated descriptive material without pausing in any way, at any time, to speculate as to
the meaning or significance of the material, or to consider its relevance
and bearing to any general idea, or to consider its applicability to any
problem or issue past or present. Even when such material is interesting, and it sometimes is, merely to cover it in this uncritical, matter-
of-fact fashion robs the material of its potential for accurate concept
formation or generalization which will be useful to students in understanding events and conditions in other times and places in which like
data appear. Simply reading and remembering the stories about Indians
in our history, no matter how many times repeated, have never insured
the development of accurate concepts about Indians or correct generalizations about the relationships between people of divergent cultures
and histories. Or, if in our haste to cover ground, we refuse to deal con-
templatively and critically with the material we are covering, the student may generalize haphazardly and may, without our help, arrive at
totally erroneous conclusions. Thus, it may be said with good reason
that the study of Indians frequently does more harm than good, teaching more untruth than truth.

The ground-covering fetish is based on the false notion that remembering is all there is to knowing or the equally false notion that one
must be well drilled in the facts before he can begin to think. M. I.
Finley, noted British historian, says about ground covering that "a mere
telling of individual events in sequence, no matter how accurately done,
is just that and nothing else. Such knowledge is meaningless, its mere
accumulation a waste of time. Instead, knowledge must lead to understanding. In the field of history this means trying to grasp general ideas
about human events. The problem is to move from particular events to
the universal; from the concrete events to the underlying patterns and
generalities."

Equally fallacious is the background theory of learning, or the notion that we must hold the facts in memory before we are ready to draw conclusions from them or to think about their meaning. This theory is at considerable variance with recognized scientific method and the ways in which careful thinkers approach an intellectual problem. The thinker or scientist frequently engages in speculation or theorizing about possible relationships, from which he deduces tests or possible facts which, if observable, verify his theory. (Some of the great breakthroughs in knowledge have come about in this way.) To say that a thinker must know all that he needs to know, let alone hold all this in memory, before engaging in thought is to completely hog-tie his intellectual development. And there is no valid reason in this respect for differentiating between a student trying to understand Indians and an Einstein speculating about the meaning of space.

What happens in our classrooms from too strict an adherence to ground covering is that the number of facts committed to memory is reduced to a relatively small number. These are the so-called basic facts which we learn, and just as promptly forget, over and over again. Thus ground covering actually works to reduce and restrict the quantity of factual information treated in our classes. What is needed instead is a vast multiplication of the quantity of factual material with which students are asked to deal in the context of reaching a reasoned conclusion about some intellectual problem. Such an enrichment of factual background will come about when we turn from our preoccupation with remembering to a more fruitful concern for drawing conclusions from facts or for testing our speculations and ideas about human events with all of the relevant data we are able to collect.

For ground covering, or remembering, we should substitute decision making, which is reflective, speculative, thought provoking, and oriented to the process of reaching conclusions. My thesis is simply this, decision making should afford the structure around which social studies instruction should be organized. The central importance of decision making in the social studies has been cited earlier. The point here is that students are not likely to learn to reach better decisions, that is, grounded and reasoned decisions, except as they receive guided and critically oriented exercise in the decision-making process.

Decision-making opportunities in the social studies classroom may run the entire gamut of difficulty, from very simple situations which take the form merely of posing questions for class consideration which require some thought and a synthesis of information supplied in a single descriptive paragraph to very complex social problems involving questions of public policy or individual behavior. Thus, in studying the Plains Indians in the post-Civil War period a low level decision could be required by asking which of the following sentences accurately, or most accurately, summarizes the difficulty continually experienced in Indian affairs: (1) The Indians were treated by the settlers as trespassers on land which they (the Indians) had inhabited and claimed as their own for centuries; (2) The Plains Indians were wanderers who knew no fixed abodes and recognized no exclusive right of anyone to own the land; (3) Renegade Indians and white outlaws were at the seat of Indian trouble (this is the Hollywood version of Indian affairs); (4) The handling of Indian affairs by the United States government was characterized by wanton disregard of Indian rights, by treachery, and by broken promises; or (5) The different manner of using the land by the Indians and the whites made agreement between the two impossible. At a higher level of difficulty a decision would be required if one asked, "Do you think General George Crook dealt fairly with the Shoshone chief, Washakie, during the military campaigns to pacify the Plains Indians? What are your grounds?" Or at a still higher level of complexity, there is the question of what should be the policy of the United States toward Indians who contest the sovereignty of the United States.

Some decisions involve essentially matters of fact. For example, suppose we are reading about the building of the transcontinental railroads in the 1870's, 1880's, and 1890's and how the government gave large grants of land and money to the railroad companies to encourage them to build the railroads. We read further that subsequently the railroads, or most of them, went into bankruptcy but also that following their construction the country experienced a great expansion of agricultural and industrial wealth whereby our exports of wheat and corn multiplied tenfold in 20 years; in the same period the value of our manufacturers' products increased 200 percent and 180 new factories were being built in Philadelphia alone. We have these and many other facts. But the decision rests in concluding what these facts mean. What do they all add up to? Which of the following generalizations accurately summarize these facts? Government subsidization of key industries brings a vast multiplication of other industries under private ownership; private investors will not take the extraordinary risk necessary to start a really new industrial development; one industrial development inevitably leads to other industrial developments; industry in which the government interferes is always inefficient and will fail in the end; private industry can never be expected to provide the transportation facilities needed for an expanding economy; government participation in industry tends to dry up the growth of private industry; industry resulting from government spending is uneconomical and is doomed to fail in the end; if the government had foregone the tax money used to aid the railroads, private individuals would have had money which they would have invested in the railroads. Clearly, the making of decisions among the alternatives listed above is essentially a matter of sorting out and applying facts until a conclusion is reached which honestly and accurately summarizes all facts that are relevant to the problem.

Other decisions, perhaps we should say most decisions, involve values as well as facts. Thus, in dealing with the issue of which of two proposed solutions to the problems of farm surpluses is best, one may conclude, factually, that government support of farm prices leads inevitably to inefficiency in agriculture and to unnecessarily high cost for food and fibre which the farm produces. This much is a factual conclusion. But this does not necessarily get us out of the woods, for one might still prefer government-supported agriculture to an unregulated agriculture because he feared the control of large agricultural corporations (which will almost inevitably follow the removal of governmental restrictions—another factual generalization) more than he fears governmental controls. The latter decision is a value judgment, though one fraught, as are all value decisions, with still further implications which could be grounded factually. For instance, in a hierarchy of values, the *greatest degree of individual freedom* may be the value sought or agreed upon by all involved in the decision. From this premise a factual investigation could be conducted of the relationship between government regulation and individual freedom on the one hand and between corporate control and individual freedom on the other. Thus, though the decision as to value is not in this way resolved, the exact issue over values is clarified by such a factual investigation of the alternatives.

If decision making is to be the focus of social studies instruction, we will need to introduce vastly larger quantities of factual information into our classrooms. Drill to the point of memory on a few basic facts will never suffice. The superficial coverage of one textbook will never be enough. The very moment that a conclusion, such as any of those suggested above, is reached tentatively, the natural demand is for more facts with which to test the conclusion. This means almost surely the introduction of large quantities of supplementary materials, with far too much content to be committed to memory. It means a reversal in the usual attitude on reading habits whereby students will be expected to read larger quantities of materials, to read them more rapidly, and to read them for purposes of getting general ideas or of locating relevant information rather than to read small quantities of material, slowly and laboriously, a few pages each day, for purposes of committing the material to memory. It may mean in the end the abandonment of textbooks and the substitution of numerous, more substantive, more informative, and more exciting books and other materials.

If the quality of decision making is to be the primary concern of social studies instruction, we must take steps to up-grade the quality of intellectual activity in the social studies classroom. Research is demonstrating the disquieting prevalence in many social studies classrooms of what is generously labeled shoddy thinking procedures. In fact, social studies classrooms seem to exhibit a quality of logic far below that exhibited in classrooms in which science, mathematics, or even English is being taught. Admitting the greater difficulty of our content, this is still something about which we cannot be complacent. Among the common errors in logic easily observed in social studies instruction is the acceptance of an assertion as if it were a fact, the confusing of fact with opinion, the validation of the truth of something on authority, the acceptance of a merely plausible explanation for a sufficient explanation, the failure to agree on the meaning of key words (frequently value laden) before engaging in an argument in which the meaning of the word is essential as, for instance, to argue over whether the first Roosevelt was a good or a strong President without first agreeing on a common meaning for "good" and for "strong," and the confusing of questions which must be referred to facts for an answer and those which defer to values for an answer. The persistent practice in our classrooms of errors in logic of the kind mentioned can lead only to intellectual confusion and irresponsibility. If we are really concerned with effective citizenship, we must not only provide the opportunity for decision making but we must see to it that decisions are made in keeping with well known rules of science and logic and that students get practice in making such decisions.

Lastly, if responsible decision making is the end of social studies instruction, we must recognize values formation as a central concern of social studies instruction. Real life decisions are ultimately value decisions. To leave a student unaware of the value assumptions in his decision or to leave him untrained in dealing with value questions is literally to lead an innocent lamb to the slaughter. Such a student could, and he frequently does, return to our fold and say, "But you didn't tell me it was this way." Or he may quickly sink into cynicism or misbelief. The question of what values he should hold probably cannot be settled in the classroom, but values can be dealt with intelligently in the classroom. The nature of the values which people hold can be made explicit, the issues over values can be clarified, and the ends to which holding to a particular value will lead can be established factually to some extent. For instance, it is possible to predict with some accuracy the factual results of valuing segregation over integration in the United States with respect to such matters as economic productivity of the American people, the respect with which America is held abroad, the effect on the efficiency of our educational system, the genetic mixing of the races, etc. Thus, it becomes possible to engage in some appraisal of the value in terms of other values held, as, for instance, world peace, Christian brotherhood, economic security and well being, national unity, the right to choose one's own friends, etc. We can compare and appraise value, to some extent, in an extended hierarchy of values from lower values, such as a preference for having one's hair cut in a segregated barber shop, to higher values, such as the belief that all men should be treated with equal respect.

To duck the question of values is to cut the heart out of decision making. The basic social problem of America today is a problem of value. In simple terms the problem may be stated as to whether we value more the survival of a free America which will require sacrifice for education, for materials of defense, etc., or whether we value more our right as individuals to spend our resources on extra fins for our cars and for all the other gadgets of conspicuous consumptions. It is not impossible to predict the outcome of hewing to either choice. It is not at all certain that our students are being prepared to make the right decision and to make it in time.

My thesis has been a very simple one. It is that quality decision making should be the central concern of social studies instruction. I could cite many renowned people as having essentially supported the position I have here tried to state. Among the ancients these would include Socrates, Plato, and Thucydides, the father of objective history. These would include the great modern philosopher Alfred North White-head and such modern critics as the economist Peter Drucker and President Robert F. Goheen of Princeton. But to quote these would continue the discussion overlong, as I suspect I may have done already. So may I quote instead a simple statement from the noted modern scientist Hans Selye, who has said that "facts from which no conclusions can be drawn are hardly worth knowing."

Some Guidelines for Changing Social Studies Education

LAWRENCE E. METCALF

A major reform of the social studies curriculum is long overdue and, hopefully, may be about to take place.[1] The purpose of this article is to discuss certain deficiencies of the present curriculum, and to offer suggestions for their remedy. Among the many deficiencies space will permit discussion only of the following six: (1) the wholly ritualistic quality of the instructional purposes offered to teachers by curriculum planners, (2) a poor and wrong solution to the problem of student motivation, (3) an inadequate and erroneous conception of problem-solving, (4) a failure to accord recognition to the newer social sciences and the continued domination of history, (5) the requirement that teachers take methods courses which do no more than elaborate upon the obvious, and (6) a tendency to treat the normative aspects of social studies instruction with the totalitarian methods of prescription and indoctrination.

Aimlessness of Instruction

Curriculum bulletins and resource units in the social studies always begin with a long list of purposes. Usually there are more purposes than any staff could achieve during a lifetime of instruction. Because these purposes are stated nonoperationally without any suggestion as to how

NOTE: This article appeared in *Social Education*, August 1963, pp. 197–201. Reprinted by permission of Lawrence E. Metcalf.

they might be achieved, propaganda analysts would call them glittering generalities. This operational vagueness is even true of those objectives which are said to be stated in behavioral terms. Clearly, behavior is broadly and roughly conceived by those who write purposes. But more to the point, the writers of curriculum bulletins and resource units seldom recommend method or content that is consistent with their poetically expressed objectives. Apparently, the practice of writing down purposes has become a kind of ritual that no teacher is to take seriously. By recourse to cant and incantation proper respect is paid to our democratic heritage. After the ceremony is over, everyone settles down to the job at hand which usually has no purpose at all other than to keep youth busy and out of mischief.

Because statements of purpose seem to have had no effect upon what teachers teach, or the way in which they teach, some reformers are now taking the position that purposes are unimportant, and that we ought to roll up our sleeves and seek improvement in courses without very much worry about our purposes. This is a healthy attitude to the extent that certain purposes are granted for the sake of working diligently on construction of the means necessary to their achievement. Unfortunately, our culture is riven with conflict, and if national goals are vague and subject to debate, some clarification of values is essential to all curriculum planning. The current debate over whether we can have both equality and excellence as educational goals is a case in point.

In 1955 this writer collaborated with Maurice Hunt in writing a social studies methods textbook in which the radical suggestion was made that the social studies pursue a single purpose.[2] It was assumed that the effective pursuit of this purpose would demand all a teacher's time and resources. The entire book was devoted to an exploration of the kind of methods, content, and evaluation consistent with this purpose in the hope that such extended treatment would give the purpose a somewhat operational meaning. It was suggested that "The foremost aim of instruction in high school social studies is to help students examine reflectively issues in closed areas of American culture."[3] Closed areas were defined as areas of belief and thought which are largely closed to rational thought. These areas abound with prejudice, taboos, inconsistencies, and perplexities. In such areas as sex, economics, religion, race, and social class, people react with their blood and common sense, and without logic and scientific knowledge. Teachers who touch upon the closed areas are expected to justify their temerity by inculcating right answers, right attitudes, right beliefs. The process of teaching in the closed areas is an amalgam of suppression, indoctrination, distortion, manipulation, prescription, and persuasion. When this sort of thing is practiced in the Soviet Union or Red China, we call it brainwashing. Its use in this country is called patriotism.

Many teachers, educators, and social scientists see nothing wrong with this kind of process. The belief that schools exist for the preservation of society, its cultural heritage, is wedded to a reinforcement theory of learning. Doubly armed they can practice the educational totalitarianism of the Soviet Union while loudly proclaiming their opposition to communism. Current attempts to teach students an "understanding" of communism exemplify almost perfectly this totalitarian philosophy. It is a major source of alarm to note that not only educators, who can use ignorance as their excuse, and publishers with the usual eye for patriotically inspired profits, but also respected social scientists have participated in this orgiastic assault upon the innocence of children and youth.[4] In place of charlatanry and incantation we need an honestly reflective study of contrasting ideologies with no suppression of knowledge as its intent or by-product. This kind of teaching would preserve that part of our cultural heritage which merits survival, and would build the only kind of patriotism compatible with democratic values.

The suggestion that the social studies limit its purposes to the fostering of reflective thought in the closed areas will not be popular with those who call themselves eclectics, and who value equally a variety of instructional aims. The trouble with many of our eclectics is that they have not included consistency as one of their philosophical criteria. A careful reading of their stated purposes leaves one with the feeling that they are not really for anything at all, since their lists of impeccable purposes are shot through with contradictory and incompatible destinations. It is fair to say that a person who wants to ride off in all directions is essentially aimless in his equestrian activity.

The single aim, reflection in the closed areas, may not be consistent with all the aims that social studies education would like to hold, but it is consistent and contributory to many of them, particularly to those that share an abode with the values of a democratic society. The responsibilities of social studies in the realm of values will be discussed more fully later in this article.

The Problem of Motivation

It is a matter of everyday observation among teachers that students are not very much interested in the social studies. Low interest is coupled with high forgetting. Attempts to solve this problem in civic apathy have tried to make a standard content interesting, easy, and attractive. Under this approach instructional materials receive a beauty treatment. The modern textbook is replete with the kind of colorful art work that one associates with the cosmetics industry. Charts, graphs, tables, end-of-chapter assists, and even teachers' manuals cope with levels of aspiration. An outstanding example of the beautician treatment of history is the hardback magazine, *American Heritage*. The trouble with this approach is that it misses the target. It is the uselessness of the content against which students have rebelled. Many of our students who dislike the social studies are hard at work on much more difficult content in their science and mathematics courses. Some of this interest in the natural sciences merely reflects the fashions of the day, but much of it expresses a genuine interest in content that, once mastered, has a wealth of meaning. Much of the content in the social studies, if properly understood by the student, has no meaning at all, and our brighter students sense this almost from the beginning of their study.

Some of the content we are now teaching would acquire meaning if its relevance to current problems and issues were perceived by students. Some of the content has no such relevance, and should be replaced by content that does. This principle does not mean that history has no value unless it is modern history. Some of the most relevant content for understanding contemporary society is to be found in the histories of Greece and Rome. A teacher can use the content of history and social science as evidence within a reflective process that tests propositions and clarifies conflicts. A student who wonders whether to believe a proposition or its opposite will be motivated to resolve discrepancy, if we are to believe recent theories of cognitive dissonance.[5] A shift from content that has become standard to one that is needed in the study of cultural disjunctions is essential to successful attempts to solve the problem of student motivation.[6]

Problem-Solving Reconsidered

The problem-solving method has never been dominant in social studies teaching and, when used at all, has seldom been interpreted, psychologically or logically, in terms that would foster intellectual growth in students. We have been wrong most of the time in our conceptions of both problem-solving and problems.

A problem is any unanswered question that can be answered experimentally. It is a perplexity felt by a student. Problems cannot be listed or handed to students on a sheet of ditto paper. It is foolish for teachers to list as thought questions those that are different in wording from questions that are said to be recall in nature. What is a recall question for one student may be a thought question for someone else. It is true that many students have in common certain perplexities that concern them, particularly in the closed areas, and these may be identified in advance as possible problems. But a part of the meaning of any problem is psychological. We create problems for our students when we are successful in questioning their beliefs to the point where they have genuine doubt as to what to believe. Without doubt, there is no problem, and all problems are in a generic sense a problem in what to believe.

Problem-solving is logical and scientific. One cannot rely upon hunches, feelings, intuitions, or even trials and errors for solutions to problems. The intuitions of students may supply them with hypotheses, but all such ideas must be tested with data before students can learn whether any of their ideas merit the status of belief. Problem-solving has been advocated by some of our eclectics as the best method for some purposes. True to their faith in variety for its own sake, they have urged other methods for other purposes without considering whether their methods and their purposes, taken as a whole, constituted a consistent theory of teaching. Research findings on the effectiveness of this method have been inconclusive, partly because its many investigators have never understood the method well enough to put it to experimental test.[7]

Social studies educators have had their greatest difficulty in their attempts to apply problem-solving to the teaching of history. A part of their difficulty has been their view of history as a chronological narrative couched in factual terms, free from an emphasis upon concepts or generalizations. Believing that there are no laws in history, they have viewed any attempt to examine reflectively the generalizations of historians as an attack upon history which would reduce the student's faith in historical knowledge. A second part of their difficulty has been the conception that a problem ceases to be a problem, once anyone has solved it. Problems, so conceived, have to be contemporary, never historical. Problem-solving in their hands is oriented to the future, to values, and to action. Under this conception, problems take the form of how can we beautify the school plant, reduce noise in the cafeteria, forestall inflation, or end the Cold War. Personal problems receive more attention than social problems because action is more feasible for one than for the other. Teachers who view problem-solving from this kind of perspective are somewhat confused by the suggestion that students be asked to solve the problem of what is imperialism, and what are its causes and effects. The understanding of imperialism is assigned to the method of assertion and recitation rather than to problem-solving.

The erroneous nature of this conception has been suggested by several uncommon sources. An excellent discussion of problem-solving in the teaching of history is available in an unpublished dissertation by Alan Griffin.[8] Another is to be found in an out-of-print work by Ernest Bayles.[9] More recent studies by Leonard Swift and by John Palmer are suggestive on the same point.[10]

History, the New Social Sciences, and the Concept of Structure

The teaching of history consumes more instructional time than any other subject in the social studies curriculum. The non-historical social sciences are seriously neglected. The new curricula of mathematics and science emphasize the importance of what Jerome Bruner has called structure. There is pressure to incorporate the same emphasis in the social studies. A recent grant from the Ford Foundation to Educational Services, Inc. is likely to apply the concept of structure to the selection of subject matter for the social studies. A movement in this direction will probably result in a larger place for the social sciences and lesser emphasis upon history because the latter is totally lacking in structure. This lack of structure is admitted by every historian who downgrades anyone who attempts to theorize about the causes of historical events.

No one can predict with certainty the outcome of this movement toward recognizing the importance of the theoretical knowledge of the social scientist. That it will dislodge history from its dominant position would appear likely. Which social science or social sciences will come to dominate is not at all clear. Any movement that recognizes the explanatory and predictive power of the social sciences, provided that it also clarifies the relevance of reflective inquiry as a method of teaching such knowledge, warrants the profession's most careful study.

The Methods Course

The methods course is under heavy fire. Unless it is revolutionized, it will probably be abolished. Much of the liberal arts criticism is justified, as methods has tended to be a course in which instructors elaborated upon the banal and the obvious. Exhortation has been high; analysis has been absent. The instructor who exhorts his students of method to ask questions that are clear and understandable is probably making no contribution to the technical competence of neophyte teachers.

It goes without saying that a good teacher will ask the right questions, and will ask them clearly. A methods course can improve the questions that students ask only by recognizing and dealing with the reasons for poor questions. Sometimes a teacher does not ask a right question because his subject-matter preparation fails to suggest it. Example: The teacher of history whose sparse background in economics makes it unlikely that he will ask questions about the effect of deficit-financing by the New Deal and New Frontier upon the size and composition of the gross national product. Similarly, a teacher who has never studied logic will fail to ask certain questions, and those many teachers who have not mastered their native tongue will always be ambiguous in many of their questions.

It is not the function of a methods course to teach economics, logic, or language. But if a teacher has a reasonable background in such subjects he can learn in a methods course how to apply this knowledge to instructional problems. Recent studies of teaching that distinguish between *definition, description, explanation,* and *justification* suggest a direction in which it would be possible for methods to develop. The proper handling of a definition is pedagogically different from the proper handling of a generalization, and likewise, the values that provide the basis for our justifications have to be handled in a special way. The teacher who is naive enough to ask a student for a true definition of free enterprise has failed to distinguish between a definition and a proposition, and is possibly slipping into his instruction some values that his students have not been encouraged to scrutinize critically. The most effective indoctrination of a totalitarian sort takes place in ways that are hidden even from the teacher. A methods course that teaches teachers an awareness of the logical aspects of instruction will not be open to the charge of conceptual void.

Normative Aspects of Social Studies

Social studies teachers believe in teaching values as well as facts. Their many objectives always include a few intents to teach students to be good. How this can be done without indoctrination has never been clear to most of us. We deplore what goes on in Russian schools. But in this country, under the revealing rubric, Know Your Enemy, students are taught to hate communism and to favor free enterprise. The only difference between what we do and what the Russians do is in the specific attitudes that schools attempt to inculcate. Both countries take a polar view on all ideological issues, and engage in emotionalisms, illogical thinking, and suppression of knowledge.

American educators who look upon dissemination of knowledge as a major purpose of public education take alarm when value commitments take precedence over cognitive obligations. "Does the teaching of certain values mean that many facts will not be taught?" they ask. They occasionally point out that a major difference between a democracy and a totalitarian culture is in the way beliefs are maintained and modified, not alone in the specific beliefs that happen to be dominant at a particular time in a particular country. They desire a kind of value education that would develop in everyone some capacity to do his own valuing. They do not find this concern or emphasis in most attempts to teach anticommunism.

A further complication is that any attempt by teachers to teach values that are not already dominant in the culture is unlikely to succeed, and there seems little point to teaching people to value what they already value, or are certain to value whether the school does anything or not. Moreover, very few teachers feel that they have the right, the freedom, the strength, or the courage to teach values that fly in the face of custom.

Perhaps a return to subject matter, a reinterpretation of problem-solving, and a new emphasis upon logic will help teachers to entertain the hypothesis that teaching people to be good is not their province. Teaching an understanding of how values affect and even distort perception is within their province. Teaching that certain values are inconsistent with other values is within their province as logicians. It is even their job to teach that some values are democratic, and how democracy is different from other systems in its effects upon human development. But no one, least of all our teachers, can tell the American people what their values are to be.

This position does not deny to knowledge a normative role but emphasizes that we teach *valuing*, not values. The role of knowledge within a process of valuing can be illustrated by a discussion of how a teacher, ideally, would handle a topic, socialized medicine. If students are to decide whether they are in favor of socialized medicine, they will find it helpful to learn what socialized medicine is, and what results from it. They will not acquire this knowledge from the free pamphlets of the American Medical Association. Neither can they learn it from any teacher who also has a specific attitude to purvey.

A fair and objective teacher will help his students find or develop a clear and non-circular definition of socialized medicine. He will also help them find data, if it is available, on the achievements and other effects of socialized medicine. He will help them to cope with the logic of those who are opponents or proponents of this institution. He will encourage them to speculate upon what the effects of socialized medicine would be if it were tried in this country. He would even ask them to rate these effects according to their desirability or undesirability. Although his knowledge of effects would give him no right to expect or demand that his students rate effects the way he would rate them, his commitment to logic would require him to expect his students to learn to rate effects according to consistent criteria. For instance, the student who favored socialized medicine, while opposing public education, might be asked to consider whether his valuing was entirely consistent. It is this building of a value structure in everyone that makes it possible for education to help youth discover who they are, and what they might become.

Some educators have expressed alarm at the idea that the concept of structure might achieve preeminence in social studies curriculum planning. They have feared that efforts to teach the structure of a subject would mean that our concern with values and needs would be lost from view. The teaching of structure is undoubtedly a threat to those who desire to teach their own values, for knowledge of the social sciences does not dictate a particular set of values. Students who possess the same knowledge may vary widely in their attitudes. On the other hand, a knowledge of the structure of social sciences has a key role to play in all valuing, and there is no conflict between those who want to teach the basic content of a field, and a process of intelligent valuing. A central assumption in reflective teaching is that attention to valuing is probably the only effective approach to the teaching of values.

Notes

1. *Time*, February 1, 1963, p. 68; also *Newsweek*, February 4, 1963, p. 56.
2. Maurice P. Hunt and Lawrence E. Metcalf, *Teaching High School Social Studies*. New York: Harper and Brothers, 1955.
3. *Ibid.*, p. 223.
4. Lawrence E. Metcalf. "Anticommunism in the Classroom—Education or Propaganda." *The Nation*. March 10, 1962, pp. 215–216; 224.
5. Leon Festinger. *A Theory of Cognitive Dissonance*. Evanston, Ill.: Row, Peterson and Company, 1957. Also Prescott Lecky. *Self-Consistency, a Theory of Personality*. New York: Island Press, 1945.
6. Robert Lynd. *Knowledge for What?* Princeton, N.J.: Princeton University Press, 1948.
7. The writer has summarized some of this research and its inadequacy in a chapter in the recently published *Handbook of Research on Teaching*, edited by N. L. Gage, and published by Rand McNally in 1963.
8. Alan Griffin. "The Subject Matter Preparation of Teachers of History." Unpublished dissertation. Ohio State University, 1942.
9. Ernest Bayles. *Theory and Practice of Teaching*. New York: Harper and Brothers, 1950.
10. Cf. Leonard Swift and John Palmer. Unpublished dissertations. University of Illinois. Also assorted papers and articles.

History in the New Social Studies

EDWIN FENTON

A decade ago, a curricular revolution began to transform the teaching of science and mathematics in American schools. During the last five years, the social studies have joined this movement. Private foundations, the government, and public school systems have financed more than 40 major curriculum reform projects during this period.[1] Organized in a variety of ways and with widely diverse objectives, these projects promise to have a marked effect on social studies programs in the schools.

In one way or another, most social studies projects involve the teaching of history. Only a few, however, particularly those organized at Educational Services, Inc., Amherst, Northwestern, the Newton Public Schools, the Cleveland Center, and Carnegie Tech, plan to develop one or more full courses in history. What they are doing—developing a new history to take its place beside the new science and math in the schools—has great significance for the historical profession.

No single element of the new history is really new; in fact, each element has an ancient lineage, at least in theory. Yet the projects are putting together a blend which is distinctively new. One aspect of the newness is the pattern in which a number of well-known elements are being assembled. Another is the translation of theory into practice in elementary and secondary school classrooms. Together, these changes imply a coming revolution in the teaching of history and of the social studies generally. Let me try to predict the nature of this impending revolution.

NOTE: This article appeared in *Social Education*, May 1966, pp. 325–328. Reprinted by permission of Edwin Fenton.

First to objectives. Although no two directors of curriculum projects would put the case in exactly the same words, most would be willing to cluster their objectives under three general headings: the development in the student of certain attitudes and values, the use of a mode of inquiry, and the attainment of knowledge about selected content. Moreover, most of the project directors would endorse the statement of objectives in behavioral terms so that their achievement by students can be measured precisely. This emphasis alone clearly distinguishes the new history from its antecedents.

The new history states many of the traditional humanistic goals of historical study in the form of affective objectives: the development of attitudes toward school and society, the development of each individual's value system, and the growth of a personal, coherent philosophy of life. The Taxonomy of Educational Objectives, compiled by Krathwohl and the Chicago group, has arranged affective goals such as these in ascending order of complexity and has suggested sound ways to state goals and to assess their attainment.[2] A number of the objectives, such as willingness to listen and willingness to respond, can be reached primarily through the way in which classes are taught, and hence imply the use of certain teaching strategies. Others—the development of a personal value system, for example—imply consideration of historical and social science content which challenges each student to reflect on his own value system. Each of the history curriculum projects involves affective objectives in a variety of ways.

As a second goal, virtually every project director emphasizes explicitly the importance of training students in the process of inquiry. This fresh emphasis has resulted in part as a reaction to the practice of requiring students to memorize facts and generalizations from textbooks. It also stems from a desire to help students learn how to discover things for themselves. One authority estimates that the new scholarly knowledge amassed in the last decade or so probably equals the total that mankind had discovered in the previous centuries of his existence. This knowledge explosion alone forces teachers to concentrate their attention upon ways to learn, in preference to an attempt to cram an arbitrarily chosen set of facts and generalizations into the heads of students.

As a part of the mode of inquiry, a number of projects are trying to identify and to teach the structure of history. We still, however, do not have consensus about the meaning of the word structure. Let me try out one idea—not a new one—on you.[3] Structure can mean the analytical questions which historians and social scientists put to data in order to make it meaningful. As we all know, facts have meaning only when the minds of men order them into patterns. As historians engage in research, they often put the implications of a social science model, a generalization developed from previous research, or an earlier instance of a similar pattern of development, in the form of an analytical question which guides their search for data. These questions generate hypotheses. The development and validation of hypotheses constitute the heart of the mode of inquiry in both history and the more rigorous social sciences. The projects are developing materials and teaching strategies to help students to learn how to interpret the past; the structure of the disciplines, phrased as analytical questions, make up an integral part of this procedure.

The projects are devoting equal attention to the process of validating hypotheses. Most directors have embraced one of the schemes for classifying cognitive skills developed during the last decade.[4] Many exercises developed by social studies projects emphasize the attainment of an individual cognitive skill, in order to give students practice with each in turn. Eventually, students can be challenged to bring their full battery of skills to bear on the sophisticated task of validating, revising, or abandoning the hypotheses they have developed, using, in the process, well-established rules of critical thinking and data that they have gathered from required reading and research.

The final group of objectives concerns knowledge of content.[5] But what content? Many decisions about selection of content follow from the two groups of objectives just cited: attitudes and values, and use of the mode of inquiry. We can, however, reach some of these objectives just as effectively with one body of subject matter as with another. So additional criteria for the selection of content becomes necessary. Generally, the new history projects, like many old ones, have chosen four: the needs and interests of the child, contemporary problems on which the past can throw light, generalizations or concepts drawn from social science disciplines, and that corpus of knowledge about a subject field which the project directors think constitutes the minimum required for a particular student audience.

Each of these three groups of objectives seems implicit in the work of most social studies curriculum projects. The projects differ in respect to objectives, however, in two major ways. First, the degree of explicitness with which directors have identified objectives varies considerably. Most of the projects have not yet incorporated into their work a written rationale setting forth objectives and discussing procedures for their attainment. Second, the rank order of the three groups of objectives varies from one project to the next. Some place knowledge of content first while others emphasize affective objectives or the mode of inquiry. Anyone who studies these marked variations soon loses all fear of the development of a single national curriculum.

What about civic education? Each of the three groups of objectives I have named implies preparation for responsible citizenship: a set of attitudes and values in keeping with a democratic credo, the ability to use a mode of inquiry, and knowledge of content—such as the history of the American Constitution—which provides information about institutional settings and other data essential to a rational decision-making process. But this threefold way of looking at objectives casts civic education in a new light. It provides a framework of discussion acceptable to both the civic education camp and the foes of what has in the past passed for citizenship training. It also provides evaluating instruments carefully devised by our best scholars which may enable us to tell when we have achieved some of our goals.

Objectives imply teaching strategies. Although each of the major history projects places more than usual emphasis upon inductive techniques, no one style of teaching can accurately describe the new history.[6] Instead, a whole range of styles is employed, from straight exposition at one end of the scale to pure discovery exercises at the other. This variety can be justified fully by our knowledge of the learning process. If a teacher wants his students to memorize a body of data for some purpose, expository techniques are probably the most efficient available. But students cannot learn to use a mode of inquiry when taught by exposition alone, nor can they practice most cognitive skills by listening to a lecture or by reading a list of skills in a text. Some of the history projects, like those of the other social studies, have become deeply involved in the sophisticated problem of trying to decide what to teach by means of each of the many available teaching strategies. Other projects seem less deeply concerned with this issue.

Both objectives and strategies imply a range of teaching materials.[7] A few seem as expository as traditional texts. At the other end of the scale are collections of data designed for discovery exercises. Between these extremes lie collections of source materials—documents, biographies and autobiographies, pieces of fiction, chronicles, case studies, and so forth. While most materials remain in printed form, many projects have developed audio-visual materials, each designed for a specific objective and for use with particular teaching strategies.

None of the history projects I have seen focuses on the study of a conventional textbook. Instead, each is putting together units or courses built primarily out of carefully selected and edited combinations of source materials and secondary accounts. Sometimes, as in the ESI eighth-grade American history course, only source materials accompanied by a sort of student workbook are used. At Newton, a great variety of public documents, biographical and autobiographical accounts, diaries, pieces of fiction, and analytical articles in both European and American history have been collected to accompany an existing short text which carries the narrative. The Amherst group is building a number of two-week problems in American history primarily from contemporary accounts, and expects later to write a brief narrative linking these units together. The Northwestern staff has developed simulation games along with a number of short exercises designed to teach students historical terms. Our program at Carnegie Tech is built around three days of readings in sources and secondary accounts followed by a summary essay which links the problem of one week to that of the next.

These objectives, teaching strategies, and materials all imply the need for a range of ways in which to deploy students for instruction.[8] Hence, a few of the projects are beginning to explore the relationships between different ways of grouping students on the one hand and objectives, strategy, and materials on the other. For example, they are trying to discover what objectives can best be attained through instruction of large groups, and which ones require independent work in the library. Most of the projects, however, seem to assume a self-contained classroom in which the same teacher meets the same group of students each day. This assumption may build unnecessary rigidity in social studies instruction.

Finally, all of what I have said implies a need for a range of evaluating instruments: objective tests, primarily to test skills, affective objectives, and content; essay tests and papers to test all of these, but particularly to rate the ability to use the mode of inquiry; and observation of students during class discussions, to test each of these objectives. The projects are developing these evaluation techniques with great care; they should be a boon to busy teachers.[9]

Several additional aspects of the new social studies deserve mention before I examine some implications for the profession of this reform movement. First, most of the projects form careful judgments about which aspects of the social studies should be taught at each level, and in what sequence they should be taught. The Northwestern Center in particular focuses on this issue, in order to make sense of the fifth, eighth, eleventh grade American history mess so as to avoid needless repetition and to ensure an integrated educational experience. Second, all of the projects provide maximum teaching aids, extending in at least one instance to model daily lesson plans. Finally, each project tries out its materials in a number of classes, and revises them as a result of the trials.

Let me suggest several implications of the new social studies for the profession to consider. The projects need constructive criticism, careful evaluation by scholars outside project staffs who will read all the material produced by a project, study its rationale and its implications for education, observe some classes where it is in use, and report responsibly to the profession. Perhaps we need a new journal devoted to critical reviews of materials for use in the schools and colleges, and to reports of research about teaching strategies.

We also need additional curriculum projects in all the social studies at all grade levels. Increasingly in the future, a wide diversity of curricular arrangements will develop as local curriculum committees make decisions for their own schools about scope and sequence. The profession should provide a wide range of materials devised for a variety of objectives and student audiences at all grade levels. Our best historical scholars should help to develop these materials. At the moment, with startlingly few exceptions, they are not doing so.

We should also suggest criteria by which teachers can decide which of the new materials, if any, to select for their students. To do this, historians must become sophisticated about objectives and about the implications of these objectives for teaching strategy, materials, pupil deployment, and evaluation. Much of the new material will come out in pamphlet form. A creative teacher will be able to make up his own course using a great variety of techniques and materials from those produced in a dozen centers. But to do this job well, a teacher must be disciplined and knowledgeable as well as imaginative. College history classrooms are a good place to start.

The new materials and inductive teaching techniques require of teachers, moreover, a better grasp of content than did courses based on the assumption that students should memorize the text. I'm sure this point is obvious. We all need in-service work now more than ever before if we are to do excellent jobs in the classroom.

These conditions challenge in-service and pre-service education programs for history teachers. I believe that teacher training programs should concentrate on content courses. Subject knowledge is indispensable to good teaching, but it is not sufficient. Teachers also need to examine objectives, teaching strategies, materials, deployment, and evaluation. The present structure of NDEA institutes in history and geography may not provide enough aid, since some scholars who run them know little about these matters. Institute faculty members who work with teachers may have to familiarize themselves with the curricular problems social studies teachers face if they wish to be maximally effective.

We must take a new look as well at college teaching. Many college historians and social scientists still teach exclusively by lecture and depend heavily on texts and monographs. They are content-centered, paying only incidental attention to the mode of inquiry or to affective objectives. But college textbook-and-lecture courses cannot provide satisfactory models of good teaching for future elementary and secondary school teachers who will be asked to employ a wide variety of inductive materials and methods in order to reach a range of goals. What can we do about the problem?

One thing we can do is develop ways to get experimental editions of new materials into the hands of college subject professors, of methods teachers, of NDEA institute directors, and of classroom teachers everywhere. We must also try to establish centers where these materials can be collected and where teachers can visit to observe a range of teaching strategies. The Office of Education plans to establish such centers soon. We must make sure that the projects contribute to them and that the history profession helps to staff and to utilize them.

A number of signs indicate that the profession is moving in some of these directions. The AHA has long maintained the Service Center for Teachers of History, which has published an excellent bibliographic pamphlet series and has sponsored a number of conferences and workshops. It is now considering a second pamphlet series which will concentrate upon the teaching of history. The Organization of American Historians, through its Study Committee on History in the Schools, has already called several meetings of representative historians and social studies teachers to assess the role of the profession in this reform movement. Several hundred historians last summer formed the staffs of NDEA institutes organized by the Office of Education for elementary and secondary school history teachers; similar institutes will be held in 1966. In addition, many professional historians have written texts for the schools, and a smaller number have devoted part of their time to one of the new curriculum projects. This summer a small group of distinguished American historians will run a curriculum project at Smith College to design a new introductory American history course for college students based on an inquiry process.

If these promising trends are to grow, history departments must recognize work with the schools as the equivalent of traditional scholarly research when they are considering promotion and tenure. Most history departments are not yet willing to do so. The proud profession of teaching, which has taken second place to the production of scholarly works, deserves equality. Once we grant research and development about teaching history equal status with traditional scholarly work, many of the problems of teaching history in the schools can be solved. Here is a challenge to the entire profession. It demands careful reflection about our purposes and a careful reappraisal of our value system. Both are long overdue.

Notes

[1] For lists of the projects, see *Social Education* 29:225–227; April 1965; John U. Michaelis and A. Montgomery Johnston, editors, *The Social Sciences: Foundations of the Social Studies* (Boston, 1965), p. 275–305; Sylvia Harrison, "A Summary of Current Social Studies Curriculum Projects" (Educational Testing Services, Princeton, November 1964).

[2] David R. Krathwohl, Benjamin S. Bloom, and Bertram B. Masia, *Taxonomy of Educational Objectives: The Classification of Educational Goals: Handbook II: The Affective Domain.* (New York, 1964.)

[3] Some social studies experts identify structure with generalizations drawn from the disciplines. See, for example, Paul R. Hanna and John R. Lee, "Generalizations from the Social Sciences," in John U. Michaelis, editor, *Social Studies in Elementary Schools* (Washington, 1962), p. 62–89; and State Curriculum Commission, California State Department of Education, "Generalizations from the Social Sciences," in Michaelis and Johnston, *Social Sciences*, p. 306–339. Others equate structure with major concepts. See Roy A. Price, Warren Hickman, and

Gerald Smith, *Major Concepts for Social Studies* (Syracuse, 1965), the latest and most significant publication among many on this subject. That structure may be identified with analytical questions is implied in Social Science Research Council, *The Social Sciences in Historical Study: A Report of the Committee on Historiography* (New York, 1954) and argued in detail in Edwin Fenton, *Teaching the New Social Studies in Secondary Schools: An Inductive Approach* (New York, 1966). Two useful discussions of structure can be found in Jerome Bruner, *The Process of Education* (Cambridge, 1960) and Joseph J. Schwab, "The Concept of the Structure of a Discipline," *The Educational Record* 43:197–205; July 1962, available also through *Professional Reprints in Education* #8001 (Charles E. Merrill Books, Inc., Columbus).

[4] Benjamin S. Bloom and others, *Taxonomy of Educational Objectives: The Classification of Educational Goals: Handbook I: The Cognitive Domain* (New York, 1956); Robert H. Ennis, "A Concept of Critical Thinking," *Harvard Educational Review* 32:81–111; Winter 1962; Byron G. Massialas, editor, "The Indiana Experiments in Inquiry: The Social Studies," *Bulletin of the School of Education: Indiana University* 39; May 1963.

[5] Two articles dealing with criteria for the selection of content are particularly important. They are: Arthur S. Bolster, "History, Historians and the Secondary School Curriculum," *Harvard Educational Review* 32:39–65; Winter 1962; and Donald W. Oliver, "The Selection of Content in the Social Sciences," *Harvard Educational Review* 27:271–300; Fall 1957.

[6] See Edwin Fenton, *Teaching the New Social Studies* and Hilda Taba and James L. Hills, *Teacher Handbook for Contra Costa Social Studies, Grades 1-6* (Hayward, California, 1965).

[7] Most of the projects have not yet published materials. A few have released experimental editions which can be obtained at addresses cited in the articles in footnote 1. In addition, a few titles based upon some of the principles of the new history have been published independently of the projects. See Van R. Halsey, editor, *New Dimensions in American History* (9 titles; Boston, D. C. Heath); Edwin C. Rozwenc, editor, *Basic Concepts in History and the Social Sciences* (7 titles; Boston, D. C. Heath); Edwin Fenton and David Fowler, editors, *The Scott, Foresman Problems in American History* (9 titles; Chicago, Scott, Foresman and Company); Edwin Fenton, *32 Problems in World History* (Chicago, 1964).

[8] See J. Lloyd Trump and Dorsey Baynham, *Focus on Change: Guide to Better Schools* (Chicago, 1961) and Judson T. Shaplin and Henry F. Olds, *Team Teaching* (New York, 1964). Also, Medill Bair and Richard G. Woodward, *Team Teaching in Action* (Boston, 1964).

[9] For sample evaluating instruments, see Bloom *et al., Taxonomy*; Krathwohl *et al., Taxonomy*; Harry D. Berg, *Evaluation in Social Studies* (Washington, 1965).

Bruner's New Social Studies: A Critique

MARK M. KRUG

Many voices have recently been raised to suggest that the emphasis on the teaching of social studies should be on the structure of history and of the social sciences. Advocates of this position take much of their inspiration and rationale from the work of Jerome Bruner. Bruner, a Harvard psychologist, maintains that each discipline can best be mastered by teaching the basic organizing principles which, according to his view, form the structure of every natural and social science. These generalizations and broad ideas help scholars, who have invented them, to organize their facts and their respective bodies of knowledge into meaningful and connected patterns. Students who study any discipline by looking at its structure are bound to find the interconnecting spiraling logic of these sets of broad organizing principles.

Bruner and his co-worker, Jerrold Zacharias, a physicist of M.I.T., contend that the stress on structure proved to be a great boon for the new mathematics and new physics and that there is no reason to doubt that the same can be true for the social studies. Consequently, both scholars, who are the leaders in Educational Services, Incorporated, an endowed corporation, are now hard at work to prepare a new social studies curriculum.

The new curriculum is to be based on Bruner's contention that "the structure of knowledge—its connectedness and its derivations that make one idea follow another—is the proper emphasis in education. For it is

NOTE: This article appeared in *Social Education*, October 1966, pp. 400–406. Reprinted by permission of Mark M. Krug.

structure, the great conceptual inventions that bring order to the congeries of disconnected observations, that gives meaning to what we may learn and makes possible the opening up of new realms of experience."[1] The implication is that learning one set of broad concepts will logically lead to the learning of a more complex set of conceptual frameworks. Bruner is confident that "any subject can be taught effectively in some intellectually honest form to any child at any stage of development."[2]

It may be of significance to note that in explicating his theory of the structure of disciplines, Bruner uses, almost without exception, examples from mathematics or from the natural sciences. His interpretation of the role and power of the organizing concepts seems to be best understood and related to the function and objectives of the natural sciences. Take, for instance, the statement of Bruner that, "Knowledge is a model we construct to give meaning and structure to regularities in experience. The organizing ideas of any body of knowledge are inventions for rendering experience economical and connected. . . . The power of great organizing concepts is in large part that they permit us to understand and sometimes to predict or change the world in which we live."[3] This statement has an obvious relevance to mathematics, physics, and chemistry. The question is whether Bruner in his work on the social studies curriculum will be able to isolate some great organizing ideas in history or the social sciences which will help the students "to understand and sometimes predict or change the world." Once this is done, it remains to be seen whether historians will be ready to accept the structure of history as finally defined by Bruner and his colleagues at E.S.I.

Bruner cannot escape the task of defining the structure of history and of other social sciences because, according to his own conception, curriculum revision calls for two initial steps, the definition of the structure of the discipline by the scholars themselves and the organization of the discovered structure into meaningful patterns of relationships for purposes of classroom instruction. This means that Bruner would have to ask historians to define the structure of their discipline. The few historians who have tried to find some order, rhythm, or structure in history have done so with limited success and usually without the endorsement of their fellow historians. Whether this task can be done by Bruner with the help of several historians who are working with him is very doubtful. The task of identifying even a small number of fundamental ideas in world history and of finding their spiraling relatedness may prove to be formidable, if not forbidding. An example of a great idea in history, cited by Bruner, "A nation must trade in order to live," is so broad and so full of fuzzy implications, that its value for classroom instruction may prove to be as useless as the generalization, "in war there is no substitute for victory" or "appeasement of aggressors does not pay."

If we are to teach the structure of history or of sociology in high school classes, scholars in these disciplines will have to agree on some list of fundamental ideas, basic skills, and methods needed and used by historians and sociologists and then show how these great ideas and skills are related to one another and how they represent the structure of history and sociology. This has never been attempted by historians or sociologists and I doubt whether many would want to try. Commenting on this question, Professor Fred M. Newmann of Harvard wrote: "Can a discipline have a structure independent of the scholars' ability to articulate it? An affirmative answer carries with it an implication that some sort of intellectual natural law transcends scholarly endeavor, unaffected by the studies of human beings, *that pre-existing structures are waiting to be discovered.* On the other hand, a negative reply suggests that the utility of structure as a concept depends mostly upon a prediction that scholars will in fact be able to articulate the structure of their field. If the existence of structure is mainly a function of the scholars' ability to construct it, then there is no logical basis for assuming that any given discipline has a structure."[4]

Suppose that some historians, even as respectable and distinguished as those who serve as advisers to Professor Bruner at the E.S.I. Project, would conclude that they have discovered the "pre-existing" structure of history. Would their "discovery" be accepted by their colleagues? Is it probable that an interlocking, logically connected, progressively complex system of fundamental ideas in history, or for that matter in sociology or in political science, could ever be identified? The basic difficulty which apparently does not exist or has been overcome in mathematics and in the natural sciences is the lack of any logical ladder of progression in the study of sociology or history. It is not absolutely essential for a high school student to have had a course in the American Revolution in order to study the Civil War. Children do learn about the Napoleonic Wars without ever having heard of the invasions and conquests of Alexander the Great. It would be rather difficult to formulate a generalization from the Napoleonic Wars which would have a logical relationship to the wars of Alexander or the conquests of Genghis Khan. The same would undoubtedly be true about the broader questions in sociology. It may be possible and profitable to study about the "apartheid policy" in South Africa without any relation, or logically discoverable relatedness, to the situation of Indians in Peru or the Negroes in America. In fact, it can be argued that any attempt, for instructional purposes based on a search for structure, to develop an organizing idea which would relate the study of these three areas would be full of loopholes and misleading.

Even granting for a moment the legitimacy of the contention that the teaching of the structure of the disciplines is the proper emphasis in education, there is a question which would naturally occur to those who have taught social studies on a high school level. Would not the teaching of the broad concepts and generalizing principles, even if taught by inventive teachers by the inductive "discovery" method recommended by Bruner, prove to be boring for many students during the long stretch of the school year? Granting that some of the students will, after engaging in an inquiry by imitating the ways of research of sociologists, political scientists, and historians, experience the "thrill of discovery," is it not sensible to assume that many other students would find this intellectual exercise boring and wasteful?

While there is no question that in the search for structure, Bruner's discovery approach is valuable and should have a place in the social studies curriculum and in the lively, dramatic study of history and the social sciences, to build the entire social studies curriculum on the structure theory is fraught with grave dangers. Much in history and in the study of human personality and group interrelationship which cannot and should not be fitted into a structure, or even related to something else, is eminently worthy of teaching to our children. The way a historian or an economist goes about his work is interesting and may occasionally be useful as a mode of inquiry in the social studies class, but equally interesting and equally important is a deductive approach by a scholarly teacher who constructs his lesson by presenting to his students for discussion and analysis conflicting conclusions reached by historians about the causes of the Civil War or about the effectiveness of the New Deal legislation.

Newmann poses a legitimate query to Bruner and his followers. "Why should a general lay population be taught to perform intellectual operations of a nature preferred uniquely by the academic profession? That is, why should all children be taught to ask and answer the kinds of questions that interest historians, political scientists, economists, etc.?"[5] It is also disturbing to note that Bruner and the Structuralists in the social studies seem to assume that history and the social sciences each have one structure, when in fact most of them may be examined in terms of several sets or patterns of great conceptual ideas.

Scholars who may eventually be induced to undertake the task of writing complete social studies curricula based on the structure theory will undoubtedly find that historians and social scientists freely borrow ideas, methods, concepts, including fundamental ideas, from one another. Professor Arno Bellack of Teachers College pointed out in his critique of Bruner's theories that "the social scientists today are characterized by a plurality of methods and conceptual schemes. . . . Instead of a unity of method or a single universal discourse, we are confronted with a vast confederation of separate areas of study. Modes of thinking and analysis differ from field to field and even from problem to problem within the same field. In time, a Bacon of the sciences that bear on social and cultural behavior may emerge, but that time is not yet."[6]

The E.S.I. under the leadership of Professor Bruner has made considerable progress in preparing a new social studies curriculum. A preliminary report on the social studies, published in 1963 by the American Council of Learned Societies and Educational Services, Incorporated, included a basic statement of policy in the preparation of a course of study in the social studies. It reads in part: "history, sociology, anthropology, economics and political science may for convenience be separated as academic disciplines, but they all deal with a single thing: the behavior of man in society. Accordingly, we propose to teach them jointly, not separately."[7] One wonders what the reaction from the academic mathematicians and natural scientists would be to a similar statement: "Mathematics, physics, chemistry and biology may for convenience be separated as academic disciplines, but they all deal with a single thing: man's attempt to understand and to control his natural environment. Accordingly, we propose to teach them jointly, not separately." The outcries of anguish and protest would undoubtedly be overwhelming. And yet, the Structuralists in the social studies do not hesitate to advocate an amalgamation of history and the social sciences and do not seem to be concerned about the protection of the integrity of these disciplines and the reluctance, if not outright opposition of most historians and of many social scientists, to a reductionist synthetic unification.

The E.S.I. group has identified 24 broad generalizations which are to be taught sequentially by using interdisciplinary insights and techniques. Here is an example of one of these generalizations.

"All societies have developed in different degrees of elaboration special institutions for ensuring conformity to other institutions [law] or changing institutions. All ultimately use the threat of force to try to ensure that conformity to institutions shall be rewarding." It is impossible to quarrel with such a broad generalization, but whether it constitutes an organizing, fundamental idea representing the structure of any discipline or the joint structure of history and the social sciences, is another matter. Most scholars would undoubtedly have grave doubts.

Apparently the followers of the structure approach in the social studies are not as cautious as the scholars in Cambridge. The new social studies curriculum published in 1965 by the Wisconsin State Department of Public Instruction, on which 26 Wisconsin educators worked for three years, set down six major concepts each for history, political science, economics, geography, and sociology. These concepts, the authors claim, are applicable to all mankind. One of the major concepts in history reads: "Human experience is continuous and interrelated. Continuity is a fact of life: there is nothing new under the sun. . . . All men, events and institutions are the outcome of something that has gone before. . . . Man is a product of the past and restricted by it."[8]

Some of the other concepts from history which, according to the Wisconsin guide, are to serve as "a means of organizing subject matter in a most meaningful pattern" are:

Every effort at reform began as the private opinion of an individual.
It is difficult to separate fact from fiction. Every writer has his biases.
Those who cannot remember the past may be condemned to repeat it.
Facts may often be interpreted in more than one way.
Nations with great power may not always use it wisely.

A similar concept in political science states. "Governments are established by men. In some situations, people delegate authority; in others authority is imposed."

One could, I hope not too irreverently, comment, "Elementary, Dr. Watson," since some of these generalizations are obvious and even trite. Several of the cited generalizing concepts in history would find little support from professional historians. Certainly, by no stretch of imagination can these statements be assumed to constitute the fundamental concepts in history constituting its structure. The more important concern is the question of how interested high school youngsters are in such high sounding generalizations and whether it is wise to build an entire social studies curriculum around them.

In the E.S.I. Report published in the summer of 1965, Bruner gives a rather detailed description of the new social studies course of study which would be given experimentally in grades 4, 5, and 6, and be entitled simply "man." "The content of the course," Bruner writes, "is man: his nature as a species, the forces that shaped or continue to shape his humanity. Three questions recur throughout, namely: What is human about human beings? How did they get that way? How can they be made more so?"[9]

The course would include a section on language, contrasting how humans and animals manage to send and receive messages, on how language is acquired by young humans and other primates, and the origins of human language and its role in shaping human characteristics. This section, says Bruner, may take a year of study. The second section of the course would deal with "tools." The objective is to give the children an idea of the relation between tools and our way of life. "Our ultimate object in teaching about tools," Bruner writes, "is . . . not so much to explicate tools and their significance, but to explore how tools affected man's evolution."[10] The study about changes in technology and the corresponding changes in society aims to fulfill one of the basic goals of the social studies program; namely, "to get across the idea that a technology requires a counterpart in social organization before it can be used effectively by a society."[11]

The crux of the matter is what is meant by the word "effectively." This statement represents one of the important objectives of the social studies as defined by the E.S.I. group. It is indeed strange and controversial. If one understands the main trend of thought of the atomic scientists as reflected in recent years in the articles that appeared in the *Bulletin of Atomic Scientists*, it is the considered opinion of our leading atomic scientists that we have failed to build a "counterpart in social organization" to deal with atomic technology. However, our society has used atomic energy "effectively" to subdue Japan, to run atomic submarines, ships, and power stations, and to create some kind of equilibrium in the world by the reality of a balance of atomic terror.

The third section of Bruner's new social studies curriculum deals with social organizations. It is aimed at explaining to the children "that there is a structure in a society and that this structure is not fixed once for all." It would seem that even our average students should have little difficulty in grasping this principle which is certainly quite obvious to them from their own gangs, clubs, and school organizations.

The fourth unit is devoted to the theme of child rearing. This study deals with the phenomenon of sentiment in human life which develops during the long human childhood and the influence of the special manner of childhood on future personality development.

The fourth and final section of this course of study aims to develop a world view and deals with "man's drive to explicate and represent his world." "Central to the unit is the idea that men everywhere are humans, however advanced or 'primitive' their civilizations." This seems to be essentially an anthropological unit aimed at proving that all cultures have inherent values and that there are no "superior"and "inferior" cultures. The objective is to combat an ethnocentric approach to world cultures.

In explaining why this unit should be taught early on the elementary school level, Bruner presents an idealistic view of world history based on the idea of the rule of reason and the continued progress, which few historians would accept. "We want children," he states, "to recognize that man is constantly seeking to bring reason [*sic!*] into his world, that he does so with a variety of symbolic tools, and that he does so with a striking and fully rational humanity."[12] Our students will be ready to accept this view only if we impose upon them and somehow enforce a total newspaper and television blackout and also frequently tape their eyes and ears so that they cannot listen to their parents, friends, and casual acquaintances. Otherwise, they may tend to believe that, unfortunately, man is not very often successful in bringing "reason into his world."

As for the methodology to be used in this new social studies curriculum, Bruner wants to use three techniques, which seem to be unique to the E.S.I. because they bear no resemblance either to the methods of inquiry in history or in the social sciences. The first technique consists of using contrast, the second is the use of especially prepared games that "incorporate the formal properties of the phenomena for which the game is an analogue." The third is "the ancient approach of stimulating self-consciousness about assumptions—going beyond mere admonition to think."[13]

Little can be said about this new methodology in the social studies because few details have been given as yet. Bruner sees "the most urgent need" to teach the students to use theoretical models which will be "rather sophisticated." Evaluation will have to await the publication of the models, and reports of their application will have to be analyzed. Enough, however, has been published to indicate that once the curriculum (which will include materials, games, films, and models, all prepared under the supervision of academic scholar), is submitted to the schools, the social studies teachers will have little opportunity to exercise their initiative and inventiveness. The traditional autonomy and flexibility of the better trained and more effective history and social studies teachers may be severely curtailed. If past experience is any guide, the more promising young people will refuse to go into social studies teaching where they would serve only as assistants to the curriculum-making and curriculum-evaluating academic scholars. Other teachers will undoubtedly offer passive or active resistance to the new packaged curriculum.

Bruner and his associates are constantly emphasizing the importance of the child "doing" mathematics or physics instead of learning about them. The student should "do" the things on the blackboards or in the laboratory that mathematicians and physicists are doing. That sounds reasonable and exciting. But how does this apply to history? Christopher Jencks, in his review of Bruner's book, *Toward a Theory of Instruction*, made an acute observation. "The analogy," he wrote, "between physics and history is at bottom misleading. The men who really 'do' history are not, after all, historians. They are politicians, generals, diplomats, philosophers. It is these people whom the young need to understand, far more than they need to understand the historians who judge them."[14]

All new curricular approaches to the social studies are basically determined by the postulated objectives. It is the objectives set by the curriculum makers that determine the content of the particular courses of study proposed.

Thus, Jerome Bruner hopes to achieve five ideals:

1. *To give our pupils respect for and confidence in the powers of their own mind.*

2. *To give them respect, moreover, for the powers of thought concerning the human condition, man's plight and his social life.*

3. *To provide them with a set of workable models to make it simpler*

to analyze the nature of the social world in which they live and the condition in which man finds himself.

4. *To impart a sense of respect for the capacities and plight of man as a species, for his origins, for his potential and for his humanity.*

5. *To leave the student with a sense of the unfinished business of man's evolution.*[15]

These objectives deserve some scrutiny. They are truly far-reaching, ambitious, and, frankly, not entirely clear. How does one "give" or "impart" respect or a "sense of respect," and how would a teacher go about measuring whether he has done so? In setting before the social studies teachers the task of stressing the power of man's rational mind (an interesting throwback to the worship of man's rational powers by the philosophers of the Age of Renaissance and Enlightenment), do we not belittle or eliminate the evidence that suggests severe limits to the use of the "powers of thought" in dealing with the human condition? Are the teachers expected to know the state of the "human condition" today and of "man's plight and his social life"? Is this not a tall order? Is this not too much to expect from high school teachers? Would not a world-conclave of scholars have a very difficult time in assessing the human condition and the very complicated plight of modern man? Why should it not also be one of the objectives in the social studies (if such basic personality changes are indeed feasible) to try to impart a sense of *dis*respect for man's consistent refusal to live up to his potential and for his *in*humanity? An effective and imaginative study of history would certainly be more likely to give the student a more balanced picture of man's virtues and follies.

The Bruner objectives, and especially the last one which aims to leave the student with a sense of unfinished business of man's evolution, have a distinct anthropological flavor. Indeed the whole proposed curriculum is anthropological in its essence. The E.S.I. approach was to be an interdisciplinary one, teaching jointly all the social sciences, but, in fact, there is little of political science in Bruner's curriculum. As for history and geography, they are virtually non-existent. It is curious that the accumulation of a body of knowledge—yes, the acquisition of related and meaningful information—is not mentioned among the objectives. This, of course, is in line with the recent trend of denigrating the importance of the transmission of accumulated knowledge. The stress is on skills, concepts, and in Bruner's terms, on "workable models." All this is based on the unproven and perhaps unprovable assumption that it is not really important to know much about, let us say, the English Civil War, about the American Revolution, the French Revolution or the Bolshevik Revolution. Bruner and his colleagues seem to say that what a future intelligent man needs to know is the basic concepts and generalizations pertaining to all revolutions, or a workable model of *a* revolution, possess the skills of critical inquiry, and when the need arises, he will merely apply the generalization, the models, and the skills to the study of any revolution he chooses to investigate.

Crane Brinton's careful study, *The Anatomy of Revolution* has failed to come up with many generalizing principles about revolutions and clearly indicated that the differences and the variables involved in the American and the French Revolutions or between the English Civil War and the Bolshevik Revolution are so great that each of these great events should and deserve to be studied separately. Even if it were possible to construct, in Bruner's words, "workable models to make it simpler to analyze the nature of the social world" and apply them to the study of revolutions, our pupils would be deprived of the opportunity of meeting and living with (through dramatic and effective teaching) such fascinating people as T. R. Roosevelt, Cromwell, Lilburne, Marie Antoinette, Dante, Lenin, and Trotsky.

Questions pertaining to the learning of a body of knowledge (carefully selected and logically connected) are rather simple. Is it or is it not important for high school graduates and college freshmen to know about the Populist Rebellion, the War of 1812, about Daniel Webster and Marcy Tweed, about the Clay Compromise, about the Teapot Dome Scandal, and about the history of Reconstruction? Is it or is it not important for high school graduates to know about Pericles and the conquests of Alexander, about Caesar, the Carthagenian Wars, about Constantine, about Genghis Khan, the reforms of Ahkbar and the wisdom of Confucius, about Voltaire, Napoleon and Waterloo? The assumption postulated here is that such—and similar related—knowledge taught in an analytical and interpretative manner is essential and worthwhile for any moderately educated man. I would shudder to think that a college freshman would have to see a Broadway play to become acquainted for the first time with the women of Troy, the complicated nature of Marat, or the tragic downfall of Charles Dilke. Historical knowledge may, of course, be gained through the partial use of Fenton's inductive method, the public controversy approach of Oliver and Shaver, the traditional chronological approach, the case-study approach, or preferably by a combination of all these approaches.

Some of the new curricula in the social studies, based on Bruner's ideas, have drastically cut the time devoted to United States history and are drawing fire from some right-wing groups. This is unfortunate and it must be resisted as an unwarranted interference with the orderly process of curriculum revision.

However, one would hope that it is legitimate to raise a voice in defense of the teaching of American history as deserving a place of importance in the schooling of young Americans. Chauvinism has no place in the school because it is destructive and because it usually leads to unbridled cynicism. But it is proper to argue that to give the students an understanding and an appreciation of the ideas that brought about the founding of this nation and the men who helped to guide its destiny, and to make them aware of the constant struggle for the improvement of the democratic process, are the proper concern of social studies teachers and of the schools. It should be stressed that America must be taught full face, with all the warts showing, and that the teachers are duty bound not to gloss over the weaknesses and imperfections of our government and of our society.

The end result of such teaching of United States history, based on integrity, scholarship, and imagination, will be a sense of pride in the unique genius of the American government and American politics. Dean James Quillen of Stanford put it this way:

> Through history a student comes to know his nation's ideals and traditions, the nature of its government, and the responsibilities of its citizens. In one sense, history is the door through which an individual can enter the edifice of his nation's culture. Without a knowledge of history, patriotism has no roots and loyalty no bonds tying it to the past.[16]

Professor Bruner has recently made his position on the place of history in the social studies curriculum in elementary schools and high schools crystal clear. We should be grateful to him for his candor, and if he and his supporters succeed in emasculating or eliminating the study of history from school curricula, no one will be able to say that this was done surreptitiously or without proper warning.

In an article in the *Saturday Review* which the editors described as a preview for his latest book, *Toward a Theory of Instruction*, Bruner relates that his work on a new social studies curriculum has led him to the conclusion that "we are bound to move toward instruction in the sciences of behavior and away from the study of history."[17] The basic reason for the need to shift from history to the behavioral sciences is that history looks to the past, the recent past, and the behavioral sciences prepare the young to grasp and to adjust to the changing human conditions. "Recorded history," says Bruner, "is only about five thousand years old, as we saw. Most of what we teach is within the last few centuries, for the records before that are minimal, while the records after are relatively rich."[18] However, Bruner continues, modern methods of retrieving and storing of information will make it possible to store masses of information and consequently, "a thousand years from now we will be swamped." Because of this specter, if I understand Bruner correctly, we ought to stop the study of history right now because, as he tells us, at that future time there would be little sense to dwell "with such loving care over the details of Brumaire or the Long Parliament or the Louisiana Purchase."

It is quite obvious that Professor Bruner never really enjoyed the study of the dramatic record of the Long Parliament, which had a decisive influence on British political institutions and British democracy, or the study of the brilliant and dramatic exercise of Presidential powers by Thomas Jefferson, whose decisions made it possible, in a large measure, for the United States to be the great power it is today. Bruner is disdainful of the record of history which includes only the recent five thousand years. He seems to be much more interested, as his anthropologically-centered curriculum clearly indicates, in teaching about the 500-million-year-old history of the evolution of mammals and man. Without in any way belittling the importance of the study of the origin of the human species, one can and perhaps should argue that the study and the understanding of those "mere" five thousand years are of crucial importance for our young generations if they are to live meaningful and useful lives and if they are to be expected to make an effort to prevent the destruction of the human race in an atomic holocaust.

Bruno Bettelheim argued that educators should ask the question about what kind of persons we want our children to be, so that they may build a new world, different from the one that we live in, "a world in which they can live in accordance with their full potentialities." Answering the question on how this objective may be achieved, Professor Bettelheim recently wrote: "Most of all, our schools ought to teach the true nature of man, teach about his troubles with himself, his inner turmoils and about his difficulties in living with others. They should teach the prevalence and the power of both man's social and asocial tendencies, and how the one can domesticate the other, without destroying his independence or self-love."[19]

History is superbly equipped to contribute a great deal to the attainment of these goals in education. It is the business of history to deal with the trials, tribulations, and the inner turmoils of man and the good and the bad in them. Effective history teachers allow their students a glimpse into the tormented soul of Ivan the Terrible and the social and asocial instincts and predilections of the Levellers.

For young people to adapt to changing conditions, Bruner argues, they must study "the possible rather than the achieved.... It is the behavioral sciences and their generality with respect to variations in the human condition that must be central to our presentation of man, not the particularities of his history."[20] Thus, Bruner made his choice. Without equivocation and without any attempt to becloud the real issue, he wants the social studies curriculum in elementary and secondary schools to be centered on the concepts and generalizations and skills from the behavioral sciences. He is willing and ready to abandon the teaching of history with its stress on the unique, the separate, and the particular. This is no place to discuss the uses of history. A. L. Rowse and Allan Nevins have done it very well. It may suffice if we observe that if Bruner's ideas on the nature, content, and objectives of the social studies should prevail, elementary and high school students would get only a little of the historical perspective they need to understand today's world and its problems.

Generalizations and generalizing concepts are helpful to scholars as ordering devices, but the world as it impinges on the minds of the young is exactly the historical world of the specific, of the unique, and of the separate. Students want to study about racial problems and about traffic laws in the cities, to learn more about the personality of the man in the White House, and about the nature of the war in Viet Nam because they are personally, specifically interested in these problems. Teachers of social studies ought to be warned that the making of the study of structure and skills—"skills in handling and imagining, and in symbolic operations"—the principal emphasis in education, as postulated by Bruner, may make much of social studies instruction boring and unrewarding. The elimination of history from the social studies would be an educational and a national disaster.

NOTE

[1] Jerome S. Bruner. *On Knowing.* Cambridge, Mass.: Harvard University Press, 1962, p. 120.

[2] Jerome S. Bruner. *The Process of Education.* Cambridge, Mass.: Harvard University Press, 1962, p. 33.

[3] Bruner. *On Knowing,* p. 120.

[4] Fred M. Newmann. "The Analysis of Public Controversy—New Focus on Social Studies." *The School Review,* Winter 1965, p. 413. (italics mine)

[5] *Ibid.,* p. 414.

[6] Arno Bellack. "Structure in the Social Sciences and Implications for the Social Studies Program," in Odegard, Hanna, Quillen, Bellack, Tyler. *The Social Studies Curriculum Proposals for the Future.* Chicago, Ill.: Scott, Foresman, 1963, p. 102.

[7] This quotation is from a mimeographed report issued by E. S. I., dated February 15, 1963, and entitled, "A Preliminary and Tentative Outline of a Program of Curriculum Development in the Social Studies and Humanities," by the American Council of Learned Societies and Educational Services, Incorporated.

[8] *A Conceptual Framework for the Social Studies of Wisconsin Schools,* Social Studies Bulletin, issued by Angus B. Rothwell. State Department of Public Instruction. Madison, Wisconsin. December 1964.

[9] Jerome S. Bruner. "Man: A Course of Study," in *E.S.I., Quarterly Report.* Watertown, Mass.: Educational Services, Inc. Summer 1965, p. 85. Also in Bruner, *Toward a Theory of Instruction.* Cambridge, Mass.: Harvard University Press, 1966, p. 74.

[10] Bruner. "Man: A Course of Study," in *E.S.I. Quarterly Report,* p. 88.

[11] *Ibid.,* p. 89.

[12] *Ibid.,* p. 92.

13 *Ibid.*

14 *Book Week.* February 20, 1966, p. 5.

15 Bruner. "Man: A Course of Study," in *E.S.I. Quarterly Report*, p. 93.

16 I. James Quillen. "American History in the Upper Grades and Junior High School," in William H. Cartwright and Richard L. Watson, co-editors. *Interpreting and Teaching American History.* Thirty-First Yearbook. Washington, D. C.: National Council for the Social Studies, 1961, p. 347.

17 Jerome S. Bruner. "Education as Social Invention." *Saturday Review*, February 19, 1966, p. 103.

18 *Ibid.*, p. 103.

19 Bruno Bettelheim. "Notes on the Future of Education." *The University of Chicago Magazine.* February 1966, p. 14.

20 Bruner. "Education as Social Invention," *op. cit.*, p. 103.

Social Studies: The Need
for Redefinition

JAMES P. SHAVER

Our common parlance is fraught with ambiguity. It is, in fact, rather surprising, considering the uniqueness in our experiences as individuals, that words carry the amount of common meaning which they do. Ambiguity serves useful functions as a source of humor in jokes and in the richness it brings to literary imagery; but it is the common meanings of language that serve as the basis for general communication. When we become involved in the discussion of matters of importance, especially as we try to persuade others of the correctness of our own positions on subjects of common interest, the ever-present ambiguity and vagueness of language become definite handicaps.

It would be difficult to find an area where word usage has introduced more confusion and frustration than in the discussion of the social studies curriculum. The lack of clear meaning for the term *social studies* has historical roots. Since the early 1900's it has provided an omnibus label for history and the various social sciences in the elementary and secondary school curriculum. (By comparison, curriculum labels such as "mathematics" and "chemistry" have clear associations with individual academic areas.) Additional confusion in meaning has been introduced by the confounding, in discussions of the social studies curriculum, of citizenship education concerns with notions about the curricular imperatives of academic disciplines. If adequate communication is to take place among the various individuals and groups con-

NOTE: This article appeared in *Social Education*, November 1967, pp. 588–592, 596. Reprinted by permission of James P. Shaver.

cerned with social studies instruction, careful attention must be given to the definition of *social studies*. More careful specification of meaning should, in addition, make more evident the bases of both disagreement and agreement among those who take differing stands regarding what should constitute the social studies program.

The term *social studies* has traditionally been defined in reference to the social sciences. That is, the *social sciences* are first defined as the scholarly fields of study of man in his social environment. (This definition encompasses history which, despite its humanistic and literary elements, is basically a systematic study of man's social past.) The *social studies* are then defined as the social sciences adapted and simplified for pedagogical purposes.[1]

This definition has perhaps done more to stifle creative curriculum work in the social studies than any other factor. For it assumes *by the very sequence of definition*—from the social sciences to the social studies—that the criteria for curriculum selection and development in social studies should come from the social sciences, not from an independent view of what the social studies should be about. The restricting effect of this definition has proved an outstanding example of the limits which language can place on our thinking. Social studies educators have become so conditioned to assuming that the curricular flow must be from the social sciences, including history, to the social studies, and that the social sciences are the only legitimate source of content for the social studies, that our curricula belie common statements of the objectives for social studies instruction.

The result is perhaps the most striking paradox of American education: We find in social studies publications an abundance of grand statements about responsibility for citizenship education and the need to educate reflective, intelligent, rational citizens to participate in the decision-making processes of a free society. Yet "social studies" curriculum projects, textbooks,[2] and classrooms reflect little direct concern with analytic concepts appropriate to analyzing public issues.

The paradox is not surprising, however, if one takes into account the subservience of educators to the notion of the social studies as adaptations and simplifications of the social sciences. The scientific commitment is to *adequate description*, not to application in practical circumstances. Moreover, the identification and communication of thought process concepts is a most difficult task. It is easier for the curriculum worker to simplify and adapt substantive content than to develop processes of inquiry and verification. Further, social scientists themselves, if one judges by undergraduate course offerings and several of the current social science curriculum development projects for the elementary and secondary school, do not regard their modes of investigation as fit matter for instruction to any but those being prepared for entry to the guild. In consequence, social studies educators are caught between uttering commitments to education for rational citizenship and perpetuating curricula which are based on criteria that seem in large part irrelevant to this objective.

A More Viable Definition

One way to resolve this objectives-content paradox would be to adopt a more adequate definition of social studies, a definition based on the long-standing commitments to citizenship education that have failed to have a pervasive effect on the character of social studies education. Such a definition should begin with the clear recognition that *social studies education is general education.* In discussing social studies, we are talking about a set of required courses, a program intended for all students. This program should, therefore, be based on a rationale that takes into account the society's goals for all youth, not just those going on to college or those who come to school with an interest in abstract descriptions of the society and its past. A reasonable focus for such a rationale in a democratic society is the preparation of students for more reflective and effective political participation in their society—a society whose central commitment to human dignity assumes that all citizens have contributions to make to the determination of public policies, and that the schools should foster the ability to participate readily and rationally.

Explicit attention to these societal assumptions leads to a more viable definition of *social studies as that part of the school's general education program which is concerned with the preparation of citizens for participation in a democratic society.*[3] Social studies is not, then, simply an offshoot of the social sciences, with content to be dictated by the interests and desires of academicians in the social sciences and history. In fact, teachers and curriculum builders willing to structure their work by this definition will need, first of all, to ask themselves, "What are the prerequisites of intelligent political participation?" rather than, "What do social scientists or historians consider to be the legitimate domains of knowledge?" And, secondly, they will need to go beyond the social sciences for their content.

This point of view does not necessarily entail the neglect of social science content. As a matter of fact, in a social studies curriculum actually geared to the education of intelligent participant citizens, knowledge from the social sciences will be of paramount importance. It will not, however, be selected or organized according to the dictates of the social scientist, but according to the demands of general education. There is, for example, no intrinsic reason why social science concepts must be taught as part of the structure of a discipline instead of being taught as they are relevant to understanding specific issues facing the society. Which of these approaches, or what combination of the two, will be most effective for teaching social science concepts is an empirical question that has not yet been fully resolved by educational research. It seems highly probable, however, that the scholar's excitement in creating structure is not akin to the feelings that students are likely to have in learning that structure. There are, moreover, research findings that indicate that John Dewey and innumerable other educators have been correct—that is, we learn that which *we* are able to use in constructing and grappling with problems of real consequence to *us* as individuals.

Those involved in curriculum work such as that carried out by the Harvard Project[4] have found that the pressing issues facing the society are of real consequence to secondary school students. Social studies teachers have too often sold the idealism of youth short by assuming that their students were neither concerned with matters beyond athletic and dating prowess, nor capable of engaging in intelligent thought and discourse about other matters. What relations with minority groups should be forced on members of the society? What are the responsibilities of the rich for the poor, and of the poor for themselves? How should we balance economic strength with humanitarian notions of equality? Such questions, critical to a pluralistic democratic society, have the ingredients to fire up adolescents who are still concerned with ideals. But one can find only rarely a curriculum built around such issues. Even American problems textbooks tend to describe the factual context of issues rather than posing the value dilemmas. Instead of pursuing issues of basic importance to the society, teachers wonder that their secondary school students seem to lack interest in discourses on the causes of the Civil War or the economic, political, and social changes leading to the Renaissance. And we despair because, at the age of twenty-one, at the height of their concern with family and occupation, young adults do not automatically make the transformation to participant citizenship.

Beyond the Social Sciences

What about the claim that we must go beyond the social sciences for concepts and content for the social studies curriculum? Political-ethical conflict is at the heart of public controversy. Choices between competing conceptions of good are the focal point of most discussions of legislation or other proposed action by governmental or other powerful social groups. Yet present social studies curricula generally ignore value conflicts as part of the neglect of the preparation of participant citizens. Moreover, the reliance of social studies educators on the social sciences for the content of instruction means a dearth of adequate conceptual tools for dealing with public controversy even when teachers do turn explicitly to the important task of citizenship education.

The social sciences do offer essential substantive concepts for describing a societal problem. It does not take great imagination to think, for example, of the contributions that social sciences such as economics, anthropology, political science, and history can make to a student's adequate comprehension of the racial segregation problems still facing our nation. At the same time, the social sciences, with their orientation toward the systematic, empirical study of social reality, have much to offer in the way of analytic concepts for determining which factual claims about a problem or a proposed solution to a problem should be accepted. The study of semantics, often included in the social science domain, has obvious contributions to make to the understanding of how language functions in controversy and to the development of intellectual strategies that might be used to clarify the language that is the vehicle for thought and discussion.

But what can the social sciences offer at the point that a choice must be made between two conflicting values? It has often been naively assumed in social studies curriculum work that the scientific method (and usually the conception of this has been extremely naive, inadequately based on the steps of thinking proposed by Dewey in *How We Think*)[5] is appropriate to solving all problems—whether factual or evaluative in their origin. Once, however, that the discussants' language has been clarified and any factual questions resolved (for example, about the consequences of different policies) and a difference over values remains, there is nothing in social science methodology that will help the citizen come to a defensible position. Beard, in *The Nature of the Social Sciences*, pointed out succinctly the powerlessness of the social sciences when faced with a choice between different courses of action:

> Here the social sciences, working as descriptive sciences with existing and becoming reality, face, unequivocally, ideas of value and choice—argumentative systems of social philosophy based upon conceptions of desirable changes in the social order. At this occurrence empiricism breaks down absolutely. It is impossible to discover by the fact-finding operation whether this or that change is desirable. Empiricism may disclose within limits, whether a proposed change is possible, or to what extent it is possible, and the realities that condition its eventuation, but, given possibility or a degree of possibility, empiricism has no way of evaluating a value without positing value or setting up a frame of value.[6]

Social studies curriculum builders must, then, draw on sources of concepts other than the social sciences if the intellectual skills taught are to be adequate to the demands of political-ethical controversy. As long as we maintain the traditional definition of social studies as the social sciences simplified and adapted for pedagogical purposes, our vision will be obscured in terms both of developing an adequate rationale for the curriculum and selecting the concepts that will be of most service to our students in confronting the crises facing society.

Obstacles to a Shift in Definition

What stands in the way of adopting a more viable definition of social studies—one that will appropriately focus attention on the task of general education and provide a more adequately comprehensive framework for the selection of the concepts to be taught? In the first place, there are certain unfounded assumptions that interfere. I have already alluded to a couple with rather recent standing. One is the assumption that if a professor derives pleasure from building conceptual structure in his academic field, students will necessarily be motivated if study of the concepts in the discipline is based on the structure. The concomitant myth is that there is some necessary relationship between the logical ordering of concepts and the psychological ease of learning the concepts.

Another assumption that interferes with curriculum reform in social studies underlies the "urn" concept of education. This approach to instruction sees students as receptacles into which data can and must be poured to be dumped back out in the near or far future as pertinent to some pressing matter. An off-shoot is the "ground-covering" fetish; that is, the notion that it is more important to finish the textbook or "cover" a particular span of history than to go into any one topic in depth. Although ground-covering has been pretty well decimated in journal articles, observation indicates that it is still a prevalent classroom practice. By the same token, although it has been shown that information is forgotten at a rapid rate when it does not fit the individual's structure for construing the world, teachers still can be heard to proclaim the necessity of covering material that *may be* of relevance later on. Depth of comprehension for a few societal problems likely to be of critical importance to the society in coming years and teaching thought process concepts thoroughly are rejected because they would take time from filling the urn with all sorts of potentially useful—and useless—information.

In fact, the curriculum research of the Harvard Project indicated that considerable economy in learning can be effected by focusing instruction on important societal issues and on the conceptual tools and information to comprehend and debate possible solutions. In the Harvard Project, two-thirds of what was traditionally a two-year U.S. history sequence was used for the analysis of problems (including, of course, the historical background of the issues studied). There were no negative effects on the learning of history and social science knowledge by our students as compared with the students in the regular curriculum. Our students did, however, show considerably greater gains in analytic ability.[7]

Another assumption that obstructs a more adequate approach to the social studies curriculum is that students learn by osmosis. That is, the belief that students will learn to think better by reading history and social science books supposedly written by "good thinkers" is patently unacceptable. In 1962, the research on the teaching of critical thinking could be summarized as follows:

> Probably the most conclusive suggestion supported by the research reviewed here is that we should not expect that our students will learn to think critically as a by-product of the study of the usual social studies content. Instead, each teacher should determine what concepts are essential—e.g., that of relevance—if his students are to perform the intellectual operations deemed necessary to critical thinking—such as, for example, the formulation and evaluation of hypotheses. Each of these should then be taught explicitly to the students. Utilizing what is known about transfer of learning, a further step can be suggested: Situations as similar as possible to those in which the students are to use their competencies should also be set up in the classroom, and the students guided in application of the concepts in this context.[8]

As already noted, our research results with the Harvard Project supported the contention that students taught to think critically will be better able to do so than those in a traditional, textbook-bound curriculum—without any loss in learning of information.

Why Do the Misconceptions Prevail?

If these contentions are true, then why do the assumptions prevail? Why are so many social studies courses still set up to teach arrays of information not organized around public issues, nor accompanied by conscious teaching for better thinking? One basic reason is the teacher's insecurity, especially in regard to his role vis-à-vis the academic professor. Teachers with years of excellent experience dealing with children and worrying about what they should be doing in the classroom feel subservient to the subject matter expert whose academic competencies lie neither in teaching children nor in making judgments about what should be taught in social studies.

Teachers are also fearful of community reaction. This fear is not entirely unfounded. Parents are not always appreciative of attempts to teach their children to think more clearly—especially when the learner begins to challenge his parents' inadequate thinking. Reactionary community groups will often protest what seems to be a departure from inculcating traditional patriotic values. This is, however, exactly where the defense of education for rational citizenship must begin—with the commitment of a democratic society to an intelligent citizenry. The claim that skepticism is being taught must be countered by appeal to the basic commitment of our society to rationality. Finally, parents may complain that their children are not going to learn the important facts which former generations learned as students. Aside from the questionable validity of much of what passes as facts in history textbooks,[9] clear grounds have already been indicated for arguing confidently that a focus on public issues and thought processes is not going to have a negative effect on the student's pool of information.

Attitudes toward history and the social sciences which bring teachers to the social studies classroom also serve to perpetuate the old assumptions. Many individuals are teaching social studies because they enjoyed the study of history. They assume that everyone should find this study interesting, and they have been reinforced in this view by their college professors. Consequently, they impose their interests on their students, often adopting the "need for a storehouse of information" as justification for the imposition. This approach usually causes little outward consternation when the students are college-bound, grade-oriented, or interested in abstract ideas. But often students branded as lacking in intellectual ability are simply not interested in history or social science knowledge for its own sake. Nor is there any reason why they should be.

In fact, teachers' reactions to students who find history as such boring reflect another reason for the continuing myths. That is, a general failure—despite much worrying about what and how to teach—to examine the basic rationale for social studies instruction. What notions about society—what it should be, what it can be, and what part the school can and should play in shaping the society—determine the teacher's curricular choices? Prospective teachers are rarely encouraged to ask these questions as part of the teacher education program. Professors of social studies education have themselves often unthinkingly adopted the restricting definition of social studies which makes the social studies the handmaiden of the social sciences.[10] It is not surprising that questions about the rationale for social studies instruction are rarely raised in the heat of teaching. By default, a curriculum is perpetuated that is too often seen by students as not only lacking in challenge, but as irrelevant to the realities of life.

Of course, teachers often do not engage in creatively restructuring their curriculum because they lack the necessary professional commitment to do so. However, even the conscientious teacher often cannot find the time or energy for curriculum building given the large number of classes he must teach, the large number of students with whom he has contact, and the many clerical and supervisory duties demanded of him.[11] The situation is not being relieved by the number of current "social studies" curriculum projects that are actually social science projects.

Prospects for Change

How likely is it, then, that a definition of the social studies based on confrontation with the most vital concern of a democratic society, the education of citizens who can intelligently perceive and reflect upon the critical issues facing the society, will become dominant and provide integrity for the curriculum? Or, put another way, how likely is it that social studies curriculum work will, in the near future, depart significantly from the notion that the academician's view of his discipline must determine the social studies curriculum, and from the view that the social sciences and history are the only relevant sources of substantive and thought-process concepts for social studies instruction?

It seems most likely that social studies courses will continue to be dominated by the same influences as in the past. New and better ways of teaching history and social science content will be devised. Many non-academically inclined students will continue to be frustrated by the irrelevance to their own lives and to the society's prevalent issues of much of what passes for social studies instruction; and academically able students will still be left to recognize on their own the germaneness of their studies to the contributions they could, and in many instances will, make to their society.

Of special importance are the teachers who are a critical link in the curricular decision-making process because they determine, whether consciously or not, what goes on in the individual classroom. As suggested earlier, they often obtain personal satisfaction from forcing their own interests in history and social science on their students. Their teacher education programs have inculcated them with the social science-based definition of the social studies. Their college experiences have all too often resulted in notions of the university professor's superiority and feelings of inferiority vis-à-vis the "academicians" (as opposed to those college professors derisively labeled "educationists" who have themselves often, apparently out of feelings of inferiority, become subservient to scholars in the social sciences and history in providing curricular leadership). In short, the frame of reference of many teachers is not likely to lead to demands for or production of startling changes in the social studies curriculum.

It is not difficult to identify outstanding teachers to whom this analysis does not apply. Unfortunately, it is doubtful that their classes account for a very large percentage of students. It is also easy to be misled into optimism by the large amounts of money being spent for curriculum development projects, and on summer and year-long institutes for teachers. Of all the nationally sponsored curriculum projects, however, very few are likely to produce rationales or materials appropriate to a definition of social studies clearly and explicitly based on citizenship education.[12]

As noted earlier, too many "social studies" projects are, in essence, social science projects. Despite the use of the term, "the new social studies," little is likely to come from these projects that will be helpful to a teacher wishing to depart from the present history-social science dominated curriculum. Not only are the projects social science based, but the academicians directing the projects are too often "scholacentric" in that they genuinely love their schools of thought and are centered on them. They find it difficult to admit the importance of other fields of study, the necessity of justifying study of their own field, or the possibility of alternative orderings of concepts from their own disciplines.[13] They are hardly likely to recognize the possibility of an alternative approach to the curriculum such as proposed here. The "scholacentrism" of even the most education-minded of the social scientists mitigates against the likelihood that their work will encourage any departure from the traditional social science-to-social studies definition of social studies.

In the present curricular climate of structure and induction, the paradoxical relationship between statements of objectives and instructional programs for the social studies will undoubtedly continue. Education for rational citizenship seems foredoomed to continue as a stepsister to history and social science instruction. Perhaps this is just as well. For, contrary to our assumptions, the intense involvement of a citizenry effectively schooled and interested in the analysis of public issues might be too disruptive to our society.

Notes

[1] This definition, the popularization of which is often attributed to Edgar Wesley through his textbook, *Teaching Social Studies in High School*, first published by D. C. Heath in 1937, stems from the work of the Committee on the Social Studies of the National Education Association's Commission on the Reorganization of Secondary Education. See, for example, Bureau of Education. *The Social Studies in Secondary Education*. Bulletin No. 28. Washington, D. C. 1916.

[2] See, e.g., James P. Shaver, "Reflective Thinking, Values and Social Studies Textbooks." *School Review* 73:226–257; 1965. A current U. S. Office of Education sponsored project at Utah State University, U.S.O.E. No. 6-2288 is aimed at developing instructional suggestions and materials for teaching concepts useful in the analysis of public controversy.

[3] Other subject areas, such as English, also claim a role in citizenship education. Undoubtedly they have an impact. Yet each has a specified area of concern—e.g., language skills, math skills—which presents its own focus for instruction, as well as problems of curriculum selection. In each case, citizenship education, especially the student's future political role, is at best of tangential, if not incidental, interest. Only social studies educators have consistently averred this as a central, direct matter of professional concern.

[4] Donald W. Oliver and James P. Shaver. *Teaching Public Issues in the High School*. Boston: Houghton Mifflin, 1966.

[5] John Dewey. *How We Think*. Boston: D. C. Heath, 1933. For confirmation of this point, see Philip G. Smith. "How We Think: A Re-examination." *The Educational Forum* 31:417–418; 1967. Also, for a discussion of the inadequacies in textbooks resulting from application of the naive concept, see, James P. Shaver, *op. cit.*

[6] Charles Beard. *The Nature of the Social Sciences.* New York: Scribner, 1934, p. 171–172. Also see Charles L. Stevenson. *Ethics and Language.* New Haven: Yale University Press, 1944, p. 30–31 and Chapter V. Also see, Charles L. Stevenson. *Facts and Values.* New Haven, Conn.: Yale University Press, 1963. Chapter I.

[7] Donald W. Oliver and James P. Shaver, *op. cit.,* Sections 1, 2, and 3 of the Appendix.

[8] James P. Shaver. "Educational Research and Instruction for Critical Thinking." *Social Education* 26:13–16; January 1962.

[9] See, for example, Harold J. Noah, Carl E. Prince, and C. Russell Riggs. "History in High School Textbooks." *School Review* 70:415–436; 1962.

[10] See, e.g., Stanley E. Ballinger's comments on methods textbooks in "The Social Studies and Social Controversy." *School Review* 70:97–111; 1963.

[11] For a more expanded treatment of this point, see James P. Shaver, "The Evaluation of Textbooks: A Continuous Responsibility." *School Review* 74:328–330; 1966.

[12] Among these few are Donald W. Oliver's curriculum project at Harvard, our project at Utah State University aimed specifically at a curriculum for teaching analytic concepts relevant to public issues, and perhaps the Sociological Resources for Secondary Schools Project of the American Sociological Association.

[13] For an excellent illustration of this point, see the conference discussions reported in Irving Morrissett, editor. *Concepts and Structure in the New Social Science Curricula.* West Lafayette, Ind.: Social Science Education Consortium, 1966.

Behavior as Objective in Education

C. BENJAMIN COX

Through uncertain, changing, and growing endeavors, issues and controversies parade endlessly. Not only is it often the case that there are unsettling questions and dilemmas, but also too often the necessary dimensions of inquiry are unknown. As a result, issues are drawn erratically and solutions are cast capriciously. In such a climate, fads offer hard competition for solidly grounded innovations, for sometimes they are indistinguishable and very often both elements are active in a single idea.

This article will attempt to examine such an idea. The supposition is that the current popularity of behavioral objectives, the idea in question, is both warranted on solid grounds and mindlessly promoted. This examination will try to discriminate between the disparate elements in the idea. The approach, in the main, will be to assess the nature, uses, and kinds of behavioral objectives following a brief survey of the sources of objectives in the curriculum.

It should be noted at the outset that the statement does not talk exclusively to social studies practitioners, though they are the target population. The assumption is made that the issues should be dealt with broadly. Their resolution, however, may be unique in each field of instruction.

I. Sources of Educational Objectives

Educational planners, including teachers and curriculum makers, are always deeply involved in the identification and clarification of their

NOTE: This article, abridged for this anthology, appeared in *Social Education*, May 1971, pp. 435–449. Reprinted by permission of C. Benjamin Cox.

goals and purposes. Objectives of every kind emerge from such planning operations, though ordinarily they reflect such limitations as the life uses of the learnings, the materials selected, the target population, the life expectancy of the plan, the nature of the bodies of knowledge used to support the project, as well as the perspicacity of the planners.

SOCIETY, KNOWLEDGE, AND LEARNERS AS SOURCES

The sources of such objectives, however, are limited. In very general terms, there are three sources of objectives for educational programs. These include descriptive and predictive statements about children and adolescents, the society, and the disciplines that provide the content of the curriculum. Largely, educational objectives are derived from organized bodies of knowledge about individuals, groups, and culture including the literature on the goals of education and the political and socioeconomic goals of the nation, the information we possess about the characteristics of children, and the literature of developmental psychology and the various disciplines from which school subjects are derived. Textbooks themselves are an appropriate source of certain kinds of educational objectives.[1]

While the extraction of objectives for the educational enterprise would seem to be quite complex, given the variety of sources from which they may be generated, it is also recondite. Atkin locates the fundamental problem as lying in the easy assumption that we know or can readily identify either the educational objectives for which we strive or the outcomes that result from whatever programs we invent.[2] Further frustrating this situation is the perplexing occurrence of often selecting for emphasis in school programs those goals that are ephemeral, sociodegradable, or trivial. While few intend to spend their energies and time in educational work committed to the trifles of the culture and to the perpetuation of the profane and the mythological, it is too often the case.

The problem grows more complex at every glance and turn. Not only must teachers and curriculum makers work with bodies of knowledge that are variant in their quality and generality and in which are embedded a remarkable range of values and predictions, but also the clientele which they serve is as variable as the society itself ranging through the spectrums of personality, intelligence, social class, color, age, and the like. Each new variable bewilders the attempts toward generalizability.[3]

CONTENT VS. BEHAVIOR

In contemporary curriculum development, there is at least one additional complication. In very gross terms, the curriculum development function in the schools has come to be dominated by two varying and, at times, antithetical cultures. On the one hand are the content scholars who represent the society's commitment to the venerable research disciplines that supply to most school subjects their life source of fact and concept. On the other hand are the evaluators, the behavior specifiers who represent in the curriculum a particular interpretation of the psychological foundations of learning.[4] The primary occupation of this statement will be with the limited task of examining the nature, the uses, and the kinds of objectives preferred by behavioristic curriculum theorists and developers, evaluators, and teachers.

II. The Nature of Behavioral Objectives

This section shall attempt to review the grounds and justifications for behavioral objectives, the effect of behavioral objectives on instructional and curriculum decisions and operations, and some prescriptive statements on the production of behavioral objectives.

THE GROUNDS IN BEHAVIORALISM AND CONNECTIONISM

The idea of behavioral objectives emerges from behavioristic and connectionist learning theories and their variants. While behavioral objectives represent a fairly simple adaptation of a fairly simple interpretation of learning, their popularity in schools is likely reflective of the utilization of behavioristic and connectionist theories of learning by educational practitioners.

For some types of learning, behaviorism offers a believable and reliable explanation. Within this concept, learning is inferred from a change of behavior. That is, "people do not learn in a general sense, but always in the sense of a change in behavior that can be described in terms of an observable type of human performance." "A successful act of learning is inferred from the fact that the individual can now do something he could not do before."[5]

The assumption is made that these statements of behavioral goals take cognizance of the individual's understanding and attitudes. While the statement emphasizes the action itself, it is assumed that the described behavior is or will be the result of the learning individual's reasoned conclusion, his disciplined feelings, and his awareness of the situation at hand.[6]

[T]here is the further implication that the change is brought about by an external force. That suggests that some instrument of the curriculum is presumed to act upon the learner as he pursues the activities of the program.

Behavioral learning, though demonstrable by a simple combination of motions and symbols, is a complex concept as expressed by the theorists.[7] For the purposes of research, evaluation, or instruction, however, the concept is too complex to deal with in all its dimensions at once. Consequently, researchers and analysts have attempted to conceptualize behavior more advantageously by teasing it apart, e.g., into affective and cognitive components, while keeping in mind the interrelations of the components.[8] The common error among the behavioral objectifiers is the neglect of the interrelations.

VIEWS AND RELATIONSHIPS OF OBJECTIVES

For the most part, behavioral objectives focus on pupil-learners, though occasionally, the teacher is identified as the behaver in the situation.

Another way to look at objectives is with respect to their contingency relationship. That is, the achievement of some objectives depends upon the prior achievement of some other objectives. This relationship may be implied by the designation of terminal and interim objectives.[9] The linear hypothesis that supports this contingency relationship between terminal and interim or en route objectives has a limited validity in social studies.... [A]n understanding of the relationship between the separate states and the central government under the Articles of Confederation would not have to precede the understanding of the relationship between the states and the federal government as defined by the Constitution. In other instances in social studies contingency relationships may be hypothesized. Students could be required as an interim objective to learn the various logical forms of explanation prior to identifying these forms of explanation in social material or judging the most adequate explanation in a given social situation.

Actually, [a]n objective maintains its interim or terminal position largely because the curriculum maker or the teacher has so designed it. From the learner's point of view, all behaviors are both terminal and interim; any learning can be thought of as an end in itself and as supporting or leading to further learnings.

SEQUENCING OBJECTIVES

Plowman deals with the questions of contingency behaviors by prescribing steps to be followed in the sequencing of behavioral objectives. This series of decisions provides for preparatory or cumulative behaviors to facilitate the performance of the terminal behavior. First, there is the decision about what the learner is to do when he has completed the sequence. Second, this terminal behavior is defined as a behavioral objective. Third, the decision is made on what preparatory tasks the learner must complete prior to his demonstration of the terminal behavior. Fourth, these preparatory, interim tasks are then cast as behavioral objectives and ordered along a continuum. If the objectives defined for this behavior system contain elements at different psychological or logical levels, then the sequencing of the behaviors should be arranged on the basis of the taxonomic or hierarchical structure that is presumed to contain the different elements.[10]

... Gagné insists that a systems approach demands attention to the motivation of the learner, the conditions in which the learning is to take place, and the transferability of the knowledge to be learned in the program. Both Gagné and Plowman emphasize decisions about assessment, an inherent aspect of behavioral objectives.[11]

The point to be made in this discussion is that in the more sophisticated statements about behavioral objectives, the idea is conceived as a complex and systematized approach to curriculum development as well as classroom instruction. Besides being means by which the teacher can infer specific learning, behavioral objectives are seen as the guidelines and signposts of the instructional program of the school.

Gronlund has attempted to encapsulate the decisions relative to the use of behavioral objectives in school programs. . . .

Behavioral Definition of General Objectives[12]

	Yes	No
Is each general instructional objective defined by a list of specific learning outcomes that describes the terminal behavior students are expected to demonstrate?	___	___
Does each specific learning outcome begin with a *verb* that specifies definite, *observable behavior* (e.g., identifies, describes, lists, etc.)?	___	___
Is the behavior in each specific learning outcome relevant to the general instructional objective it describes?	___	___
Is there a sufficient number of specific learning outcomes to adequately describe the behavior of students who have achieved each of the general instructional objectives?	___	___

DEFINITION OF BEHAVIORAL OBJECTIVES

In this section a working definition of behavioral objectives will be attempted. Generally speaking, objectives of any ilk serve similar purposes in curriculum and in instruction. They are primarily destinations or intended states toward which the educational process is to tend. They declare the hoped-for conditions, the expectancies, the anticipated consequences of the educational system. Within this definition, behavioral objectives are a subclass of the class concept objectives. As such, they are presumed to function within the curriculum as would objectives of any definition. The argument is, however, that objectives of the garden variety are possessed of ambiguity and vagueness.

Broudy insists that the basic import of the move toward behavioral objectives is objectivity rather than behaviorality. Primarily, he says, "the motive is to exorcise the evils of fuzziness and idiosyncracy from subjective judgments."[13] The high priests of behavioral objectives go a step further in their stipulation, however. They assert that the only way to achieve clarity in statements of objectives is to couch them in behavioral terms. Such a statement, according to Gagné, is an operational definition "that communicates reliably to any individual... the set of circumstances that identifies a class of human performances." These operational definitions, according to Gagné, are comprised of four basic components: (1) a verb denoting observable action; (2) a description of the class of stimuli being responded to; (3) a word or words denoting the object used for action, unless implied by the verb; and (4) a description of the class of correct responses.[14]

MEANINGFULNESS VS. WORTHWHILENESS

A major objection to the idea of behavioral objectives is a reaction to the dogmatic insistence that objectives having observable and measurable behavioral counterparts are meaningful and worthwhile. The requirements for stating behavioral objectives have the effect of shifting objectives toward the trivial. Typical criteria necessitate overt behavior, the prediction of situations which the learner must respond to, and an evaluation procedure. It is doubtful whether the application of these criteria alone will result in significant statements of instructional goals.[15]

... Raths declares the criteria proposed for behavioral objectives lead to statements that are more specific than teachers use in practice.[16] Critics Eisner and Haberman believe that only the simplest of aspects of instruction are readily stated in behavioral terms. The dynamics of classroom interaction are much too complex and reflect too many important affective considerations to be predicted by specific behavioral objectives.[17]

III. Uses for Behavioral Objectives

BEHAVIORAL OBJECTIVES AS AN EMPIRICAL BASE

The popularity of behavioral objectives has grown with the increasing demand for the development of an empirical demonstration of educational improvement. Credibility and accountability are the new clichés which couch the demands made upon teachers, schools, and curriculums by parents, newly militant groups, and society itself. Either procedures for laying an empirical foundation must be developed and marketed widely or believable reasons for not doing so must be forthcoming.

The behavioral objectivists tend to see effectiveness and efficiency as the twin criteria of improvement. Reflecting these criteria, instruction is viewed as basically the management of the conditions of learning pointed toward producing the greatest possible change in performance in the shortest possible time. Linked to this definition of instruction is the dictum that clearly stated behavioral objectives are the essential first step towards sound instructional design.[18] The road to an adequate response to the demands of the society for an empirical demonstration of improvement in education is paved with behavioral objectives.

[T]he behavioralists propose to lay stepping stones of consistent reliability and dependability. They opt for the direct measurement of outcomes, according to Gagné, to insure that instructional objectives have been met.[19]

APPLICATIONS OF BEHAVIORAL OBJECTIVES

Proponents of behavioral objectives assert that in the classroom the motivation and performance of the student are directly related to his knowing what to do and how well he did. Students shouldn't have to guess; they will waste time studying the wrong things.[20]

[T]he use of behavioral objectives in classrooms is differentiated for extemporaneous and predesigned instruction. Ordinary classroom interaction is considered by Gagné as extemporaneous inasmuch as decisions concerning the direction of discourse are made in response to unanticipated events. Predesign, on the other hand, is a general characteristic of mediated instruction which is less flexible and subject to more prior decisions concerning expected performances.[21] [Moreover], behavioral objectives can help the teacher design appropriate test items and discriminate among relevant and irrelevant test items.[22]

Haberman identifies seven advantageous uses of behavioral objectives in the design of curriculum and in the instruction in classrooms as well as in the training of teachers and in the process of research.

1. Behavioral objectives give both teachers and pupils a *clear sense of purpose.*

2. Behavioral objectives facilitate the fragmenting of content into *meaningful and manageable* pieces.

3. Behavioral objectives facilitate the *organizing of content* into hierarchies and therefore instructional sequence.

4. Behavioral objectives simplify *evaluative procedures.*

5. Behavioral objectives simplify the *training of teachers.*

6. Behavioral objectives *clarify the relevance* of particular pieces of instructional material.

7. Behavioral objectives open the educative process to *research and planning.*[23]

In the next section some of the more critical detriments of behavioral objectives in the process of education will be analyzed.

DETRIMENTS OF BEHAVIORAL OBJECTIVES

Opposition to the employment of behavioral objectives in the schools ... [is] grounded largely in the claim that devotion to specific goals in the process of education precludes attention to other important matters in education. Raths expresses this objection in terms of the typical values of teachers. The requirements of specificity now being advanced by Mager, Popham, Walbesser and others, he asserts, are in direct conflict with the traditional values of teachers. Teaching for such limited goals is not only an unappealing task for classroom teachers, but also is antagonistic to their spirit of humanitarianism and, in addition, runs counter to their values of intellectualism.[24] [I]n this view, teachers are seen as perceiving themselves as intellectuals who prefer to deal with specific content and information primarily as a means to clarify the powerful ideas of a general nature in the culture.

The incorporation of this new master in the classroom, the behavioral system, produces a mechanical pedagogical style on the part of the teacher and results in his loss of spontaneity in his work with students.[25] As expressed by Broudy, behavioral objectives put a premium on teaching information and on the rote recall of definitions, rules and principles, particular operations, and the solution of problems having only one solution.[26] As a result, those outcomes that are identified only with difficulty or are rarely translated into behavioral terms will tend to atrophy.[27] The overemphasis on the replicative use of knowledge has had the unfortunate consequence of making relatively unpopular within the educational system the interpretive, associative, and applicative uses of knowledge, though these are particularly important in life after school.[28]

Broudy further claims that our excessive concern with behavioral objectives is accompanied by a belittling of the important life-use aspect of schooling embodied in the concept of tacit knowledge. Tacit knowledge, according to Broudy and Polanyi, is a kind of social wisdom made up of a mysterious amalgam of once known, but unattended specifics that allows one to judge, to understand, or to explain without being able to recall the particulars that support the judgment....[29] Broudy does not appear to claim that attention to behavioral specifics prevents the appearance of tacit knowledge; but he is suggesting that excessive attention to one aspect of learning precludes an appropriate interest in the development of the other.

... Atkin declares that the early articulation of behavioral objectives by the curriculum developer limits the range of his exploration. The curriculum developer becomes so committed to designing a program that will achieve these particular goals that he is unable to see the delicate and fascinating opportunities that shimmer fitfully in the periphery of his vision.[30]

Popham listed the 11 most common objections raised against the employment of behavioral objectives in the schools. To each of these criticisms he expressed his own response as a strong proponent of behavioral systems in curriculum and instructional programs. Epitomizations of the 11 criticisms and Popham's responses are paralleled in the columns following....[31]

Reasons given in opposition to behavioral objectives	Popham's responses to the objections
1. Trivial behaviors are easiest to operationalize. Really important outcomes will be underemphasized.	1. Explicit goals allow easier attention to the important goals.
2. Prespecification prevents teacher capitalization of unexpected instructional opportunities.	2. Ends do not necessarily specify means. Serendipity is always welcome.
3. There are other types of educational outcomes that are also important, e.g., for parents, staff, community.	3. Schools can't do everything. Primary responsibility is to pupils.
4. Objectively, mechanistically measured behaviors are dehumanizing.	4. Broadened concept of evaluation includes "human" elements.

Reasons given in opposition to behavioral objectives	Popham's responses to the objections
5. Precise, preplanned behavior is undemocratic.	5. Society knows what it wants. Instruction is naturally undemocratic.
6. Behaviorally described teaching is not natural, is unrealistic of teachers.	6. Identifying the status quo is different than applauding it.
7. In certain areas, e.g., fine arts and humanities, it is more difficult to measure behaviors.	7. Sure it's tough; but still a responsibility.
8. General statements appear more worthwhile to outsiders. Precise goals appear innocuous.	8. We must abandon the ploy of "obfuscation by generality."
9. Measurability implies accountability. Teachers might be judged on their ability to produce particular results rather than being judged on many bases.	9. Teachers *should* be held accountable for producing changes.
10. It is more difficult to generate precise objectives than to talk of them in vague terms.	10. We should allocate the necessary resources to accomplish the task.
11. Unanticipated results are often most important. Prespecification may cause inattentiveness.	11. Dramatic unanticipated outcomes cannot be overlooked. Keep your eyes open!

IV. Kinds of Behavioral Objectives

STRUCTURING BEHAVIORAL OBJECTIVES

One attempt to provide a structure by which behavioral objectives can be sequenced is Gagné's hierarchy of learning types. Gagné hypothesizes that there are several types or levels of learning that can be ordered along a hierarchy whose controlling concept is complexity. At the base of Gagné's hierarchy is *signal* learning or conditioned response. At the second level is *stimulus response* learning or precise response to discriminated stimuli. The third type of learning is the *chaining* of stimulus response bonds. At Gagné's fourth level, *verbal associations* or verbal chains are formed. Next is *multiple discrimination*, defined as very complex stimulus responses. At a still higher level is *concept learning* where the individual learns a common response to a class of stimuli. At the seventh level chains of concept are put together in the performance of *principle learning*. Finally, at the apex of Gagné's hierarchy is *problem solving.* This level of learning requires that the individual manage a number of internal events called thinking.[32]

Plowman lists 14 types of learning sequences which could serve to establish the sequence in behavioral systems. His list is included here as evidence of the variability possible in the design of these systems.

Types of Learning Sequences[33]

1. Fact #1 → Fact #2 → Fact #3. . . .

2. Fact → Concept

3. Concrete Experience → Abstract Representation of Experience

4. Skill #1 → Skill #2 → Skill #3. . . .

5. Maturative or Developmental Level #1 → #2 → #3. . . .

   Personal or Societal Developmental Task #1 → #2. . . .*

6. Level of Awareness #1 → #2 → #3. . . .
   6.1 Through sensitizing a person to his environment.
   6.2 Through sensitizing a person to relationships among persons, among institutions, and among data.
   6.3 Through multi-sensory experience.
   6.4 Through using and developing all the senses.

7. Level of Rationality #1 → #2 → #3. . . .
   e.g., Comprehension and proposed solution to problem.
   7.1 Using additional facts, possibly from different subject-matter disciplines, to achieve successively higher levels of comprehension.
   7.2 Formulating more sophisticated definitions of the problem.
   7.3 Generating a number of possible solutions to the problems.

8. Ways of gathering data, solving problems, or of bringing about change.
   8.1 Various strategies and processes, usually starting with gathering data and organizing it in some way and ending with either verification of solutions or institutionalization of an innovation.

9. Knowledge → Comprehension → Application → Analysis → Synthesis → Evaluation†

---

*Robert J. Havighurst, *Developmental Tasks and Education,* New York: McKay, 1952.
  †See reference Bloom *et al.*

10. Cognition → Memory → Divergent Thinking → Evaluative Thinking**

Creative Process††

11. Preparation → Incubation → Illumination → Revision

Creative Skill

12. Awareness and sensitivity to a situation → Cognitive reordering of elements of the situation → Search model formation → Verification of product and worth of product and testing

13. Conceptualizing an object of art → Preparing a plan → Selecting medium and materials

Choosing tools → Producing an object of art → Evaluating the product

Leadership

14. Getting other persons to engage in an activity or to carry out a task with few or no objections or interruptions.

Planning → Motivating → Organizing → Coordinating → Protecting Followers → Evaluating

**J. P. Guilford, "Creativity: Its Measurement and Development," *A Source Book for Creative Thinking*, edited by Sidney J. Parnes and Harold F. Harding. New York: Scribner's, 1962.

††Graham Wallas, *The Art of Thought*, New York: Harcourt, Brace & World, Inc., 1926. From E. Paul Torrance, *Guiding Creative Talent*, Englewood Cliffs, New Jersey: Prentice-Hall, Inc., 1962, p. 17.

THE COGNITIVE TAXONOMY AS STRUCTURE

Among the types of learning sequences identified by Plowman is the cognitive taxonomy developed by Bloom and nearly three dozen of his examiner and evaluator colleagues across the United States.[34] The taxonomy has proved of special value in the evaluation process and has remarkably direct application for the curriculum maker or the teacher attempting to design behavioral systems for classroom employment.

Gronlund has applied the cognitive taxonomy to the statement of general instructional objectives and specific learning outcomes. The vertical components of his table reproduced [in part] below reflect the six categories of cognitive objectives: knowledge, comprehension, application, analysis, synthesis, and evaluation. The verbs on the right-hand side of the table refer to specific behaviors sought for in the cognitive realm. A behavioral objective in the cognitive domain would begin appropriately with one of these verbs.

**Examples of General Instructional Objectives and Behavioral
Terms for the Cognitive Domain of the Taxonomy**[35]

Illustrative General Instructional Objectives	*Illustrative Behavioral Terms for Stating Specific Learning Outcomes*
Knows common terms Knows specific facts Knows methods and procedures	Defines, describes, identifies, labels, lists, matches, names, outlines, reproduces, selects, states
Understands facts and principles Interprets verbal material Interprets charts and graphs	Converts, defends, distinguishes, estimates, explains, extends, generalizes, gives examples, infers, paraphrases, predicts, rewrites, summarizes
Applies concepts and principles to new situations Applies laws and theories to practical situations Solves mathematical problems	Changes, computes, demonstrates, discovers, manipulates, modifies, operates, predicts, prepares, produces, relates, shows, solves, uses
Recognizes unstated assumptions Recognizes logical fallacies in reasoning Distinguishes between facts and inferences	Breaks down, diagrams, differentiates, discriminates, distinguishes, identifies, illustrates, infers, outlines, points out, relates, selects, separates, subdivides
Writes a well organized theme Gives a well organized speech Writes a creative short story (or poem, or music) Proposes a plan for an experiment	Categorizes, combines, compiles, composes, creates, devises, designs, explains, generates, modifies, organizes, plans, rearranges, reconstructs, relates, reorganizes, revises, rewrites, summarizes, tells, writes
Judges the logical consistency of written material Judges the adequacy with which conclusions are supported by data	Appraises, compares, concludes, contrasts, criticizes, describes, discriminates, explains, justifies, interprets, relates, summarizes, supports

THE AFFECTIVE TAXONOMY AS STRUCTURE

Potentially useful in subject areas as value tumescent as social studies is the taxonomy of objectives in the affective domain produced by Krathwohl, Bloom, and Masia in association with the evaluators who had helped on the cognitive taxonomy. To date, the affective taxonomy and affective goals in general have received comparably less coverage in educational literature. The reasons for this relative neglect are fairly evident. The absence of a general affective theory presents a major obstacle in identifying, observing, and measuring affective behaviors.[36]

Also an aura of privacy tends to enshroud the realm of the affective. Persons in this culture are expected to claim the right to their own opinions, many of which are laced with affect. Not only are attitudes, appreciations, tastes, feelings, interests, opinions, values, and the like thought to be private possessions, but also they are viewed as almost inviolable. Teachers are taught to abhor indoctrination and to resist making wholesale assaults on their students' values.

The behaviors of the affective realm seem to be more elusive and ephemeral than the behaviors of the cognitive realm. The child can be asked his attitude (an approach not essentially different than that used in assaying his knowledge); but he may not know it, or he may not be able to verbalize it, or he may not want to tell it.[37]

[A] cognitive objective is always a *can-do* response, while an affective objective is always a *does-do* response. Behaviors of the can-do variety are traditionally and relatively easily triggered and evaluated. But behaviors of the does-do variety, while highly valued, tend to be more difficult to trigger reliably and standardize.[38]

Gronlund has applied the affective taxonomy also to the statement of general instructional objectives and specified learning outcomes. The vertical components of his table refer to the five categories of affective objectives, receiving, responding, valuing, organization, and characterization, as defined in the taxonomy. As in the exemplary table for the cognitive domain, the verbs on the right-hand side of the table refer to appropriate behaviors sought for in the affective realm.

Examples of General Instructional Objectives and Behavioral Terms for the Affective Domain of the Taxonomy[39]

Illustrative General Instructional Objectives	*Illustrative Behavioral Terms for Stating Specific Learning Outcomes*
Listens attentively	Asks, chooses, describes, follows, gives, holds, identifies, locates, names, points to, selects, sits erect, replies, uses
Shows awareness of the importance of learning	
Shows sensitivity to human needs and social problems	
Completes assigned homework	Answers, assists, complies, conforms, discusses, greets, helps, labels, performs, practices, presents, reads, recites, reports, selects, tells, writes
Obeys school rules	
Participates in class discussion	
Completes laboratory work	

Illustrative General Instructional Objectives	Illustrative Behavioral Terms for Stating Specific Learning Outcomes
Demonstrates belief in the democratic process Appreciates good literature (art or music) Appreciates the role of science (or other subjects) in everyday life	Completes, describes, differentiates, explains, follows, forms, initiates, invites, joins, justifies, proposes, reads, reports, selects, shares, studies, works
Recognizes the need for balance between freedom and responsibility in a democracy Recognizes the role of systematic planning in solving problems	Adheres, alters, arranges, combines, compares, completes, defends, explains, generalizes, identifies, integrates, modifies, orders, organizes, prepares, relates, synthesizes
Displays safety consciousness Demonstrates self-reliance in working independently Practices cooperation in group activities	Acts, discriminates, displays, influences, listens, modifies, performs, practices, proposes, qualifies, questions, revises, serves, solves, uses, verifies

THE RELATIONSHIP OF THE COGNITIVE AND AFFECTIVE

The dichotomization of behavior into cognitive and affective realms, as practiced in the above discussion and in most of the literature, is a conceptual convenience. It reflects a human incapacity for dealing simultaneously with all aspects of behavior at an adequate level of sophistication. Underlying this analysis is the assumption that somewhere it can be put all together.

Teachers are poignantly aware of the relationship between motivation and learning. Motivation, a concept that reflects many affective particulars, is a major way that the affective domain is used as a means to the cognitive. As Krathwohl expresses it, the influence of hedonic tone on memory and learning is appreciable.[40]

Teachers often intuitively use cognitive behaviors and the achievement of cognitive goals as a means to attain affective behavior. For example, a teacher who challenges his students' beliefs or discusses issues in class may be satisfied with the interaction only when students commit themselves emotionally to a point of view or ground their opinions in a value position. Sometimes cognitive objectives are prerequisite to affective goals. For example, an appreciation of art or music at a sophisticated level would need to be preceded by an understanding of art and music, at least at the level of analysis.[41]

One attempt to draw these two realms together in the evaluation of students is seen in the performance scale of Leppert and Payette.[42] In this instance the affective is represented by the concept willingness while the cognitive is represented by the concept ability. The specific behaviors intended are categorized under the general behaviors of communicating, thinking, and acting.

Directions: The assessment of the person's behavior may be made at any point along the scale. H represents High; M, Medium; L, Low. Check ( ) the appropriate point on the scale for each of the behaviors observed.

Willingness to Communicate

The person described

1. shares facts   H / M / L

2. shares personal beliefs about people and institutions   H / M / L

3. shares interpretations   H / M / L

4. shares personal experiences   H / M / L

5. shares vicarious experiences, i.e., learning based on the experiences of others   H / M / L

6. shares rating experiences   H / M / L

7. shares feelings   H / M / L

Ability to Communicate

The person described communicates

8. clearly rather than vaguely   H / M / L

9. accurately rather than erroneously   H / M / L

10. freely rather than reluctantly   H / M / L

11. sensitively rather than insensitively   H / M / L

12. deliberately rather than compulsively   H / M / L

Willingness to Think

The person described

13. formulates hypotheses   H / M / L

14. defines terms   H / M / L

15. examines how terms are used   H / M / L

16. searches out all related information   H / M / L

17. establishes logically necessary
    conclusions   H / M / L

18. rates events on the basis of standards H / M / L

19. identifies values pertinent to social
    issues or problems   H / M / L

Ability to Think

The person described

20. tests hypotheses, beliefs, conclusions
    against appropriate information   H / M / L

21. tests the adequacy of terms by
    reference to customary usage by
    offering explicit reasons for new uses
    of terms.   H / M / L

22. applies tests to determine whether
    conclusions follow necessarily from
    the reasons provided in an argument   H / M / L

23. revises conclusions as required by
    new information   H / M / L

Willingness to Act

The person described

24. participates in the resolution of
    issues and problems   H / M / L

Ability to Act

The person described

25. acts consistently with tested beliefs   H / M / L

26. stresses negotiation rather than
    arbitrariness   H / M / L

Summary

This statement has looked primarily at the description, uses, and kinds of behavioral objectives. While arguments for and against behavioral objectives have been offered, it is presumed that neither a conclusion that they are either good or bad nor the judgment that they should or should not be used can be made on the basis of this review. If the teacher decides to employ behavioral objectives in his teaching, there are significant hazards which he should attempt to avoid. If he decides, on the other hand, that he should not make use of behavioral systems in his classroom, then for him, too, there are significant perils to which he should attend.

Perhaps the issue is prematurely drawn that requires the teacher at our present level of understanding to choose either one option or the other. Rather, the teacher should ask himself what goals the employment of behavioral objectives will enable him to achieve and to what extent he wishes to commit his teaching to those goals.

NOTES

[1] Paul D. Plowman, *Behaviorial Objectives,* Chicago: Science Research Associates, 1971, p. xxiv.

[2] J. Myron Atkin, "Behavioral Objectives in Curriculum Design: A Cautionary Note," *The Science Teacher,* 35:28, May, 1968.

[3] Hilton M. Bialek, "A Measure of Teachers' Perceptions of Bloom's Educational Objectives." Paper presented to AERA Annual Meeting. New York, 1967. See also William D. Johnson, "Use of Behaviorally Stated Educational Objectives," mimeo., University of Illinois, 1970, p. 3.

[4] Atkin, *op. cit.,* p. 29.

[5] Robert M. Gagné, *The Conditions of Learning,* New York: Holt, Rinehart and Winston, Inc., 1965, p. 172.

[6] Harry D. Berg, editor, *Evaluation in Social Studies.* Thirty-fifth Yearbook of the National Council for the Social Studies. Washington, D.C.: NCSS, 1965, p. 158.

[7] David R. Krathwohl. Benjamin S. Bloom, and Bertram B. Masia, *Taxonomy of Educational Objectives: Handbook II: Affective Domain,* New York: David McKay, Inc., 1964, p. 45.

[8] *Ibid.,* p. 46.

[9] F. Coit Butler, "Preparing Instructional Objectives," mimeo., American Institutes for Research, 1968, p. 8.

[10] Plowman, *op. cit.,* p. 31.

[11] Gagné, *op. cit.,* p. 263.

[12] Norman E. Gronlund, *Stating Behavioral Objectives for Classroom Instruction,* New York: The Macmillan Company, 1970, pp. 51–52.

[13] Harry S. Broudy, "Research and the Dogma of Behavioral Objectives," mimeo., University of Illinois, 1969, p. 1.

[14] Gagné, *op. cit.,* pp. 242–243.

[15] Louise L. Tyler, "Symposium on the Instructional Objectives Controversy." Paper presented to AERA Annual Meeting, Chicago, 1968, p. 4.

[16] James D. Raths, "Specificity as a Threat to Curriculum Reform." Paper presented to AERA Annual Meeting. Chicago, 1968, mimeo., pp. 3–4.

[17] Elliot W. Eisner, "Educational Objectives: Help or Hindrance?" *The School Review,* 75:250–260. Autumn, 1967. Martin Haberman, "Behavioral Objectives:

Bandwagon or Breakthrough?" *The Journal of Teacher Education*, 19:91–94. Spring, 1968. See also William D. Johnson, *op. cit.*, p. 1.

[18] Butler, *op. cit.*, pp. 9–10.

[19] Gagné, *op. cit.*, p. 260.

[20] Butler, *op. cit.*, p. 2.

[21] Gagné, *op. cit.*, p. 251.

[22] Robert F. Mager, *Preparing Instructional Objectives*, Palo Alto: Fearon Publishers, 1962, pp. 33, 37.

[23] Haberman, *op.cit.*: see also Johnson, *op. cit.*, p. 1.

[24] Raths, *op. cit.*, pp. 3–4.

[25] Atkin, *op. cit.*, p. 29.

[26] Broudy, *op. cit.*, p. 1.

[27] Atkin, *op. cit.*, p. 28.

[28] Broudy, *op. cit.*, p. 2.

[29] *Ibid.*, p. 7.

[30] Atkin, *op. cit.*, pp. 2–3.

[31] W. James Popham, "Probing the Validity of Arguments Against Behavioral Goals." Paper presented to AERA Annual Meeting, Chicago, 1968, pp. 1–7, *passim.*

[32] Gagné, *op. cit.*, pp. 58–59.

[33] Plowman, *op. cit.*, pp. 34–35.

[34] Benjamin S. Bloom, editor, *Taxonomy of Educational Objectives: Handbook I: Cognitive Domain*, New York: David McKay Company, Inc., 1956.

[35] Gronlund, *op. cit.*, p. 21.

[36] Berg, *op. cit.*, p. 119.

[37] *Ibid*, p. 164.

[38] Krathwohl, pp. 60–61.

[39] Gronlund, *op. cit.*, p. 23.

[40] Krathwohl, *op. cit.*, p. 57.

[41] *Ibid.*, pp. 55–56.

[42] Ella Leppert and Roland F. Payette, "Description of Student Performance Aspects," mimeo., University of Illinois, 1970–71.

The Revival of Civic Learning

A Rationale for the Education of Citizens

R. FREEMAN BUTTS

When I saw in the program the title of the talk that Chuck Quigley had assigned to me, I was reminded of a friend of mine, Karl Bigelow, a long-time colleague at Teachers College, Columbia. Bigelow is a New Englander in speech and manner and an Anglophile in interests, as well as a voracious reader of dictionaries, encyclopedias, the *Whole Earth Catalog*, and all sorts of other esoterica. When he was director of the Commission on Teacher Education of the American Council on Education in the 1940s, he would take a secret delight in speaking with a straight face of the "rāshunalē" of teacher education, as if everyone knew that *that* was the way the word rationăle *should* be pronounced. And of course it is—according to the *Oxford English Dictionary*. Even *Webster's Unabridged Dictionary* gives "rāshun-alē" as the second preferred pronunciation. After due consideration, however, I have decided to follow *vox populi Americana* and stick to rationăle. So you will listen to *what* I am trying to say and not how I am saying it.

The important thing, I suppose, is not the word's pronunciation but its meaning. Here, both the OED and Webster agree. One meaning is the exposition of the principles of some phenomenon. The other is the underlying reason or rational foundation for anything. Since Webster says the first meaning (an exposition of principles) is now rare and since I have only a few minutes, I am going to concentrate on the second

NOTE: This selection, delivered as an address at the 1978 National Conference on Civic Education, appeared in *Social Education*, May 1979, pp. 359–364. Reprinted by permission of R. Freeman Butts.

143

meaning, and try to say something about the fundamental reasons why we should be concerned about the education of citizens and especially at *this* time. I shall concentrate on three reasons:

1. the argument from history

2. the need to counteract the rising mood of pessimism and aliena-tion concerning government and schooling; and thus the need to redirect educational priorities in the face of academic indifference or preoccupation with other goals or institutions

3. some hopeful signs that *now* is the time for what I would like to call a revival of the civic learning

(1) The Argument from History

I have written a good deal recently about the history of civic education— a chapter in the National Task Force Report on *Education for Respon-sible Citizenship* (sponsored by the Danforth and Kettering Foundations) and at greater length in my just published book, *Public Education in the United States*. I shall not try to summarize the substance of 200 years of history, but let me make a few generalizations.

First, I remind you that the fundamental reason why the founders of this Republic proposed universal common schooling was the *political* reason that education of the public was essential for a democratic so-ciety devoted to liberty, equality, popular consent, and personal obliga-tion for the public good. Universal education was not primarily to serve the self-fulfillment of individuals, or to develop the mind for its own sake, or to prepare for a job, or to get into college. The prime purpose was the welfare of the Republic, which would not survive or prosper apart from an educated citizenry.

I believe that this generalization holds good for the future of the Republic as well as for its founding. I believe that the fundamental ratio-nale for the education of citizens is the regeneration of a sense of demo-cratic political community among each new generation of Americans. This sense of political community should rest upon a common commit-ment to the basic values and ideals of constitutional government as these are denoted by the concepts of liberty, equality, popular consent, justice, and personal obligation for the public good. These values the founders embodied in the Declaration, the Constitution, and the Bill of Rights. The most fundamental purpose of universal schooling is the polit-ical goal of empowering the whole population to exercise the rights and cope with the responsibilities of a genuinely democratic citizenship.

Having said this, we must add that our problems just begin. Even if there is agreement on such a generalization, the consensus may quickly fall apart when it comes to defining just what kind of civic education should go on in schools. For 200 years we have struggled with the dilemma of politics and education. On one hand, we believe that education is fundamental to the health and vitality of an ideally democratic political community and that therefore schools should educate for citizenship; yet we do *not* believe that schools ought to be involved in "political education" or inculcation of partisan political ideas. Some even go so far as to say "It is undemocratic to indoctrinate for democracy."

The reasons for the persisting dilemma and lack of consensus over the *means* of civic education, if not the broad goals, arise from our history. I read this history of the civic role of education as a product of the interplay and tensions arising from three major elements in American life:

(a) The cohesive value claims that I have mentioned as undergirding the overall political community and long-range constitutional order; (b) the differentiating value claims of the pluralisms that give identity to the various groups or segments in American society (religion, ethnicity, race, and localism or regionalism); and (c) the drive toward modernization that has wrought deep changes in rural, agricultural, and traditional societies all over the world for the past several centuries (the mobilizing and centralizing power of the national state, the industrialization and technicalization of production of goods, whether impelled by capitalistic or socialistic forces, the urbanization arising from the magnet of city life, and the secularization of knowledge and intellectual life arising from science and empirical approaches to social problems).

These are vast and complicated historical movements that cannot be dealt with in a few minutes. But let me give just a few examples of the way they complicate the fundamental rationale for civic education. Although proponents of civic education in the schools usually agree in the appeal of their rhetoric to the cohesive value claims of political democracy, they often disagree in their underlying legitimacy or rationale. Some have appealed to the authority of a particular religion (say, Protestant Christianity), or morality (Puritanism), or ethnicity (Anglo-Americanism), or race (white superiority), or localism (states' rights). In such cases some pluralistic segments have sought to use the public schools to promote *their* particular versions of democratic political values.

When other pluralistic segments grew stronger or resistant, they sometimes sought to break away from the cohesive claims and establish their own schools and thus promote their own religious values and languages as the basis for building a sense of particularistic community. When the pluralistic pulls to differentiation grew strong enough to seem to threaten the cohesion of the overall political community, appeal was then often made to the claims of modernization (national unity, national strength, manifest destiny, economic development under free enterprise). Thus were injected into the civic programs of the schools an overweening emphasis upon patriotic loyalty, even a chauvinism and conformism stifling to dissent.

As a result of this persistent three-way pulling and hauling among the claims of a common democratic polity, of freedom for a variety of segmental pluralisms, and of an aggressive economic and nationalistic modernity, the civic education programs of the past have vacillated between two didactic extremes: those motivated by a strong moral, national, or nativist fervor which tended to give civic education a tone of preachy or pugnacious patriotism: and those that would at all costs avoid political controversy in the schools and thus would turn civic education into pedantic, pallid, platitudinous, or pusillanimous textbook exercises.

So where do I come out? Obviously, I do not recommend either of these extremes. And we cannot simply go back to the proposals of the founders of the Republic in the late eighteenth century or the founders of the common schools in the early nineteenth century. Society and government, and thus the nature of citizenship, have changed drastically in the past 200 years. Simple literacy in the 3R's for elementary school white boys is obviously not enough. Simple history as proposed by Jefferson or the elements of civil government as proposed by Washington are not enough. Vague preachments on the glories of an undefined liberty are not enough. Textbooks should not be left largely to politically conservative or neutral authors, as they have been in the past. Didactic appeals to moral, spiritual, or political principles upon which everyone can agree, as Horace Mann proposed, cannot give us the knowledge we need; yet in a pluralistic society the schools cannot become "theatres for party politics" designed to indoctrinate in particular, partisan economic or ideological platforms.

Somehow we must surmount Horace Mann's dilemma in which he insisted that schools stress the understanding of the constitutional regime but only so far as there is consensus within the community as to what the Constitution means. He argued that on matters of controversy the school is not a proper forum for discussion. Today, that would mean that the most crucial elements of civic education should be left to the family, voluntary groups, political parties, business, labor, the press, or, more particularly, to Walter and Roger, John and David, and Harry and Barbara. We must find a way to surmount Horace Mann's solutions which became the pattern for most social studies teaching for more than a century.

So, if we are not to give up on the schools entirely as forums for study of controversial public issues, we must find ways to avoid their subservience to the extreme pluralistic claims and extreme nationalistic claims. In doing this we should draw on our historical tradition, which stressed the role of education in social reform and human welfare rather than the narrow and restrictive fear of the alien and the foreign and the different. We should learn from our tradition of generous, cosmopolitan, and humane assimilation of vast numbers of immigrants with sympathetic respect for their traditional cultures, rather than from the dreary record of the anti-Catholic, anti-foreign, anti-radical, and Anglo-superior stance of so many of our schools of the past. We need to re-enforce the older confidence in the capacity of the Republic to accept great diversity and pluralism as a basic characteristic of a genuinely democratic political community. And we should draw sustenance from our political tradition which recurrently called upon government to take the lead in social reform when voluntary effort proved to be indifferent or unsuccessful (in the reform of prisons, sweat shops, child labor, women's suffrage, civil service, universal education, and, more recently, the efforts to dismantle segregation in the schools, equalize financial support of education, and open up access to those disadvantaged by poverty, race, or ethnic or linguistic background). Compensatory education, affirmative action, and the other recent efforts to achieve a more secure freedom and equality of rights by governmental action should be viewed as essential for the health of the Republic and thus as essential to civic education, rather than as solely for the advantage of individuals in getting a job or getting ahead. The impact of the Bakke decision on the role of government is yet to be determined; half of it said that the state university may act to consider race in admissions; the other half said that Bakke had been illegally excluded because of his race.

I know that the view that government and schooling should be looked upon as primary instruments to "form a more perfect union, establish justice, promote the general welfare, and secure the blessings of liberty to ourselves and our posterity" is not very popular just now. This brings me to my second point in the rationale for civic education.

(2) The Rising Mood of Pessimism and Alienation Concerning Government and Schooling, and the Preoccupation of Public and Profession Alike with Other Goals and Other Institutions of Education

Without seeming to sound apocalyptic, I believe that we may be coming to a peculiarly important juncture in the history of American education. It is, of course, imprudent to try to predict the future; but let me simply remind you of some aspects of the mood of the late 1970s, stemming perhaps from the prior decade of the Vietnam War, Watergate, campus unrest, corruption in quiet places, violence in the schools, etc.

The signs greet us on all sides: cynicism and skepticism about the role of government; alienation and exasperation with public institutions and public officials, including school officials and organized teachers; a simplistic and self-serving complaint by big business about "big government" and an undignified scramble by politicians to echo "me too"; and the taxpayers' revolts, often directed at the schools because taxpayers could make their voices heard most directly by voting down school bond issues and budgets (three out of five in the early 1970s).

Then came Jarvis-Gann and Proposition 13 in California last June, which set off all kinds of schemes to lower property taxes with apparently little thought or concern for what might happen to public services, including the schools. All this comes at a time when the educational graphs all seem to be on the decline: decline in budgets, decline in jobs, decline in enrollments, decline in test scores, decline in confidence that schools make much difference. All this feeds the public mood to curtail schooling if need be, but certainly gives support to a back to the basics movement, which, among other things, would appear to be less expensive than all those education fads and frills which have padded school budgets with fat during recent years. And, besides, it is argued, we could probably improve the achievement and discipline of the schools if we lowered or did away with compulsory attendance laws. In this way we could get rid of all those trouble-making kids; let the schools get back to their real academic tasks, and thus reduce the violence, the vandalism, the drugs, the sex, the fear, and the crime that beset so many schools.

I do not mean to make light of the public disaffection toward governmental and educational institutions, nor to claim that the malaise is entirely uncalled for. It must be taken into account as we look to the future. But perhaps even more unsettling in the long run may be the pessimistic mood *within* the academic world and *within* the teaching profession itself. For if the academics and the professionals succumb to a pessimism about government and schooling along with the public, what can we hope for from the students and the children?

The malaise about government and schooling comes from both the right and the left of the academic community. Neo-conservative scholars in economics and sociology have gained a new respectability. A recent sign of this is the article in *The New York Times Magazine* for July 23, 1978 called the "Right-Thinking Think Tank," describing such luminaries of the Hoover Institution at Stanford as Milton Friedman (father of the school voucher idea and strong supporter of Jarvis-Gann) and its ties with the right wing of the Republican Party, especially through its director, Glenn Campbell. The new respectability and political influence of academic conservatism of which *The Times* article speaks generally side with private effort, rather than governmental, in the school and in educational as well as economic fields. While the Hoover Institution flourishes, such liberal think-tanks as the Center for the Study of Democratic Institutions at Santa Barbara find it hard to stay afloat.

The move toward private effort in schooling, rather than government support and control through public institutions of education, runs a gamut from the Moynihan-Packwood effort to get the Senate to provide tuition tax credits for private elementary and secondary schools as well as colleges to the effort of Protestant Fundamentalists who are suing in Kentucky to prevent the state from imposing *any* kind of standards upon their private religious schools as a violation of the First Amendment. They do not want their schools accredited nor their teachers certified.

The irony is that while the fad for reducing local property taxes for public schools spreads like wildfire fanned by Proposition 13, the overall result may just be that the states and the Federal government will be importuned to exert more control over public schools and to give *more* support to private education as proposed in Washington by Senator Moynihan. The left-hand purse knoweth not what the right-hand purse may be doing. And the rationale for taking government out of the education business is not confined to small fundamentalist religious groups. It is the main theme of respected scholars within the academic and educational professions. Robert Nisbet, Columbia sociologist (formerly from California), speaks of the *Twilight of Authority* of the historic liberal state, which he hopes will be replaced by a return to kinship, localism, voluntary association, and a recovery of the central values of social and cultural pluralism rather than those of the national political community. Schooling should also be returned to these non-governmental auspices.

Similarly, in the philosophy of education the pessimistic mode about a common civic education is apparent from a conservative point of view. In a recent book called *A New Public Education*, Seymour Itzkoff of Smith College feels that the legitimate authority for education lies not in the cohesive values of political community but that "the best hope for an enlightened, rational society lies in the natural diversity and pluralism of communities and groups that have been given an opportunity and the wherewithal to develop schools of their own choice, a new but equally public educational system."[1]

The practical meaning of this is voucher or tax credits for ethnic groups, cultural groups, religious groups, and all kinds of "natural" groups to run their own schools. Ted Sizer, former dean at Harvard and now headmaster at Andover, argues for "a smorgasbord of schools" to recognize the increasing importance of interest groups that rest on racial and ethnic origin. And a brand new book by Jack Coons and Steve Sugarman of the Law School at Berkeley, called *Education by Choice*, is a persuasive argument for *family* control of education supported by public funds. This book is hailed by Andrew Greeley, director of the Center for the Study of Ethnicity in Chicago, as "possibly a fatal blow to the oppressive bureaucratic monopoly exercised by the public schools."

The pessimistic mode about the role of schools in civic education is even more pronounced among historians of education, especially those of a radical persuasion. I have recently returned from a symposium conducted by Research for Better Schools in Philadelphia on the history of education and its meaning for the education of citizens. The malaise of three radical revisionist historians of education was clear. Clarence Karier of the University of Illinois reads the history as the steady victory of the totalitarian state over individual freedom, and the schools have always been a party to this victory of the state. The schools should *not* teach loyalty to the government or the Constitution. So he is pessimistic about the role of schooling in citizenship education. Marvin Lazerson of the University of British Columbia finds that citizenship education has not permitted root differences among cultural groups to be thought of as legitimate differences, so *he* is pessimistic that citizenship education can be reconceptualized unless the state itself is reconceptualized. I take this to mean that the historic liberal state must be "reconceptualized" along socialistic lines. And Michael Katz, now at the University of Pennsylvania, finds the essence of our history to be a conflict of social classes; the schools always on the side of the upper classes, imposing *their* middle class values upon a reluctant lower class. So the schools should be value neutral, and simply teach the basic academic skills. He is *not* in favor of deliberate programs of civic or moral education, because they are bound to be used to maintain the present exploitative, class-based status quo.

While this mood of pessimism about government which is the prime object of civic education and about the role of schooling in promoting civic education gains adherents in schools of education, what are the schools and the teachers of teachers going to do about it? If I were in a cynical mood and not attending this conference, I might argue that the schools are so preoccupied with other educational goals than citizenship and the teacher educators are so preoccupied with all sorts of educational institutions other than the schools that there is little hope for a revival of civic education.

I could point to the disarray in the social studies, where electives have reduced attention to history, civics, and government. So much so that the National Assessment shows a marked decline in students' political knowledge between 1970 and 1976. Incidentally, that report was almost totally ignored by the press. *The New York Times* gave a whole column to the NAEP report on decline in *science* tests, but only three or four sentences to the civics test results. I could, of course, point to the fascination with "back to the basics." The profession as well as the public seems to have forgotten that the original purpose of universal literacy was to enable all the citizens to exercise their civic duties properly, rather than to enable them to get jobs.

I could point out how the spread of competency-based education and CBTE seem to have had extremely little to say about civic education, and how professional organizations like NEA, ASCD, and AACTE are focusing on multicultural education, cultural pluralism, and bilingual education but saying little or nothing about civic education. The current fashions in avant-garde pedagogical circles have to do with personalized learning, individual learning, sex education, drug education, career education, consumer education, energy education, ecological or environmental education, and, above all, alternatives to *all* of the above.

These are all very important public issues and deserve careful attention; but I submit that they downplay the *political* values that underlie them, the *political* knowledge required to understand them, and the *political* skills required for citizens to have some effect upon their solution. Meanwhile, it is currently fashionable to downplay what *schools* can do when compared with families, communities, churches, neighborhoods, museums, camps, libraries, and, above all, TV. A recent issue of the *Teachers College Record* is given entirely to articles on the family and the community as educators, with little or no attention to the distinctive role of schooling in American society.

But I am *not* in a cynical mood nor am I in a pessimistic mood, and that brings me to my third and final point.

(3) It's Time for a *Revival of the Civic Learning in the Schools*

We all know that the term and even the idea of "citizenship education" is often greeted by yawns of indifference among teachers and especially among university academics. It was not so long ago (1962) that the Executive Secretary of the American Political Science Association argued that knowledge of political science in secondary schools had very little to do with the making of good citizens and that such beliefs rested on distorted conceptions of how citizens are made and what democracy requires in an age of expertise and specialists.

We know, too, that didactic moral instruction and outward ceremonies of patriotism through pledges of allegiance, loyalty oaths, salutes to the flag, and patriotic songs have lost their savor among academics at all levels of formal education. Within half a century, two or three hot wars and the Cold War have made the academic and scholastic world very uneasy about patriotism, long considered at the heart of the rationale for citizenship education.

Meanwhile, in 1971 the Committee on Precollegiate Education of the American Political Science Association reported on a survey of civic education in the schools[2]:

> [It] transmits a naive, unrealistic, and romanticized image of political life which confuses the ideals of democracy with the realities of politics. (p. 7.)
> In summary, the majority of civics and government curriculum materials currently in use at all grade levels either completely ignore or inade-

quately treat not only such traditionally important political science concepts as freedom, sovereignty, consensus, class, compromise, and power
but also newer concepts such as role, socialization, culture, system, decision making, etc. (p. 10.)

This was quite a turnaround for APSA in a decade. Now the Precollegiate Committee is in the process of producing an extensive volume of
readings on political education. And a vast literature on political socialization has been developing during the same period which needs to be
plumbed for its value in improving civic education in the schools.

Meanwhile, the humanistic side of political philosophy and moral
philosophy has received a renaissance in such diverse and influential
works as those of John Rawls' *A Theory of Justice*, Robert Nozick's
Anarchy, State, and Utopia, and of the Institute for the Study of Civic
Values. Thus, both from the behavioral and empirical approach and
from the philosophic approach, there are new bodies of learning in
political science that can inform new approaches to civic learning in the
schools.

There are signs that the other social sciences are also moving down
from their lofty disciplinary perches of the 1950s and 1960s to apply
theory to practice. Nathan Glazer has stressed this point in a recent
article in *The Chronicle of Higher Education* (July 31, 1978):

> [The social sciences] have moved from a stance toward the world that
> emphasizes detached observation and analysis to a stance in which ob-
> servation is increasingly mixed with participation, analysis with judgment
> and advice. The social scientist relates to institutions less as an unin-
> volved scholar seeking general truth than as a participant whose con-
> cerns are close to, intermixed with, the concerns of the practitioner.[3]

Presumably this is because they both share the same concerns in
their general role of citizen. Why has this shift of intellectual orientation
among the disciplines taken place? Glazer gives three reasons: the enormous expansion of government in many spheres; radical changes in
such institutions as schools, hospitals, prisons, and social work agencies;
and the fact that the growth and change in government and other
institutions have become increasingly problematic, something to be questioned, challenged, and defended. This shift from theory to practice has
affected both conservatives and radicals in sociology:

> Social change—seen in the past as consisting of such processes as tech-
> nological change, cultural lag, social movements, and revolution—now is
> increasingly felt to result from change in the behavior and scale of gov-
> ernment and in the service institutions that had become so large a part of
> government activities.
>
>   And so today, schools, prisons, hospitals, housing, and public administra-
> tion are now all considered as linked deeply to and implicated in the
> structure of society. *They reflect and shape its values, creating the world
> we all live in* . . . . (italics added)

I think a necessary adaptation of the social-science disciplines to a changing world is taking place, a world increasingly created by law, regulation, judgment, and large organization, as against the atomic action of individuals and small organizations.[4]

I don't agree with Nathan Glazer on much of his outlook, but I think he has made some very acute points in this article. Similar points could be made with regard to history. Robert Kelley points out how historians are finding that the cultural politics of pluralism are more revealing than the older theories of class conflict and economic materialism. And, above all, psychology has developed an enormously important approach to questions of moral and civic development.

My point is that the world of scholarship now has more to offer the schools in a renaissance of civic learning than has been the case for 30–40 years. The disciplines are once more concerned in a way that they have not been since the New Deal and the Fair Deal of the 1930s and 1940s.

And I believe that there are now at least a few signs that the practical world of affairs may be more receptive than at any time since the early 1960s to promote the importance of schooling after a long period of malaise and uncertainty about its values. Robert Wood, a former university president who has been appointed Superintendent of Schools in Boston, argues that the schools are the linchpin or the keystone for the regeneration of urban life. After a long and exhaustive study, Gary Orfield argues that school busing, after all, is the only way to desegregate American society in our lifetime. And federal judges in Los Angeles and Dayton have agreed in their recent decisions. The *Harvard Educational Review* for May 1978 reports several evaluation studies of Headstart and Follow-Through, some of which are more optimistic concerning the influence and effect of such government-supported projects than was the popular opinion of researchers a few years ago. A new era of concern for international education may result from the U.S. Commissioner's interest, from a Presidential Commission on International Studies, and from the new stance on behalf of human rights throughout the world which has been taken by the President, the Secretary of State, and the U.N. Ambassador. Recently the *San Francisco Chronicle* described a report to President Carter being made by 14 federal agencies called "Global 2000 Study," which warns that overpopulation, ecological problems, and environmental conditions will endanger world peace and security more than will outright war. The point is that the technological resources are available to solve many of the ecological problems and to save productive land, forest, and sea; but the real problems are the institutional and *political* barriers. It may just be that the political education of the American people on such matters will be a critical factor in whether or not the international political barriers prove to be insurmountable.

And as we look ahead, the time seems all the more appropriate for a revival of civic learning in the schools as we enter the 200th anniversary of the decade between 1776 and the forming of the Constitution in 1787, its adoption in 1788, its operational beginning in 1789, and the adoption of the Bill of Rights in 1791. Significantly, celebration of this Bicentennial of the Constitution is being planned by a joint committee of the American Historical Association and the American Political Science Association. The effort is being called "Project 87." It will be conducted in three stages. The first, from 1978 through 1980, is being devoted to scholarships, fellowships, seminars, and conferences to study anew the Constitution's relevance and adequacy for the present. The second stage, beginning in 1981, will focus on improving teaching about the Constitution in elementary and secondary schools and in producing public television programs. The third stage, culminating in 1987, will engage the broadest possible public participation in discussions of the Constitution.

Thus, this conference comes at a peculiarly strategic time to take account of the historical setting, to meet the challenges of political pessimism, alienation and disaffection, and to capitalize on the signs of awakening to the primacy of the civic role of the schools, which was their oldest innovation and could again be their newest innovation. I hope that we can learn something from Project 87, and I am sure that it can learn a great deal from the assembly of civic projects gathered here this week. Each of these projects will captivate you in its own way. Each, I imagine, will be learning something from the other projects and from you as participants.

When I speak of the revival of civic learning, I am purposely relying upon the multiple meanings of "learning." In history we speak of the Revival of Classical Learning of the twelfth-thirteenth centuries, prelude to the Renaissance. "Learning" in this sense is a corpus of knowledge and scholarship which informs and challenges the highest reaches of the intellectual, the moral, and the creative talents of humankind. Thus, it symbolizes our connection with and our reliance upon the major disciplines of knowledge and research, what my late colleague Lyman Bryson once called the reliance upon "significant truth rather than plausible falsehood or beguiling half-truth."

But "learning" also signals our concern for and our reliance upon the most significant ways in which learning takes place among individuals at different ages and stages of development and in all the contexts of modern life. Thus, learning symbolizes our efforts to improve all those skills and experiences which will motivate and enhance the realistic involvement of students in their own learning experiences relating to the political processes and the moral judgments that underlie the political system. Thus "the civic learning" embraces the long range and fundamental values of the political community; a realistic and scholarly knowledge of the working of political institutions and processes; and the skills of political behavior required for genuine political participation in a democracy.

I like the way Charles Frankel recently put the matter in an article on the humanities entitled "The Academy Enshrouded" (*Change*, December, 1977):

> In every generation in which the humanities have shown vitality, they . . . have performed an essential *public, civic, educational function*: the criticism and reintegration of the ideas and values of cultures dislocated from their traditions and needing a new sense of meaning. This is what humanistic scholars did in fifth- and fourth-century Athens, in the thirteenth century . . . in the Renaissance, and in the nineteenth century. Can they perform this function now?[5]

In answering Charles Frankel's question, I propose that the keynote of this conference be that *we* are indeed determined to perform an essential public, civic, educational function. We propose to give a new sense of meaning to the ideas and values which have been dislocated from our traditional civic community. We signalize here a revival of the civic learning.

NOTES

[1] Seymour W. Itzkoff, *A New Public Education*. New York: David McKay, 1976, p. 308.

[2] American Political Science Association, Committee on Precollegiate Education, "Political Education in the Public Schools," reprinted from *PS*, Newsletter of the A.P.S.A., Summer 1971, Vol. IV, No. 3, 1971.

[3] Nathan Glazer, "Theory and Practice in the Social Sciences," *The Chronicle of Higher Education*, July 31, 1978, p. 28.

[4] *Ibid.*, p. 28.

[5] Charles Frankel, "The Academy Enshrouded," *Change*, December 1977, p. 64. (Italics added.)

III.

The World Scene

MARK TWAIN ONCE WROTE: "They spell it Vinci and pronounce it Vinchy; foreigners always spell better than they pronounce." Pronunciation is only one of many aspects of life in other countries that present problems to Americans. As a result, teaching about other lands and peoples continues to be a difficult task for American educators. Fortunately, there are those who are willing to accept the challenge.

Thus, at any given day in the school year, teachers might be instructing about the history of Canada, Mexico, Argentina, Britain, Greece, Israel, Iran, India, China, the Soviet Union. An up-to-date atlas—revised annually—is a must! Words, too, dance in and out of the center of our attention. So, terms describing our planet have changed from "national" to "international" to "global" to "spaceship earth." Regardless of how the world is viewed, however, the demand by social studies teachers for materials about other parts of the world has remained heavy.

This section of the anthology focuses on different lands and different peoples. It begins with the article "Egypt—and the Case for 'Baggage'" by Josephine Mayer, who, as early as 1938, felt that it was necessary to warn against forsaking the minutiae of history. "The smallest detail," she observes, "may turn out to be important." Then she reaches beyond the customary salute to *The Book of the Dead*, the *Rosetta Stone*, and the *Edwin Smith Papyrus* and reminds us of the ancient story-tellers in the taverns of Thebes, the sayings of the vizier Ptah-hotep, and the lyrics of Egyptian lovers. It is clear that Mayer, who was an experienced teacher and historian, feels that she is stronger carrying her "baggage" than traveling without it.

There have been a number of statesmen—Winston Churchill and John F. Kennedy come to mind at once—who also possessed literary skill. Few, however, had the writing gifts of Carlos P. Romulo, who served as president of the United Nations General Assembly, Philippine ambassador to the United States, and president of the University of the Philippines. In "Our Consciousness of Asia: An End to Innocence," he invites readers to see Asia "like a book open in the sun." "The text should not be too blurred to read even now; the leaves are perhaps crisp from overexposure in the sun, but certainly it is a book to leaf through and perhaps to read." Romulo's reading of the book is distinctive and worth considering carefully.

The American poet Robert Lowell once remarked, "Our culture is so heroically receptive, so willing to imagine that every straw in the haystack is a needle, that the real needle cannot be discovered." In examining aspects of Canadian literature in "Adam's Inventory," D. G. Jones of the Université de Sherbrooke, Québec, seems well aware of the significance of Lowell's comments when applied to Canadian culture. Jones therefore searches carefully for the central meaning of literary efforts in his country, and he does so by recognizing that "to give tongue to the mute, to make the unconscious conscious; to transcend the opposites and unite what is divided by particularity and death; to transform a chaos of random particulars into a cosmos, isolation into communion, such is the ultimate role of the imagination. . . ." Jones's inventory reveals order not chaos, and his analysis leads to a dream of universal communion.

Economist Barbara Ward always had a way with words. Thus, in her article "Urbanization: A Worldwide Process," she states that the process of modern urbanization can be compared to dropping a jellyfish from a great height; that some fifty-block apartment complexes are places where children are supposed to grow up between heaven and earth and never reach the ground; that the grand dukes unknowingly contributed to the Gross National Product by building unnecessary castles that are now tourist attractions; that if the population increases greatly in a Green Belt, an area of trees and parks encircling a city, the Belt becomes a halter around your neck; and that anyone who reads Dickens should know that pollution in the grand manner was demonstrated in his city novels by having characters with gin-blue faces stumble through the thick fog until they met their death by tumbling into the river. Barbara Ward's efforts to convince seem effortless, and her concluding observations underline the need for reform of urban life. "There is the possibility that we are creating an environment so hostile that to survive at all man might essentially have to stop being human," she declares. Her words become a stimulus to action.

Consider the problems. First, to deduce a logical location for the safe anchorage of a king's ships in case of northern winds. Next, to explore by submarine the waters around a small island north of Crete. Then, to fly by helicopter to attain a photographic coverage of the island. And the results? Most satisfying, according to oceanographer Jacques Cousteau, who explains what happened in "Jacques Cousteau Comments on Current Archeological Exploration of Greek Waters."

The section concludes with "Dismantling Apartheid," views expressed by Nobel Prize Laureate Desmond Tutu. "We shall be free," Archbishop Tutu declares, "and we will remember who helped us to become free." It is a declaration that rings throughout the world today.

Egypt—and the Case for "Baggage"

JOSEPHINE MAYER

I

Clambering from *history* to *the social sciences,* the study of the past has cached along the way some of its most colorful baggage. The abandonment was not deliberate. It came about quite naturally. As related sciences and pseudosciences crept in, something had to be discarded; the pack must be kept to a decent weight. Particulars gave way to formulas, personalities to generalizations. Statistics brushed aside the curl of a mustache, the set of a hat. Perhaps this should be so. But the fact remains (or at least the suspicion remains) that while much that is indispensable in understanding human development has been added, much that would deepen this understanding has been thrown out.

If we believe that in history teaching "the really interesting and essential thing is to enter into and trace the changes that have passed upon the human mind,"[1] we are committed to salvage operations. We must recover the bundles and examine the minutiae. For ideas cannot be separated from the people who hold them, and a people cannot be perceived unless the particular traits and qualities that distinguish them from all other peoples are thrown into sharp relief. In this process the smallest detail may turn out to be important. Today's ubiquitous sack suit, for example, proclaims the triumph of the bourgeoisie. It furnishes a goodly part of humanity with covering, and provides the modern business man with antecedents as well. According to Miriam Beard,[2] his trousers, and even his drab jacket and stiff hat, derive from that medieval freebooter, the Venetian merchant. The theatre has had a hand in per-

NOTE: This article appeared in *Social Education,* May 1938, pp. 307–312.

petuating his costume. As *Pantalone*, stock comedy figure of the *commedia dell' arte*, he walked the boards arrayed in a strange nether garment borrowed from "his best customers," the Turks and Saracens. Transported to France by a daughter of the Medici, *Pantaloon* amused the aristocrats, won the leading part in Molière's *Le Bourgeois Gentilhomme*, survived the revolution, and, grown vastly in dignity and importance, fastened the trouser, emblem of trade, on a complacent world.

While the fortunes or misfortunes of traders seem far removed from the life of a poet and saint, there is in either case the same necessity for procuring and using significant detail. And besides, St. Francis, son of Messer Piero Bernardone of Assisi, was merchant-born and merchant-bred. Originally he had been destined to carry on his father's business, and to deal in woolen cloth "of diverse colours." The simplicity of his later dealings, his tenderness, his humility, his courage in casting aside "the props of property" and, with his followers, walking propertyless upon the roadways of the world—in short, St. Francis himself—is in danger of being lost to us. He disappears beneath the usual discussion of the Franciscan movement and the bare sentences about its originator. There is nothing in them to account for his popularity among countless generations of peasants or the esteem in which he is held today, or to explain him as "the poet who was practically the founder of medieval and therefore of modern art."[3] The brief notice that he loved all creatures even "brother worm," that he wrote songs of praise to God in the Italian vernacular, that his "Canticle of the Sun" has come down to us, that he sometimes pretended to be playing the viol "all the while singing a joyous French song about the Lord" fails to bring him to life because there is no life there. But there is in that joyous French song (if we could only hear it), and in the frescoes which Giotto painted in the churches of Assisi (which we can see), and in the tale of the deal which St. Francis made with a rather rough wolf. And in his words: "Praised be my Lord God, with all his creatures, and especially our brother the sun, who brings us the day and who brings us the light; fair is he, and he shines with a very great splendour."

Helen Waddell in *The Wandering Scholars*[4] speaks of the furniture of a man's mind. The mind in question was thirteenth century, its furniture classical or pseudo-classical. The style of its chairs and tables does not concern us here, but the type of inquiry does. Delving into men's minds, especially into the minds of men long dead, is a task for scholars. The fragments which they unearth, and which come forth so fresh and dustless, are of immense value in re-creating the past. We may say, as did Milton, that they enable us "to be present as it were in every age, to extend and stretch life backward from the womb." In the three hundred years since Milton life has been stretched backward an astonishing distance. Today the man of the Stone Age begins to emerge, and his art (certainly very near his mind and spirit) to gain some acclaim.

Of particular interest, then, is the statement that a forthcoming volume of world history is an account of *peoples* and their *ideas*.[5] Set down before its text are these lines from Walter Pater: "Nothing that has ever interested living men and women can wholly lose its vitality—no language they have spoken, nor oracle beside which they have hushed their voices, no dream which has once been entertained by actual human minds, nothing about which they have ever been passionate, or expended time and zeal."

The people of ancient times have suffered most from the vogue for condensation. While the researches of the last century have brought new life to the past, in school texts the results are reduced to pitifully general terms. No summary of what has interested living men and women, no catalogue of their art can be anything but dreary. Too often has Homer been resolved to a bust with a beard, the dramas that excited the Greeks to a compendium of authors and titles. The student would be hard put to it to tell why seven cities claimed great Homer dead.

Yet Homer still lives to those who know his words. T. E. Lawrence, in the foreword to his translation of the *Odyssey*,[6] says of the man: "In four years of living with this novel I have tried to deduce the author from his self-betrayal in the work. I found a book-worm, no longer young, living from home, a mainlander, city-bred and domestic. Married but not exclusively, a dog-lover, often hungry and thirsty, dark-haired . . . he loved the rural scene as only a citizen can. No farmer, he had learned the points of a good olive tree. He is all adrift when it comes to fighting, and had not seen deaths in battle. He had sailed upon and watched the sea with a palpitant concern, seafaring not being his trade. . . . Yet this Homer was neither land-lubber nor stay-at-home nor ninny."

And we can turn to the "book-worm" himself: "'Come, tell me now this also, god-like Homer: what think you in your heart is most delightsome to men?' Homer answered: 'When mirth reigns throughout the town, and feasters about the house, sitting in order, listen to a minstrel; when the tables besides them are laden with bread and meat, and a wine-bearer draws sweet drink from the mixing-bowl and fills the cups: this I think in my heart to be most delightsome.'"[7] To get a sense of Homer is not too difficult. It takes time (but not four years), and the conviction that for this Greek and his tale of Troy portrait and paraphrase will not do.

These words of Homer do not strike us as strange. Conviviality seems natural in the Greeks. Few of us, however, think of the Egyptians as "a bright merry people who loved wine and music and feasting."[8] And yet they were, as their writings and the paintings that enliven their tombs clearly show. Mummification was not their sole occupation nor even their principal diversion. Neither is *The Book of the Dead*, a collection of magical hocus-pocus, their only contribution to literature. Inventors of the short story as well as the calendar, they were the first people to have a literature of entertainment. Story-tellers held forth in the taverns of Thebes a thousand years before Homer sat sipping his sweet wine. Snatches of fabulous tales shortened the homeward road for thousands who by day toiled to raise the pyramids. The sayings of Ptah-hotep had become proverbial by the time Abraham led his flocks and his family into the land of Canaan. If we place the greatest period of Egyptian literature in the Old Kingdom, as some scholars do, then the height of her writing was reached forty-five hundred years ago. Manners and morals, religion and poetry, medicine and surgery, history and legend, education and philosophy, all are represented in the records recovered for us in recent years. Nor must we rely on these alone for the details that make Egypt live again, for the highly colored reliefs of tombs and temples are equally revealing.[9]

II

Across these centuries the Egyptian by his own words reveals himself with startling candor. To the young men of Memphis, Ptah-hotep, vizier of an early Pharaoh, offered shrewd counsel gained through a long and profitable life:

> If thou be wise marry. Love thy wife sincerely. Fill her belly and clothe her back. Oil is the remedy for her body. Make glad her heart all thy life. She is a profitable field for her lord.
> If thou art a guest at the table of one who is greater than thou, take what he may offer thee as it is set before thee. Fix thy gaze at what is before thee, and pierce not thy host with many glances, for it is an abomination to force thy notice upon him. Speak not to him until he biddeth thee, for one knoweth not what may be offensive; but speak when he addresseth thee, for so shall thy words give satisfaction.
> Bend thy back to him that is over thee, to thy superior in the administration; thy house shall abide by reason of his substance, and thy recompense shall come in due season. Evil is he who resisteth his superior, for one liveth only so long as he is gracious.

Ptah-hotep was third in the line of Egypt's great sages. Before him came Imhotep, versatile vizier of King Zozer, and Prince Harzozef, son of the mighty Khufu. Their words have been lost, but perhaps it was their thoughts he uttered in this advice to Egypt's intelligentsia: "Be not arrogant because of thy knowledge, and be not puffed up for that thou art a learned man. Take counsel with the ignorant as with the learned, for the limits of art cannot be reached, and no artist is perfect in his excellence. Goodly discourse is more hidden than the precious greenstone, and yet it is found with slave girls over the millstones."

Reflecting what Breasted calls "a carnival of destruction," the writings of the Middle Kingdom show a tendency towards pessimism. The chaos that followed the breakup of the Old Kingdom turned the author in on himself as it turned the common man to the protection of petty princes. Gone was the faith in unassailable monarchs so marked in the time of Khufu and Khafre, and the confidence with which an earlier Egypt faced the new day. Revolution had left its mark; the cry of this writer was the cry of all Egypt:

> Behold, he that possessed wealth now
>   spendeth the night athirst;
> He that begged of him his dregs is now a
>   possessor of wine-vats.
> Behold, they that possessed clothes are
>   now in rags;
> He that wove not for himself now pos-
>   sesseth fine linen.
> Behold, he that had no shade is now the
>   possessor of shade;
> The possessors of shade are in the blast
>   of the storm.
> Behold, he that had no knowledge of the lyre now possesseth a harp;
> He to whom none sang now vaunteth the Goddess of Music.
> Behold, cattle are left to stray, there is
>   none to herd them;
> Each man must fetch for himself those
>   that are branded with his name.
> Behold, he that was bald and had no oil
> Has become a possessor of jars of sweet
>   myrrh.
> Behold, she that had no box is now a pos-
>   sessor of furniture;
> She that beheld her face in water now
>   possesseth a mirror.
> Behold, noble ladies go hungry;
> What was prepared for them goes to sate
>   the butchers.
> Verily the children of princes are dashed
>   against the walls.

Out of these evil days comes an early consideration of "to be or not to be." The decision of a man to destroy himself is vigorously opposed by his soul or *ba*. Death is evil, it declares, and survivors lax about furnishing the deceased with the necessary supplies of food and drink. "Those weary ones who die upon the river-bank have none to care for them," the *ba* argues. "And the water and the sun's heat alike destroy them; and the fishes of the river's bank have converse with them. Enjoy thyself and forget care." But the man longs for death:

Death is in my eyes today
Like the scent of myrrh,
Like sitting beneath the boat's sail on a breezy day.

Death is in my eyes today
Like the smell of water-lilies,
Like sitting on the bank of drunkenness.

Death is in my eyes today
Like the desire of a man to see his home
When he hath passed many years in captivity.

Egyptians were frank about the joys of soldiering, or at least the school-masters were. When the period of Empire and the "age of chivalry" descended on Egypt, the teacher's task became increasingly difficult. Then, as now, it was hard to hold boys in school against the lure of a uniform and the prospect of glory. While the officers of Egypt practiced with their great bows in full sight of the squatting youngsters, the class was forced to write: "Come, let me tell thee of the woes of the soldier. He is hungry, his body is worn out, he is dead while yet alive. His commanders say to him, 'Forward, brave soldier, win for thyself a good name.' But he is half-unconscious. In the village are his wife and children, but he dieth and doth not reach it."

With the Empire and its line of conquerors came the high point of the martial song, and, quite naturally, of the love lyric. Frank delight in physical beauty and a heightened enjoyment of nature are characteristic of the Egyptian lovers. The "brother," or lover, prays to the Golden Hathor, goddess of beauty and pleasure, as a later lover might have prayed to Aphrodite; while the "sister" in the presence of her beloved inhales the breath of Amon. The "sister" speaks:

There are *saamu*-flowers in my wreath.
One is uplifted in their presence.
I am thy first sister.
I am unto thee like the acre
Which I have planted with flowers
And all manner of sweet-smelling herbs;
And in it is a pool which thy hand has digged.
In the cool of the North Wind,
It is a lovely place where I walk,
Thine hand upon mine, and my body satisfied,
And my heart glad at our going together.

By 1100 B.C. the end of Egypt's long run was in sight. Although it was scarcely fifty years since Ramses III had put down the turbulent sea peoples and reasserted the suzerainty of Egypt in Syria, an envoy of the Two Lands now stood powerless before Zakar-Baal, Phoenician prince of Byblos. Wenamon had been sent to Syria to fetch timber for "User-het," the god Amon's sacred barge. But no longer could a representative of Egypt command respect from the potentates of Syria, or secure cedar from the forests of the Lebanon. Wenamon was haled before the prince:

> Zakar-Baal: On what business hast thou come?
> Wenamon: I have come after the timber for the great and august barge of Amon-Re, king of gods. Thy fathers did it, and thou wilt also do it.
> Zakar-Baal: I am neither thy servant nor am I the servant of him that sent thee. If I cry out to the Lebanon, the heavens open, and the logs lie here on the shore of the sea. What then are these miserable journeys which they have had thee make?
> Wenamon: O guilty one! They are no miserable journeys on which I am. There is no ship upon the river which Amon does not own. For his is the sea, and his is the Lebanon of which thou sayest, "It is mine." He is indeed what he once was, while thou standest and bargainest for the Lebanon with Amon, its lord.

In spite of his faith in Amon and Egypt, the messenger of Pharaoh left Byblos without the timbers. Pursued by the outraged prince of Dor, he was helped out of the harbour by Zakar-Baal. Escaping to Cyprus, he was sheltered by the queen, but what happened to him afterward we do not know for the papyrus is badly damaged and the conclusion of Wenamon's report is lost.

The contemplative teaching of Amenophis also foreshadows the end of the kingdom of the Pharaohs. Tranquility, the quality which Amenophis urges upon his little son, is curiously un-Egyptian. In the great days of the great Thutmose few would have paused long enough to listen to their "heart's counsel." But this late book of Egyptian wisdom is concerned with piety rather than practical considerations, with contentment rather than self-seeking:

> The truly tranquil man, he setteth himself aside,
> He is like a tree grown in a plot;
> It grows green, it doubles its yield,
> It stands in front of its lord,
> Its fruit is sweet, its shade is pleasant,
> And its end is reached in the garden.

NOTES

[1] Viscount Bryce in *World History* (London: Oxford Univ. Press, 1919) says: "To describe the external causes and processes by which material civilization has advanced ... is possible for a writer of high selective skill and the faculty of condensation. But the really interesting and essential thing, the vital part of history, is to enter into and trace the changes that have passed upon the human mind."

[2] *A History of the Business Man*. New York: Macmillan, 1938, pp. 101–102, 114.

[3] *Giotto, The Legend of St. Francis.* The Assisi Frescoes copied by E. M. Cowles with a foreword by G. K. Chesterton. London: Dent, 1931, p. 7.

[4] New York: Holt, 1934, p. ix.

[5] Carl Becker and Frederic Duncalf, *Story of Civilization,* to be published by Silver, Burdett, New York, in May, 1938.

[6] New York: Oxford Univ. Press, 1932.

[7] H. G. Evelyn-White, *Hesiod, the Homeric Hymns and Homerica.* London: Heinemann, 1929, p. 573.

[8] T. E. Peet, *A Comparative Study of the Literatures of Egypt, Palestine, and Mesopotamia.* London: Oxford Univ. Press, 1931, p. 7.

[9] The selections from Egyptian writings are taken from *Never to Die, The Egyptians in Their Own Words,* with commentary by Josephine Mayer and Tom Prideaux, to be published by the Viking Press, New York, in May, 1938.

Our Consciousness of Asia:
An End to Innocence

CARLOS P. ROMULO

If I may be allowed to express my personal sentiments, let it be of record that my joy over having been given this privilege to address you on this occasion is not unadulterated by impressions of the last few weeks that I cannot shake off. The press of Seattle might not have carried any news about it, but we have had a recent catastrophe in my country. Early this month, an otherwise kindly Nature has allotted thousands of my countrymen their share of misery.

President Ferdinand Marcos and I flew to the Bicol Peninsula on Luzon to visit the worst-hit areas of the country, and the mission was not at all comforting. We assessed the damage left by the two-day blow of a wild Pacific storm that packed winds of over 200 miles per hour in velocity.

An exhibit without the ribbon-cutting ceremony. The first sunny day since the terrible winds and rains naturally exposed the shambles and wreckage all over this little town in Bicol Peninsula. My first concern, as Secretary of Education, was to look into losses in terms of school property and the public school system in that area.

As I said, it was a rather sunny day, and to our great distress President Marcos and I viewed an astonishing exhibit of school books laid out in the sun to dry—row upon row of them, some too wet to be really salvageable, others torn and limp even as they were spread on a platform.

NOTE: This selection, an address delivered at the 47th Annual Meeting of the NCSS, appeared in *Social Education*, March 1968, pp. 229–232.

We in the warmth of this hall cannot perhaps grasp the impact of this exhibit which was attended, not by a ribbon-cutting ceremony, but by the fury of Nature, a fury that nullified years of hard work and struggle on the part of the people of my country.

I advert to this incident, realizing that the brochure listing the activities of the 47th Annual Meeting of the National Council for the Social Studies is almost entirely supported by advertising from book companies all over America. It should not then be difficult for me to invite your attention to see Asia, as it were, like a book open in the sun. The text should not be too blurred to read even now; the leaves are perhaps crisp from overexposure in the sun, but certainly it is a book to leaf through and perhaps to read.

Your Asia and Mine

Fifteen years ago a *Saturday Review of Literature* writer made the following reminder:

1. Most people in Asia will go to bed hungry tonight;

2. Most people in Asia cannot read or write;

3. Most people in Asia live in dire poverty;

4. Most people in Asia have never seen a doctor;

5. Most people in Asia have never heard of democracy;

6. Most people in Asia have never known civil rights;

7. Most people in Asia believe anything different could be better than what they have and are determined to get it;

8. Most people in Asia believe that freedom or free enterprise means freedom of colonial or western forces to exploit Asians;

9. Most people in Asia distrust people with white skins;

10. Most people in Asia are determined never to be again ruled by foreigners.

Perhaps today, it is a matter of personal idiosyncracy whether one could change the phrase "most people in Asia" into "more people than before in Asia. . . ." So this I would say: If life as it is lived today in Asia were an open book for all of us to read, what illumination or revelation would arise from its pages? Assuming that the ten points given are still true, what interlinear details have to be attended to and understood?

To begin with, it has not been easy to read Asia. The book, in other words, has been there all the time and has been opened, the text has been clear, the encounter between reader and text has been dramatically recounted by history. It was an encounter attended by expediency and violence, by pride and aggression, by power and lack of power, by peace and more longing for peace. The era of colonization was not without its symbolic meaning in the conquest of the seven seas that had been also the quest for spices and gold. From the crow's nest of a thousand ships, the lands of Asia had risen literally at the end of the rainbow—where awaited, so human fancy constructed, the fabled pot of gold. The adventurer became the conquistador, and he had bested, ironically, the defenders of the land that had been the birthplace of gun powder. Western invention and organization subsequently cut up Asia, not so much into spheres of influence, as into enclaves of progress, whilst with profound interest Hindu mysticism and Buddhist thought viewed the planting of a Christian ethos, whose tender stem, Charity, rising from the new soil, had yet to be given fuller nourishment.

Children of Nature

The farmer in his rice paddy, the fisherman and his outriggered boat, the little shopkeeper at his counter with its thatched roof barely three feet above his head, the boy with his water buffalo, the mother with her youngest child astride her hip as she strode off in the sun with vegetables in a basket on her head from market day in town, the betel nut chewing uncle with his fighting cock under his arm—Asian humanity, in short, lived through those years of conquest and colonization, even of exploitation, and survived the way humanity has always survived: as essentially a child of Nature. In the meanwhile the West, too, fought its wars and fought out its claims for peace, refining even its concept of government and other social institutions, and with its genius creating a civilization that was soon to discover science and technology and evolve a world entirely apart from the rest of mankind.

With time the issues of supremacy and power became more paramount and could not be contained until more appropriately crusading wars were fought. The same genius which centuries ago conceived the world to be round discovered the power in the atom, and the implications of this discovery brought on yet larger issues of survival—not only in terms of powerful nations, but in terms even of the weak and small. Thus science, now supreme in its pinnacle, has come to dictate to the world and its century a new morality, leavened by the Christian law of charity, and threatening total extinction if its ideals are unheeded.

Aspirations Versus Change

To read the book of Asia today is to find many chapters describing landscape with storm clouds aloft. For so long this Eden underwent defoliation. Nature has given its peoples a land mass enjoying a winter-free climate; yet discontent is written on these peoples' faces. No sooner was the boy on his water buffalo's back out from the field than he was hied off to school. There are over 7,000,000 of them in my country; 624,300 in Cambodia; 7,000,000 in Thailand; 12,000,000 in Indonesia; and many millions more elsewhere according to 1960–61 figures. But of Asia's population, 87 percent is rural, and with the 13 percent in urban areas the high rates of unemployment and dependency have appeared to be standard features of the economic scene.

The West has known all this and watched and calculated, even envisioned, an era in which peace and progress might be demonstrated on the drawing board. This is the same visionary West that has been steeped in the arts of war and bigger wars, that has realized that since war begins in the minds of men, more so must peace emerge from the same source. Thus concepts of assistance, of the rich nation helping the poor nations, have been and are continually being evolved. American billions have been brought in to bear witness to this new calculated, programed concept of neighborhood. With political withdrawals, as the British have demonstrated in Malaya and Singapore, have arisen new problems of responsibility for cultural and economic leadership in the region.

Disraeli, along with ancient Chinese sages, has held the inevitability of change, and in a progressive society, he reminds us, change is continuous. In this light Asia's plural societies have seen continuous change, and as progressive, in fact, as we are willing to grant. India's untouchables are no more, and the transistor radio is the peasant's companion through the changing seasons of the rural year on millions of Asia's farms.

But all change begins individually even as it assumes later on a collective, national, and international, character. Walt W. Rostow, speaking in terms of economics, has contributed to modern vocabulary the phrase, "the take-off stage." In a larger sense, all of Asia is at a take-off stage—planned or unplanned, sometimes spontaneous, but never casual or painless—a departure from its pasts into a long present. I like to think that the plurality of these pasts are the very roots of the emerging singularity of the present.

The lingering recollections of a colonial heritage and the complex political confusions of the present and their inevitable moral implications are what today is writ large on the opened book of Asia. Imbalances between population and productivity, between current and traditional values, and finally, between illusion and reality, between fact and dream—these have been translated in many languages: Khmer,

Tagalog, Burmese, Lao, Malay, Iban, Waray, and many more than 30 other vernaculars. To read Asia, to be truly sensitive to the new awareness of its people and their aspirations, is to have the skills of a linguist, an economist, a political scientist, a demographer, and yet many other skills. But there are other pages ahead.

The Grand Dilemma

While the colonist's Asia is becoming transformed into the economic planner's developing societies, for all of us a dilemma has arisen. What with our background of history and the sudden encounter, comparatively speaking, with the technology that science has evolved, and further, with the new morality that the richer nations have been inspired to adopt, we are nevertheless impatient over the slow rate of progress, and ours is an impatience all the more keen as efficient gadgetry and quality consumers goods cannot be concealed from our knowledge and desire, or have never been intended, in the first place, to be so concealed. Ours is an impatience so harassing because of the shrinking distance between centers of progress and the marginal swamps where our populations thrive; an impatience that is frustrating because of our respect for human lives and reflected in the growth of population; and, finally, an impatience that overwhelms us with anxiety because all this development to which we aspire in Asia may not and should not be achieved at the expense of our traditions and our way of life.

Economic planners speak of patterns of development, and UNESCO experts tell us that if "economic development is to take place in which the best of modern techniques are to be developed in a framework of institutions and skills close to the economic environment of the region, growing from existing patterns and skills rather than from the blanket impositions of Western organizations and practices, there must be a corresponding reaction from educational development." And indeed in Asia, we have evolved an extensive educational machinery, the output of which will project a new Asia in the very near future.

Already in the Philippines, for example, we have brought college education to almost 1 percent of the entire population, a figure higher than that obtaining in the United Kingdom. Burma will have by 1975 a ratio of one doctor to six thousand people as against one to 14 thousand in 1962. Malaya expects to meet its need of technicians by 50 percent in the early 1970's, possibly with a technician-engineer ratio of 3:1. Thailand's universities expect an annual output of two thousand specialists in agriculture, medicine, and industry, on the premise that there should be at least three scientists behind every agricultural field officer and from four to five physical scientists behind every engineer and industrial chemist.

The Third Asia

This is development, and much more is going apace all over Asia. But I dare say that a third Asia is fast emerging as well—the Asia of culture, the Asia from which the traditions we hold are rooted and in which the ways of life we cherish are immortalized. I have never for a moment doubted that on the chopping board of the ruthless interaction of economic and political factors our traditions and ways of life are due for a shattering; but I do know that these are less subject to any one man's will, or even to institutional direction. The hundreds of Peace Corps Volunteers in my country, for example, are learning much more from us than what our society is benefiting from them, which is in the very nature of things. Who built the temple caves of Ajanta, who conceived their art but Indian culture in large? And so they stand, to delight continually and give us a renewed sense of wonder—even as my Peace Corps friends go home someday a little wiser, having shared America with our younger generation, yet leaving essentially the hard core of Philippine life very much as it is.

Not that we are stubborn to change, but the area of culture and art are the sectors least manageable for change—that is, as I say, if management is at all necessary. A hundred cities in Asia today—Hongkong, Kyoto, Tokyo, Kuala Lumpur, Taipeh, Makati, and Manila—are seeding grounds of a new era in which the new and the old meet, where pop art and electronic music are as valid as the shepherd's flute and the gong as vehicles for the expression of man's spirit; where the bamboo footbridge is as essential to our sense of landscape as the monorail system with all its speed; where the thatched roof is as soothing to our sense of form as the skyscraper.

I must invite you to a sensitiveness about Asia in these terms. We have been for so long rudely materialistic in regard for our part of the world. We have—at best, some of us—regarded Asia with an innocence that warms the cockles of the practical heart. It gives us comfort to watch a *noh* play and a *bharata natyam* dance secure in our feeling that this experience belongs to that part of us unrelated to everyday life. The *Haiku* and the Philippine *kundiman*—what have these to do with the manpower needs of industrialized Japan and developing Philippines? In fact, this is a question we do not ask. It is in the nature of our innocence to read only the symbols on one side of the coin. We are dead to that part of the human spirit that deals with myth, poetry, and beauty—in our effort to understand how many man-hours will be saved if so many odd hectares of pineapple land were plowed over by tractors which we would manufacture and sell to governments under trade arrangement meticulously worked out by treaty experts and economists.

The situation reminds me of a story that the art critic, Clive Bell, has told. It concerns a Greek freeman in the days of Serverus. A clever craftsman, comfortable, intelligent, his master having been Epicurus, he awoke each morning "to a quiet day of ordered satisfaction. The prescribed toll of exacting labor, a little sensual pride, a little rational conversation, a cool argument, a judicious appreciation of all that the intellect can apprehend. To the Greek, it seemed that the breath of life had blown through the grave, imperial streets. Yet nothing in Rome was changed. The same waking eyes opened on the same object; yet all was changed. All was changed with meaning. New things existed. Everything mattered. In the vast equality of religious emotion, the Greek forgot his status. His life became a miracle and an ecstasy. As a lover wakes, he awoke to a dull day full of consequence and variety. He had learned to feel and because he felt a man must live, it was good to be alive."

The West knows how good it is to be alive and knows that Asia is anxious over a future which must be lived together in peace and plenty with all the world, the West included. But the West must needle its conscience with the certainty that there is a spiritual need that longs for satisfaction, a way of looking at Asia that can unfold areas of cooperation. I submit that that need might find expression in a new era of recognition and patronage—in that life in Asia which is in the imagination of its peoples, the life of Art. I submit that in articulating this support we grow in knowledge and appreciate Asian courage and dreams for its place in the modern world.

Let it be understood that this is beyond economics and politics, beyond power and play and industrial cartels. But to paraphrase Clive Bell, "It seems reasonable . . . to seek in Art what [we] want and Art can give. Art will not fail [us]." And we will find, like the Greek of his story in the days of Epicurus, "that emotional confidence, that assurance of absolute good which make of life a momentous and harmonious whole. Because the aesthetic emotions are outside and above life, it is possible to take refuge in them from life."

Towards Creativity

To realize this is to meet an Asia with its ancient composure, its variety and vitality, and, as Clive Bell expressed it, to return "to the world of human affairs equipped to face it courageously and even a little contemptuously. . . ."

The Chinese poet, Li Po, has perhaps dramatized this thought of the new Asia I am inviting you to see, and I quote from a translation of one poem:

> Here! Is this you on the top of Fan-Kuo Mountain,
> Wearing a huge hat in the noonday?
> How wretchedly thin you have grown!
> You must have been suffering from poetry again.

Perhaps this is the affliction which today the West needs, better to see in Asia a likeness of itself—a contamination of that virus of Beauty which we have tended to regard like the common cold. But this indifference should be past, and like all the dead, as a Chinese poem tells us, with them "we cannot converse. The living are here and ought to have our love...."

It is with this thought then that I should like to invite an enthusiastic, perhaps even an aggressive, involvement of the Western mind in the arts of Asia. I mean by this not the casual, cursory interest of the tourist, but the disciplined quests of the scholar. I mean by this a probe into the creativity of the Asian mind in the past and the rediscovery of the principles that would usher in a new creativity for our present. This is an invitation to institutes of Asian studies, one of which we have at the University of the Philippines, to make the cultures of Asia available and comprehensible to as wide a public in the West as possible. This is an invitation to international organizations, art councils, instrumentalities of the UNESCO, and the like, to a programed exchange of artists between the West and the East. One such international program for writers, for example, has been started at Iowa. We may well have in the future our own creative arts center in the Philippines. This is an invitation to share with the rest of the world the dances and music of India, Malaya, and Indonesia, and perhaps the creation of new forms of harmony of sounds employing, to be quite avant-garde, the clatter of the abacus as well as the boom of the gong. Already this is being done by some of our artists-composers in the Philippines, and their work will need the opportunity to be heard one of these days. Then again, this is an invitation for the West to share our interpretations on canvas, as varied as cultures will permit, of the quality of our sunshine. And for the West, to be involved in these is to see Asia not as a combination of markets and the Taj Mahal, nor mere suppliers of rubber, hemp, tin, and tungsten, to be roused as rabble against the evils of free enterprise; but to see Asia as a creative force, unique in its ancientness, but youthful and visionary in its hopes for a better world.

Adam's Inventory:

Aspects of Contemporary Canadian Literature

D. G. JONES

I stumble over the centuries'
exposed root
lost in my own
> *particularity*

(patterns I deny
and that
is part of a pattern).

> George Bowering,
> "Circus Maximus"[1]

George Bowering is a young Canadian poet who lives in Montreal and cheers for the Expos, the new major-league ball club. His refusal to see things in neat patterns may well serve as a warning to the reader and also as a sign of the times.

Since World War II, Canadian literature has developed enormously, both in English and French. It is studied in university courses which a generation ago did not exist. With poets of the stature of Irving Layton, Alain Grandbois, Anne Hébert, critics of the stature of Northrop Frye or Marshall McLuhan, it has created a cultural climate sufficiently rich to sustain or generate within itself a fairly varied and vital growth. One may trace such internal or familial lines of influence as that of A. M. Klein on Irving Layton, of Layton on Leonard Cohen, of Cohen on young writers in the universities and in the coffeehouses. Whereas the relationship between English and French culture was, until yesterday, precisely characterized by the title of Hugh MacLennan's novel *Two Solitudes* (1945), the intense literary activity combined with the political aspirations of Québec has sparked a burst of translations and invited a

NOTE: This article appeared in *Social Education*, October 1971, pp. 595–601. Reprinted by permission of D. G. Jones.

dialogue whose potential consequences have scarcely been imagined. And amid these indigenous activities, the writers in both languages have become more intimately engaged with the imagination of American writers and the American people.

A Developing Myth of the Creative Word

It is impossible in a single article, especially if it is to contain substantial quotations, to do more than touch on certain aspects of this development. Even so, I have been forced to leave aside any real discussion of this development in French. I have attempted, in spite of Bowering's warning, to isolate a pattern of themes. In its most general form, and again in defiance of certain poets, we might characterize the theme as a developing myth of the Creative Word. It is announced by Anne Hébert in her essay, "Poésie: Solitude Rompue," when she writes:

> Our country has arrived at the first days of creation. Life here is to be named and discovered: the obscure features we possess, the silent heart that is ours, the whole landscape extending before us, waiting to be inhabited and possessed, and the confused words that issue in the night, all these seek to find expression in the light of day.[2]

These lines, along with others in Miss Hébert's poem on the mystery of the word, could serve to introduce the theme of much English-Canadian writing as well. It may be implicit in the naming of concrete particulars or explicit in the myth of Adam or the Incarnate Word. It may range from the simple taking possession of one's immediate world by means of the word, through affirming a collective identity, to articulating a vision of reality in which the fully realized man is at home in the universe, in which Nature and Man are as harmoniously one as the perfect lover and his bride. It is such a vision that frequently haunts the songs of Leonard Cohen, his poems such as "You Have the Lovers," where the speaker enters a room that has been locked through many years of banal existence, of marriage and children and departures, of gradual aging and isolation, to discover a tangled garden has grown up around the bed of the lovers and the lovers themselves become hopelessly confused:

> Her hair and his beard are hopelessly tangled.
> When he puts his mouth against her shoulder
> she is uncertain whether her shoulder
> has given or received the kiss.[3]

And when the speaker lies down with the lovers, wondering how many multitudes are lying beside him, he too becomes part of that embrace. There is a moment of pain or doubt, but "a mouth kisses and a hand soothes the moment away." He is made one flesh with the girl or the garden, and "All her flesh is like a mouth." He becomes, we might say, one with the world, or with the Word made flesh. Here we approach what Frye and certain poets influenced by Frye would call the world of archetypes and traditional myth. But perhaps we should start at the opposite pole and with another range of influence.

Originally from Vancouver, George Bowering reflects the influence of such American poets as William Carlos Williams, Charles Olson, Robert Creeley, or Jack Spicer, which helped to create a whole new literary scene on the West Coast during the early Sixties. The influence of Pound and Williams was already apparent in some of the work of Raymond Souster, Louis Dudek, and Irving Layton in Toronto and Montreal. In the Maritimes a similar spirit shaped the poetry of Alden Nowlan, one of whose poems records a drunken telephone conversation with a friend in Maine, during which he learned of Dr. Williams' death. With its emphasis on open forms, the rhythms and diction of speech, immediate observation and individual and local history, this influence has a strongly marked character. It has occasionally been viewed as one more example of the American domination of Canadian life. But, though hostile to some aspects of what might be called the older tradition of Canadian poetry, this "American" influence has had the converse effect of leading the Canadian poet to a more intimate exploration of his particular reality. Following Williams' dictum, no ideas except in things, it is suspicious of the generalizing tendency of conventional myth, metaphor, or thought and appeals to the concrete and the particular. Exactly, says John Newlove, another West Coast poet, in his poem, "I Talk to You":

> To whom shall I talk except
> my exhaustive self? To whom indicate
> the shape of the house I inhabit,
> or the brain and the leg, the pressures
> behind the bony skull, the leg's hairs,
> the moulding on the front-door stairs.
> To talk to myself expecting an answer,
> expecting a credence, confessing
> insaneness in this dialogue—
>
> is this to be mad? To sound foolish,
> to sound foolish, to be mad to say,
> to say the convulsive illegible world
> is how? and demand a reply.
>
> To be mad, to be mad, unangry, to sit
> sour in the old wooden chair
> and run across the unmoving world
> without pity, with only the wild regret
> at not to know? To be mad for an answer
> knowing there is no answer, except
> in peculiarities and particularities?

> The chair: what sort of sunny wood
> its back is made of; the leg's shape
> and not the brain's. And whom to talk to;
> and whether it is fit to whisper or to shout.[4]

Whether it is Newlove or Bowering on the West Coast, or Nowlan on the East Coast, or Raymond Souster in Toronto, or Al Purdy who ranges from sea to sea, these poets all exhibit a similar preoccupation to say, tell, or articulate the convulsive illegible world in its manifold particularities and peculiarities.

Ironically, despite their opposition to the older generation and to any of their contemporaries who make deliberate use of poetic convention or myth, these poets are fulfilling the central role of the poet as defined in essentially mythical terms by A. M. Klein in the 1940's. In his "Portrait of the Poet as Landscape" Klein lamented the depreciation of the poetic imagination and the disappearance of the poet in an overwhelmingly secular and utilitarian culture. No longer informed by the religious or poetic imagination, the world becomes a wilderness, a sea, in which the poet lies like a drowned Lycidas. Yet this situation could only reveal more clearly the vital role of the poetic imagination, to say the illegible convulsive world and to shape the flux of life into an articulate human order. The poet must be:

> the nth Adam taking a green inventory
> in world but scarcely uttered . . .[5]

In making such a green inventory, many of the poets of the Sixties are meeting a related but more particular demand. It was made nearly 30 years ago by Patrick Anderson in his "Poem on Canada." In a witty and vivid retelling of Canadian history, Anderson portrays the land as an unhappy bride whose individual character the bridegroom ignores, as a mirror into which he looks only for the confirmation of his own preconceived ideas. He is a colonial. And until he is prepared to recognize the intimate life of the land in all its variety and particularity and to give voice, in effect, to his own unconscious life, it will remain America's attic, a cold kingdom, an undanced dance; the Canadian will continue to lack a sense of national identity. The same idea is echoed by F. R. Scott ten years later in his "Laurentian Shield":

> Hidden in wonder and snow, or sudden with summer,
> This land stares at the sun in a huge silence
> Endlessly repeating something we cannot hear.
> Inarticulate, arctic,
> Not written on by history, empty as paper,
> It leans away from the world with songs in its lakes
> Older than love, and lost in the miles.[6]

Scott went on to predict that the land would find its voice when it had chosen its "technic." Submitting technology to a humane purpose, he foresaw a fruitful union between man and the land, whereupon the emptiness would be filled with neighbourhood. But his optimism may have been premature.

Examining five outstanding Canadian novels in his 1960 article, "Wolf in the Snow," Warren Tallman was impressed by the extraordinary picture of isolation and frustration which they presented, whether set on the prairies or in the Maritimes or in Montreal.[7] Again, it is to be explained by the attempt of the established community to maintain social, moral, or religious values that fail to countenance let alone cultivate much of the actual, often crude life of the community, and beginning with their own most instinctive or spontaneous impulses. Much that was crude remained crude; much that was vital remained frustrated and mute or became vocal and violent.

The discussion continued with the approach of the 100th year of Confederation. Canadians, some argued, whether in religious or secular matters, have been inveterate colonials, borrowing their language or technic from England or France or, more recently, from the United States, and imposing that order on the life of the land rather than generating their own authentic order from out of that life. Thus the curious figure who appears in Margaret Atwood's poem, "The Progressive Insanities of a Pioneer," who stands in a vast unenclosed space shouting, "Let me out!" Imprisoned in his own preconceived order, his cabin or ark in the wilderness, he finds that:

> Things
> refused to name themselves; refused
> to let him name them.
> The wolves hunted
> outside.

It might have been otherwise, says Miss Atwood in this ironic portrait that appeared in 1967, the very year of Expo and the Canadian Centennial:

> If he had known unstructured
> space is a deluge
> and stocked his log house-
> boat with all the animals
> even the wolves,
> he might have floated.[8]

Cataloguing the Wilderness

Even as Miss Atwood was developing this theme in her more abstract, deliberate symbolic or allegorical fashion, the other poets mentioned were busy cataloguing the wilderness, stocking the Canadian houseboat with the excluded fauna and flora, admitting them to the white center of consciousness. Souster's caged animals, dead birds, blind men, lame men, bums, and prostitutes; Nowlan's Indians and shack-dwellers; his farm-boys wracked by desire and the wrath of a Calvinist God; his own youth in which he and his sister wore gold, azure, and purple under-pants made from the cloth papa stole from the local cotton mill; New-love's drunken father, whom he loves despite his desertion of the family; Purdy's failed farms, broken carvings by inept Eskimo carvers; his '48 Pontiac and the girls he made love to in the back seat; old Alex, so gross, mean, hypocritical, especially when drunk or when spouting the Bible, that no one could love him or mourn his death any more than they could love or mourn a disease, but whose "hate was lovely,/ given freely and without stint," whose very smallness made others feel noble "and thus fools," who will be forgotten like a bruise, though "when he was here he was a sunset."[9] Their green inventory covers the past and the present, the city and the country, the failures and the successes, the crude and the delicate, the good and the bad, even the wolves. And as the list grows so does the poet's sense of his own authentic and independent life. As John Newlove puts it at the end of a long poem on the North American Indians called "The Pride,"

> we stand alone,
> we are no longer lonely
> but we have roots,
> and the rooted words
> recur in the mind, mirror, so that
> we dwell on nothing else, in nothing else,
> touched, repeating them,
> at home freely
> at last, in amazement.[10]

Rarely does the English-Canadian writer go on to give to such a statement the explicitly political and nationalistic definition that it is frequently given in French. It nonetheless implies a new sense of a collective identity. And the kind of self-recognition and self-affirmation we detect here is not limited to John Newlove's "The Pride," or to the work of isolated poets. Something of the same movement towards self-discovery and a new assurance can be traced in the development of the novel.

Literary Confirmation

The better known of the established writers of prose fiction, from Leacock, through Mazo de la Roche and Morley Callaghan to Hugh MacLennan, have identified with central Canada, Ontario, and Québec although MacLennan, who was born in the Maritimes and located two of his novels there, is something of an exception. But a surprising num-ber of outstanding individual novels have come out of the prairie provinces of the Canadian West, and viewed in sequence they may serve to confirm the movement we have described.

From the early novels of Frederick Philip Grove to Margaret Laurence's *Stone Angel* we are presented with a variety of attempts to impose a strict order on the life of the land or on its inhabitants. That order, whether primarily practical or social or religious, or some combination of the three, tends to be exclusive or even a mere façade, and almost invariably it produces frustration and ends in defeat. It divides man and woman, the older generation from their children; and the young, for good or ill, attempt to resolve the conflict by getting out. John Elliott in Grove's *Our Daily Bread* (1928) tries to establish a patriarchal order conceived on the biblical model of Abraham and his sons, but he dies alone in the deserted and practically ruined farmhouse. Abe Spalding in *The Fruits of the Earth* (1933) tries to establish a similar but highly mechanized farming empire; he learns to temper his puritanical will, but only after one of his sons dies, his daughter conceives an illegitimate child, and his wife threatens to leave him.

In the small classic, Sinclair Ross's *As for Me and My House* (1941), the conflict is internalized in the Rev. Philip Bentley, a would-be artist who himself serves to support the false façade of the small-town prairie community as the minister of a church in which he does not believe; and he is aided in the task by his wife, who in helping her husband alienates herself. The intense frustration and sterility of their lives is relieved only when Bentley's own nature revolts; he is seduced into an affair with a young woman in his choir, and he fathers an illegitimate child. The conflict is resolved on a positive note when the girl dies, Mrs. Bentley accepts the child, and they start anew by getting out of the town and out of the Church.

The conflict is externalized and becomes more decidedly comic in W. O. Mitchell's *Who Has Seen the Wind* (1947). Though centered on the growth of Brian O'Connal from childhood to young manhood, much of the action turns on the conflict between the hypocritical and sterile forces of the small-town establishment and those who represent both the life of the land and the life of the mind. Nature's violent revolt is as comically symbolized by the explosion of an illicit still that has been hidden in the very basement of the establishment church, as by a tornado that singles out the property of the establishment figures, making them pay for their sins to the tune of $50,000. The novel ends with the young man leaving town to attend the university, but with the optimistic suggestion that he will return to establish a more inclusive and vital regimen, to cultivate rather than confront the land as an agronomist or dirt doctor.

Two quite different novels, Adele Wiseman's *The Sacrifice* (1956) and Sheila Watson's *The Double Hook* (1959), develop the same basic theme in more complex terms, intensifying the violence and pointing to a more profound resolution. *The Sacrifice* follows the pattern of the realistic novel, gradually unfolding the story of a Jewish immigrant family in Winnipeg; whereas *The Double Hook* adopts the more explicitly symbolic strategy of romance, the drought-ridden and fear-ridden community in the foothills of Alberta clearly becoming a kind of rural "Wasteland." Both novels, however, tell of the attempt to maintain an exclusive vision and order of life, static and designed to shut out whatever is dark, irrational, or dangerous. The result is again a certain frustration, sterility, and consequent violence. The hero in both cases is driven to murder; fire razes the synagogue in *The Sacrifice*, killing the protagonist's only remaining son; fire razes the house of the protagonist in *The Double Hook*, killing his sister and destroying the mortal remains of his mother. But both books end positively with an affirmation of a more inclusive vision. The grandson in *The Sacrifice* comes to terms with his grandfather, the murderer, recognizing in the old man's hands the inevitable duality of life or what Alan Watts has called the two hands of God. Similarly Sheila Watson's characters arrive at the understanding that to hook the glory you must hook the darkness too, and the more you fish for the glory, the more you must comprehend the darkness of life.

A similar pattern and, at least implicitly, a similar point emerge from a major novel by Margaret Laurence called *Stone Angel* (1964). At first the central character rejects her father's Presbyterian world of weights and measures and practical success and in defiance of all propriety marries the dancing, swearing, improvident Bram Shipley, only to leave him again and serve those proper values into a sterile old age. Then, however, in the penultimate gesture of her life, she abandons them once more and at the expense of all dignity, health, physical or psychological security enters into a more vital communion with her fellow man in a kind of wild garden. The book ends in a hospital scene but with a hymn of praise.

The exuberant tone of *The Words of My Roaring* (1966) and *The Studhorse Man* (1969), both by Robert Kroetsch, an Albertan presently teaching in New York State, may be partly ascribed to the fact that his characters embody from the outset an inclusive view, accepting in themselves both the crude and the refined, the mortal and the vital, and affirming themselves and their world with a Homeric gusto that is both physical and spiritual—or perhaps I should say, verbal and sexual. Not the depression, not even death, can defeat Hazard Lepage, the studhorse man. His stallions go on to a royal if quite unforeseen new career, and his name is perpetuated if somewhat irregularly in a daughter, Demeter.

Identification with the Whole of Life

"In a sense," says Kroetsch, "we haven't got an identity until someone tells our story. The fiction makes us real."[11] In part what such fictions articulate is our identity as Canadians, but they point beyond any national character towards an identification with the whole of life, towards what Frye calls the apocalyptic vision of Nature contained in the image of Man. It is such an inclusive or universal vision that Jay Macpherson, following Frye, envisions in her poem, "The Anagogic Man," where old Noah becomes identified with his Ark and with the whole of the creation it contains.

> Angel, declare: what sways when Noah nods?
> The sun, the stars, the figures of the gods.[12]

The inventory becomes invention, the creation of myth. It is the myth that makes us real. And the happiest myth is one in which man may affirm the whole of life while affirming himself. As Hugh MacLennan wrote in his most profound novel, *The Watch that Ends the Night*, "It came to me . . . that to be able to love the mystery surrounding us is the final and only sanction of human existence."[13]

To give tongue to the mute, to make the unconscious conscious; to transcend the opposites and unite what is divided by particularity and death; to transform a chaos of random particulars into a cosmos, isolation into communion, such is the ultimate role of the imagination, the poet, the Word. If one of the chief Canadian poets, Irving Layton, appears to speak with a kind of arrogant exuberance, it is because he speaks as the poet, in terms of this larger office. That is, despite his hostility towards Frye and towards myth, he speaks as a mythical figure. His inventories in "Composition in Late Spring," "The Birth of Tragedy," "The Cold Green Element," or "A Tall Man Executes a Jig," are not those of the local shopkeeper named Irving Layton, nor of the Canadian, but Adam's inventory. He speaks for vitality, an imaginative vision that does not die when Irving Layton dies, so that even as "living things arrange their death," the speaker is aware that "someone from afar off/ blows birthday candles for the world." And, in his role as poet, he may rejoice:

> And me happiest when I compose poems.
> Love, power, the huzza of battle
> are something, are much;
> yet a poem includes them like a pool
> water and reflection.
> In me, nature's divided things—
> tree, mould on tree—
> have their fruition;
> I am their core. Let them swap,
> bandy, like a flame swerve.
> I am their mouth; as a mouth I serve.[14]

Art may transcend division, pain and tragedy, but as Layton notes elsewhere, it does not negate them or make them disappear. They loom large in any contemporary inventory, not only because they are radical features of all existence but because, partly in an attempt to shut them out, western man has succumbed to the progressive insanities of Miss Atwood's pioneer. We have created a battleship instead of an Ark. Our urban, commercial and technological world is informed by a highly aggressive and highly exclusive vision. Increasingly, the kind of world we live in, and its peculiar frustrations and violence, cannot be characterized in terms of a distinctly Canadian or distinctly American past. The corrosive effect of this common culture on all local and national traditions, its global sweep, is vividly dramatized by one of the most provocative of the young writers, Dave Godfrey, in his novel *The New Ancestors* (1970), which is set neither in Canada, nor in the United States, nor in Europe, but in an Africa crisscrossed by international pressures.

Increasingly what our inventories reveal is a world of demonic cities. As in Layton's "The Improved Binoculars," their inhabitants rejoice to see them razed by fire, calling "Only for more light with which to see/ their neighbour's destruction."[15]

At this point, the Canadian writer joins with the American in his resistance to the world of Moloch as portrayed in Allen Ginsberg's "Howl." Another article could be written on the images of violence and destruction in Canadian poetry of recent decades, both in French and in English. These images have found literal echoes in the political life of both Canada and the United States, in the riots in the streets, in the bombings, the burnings, the murder of individual men and women. But that is to confuse literature and life. The house which the writer is engaged in destroying is a cultural house; he does not aim at the death of the individual men but at the death of an image of Man. The fundamental revolution must be a revolution in our cultural vision, a revolution of the imagination. And having shaken off or demolished an overly narrow vision, we come back to the perennial task of articulating a more inclusive and satisfying one. As Margaret Avison says, we must learn to see with the "optic heart." Or as one young poet, Raoul Duguay, writes in Québec, we must blow up an obsolete order not with the A Bomb or the H Bomb but with the bomb of the five senses.

If we are to delight in ourselves, if we are to love the mystery surrounding us, to cultivate it as a garden instead of attacking it as a hostile wilderness, we must articulate a vision so inclusive that it will contain and nourish all the particularities and peculiarities. Amid the contemporary violence and confusion we continue to be haunted by that dream of universal communion, by Leonard Cohen's image of the lovers in the tangled garden behind the locked door. And despite the fatigue and what Susan Sontag has called the great weight of suspicion we feel towards language and the power of the word, contemporary Canadian writing betrays an unwonted confidence in the imagination, in the power of poetry to unlock that door.

NOTES

[1] George Bowering, "Circus Maximus," *The Silver Wire*. Kingston: The Quarry Press, 1966, p. 38.

[2] Anne Hébert, "Poésie: Solitude Rompue," *Poèmes*. Paris: Editions du Seuil, 1960, p. 71. (My own translation)

[3] Leonard Cohen, "You Have the Lovers," *The Spice-Box of Earth*. Toronto: McClelland and Stewart, 1961, pp. 32–33.

[4] John Newlove, "I Talk to You," *Moving in Alone*. Toronto: Contact Press, 1965, p. 71.

[5] A. M. Klein, "Portrait of the Poet as Landscape," *The Rocking Chair*. Toronto: The Ryerson Press, 1948, p. 55.

[6] F. R. Scott, "Laurentian Shield," *Events and Signals*. Toronto: The Ryerson Press, 1954, p. 16.

[7] The novels discussed by Tallman are W. O. Mitchell, *Who Has Seen the Wind*; Sinclair Ross, *As for Me and My House*; Hugh MacLennan, *Each Man's Son*; Ernest Buckler, *The Mountain and the Valley*; and Mordecai Richler, *The Apprenticeship of Duddy Kravitz*.

[8] Margaret Atwood, "The Progressive Insanities of a Pioneer," *The Animals in that Country*. Toronto: Oxford University Press, 1969, pp. 36–39.

[9] Al Purdy, "Old Alex," *The Cariboo Horses*. Toronto: McClelland and Stewart, 1965, pp. 57–58.

[10] John Newlove, "The Pride," *Black Night Window*. Toronto: McClelland and Stewart, 1968, p. 110.

[11] Robert Kroetsch, quoted from a MS. which has since been published in a collection entitled *Creation*. Toronto: New Press, 1971.

[12] Jay Macpherson, "The Anagogic Man," *The Boatman*. Toronto: Oxford University Press, 1957, p. 56.

[13] Hugh MacLennan, *The Watch that Ends the Night*. Toronto: Macmillan, 1959, p. 372.

[14] Irving Layton, "The Birth of Tragedy," *Collected Poems*. Toronto: McClelland and Stewart, 1965, p. 64.

[15] *Ibid.*, p. 94.

Urbanization:
A Worldwide Process

BARBARA WARD

"Urbanization" is an overwhelming topic for a speech; complete details would keep us here all night. So I hope you won't feel even more overwhelmed when I confess that urbanization *per se* is not exactly what I am going to talk about. I chose the topic primarily as an all-too-evident symbol of a much wider process which may change the course of the human race, and which we all must realize is happening throughout the world.

This is the process by which man is building up an environment that is gradually replacing the natural environment in which he first became human—a very extraordinary and a very risky occupation. There is no turning back, because he is certainly not going to give up the science and the technology that have given him such power. But he is presently developing this new environment only to serve the idols of the tribe and the idols of the market—nationalism and consumerism. And if he continues to use this power so blindly, the environment he is going to create for himself is going to be about as lethal as a den of saber-tooth tigers. (In fact, our roads are already inhabited by steel monsters that are far more lethal than saber-tooth tigers.)

With such warnings before us, we must look forward over the next 50 years; we must reexamine our extraordinary technological environment in which nature recedes, human relationships become more and more televised, and all those natural processes of our mountains and of

NOTE: This article, based on an address delivered at the 50th Annual Meeting of the NCSS, appeared in *Social Education*, January 1972, pp. 21–28, 94.

our seas move back a little from our direct experience. For our scientists and our poets are beginning to warn us that man may soon have to choose between two courses of change in order to survive: either he will have to evolve into a completely different race, one a little like the machines that now dominate him, or he will have to redesign the Technological Order entirely, drawing enormously on all his resources of imagination and poetry and life and love.

If such a decision has to be taken, it will, of course, be the young among us who will probably make the crucial choices and who will certainly have to live with the results. That is why it is so important that you teachers be aware of what the environment of humanity is today—and how it got that way. For it is you, the teachers, who have the incredible task and privilege of saying to the young mind, "Look at the social environment in which you are going to live." Of all the teachers the world has known, I would say that you face the most acute responsibility, a frightening but exciting challenge on which the fate of the planet quite literally may rest.

That is why I want to make it clear that when I talk of urbanization I am not just speaking of a modern way of life which we may find personally inconvenient or unaesthetic or even unhealthy. I am speaking of urbanization as the symbol of the nonnatural environment which is becoming the daily habitat of nearly the entire human race, an environment that we *have* to keep but also *have* to make human or else it will destroy us.

Cities in Historical Perspective

As teachers of social science, you know that no phenomenon should be examined outside its historical perspective, that we can learn much about what a thing is by studying how it developed. Certainly, this is true of urbanization, for one of the troubles about our man-made, urban environment is that it has developed in such a haphazard fashion.

The city, of course, appears throughout recorded history. The very word "civilization" comes from the "civil," the "civic," the "city." For the city has always been regarded as the center of civilization, of urbanity. The city, in this sense, has been one of the great continuing symbols of human thought, one of the recurring images of human poetry: the idea of Jerusalem coming down like a bride from heaven; the idea of Rome—the first Rome, the second Rome, the third Rome; the idea of Byzantium, which inspired Yeats to picture the whole of human experience in the microcosm of the city. And the city in this sense was not just an image; it was reality. All through these earlier centuries there were these small centers of high literacy and high art and high achievement. Some height of civilization, the flowering of the animal that is man, was achieved in these tiny enclaves. And when you think what was produced by a center like Athens, which was not much larger than Bridgeport, you can understand why the city goes to the roots of man's imagination; you realize how incredibly important it has been for the development of the fully human society.

But then came the new order, the order of science and industrial technology, and the cities became something quite different. They were still called "cities," and, in some cases, the geographic location was the same, but they were no longer small enclaves of high civilization. They were an entirely new *kind* of center in which, for the first time in history, man's basic work was brought in from the forests and fields into the factories. And they "growed" and "growed" and "growed," just like Topsy.

In these manufacturing cities, the concentration of men in the new factory system created the growing internal market, thereby creating more jobs. Then it became infinitely more convenient for *more* industry, *more* factories to come where there were already workers and supplies and transport nodes. So, before long, the cities began to act like a vortex, sucking in and sucking in ever more people and the artifacts of their work and lives. And it was this haphazard pull that determined the growth of the cities.

Flaws Stemming from Haphazard Growth

This is what we must always remember about the process of modern urbanization—it has been incredibly haphazard. Since we call it a process, it sounds rather orderly. But it has actually been more like dropping a jellyfish from a great height. In fact, it is even inaccurate to speak of the *urban* process, for the factors that shaped it have been the factors of industrialism and technocracy; the cities that developed were coincidences, by-products.

With such haphazard growth, it is not surprising that the industrial cities developed with four or five major flaws, which, I think, they still have—although in rather different forms.

The first, of course, was that the unplanned, unscientific concentration of people led to the most unbelievable pollution. We sometimes think of pollution as a recent phenomenon, but anyone who has read Dickens knows that all his city novels begin with thick fog through which people with gin-blue faces tumble until they fall into the river and die instantly. This was pollution in the grand manner; it was produced by this boiling up of uncontrolled concentrations of people as a by-product of the industrial process.

Another impact of this sudden urbanization was the incredible prevalence of disease. You cannot read a Victorian novel without encountering the death scene in which someone—usually the upstanding young husband—dies conveniently of typhoid. Why typhoid? Well, typhoid was a fact of life in every stratum of society—even the Prince Consort died of it. Cholera, too, swept through American and European cities with great regularity until the 1860's. Both diseases were certain to be prevalent in polluted cities where sewage systems had not yet been invented. Only toward the end of the century, when public health measures were instituted, did the cities become safer places to live than the countryside.

So the first flaws we see in the cities of technocracy are the pollution and disease caused by mixing an enormous increase in urban population into a burgeoning industrial structure, and then leaving everything to chance.

The second set of flaws showed up in the economic structure of the urbanized society. It is quite interesting how a society's economics develop. People usually think of economics as being tremendously mathematical and scientific, but actually it has profound cultural roots. One of the most culturally determined elements is how costs are determined, and from the beginning of the Industrial Revolution costs in the urban situation got out of control in two ways.

The first was that no one noticed what was happening to land prices until they were distorted beyond all reason. Industrial cities required land—land for expansion of factories and land with the mineral resources to fire them. Urged on by speculators, land prices skyrocketed. What had been a cozy little farm became property worth 100 times its former agricultural value. Yet, in the absence of any cultural determination to the contrary, the original owner did not need to contribute anything to the new industrial society except willingness to rent or sell for the highest price he could get. By the time that Henry George argued that the increment of gain simply must be taxed, the private land market had spiraled upward beyond control. Once land prices reached such heights, the whole urban building program became perverted because it was impossibly expensive to provide decent housing for the masses of city dwellers.

Meanwhile, of course, the burgeoning urban centers attracted more and more vehicles—commercial and personal. First they were horse-drawn; then came the steam-driven railway, and then the onslaught of the automobile. But because country carts had always been allowed to go down village streets free, no one thought to make this vast increase in traffic pay for itself.

Today we see the ultimate distortion of these haphazard decisions in our inner cities where land is so expensive that the poor can only be housed in fifty-block apartment complexes where children are supposed to grow up between heaven and earth and never reach the ground. Even prestigious offices must be placed in hideous trade towers. But one inch away from those trade towers is the street, and *there* a huge station wagon can drive forever and ever, yet pay nothing for occupying the space. When you think about it, this is fantastic: the market divides itself by one inch down the road. One part is so expensive that we cannot rehouse the poor; the other so free that we cannot keep traffic moving. Yet the root cause of this anomaly is almost pure chance—the fact that nobody noticed that the cities were happening.

Another historical chance, which is just as important for modern economics and was equally culturally determined, is our curious separation of industrial from social costs. For example, during the earliest days of the Industrial Revolution, wool manufacture depended upon water power. Now water power in those days was something that had to be taken where it occurred naturally—usually out in the countryside. To get enough workers to live nearby, the manufacturers often had to provide some social inducements. Therefore, in Britain, nearly all the early wool industrialists were the builders of small towns and the providers of small amenities; the same was true in New England.

But the invention of steam power changed this. Factories could be built almost anywhere, and much larger concentrations of workers became possible, even necessary. It was convenient for industrialists to share installations, to be close to the processors of raw material, to have an immediately accessible market. Production and marketing became ever more elaborate, ever more interlocking. Such a system demanded a large pool of laborers, but since these workers were used by many different employers, no one was particularly responsible for bringing them together and no one assumed responsibility for their social welfare.

Thus, although the social costs of the labor force are clearly part of the full cost of the industrial process, they became totally divorced from the cost charged to the consumer. All that was passed on to the consumer were wages, capital investment, the cost of materials and management, and profits—not housing, not education, not urban services. In other words, on the one hand, there was the industrial system concentrating people but not, in itself, accepting responsibility for the results; on the other hand, there were burgeoning urban societies that were not ready for this impact. The immediate consequences were the horrors of Dickens' London, the horrors of the cities described by Balzac.

Phase II of Urbanization Process

But after 40 to 50 years, the most evident of these horrors were overcome. This period might be called Phase II of the urbanization process—approximately 1880 to 1945. During Phase II there evolved something of an effective city government, a working drainage system, an end to pollution, the beginnings of some kind of control in these cities.

The fight wasn't easy for, by that time, the pattern had been established that industry made the mess and society cleaned it up. And society, then as now, was very reluctant to pay and did as little as possible. (Today, when we denounce industry for polluting or government for being too slow to clean it up, we must remember that we are in a great tradition. The true problem lies in the cultural chances which formed the early cities. We can only hope that we will have learned from experience and will do rather better now.)

Nonetheless, men like Chadwick and women like Florence Nightingale did lead a very effective revolution against early pollution. One reason for their success was, of course, that pollution and resultant disease did not respect class lines, and you do tend to clear up what hits you rather closely.

But there was more to it than that. An incredible liberal drive of urban reform did grow up in the late nineteenth century. It not only produced the control of the worse forms of pollution; it also went into model building for the industrious poor (in those days you had to be good to be helped). In addition, there were the exploratory beginnings of an urban philosophy, which produced ideas such as garden suburbs, new towns, and, in a few countries, government control of the land market. So there were breakthroughs in the concept of how you organize a decent city, there was a movement away from the extraordinary haphazardness of early urbanization.

Some of the reformers' ideas dealt with a result of the early industrial cities which I have not yet mentioned, but which haunts us still. That was the attempt of the middle class to get away from typhoid and cholera and other horrors—the suburbs.

It is very interesting to examine a modern city, such as London, which has grown up around one of the pre-urban cities. It is like a fossil with various layers showing how the city developed. At the core is the inherited city of the aristocracy, which is now a great tourist attraction. (Little did grand dukes know what they were going to contribute to the Gross National Product merely by building unnecessary castles.)

Also at the core, down by the river, are the worst of the slums, the dwellings of whatever group is currently at the bottom of the economic ladder. Then back go the suburbs. First the suburbs that you could reach by carriage. Then the suburbs that you could reach by the new train. Then, lurking out beyond the wall, the suburbs you could reach by the motor car.

These "geological layers" show that, almost from the beginnings of the technological city, many people have felt that they wanted to get away from it as soon and as often as they could. But since the escape routes, the suburbs, developed in as haphazard a fashion as the city itself, this drive rapidly produced an urban population with the movements and the habits of the ant heap. (The image is not original; it is the one the astronauts use about our modern cities viewed from afar. Morning and night they look exactly like ant heaps being kicked—which is scarcely surprising when you consider that in London public transport alone moves three to four million people every week day, a figure equivalent to most of the population of South Vietnam. Of course no one would try to move that many people in a two-hour period on a national basis, but every great metropolis does it, though not with any great comfort or humanity.)

Thus, as the cities grew, the pressures to get out became as great as the pressures to get in. And soon these opposing, unregulated pressures began to produce the phenomenon of urban sprawl—something that was neither city nor country but just went on and on and on.

One consequence of this was that people were no longer seeing nature at all. And yet, long past the time when escape from the city was a positive health measure, people continued to show the most passionate addiction for getting to the seaside or the countryside in the summer and on weekends. This lemming-like surge away from the urban, this desperate search for the non-urban, seems irrational at times; it suggests that, lurking under the carapace he is building for himself, man still desires—even requires—contact with something soft and moving and non-technological—a wave or a mountain or a tree.

This need for contact with nature was another of the factors that the early urban philosophers began to take into account during Phase II of urbanization. Between the two world wars, concepts such as the conservation movement, the garden suburb, and the Green Belt movement around London began to pick away at the edges of the results of haphazard technological growth.

Between the wars, also, countries such as Britain did very largely reduce the slums, the areas in which misery was perpetuated for generations by the sheer hopelessness of the housing in which children had to grow up. The concepts of new towns, of metropolitan areas, of urban planning were also introduced.

And so, for a time, it looked as though some rationality, some cohesion was about to be introduced into the urban process, which had grown so haphazardly, as the result of so many other factors.

Phase III

But then we come to Phase III, which is where we are now. And, unfortunately, we are discovering that a lot of the Phase II solutions were based on assumptions which have proven to be wrong.

There are a number of reasons for this. First of all, population, which had stabilized before the First World War, began to increase quite rapidly after the Second World War, at least for a time. So a great many of the solutions that had been postulated upon a stable population no longer worked. For example, a Green Belt works only if the population is not increasing. If it is, the Belt becomes a halter around your neck. In London people just jumped over and urbanized on the far side, giving over the Green Belt to the most melancholy collection of hen farms.

As population pressure negated the purpose of the Green Belts, it also ruined the tidy schemes of new towns and urban renewal, which the planners had counted on to keep urban life human. The burgeoning pressure of people searching for living space outmoded plans while they were still on the drawing boards; the new towns were sucked into the ever-widening circle of bedroom communities. Inexorably the rings of suburbs grew. London had been the first city whose tentacles threatened to meet those of its neighbors, but after World War II this became a universal phenomenon. The Low Countries are now almost completely urbanized. Even a nation such as the United States, with a tradition of the boundless frontier, is well on its way to such attractive metropolises as Bos-Wash on its East coast, San-San on the West, and Chi-Pitts in the middle.

The second surprise, in many countries, was a very large migration of people out of rural poverty into the cities. The best known example of this phenomenon is the one you live with in the United States—the great migration of Blacks from the rural South to the cities of the North. An almost exactly parallel movement is occurring in Italy where the Sicilians have decided to go North—partly because the promise of employment is there, partly because the means of going to America have been somewhat restricted, partly because of the lure of the city in a technological society. Britain is experiencing an urban influx in quite a new way, with peoples coming in from the West Indies, inducing a kind of cultural exchange which no one had foreseen. And France is witnessing an enormous flow of Algerians into the Parisian regions.

In every case the employment opportunities open to these poor, often unskilled people are the jobs no longer desired by local people. And these unemployed or under-employed newcomers have taken up their homes primarily in the central cities, in rundown districts which the planners had hoped to renew or to phase out.

Such movements into the central cities are re-creating the migrant conditions which everyone thought the nineteenth century had seen the end of. Nor is it the merely physical conditions that are the same; social attitudes about the inferiority of the newcomers are recurring—attitudes that recall the "joke" of the 1840's, that "God invented the wheelbarrow to teach Paddy to walk on his hind legs."

Such social fears hasten the flight of the middle classes to the ever-growing suburbs, increasing the physical deterioration of the central core. And so the idea that Phase II had seen the solutions to the worst problems of slums has proved untrue.

The third unlooked-for factor in today's urbanization process is the reappearance of pollution. Twenty years of unparalleled affluence, coupled with the ignorant notion that air and water are in unlimited supply and endlessly self-cleaning, have induced habits of pollution that would make the nineteenth century envy us. Again, it is a problem of not noticing where we have been headed, of not stopping to consider the probable results of combining an increase in population with burgeoning dependence on the motor car, the extraordinary chemical revolution, and a belief in the power of packaging practically everything in cellophane and plastic. And suddenly the air in our cities is actually lethal and Lake Erie is dead.

The cause, again, is our haphazard building of society. The separation of the costs of industry from the cleaning up of industry—a separation as old as the industrial system itself—has been applied to twenty years of the most fabulous prosperity, combined with the technological and chemical revolution. And that has put us back with the kind of environmental problems that the Victorians thought they had cleared up. About our only triumph is that, so far, typhoid and cholera have not come back. But if we go on as we are now, I'm not too sure that they won't.

For typhoid and cholera *are* endemic in some of the world's urban areas. And here we come to the true challenge of the next fifty years. The problems of the developed, Atlantic world are, after all, within the reach of our solutions, considering our resources and the technological knowledge we can draw on.

But once you move away from that core of countries that industrialized in the nineteenth and early twentieth centuries, then you find true trouble. This two-thirds of the world—Latin America, Africa, Asia—is now urbanizing *more* rapidly than the nineteenth century ever did: population there is growing at twice our Victorian level; the cities are growing four to eight times as fast as population. Even more critical, the industrial work force is growing twice as fast as did that of the nineteenth century. And this tornado of people coming into the cities round the world, coming there ahead of the jobs to employ them, coming at a time when technology demands capital and not unskilled labor, form the violent centers of misery and collapse on our planet. The problems are so great as to make the Victorian situation look really cozy, so great that the urban guerrilla looks to become one of the features of everyday life, just as bandits were features of the late Middle Ages and of China's crises of famine and disruption.

The reason for this intense urban crisis in the developing world is that the cities, in a sense, have come ahead of development. They were built in colonial times as entrepreneurial centers, as ports to serve Atlantic trade, not to feed and develop hinterland. Today, quite suddenly, the entire purpose of these huge centers has changed, without time for structure and institutions to evolve gradually. The problems these cities face are far worse than ours were or are, because they are, in a sense, facing all the problems and forces of the West's urbanization Phase I, II, and III simultaneously.

One reason for their crisis is the same as in the developed lands—the well-publicized population explosion. Another is the phenomenon we have already examined on the fringes of Western society—the massive movement of the rural poor into the cities—cities which offer employment only to skilled labor, cities in which the institutions of environmental good health have yet to be installed, cities in which housing is so desperate that people sleep on the streets, cities which are not able to cope with the sheer influx of humanity.

A third similarity is that the developing lands are inheriting our economics along with our technology—an economics that, as we have seen, ignores social costs.

Thus, although the Third World problems are more intense, more difficult of solution, there are threads of common experience running between Chicago and Rio, between the suburbs of Paris and the outskirts of Calcutta, between the slums of Milan and those of Hong Kong. This is the skein of an urbanization that is threatening to become lethal, this is the web of the ultimate mismanagement of the Technological Order.

What Can Be Done?

What can be done about it? First of all, I think one must point out that our urban challenge is producing, as did that of the nineteenth century, a whole range of new ideas and new possibilities.

First, there is the work being done by urban specialists on the concept of the neighborhood. This theory seeks to break away from urbanization as a mere byproduct of industrial forces and to concentrate on building cities that are a positive response to human needs. The first priority—which is of great interest to teachers—is given to the idea of what human beings need during the "nesting period," the time when the children are growing up, going to primary school, getting their first social experience. Since this seems to be the most critical stage in the development of human beings, the planners are concentrating on it in their attempt to build neighborhoods. And since we have all seen how impossible it is to train children whose whole experience of life has been in the violent, dangerous, corrupted urban ghettos, I believe that giving first priority to the building of a "nest," which human beings need in order to become human, is one of the great breakthroughs in architectural and urban theory.

Secondly, there is renewed, more sophisticated interest in the concept of the new town and the new city. A French plan may be taken as example, although similar experiments are proposed in Scandinavia and the Netherlands. All along the Seine the French are attempting to decentralize a haphazard pattern centered almost entirely on Paris. They plan a series of subsidiary cities, including a new one near Rouens; this will be the first experiment to see if environmental answers can be built into industrial cities. In other words, their planners say, why not build a city in such a way that the environmental solutions are part of its very structure?

A third area of experiment, which has interesting applications for both developed and developing countries, is that of urban "gravitational fields and counterpulls." The basis of this scheme is acceptance of the fact that mere *fiat* will not stop haphazard urbanization. The Russians tried that as early as 1932 when they prohibited further growth in Moscow and Leningrad. At that time each city had approximately two million inhabitants: today Moscow has over seven million and Leningrad nearly four million, despite all the prohibitions. So, if even Russian bureaucracy cannot overcome the sucking pull of the metropolis, perhaps it can be neutralized by establishing *another* urban center close enough to attract some of the incoming population, but distant enough to avoid becoming just another satellite or suburb.

Such a scheme has been put forth in detail for southeast England, which already contains thirty percent of the nation's population and may shortly contain eighty percent. To counter London's pull in this area, the British plan proposes deliberately encouraging the growth of three small towns already in the region. With the insights of modern planning and the possibilities of new construction, these could be developed as true urban centers (rather than bedroom communities) in which people would want to live and work. And three such centers, on the edge of London's gravitational field, would act as counterpulls, checking the growth of the metropolis but enhancing the planned development of the entire region.

All these ideas are creative responses to the crises in which we live. They are, I think, linked to another field of thought which is relevant to the urban situation: getting new concepts of cost/benefit ratio into our economics. We have already seen that our price system grew haphazardly from cultural influences that predate the Industrial Revolution and have little relation to the realities of a technological, urban society.

But other price structures are possible, and today they are actually being considered, at least in the abstract.

Suppose that the consumer had to pay even part of the true social costs of production? I think the Western habits of high mass consumption might undergo some changes.

Suppose that the buyer had to pay the true cost of the cellophane packaging he purchases? (This is an area where a few governments are beginning to make the first inroads, despite the wails of those who produce those pretty packages.) Quite soon we would see at least some reuse of our newsprint.

Suppose the automobile owner had to pay for the space he uses at a rate equivalent to that paid by the person who wants an apartment or an office? The proper cost of bringing a motor car into Manhattan would be something like $5000 a day. Enforcement of such a rate would bring about the creation of a decent system of public transport very quickly. And, if we had a moderate land market, a city like New York would certainly move on constructing decent housing in Harlem before it built any more monstrous trade towers.

So, at least among the economists and the planners, there are hopes of an increasing rationality. And intimately connected with such hopes for a rational economic structure is the new concern for the environment. I am happy to say—especially with the United Nations Conference on the Human Environment coming up in June, 1972—that this seems to be a deepening concern. In country after country, as public interest in conservation increases, there is a growing idea of absolute protection for parts of the land, absolute prohibition of certain forms of development.

In addition, concern for the environment may lead us away from the historically conditioned separation of social costs from economic costs. Since the Industrial Revolution consumption has been subsidized continuously and outrageously by society and by nature. Poor old Mother Earth—the biosphere as we call her now—has been left to pick up the pieces. Well, the dear old lady has done her best, you must admit. For 150 years we've larded her with filth and dirt, with scraps of everything we didn't want—in part because we had no calculus of social costs, in part because no one has assumed responsibility for protection of the total human environment. Take, for example, the recent discoveries in Scandinavia. For some time there have been megadeaths of fish and birds along the North Sea coast, and no one knew why. Now we learn that plastic manufacturers from West Germany and Britain have been hiring boats from Scandinavian ports, loading them with small canisters containing the most poisonous effluent of plastic production, and dumping them into the North Sea. So now we do know what is probably causing the deaths, but we can't stop it. The discharge of poisonous wastes is regulated or prohibited *within* most European countries, but as the effluent was dumped beyond the twelve mile limit, it's nobody's responsibility, nobody's jurisdiction.

Now that's the kind of separation of true costs from economic costs which has to stop before we can get decent cities—and perhaps before we can have an environment in which man can survive at all.

Another example of our desperate need for planetary responsibility is the testimony of Thor Heyerdahl, who reports that the surfaces of the oceans, hundreds of miles from land, are increasingly covered with garbage and gunk. Yet it is out on the surface of the oceans that tiny organisms called phyto-plankton produce one-quarter of the oxygen supply used by the human race. One remembers those glorious words of Keats, "The moving waters at their priest-like task/Of pure ablution round earth's human shores." And what do the tides wash in today? Oil slicks or worse!

So, although I'm not a doomsday ecologist, I think we must face the fact that there is such a thing as the point of no return. Behind the processes of supposedly cost-less production, behind our haphazard urban growth, behind our separation of true social cost from our distorted price patterns, there is the possibility that we are creating an environment so hostile that to survive at all man might essentially have to stop being human. It is often safer to listen to the poets rather than the calculators. And the poets among us, particularly those poets with an interest in biology, are most seriously disturbed. Man, they say, was molded by the earth, by the free air and clear water, by the forest in which he lived for so long that the garden of Eden still haunts his imagination. And, the poets ask, if we continue to create environments as ugly, as dangerous, and as cut off from nature as those we are building now, can the human species survive?

This, surely, is a tremendous challenge for teachers. You are the ones who see, year by year, the next generation coming up still fresh, still ready to contribute to the experience of living on this planet. You are the ones who can make them see that the way to the good life lies in the way in which they respect the biosphere, the way in which they learn to see the physical and social unity of the planet, the way in which they see the problems of races and of policies in the cities as part of the whole human experience in which we are all involved.

And if you grasp this opportunity and use it well, I think your next fifty years will be very well spent.

Jacques Cousteau Comments on Current Archeological Exploration of Greek Waters

One of the most exciting expeditions of my life to date is the current archeological exploration of Greek waters, where we are looking for remains of lost civilizations as well as looking for archeological lessons from antiquity generally. I am going to recall this because I think it is typical of the mental mechanism of exploration. Our research vessel *Calypso* arrived in Crete; and we docked in the harbor of Heraklion, on the north coast of Crete near Knossos. A violent North Sea storm, the wind named "Meltem," made our situation almost intolerable inside the harbor, in spite of the fact that we were sheltered by a modern jetty built of concrete. Then, as a sailor, I started reasoning that in antiquity the tiny primitive harbor of Knossos could not have protected the ships of King Minos from Meltem. Looking at a map, I deduced that the only safe anchorages in case of Northern winds were to be found on the south coast of Dhia, a small island lying only eight miles north of Crete. That was a deductive standard mental process called "vertical thinking."

We explored the waters around Dhia, in depths ranging from 20 feet to 300 feet, with divers and our exploration submarine. We discovered six ancient shipwrecks ranging from the 16th century A.D. to the first century A.D. The ships were carrying bronze guns, copper and silver-ware, hundreds and even thousands of amphorae, and dozens of large blocks of marble, some of them ornate or sculptured. They may have been the remains of a stolen palace or a stolen temple transported in parts, like the famous Hearst Castle.

NOTE: This selection, an excerpt from NASA EP 125, which was prepared from a transcript of a panel discussion, appeared in *Social Education*, April 1977, p. 277.

We were about to leave when my chief diver, Albert Falco, asked me to let him have a last swim near shore. He snorkeled in the bay of St. George in Dhia while we were warming up the motors to sail away. He came back reporting that he found a strange heap of stones of colossal stature—nothing much, after all, a few stones or maybe . . ., maybe something unexpected. This last-minute find, vague and dubious, did not fit into our program. We were to explore the southern coast of Crete. I hesitated for one minute and then I stopped the motors. There was no committee I had to report to for a change of program.

There was no logic for abandoning our initial program. Falco's hesitant report appeared to be uncorrelated with our aims. Forty years of exploration had repeatedly proven to me that the deductive process of thinking—vertical thinking—although it is a powerful tool, rarely leads to a breakthrough discovery. Independently, lateral thinking, the process by which the mind scans events or facts that are apparently uncorrelated to investigate whether in reality they could be even remotely correlated, has often led us and many others to important breakthroughs. What followed is endless. The heap of stones proved to be a large submerged manmade harbor of probably Minoan origin. Then—back to vertical deduction this time—we thought that if there had been a harbor on that desolate piece of rock (the island of Dhia), then there also necessarily had been human settlements. Our helicopter made a photomosaic coverage of the island, revealing several villages or towns and a huge Cyclopean fortification system, totally erased today. We could only see traces of its foundations on the photographs, taken with low Sun for contrast. Minoan fragments of pottery and at least one Minoan idol on land were found before an excavation was made.

A full-scale underwater excavation of the harbor—a three-month effort—confirmed all our theories. Five thousand years ago the island of Dhia was a paradise covered with woods and refreshed by large rivers, a paradise where Theseus eloped for a famous honeymoon with Ariadne, daughter of Minos, after he killed the Minotaur. Then the island was progressively deforested to build or repair ships and to cook dinners in the thousands of homes. Dhia succumbed, probably 4000 years ago, from overpopulation—a lesson of ecology from antiquity. Then 500 years later, the explosion of the volcanic island of Thera, better known as Santorini, raised a 300-foot-high tidal wave that washed clean the island from its fortifications, villages, towns, walls, harbors. Ever since, Dhia has remained a desolate rock. This major discovery is going to lead, certainly, to decades of very difficult and systematic excavations on land. Then it was no more our business and we went on to some other discoveries.

Dismantling Apartheid

DESMOND TUTU

On December 4, 1984, Nobel Peace Prize Laureate Archbishop Desmond Tutu presented his views on apartheid to the U.S. House Committee on Foreign Affairs Subcommittee on Africa. His comments are presented here in full.

Mr. chairman and members of the committee, thank you very much for your very warm welcome and your words of congratulations. Thank you, too, for the great honor of addressing your influential subcommittee.

May I pay warm tribute to yourself and your colleagues for your commitment to the struggle for a just and truly democratic and nonracial society in South Africa, the hope of all of us who have the vision of a new kind of society in that beautiful but so sadly tortured land.

May I add a special word of appreciation to those Members of Congress and others who have been participating in the protests at the South African Embassy and the South African consulates throughout the United States in the Free South Africa movement. I hope that we note this is a peaceful, nonviolent strategy to effect changes in the policies of the U.S. Government and within South Africa.

The oppressed in South Africa and the lovers of freedom there are deeply thankful for this demonstration of solidarity with the exploited, the voiceless, and the powerless ones. The protest is not, might I point out, anti-South Africa. It is decidedly antiapartheid, antiinjustice, antioppression, which are not the same thing.

It is one of the ironies of the South African situation that I can here, in this great and free land, the land of the brave and home of the free, address so august a body as this; and yet, in my own country, the land of my birth, I would not be able to speak to a comparable body because I and nearly 23 million other black South Africans are victims of the politics of exclusion.

NOTE: These comments appeared in *Social Education*, September 1985, pp. 453–456.

Here I am, a bishop in the church of God, 53 years of age, who some might even be ready to risk calling reasonably responsible, and yet I cannot vote in my motherland; whereas, a child of 18 years of age, because she is white, and only very recently colored and Indian, can vote. More of this later.

Mr. Chairman, I should have come to this country at the beginning of September to start my sabbatical of four months as a visiting professor at the General Theological Seminary in New York. My wife and I had to postpone our departure from South Africa because of the heightening crisis there. I called on the then South African Prime Minister, Mr. P. W. Botha, now state President, and other senior cabinet ministers, to meet with church leaders to try to deal with what I feared was likely to be a tragic situation. Mr. Botha did not respond, though a delegation of church leaders was able to wait on two senior cabinet ministers.

I have still tried to engage the South African Government in dialogue, despite their unrelenting efforts to vilify and discredit the South African Council of Churches and its employees, despite the government's strictures that we were fomenting revolution at a time when the government was allegedly embarking on the road to reform. We reckoned the situation was too serious to try to be scoring debate points, and subsequent events have borne out our apprehensions.

The Nobel Peace Prize is a global indication of the South African Council of Churches and those associated with it that the world recognizes that we are true agents of justice, of peace, of reconciliation, and that we in the South African Council of Churches stand between South Africa and disaster.

We had an emergency meeting of the South African Council of Churches Executive Committee and leaders of the SACC member churches. We visited some of the trouble spots. I accompanied those of the meeting who went to Watervill, a black township.

We visited one home where the old lady there said she looked after her grandson and the children of neighbors whilst their parents were at work. She told us that one day the police chased some boycotting black schoolchildren who disappeared among the township houses. The police then drove down her street. She was in the back of the house, in the kitchen. Her charges were playing in the yard in front of the house. Suddenly her daughter dashed into the house, calling to her to come quickly.

She says she rushed into her living room. Her grandson had fallen just inside the door, dead, shot in the back. He was 6 years old.

A few weeks later a white baby was killed in a black township. Two such deaths, Mr. Chairman, are two too many—the high cost of apartheid.

The new constitution is an instrument of the politics of exclusion I referred to earlier. Seventy-three percent of South Africa's population, the blacks, have no part in this constitution, which mentions them quite incredibly only once. How could this be seen as a step in the right direction? How could this be regarded as even remotely democratic? Its three chambers are racially defined. Consequently, racism and ethnicity are entrenched and hallowed in the constitution.

In the parliamentary committees the composition is in the ratio of four whites to two coloreds to one Indian, and even if your arithmetic is bad, you know that two plus one can never equal let alone be more than four. Thus white minority rule is perpetuated and entrenched in this constitution. Coloreds and Indians are being co-opted to perpetuate the oppression of the vast majority of South Africa's population.

Mercifully, they rejected this monumental hoax to hoodwink the world into thinking that South Africa's apartheid-mongers are changing—for only 20 percent of colored and Indians participated in the August elections. It has been a dangerous fiddling, while our Rome burnt.

The oppressed have protested this politics of exclusion and they have done so peacefully. They have staged stayaways and demonstrations against the new constitution, against sham black local government, against increases in rent, against increases in the general sales tax, against the inferior education foisted on blacks. The South African Government has reacted violently and with a mailed fist—against a popular and mass movement of peaceful protest it has reacted with violence.

It has detained the leaders of the election boycott movement. It has arrested the leaders of the trade union movement who staged the most successful legal strike for political reasons, all without due process, without preferring charges, and having the evidence tested in open court. The writ of habeas corpus in many instances no longer exists in South Africa.

Last week 12 people were arrested for protesting legally and peacefully by displaying banners and picketing, and these included people of the caliber of John Dugard, a law professor at Witwatersrand University and the director of the Center for Applied Legal Studies. Journalists have been subpoenaed under the International Security Act to testify against the organizers of the stayaway. This is a country that is lauded as being the bastion against communism, as the upholder of Western white Christian civilization and its values.

I have said that blacks deplore communism as being atheistic and materialistic. But they would regard the Russians as their saviors, were they to come to South Africa, because anything in their view would be better than apartheid, for the enemy of my enemy is my friend. When you were in a dungeon, and a hand is put out to unlock the door and get you out, you don't ask for the credentials of the owner of the hand. After all, the West was not too finicky in accepting the Russians as allies against Nazism.

Twenty-four blacks were killed during that two-day strike in November. Six thousand were sacked from their jobs. There was not a squeak of protest from the Government of this country. When a priest in Poland was missing, and then his body was found, there was an outrage in this country and the media quite rightly gave it all extensive coverage. When 12 black South Africans are killed by the South African police, and 6,000 people are sacked, you are lucky if you get that much coverage. There was no expression of outrage and concern. That is part of constructive engagement.

I believe we are being told that this administration is not being soft on apartheid. Heaven help us when they do decide to be soft.

Would the reaction and the silence have been so deafening if the casualties had been white? Would the reaction and the silence have been so deafening if the casualties had for instance been Jewish?

The South African Government has uprooted over 3 million blacks and dumped them as if they were rubbish in Bantustan homelands and not even an uncustomary protest by the State Department could stop them from uprooting 300 families from Mogopa. Just now a community, the people of Kwangena in the eastern Transvaal, face the threat of being uprooted. It is the same community, one of whose leaders, Saul Mkhize, was killed protesting the removal of his people from Driefontein.

Mr. Chairman, we are being turned into aliens in our fatherland, because an alien cannot claim any rights, least of all political rights. They don't know that I am a South African, for I travel on a travel document that describes my nationality as undeterminable at present. The South African Government with impunity, in the full glare of international publicity, is dealing callously with the women of the KTC squatter camp near Capetown, where their flimsy plastic coverings are destroyed every day so that these women are reduced to sitting on soaking mattresses with their household effects strewn around their feet, and whimpering babies on their laps in the bitter Cape rain because they want to be with their husbands, they want to be with the fathers of their children, and it is illegal for them in this Christian Western civilized country, to lead a normal, stable family life.

This is the kind of system that those who invest in South Africa are purchasing. This is the kind of system that the Reagan administration's constructive engagement is encouraging and supporting, encouraging the white racist regime into an escalating intransigence and repression.

It is no use for South Africa entering into nonaggression pacts with foreign countries when it carries out acts of aggression against its own civilian population, when it sets the army on defenseless civilians. It is no use having détente only for external consumption when the South African Government refuses to talk with our real leaders inside the country and those in exile. For the problem of South Africa is not outside that country. The problem of South Africa is inside South Africa.

The problem of South Africa is the system, the repressive and unjust system of apartheid.

Mr. Chairman, our people are peace loving to a fault. They have sought to change South Africa's racist policies by peaceful means since 1912 at the very least, using conventional peaceful methods of demonstrations, petitions, delegations, and even a passive resistance campaign. As a tribute to this commitment of our people to peaceful change, the only two South Africans to have won Nobel Peace Prizes are both of them black.

The response of the authorities, as I have said so many times before, has been police dogs, tear gas, guns, death, detention, and exile. Protesting peacefully against the pass laws, 69 of our people in the Sharpville 1960 march were massacred, most of them shot in the back, running away. In 1976 our children protested peacefully against Bantu education, singing songs in the streets, and over 500 people were killed. Many of our children are in exile, most of whose whereabouts are unknown to their parents. Now in the most serious protest against apartheid, nearly 200 of our people have been killed, most by the authorities who are using the army, as I have said, against a peaceful civilian population, and the West does not appear to care.

Constructive engagement goes on. Namibia we were told four years ago would be independent because of constructive engagement. Namibia, four years later, is not independent. The United States has provided a recalcitrant South Africa with a further reason for dragging its feet by linking Namibian independence with the withdrawal of the Cuban troops from a sovereign state, Angola, and in the meantime people are dying, people are suffering needlessly.

Constructive engagement has worsened our situation under apartheid. Four years ago I said this policy was an unmitigated disaster for us blacks. Four years later I have no reason to alter my original assessment despite what Dr. Chester Crocker is reported to have said.

It is giving democracy a bad name, just as apartheid has given free enterprise a bad name.

Mr. Chairman, we are talking about a moral issue. You are either for or against apartheid, and not by rhetoric. You are either in favor of evil or you are in favor of good. You are either on the side of the oppressed or on the side of the oppressor. You cannot be neutral. Apartheid is evil, is immoral, is un-Christian, without remainder. It uses evil, immoral, and un-Christian methods. If you have supported the Nazis against the Jews, you would have been accused of adopting an immoral position. Apartheid is an evil as immoral and un-Christian in my view as Naziism, and in my view, the Reagan administration's support and collaboration with it is equally immoral, evil and totally un-Christian, without remainder.

In court you are guilty as an accessory before or after the fact. Constructive engagement is saying blacks are dispensable. Why should this administration respond so quickly and so decisively when something is done against Solidarity in Poland, applying sanctions at the drop of a hat, and yet when similar treatment is meted out to black trade unions in South Africa, all we get is convoluted sophistry.

America is a great country, with great traditions of freedom and equality. I hope this great country will be true to its history and its traditions, and will unequivocally and clearly take its stand on the side of right and justice in South Africa, for what the United States decides and does has a crucial bearing on what happens in other lands. Many lives will be saved, many blacks will be won for democracy in South Africa if the United States is true to her real self.

I said four years ago that to protest constructive engagement I would not see any representatives of the Reagan administration. I relented because I thought I could persuade them of the folly and the danger of constructive engagement, and because of an educational program for black South Africans in which I was involved.

I have failed to persuade Dr. Crocker, a good and very intelligent man, and others. So I want to state here that I will not see anyone of the Reagan administration as of today unless constructive engagement is abandoned. I may see the President of this country or the Secretary of State if they do invite me to meet with them.

Mr. Chairman, I am deeply saddened. What have we still to say which we have not said? What have we still to do which we have not done to persuade people that all we want is to be recognized for who we are, human, created in the image of God?

How must we say that we don't want to drive white people into the sea, that we want to live amicably with them in a nonracial, a truly democratic South Africa?

I hope this great country, with an extraordinary capacity sometimes for backing the wrong horse, will for once break that record. Will you please for a change listen to the victims of oppression? We shall be free, and we will remember who helped us to become free.

That is not a threat. It is just a statement of fact. We want so desperately, so eagerly, to be friends of the United States, after South Africa is liberated, for all its people, black and white, as it shall. Thank you.

IV.

The Literary Touch

ON THE COVER of one issue of *Social Education* were these lines by T. S. Eliot:

> We shall not cease from exploration
> And the end of all our exploring will be
> To arrive where we started
> And know the place for the first time.

It is not unusual for the journal to feature the words of a poet. Throughout the years, *Social Education* has reprinted works by a number of distinguished writers of literature: Ray Bradbury, Langston Hughes, Judith Merril, Isaac Peretz, and others. In addition, the journal published original poetry, satire, essays, and fiction by other writers. In doing so, *Social Education* demonstrated that there was a close and meaningful connection between social studies and "the literary touch."

Informal accounts of one's experiences as a teacher have delighted readers for years. One thinks at once of Jesse Stuart's *The Thread That Runs So True*, or the whimsical tales of Bel Kaufman. The first article in this section, "The Moonshine Curriculum" by Professor Richard E. Gross of Stanford University, is in that tradition. A conscientious educator visits a four-room school in a barren, scrub pine area of the Florida panhandle and declares, "The school is life." This comment seems reasonable enough. But how can one explain the joyousness of his final remark: "Down the hatch!"?

Beatrice Laskowitz Goldberg, the author of "She Is Risen," has an interest in both art and poetry. In her poem, which focuses on a visit of children to an art museum, the sight of a vivid painting by Gauguin and spontaneous thoughts about the rules of society merge to produce an unexpected question. It is a plaintive question and, in its sadness, all the more disturbing.

William Sayres, a member of the faculty at Teachers College, Columbia University, served as an adviser on a technical assistance team in the Ministry of Education in Afghanistan. Living in that country, he may have been able to obtain a unique perspective from which to view the educational developments in the United States. One result was a series of satirical pieces entitled "From the [Until Now] Unpublished Files of Mr. Harry Wesley," one of which is presented here. Tempted as they were to do so, the editors of *Social Education* never discussed their own problems with the mysterious Mr. Harry Wesley.

Clara Mannheimer Glasser, who resides in Florida, has always lived close to the sea, and from what she describes as "old taproot ocean" she has drawn the rhythms that permeate her sensitive poetry. In "Morning," she speaks of "shucking to the salted air a sense of self and solitude." Yet, as in all of her writing, there is the strong impression that a part of her will always remain uniquely her own.

On occasion, *Social Education* found some author's writing so delightful and so relevant to social studies that it warranted reprinting in the journal. Such was the case with "Jefferson's Document Needs Work." It is a piece written by an anonymous author at the Agency for International Development and passed along to Mike Causey, columnist of "The Federal Diary" in *The Washington Post*, who passed it along unknowingly to an editor of *Social Education*, who passed it along to his readers. It is a triple bypass that gets to the heart of a seriocomic matter.

The concluding selections, presented under the title "Reflections on Time," were written by Daniel Roselle, the third editor of *Social Education*. They are all concerned with some aspect of time—its quality, its duration, its impact on the lives of human beings. Appearing on the editorial page of various issues of the journal, the four pieces were part of an attempt by the editor to replace formal expressions of opinion on transient matters with personal reflections that might be of more lasting interest to readers. Thus, "The N-9 Bus" is based on personal experiences but, as the author suggests, it is a bus that every person rides.

The Moonshine Curriculum

RICHARD E. GROSS

"The story of the 'Moonshine Curriculum' is factual," the author writes. "It took place as recorded except, of course, that the school goes unidentified and the names of the two instructors have been changed. While the conditions it reflects are happily disappearing, unfortunately they can still be found in isolated, rural school situations throughout the entire United States, not only the South. I certainly did not write the piece to make fun of anyone or any place; my hope is, rather, to illustrate certain key curricular issues."

The school was the typical square, grayish wood building with a vestigial steeple. It was set in a clearing in the woods, just as were the homes of most of the pupils that dotted this barren, scrub pine country in the Florida panhandle. It was a four-room, four-teacher school; the principal taught grades seven and eight, and the other three instructors each also handled two grades in single rooms. Two of the teachers had recently enrolled in an in-service course which called for them to come to the university campus twice a month, and for a university consultant to spend a day with them at their school once each month.

The in-service class had a large enrollment, spreading from south Georgia throughout northwest Florida. The two-way arrangement kept their university instructor on the leap. So, when my colleague heard that I would be traveling in this out-of-bounds direction, I was drafted to make the initial field service visit with Mrs. Wynn and Miss Potter.

According to my reference card, Miss Potter was working on a project to improve the diet and hygienic habits of the pupils in this pellagra-hookworm region. One facet of her program involved a school garden; another included food and health units and lessons for various grades; another aimed at providing a balanced hot lunch, and parental instruction was emphasized for the various mothers who came in from week to

NOTE: This article appeared in *Social Education*, October 1957, pp. 255–256, 266. Reprinted by permission of Richard E. Gross.

week to prepare the noon meals. I wondered how Miss Potter was progressing against the entrenched tradition of black-eyed peas and fatback.

As my car bumped along the dirt approach road I also noted the too-brief statement of Principal Wynn's project—"curricular revision." Well, we would see. One never knows what he will find in such small, isolated, rural schools. I had previously discovered some of the finest, unpublicized, "core" teaching one could ever hope to observe. (Perhaps when these arrangements rise out of necessity, there is more chance for success.) I had also recently visited such a building where the principal had been run off by the students just minutes before my arrival. I found most of the temporary victors in this real battle of learning enjoying themselves gambling with playing cards, provided in multiple decks for each room as the first contribution to educational improvement by the P.T.A.! Undoubtedly Mrs. Wynn's school would be in need of curricular alterations of some nature. What school isn't?

As my car rolled to a stop in front of the school, I glanced at my watch.

"Too early for lunch," I thought to myself. "It must be recess time." Barefoot children were all about the premises, playing on the steps, in the clearing, and about the fringes of the piney wood. I gathered my brief case and stepped toward the building. A strong wind carried the smoke and pleasant smell from a nearby sawmill and turpentine works, which along with the fishing provided most of the employment in the locality.

"I'm Dr. Gross," I explained to a questioning youngster. "Where can I find the principal?"

"She ain't here," was the hesitant answer.

"Besides," added another, "no one is sick here anyhow, see."

A figure appeared at the school door with bell in hand and I soon had introduced myself to Miss Potter. She exclaimed, "Oh, you couldn't have come on a worse day. One of the school trustees died and the funeral is this morning. Mrs. Wynn went to represent the school and the other two teachers are his kinfolk, so I'm left alone with the whole school!"

I pointed to the bell, "Is recess over? I'm looking forward to observing how you spread yourself into four rooms at one time and teach grades one through eight."

She replied cautiously, "I was just fixin' to call them in if your car was Mrs. Wynn's car and the other teachers. I tried to keep the kids all busy early this mornin' but they got pretty rambunctious so I had to let them out for the rest of the mornin'. You know, I can watch those little folks a lot better out here and they'll do a lot less damage."

She set the bell on the top step and we walked toward the school garden. Miss Potter was having problems with her project. I was informed that only yesterday most of the children had refused to eat the strange carrots at lunch and thereby wasted most of the school crop. Besides, this real-life evaluation proved the inadequacy of the new-vegetable emphasis in her food unit. I turned to a little blond urchin in faded gingham who was following us and asked, "Did you eat your carrots yesterday?"

"No," she answered quickly. "I'm like the rabbits that gits into the garden most nights. They knows what's good—just eat the greens and peas!"

Miss Potter nodded in sad agreement. Her project just wasn't developing as envisioned. One of the mothers who cooked that lunch had said she'd never seen such queer-shaped sweet potatoes!

Miss Potter seemed quite nervous. She glanced at the groups of children playing about the clearing and then invited me to come into the school. As we entered I overheard one little girl say, "Yo' all know he's from Tallahassee." Her schoolmate sighed, "I've never been there. Wonder what it's like in a big city?" As we walked down the squeaky floored hall toward Miss Potter's room I shook my head over the isolation that marked these children in this community. I was reminded of the boy who was reciting a geography lesson in a nearby school. The teacher had asked for the four seasons and he sagely listed, "'Possum, fishin', duck, and deer."

I asked Miss Potter if I might see the children's work on their food unit. I commended her on the bulletin board but was certainly not impressed by the odd-shaped and off-colored fruits and vegetables drawn by the pupils; but then, many of them had never seen some of the produce they were drawing. Miss Potter was at the open window watching the children outside. Suddenly she turned to me.

"Dr. Gross, haven't you overheard or noted what's going on out there? I just don't know what to do or if I should tell Mrs. Wynn what has happened." I walked to the window to take a more careful look into the bushes.

Nothing seemed seriously wrong at first observation. I then noted, however, that pupils of very different ages were all playing with one another. Indeed, the bulk of the children were participating in what seemed to be a large-scale, organized, playground-wide sociodrama! As I watched further, the pattern of this extemporaneous reality practice suddenly took on meaning. There were buyers and sellers—and it was a furtive exchange. There were producers too—cooking, stirring, and bottling. This process was conducted behind some protective bushes; guards seemed to watch the approaches. Immediately below us several third graders who had just made an imaginary purchase were already in a highly elated condition. Suddenly, out of the woods a party of sixth-grade State Beverage Department agents surrounded the area of the still. A pitched battle ensued between them and the defenders, boys and girls who were not going to give up their "juice" to the "revenoo-ers"!

Miss Potter was becoming paler by the second.

"Oh, Professor, I am so embarrassed; but you see it's their daddies' main extra-curricular activity! And these children don't know of much else for exciting play." My mind flashed back to my own boyhood days in Capone's Chicago. We had played somewhat different parts of a related game—and on the schoolgrounds too! I laughed heartily.

"'The school is life,'" I quoted. Then I pointed to a child's textbook left open on the well-worn desk.

"Is this their current social studies?" I inquired.

"Yes," she replied. "This group is studying the ancient fertile crescent."

My point went completely over her head. She decided, "Oh, I just have to stop this. I guess I better call them back in."

A car could be heard approaching up the road.

"The funeral must be over. Should I tell Mrs. Wynn about this?" she pleaded.

"Well," I replied, "you know Mrs. Wynn and I don't. How will she react to your having released the whole school all this time as well as to a report of the dramatic play that evolved?"

"I'm not sure about the first," her voice rose in alarm. "But, oh that game; she's a very religious, non-drinkin' woman. . . ."

"She may understand why they did it even if she does commute to this job every day," I added. I had picked up Mrs. Wynn's reference card once more and noted her home address in a larger community about twenty miles away. The words "curricular revision" took my eye again.

"Miss Potter, do you know just what kind of a curriculum project Mrs. Wynn has been working on for this course?"

"She started several," Miss Potter explained, "but they haven't developed. Lately some parents requested a greater academic emphasis in the upper grades so I think she is trying to find a way to work some Latin into grades seven and eight. Although I don't know who would want to take it or who could teach it."

Mrs. Wynn's car came to a loud and dusty halt. She emerged, looking quite large and disturbed, and peered simultaneously at her watch and the frolicking children. "You know, Miss Potter," I whispered to my companion, "in light of the total situation I think you and I should keep this moonshine curriculum to ourselves."

Raising her hand in a mock toast, she smiled for the first time. "Here's to you," she said.

I returned the pledge, "Down the hatch!"

She Is Risen

BEATRICE LASKOWITZ GOLDBERG

Ten years ago I lectured to a class
Of Harlem children, come to see the world
Of art made public in a great museum.
I chose, as I had chosen in the past
For ones so young (of six and seven years),
A subject for our slow meanderings.
"Let's see the Mother and the Child in art.
Let's see, as artists of the past have seen,
All loving mothers, and their children, here
Upon these walls, inside these frames.
The same, sweet subject, from the far and recent past."

All smiles and romping, as they held the arms
Of sweaters dangling, and the legs of stools,
They said they'd come and follow me around.

More sobered now, with looking, we went by
An Empress with her son upon her knee—
A solemn kingling from the Byzantine.
His nimbus golden, and his sky the same,
He hushed our speaking with his golden eye.

We were more free a hundred years away,
In time proceeding through the Renaissance.
The babies dimpled and the mothers smiled.
The sun shone smiling on the Tuscan hills.
The child stood freely on the balustrade,
Her hand but lightly holding, lest he fall.

NOTE: This poem appeared in *Social Education*, January 1969, p. 39. Reprinted by permission of Beatrice Laskowitz Goldberg.

And all around were springtime leaves and buds,
Some bursting, as he burst from infancy.
He played with grapes; she would not see. She smiled.
They were not yet the wine of martyrdom.

And so, at last, upon the bright Gauguin,
The final family—mother, child, and friends.
Here was an island brilliant in the sun:
A second Eden, jungled in the light.
Here was the mother, brown and glistening.
Here was the baby, browner on her arm.
"And this is Mary. This is Jesus, here."
I showed the tracings of their halos, drawn
Against the ripeness of the hills and sky.

There was a stillness in my audience,
Come down from Lenox Avenue to see
Some beauty in a city lived in stone.

One hand was raised in question—one for all.
One small, brown hand upon a browner arm.

"And that is Mary? That is Jesus, there?"
His eyes were wondered wide with hope and fear.
"They are," I answered, and his brow was knit
Into a trouble, terrible and proud.
I waited, as he stood to make the words
That came so slowly clear: "Is that allowed?"

Where is he now, my visitor, my friend?
What alley; stoop? What furnace room? What school?
What car; what office in the day or night?
Where has he gone? Where will he go—that boy
Who had a Yes, however brief in time,
When he was young, and questioned, and could say:
My love-white Mother could have mothered God.

From the [Until Now] Unpublished Files of Mr. Harry Wesley, OEEO

WILLIAM SAYRES

Mr. Harry Wesley, Director
Office of Equal Educational Opportunity
State Education Department

Dear Mr. Wesley:

This is to direct the attention of your office to certain developments related to our local Equal Educational Opportunity program.

In order to provide a setting conducive to the effective implementation of the program, we have taken steps to alleviate the handicapping effects of de facto segregation. That is to say, we have arranged to have, through bussing, an equitable mix of ethnic elements in each and every Freelawn school.

As you may or may not know, Mr. Wesley, the City of Freelawn consists of six wards, each with its own comprehensive school. Unfortunately, the settlement pattern of Freelawn has led to the concentration of particular ethnic groups in some wards and of other groups in other wards. As the State Education Commissioner has pointed out, this is an unhealthy situation from an educational as well as social standpoint, since each school has had a disproportionately high representation of some groups and a disproportionately low representation of others.

This is not, you will agree, a proper training ground for effective participation in a democratic society.

NOTE: This selection appeared in *Social Education*, December 1970, pp. 917–920. Reprinted by permission of William C. Sayres.

I enclose a reprint of the Commissioner's speech of October last, "Meeting the Challenge of Ghetto Education." You will note that he says: "Much as we may resist the idea of bussing our children to schools in other neighborhoods, it is my conviction that, if the alternative is ghetto education, then we must be prepared, as good Americans, to bus." The Commissioner certainly does have a way with words, doesn't he, Mr. Wesley?

We in Freelawn were the first to respond to the Commissioner's message, that is, among the first. We recognized that we could not expect to have an effective educational program unless and until our pupils could take part in the learning process shoulder to shoulder with their fellow American pupils of other antecedents and persuasions.

The principal groups of Freelawn are: Whites of English-Scotch descent, Whites of Italian (Sicilian) descent, Whites of Armenian descent, Negroes, Puerto Ricans, and Japanese. Once we had established how many pupils of each group lived in each ward, it was child's play for our 650 computer to work out the bussing pattern which would ensure effectively blended enrollments in each school.

The system is deceptively simple: 42% of the pupils from Ward 1 attend the Grant School; 37% of the pupils from Ward 2 attend the Woodward School; 64% of the pupils from Ward 3 attend the Jackson School; 79% of the pupils from Ward 4 attend the Blaine School; 27% of the pupils from Ward 5 attend the Coolidge School; 46% of the pupils from Ward 6 attend the Grant School; 28% of the pupils from Ward 1 attend the Tyler School; 34% of the pupils from Ward 2 attend the Blaine School; 18% of the pupils from Ward 3 attend the Coolidge School; 21% of the pupils from Ward 4 attend the Grant School; 22% of the pupils from Ward 5 attend the Woodward School; 23% of the pupils from Ward 6 attend the Blaine School; 16% of the pupils from Ward 1 attend the Jackson School; 29% of the pupils from Ward 2 attend the Grant School; 12% of the pupils from Ward 3 attend the Tyler School; 19% of the pupils from Ward 5 attend the Grant School; 14% of the pupils from Ward 1 attend the Coolidge School; 6% of the pupils from Ward 3 attend the Woodward School; 15% of the pupils from Ward 5 attend the Blaine School; 11% of the pupils from Ward 5 attend the Jackson School; 6% of the pupils from Ward 5 attend the Tyler School; and 31% of the pupils from Ward 6 attend the Woodward School in the morning and the Jackson School in the afternoon.

You must not suppose, Mr. Wesley, that completion of the research was automatically followed by implementation. This has been one of the chronic frustrations of my job: the reluctance of some people to act on the results of research. You would think they would be grateful to have the facts, but instead they persist in their anti-scientific attitudes and act on the basis of emotionalism and expediency. That is no way to act. They cannot act that way and expect to be effective in the long run.

Nevertheless, reason has prevailed and our plan has at last been put into operation. While busses go astray now and then, on the whole the system is working out quite smoothly and effectively.

A problem has, however, arisen. Without consulting us, a Mrs. Clara Vickers of Ward 3 has moved to Philadelphia with her three children.

Naturally, this throws the whole pattern off. Our system has been designed so systematically that such a change in any one part of it affects the rest of it. We have written to Mrs. Vickers, but she refuses to come back. She is a good example of an anti-scientific person who has no consideration.

Meanwhile, our proportions are all askew. We thought of recalculating the pattern and giving out new bussing assignments, but it has taken us so long to overcome confusion over the present assignments and to get the system running well that we have been looking for a less disruptive solution.

We have put the problem to our 650 computer, and have determined that the least disruptive method would be to reestablish the previously existing proportions. This can be done by selective relocation of families with matched characteristics. As a matter of fact, only two relocations will be required: If Mrs. Rose Anne Bennington moves out of Freelawn, and if the Peter Dunhill family moves from Ward 2 to Ward 6, no other adjustments will be necessary.

We have talked with Mrs. Bennington and with Mr. and Mrs. Dunhill, and I regret to report that they have been most uncooperative. Mrs. Dunhill in particular was quite rude. They simply do not see the larger picture.

There is a very good chance that we can have the Bennington property condemned, but since the Dunhill property is fairly new our approach must be different with them. We might be able to have the house jacked up, put on rollers, and moved to Ward 6 while the Dunhills are away on vacation, but Mrs. Dunhill does not strike me as a person who likes being surprised in this manner.

(If we were able to move the house, Mr. Wesley, would funds from your office be available for this purpose?)

We would very much appreciate any advice you can give us. Is there any possibility that you could come down here and talk to Mrs. Bennington and the Dunhills?

Under separate cover I am sending you a copy of a study I recently completed on the subject of horizontal teacher-pupil relationships.

Sincerely,
Robert M. Weatherby,
Research Associate
Freelawn City School District

Mr. Harry Wesley, Director
Office of Equal Educational Opportunity
State Education Department

Dear Mr. Wesley:

Since last September, I have served as President of the new Archer Community College which, if I may say so, constitutes a unique experiment in Education for Social Maturity. Thanks to the very generous subsidy provided by your office, we have made available to the children of economically impoverished families of the area an educational environment consecrated to the search for personal and social relevance.

At Archer, we have done away with the repressive rigidities of the archaic conventional curriculum, which has proved to be so poorly adapted to the needs of the new generations. Among the excess baggage, if I may use the phrase, that we have discarded are entrance requirements, the credit system, examinations, grades, class attendance regulations, compulsory homework, reading lists, a fixed set of courses (students may participate in the development of their own courses or, if they prefer, engage in educational experiences that do not involve coursework), dormitory hours (though most students are within commuting distance of the college, we provide coeducational dormitory facilities in order to maximize constructive opportunities for group living), and all externally imposed rules of dress and conduct (believing as we do that social growth and responsibility must come from within; we are, after all, dealing not with elementary school children but with young adults).

In keeping with our students' keen sense of moral outrage over the lack of justice and meaning in our society (an outrage so incisively expressed that I must send you some recent issues of our underground newspaper: I have seen no other publication that so beautifully and poignantly captures the "Now" spirit of total hopelessness, despair, and bitterness: truly a memorable cry from a crushed soul!), we do not permit on campus any recruiters from the Army, Navy, Air Force, business firms associated with a product that may have military applications, organizations without blacks in executive positions, manufacturers of insecticides, industries that pollute air or water, or companies with unsatisfactory strike settlement records. It may be unnecessary to add that we do not have an ROTC chapter here.

In view of all the strides we have felt we were making, it is personally and professionally embarrassing to me to have to report that, since last Friday, I have been locked out of my office.

It is true that in the past I have voiced a certain amount of sympathy for students who feel they must resort to sit-ins. When appeals through established channels fail, and the provocation is sufficient, who can honestly condemn those who seek redress through means which, if not orthodox, serve to dramatize and ultimately alleviate the plight of the aggrieved?

However, this sit-in is not by students. It is, I am chagrined to say, by their mothers.

Not *all* the mothers of our students are taking part. But those who are involved are, I must say, behaving in a most unmotherlike way. They are trying to undo all the good we have done.

They have presented me with a list of *non-negotiable demands!* These include accredited courses given by teachers with professional training, periodic examinations, the grading of student performance, regular attendance of classes, basic reading requirements, and supervision of student conduct in accordance with what I can only describe as a neo-Victorian code. Have you ever heard of such a thing?

We have done our best to avoid publicity, but I am afraid the press now has the scent, and soon enough we may be swamped by the mass media. And who can tell what distortions will be spread?

At first, we were inclined to treat the matter as a joke, but these ladies are not to be taken lightly. Unfortunately, among their number are several members of the Women's Liberation Movement who are, to put it bluntly, formidable. Most of our students, however forcefully they may attack other targets, seem reluctant to tangle with their mothers, particularly mothers so aroused. Our campus Weatherman faction did press for a confrontation and was, to the surprise of many, routed with ridiculous ease . . . with umbrellas and hatpins!

We have tried to establish a dialogue with these mothers, but they have made it clear that they want to put an end to our *system.*

Mr. Wesley, what can we do? Do you think we should appeal to the Attorney General?

Sincerely,
Rutherford D. Haley

Morning

CLARA MANNHEIMER GLASSER

6:15 in gloom
Along the pie-crust beachline, where the eye
Delicately selects the firmest sand between
Rank mops of raggy seaweed, wrapping homely artifacts
Of Pabst cans, tinfoil, plastic cups
Along with shrimpboat markers,
Sea-swollen derelict slats sporting wicked nails.

Up there those paper silhouettes of gulls float
Like perfect peers of space. But,
I have seen them brake and land
Screaming cheap insults, voracious, adder-necked,
Not one of these a Jonathan.

Time for sunup
Where that sullen bloody ball on slate swells,
Flaring blond-on-rose,
An unbound sash unfurled
Waves westward.

Time in all the world to possess it all
Before the sleeping bags disgorge the Beachniks,
Crawling out from under dreams of home,
Shucking their jeanskins
And, holding high their surfing shields,
Assault the clotted foam, so rich in jellyfish,
Sea grape and men-of-war.

NOTE: This poem appeared in *Social Education*, April 1973, p. 291. Reprinted by permission of Clara Mannheimer Glasser.

I too divest myself, shucking to the salted air
A sense of self or solitude,
A bright thought I might have saved or clung to prayerfully
Had I a pen to note it. Where?
On my soiled greedy palm, tarred and sand-stuck
From scrabbling in effluence of broken shell,
Searching for one perfect form?

I let it go. It may return
As do the storm-marred conchs tossed back
To drag awhile by swell and tide,
Yet humbly wash ashore again, bedecked in coraline
Mutated and re-formed.

Time to go. One dawn I found a rarest cowrie shell
That in the past had served to buy a bride or ransom slaves.
Meanwhile, from this old taproot ocean
I have sucked more than my share
Of a whole new yellow day.

Jefferson's Document Needs Work

MIKE CAUSEY

Suppose the Founding Fathers assembled in Philadelphia to hammer out a new form of government had been forced to contend with a 1976-style bureaucracy? Chances are that instead of preparing for the July 4 Bicentennial, our biggest national holiday would be the Queen's Birthday.

For a glimpse of what-might-have-been, consider the following allegedly worked up by some fun-loving, but anonymous, type at the Agency for International Development. AID has one of the most talented collection of writers, editors, artists and photographers in government. Also, we got this free from them.

Somebody at AID, without the intestinal fortitude of John Hancock who signed his name, big, worked up this example of what Thomas Jefferson and company would face today, if they had to run a draft of a "Declaration of Independence" past bureaucrats, technocrats and lawyers for approval. This, the AID people say, is what Jefferson's rejection slip might read like:

"Dear Mr. Jefferson: We have read your 'Declaration of Independence' with great interest. Certainly, it represents a considerable undertaking, and many of your statements do merit serious consideration. Unfortunately, the Declaration as a whole fails to meet recently adopted specifications for proposals to the Crown, so we must return the document to you for further refinement. The questions which follow might assist you in your process of revision.

NOTE: This column appeared in *The Washington Post*, August 28, 1975. It was reprinted in *Social Education*, February 1976, p. 121. It is reprinted here by permission of *The Washington Post*.

"1. In your opening paragraph you use the phrase 'the laws of Nature and Nature's God.' What are the criteria on which you base your central arguments? Please document with citations from the recent literature.

"2. In the same paragraph you refer to the 'opinions of mankind.' Whose polling data are you using? Without specific evidence, it seems to us, the 'opinions of mankind' are a matter of opinion.

"3. You hold certain truths to be 'self-evident.' Could you please elaborate? If they are as evident as you claim, then it should not be difficult for you to locate the appropriate supporting statistics.

"4. 'Life, liberty and the pursuit of happiness' seem to be the goals of your proposal. These are not measurable goals. If you were to say that 'among these is the ability to sustain an average life expectancy in six of the 13 colonies of at least 55 years, and to enable all newspapers in the colonies to print news without outside interference, and to raise the average income of the colonists by 10 percent in the next 10 years,' these would be measurable goals. Please clarify.

"5. You state that 'whenever any Form of Government becomes destructive to these ends, it is the Right of the People to alter or to abolish it, and to institute a new Government. . . .' Have you weighed this assertion against all the alternatives? Or is it predicated solely on the base-instincts?

"6. Your description of the existing situation is quite extensive. Such a long list of grievances should precede the statement of goals, not follow it.

"7. Your strategy for achieving your goal is not developed at all. You state that the colonies 'ought to be Free and Independent States,' and that they are 'Absolved from all Allegiance to the British Crown.' Who or what must change to achieve this objective? In what way must they change? What resistance must you overcome to achieve the change? What specific steps will you take to overcome this resistance? How long will it take? We have found that a little foresight in these areas helps to prevent careless errors later on.

"8. Who among the list of signatories will be responsible for implementing your strategy? Who conceived it? Who provided theoretical research? Who will constitute the advisory committee? Please submit an organizational chart.

"9. You must include an evaluation design. We have been requiring this since Queen Anne's War.

"10. What impact will your program have? Your failure to include any assessment of this inspires little confidence in the long-range prospects of your undertaking.

"11. Please submit a PERT diagram, an activity chart, and an itemized budget.

"We hope these comments prove useful in revising your 'Declaration of Independence.'

"Best wishes, Lord North.

"P.S. Could you please enclose vitae of the signatories? We need them for our files.

"P.P.S. We note that you have not included a logical framework matrix listing underlying assumptions, and end of project conditions. Please submit with your revised paper."

Reflections on Time

Family

He stood at the top of the key with his arms high above his head. The ball came in to him at just the right angle, and he pivoted to the left and hooked a shot toward the basket. The ball rolled around the rim, hung there—and fell out. "Rebound!" shouted a frantic cheerleader. "Reeeeeebound!" He moved in fast, grabbed the ball in midair, faked with his shoulders, and sank his shot off the backboard. Roosevelt High School was in the lead again.

And you sat in the gymnasium and wondered when you would ever find the time to read Jean Piaget's *The Psychology of Intelligence* or the Ned Flanders/Anita Simon article on "Teacher Effectiveness" or the B. M. Morrison doctoral dissertation on "The Reactions of Internal and External Children to Patterns of Teaching Behavior" or the latest pronouncements of Jerome Bruner....

She rose on her toe in an Arabesque Penchée, glided gracefully into an Attitude Devant, and turned with all the joy and spirit of a developing young ballerina in the Melinda School of Ballet. It required little imagination to visualize her as a future Eurydice in *Orpheus* or a Sylvia in *Sylvia Pas de Deux* or even an Odette in *Swan Lake*.

And you sat in the ballet school and reminded yourself that, after you had read the Leo M. Franklin Memorial Lectures, you had intended

NOTE: These four vignettes appeared in *Social Education*, April 1973, p. 259 (Family); January 1974, pp. 3–4 (Reunion); October 1975, p. 343 (The N-Bus); and October 1979, pp. 408–409 (Have a Nice Day, François Villon). Reprinted by permission of Daniel Roselle.

to make an in-depth study of the points of view of historians Goldwin Smith of Wayne State University, A. L. Rowse of All Souls College, Oxford, and J. H. Hexter of Yale University. You had not done it. All that you needed was time . . . just time. . . .

She stood smiling shyly with the other Second Graders who were singing the Alphabet Song and waited impatiently for her turn. Then she grasped her hands tightly to the sides of her dress and sang: "'G' is for gardens—And flowers in a row; After a rain—You just watch them grow."

And you sat with the other parents on Visitors' Day and remembered that you still had not had the time to read Milton Klonsky's latest anthology of verse. James Agee's "Variation 4"; John Berryman's "185," "263," "149"; Jack Kerouac's "201st Chorus"; and Ian Hamilton Finlay's "XM Poem" would have to wait. Indefinitely? . . .

She handed you a shopping list with the advice that the Canned Fruit could be found in Aisle 3, Dry Cereal in Aisle 6, Paper Toweling in Aisle 8, and Premium Cat Food on the bottom shelves of Aisle 11. Then she wheeled her cart away and disappeared in search of Heads of Lettuce, Brussels Sprouts, and, if the Fates were kind, Lean Ground Beef.

And you pushed your own cart slowly down the aisles of the supermarket and recalled that you had not analyzed the latest data on concept formation in experiential instruction or affective determinants of psychosomatic policies or divergent and convergent elements of the interrogative process. And you knew that you must find the time to do so shortly. Time . . . always time . . .

But there was no time. You seemed to be living in a universe of chaos, not cosmos—a Giorgio de Chirico or Max Ernst world of metal braces on children's teeth, P.T.A. meetings in straight-backed chairs, stationwagons loaded with screaming children in bathing suits, and a room filled with once-precious but now burned out and irreplaceable minutes. No time at all.

And then one night you returned home very late from work and, just as you headed for the study and your books, a tiny voice fighting off sleep called out from the second-floor bedroom: "I stayed awake to say Good Night, Dad. Good Night!"

And you understood again why family is more important than time.

Reunion

My daily equation was time + ambition + pride = success. There were miniscule variations, of course, but in general the pattern of my behavior (I dislike the term "life style") was set. I arose at 6:10 AM exactly, listened to the 6:30 AM news report, caught the 7:25 AM bus, kept my 8:15 AM appointment for breakfast, and was at my desk promptly at 9:15 AM determined to make up for lost time. So it went every day—always a Vonnegutian time machine and never a Proustabout. The present was my soul concern, the past discarded, the future disregarded. I sought (and found in each day's ticking of the clock) not the ineffable of the ever but the measurable of the now. Call me Relevant Man, Ishmael, and can the nonsense about a great white whale.

And then one day "Smoky" Hamilton's newsletter for 1973 arrived and, by listing the names of one-time G.I.'s who had died, reminded me that I had not attended a reunion of the 30th Infantry Division Military Police Platoon for twenty-eight years. Time, he said by saying nothing, was getting short. Since the end of World War II in 1945, "Smoky" wrote, Torris Ashurst of Eatonton, Georgia, had died, and so had Mel Channell, Greensboro, Georgia; Mac Griffin, Ellijay, Georgia; Warren Jaudon and Otis Newton, Springfield, Georgia; Homer Johnston, Barnesville, Georgia; Mitchell Peak, Albany, Georgia; James McMillan, Hephzibah, Georgia; and others from towns like Leaf, Mississippi, and Paden City, West Virginia. Twenty-nine men in all, not counting anyone on the list of "Addresses Unknown."

So I said thehellwithit and took the morning plane out of Washington, D.C. to the reunion in Macon, Georgia, and enroute I drank champagne and picked up a magazine and read descriptions of the food in San Francisco restaurants ("*L'Odeon*—Lacy crystal chandeliers overhead, leopard carpeting and, on the table, Mediterranean marvels. Exotic Greek dishes of lamb or seafood, spectacular crepes dessert") but I (barbarian!) kept thinking only of tasting once again hot Georgia grits. H.L. Mencken was wrestling with Andy Griffith and losing, but by the time the plane reached Georgia, I did not give a damn about either of them.

Then Macon. I was carrying my suitcase up to the reunion motel when I ran into the first group of our men, six ex-G.I.'s whom I had not seen for over a quarter of a century: "Dude" Mullis, who had lost most of his hair and some of his teeth, but none of his wit; Joe Yelenosky, armed with a camera to record the new, and an extraordinary memory to recall the old; George Denton, his straw hat perched forward on his head just as he had worn his army cap when making assignments at the Command Post during the war; C.C. Burch, bigger than he had been the night he showed me how to patrol the beat in Boomtown and survive; Bob Lodi, an unreconstructed Yankee like myself, who had come all the way from Boston for the reunion; and "Smoky" Hamilton himself, who had kept the Platoon together through the years. All six of them were older, grayer, broader, different, and all of them were the same as they had always been.

And then came the wild handshaking and the slugging of backs and the patting of paunches and the drinking of beer and the remembering . . . EEE—YOW!

Remember Camp Blanding, where "Racehorse" Green and "Stem" Coogle would car-wrestle with the bumpers of their jeeps locked together like antler horns?

Remember Isigny, where John Sullivan calmly sipped Calvados and recited poetry while antipersonnel bombs ripped holes in our helmets?

Remember Cambrai, where Joe Peters, directing traffic at an intersection, waved a retreating German vehicle into line with an advancing American column, not knowing that it *was* German until it had moved down the road and been filled with bullets?

Remember Neuenkirchen, where Warren Jaudon and Fred Lee, after capturing one German in a haystack, decided to prod the hay with their rifles—and dug up 17 more?

Remember Paris and Dick Forrester's comment after a three-day pass to that city: "Three more days would have killed me!"

Most of the events were true, some were exaggerated, and a few had never happened at all. But there were infinite beers to drink at the motel and countless moments to relive and now-familiar faces everywhere, and after awhile it did not matter what was being said but only that we were hearing it together.

I do not know exactly when it happened (perhaps it was when "Smoky" was showing his slightly blurred films of past reunions and began to run them forward and backward), but somewhere between 11:86 PM and 1:92 AM I lost all sense of time. "Time present and time past are both perhaps present in time future, and time future contained in time past," T.S. Eliot had written, and I understood him far better now than in the days of Professor Tynan's seminar. Delicious timelessness—time without minutes, time without schedules, time without beginnings, time without ends, time reaching forward and backward and inside and outside and nowhere and everywhere. And with the death of structured time came the death of petty things: ambition, pride, success. And with the death of time came life.

This sense of timelessness stayed with me for the remainder of the Macon reunion: through the loud silences for those killed in action, through the ceremonial folding and packing of the Platoon banner, through the sweat-in-hand resolutions to keepintouchandwriteoftenand-visitifyougetachanceyounogoodbastard. It stayed with me during the return flight home. It would, I was certain, stay with me forever.

The next day I arose at 6:10 AM exactly, listened to the 6:30 AM news report, caught the 7:25 AM bus, kept my 8:15 AM appointment for breakfast, and was at my desk promptly at 9:15 AM determined to make up for lost time. It must have been close to noon when I could have sworn that I heard someone far away laughing at me—in a southern accent.

The N-9 Bus

The 6:55 A.M. N-9 bus leaves Montgomery Mall in Maryland promptly any time between the hours of 6:55 A.M. and 7:20 A.M. depending on the experience, sense of direction, and mood of the driver. Its destination is

Washington, D.C., and it carries on board about 40 passengers who, in general, are affluent, ambitious, and amiable. Except for Logan, who sits huddled against a window, his breath smelling of Old Forester, and who does not give a damn.

There is Harold the speechwriter and Morris the lawyer and Al the dentist and Shirley the chemist and Philip the physicist and Joan the economist and Frank the linguist and Bob the merchant and Marge the statistician and Wilson the engineer. And, of course, there is Logan, a musician who claims he has papers to prove that his ancestry goes back to one wild night between Orpheus and Eurydice, and who is sometimes seen carrying a whiskey-scented French horn under his arm.

But though they talk loudly about gasoline prices and other national disasters, or circulate Art Buchwaldian rumors about the football that President Ford keeps hidden in his desk, or rant at the madness of Arthur Burns' latest contradictory remarks about business cycles, each of the passengers sits alone. *Is* alone. And their isolation from each other is as marked as their pretense at unity.

The passengers in the N-9 bus sit surrounded by signs of loneliness: "No Smoking Please"—"Please do not talk to me while I am driving. Safe operation of this bus requires my full attention."—"Emergency Exit Instructions—Located in Center of Next Window"—"Super M Menthol 100's Hermetically Sealed in Airtight Packs"—"Air Force Jobs. Call 800-447-4700. Toll Free"—and, for the desperately lonely, "Come to Ringling and Barnum and Bailey Circus. Unparalleled!"

And as they sit alone they read alone: *The Washington Post, All Creatures Great and Small, The Bankers, The Wall Street Journal, The Eco-spasm Report*, and Tom Wicker's *A Time to Die* ("There's always a time to die," Herman Badillo said, "I don't know what the rush is.").

Meanwhile, the N-9 bus travels down Route 495 Beltway, turns off at Glen Echo, and, despite its rich cargo, moves along Canal Road with more of a Ken Kesey bounce that a Rockefeller rock. It rounds the corner at Key Bridge, weaves its way through Whitehurst Freeway, and comes down K Street in the District, where it merges with scores of other buses in the morning's traditional tangle of N-9 L-32 V-16 M-28 H-05 S-15.

Here the N-9 bus discharges its passengers in ones and twos and threes, and they disappear—alone—into the city in a flutter of swinging briefcases and tilting hats. The last words that they hear are forgettable for they are for the forgotten: "Have a good . . .," "Give 'em. . . .," and "See you." Except for Logan, who generally lurches out of the bus to the accompaniment of "Steady as she goes!"

Has Barbara Ward ever ridden on an N-9 bus? A scholar can be an omniscient passenger on a spaceship earth moving gracefully through a galaxy of spotlighted lecture platforms. But can she unite the passengers on *one* bus?

Did Arthur Eddington ever ride on an N-9 bus? A scientist can explore the intricacies of abstract structure. But can he achieve the unification of passengers by theories of relativity? (Has Logan ever heard of isomorpheme and intrinsotheme? Does he care?)

And when Eugène Ionesco dramatized the absurdity of the absurd (*Quelle est la morale? C'est à vous de la trouver.*), did he not also brutally widen the gap between passengers?

The N-9 bus. It all comes down to that. Unite the bus and then the town and then the state and then the world. But first the bus.

And then one day it happened. At 6:55 on Wednesday morning, September 3, 1975, there was no noise on the N-9 bus. No shouting. No reading. No laughing. Most important, no separateness. Each passenger sat silently and in that silence merged with all the rest and in that merging formed a common bond and in that bond brought an end to isolation. The passengers on the N-9 bus were united at last.

A whisper did it.

"Logan died last night," one passenger whispered to the next, "Logan died."

Lo-gan d-i-e-d.

That was the way the passengers on the N-9 bus learned the only thing in the world that bound them and all human beings together. And, although they were frightened, they were lonely no longer.

Have a Nice Day, François Villon

François de Moncorbier, better known as François Villon—vagabond, thief, and poet—was born in Paris, France in 1431, the same year that Joan of Arc was burned at the stake; and, as far as anyone knows, he is still alive today. That is to say, there is no record of Villon's death; and, adhering to the importance of statistical confirmation of human behavior, I am tempted to give him the benefit of the doubt. Thus, setting aside the logic of Burckhardt, Haskins, and Huizinga, it can be said that Villon lives! (Is this fantasy too tolkien to be talked about? Very well, then, modify it: Villon lives, if not in flesh, at least in spirit.)

As a student, I first met François Villon as he faced the gallows for an unspeakable, if unspecified, crime against the criminal; and I heard his voice in these lines:

> Frères humains qui après nous vivez,
> N'ayez les cuers contre nous endurcis,
> Car, se pitié de nous povres avez,
> Dieu en aura plus tost de vous mercis.
>
> Vous nous voiez cy attachez cinq, six;
> Quant de la chair, que trop avons nourrie,
> Elle est pieça devorée et pourrie,
> Et nous, les os, devenons cendre et pouldre.

De nostre mal personne ne s'en rie;
Mais priez Dieu que tous nous vueille absouldre.

(Brother men who live after us, do not harden your hearts against us, for if you have pity on us poor sinners, God will sooner have mercy on you. You see us hanging here, five, six; as for the flesh, which we fed too well, it has long ago been eaten and rotted, and we, the bones, are becoming powder and dust. Let no one laugh at our affliction, but pray to God that he should absolve us all.)

And I, who could trace my ethical ancestry back to the prophet who had raised the Tablets on the Mount, was affronted by Villon's words. Why had he called me brother? Why had he sought absolution for me? Why had he expected me to feel a sense of unity with him?

As a teacher, I felt the presence of Villon next during mandatory study of the Thirty Years War, when, condemned by the political decisions of the Holy Roman Emperor, King Christian IV, Gustavus Adolphus, and the incomparable Wallenstein, thousands of human beings were slaughtered in the name of religion. For just a moment, I thought I saw the shadow of François Villon as he mourned for the victims and wept and cried out: "Frères humains! Frères humains!" But I did not understand the meaning of his words.

Then, as a novice biographer exploring the records of Salem, Massachusetts, I caught a glimpse of Villon again during the 1692 witchcraft trial of Bridget Bishop, charged with causing a sow to have fits, with bewitching money into disappearing, and with having upon her body a preternatural teat that disappeared in three hours. When they hanged her, Villon, mingling like a madman with the crowd, could not be restrained. "We are one!" he screamed. "We are one!" But I heard his words without listening to them.

I do not know why it took me so long to understand what Villon was saying. Almost a decade. Perhaps it was because of the widespread acceptance of Robert Ardrey's twentieth-century absurdity that human beings are predators whose natural impulse is to kill, which, even if it were true, is not the point at all. The key to human behavior is not that some human beings kill and maim and destroy; or that when they do not, life itself serves as implacable Inquisitor. *The significant point is that misery—however tragic it may be—is still a basic factor uniting all human beings.* Villon was right. Misery—cold, hard, universal—is often more binding than joy—warm, soft, individual, so ephemeral that, lest we forget, it must be marked in red on calendars or celebrated by the glow of painted candles. Misery "Frères humains!"

Listen to the words of Hans Castorp in *The Magic Mountain* as he struggles to come to terms with life and death: "Now I know that it is not out of our single souls we dream. We dream anonymously and communally, if each after his fashion." Precisely. And life (no dream by any measure!) shapes and patterns our realities not through tinselled, individual, Hallmarked pleasures, but through the miseries that every human being must inevitably face in every generation—anonymously and communally. We are one because we are not one.

I wish that American students could be taught this fact, particularly those in suburbia. I wish that their world could transcend the Saturday morning superheroes on T.V.; the jingle of BurgerkingandI; the shifts in hair styles and TransAms; the paper streamers fluttering in the trees after varsity victory; the Student Government debate on whether to hold the all-school prom in the gym or at the Hilton; the pursuit of individual pleasures which, however joyous they may be, lead only to new pursuits. I wish that the illusion of technique did not take precedence over the core of Being. I wish that American students today were different from the students of my own generation. I wish.

Why do some educators and many parents filter out the darkness, rather than the light? Why do they assume that the good society can be developed only by focusing on individual pleasures, rather than on harsh realities common to all human beings? Why do they shield children from unpleasant facts that could be their best defenses? Why do they not see that unity comes by understanding that while joys are particularistic and temporal, sorrows—and ultimate human destiny—are universal and cannot be assuaged by soothing imperatives to "Have a nice day!" Why can't they understand this?

John Cheever understands it today, although some of his characters do not; Steinbeck came close in *The Grapes of Wrath*; and even pragmatic Lincoln had to resort to a quotation from *Macbeth* to universalize experience. It took Douglas Wertheimer to suggest that ultimate unity can be derived from ultimate tragedy. Remember?

> Let not the atom bomb
> Be the final sequel
> In which all men
> Are cremated equal.

Please do not misunderstand. I am not demeaning or denouncing popular pleasures. Indeed, I derive a kind of morbid pleasure of my own from wondering whether the Love Boat will sink during its next cruise, carrying to the bottom of the sea all those smiling teeth of the captain and his staff; and, late in the month, I am not averse to ordering an occasional Big Mac, although I am still somewhat embarrassed when compelled to identify ground meat as an old pal o' mine.

If, however, we seek to develop a society and a world in which human relationships are based on more than fantasies, we will have to recognize and accept the realities of human existence. The myth of Sisyphus is a myth—but not to Sisyphus. Have a nice day? No. Have a day? That's more like it!

V.

Freedom and the Crucible of Dissent

THE HISTORY OF DISSENT reaches far into the past. Plato dissented from the prevalent view of the value of Homer. Plutarch expressed negative opinions about the achievements of Herodotus. Handel preferred his cook's counterpoint to that of Gluck. And Debussy disagreed with those who liked the piano music of Beethoven.

Censorship, too, has a long history. In 1918 the U.S. War Department withdrew seventy-seven books from circulation in the military camps. Twenty-five years ago the writings of J. D. Salinger, George Orwell, Thomas Mann, and John Steinbeck were already being attacked, as was *The Good Earth* by Pearl Buck. And today the contents of some children's books and school books are being severely criticized.

This section of the anthology presents articles on "Freedom and the Crucible of Dissent." A reading of the selections demonstrates that, whether they occurred in the past or in the present, disputes about freedom of expression and thought raise similar questions on the rights and responsibilities of human beings.

In the first selection, "A Study in Censorship: Good Concepts and Bad Words," Harold Rugg, who was on the faculty of Teachers College, Columbia University, writes: "Although six to eight million Americans have buzzed with questions about Rugg and his books since 1939, the entire phenomenon is a record of controversies initiated and kept alive by a few hitherto unknown persons standing in strategic places and with access to powerful national means of communication and community action." Why, asks Rugg, citing an instance of censorship, can one teach "America—a land of opportunity," but not "America—a land of opportunity for many, but not a land of opportunity for all"? Rugg's conclusion—that to keep issues out of the school program is to keep thought out of it—is as boldly presented as the red carnation he often wore in his lapel when teaching.

In his work Merle Curti of the University of Wisconsin, Madison, combined the best attributes of the scholar with those of the teacher. Thus, his achievements were recognized not only by a Pulitzer Prize for his book *The Growth of American Thought* but also by numerous accolades for his coauthorship of a best-selling textbook on American history. In "The Responsibility of the Teacher in Times of Crisis," Curti poses a difficult question: What is our responsibility to our country and to the canons of our craft if there is conflict between these canons as we understand them and the demands of patriotism? His answer brought forth a variety of favorable and unfavorable responses from the readers of *Social Education*.

In "Dilemmas of a Textbook Writer," Henry Wilkinson Bragdon, coauthor with Samuel P. McCutchen of the highly successful textbook *History of a Free People*, candidly presents an author's views of what happened in the writing and development of one textbook in American history. According to Bragdon, "the care and feeding" of the textbook became his principal occupation. His analysis of his experiences and the extent of his freedom with Publishers, Patriots, Pedagogy, and Conscience makes clear that certain widely held beliefs about textbooks, textbook publishers, and textbook authors may have to be revised.

In April 1970 United States and Vietnamese troops entered Cambodia. According to American officials, the primary purpose of this "incursion" was to attack North Vietnamese supply depots that were located there. Deeply concerned that such actions might widen the war, college students on many campuses participated in antiwar protests. On May 4, during the confusion of a demonstration, four students at Kent State University in Ohio were killed when a National Guard unit opened fire.

Harris L. Dante was chairman of the Faculty Senate at Kent State University from April 1, 1969 to September 1, 1970. Thus, he was in close contact with events on the campus, and his comments in his article, "The Kent State Tragedy: Lessons for Teachers," are based on personal observation and intimate knowledge of the situation. At the 1970 Commencement of the university in June, Professor Dante, reflecting on the events that he discusses, declared: "This convocation is indeed a commencement—a beginning of a new era for all of us who are identified with and have affection for and loyalty to Kent State University."

In 1982, Murry R. Nelson and Patrick Ferguson, representing *Social Education*, asked the following questions:

- Is it proper to prohibit high school students from reading certain books?
- Should instructional materials used by teachers reflect the dominant views of the community?

The responses of Jack Anderson, nationally syndicated columnist; Max Hocutt, who served as chairman of the department of philosophy at the University of Alabama; John Irving, author; Ruth B. Love, then general superintendent of schools, Chicago Board of Education; Newton N. Minow, former chairman of the Federal Communications Commission; and Leo M. Yambrek, a member of Eagle Forum who was instrumental in convincing the Alabama Board of Education to remove six social studies textbooks from an adoption list, reflect a variety of points of view. *Social Education* thus provided its readers with another opportunity to choose from several strongly held and conflicting positions.

A Study in Censorship:
Good Concepts and Bad Words

Harold Rugg

I have read Dr. Anderson's article in the January, 1941, issue of this magazine with great interest and agreement. Since my own work has been one of the chief targets for the attack of the self-appointed censors in the schools I should like to generalize and extend Dr. Anderson's discussion a bit, supplying some additional factual details. But first I wish to join him in a categorical denial of the ridiculous charges made against teachers and writers in the social studies. There is not the slightest vestige of truth in them. It is to be regretted that a situation can be built up in our country in which it becomes necessary to deny charges of this kind. I do so only after years of silence and at the urgent request of teachers, colleagues, and friends. Those who know me and those who *have* read and understood my books—and these include tens of thousands of students and teachers and parents who have used them for almost twenty years—know that the statements made against them do not describe my philosophy or my work.

The present attack on liberalism in education is not the first of its kind. It is true that this one is nation-wide, more virulent, and promises to last longer and to set back the work of the schools more than any previous one. But it *has* happened before. Five times since the World War a wave of censorship has rolled up on the schools.

As I write there stands behind me a four-foot shelf of manufactured conflict about "un-Americanism" in the schools. It is a twenty-year documentary record—newspaperclippings ... articles and cartoons from

NOTE: This article appeared in *Social Education*, March 1941, pp. 176–181.

national magazines ... scrap-books and folders ... pamphlets, bulletins, and official reports ... chapters clipped from books ... transcriptions of records of hearings and court actions ... stenographic records of Hearst newspaper interviews ... and whatnot.

Does it indicate nation-wide popular protest? It does not. Although six to eight million Americans have buzzed with questions about Rugg and his books since 1939, the entire phenomenon is a record of controversies initiated and kept alive by a few hitherto unknown persons standing in strategic places and with access to powerful national means of communication and community action.

Let there be no doubt about the general staff of the patrioteers now invading education. Eight hitherto unknown persons of almost no prestige or influence have made the attack and are artificially keeping it alive:

1. Merwin K. Hart, of Utica, New York, and New York City; executive of his personally organized New York State Economic Council.

2. Bertie C. Forbes, of Englewood, New Jersey, and New York City; for many years a columnist for the Hearst newspapers, and publisher of his own magazine, *Forbes*.

3. Major Augustin G. Rudd, of Garden City, Long Island, New York; former U. S. Army man, business executive, and active in the American Legion.

4. E. H. West, of Haworth, New Jersey, and New York City; business executive; active in the American Legion; zealot for rooting out "un-Americanism" in the schools.

5. Major General Amos A. Fries, of Washington, D.C.; retired U. S. Army man; editor of *Friends of the Public Schools*, a periodic bulletin frequently attacking the work of certain public schools.

6. Elizabeth Dilling, of Kenilworth, Illinois; wealthy author and publisher of *The Red Network*; lecturer on "Un-Americanism" and the danger of communistic tendencies in America; one of the chief "stirrer-uppers" of tension and suspicion.

These few persons make up the spearhead of the present attack on the schools. To them must be added at least two professional writers who have written and published articles against the schools in national mass-circulation magazines:

1. George E. Sokolsky, of New York City; wrote three articles in *Liberty* in 1940, reaching millions of readers and causing unrest and suspicion about the schools.

2. O. K. Armstrong, of Springfield, Missouri; active in the American Legion; writer of "Treason in the Textbooks," which appeared in the *American Legion Magazine*, in September, 1940.

The influence of these persistent enemies of liberalism working alone as individuals would no doubt have been insufficient to stir up suspicion the country over. But their present success is due in large part to the fact that they have had access to the facilities of national agencies, the principal ones being:

1. The Hearst newspapers with their affiliated syndicated features, reaching many millions of readers, daily and weekly.

2. National patriotic organizations with memberships totalling several millions.

3. Several of the largest and most powerful national business organizations with vast sums of money set aside to carry on such kind of "reform" work.

4. The American Parents Committee on Education formed by Hart, Rudd, *et al.* in the spring of 1940. Their office distributes reprints of articles and other materials dealing with liberalism in the schools.

In spite of the provincial nature and influence of these individuals—I suspect nobody regards them as competent students of American civilization or public opinion—they have succeeded in stirring up unrest in hundreds of communities and fear in thousands of teachers and administrators. I have explicit proof of this—from actual personal participation in several community controversies; from the written and spoken statements of teachers, administrators, and citizens interested in the schools; from histories back of the elimination of the Rugg and other books and of *Scholastic* and other magazines; and from school administrators' and teachers' confidential communications—"they must sit tight" until "things blow over" and "get less hysterical."

Good Concepts and Bad Words

Almost from the beginning of my work in preparing school materials it was evident that to get a sound and clear description of society into the school required more than my own capacity to understand that society myself and to write it clearly and with the greatest possible objectivity. It required parents' cooperation in helping to build understanding in our young people. Would they give it? Would other citizens, especially those of the community who have prestige and leadership, go along with us on the idea? Could they be brought to see the importance of young people confronting social conditions and issues squarely and digging to the very roots of our changing culture?

As the years passed, I became more and more convinced that democracy could not survive the attacks upon it unless young Americans came to a thorough understanding of the world in which they were living. The democratic process in America, I was sure, could not be guaranteed unless our youth were introduced to the full story—the deficiencies as well as the achievements of our society, the problems and issues as well as the narrative of adventure. Would adults in the community share this view?

It was not long before we found out. Throughout the years thousands of parents have read the books along with their children. Reports from them have come continuously, and these show that they themselves have become aware of the urgency of having a real description of society in the schools. It is not these who have voiced the protest against the ideas presented. It is the small group of self-appointed censors, to whom I have referred. They took it upon themselves to criticize the content, approving some ideas and some words and condemning others, all in terms of their own interests, prejudices, and philosophy. Increasingly we saw that certain indispensable ideas came to be the nub of the attack. These ideas I have called "the good concepts" and "the bad words." The table on the following page illustrates some of them.

Were these ideas, these concepts, dangerous to youth, as the critics said? In the light of twenty years of documentation these are my conclusions concerning them:

First, every concept in both lists is indispensable to a real understanding of American life—the country's magnificent achievements, its vast potentiality for an abundant physical and spiritual life, certainly; but also its deficiencies and problems. All are needed that men may understand.

Second, the ideas listed on the left called "Good Concepts" arouse no opposition at all. The patrioteers as well as the merchants of conflict think they are grand; in fact they constitute the bulk of their own verbal stock-in-trade. America to them is portrayed only in these terms.

Third, the concepts listed on the right, called "Bad Words," simply can not be introduced into the school, in any form, without arousing the bitter opposition of certain special- interest groups—persons like Miller of the 1921–1926 witch-hunt and the Forbes-Hart-Rudd-West combination of today. It can be seen from my story that although these persons are very few in number and inconsiderable in prestige, they are powerful in influence. They can and do try to prevent materials that speak "the bad words" from being used. Furthermore, the ideas are such that they can not be camouflaged with "good words." The ideas must be made clear, and as soon as they are, no matter how phrased, they become "bad"—"subversive," "un-American," "poisonous," "treason"—or whatnot.

Fourth, the evidence is clear that the preponderance of our thinking citizens who do not have personal axes to grind by censoring the schools are actually well-disposed toward having all of the indispensable ideas for understanding presented to their children. Indeed, after studying the problem, they welcome—no, insist on—it. I draw a clear line, therefore, between the vast body of reasonable and well-intentioned citizens and the little corporal's guard of self-appointed censors of the schools.

Some "Good Concepts"	Some "Bad Words"
American life—a high standard of living.	America, highest standard of living in the world and potentially a land of plenty, is, compared to its potentialities, a depressed society.
The individual should have full liberty of action to make the most of himself.	"My freedom stops where my neighbor's, or the public's, good begins."
America—a land of opportunity with a ladder of opportunity for those who compete, work hard, and persist.	America, a land of great opportunity for many, but—today not of equal opportunity for all.
The American system of free enterprise.	Free competition balanced by government controls over economic enterprise for the general welfare.
The Founding Fathers—brilliant and devout patriots.	The Founding Fathers, brilliant and devout patriots—men of property who made a constitution difficult to change.
The free play of private ownership.	Private ownership except where public ownership is necessary to guarantee public welfare.
Unrestricted freedom to develop natural resources.	In parts of America land and people were exploited, eroded, and wasted by too uncontrolled freedom.
Scientific management in industry.	Accelerating technological unemployment.
The American constitution one of the world's greatest state papers of democratic government.	The "economic determination of the Constitution."
Democracy as the American way of life. Initial swift development of the continent a magnificent achievement, but necessarily not planned.	The characteristics of socialism, communism, and fascism compared with those of democracy. To prevent the recurring break-down of the economic system it must be planned.
Resourceful people, each looking out for himself. A sense of equality, absence of class lines among the people. "I'm as good as you."	Our people exhibit vast individual differences, energy, intelligence, ambition, and other traits.

"You Can't Say That!"

The lists deserve careful study. Note that one can talk about the "free play of private enterprise," but not about "controlling the free play of private enterprise in the public interest."

One can describe the founding fathers as "brilliant and devout patriots" but not as "the founding fathers, brilliant and devout patriots, men of property who made the Constitution difficult to change."

One can praise the Constitution as "one of the world's greatest state papers," but one can not say or imply any "economic determination of the Constitution," even though the monographs of Charles A. Beard and others are now accepted as valid documentary evidence.

One can teach "America—a land of opportunity," but not "America—a land of opportunity for many, but not a land of equal opportunity for all"—even though proof that it isn't glares at us from 10,000 communities and 10,000,000 poverty-stricken families.

One can speak of "scientific management in industry"; but "technological unemployment"—that's bad! I need not go on; the reader can multiply the examples manyfold.

It becomes clearer and clearer, then, just what the liberal-baiters will not have in the schools. They will not have (1) anything that even approaches a questioning of the complete purity of motives and behavior of the founders of our country or the leaders of the past; (2) anything that questions contemporary American life; (3) anything that presents negative aspects of American history or development; (4) anything that portrays social change; and (5) anything that deals with controversy. "Such things must not be brought into the school!" they say. These guardians of "everything rosy" know well, of course, that our young people are confronted with striking examples of social change every day of their lives. They themselves engage in the discussion of matters of controversy in public and private life. As for the deficiencies in American life, it is hardly necessary to remind ourselves of the fact that youth's eyes and minds are open to evidences of them on every side—in their homes, on the streets, in the playgrounds, in the movies, wherenot; they read and hear about them in the newspapers and magazines, and over the radio. But, say the attackers, our young people may not talk about such things in the classroom, shouldn't even think about them. They must not question American life, its heroes of the past or present. The function of education is to build in youth an admiration for things-as-they-are. The school is to be used to buttress the *status quo.*

The first lesson that I learned, then, from the self-appointed censors in our schools was that in dealing with the materials of education one must distinguish sharply between the Good Concepts and the Bad Words. Even the good concepts become bad words, of course, in the minds of the attackers.

How to Introduce the "Bad Words"?

The second lesson deals with the question which then faced us: How shall we handle the ideas called "The Bad Words"? They can not be camouflaged; they must be clarified. One step in this direction is the launching of a vigorous campaign of adult education. The local community leaders, along with superintendents, principals, and teachers, must take the chief responsibility and carry the community along in advance of the use of controversial issues in the schools. If the study of the ideas underlying the culture is undertaken by the adult population there will be no fears about them or rebellion against them, because the people will have come to understand.

The other step must be taken by the teachers, curriculum organizers, and writers of the materials. They must make meticulous distinction between "history" and "hypothesis." Some concepts are so firmly established and so fully documented by research data that they can be taught as history. On the soundness of these the total body of historians stand, a solid phalanx of support. Other concepts and generalizations, while confirmed by some buttressing evidence, still do not command the full support of all the competent students of society. Where there is still some doubt about their validity, the tentative conclusions must be recognized and deliberately pointed out in the text of the materials. Those which have been established by history should have all the supporting evidence in place.

With regard to the hypothetical concepts, they too must be brought into the school, but must be presented as hypotheses, with all evidence for and against included. They must be introduced as questions and treated as problems for investigation and thorough discussion of all sides. These are the concepts which frighten the timid soul and enrage the representatives of special interest groups which feel that they are being attacked.

Thus it seems to us that the distinction between fact and theory, history and hypothesis, becomes increasingly clear to young people if so presented in the materials for study.

Shall We Have Controversial Issues in the Schools?

Another example of the content that the patrioteers will not permit in the schools is that which deals with controversial issues and problems. It is my thesis that if we are to have consent in a democratic people it must be built upon the study of controversial issues, because such study is the intellectual foundation of the schools. One of the chief planks of my program is that the young people shall be urged constantly to *take thought before they take sides*, but it is obvious that to "take thought," to make choices, they must confront the alternatives set out clearly before them. How else can human beings practice decision-making than by confronting issues! *To keep issues out of the school program is to keep thought out of it.* Issues are the very nub of the psychology of consent. Indeed, the psychology of learning inevitably leads to the conclusion that the whole intellectual program of the school must be organized around issues if the school itself is to be a practicing democracy.

Of course, I am not unmindful of the fact that most human events are to a certain extent episodes in censorship. The very nature of the development of personality in social groups tends to bring that about. The culture itself, by virtue of the child's membership in certain face-to-face groups (such as being born into a family of given political-economic-social-religious orientation, and growing up in similarly "censored" play groups, school and church groups, whatnot)—the culture itself, I say, presents to him a definitely censored world. But this is naive censorship, the kind of limitation which is inherent in heterogeneous groups of multitudinous and varied pressures.

We recognize also that there is a kind of conscious, deliberate censorship in times of crisis, which can be justified as being "in the public interest." It is imposed for the public good by officials elected for the purpose. They are subject to recall by the general body of electors whenever the need disappears. This kind of deliberate censorship is not opposed to democratic government in action, though its constructive usefulness does depend upon the wisdom, competence, and honesty and personal disinterestedness of the censors.

Censorship and Social Danger

Finally a brief word about the question of censorship. Let us not fail to discriminate clearly between censorship and the proper expression of the opinions of any group of our people concerning what shall be taught in the schools. There is no opposition to the latter; in fact, active interest and expression on the part of all citizens in the education of their children should be encouraged. I hold that true democracy can not be carried on unless such expression is actually heard from all sectors of the population. From *all sectors,* I repeat. Throughout twenty years of making new social science materials for the schools this has been my guiding principle.

But to censor is to withhold. It is for one sector of the population, by virtue of its prestige and power, and hence its control over the agencies of communication, to withhold data needed for the total group to carry on social life efficiently and cooperatively. Whereas to propagandize is positively to *distort* the data that are necessary for group decisions and the enhancement of social welfare, to censor is to withhold such data altogether. As Lippmann has well phrased it: it is to erect a barrier between the event and the public. It is to transform a public event into a private one. It is the artificial creation of privacy.

The Truly Subversive Enemies of Democracy

But for minority groups to attempt to censor the citizen's world in a democratic society, and particularly in a time of crisis, is a matter fraught with great danger. It is to destroy the only instrument which can make democracy work. So I say to the self-appointed censors of education: Censor the schools and you convict yourselves by your very acts as the most subversive enemies of democracy. Censor education and you destroy understanding . . . you instate bias . . . you give free reign to prejudice . . . finally, you create fascism. Nothing but an education in the whole of American life will build tolerant understanding in our people and guarantee the perpetuation of democracy.

The Responsibility of the Teacher in Times of Crises

MERLE CURTI

Freedom of inquiry, of publication, of discussion, and of teaching have been suppressed in totalitarian states. They tend to be controlled—and that means a degree of suppression—in any country during a war. In the long run, or the final balance, do teachers serve best in times of crisis by becoming frank propagandists, surrendering our freedom and abandoning our critical and scholarly procedures, or by trying to maintain, to the extent that any human beings can, our independence and our professional techniques?

The present emergency is neither the first nor the only one in the history of modern civilization. But the present emergency is, unquestionably, a very grave one. It has made itself felt in every American city and hamlet. Tensions have become sharpened. Passions now run high—and threaten to break all dams as the crisis deepens.

It is already clear that the emergency has directly affected the mood and the conditions of our teaching. In *Minersville School District v. Gobitis* the Supreme Court has declared that no minority has any legal, or, for that matter, moral, right to reject any provisions whatever, wise or foolish, which the state makes for the promotion of patriotism and national unity. New propagandas knock at the classroom door—more subtly disguised than the propagandas with which we have wrestled in academic exercises. The problem of maintaining even some part of objectivity, of dispassionate analysis, of calm and honest thinking, has already become difficult, and every sign points to the likelihood that it will become yet harder in the days ahead.

Some, indeed, have in effect already said that any effort to be neutral before the issue of war and peace, of the American in contrast to competing ways of life, is little short of treason. But many of us still feel that

NOTE: This article appeared in *Social Education*, April 1941, pp. 251–254. Reprinted by permission of Merle Curti.

the social studies teacher must find some way to promote the larger national purposes and yet at the same time keep a free mind, to search no less patiently for the facts, to analyze their meaning with no less dispassion. This is our dilemma. How, under what circumstances, can it be resolved? What is our duty? What is our responsibility to our country and to the canons of our craft if there is conflict between these canons as we understand them and the demands of patriotism? What should we try to do? What are we apt to be permitted to do?

I have no final answers to these questions. But I do think that we must at the outset face certain facts—and I choose the word deliberately. But facts and faiths are never entirely divorced. Let me, therefore, first express an act of faith—but an act of faith in support of which as an historian I could marshal plenty of facts.

To begin with, I reassert my faith that a free mind, and freedom itself, are still important ends. Many, impressed by the crying need for a greater measure of both personal and national security, have insistently urged that freedom is only a means to a more important end—security, abundance, and what has been so often, and so vaguely, called the American way of life. These people argue that we may under certain conditions set aside freedom as a means of attaining the good life. According to them we may do so if it jeopardizes the end of security, whether social or, in a larger sense, national. We have heard the argument (and how plausible it is!) that the amount of freedom possible in any situation is directly related to the amount of security: if economic lines are not tightly drawn, if there is a good measure of security in the shape of jobs, credits and national safety, then freedom will flow like water from a bounteous spring; and that, on the other hand, when this general security is in hazard, then freedom contracts.

I defer to no one in my conviction that we must indeed have, if we are to live, vastly more security than the masses of our people have enjoyed, and than any nation has felt. I disavow any sympathy for those privileged interests which, in the name of liberty, seek only to consolidate their own blessings while letting the rank and file of plain people shift for themselves as best they can. But I am also convinced that if we forfeit freedom—by which I mean, roughly, the civil liberties—as a means to a larger and better life, we are endangering the goal of any true security. We are also risking freedom—one among other values—as an end. Does not the experience of all the totalitarian countries prove that much at least?

Let me put this in other words. We have, as a group, long debated the issue of subject matter versus method in the social studies. Most of us have come to agree that each is important—that, indeed, each is indispensable and that the two are inseparable. Emphasizing method alone is conducive to superficial verbiage. Subject matter as such comes dangerously near being useless information. Likewise in the larger world of social and economic actualities the forces themselves and the methods of controlling them are each of indispensable importance in the grand scheme of things.

Let us, however, suppose that an emergency arises in which it is necessary to give priority either to the content in the large social framework, or to the methods by which this content is to be understood and directed. We may well be asked, in order to save democracy, to sacrifice the method of freedom of inquiry, of tolerance of an opposition that threatens to destroy all democratic values, including the free mind itself. We will be told that in this sacrifice and this alone lies salvation. We are in fact already being told that if democracy is to survive in a terribly, brutally hostile world, its friends must submit to discipline, to restraint, for the ultimate security of democracy itself. If we enter fully or in part into the rapidly world-engulfing war we shall surely be told that we must abandon, for the time, the fact-searching, critical mind: that we must denounce all that opposes, or seems to oppose, what is being done by majority will at the moment. This is abandoning method for the subject matter. The subject matter—in this case democracy—will, of course, be emotionally charged as a highly desirable good struggling for its very existence.

I submit that such a choice is one fraught with grave dangers to democracy itself. I submit that, in such a dilemma, in such a crisis, the means, freedom, is even more important than the end, democracy; for democracy grows only out of freedom. Moreover a static democracy, in the world we have, is a contradiction in terms. Such democracy as we have could hardly have been achieved without the method of freedom, without keeping open the channels of inquiry, of communication, of scope for trial and error, of adaptation to new situations. Only by preserving the method of freedom to meet new situations in a volcanic world can we prevent crystallization—only by the method of freedom can we insure growth. And without growth democracy can have no life.

At one time I should have said that the amount of freedom of inquiry and discussion possible in any society is directly proportional to the amount of economic security. In view of what seems to be taking place in the totalitarian lands I must dissent from my own earlier conviction: for freedom does not seem necessarily to have followed in the wake of such economic security as Russians and Germans appear to enjoy. And in view of what is happening in England I feel compelled still further to revise my earlier views. All the world knows that England is desperately insecure—that she is fighting against tremendous odds for the means of life, indeed for her very existence. Yet the value of free inquiry and discussion is so ingrained, apparently, in the culture that the universities have not been muzzled. Conscientious objectors have not been hounded and tortured: indeed, it even appears that they have been permitted to teach in English schools on condition of not advocating in the classrooms a doctrine that would reflect on the brothers and fathers of school children. In other words, what England is doing seems to prove that even in times of great personal and national insecurity a considerable measure of freedom is possible. It seems to be possible if it is sufficiently well-rooted as a value in the culture, just as it is impossible for freedom to accompany security—personal or national—where its roots do not reach deeply into the culture. Now education is, of course, only one factor in the making and transmission of cultures. It reflects the material bases of the culture—but it also changes and conditions it in so far as it selects and emphasizes certain values existing in the culture at the expense of certain contrary values.

As teachers of the social studies we have responded to certain values in our culture, because we believe them to be a necessary part of democracy. It is now our major responsibility to hold to the canons of our craft—to maintain an open and inquiring mind, dispassionate analysis, sanity, and a reasonably honest adherence to the rules of the game in the democratic process of give and take. It is our responsibility to do our utmost to combat influences which make these things impossible. We must do so now, while there is yet time, if there is time. And we must furthermore do all in our power to help our pupils and each other to think—not merely to feel. If we are not willing to do this, or at least to try to do it, then we must confess that the democratic conception—and I may say the scientific conception—of human nature to which many of us have all along held has been wrong, and the totalitarian one right. For while admitting the power of irrational instincts and drives in what we call human nature, we could hardly have achieved our present state—with its infinite beauty and its infinite brutality—had we not possessed the power to solve problems with the aid of past experience, in other words, to think rationally. And this small but precious rationality is like a tender flower which can only survive and grow in soil which is not given over to rank weeds. It can not grow in a soil of irrationality, of emotion, of hysteria, of obedient acceptance of mere authority, even if invoked in the name of security.

To be concrete, what can we as teachers of the social studies do beyond trying our best to keep faith with the highest ideals of our craft when the odds are greatly against us? We can, for one thing, strengthen our faith by recalling in how many instances patriotism has been merely a cloak for insuring the maintenance of a status quo. We can, in pondering on Mr. Justice Frankfurter's majority opinion in the Minersville flag-saluting case, ask ourselves and others, to what end such discipline? Is it to preserve and strengthen the best, or the least desirable elements in our national traditions? One method we might try is this. We can, in our classrooms, consciously present highly emotional situations, in which, of course, our students will fail to think. We can then, by questions and class discussion, help them to see how and why they failed to think.

Such a Socratic method is, it seems to me, of vast importance; for whatever thinking is to be done on public issues will no doubt have to be done in a highly emotional setting.

By some such methods and in various other ways we can do better than we have done the job of helping young Americans to love America as a democracy. This can not be done by making blind conformists or blind enthusiasts of them, nor by instilling into them devotion to any status quo under the mask of devotion to national security nor even by drawing a veil over our national sins. We can, without betraying the method, at least, of the social studies, emphasize with renewed conviction all that is best in American life—and, moreover, all that is best in the promise of American life. And that, I think, includes continual emphasis on freedom as a method, as well as freedom and security as ultimate ends. It is certainly our sacred responsibility to give no sanction to the totalitarian doctrine that the state can do no wrong. We must train our boys and girls to be thinking citizens of a growing democracy.

But freedom as a method does involve discipline. It involves responsibilities. To achieve democratic discipline we need not accept Archibald MacLeish's indictment of the awakened writers who taught us to regard the last war as a mistake and a calamity. But we must, in and out of season, ask carefully and tirelessly what effects given positions on social questions are apt to have, and are having on the purposes and values which they are alleged to possess. Our responsibility is to discipline ourselves by refusing to accept at face value what the majority is saying—or what dominant pressure groups are saying for the majority. If there are saboteurs among us—those who use their positions to dislocate the process, then, if the danger they present is reasonably, not emotionally, clear and present, to use Mr. Justice Holmes' words, there should be no place for them in the teaching profession. No one better expressed the delicate problem of balancing discipline and freedom in great crises than Lincoln: Must a government of necessity be too *strong* for the liberties of its people, and too *weak* to maintain its own existence? Without such disciplined freedom for testing and for truly sharing decisions how can the democratic process function—especially in national crises with all their tension and emotion?

Let us, then, grant that this is the kind of discipline, this the responsibility, we should cultivate in ourselves and in our pupils. We may not be able to do it; or we may be able to do it only in small part. But do we want to abandon the will to do it even though the emergency be yet greater than it threatens to be? There are signs that our leading intellectual guides, many of them, are abandoning the value of freedom as a means. If we abandon it, even for the time, it will be hard to recapture. And we should have, certainly, to return to it some day, if we are to solve by reason rather than by force the problems that will surely, surely be born of the times to come.

Dilemmas of a Textbook Writer

HENRY WILKINSON BRAGDON

Nearly twenty years ago I signed a contract to write an American history text for senior high school students. A Macmillan officer remarked at the time that this could be a full-time job. And that is almost what it has become. The care and feeding of this text, *History of a Free People*, is my principal occupation. It took over four years in the writing. It has been revised five times, and I am now working on still another edition. Macmillan has surrounded it with a flotilla of eleven paperbacks; I wrote one and helped to edit the rest. Six more paperbacks and a two-volume edition are in the works. There is a continuous stream of correspondence from teachers and students, usually critical, sometimes angry. There are attacks from both the right and the left. One has to develop a thick carapace. What bothers me most is not the work, nor that I often wish I were back in the classroom. nor the critics, but that I have never resolved certain practical, pedagogical, and moral dilemmas.

I shall analyze these and other problems and deal successively with Publishers, Patriots, Pedagogy, and Conscience.

Publishers

I have sometimes seen in print statements to the effect that textbook writers are simply marionettes, with the publishers pulling the strings, that publishers tell us what to write, how to write it, and surround us with taboos as rigid as those that bedevil television. Here, for instance, is

NOTE: This article appeared in *Social Education*, March 1969, pp. 292–298. Reprinted by permission of Jane Bragdon.

an article, "Textbooks and Trapped Idealists," *Saturday Review of Literature*, January 18, 1964, by Frank G. Jennings, one of its editors. According to Mr. Jennings a textbook is likely to germinate in the mind of a book salesman, and then to be hatched corporately by the staff of a publishing house, whose first concern is that it shall offend no segment of the textbook buying public.

All I can say is that this was not the way it was with this book. I was approached by a Macmillan Vice President in charge of the school section, Richard Pearson, and asked if I'd like to try my hand at a high school textbook. After thinking it over, I said yes, but that I was interested only in a certain kind of book—one with a chronological arrangement instead of the then fashionable topical approach; one that reduced the colonial period to a single chapter; one that centered on politics and political ideas. Macmillan accepted these and other later ideas presented either by me or by the coauthor they found to work with me, the late Professor Samuel P. McCutchen of New York University. We were assigned an excellent editor, Mrs. Dorothy Arnof, and she worked so closely with us that she became in effect a third author. Macmillan advised us about certain technical matters—whether pages should have one column or two, for instance—and decided on the format. But in all big things we made the decisions. This took courage on the publishers' part because their initial investment in plates, maps, illustrations, charts, and other production costs was not less than $250,000.

The text was being written at the height of the McCarthy era, but Pearson told us to forget it, that this would have passed by the time the book came out. He kept sending me books on civil liberties, such as Alan Barth's *The Loyalty of Free Men*, and throughout our book civil liberties received emphasis greater than in most texts. The very title, selected by the publisher, was meant to be a kind of rebuke to McCarthyism. The first title more or less agreed on was *United We Stand*—defiant, shoulder-to-shoulder; it was changed to *History of a Free People* to get across the idea that freedom was a good to be cherished.

I don't say there were not restraints that irked me. At first I was expected to submit to a curriculum expert who tried to get me to write prose according to a series of formulas—I should, for instance, limit myself to the first 5,000 words in the Thorndike word list; sentences must be short; I should avoid compound sentences, so the semicolon was *verboten*. I soon found I could not stand this, told Pearson so, and he called off the expert. And yet she had done me good in that she forced me to wonder constantly whether I was communicating meaning to eleventh graders.

I found writing a textbook the most difficult form of composition I have ever attempted. This derives partly from the necessity for compression, which I shall deal with later, partly from not knowing what course to steer between the Scylla of writing over the readers' heads and the Charybdis of underestimating their intelligence. Then too I was writing for a most varied audience, composed of intelligent and interested students, apathetic and unintelligent students, teachers, consultants, and in the background my professional colleagues. Recently while acting as consultant for a publisher I had occasion to criticize the style of the manuscript of a projected American history text. My advice to the authors—and I admit this is a counsel of perfection—was as follows:

Don't Write Down! .... *Write as though you were writing for a mature audience consisting of at least four persons:*

> a dull, uninterested person whose attention you want to attract and who has difficulty in comprehension;
>
> a bright, knowledgeable person, whose intelligence you don't want to insult;
>
> a highly respected English teacher, who used to tear your schoolboy compositions apart;
>
> an historian who is going to grade you on whether you are to keep your membership in the historical fraternity.

One taboo Macmillan did insist upon: the Civil War had to be called The War Between the States. This concession to the Southern market irritated me, and I demanded that Macmillan prove it was necessary. So they polled their eleven southern sales offices; every one of them solemnly stated that a textbook that used the term Civil War could not be sold south of the Mason-Dixon line. I gave in. Texas, I thought, was worth a mass. This is one occasion where the publishers in effect forced me to do something I disliked. The only other point at which I was pressured was in just the reverse direction—I must mention certain members of minority groups, such as Crispus Attucks and Haym Solomon. But that was all—nowhere else was I told what to put in or keep out.

It would be disingenuous of me to maintain that I am not influenced by certain unspoken barriers. I cannot remember offhand any that influenced me in writing *History of a Free People*, and so take an example from a book on constitutional rights that a colleague and I have just completed.[1] In it we put students to close examination of recent Supreme Court decisions. In discussing right to counsel we chose *Escobedo v. Illinois* (1964) over *Miranda v. Arizona* (1966), even though the latter was more recent and perhaps more controversial, simply because Miranda dealt with a case of rape, while Escobedo was accused merely of being an accessory to murder. According to the peculiar mores of American society, which naturally permeate schools, children may contemplate any kind of violence so long as sex is not involved.

Furthermore, one cannot get away from the Confucian proverb: "The superior man knows what is right; the inferior man knows what will sell." I'd be happier about *History of a Free People* if it were not so obviously designed as an article of commerce. Every two years or so there is a new cover, like the changing radiator grilles on new cars. There are so many illustrations, chapter-end activities, bibliographies, appendices, maps, and diagrams that students may complain that the book is too heavy to carry home. But there is no help for it. Some other texts are horrendously even bigger, and I am assured that this increases their sales.

The evidence I get through Macmillan salesmen is that Mr. Jennings is too often right when in the previously quoted article he wrote:

> Textbooks are accepted or turned down because they are profusely illustrated, because they have lavishly colored covers, because they are larger or smaller than the ones in use, because they are written by people with the right kinds of names, coming from the right schools, in the right part of the country. Sometimes they are accepted or rejected, because it is very late on a dreary Friday afternoon.

To give an example from our experience. An adoption board in a city that shall be nameless was divided three to three as to whether to adopt our book or that of a competitor. No compromise was possible. So they finally decided to test which book was more durable—textbooks are supposed to stand up to the wear-and-tear of daily use for from three to five years. Those who liked our book better threw the other one at the wall, taking turns with the others throwing ours. Eventually the cover came off the other book and we got the adoption.

Patriots

Back of the idea that timid publishers are constantly telling writers "You can't print that," is the notion that pressure groups, especially those of self-dubbed "patriots," will drive from the market any books that aren't a bland, homogenized mixture of pap and uplift. There is substance to this notion. In the 1940's rightists attacked a series of junior high school texts written by Harold Rugg of Teachers College, Columbia, as being leftist and un-American. Based on the idea that students in sixth, seventh, and eighth grade should know the historical background of contemporary issues and should learn to discuss them, the Rugg texts were the best in the market. But in not more than five or six years the patriots won; Rugg's books disappeared from schools.

The patriots are still at work. Look at the illustration from the cover of *History of a Free People*. See—that's the fascist eagle holding the communist sickle. A certain Congressman Utt from California said so; and students in Santa Barbara schools were told by frightened parents not to take the book home. The same crazy notion turned up in other California towns, and in other states. The publishers had to issue a release to let agitated teachers and school superintendents know that this eagle came from an index of American design published in 1840.

More dangerous than the kooky charge by the California Congressman was the one by Holmes Alexander, a columnist said to be syndicated in 300-odd newspapers. Among other things, Alexander accused me of "clayfootery" and to prove it quoted *History of a Free People* as follows:

> (General George Washington) lost more battles than he won .. (and) sometimes annoyed men by his stiff manner and a tendency to talk and write as though all were lost.

"This," remarked Alexander, "about the indomitable man who refused to be beaten!" To show the extraordinary mendacity of his attack here is the whole paragraph (with Alexander's quotes in bold type):

> Washington was undoubtedly the greatest American asset, even though he **lost more battles than he won.** He may have been mistaken in training his army in strictly European lines. He **sometimes annoyed men by his stiff manner and a tendency to talk and write as though all were lost.** But no man did more to win the war. While British commanders often returned to England for the winter, Washington's devotion to duty was such that he saw his home at Mount Vernon only once during the war, and then only for a few hours. He alone commanded sufficient respect to keep the Continental Army in being. Often soldiers remained with the army, even when they were unpaid and their enlistments were up, because, as one of them used to tell his grandchildren, "He was a fine man, General Washington—he was everything a man should be."

Alexander went on to accuse me of trying to create a younger generation "without heroes, without respect for their country, and without emotional patriotism." He concluded by remarking that "some people in the textbook business are doing the work of our enemies." I consulted a lawyer on this one. He consulted other lawyers and they thought that I had grounds for libel. But Macmillan advised against it. They said I'd lose my shirt in lawyer's fees, that they'd see to it that Alexander was answered, and that the assault was so extreme it would boomerang.

There is evidence that they were right. Alexander was rebutted by several letters to the editor (including one by a former student of mine), and there was no evidence that sales were adversely affected.

Then there is an evaluation of our book put out by an organization called "America's Future, Inc." On the face of it this is a reputable organization; most of the committee that run it are men of academic standing, including Felix Morley, former President of Haverford College, and professors from Kenyon, Yale, Northwestern, and Minnesota. They have issued an evaluation written by E. Merrill Root, who previously had embarrassed Professor McCutchen and me by praising our text in a book called *Brainwashing in the High Schools*. Later he changed his mind. He wrote, in part:

One half of it seems so good that the other half ought to be better. It seems as if two different authors had written a different half, without benefit of collaboration. [He apparently thought that I, from conservative Phillips Exeter Academy, wrote one half, and McCutchen, from suspect NYU, the other.] The half that deals with the earlier history of America is excellent, while the half that deals with modern history is weak and fallible. There seems a sort of schizophrenia between the two halves. . . .

Some criticisms of the latter part of the book are that we do not suggest that "people in power" deliberately failed to warn the military and naval commanders at Pearl Harbor because they sought war with Japan; that we do not assert that the Bonus March was "Communist-inspired"; that we entitled a chapter "The Affluent Society," thus revealing a "liberal" slant. So, concludes Root:

The impact of the book, especially since the first half seems to validate the book, is to lull the student into acceptance and then to indoctrinate him with "liberal" superstitions, a "liberal" mood of anti-anti-Communism, and a soft sentimentality toward collectivism.

Root obviously suspects conspiracy.

The publishers tell me not to worry about the right-wing attacks. There is no appeasing the so-called patriots, who are often paranoid and unreasonable people. There is greater danger, even from an outright dollars-and-cents point of view, in knuckling under to them than in ignoring them. So I do not feel especially threatened by thunder from the right. As a citizen I am frightened by the Birchers and the Minutemen and the Citizens' Councils, because I was in Germany in 1929 when Hitler was considered a joke, but as a textbook writer I do not consider myself peculiarly vulnerable.

Pedagogy

So, as I work at successive revisions of *History of a Free People,* I do not feel controlled or threatened by anybody. I have only myself to blame if the book is less good than it ought to be—there are no convenient scapegoats anywhere I look. My present concern lies in two areas—pedagogy and conscience.

Regarding pedagogy, there is widespread opinion that history textbooks and courses taught from them are *ipso facto* to be deplored. My friend, the ubiquitous Charles Keller, expressed this view in a talk to teachers at Manhasset, Long Island, in September, 1962:

Current textbooks and their excessive use are both bad. . . . Textbooks take the fact-by-fact approach. They *tell* students things in a way and an order which the author has decided—too frequently with his eye, or that of his publisher, on getting adoptions in as many school systems as possible. The textbook-learning teacher gives students little chance to figure things out for themselves.

I have been intermittently engaged in producing new social studies materials for an organization called Educational Services, Inc. (now Educational Development Corporation). The very concept of a single text was anathema at ESI (EDC). We produced games, documents, pamphlets, packets of stuff, maps, pictures, movies, simulations, artifacts, and I don't know what all, but nary a single volume that could be labelled a textbook.

I sympathize with this approach. Textbooks encourage the idea that history is something to be memorized and regurgitated. Too many teachers never go beyond the text and simply put students to learning the answers to the questions in the chapter-end activities. There is abundant evidence, alas, that too many teachers concentrate on picayune facts. The Macmillan salesmen almost unanimously report that teachers want more military history, and for all I know *History of a Free People* may sometimes lose out because it minimizes the details of wars. I have seen tests based on my text that demanded nothing but a knowledge of details. All this bears out what Henry Adams meant when he said that "nothing in education is so astonishing as the amount of ignorance it accumulates in the form of inert facts."

As long as the textbook is the chief pedagogical tool in high school history courses, just so long are those courses likely to be a dreary business of read-recite-test, read-recite-test.

Another difficulty with basing a course on a textbook is that it tends to make everything seem equally important, while if you want to excite students about history and give them a real sense of the past, with a sophisticated awareness of the complexity of events, it is necessary to do a certain amount of "postholing"—settling down and going into a period or a topic in depth, or setting students to their own explorations.

A textbook does not *force* bad teaching. A reasonably imaginative teacher or curriculum maker will put it in its place, will use it to give an overview, or simply for reference. Here it is useful. To try to do without it is like moving into a wilderness area without a map.

Furthermore, we have tried to break down the Procrustean influence of the textbook in various ways:

1. In a Teachers' Annotated Edition we constantly urge teachers to get students to look beyond the daily assignments. In a bound-in set of suggestions we adjure them not to abuse the textbook by treating it simply as a repository of inert knowledge, but instead devise "attack strategies" that will "actively engage students' minds."

2. Dorothy Arnof has edited a book of readings, *A Sense of the Past,* especially designed to appeal to the average student, as well as to the able one, and to get across the sense that history deals with people. A friend of mine teaching slow students in a junior high school found that they enjoyed being read to out of this book.

3. For able students, we have put out ten paperbacks: *Frame of Government*, a close textual study of major constitutional documents, and nine books of *Perspectives in American History*, "postholing" and combining lively narrative, documents, and historical interpretation.

But too many teachers will not look beyond the text, too few school boards will invest in extra paperbacks for history classes, so one is driven inexorably back to the proposition that the textbook itself must contain antidotes to the pedagogical poison it may transmit. We have attempted this in various ways:

1. In each chapter there is an informal sketch of some usually minor figure of the time, written in such a way as to be read simply for interest. (In the Teachers' Annotated Edition we urge that they do not test on these.)

2. Each section of the book is prefaced by a little essay, which we privately call a "Vista," designed to induce the reader to look up and away from the ordered expository narrative. Here is the beginning of a vista entitled "Moods," prefacing a section that runs from the First World War through the Great Depression:

> Perhaps there is no more vivid experience in life than the sudden remembrance of things past. What brings this on is hard to say—sometimes a sound, such as a distant train whistle or the song of a bird; sometimes a smell, such as the scent of lilacs or a wood fire. For a moment you remember what it was like to be three years old and reaching up for the hand of a grown-up, or six and getting water up your nose at your first swimming lesson.
>
> In the history of nations, as in the lives of individuals, different periods have characteristic moods. The progressive period of the early twentieth century was one of high purpose. The delegates to the Bull Moose convention in 1912 chanted "Onward Christian Soldiers," and Woodrow Wilson called his inaugural "a day of dedication." The spirit carried on into the World War: America was joining in a crusade to "make the world safe for democracy." And there was the poignant gaiety of the doughboys singing "Over There" as they marched to the ghastly slaughter on the Western Front.
>
> With the coming of the twenties, there was an abrupt change. A new mood of disillusionment was reflected in two war plays, "No More Parades" and "What Price Glory?" The cynics' prophet, magazine editor H. L. Mencken, never tired of ridiculing the great American "booboisie." Crazes came and went. . . .

3. We have inserted into the text short italicized questions that suggest further study or provoke discussion or at least induce the reader, as I have already said, to look up and away. Here are two:

> Question: *Young people who have not reached voting age are subject to sales taxes, excise taxes, and income taxes. Have they a legitimate grievance under the principle of "no taxation without representation"?*
> Question: *How near must a person be for you to be able to see the whites of his eyes?*

We have devised still another means of trying to promote active learning, but I shall not detail them further. For better or worse, these are gimmicks, and I am not sure that they or anything the writer can do will take the primordial pedagogical curse off a textbook. Perhaps the very writing of a textbook is an immoral proceeding on the ground that it contributes to the mental delinquency of minors. And this brings up the last and most difficult set of problems that I lump together under the heading *Conscience.*

Conscience

Here I might start with what is on the surface an innocent question: what should be the length of a textbook? Presumably a school text should be short, so as to leave students free for other endeavors. We had it written into the original contract that the basic narrative should not exceed 225,000 words—this was 50,000 words shorter than any competing text. But brevity creates a whole series of problems. To make a text brief you must leave things out. I thought, for example, of omitting all formal reference to literature or the arts because these cannot be treated in any really informative way. But at a dinner of school art teachers I was persuaded that to omit mention of the arts was to imply they were not important, so I had somehow to work them in, in a way that I found unsatisfying because so superficial. And this danger of superficiality runs all through. To shorten you must simplify, and you inevitably falsify, since history is never simple. Simplification, furthermore, may do students long-time harm by leading them to expect oversimple explanations for contemporary phenomena, or pat solutions to contemporary problems.

A columnist in the *Baltimore Sun* took *History of a Free People* apart for its descriptions of McCarthyism and the school desegregation decision of 1954, saying that they were so brief and colorless as to be worse than useless. When I went back to the passages involved, I had to agree. And yet I had not deliberately pulled my punches. It was simply that I was writing within a strict word limit that handicapped me in attempting to give anything like a feeling for the topics concerned.

In short, I've come right up against the question whether a one-volume history of the United States does not have to be so compressed that it cannot tell the truth.

Then there's the problem whether any individual—I don't care who—is equipped to write a history of the United States, in one volume or fifty. No one knows enough. The fundamental morality of the historian is that he do his own digging and make his own assessment of the sources. But obviously no man can do that for more than a small fraction of the whole field of American history. So the textbook writer, no matter how much he knows, must rely for the most part on secondary sources. He is always in effect plagiarizing other men's works. Nor does he always know which ones to plagiarize. For instance, when I was writing the last major revision there was a dispute going on about the War of 1812. Some years ago various historians, especially J. W. Pratt, presented the notion that it was a "war of agrarian cupidity," brought on by western and southern War Hawks with designs on Canada and Florida. Now historians pooh-pooh the Pratt thesis but disagree among each other. I could not go over all the evidence to find out which one to follow. What to do?

When preparing this last edition we did what we could to remedy the fact that I was a single fallible individual. We hired scholars of high repute to go through the text and say where it was lacking and where it was in error, also to tell me what books to read to overcome my ignorance. Still, I was always skating on thin ice.

Then there is the matter of commitment, to which Frederick S. Allis gave his attention in an excellent essay, "The Handling of Controversial Material in High School Texts in American History," published in Volume 72 of the *Proceedings of the Massachusetts Historical Society*. Allis examined in detail three texts, including *History of a Free People*, to see how they handled sensitive topics. Our text emerged with a bit more credit than the others, but it by no means escaped impeachment for "neutrality and lack of commitment." Even when we did commit ourselves, Allis accused us of doing so by indirection, either by quoting what others said or by mere emphasis.

I certainly feel free now to commit myself on any and all issues. And recent editions are more outspoken than earlier ones in certain areas—such as the three centuries of injustice to the Negro. As the great-grandson of four militant abolitionists, I never intended to pussyfoot on this matter, but the Negro revolution has educated us all in this regard and has made us realize the way we have made the black the "invisible man" in American history. Still, it is not easy. Take this passage:

> In May, 1963, the Reverend Martin Luther King organized peaceful demonstrations against segregation practices in Birmingham, Alabama. Men, women, and children participated. When hundreds were jailed

> violence broke out. King and his followers seemed to have won conces-
> sions, but white extremists exploded bombs among Negro groups, trig-
> gering an outbreak of Negro violence. . . .

That passage was enough to get our text thrown out of Birmingham. And in a way there was justice, because I made one blooper, one un-provable statement, when I said that the bombs were thrown by "white" extremists. I happen to think the bomb-throwers were white, probably you do too, but the Birmingham authorities said I was jumping to con-clusions. I was condemning whites without due process.

The most difficult aspect of the question of commitment is how and how far to make a conscious effort to inculcate values. It is an ines-capable function of an American history text that it affects students' attitudes toward their society. A traditional method of doing this is to get across the idea that everything American is better. A text that en-joyed a vogue fifteen or twenty years ago opened with a section entitled something like "Our America" which was a paean of praise to the United States and its superiority over the USSR. It told how much better we ate and dressed, how well we were educated, how we stood in the world as paragons of all that was right and just. This is one extreme, and I think it self-defeating, since it fails to equip students with the idea that there can be need for change or reform, and by inference assumes that foreign nations are inferior. The other extreme is represented by a sociologist we hired as a commentator. He regarded any suggestion that American society might be better than any other in any way as leading to cultural chauvinism. Somehow I cannot go along with this. I feel that there is a mandate to a textbook writer to attempt to instill a sense of commitment to this country, free of condescension or false pride, a patriotism that looks to the past traditions of America to attempt to right present injustices.

Up to now what we've done in this text is to present ten themes of American history, such as economic opportunity, a mobile population, concern for the welfare of others, making clear that these are not neces-sarily uniquely American, nor ever fully realized. "Taken as a whole," we say, "the history of the United States has been that of a bold and excit-ing experiment in founding a society on faith in human intelligence, human freedom, and human brotherhood. So far this experiment has been a success. Its future success depends on the intelligence, good will, and sense of responsibility of coming generations." In the new editions I have toned this down a bit, and the book ends with an assessment of how far we have achieved our stated ideals and how far fallen short. But I'm still uncertain. Go too far in the direction of indoctrination, and you lay the ground for future disillusion: fail to make any effort to inculcate a sense of what America has meant in the world, and you lose a good deal of the purpose of studying our past and may contribute to the all too common sense of alienation. I can only say that my intention runs with what Alfred North Whitehead once wrote:

> The art of a free society consists first in the maintenance of the symbolic code; and secondly in fearlessness of revision, to secure that the code serve those purposes which satisfy an enlightened reason. Those societies which cannot combine reverence to their symbols with freedom of revision, must ultimately decay either from anarchy, or from the slow atrophy of a life stifled by useless shadows.[2]

Notes

[1] Henry W. Bragdon and John C. Pittenger, *The Pursuit of Justice: An Introduction to Constitutional Rights.* New York: Macmillan, 1969.

[2] *Symbolism: Its Meaning and Effect.* New York: Putnam, 1959, p. 88.

The Kent State Tragedy:
Lessons for Teachers

HARRIS L. DANTE

In the seventeen months from April 1, 1969 to September 1, 1970, Harris L. Dante served as chairman of the Faculty Senate at Kent State University. His observations and conclusions concerning events at that institution are particularly important for their authenticity and perceptiveness.

Anyone who lived through the nightmare of the Kent State tragedy with its resulting confusion and tension extending through last summer may very well wish for an end to any further discussion of the issues, many of which will never be resolved. There will be no attempt here to go back over the ground that has already been traversed by numerous official and unofficial investigations. Moreover, there are many articles, reports, and books, both already published and projected, dealing with the events of May 1–4 as well as with what led up to the fateful shootings and subsequent developments, which will deal with the Kent affair in much more detail and authority.

There are, however, some lessons to be learned for all Americans that may have special meaning for social studies teachers. One might add parenthetically that at least one salutary, although equally tragic result, was the fact that the killings at Jackson State would have received even less notice than they did if the tragedy there had not been preceded by the events at Kent State. Nor should one lose sight of the obvious truth that there are riots and then there are riots. The recent football disturbances in Columbus, Ohio, caused far more property damage to local merchants, and involved more persons than did the downtown disturbances in Kent. But then boys (of all ages) will be boys and, after all, OSU *did* defeat Michigan. Furthermore, it has been observed that the most serious campus rioting occurred in 1962 when the University

NOTE: This article appeared in *Social Education*, April 1971, pp. 357–361. Reprinted by permission of Harris L. Dante.

of Mississippi attempted to integrate James Meredith. In this case hundreds of students were involved, hurling not only rocks but firing shotgun blasts at a beleaguered group of federal marshals. It took an army of about 13,000 troops to restore order at a cost of hundreds of thousands of dollars, and not one student was killed. Apparently riots that are on behalf of causes that are approved by the majority of the community are just good clean fun or at least justifiable, if not legitimate.

Kent State in Perspective

What happened at Kent State could have happened on any other large college campus. There is evidence that there was an outside cadre of revolutionaries who had singled out Kent as the place for confrontation with Middle America. The reasons why it began and developed as it did are certainly complex, with outside events, particularly Cambodia, acting as catalysts. That Kent was the place was accidental, and the events that moved from a downtown fracas on Friday to death on the campus on Monday were due to a series of incidents that might have been contained. It would certainly have been more rational for campus disruption to have occurred at any one of a number of other Ohio campuses.

The tragedy became even more difficult to bear as an aroused public placed the blame on the University community. No university in Ohio and few in the nation had taken more significant steps to prevent disruption. Some of the programs that had been in operation during 1969–70 and earlier were the Human Relations Center, the Afro-American Studies Program, a Black Cultural Center, the Faculty Senate, the Student Senate, and the Faculty Ombudsman. The office of Student Ombudsman was established this past summer. All of these offices and programs have been high on the list of demands at other institutions. In addition, at Kent State both the Chairman of the Faculty Senate and the Chairman of the Student Senate were and are *ex officio* members of the Board of Trustees, a Faculty Senate committee advises on the total University budget, student advisory committees were established in every College, there were student representatives on curriculum committees, and a Faculty Senate/Student Senate Liaison Committee was in operation. Moreover, other state institutions in Ohio had experienced much higher property damage and far more injuries to law enforcement officers than at Kent State.* Those who led the cry for law and order quickly forgot that in

---

*Without approving of the burning of buildings, it should be pointed out that the ROTC building was a tempting target for an anti-war crowd or a symbol to be attacked by a small band of extremists. It was a one-story "temporary" wooden structure erected in 1947 to meet the immediate enrollment increases following World War II and should have been removed twenty years ago.

the Spring of 1969 the administration, making use of the Highway Patrol, had handled an SDS disturbance with minimum property damage (one door) and with no injuries. At that time the administration came under criticism for being too harsh, as more than fifty students were arrested (some were later declared innocent by the Court) and the leaders given jail sentences of several months.

Journalists and others who have come to Kent expecting to find the campus a center for New Left activists have been disappointed. The faculty is strong in many areas† but essentially conservative, while the student body represents mid-western middle-class suburbia, in spite of the geographic location of Kent which is surrounded by large urban centers. Still the indifference of the campus has been partly overcome by the reactions of the public and the spotlight of numerous investigations and reports, so that many students have become radicalized although committed to non-violence.

The first reactions to the tragic events of May were shock, confusion, despair, and fear for the future of the University, which was kept closed under a Court injunction. There were times when it seemed that unfounded rumor and panic would prevail, that a tragic situation was being used to secure demands, even to settle old scores. The President of the University, Robert I. White, who had the support of the overwhelming majority of faculty and students, who had always had good rapport with the legislature, and who apparently had been regarded with affection by many townspeople, suddenly found himself the object of merciless attack and abuse from all sides. Recognized in academic circles as one of the most democratic and able university administrators in the nation, he must have wondered where all of his friends had gone. Some of the more responsible legislative leaders refused to be stampeded into the most extreme type of punitive legislation but there was very little public support of the University and its President from any source. In the Fall quarter of 1970 Kent State University is alive and well with the entire university community pledged to non-violence and with tensions lessening with townspeople and other critics. Enrollments did not suffer the predicted decrease but instead increased to more than 21,000 students, with the faculty and student body brought more closely together.

Six Conclusions: A Personal View

In the seventeen months that I served as Chairman of the Faculty Senate, from April 1, 1969 to September 1, 1970, I learned a great deal. Some of

† The four University Professors, all distinguished scholars in their fields, are: Harold M. Mayer, Geography; August Meier, History; Richard S. Varga, Mathematics; and Howard P. Vincent, English.

the conclusions that I reached will, hopefully, have some special significance for teachers of the social studies.

1. The value question is perhaps the most important and difficult problem to which social studies teachers need direct themselves. If there was ever any evidence needed that accidents often determine events, that society is irrational, and that people believe what they want to believe in spite of factual proof to the contrary, it was made quite clear by the Kent State experience. There were those who had always sworn that the FBI was a super-efficient law enforcement agency, with J. Edgar Hoover at God's right hand, who, because they did not agree with the findings of the FBI Report, suddenly declared the FBI mistaken, naive, and an ineffective organization.

One very vocal critic of the University testified before the Scranton Commission that she could no longer take her children to any of Kent's three movie theaters because they offered nothing but films dealing with sex and violence, catering to the college students who were their chief patrons. Obviously the Kent movie houses have no monopoly on cinemas dealing with sex and violence, and the fact is that on the very day this testimony was given a Disney production, "The Boatniks," was being featured at one of the local theaters.

In the understandable frustration of fearful citizens and enraged taxpayers, who witnessed young men and women (whom they regarded as quite privileged to have a college education) engaging in destroying property, it was quite easy to subscribe to a conspiratorial theory or to blame society's ills on the permissiveness of the University. Many persons accepted the view of one public official that the trouble with Kent State was that "*All* of the faculty are communists."

The central question for social studies teachers would seem to be the problem of how to go about changing attitudes. We can subscribe to critical thinking as *the* method and certainly we must rely on factual evidence, in as far as it can be established, unless we are to return to superstition, but we need to give far more attention to the affective domain. Students must be encouraged and challenged to examine the basis for their beliefs, and priority must be given to the establishment of criteria and agreements on the core values of our society. The facts will be of little use to us unless we are willing to subject our prejudices to rational examination.

2. The polarization and threatened disintegration of our society is much more serious than we realize. I made what I thought was a moderate statement on television in which I merely noted that young people today are trying to tell us something, that we should listen to them, and that when they believe no one is listening, particularly when they feel there is no dialogue with their government, they become frustrated. As a result I received many hate letters from all over the nation. Many said the only mistake made by the National Guard was that they did not shoot the faculty. Others felt that more students should have been killed. Several were from persons who observed that they were glad their parents had been too poor to send their children to college where they would have been exposed to professors of my ilk. Others suggested that I should leave the country.

The President of the University had to bear the agony of thousands of such letters, many of them blaming him personally for the deaths of four students. The tragedy is that many of these views were shared in one degree or another by many so-called "good" people or "enlightened" citizens who should have known better.

3. *The failure of many persons to understand the true nature of a university or the meaning of academic freedom makes it imperative that all academicians learn how to communicate with the man in the street, and that we be constantly mindful of the responsibilities that are part of our professional obligation.* In a time when the Bill of Rights would have tough sledding in the public opinion polls and even in legislative chambers, the university must remain a sanctuary of freedom and of free but responsible expression. Any successful educational system attempts to civilize man to make him more rational and to increase his wisdom. In the words of Robert Maynard Hutchins: "This is why a good educational system is constantly at war with the culture that is, with the prevalent habits and opinions of the day. Of course, any good educational system reflects the culture. But every good educational system aims to refine and improve the culture."

These views are dimly understood, if they are not actually opposed, by many laymen. It was July when a group of six faculty members sat down with six leading citizens of the city of Kent to see if a statement of support for the University could be put together. In our first session we were asked such questions as: "When are you going to get that place up there under control?". When we asked, "What do you mean by 'control'?", we began to engage in a meaningful dialogue. It was four sessions later and the end of July before we could agree upon a published statement; and in it, as we had been advised, we could not use the term "academic freedom" because to the average citizen that simply means license to do what you damn please.

The same charge of irrationality can, of course, be leveled at left-wing extremists. If it is really believed that our society is so corrupt and ineffective that there is no possibility for reform within the system, then there is nothing left but revolution. Such a revolt would lead only to extermination of the revolutionaries and repression of the entire society. Moreover, these extremists have given few clues as to the kind of brave new world they have in mind.

The university must remain a forum for the study and expression of unpopular ideas and minority views. One of the major criticisms made of the administration was the appearance of Jerry Rubin on the Kent campus last spring. He did not use any university facility but spoke outside to an audience of several hundred students. Rubin was a very ineffective speaker, was heckled, and his statements received very little support. It is doubtful if he influenced anyone. If we had tried to prevent him from speaking or if he had been driven off the campus, we would have had rioting similar to what was experienced at the University of Illinois over Kunstler. A few days later Ralph Nader spoke to an overflow audience in the University Auditorium as part of an Environmental Week Program and, as I later told the Ohio House Judiciary Committee, he is a much greater threat to the Establishment than Jerry Rubin, but he works within the system and has a short haircut.

4. *Social studies teachers need to have their students engage in a critical analysis of the news media.* On balance the American press does a fairly adequate job of informing the public; at least some approach to the truth can be found if the citizen is willing to dig for it and if he has learned the limitations of the sources of information. The Kent State affair eventually was handled with some degree of insight by the leading metropolitan newspapers, especially the *Akron Beacon Journal,* which used top reporters of the Knight chain in the first extensive study of the tragedy with conclusions that were largely supported later by the FBI Report and the Scranton Commission. Many smaller papers, and at times the larger ones too, reflected the local prejudices. Apparently some editors believe that freedom of the press means opening the "Letters to the Editor" columns to any prejudiced and uninformed person to express an opinion no matter how inaccurate and damaging it may be.

It is doubtful if any society can stand the kind of instant reporting that we get from the daily news media. A television crew will film for two or three days to get seven minutes on the evening newscast, or one statement is lifted out of a thirty-minute interview. The selection process that is part of the editing for a television program, and the newsroom choice of what news items are to be chosen from the ticker tape that seemingly flows on and on, carries a serious responsibility. The television camera often focuses on much that needs to be brought to view but it can also make a crowd of fifty look like five hundred.

Controversy is more interesting than normal processes, and reporters instinctively are more alert in seeking it out. In televising interviews regarding the events that occurred in the city of Kent, public officials and businessmen were found who stated that if it had not been for police action the students would have burned down the entire city. It is true that this was really believed by many citizens but to my knowledge the opposite view, particularly in regard to the events downtown on Friday night, was never shown. The fact is that half of those arrested for Friday's disturbance were not students, and some have said the officials and police overreacted to the situation. A prominent local druggist who was mayor of Kent for four years prior to January, 1970 could have given a viewpoint more sympathetic to the students and more critical of the way the incident was handled, but he was not interviewed on this point even though such an interview was recommended.

Teachers must help students learn how to analyze critically the sources of information, to distinguish between reporting of the news and editorializing, to note the distinction between responsible reporting and unethical unreliability, to recognize the limited perspective of piecemeal daily reporting of the news, and to learn how to separate information that will contribute to substantive understanding from the trivia which is both irrelevant and confusing. Social studies teachers need to get above the level of "I seen it in the papers" and make use of the unpopular, critical, and more authoritative journals. If students do not get acquainted with this kind of material in school, when will they ever do so?

5. *There is a need for all educators to stand together against the anti-intellectual, anti-educational attitude that has developed in the nation, resulting in punitive legislation, loss of faith, and lack of support of education.* At the same time we need to be responsible professionals, to promote understanding, and to bring together the diverse forces in our society.

In the faculty lounges of many public schools the same "they should have shot more of them" attitude that was being expressed by many laymen could be heard stated by teachers. The permissiveness of the University was blamed for student unrest, and all of the defects of our universities were proclaimed. It should not be too much to expect that teachers, who are themselves college graduates, should understand the purpose of a university better than others, and that they would have learned to base their judgments on fact, while not being too hasty to condemn others who teach.

I have no respect for the college professor who blames his failures as a teacher on those who had the student at earlier levels. This is a futile exercise which eventually gets down to the kindergarten teacher who puts the blame on the child's family. Naturally, the mother blames the father's side of the house, so it ultimately reaches back to dad and his ancestors.

The current taxpayers' revolt against schools is more than a failure to realize that most tax dollars go to pay for past, present, and future wars, or a result of the property owner bearing more than his share of the burden. There is a feeling that the public is not getting its "money's worth" for its support of education. It should be obvious to educators, at least, that the costs of reaching the American ideal of a quality education for all requires the kind of effort the public has not been willing to make. We are a wealthy nation. A trillion dollars GNP, even though it is an inflated figure, is a lot of money. It means that all mass expenditures in this country are big. Teachers should not let the public be deceived by absolute dollar amounts devoted to education but should break it down on a comparative per capita basis or measure it against expenditures for something trivial—say, chewing gum, jewelry, or greeting cards. We have always spent more on the three C's (candy, cigarettes, and cosmetics) than on the three R's, more on recreation than on total public education. Perhaps the public ought to know also what a separation of auxiliary costs (bus transportation, etc.) from purely instructional costs would reveal. Of course, money isn't everything, but as Ohio's new governor, John Gilligan, has remarked, "It will do until something better comes along." My point is that the education profession cannot afford debilitating divisions within its ranks, and teachers need to be able to explain the facts about educational costs to the taxpayer.

At the same time we do need to be responsible professionals and to remember that we are public servants whose first obligation is to provide a meaningful educational experience to our students. There is a need to reform, to cleanse our ranks of incompetents, to change, and to innovate. The shocking differences in educational opportunity need to be wiped out, our curricula made relevant, and our educational institutions humanized so that they are no longer the institutions of repression as described by Charles Silberman.

6. *People are ready to take advantage of a crisis to further their own ends.* Politicians are reluctant to support education against the popular tide or are willing to shape educational planning and support to meet political ends. Businessmen hesitate to take what might be an unpopular stand. Faculty members are willing to risk the future of a university in their goal to politicize the educational process and to bring about change. In addition, students want to rap when they often have little knowledge with which to rap.

It is because a university is basically decent and dedicated to reason that it is particularly vulnerable. We need to recognize how fragile it is and how easy it would be to attack it and destroy it. Any university today is caught between contending forces in our troubled society, yet the university as an institution cannot be all things to all men.

Neither the flag nor one's hair style should become symbols of ideological differences. Some day the desperate problems of our time will lessen, when our society determines to unite together in resolving them. This will occur sooner when we focus less on the GNP as a quantitative figure and give more of our energies, talents, and resources to improving the quality of life. In this undertaking, the kind of educational program we have will hasten the day when the people of our nation, including our youth, will renew their faith in our political system without which neither our government nor society can survive.

Social Education Asks:
Is it Proper to Prohibit High School
Students from Reading Certain Books?

Should instructional materials used by teachers reflect the dominant values of the community?

Prepared by MURRY R. NELSON and PATRICK FERGUSON

Jack Anderson, Nationally Syndicated Columnist

I've never written a dirty book nor do I ever wish to read one. But as an investigative reporter, I cannot tolerate censorship of what I read or anyone else reads or what I write or anyone else writes.

As a father and a grandfather, I find the tawdry smut available to American youngsters on the pornographic bookstands abhorrent. Salaciousness, like bad money, drives out the good. It perverts honest literary effort.

I insist, however, that self-appointed moralists must not be allowed to burn books, no matter how well-intentioned the censors may be. High school students have the right to read books available to adults. To impose taboos on their library shelves is to confine them to an adolescent expurgitica of ignorance.

Denying them books that some would like to censor won't produce a Sir Galahad in this age of obscene graffiti on toilet walls. Too often, it produces a teenager who can't cope with the realities of growing up.

Without question, the teachers of our children bear a responsibility for what they teach. They should educate within the mainstream of American ethics and ideals. This should not, however, preclude them from raising challenges to shibboleths in our cultural values. Our children need teachers in the classroom, not just parrots.

NOTE: These responses appeared in *Social Education*, April 1982, pp. 267–272.

Max Hocutt, Professor and Chairman, Department of Philosophy, University of Alabama

Is it proper to prohibit high school students from reading certain books?

This is not a simple question. It will look simple to people trying to protect their children from smut and alien ideas, and it will look simple to people trying to protect the public schools from self-appointed censors, but it is not simple. The question calls not for an answer but for an analysis, not so much of the question as of the situation which has produced it.

Why are we being asked this question at this time? Because there is a bitter struggle for control over the public schools. On one side of the struggle are fundamentalist Christians with conservative moral beliefs. Fervently convinced that the public schools are indoctrinating their children with secular theology and libertine morality, they want the authority to decide what ideas and values their children may be taught. On the other side of the struggle are the people who already enjoy control over the content of the curriculum and the conduct of the classroom. Content with their own authority, they are reluctant to share it with any rival. To be asked this question at this time is, therefore, to be asked to choose between one of these groups and the other.

It looks to me like a choice between the devil and the deep blue sea. I can think of no defense for compelling the children of fundamentalist Christians to learn doctrines and attitudes abhorrent to them. The Constitution wisely guarantees to each citizen freedom of worship and speech. On the other hand, I do not think that we can give fundamentalists power to decide what other people's children may learn. The Constitution also wisely prohibits the establishment of a public religion. So, I do not want either to grant censorial authority to the fundamentalists or to continue making them support and send their children to schools of which they disapprove.

What is the alternative? To let not only the Moral Majority but all others who wish to do so spend their own money on schools of their own choosing. We should let every parent select the education that he thinks best for his own child, and we should give nobody the right to dictate how another parent's child will be taught. So, we should return to taxpayers the money we now extort from them in support of the dissemination of ideas they regard as evil, leaving them free to fund schools that teach doctrines more to their liking. To the poor we can give educational vouchers of which they can make similar use. Thus granting everybody liberty to choose his own education seems to me to be preferable both to preserving for current officials and to granting to new censors the authority to decide what ideas and values other people may learn.

Could we not make arrangements within the public schools for some students to be taught in one way and others to be taught differently, according to their parents' wishes? I do not think so. Besides fundamentalist Christians, there are socialists, Buddhists, libertarians, Muslims, and so on. No school system could afford to provide all of the many diverse curricula that would be required to satisfy all of these groups. Any system that tried to do so would soon lose all definition and character. One of the worst features of recent public education is that it has tried to be all things to all people. In consequence, nobody has received a very good education in anything. Far better to have separate schools serving distinct clientele well than to have a single system serving everybody badly.

What about equal time for opposing points of view—say, half-time for Darwinism and half-time for Creationism? That won't work either, for several reasons. First, it would still require people to learn alien doctrine. Second, as the communications networks are discovering, it is impossible to give equal time to all points of view; there are too many of them. Third, such attempts at impartiality themselves constitute indoctrination in a false doctrine, the belief that one point of view is as good as another. Far better to have many schools, each teaching its own brand of truth, than to have one system teaching the falsehood that there is no truth.

Really, there is no solution within the public schools to the problem of ideological conflict. A functioning public school system presupposes a populace essentially unified religiously and politically. Where disunity exists, maintenance of a free society requires that citizens be allowed and enabled to choose between the public schools and private alternatives.

John Irving, Author

Under NO circumstances do I think it proper to prohibit high school students from reading certain books. There is ample historical evidence that there is no such thing as a little harmless censorship.

As to whether instructional material used by teachers should reflect the dominant Culture, teachers (presumably) are prepared to judge the Culture for themselves; parts of what is dominant in Culture, at any time, are valuable and interesting; other parts aren't worth anyone's time. Teachers, and students, need continually to assess what's valuable—in and out of Culture.

No one should decide for students what they shouldn't read; no one should decide for teachers what they should teach.

Why is America, under the banner of a new, morally self-righteous conservatism, suddenly endorsing ideas that are so plainly un-democratic?

Ruth B. Love, General Superintendent of Schools, Chicago Board of Education

Do you think that it is proper to prohibit high school students from reading certain books?

The concept of freedom of expression must be considered as essential in our schools if our students are to become independent-thinking, well-informed citizens who can function effectively in society. In the educational process the high school should be a place where open discussion and free inquiry are promoted. Within the framework of sound educational goals and objectives, it is the responsibility of the school to ensure the students' freedom to read and receive information, or, as Mr. Justice Douglas has termed it, the students' "right to know."

As educators, it is our obligation to offer students a broad range of reading materials which present diverse points of view and have varied appeal. Reading stimulates the intellectual growth of students and aids in the development of their ability to make intelligent judgments and to recognize literary and aesthetic values. I believe that First Amendment protection in the educational environment precludes denying students access to a particular book.

Should instructional materials used by teachers reflect the dominant culture?

Instructional materials should be selected according to a variety of criteria, including readability, accuracy, currency, and freedom from racial, ethnic, religious, and sexual bias. Since our society is multicultural in nature, it is the obligation of our educational system to provide students with materials which foster a respect for and an understanding of our cultural pluralism. The materials should reflect the basic philosophy of a democratic society, be realistic in approach, and maintain well-balanced presentations portraying similarities and differences of various groups.

While we recognize that the needs, interests, and values of the local community are a basic consideration in formulating the educational goals and objectives of the school, we must also recognize our cultural diversity and provide instructional materials which express this diverse nature of our society.

Newton N. Minow, Former Chairman of the Federal Communications Commission. He is now a senior partner in the law firm of Sidley and Austin, Chicago.

Do you think that it is proper to prohibit high school students from reading certain books?

A prohibition on reading is a prohibition on learning, thinking and growing.

If reading is prohibited by any source of authority other than the parent in consultation with the student, it is a flagrant violation of First Amendment protection afforded expression and self-expression. There can be instances in which educators and librarians, in the exercise of their professional judgments, justifiably believe that certain materials should not be purchased by the school, or assigned by the teacher or otherwise made generally available in the library to all students. However, the right to read is only as valuable as the range of reading materials available to a reader. It is a right which must not be arbitrarily shackled. We should encourage young people to read widely and critically. Prohibitions foster fascinations; they do not protect a student from anything except the broad exposure necessary to become a mature and educated citizen.

Should instructional materials used by teachers reflect the dominant culture?

The dominant aspect of American culture is its diversity. Therefore, I believe a teacher's instructional materials should reflect the dominant culture—in all its variety. Our schools are places where learning should be based on the greatest amount of information—facts, philosophies, arguments and points of view—that we can communicate to students. As students study, they learn to analyze critically and to discern the sometimes subtle differences between good and bad, right and wrong, logic and nonsense and social and anti-social. They cannot do this in a womb of homogeneous thought. One of the most important roles of schools and teachers is to expose and instruct our young people in those parts of the dominant culture with which they are the least familiar.

Leo M. Yambrek, a Graduate of Western Michigan University and an Industrial Shift Foreman in Sheffield, Alabama; a Member of Eagle Forum and Instrumental in Convincing the Alabama State Board of Education to Remove Six Social Studies Textbooks from the Adoption List Recommended by the State Textbook Committee for 1981–1987.

Do you think that it is proper to prohibit high school students from reading certain books?

Questioning whether it is proper to prohibit high school students from reading certain books seems to be a backwards argument to the question of whether it is our legal and moral responsibility to ensure that high school students are reading the "best that has been known and said."

There has been a skillful use of rhetoric by certain pseudointellec-
tuals in the fields of publishing, national news media, and the educational establishment to distract concerned parents and taxpayers by
placing them at a psychological disadvantage and labeling their concerns as censorship, prohibition, bookburning, and textbook activism.
Barbara Morris, author of *Change Agents*, has stated that the issue of
offensive textbooks is just a symptom and censorship is a smoke screen
to drum up support for a dying school system.

As my wife and I have dared to become involved in the academic
education of our children instead of merely confining ourselves to the
socialization and extracurricular activities, we have found that our
children are being taught WHAT they must think and not HOW to
think. The tendency of today's textbooks is to supply knowledge from a
vacuum. For example, the presentation of evolution as a fact in Social
Study texts, distorting biblical doctrine, falsifying history, and shrinking
chronological facts out of sight are paramount in textbooks today.

Recently we have observed this same trend of relevancy and cultural acclimation in English Language texts. Many texts reviewed at a
recent textbook hearing in Alabama contained nonacademic material
that concentrated on psychosocial teachings of subversion and rebellion
against authoritative figures. Also many of the texts were written on a
low reading level for the grades they purport to teach and therefore
would not challenge a student to learn. Furthermore, some texts fostered the studying of cultural studies of Hobo signs, the latest dance
crazes, and the current Women's Equity movement, thereby indoctrinating the student in the author's biased philosophy.

If our children are to be exposed "to the best that has been known"
and if they are to have an education with a high degree of vitality, why
is there such a plethora of schoolbooks that foster behavior modification, situation ethics and hostility towards the American family?

We as concerned parents are absolutely right in our endeavor to try
to alter and change the nonacademic substance within our children's
textbooks and curriculums. Is it not a public education where everyone
should have the opportunity to participate freely and advance their
proposition? In reality we have a forced indoctrination by a selective
group choosing the criteria to be taught, choosing the material, choosing and developing the curriculum.

First, where do the rights of the parent and child to obtain an un-
biased, balanced and intellectually free education come in? These rights
do not exist in the compulsory public school education where quantity
is the priority and quality is the shrinking factor. In reality what we have
is a cosmetic trend of education rather than an education of substantive
nature!

What we are trying to do is to find a way out of the decaying walls of the public school system. But we are being charged by the opposition as trying to do something radical. It is not we who are the revolutionists but those in the field of academia being led by a very small group of rebellious disturbed individuals who have been clever enough to hide the real problem of a "dying public school system."

John Coyne has depicted the problem in a highly astute manner when he stated in his book, the *Kumquate Statement:* "There is anarchy in the groves of academe . . . . there is an intellectual order of settled antagonists that are against American institutions that presently rules academe." He also stated the very nature of intellectualism in academic inquiry has a leading tendency to assume that there are no truths. That every question is still an open question to be answered and everybody who has a position, point of view, or value that they hold dear is to remain open because there may be another truth to be found in the near future that substantiates their opinion. When the educational systems propagate opinion and sincerity as valid and factual, they have truly reached the "Age of Unreason." There must be reasonable limitations set. One reasonable limitation is to promote the intellectual nurturing of our children by transmitting the traditional basics of reading through phonics, writing and arithmetic within the moral and ethical framework of the Constitutional Republic.

Nurturing the child's intellect cannot be when one selects a concept such as a child should be able to read anything, especially when the term "anything" is one of a biased conceptualized philosophy. Anyone who proclaims a child's physical and psychological makeup cannot be affected in an adverse manner by what he or she reads is one of three things: completely incompetent, out of order, or stupid. If you believe that students cannot be adversely affected by what they read, you must also believe that they cannot be intellectually enriched by what they read, which is totally ridiculous!

Does freedom of educational speech mean that there are no limits? Does it mean, for example, that educators are free to expose children to information which might threaten the health, welfare, psychological and intellectual makeup of the child? The First Amendment is not an absolute; we cannot slander, defame and walk out in public naked. The potential dangers of public school educators to be guaranteed against interference and also effectively shielded from parents' and taxpayers' supervision represent a "massive power center." Such power, when handled licentiously, is capable of inflicting damage on our children, on our families and on our national freedom of speech. The great statesman, Benjamin Franklin, once said, "Abuses of the freedom of speech ought to be repressed, but to whom do we dare commit the power to do it?" Today it certainly is not one select group—as we have had in the selection of textbooks and the education of our children—such as the educators. The hard-working, taxpaying citizens and parents should be afforded every opportunity to speak freely and decide what goes into the minds of their children through public school education. We must remember that a librarian and a classroom instructor can censor more from a student in one week than any right wing or left wing group can in a year.

VI.

On Values and Morality

NO AREA OF SOCIAL STUDIES EDUCATION is more controversial than that of "Values and Morality." Questions heatedly debated include: Should students be deliberately taught to accept the principal values of a nation? Should students be encouraged to make their own judgments about the right and wrong of the values of their nation, even though some of their judgments might be opposed to such values? Should courses be taught with as much objectivity as possible, no distinctions being made between what is considered to be morally right and morally wrong? Should teachers and students be permitted to analyze freely every area of life of a nation and to criticize those values of which they do not approve? Should teachers concentrate on the task of imparting knowledge to students and keep out of the classroom any discussion of values and morality?

Values, as sociologist Robin M. Williams, Jr., points out, "are not the concrete goals of action, but rather the criteria by which goals are chosen." Morality, a term difficult to define in a way that is satisfactory to everyone, includes the codes of values, the principles of conduct, and the specific behavior of individuals and groups.

But the questions persist. *Whose* values? *Whose* morality? Plato's? Aquinas's? Kant's? Or the morality of each country? Each community? Each individual? And the debate goes on.

Any examination of American values and morality would seem to require some consideration of "Yankee Individualism," which, according to

Claude M. Fuess, the author of the first article in this section, manifests itself in such virtues as "resourcefulness, originality, thrift, integrity, simplicity, and stability." A headmaster of Phillips Academy in Andover, Massachusetts, and a biographer of such diverse personalities as Daniel Webster and Calvin Coolidge, Fuess admits that "Yankees are not, of course, all alike, but differ among themselves." Not every Yankee echoes the couplet: "Come weal, come woe/My status is quo!" Fuess is equally convinced, however, that "the Yankee, whether in Vermont, or Wisconsin, or South Dakota, is a type which we can ill afford to lose in a period when uniformity is a national peril."

For years Professor Earl S. Johnson of the University of Chicago presented innovative ideas in the field of social studies education, and his students disseminated his views widely. In "Reflections on Teaching the Social Studies," Johnson does not hesitate to disagree even with Socrates. Knowledge is *not* virtue, he declares. Then, with literary grace, he explains the reasons for his position.

The cognitive-developmental approach to moral education, Lawrence Kohlberg has stated, had its origins in Socrates' Athens, and "the research of my colleagues and myself has helped give the Socratic vision contemporary credibility." Some of the ideas of Kohlberg, a professor of education and social psychology at Harvard University, are outlined in his article, "Moral Development and the New Social Studies." When applied to the teaching of social studies, these ideas created considerable controversy. The controversy continues today.

In 1970 the program *Man: A Course of Study* was published. A course for upper elementary-school children, it focused on the study of human behavior and concerned itself with three questions: What is human about human beings? How did they get that way? How can they be made more so?

The teaching of *Man: A Course of Study* set off a national debate in the United States between those who hailed the course for its anthropological approach and ability to stimulate the thinking of students and those who criticized it for stressing moral relativism and leading children to accept bizarre human behavior as normal.

The public soon became actively involved in the discussions. In time, the debate reached the United States Congress, where Congressman John B. Conlan (R-Arizona) played a major role at committee meetings in attacking the controversial program. Peter B. Dow of the Education Development Center, Cambridge, Massachusetts, who became director of the program in 1966, was one of its strongest defenders.

The opposing views of John Conlan and Peter Dow are presented in the next selections, "The MACOS Controversy." Both men begin and conclude their presentations at opposite ends of a spectrum, and their candid comments reflect the sharp disagreements generated by the controversy.

If there were a Hall of Fame for the best cartoons depicting children in schools, surely the drawing of Miss Peach's class reciting the Pledge of Allegiance belongs in it. Remember the pupils' words?

> I play the legions
> To the Flag
> And to the public
> Sandwich it's for
> One action
> Invisible
> With library
> And just is for all.

"How Do We Stand with the Pledge of Allegiance Today?" asks Hyman Kavett, at the time associate professor of education–social studies at Richmond College, City University of New York, in the final article. His conclusion and his recommendation are as provocative today as they were a decade ago.

Yankee Individualism

CLAUDE M. FUESS

I am somewhat embarrassed in talking on Yankee Individualism in the presence of that sterling and representative Yankee, Mrs. Dorothy Canfield Fisher. But when I recall that she is herself a native of Lawrence, Kansas, I take heart, for I was born in the Mohawk Valley, and never saw New England until I came east to college. Speaking here, in the shadow of the Custom House, I feel like James Boswell, who said, on his first meeting with the Great Lexicographer, Dr. Samuel Johnson, "Sir, I do come from Scotland, but I cannot help it!" Ladies and Gentlemen, I do come from Central New York, but I cannot help it! So I, who am not a Yankee by birth or by name, am glad to remember, furthermore, that even a double-dyed Yankee like Robert Frost was born in San Francisco.

Some years ago, through an accident to which those who talk too much are occasionally liable, I found myself the target of violent denunciation. I had delivered an address on the "Vanishing Yankee," in which I had attempted what I thought to be a sympathetic appraisal of certain Yankee traits. For this I was promptly called to account by a few relatives of the Late George Apley, who apparently preferred eulogy to analysis. From one source, however, I received much comfort. A Polish tobacco grower with an unpronounceable name wrote me from Hadley, Massachusetts, saying, "I read your article on the Vanishing Yankee with great delight; and I just thought I ought to tell you that I married one. She hasn't vanished yet, and she has made me a better wife than I expected."

NOTE: This article appeared in *Social Education*, March 1947, pp. 103–106, 137.

This confession, from an acknowledged "foreigner," led me to reflect that the Yankee spirit may be marching on, like John Brown's soul, while the type itself is mouldering in many an abandoned graveyard. The Acropolis at Athens is a ruin, and "the grandeur that was Greece" has become a memory. But the words of Plato and Sophocles animate our modern culture, and the art of the Aegean peninsula has influenced the architects of our courthouses and libraries. Through some such transformation the Yankee, though he may be vanishing in New England, though his rock-strewn pastures may be covered with alders and poplars, has left a deep impress on our civilization.

Whatever his weaknesses in provincialism, parsimony, and lack of artistic taste, the Yankee was always an individualist, and New England has had its full share of characters as "crusted" as in any of the novels of Thomas Hardy. The central figure in Robert Frost's poem, *The Code*, is a helper in the hay-fields, who, when his "townbred" employer urges him to take pains with cocking the hay, suddenly thrusts his pitchfork in the ground and marches himself off home. A third man, who knows the Yankee, says to the owner:

> You've found out something.
> The hand that knows his business won't be told
> To do work better or faster—those two things.
> I'm as particular as anyone;
> Most likely I'd have served you just the same,
> But I know you don't understand our ways.

"Our ways!" The true Yankee has his peculiar code and pride, from which he cannot, will not, be deflected. Only too often he re-echoes the famous couplet:

> Come weal, come woe,
> My *status* is *quo*!

Everybody acquainted with New Hampshire and Vermont has learned from experience that you cannot engage a native to work for you by just offering him a good wage. He must be treated as an equal, pleaded with perhaps, if you expect him to be "your man." If you win his respect, however, he will follow you to the end. He prefers to loaf rather than toil in what he regards as a menial capacity or take a job beneath him. During this past summer I was for a time in a New York border village filled, as so many such communities are, with Yankees as "tart" as anybody in Vermont. The Mr. Green who came one day to do chores, out of loyalty to my wife, was seeing me for the first time, and I noticed that he watched me carefully as I sawed off the lower branches of the pines. A friend in the town asked him the next day if I was a good worker. "Yes," he admitted, rather grudgingly, but honestly, "He works pretty hard. But he didn't have breakfast the other day until eight o'clock!"

It is part of his individualism that the True Yankee distrusts pompousness and arrogance,—that he does not like "stuffed shirts." It must have been a Yankee trait in the Englishman, Charles Lamb, which led him once to go up to an obviously self-satisfied pedestrian and ask, with his inimitable stutter, "I b-b-beg your pardon, but are you any one in p-p-particular?" Many an urban rusticator in a New England hamlet would be astonished if he knew what those whom he calls the local peasantry know and say about him. They have no sense of inferiority. On the contrary, they quickly discern all the weaknesses of the alien, and use them for their own purposes. A visitor in one of these communities has to prove his worth before he can be accepted; and nobody will be more aware than his neighbors if he shows any superciliousness or pretence, or tries to "put on the dog."

The slogan, "Everybody's doing it!" is likely to make a Good Yankee move in the opposite direction. The Yankee is stubborn—or, if you prefer it, obstinate—in his reactions and rather enjoys being out of step. If I recall correctly, Vermont was one of the two states which voted for Taft in 1912; and it resisted the Democratic movement even in 1936, during a campaign of which it was said, "If Landon had made two more speeches Roosevelt would have carried Canada!" It does not disturb a Yankee to be one of a strong silent minority; indeed it rather strengthens his confidence in himself. Like the Highland Scots, he is always willing to espouse a Lost Cause, and his causes have not always been lost. Did he not resist to the end the encroachments of aggressive Yorkers on his Green Mountain Grants?

The Yankee insists on managing his private affairs, in taking care of himself, and consequently he is seldom "on the town." He loves his freedom of speech and of action. I have seen in a New England Town Meeting a farmer argue forcibly without the slightest evidence of servility or fear against the president of the local bank which held a mortgage on his property. Few Yankees feel that the world owes them a living. They go out and make it. A genuine Yankee would certainly resent being told that he could lay only eight hundred bricks a day. He might please to lay only five hundred, but he would never abandon his right to be more energetic if he chose to do so.

As a corollary the Yankee, no matter how meagre his income, hates to be in debt. He patterns his outgo on his intake, and usually has a little cash tucked away for an emergency. The late Colonel John C. Coolidge, whose income was seldom as much as $2,000, left at his death bank books containing an aggregate of $58,000—the savings of a lifetime. Out of his small salary he always planned to put aside a few dollars each month, and, once deposited, the money continued to draw interest and was never spent. There *are* good citizens who prefer to enjoy their money while they are still alive. But I venture to think that Colonel John derived as much satisfaction from the thought of that nest-egg as he would have had if he had maintained a yacht. That is the Yankee nature! And it is a phase of Yankee individualism.

As a horse-trader the Yankee has always been famous—and notorious—and his ability to handle himself in any financial transaction has rarely been doubted. His confidence in his ability to hold his own in competition is not often shaken. Mr. Frederick F. Van de Water, in his charming book, *A Home in the Country*, tells us how, when his wife and he were thinking of buying a house, "a sunny, kindly old gentleman was changed in a twinkling into a bargaining Yank, vigilant, shrewd." Mr. Van de Water explains that the excited maneuverings of a business deal are more than just financial transactions to "an old line Vermonter." "Purchase and sale comprise an odd, intense game into which he throws himself wholly and unscrupulously, and expects the like dedication and lack of mercy from his antagonist." This again is a manifestation of individualism—the matching of wits in a duel with an opponent!

The True Yankee has an instinct—with which I sympathize—for leaving people alone. His passion for gossip is, it is true, ineradicable, and the housewives spend much of their time at the windows, watching what is going on, or, in these modern days, at the party line telephone. But disliking interference, the Yankee resents paternalism even from a Republican administration. In order to survive, he has been compelled to be independent, reticent, and cautious, and he has learned to rely upon himself. Some one has remarked, "Not until you ask for it, and then only with the greatest reluctance, will a Yankee trespass on your individuality by telling you how to do something." And yet at the same time—and this is not a contradiction—he wishes to be a good neighbor. "Our community," said a friend of mine, "is a place where everybody talks about you when you are well and calls on you when you are sick." Seldom have I known such kindness as has been shown in one Yankee town towards persons who were ill or in distress.

Yankees are not, of course, all alike, but differ among themselves. One of my family had an old family retainer who did errands and raked up the leaves until he was past eighty. The head of the house was Lawrence B. Cushing, a descendant of the colonial aristocracy. Every morning when they met, the ancient servant said, "Good morning, Lawrence," and the employer responded, "Good morning, Mr. Pettengill!" Each was doing his proper share in the exchange of courtesies. But I have known Vermont Democrats who were proud of their dissent from their Republican relatives. "This," commented Edmund Burke, "is the very dissidence of dissent." Mr. Justice Holmes, whose dissenting opinions are now part of our legal heritage, was Yankee through and through, as his biographer indicates in the title of her book. It is the glorious privilege of Yankees, as it of Irishmen, to differ honestly and courageously and fiercely with one another. To listen to Yankee politicians as they discuss at Town Meeting the problems of sewage or road construction is to be at the very heart of American democracy.

The primary Yankee virtues are resourcefulness, originality, thrift, integrity, simplicity, and stability; and I submit that these are qualities badly needed in a world in which docility, extravagance, exhibitionism, suspicion, and greed are altogether too common. The Yankee has his weaknesses—I myself have commented on them more than once—but imitation has not been one of them. Whatever he has done, he has usually been himself; and for that blessed attribute I can forgive him his insensitiveness to beauty, his insularity, his excessive prudence, and his disturbing taciturnity. Perhaps even his silences, in an era when every public man is so voluble, may be reckoned as a virtue. A community made up solely of Yankees would perhaps be a little depressing. But Yankees and the Yankee spirit are needed to keep alive the idea that a man's soul is his own—and that he need not be managed or converted or reformed. I agree with the commentator who said, "Whatever changes are coming, the Yankee, I am convinced, will be the salt of whatever civilization he is a part."

Yankee individualism is deep rooted and persistent; and it is not remarkable, therefore, that he has carried this tradition on his migrations out of New England, across the continent and even into the tropical areas of Miami and Pasadena. On some of my tours I have been astonished—and pleased—to find in Ohio, in Minnesota, and even in Oregon the same white town hall, the same pillared church, and the same Yankee spirit that are part of Vermont's inheritance. As in the case of Athens, while Yankeedom may have been on the decline among its sources, it has leavened a vast area to the West. How often I have detected, beneath the expansive words of those who have been praising the California climate, an undertone of nostalgia for the east winds and the infinite variety of New England. As for Florida, it is dominated by retired Yankees, pitching horseshoes, playing checkers, and maintaining in their voluntary exile the mood of the cracker-barrel and the country store.

During the last quarter century, Yankee individualism on its own soil has been exposed to attack from many quarters, and it is marvellous that it has retained any vitality. The contemporary forces making for standardization are so potent and far reaching that they have affected even the most isolated hamlets. Unless one is really familiar with life in tiny mountain villages, he cannot understand how effectively the radio and the movies have carried urban ideas and ideals into the country. Fred Allen and Jack Benny, Charlie McCarthy and Frank Sinatra, Ingrid Bergman and Mae West, are as well known in Plymouth Notch as they are in the Algonquin Hotel; and Bette Davis actually spends her summers in Franconia. I have seen on Vermont streets on Sunday mornings hats fully as ridiculous as those which could be observed on Park Avenue.

A "wisecrack" which originates on Broadway is far up among the river valleys in twenty-four hours. All this makes for a monotony of tastes, for a unanimity of opinion, which violates essential principles of Yankeedom.

The easiest method of fostering mediocrity is to get everybody thinking in the same way, for without differing views there can be no honest test of what is true and good. The very unity of the German nation under Hitler was the prelude to its destruction. Individualism means freedom. The virtue of non-conformity is that it compels conformists to examine what they believe. Individualism, with its indifference to temporary popularity, is a quality which should be encouraged. And if it is genuine, it can never be completely crushed.

Now I am not claiming that Yankeeism is the only influence in this country working against uniformity. But I do declare that a little healthy Yankee spirit infused into other races can do them no harm. Personally I have no faith in pure Aryan stock as the indispensable solvent for our problems. For good or for evil, we are a mongrel people, and our extraordinary ancestral blends are among the sources of our strength. When Yankees marry Poles and Swedes and Irish and French, the consequences, measured in children, are likely to be good. When or if an Endicott weds a Groblewski or an Adams a Murphy, the mixture of blood may revive certain dormant attributes in both. I am told by rose growers that if a bush is left to itself for three or four years, it inevitably deteriorates, reverting to its primitive original, and that the proper method of growing beautiful blossoms is to graft them almost from year to year. Such a procedure in biology may mean that the best features of Yankee individuality may be perpetuated in families whose names have no Yankee sound. Strictly speaking, a hybrid is an offspring of a tame sow and a wild boar—but the result, I am told, is not to be despised!

The type of Yankee depicted by A. B. Frost or Joseph C. Lincoln, with gaunt bearded features, a drawl, a caustic humor, and complete independence, cannot last forever. Occasionally nowadays an artist finds such a survival and uses him for his own purposes. In Hollywood there are always hanging around the sets men who can be cast as Uncle Ezra or Cousin Hiram—specialists who have modeled themselves on caricatures of Yankees. But the people who have tried to imitate Calvin Coolidge have never done very well at it. Once, when Mr. Coolidge was sitting in his swivel chair in his White House office, a little group of newspaper men were discussing great orators. Finally one of them said in a loud voice, "Well, last week I heard Jim Watson of Indiana make a brilliant speech to his constituents. As he closed, he cried, 'And now, my friends, you have heard the facts as well as I can explain them, and you can vote for me or go to Hell.'" Nobody thought that the President was listening. But he did swing his chair slowly around and said, in his nasal tones, "It was a difficult alternative." Only a Yankee could have made a remark like that.

But the individualism of which I am speaking need not show itself in clothes or accent. The progeny of these mixed marriages will not say, "I swan!" or, "Gosh all hemlock!" and the ladies will not grow up to be angular spinsters, like those in the books of Mary E. Wilkins, with a propensity to gossip and acid repartee. But they may form their own opinions and hold to them, and they may develop the exasperating but salutary habit of asking at crucial moments, "Why?" or "What for?" When propaganda is being spread abroad by pressure groups in the manner so common in 1946, these individualists may have the courage to cry, "Stop a minute! Are you giving us food—or poison?" They may even possess the courage to halt pork barrel legislation by asking, as Coolidge used to do, "Where are you going to get the money?"—incidentally always a good Yankee question! Or they may even invoke Dwight W. Morrow's famous Rule Number 17, "Don't let's take ourselves too seriously!"

If any Southerner present objects to this laudation of Yankee virtues, permit me to say that the same plea for the preservation of individualism may be applied to Dixieland. Let the Gone-with-the-Wind Girls *continue* to say "You-all" and prefer mint juleps to hard cider. It will be a colossal disaster when life along the Suwannee River is the same as that on the banks of Lake Sunapee. Bombazine and crinoline each belongs in its own proper section, and Vermonters and Kentuckians ought never to be too much alike. I don't know very much about the Georgia "cracker" except that he has his own ways of doing things—or not doing them—and that I should hate to see him masquerading in store clothes. When all the Kentucky Colonels are dead, that will be a sad day for picturesque America.

The Yankee is not always a farmer, shut off among the lonely hills. Sometimes, like John Quincy Adams or Calvin Coolidge, he escapes to a broader world, to remain there still an individualist. Daniel Webster, although altered by success and perhaps corrupted by rich living, remained a New Hampshire Yankee to the end. Sometimes, like Mark Hopkins, he has become an inspiring teacher, or like Oliver Wendell Holmes and Harlan Fiske Stone, a distinguished jurist. Again, as in the cases of Thoreau and Emerson, he has entered the field of philosophy. Of course he has gone into business and often achieved amazing success through his resourcefulness; and he has even, like Horace Greeley, spread Yankee doctrines through the daily newspaper.

It would be easy to call the roll of hundreds of Yankees who have made their mark in cities across the continent, far from their native Yankee soil. I sometimes think that the type was never better illustrated than in John Garibaldi Sargeant, of Ludlow, Vermont, whom Coolidge made his Attorney-General—six feet, five inches tall, slow moving and slow talking, with a dry and sardonic wit, a lawyer whose reputation had spread through his own state. He came to Washington in 1925, on a bright sunny day, carrying his "goloshes," with true Yankee caution, in a paper bag. Although he never was really happy in the national capital transplanted from his Vermont environment, he won the respect of all the politicians who tried in vain to seduce him with their professional wiles. Among sophisticated statesmen he remained during his term of office the simple, independent, unspoiled Yankee who had his job to do; and when it was over he returned, probably with joy in his heart, to his Ludlow clients and the hills which he had never ceased to love.

Yankee individualism has its irritating qualities, especially when it is openly on the unpopular side, and it is often shown in that kind of stubbornness which resembles inertia, suspicion, or stupidity. But it is a valuable ingredient in a democracy, where all shades of sentiment need expression. It has furnished inspiration to artists, novelists, and dramatists, and has provided the material for Ethan Frome, Jethro Bass, and *Desire Under the Elms*. It is picturesque, persistent, and provocative. And the Yankee, whether in Vermont, or Wisconsin, or South Dakota, is a type which we can ill afford to lose in a period when uniformity is a national peril.

Reflections on Teaching
the Social Studies

EARL S. JOHNSON

It is my belief that the central issue in the teaching of the social studies is the "fact-value" issue—the relation of social knowledge to belief. Socrates stated this same issue as the relation of knowledge to virtue. But Socrates held that knowledge *is* virtue, a position which I cannot accept. That knowledge may be an *aid* to man's being virtuous, I would readily accept.

If we should say that the social sciences, from which the social studies take their content, are disciplines with the methods of the natural sciences and the subject matter of the humanities—poetry, *belle lettres*—we would be half right and half wrong. Hence, the statement needs two important modifications. *First*, the method of the social sciences brings knower and known together in ways unlike those which obtain in the natural sciences. This distinction is made simply and convincingly by Wilhelm Dilthey. For him, the method of the natural sciences is that of *anschauen*, literally, "looking at from the outside," while the method of the social sciences is that of *erleben*, literally, "re-living" the experience of other human beings. *Second*, and a consequence of the difference between *anschauen* and *erleben*, sympathy which is quite inappropriate in the study of the objects of physical nature—stars, atoms, or rocks—is an indispensable factor in the study of the objects of human nature.[1]

It is, then, the affinity which the method of the social sciences bears to humanistic materials—materials about which the social scientist can experience sympathy—that is the focus of my concern.

NOTE: This article appeared in *Social Education*, December 1960, pp. 351–353.

Let me put the problem in the words of the late Professor Robert Redfield. To the question, "What do the social sciences and the humanities have in common?" he answers, "They have humanity in common."

> Humanity is the common subject matter of those who look at men as they are represented in books or in works of art, and of those who look at men as they appear in institutions and indirect-visible action. . . . As physics is concerned with energy and matter, and biology with organisms and life processes, so social science is concerned with the way men and women feel and think and act. . . . What matters to us all, what we live for, is sympathy, understanding, imagination, reason, tradition, aspiration, and personal and human association.[2]

Thus, as Professor Redfield observes, the social scientists are closest to their materials when they are concerned with feelings, sentiments, opinions, standards, and ideals. This principle is true, he tells us, when the economist speaks of economic policy, for in this term he is really dealing with what somebody intends to do. Likewise, when the political scientist talks about the political machine. It is only figuratively a machine; it is really people with hopes, ambitions, intentions, and understandings.

I wish now to submit additional evidence, some of it cast in poetic form, of the truth that the social sciences and the humanities have humanity in common. I wish, in these illustrations, to suggest that there is something besides objective knowledge. This "something besides" is implied in Pascal's aphorism that "the heart hath its reasons which reason does not know."

I turn first to Alfred North Whitehead who, in writing about the teacher, said that "it is for him to elicit enthusiasm by resonance from his own personality and to create a larger knowledge and a firmer purpose." These, "a larger knowledge" and "a firmer purpose," symbolize, for me, the "something besides" of my concern.

I turn next to Keats:

> Through no great minist'ring
> reason sorts
>   Out the dark mysteries of human
> souls to clear convincing;
>   Yet there ever rolls a vast idea
> before me, and I glean therefrom
>   My liberty.

Now, a verse from a poet whose name I do not know:

> Knowledge, we are not foes
> I seek thee diligently,
>   But the world with a great wind blows,
> Shining, and not from thee.

Next some lines from Tennyson's "In Memoriam":

> Who loves not knowledge? Who shall rail
> Against her beauty? May she mix
> With men and prosper! Who shall fix
> Her pillars? Let her work prevail.

After this, omitting six lines and prefaced now with an implied "but," Tennyson continues:

> What is she, cut from love and faith,
> But some wild Pallas from the brain
> Of Demons? Fiery-hot to burst
> All barriers in her onward race
> For power . . .

And then these lines:

> A higher hand must make her mild,
> If all be not in vain; and guide
> Her footsteps, moving side by side
> With wisdom, like the younger child.

One more illustration of what I have called "something besides" objective knowledge which is the presence and importance of humanistic elements in human behavior. This I take from Dr. Glen Olds.

> Facts become pertinent to conduct when their meaning engages decisive human concern and this, in turn, is the effect of the clarity with which human beings embrace a philosophy and dedicate themselves to a faith that undergirds their system of values.[3]

Dr. Olds seems to be saying that men are not motivated by facts save they illuminate some values.

May I now tell you what these representations of the fact-value issue mean to one who has been a teacher and student of the social studies for more than 40 years. It is this: science used in the study of human beings is both a tool and a guide but that to which it guides lies not with science but with human passion and concern. Thus I would affirm the interdependence of the social and the humanistic which is the substance of the relation of facts to values.

In this view, the ultimate task of the social studies is to instruct and humanize the emotions. Likewise, in this view, the scientific attitude may be seen as full of passion; that is, as much a function of one's whole being and not merely the so-called intellectual part of him, as any other approach to human action. How meager, then, the view that the task of the social studies is to provide students with something called "the facts" without asking about the values of which they *are* the facts!

This all runs counter to the prevailing view, which is that it is the task of reason to do away with emotion. The facts are that all reflective experience has both an intellectual and an emotional content. It was

John Dewey who taught me that "there is no thought lest it be enkindled by an emotion." Furthermore, there is a rationality of feeling as well as a rationality of thought, for a thought is rational when it fits accurately the situation to which it refers. So, too, a rational emotion. Irrational thoughts and irrational emotions are, on the contrary, those which do not accurately fit the situations to which they refer.

I believe we ought to ponder soberly the true relation between intellect and emotion lest we take the mistaken view that it is the function of the intellect to dismiss the emotion. But such a view makes no sense for, if there is no emotion—no *conviction*—there is no need to turn to the intellect to instruct us how best to be responsible toward those matters which stir our emotions. If there is no emotion for the intellect to direct and discipline it can be engaged only in doing something with the greatest exactness, the most faultless reliability, and the nicest precision concerning matters which are not at all important. This would, indeed, be "scientism" at its best—or worst!

Guided by the view which I have sought to set forth, I wonder what would happen in a social studies class if the teacher should say, "Today, we are going to examine our faith—that in which we believe"—I mean, of course, our sociological rather than our theological faith!

May I now suggest some of the objects to which our students' faiths attach, as well as those areas of their experience in which those faiths—some of them at least—are probably already subject to considerable doubt and uncertainty.

> Faith in "father and mother know best," or "I'm old enough to go it alone"—with, of course, a hidden subsidy of both affection and cash.
> Faith in the politics and economics of the frontier in our twentieth century urban-industrial society.
> Faith in the view that "the facts speak for themselves."
> Faith in uncorrected common-sense unaided by any of the cautions and skills of science.
> Faith in opinions though they have no reliable facts to support them.

If the examination of the validity and usefulness of such articles of faith as these should result in the social studies being conceived as *moral* studies—which, of course, they are—the bearing of the facts-of-life upon the values-of-life might be illuminated and served. Our students might also come to understand that the ultimate task of the social studies is to aid in the making of choices between alternative values and that these, in the long run, are the stuff of both character and conduct. Thus, they might come more fully to understand the wisdom of the poet Shelley that the moral sciences only arrange the elements which poetry creates—with poetry interpreted, as I am sure Shelley meant, to refer to the human imagination at its best in whatever form expressed.

Let me make it clear, though, that such a view of the teaching of the social studies does not commit the teacher to giving students "right" moral answers. It is rather, in the words of the Persian poet, Kahlil Gibran, that of leading them to the "threshold of their own understanding" which they would test in the light of the demands of democratic humanism.

That this view of the teaching of the social studies involves great risks I am sure we all recognize—as indeed all purposive teaching does. There is, for our students, the risk that they may discover that they have no faith, no mortar wherewith to hold together the bricks of their values. They may discover that in its place they have only opinions subject, as may well be the case, to the vagaries of the winds of their gang, their club, or their clique.

For us, their teachers, there is the risk of being charged with the evil of introducing young minds to controversial matters. From this risk there is no protection unless it be the divorce of facts from values, in which case any fact is as good as any other and none is to be other than rote-learned.

I list no other risks, but now ask what might be the outcome, what might be both learned and *believed*, if the social studies were conceived as moral studies in the sense I have suggested. Such facts and beliefs as the following might, I should devoutly hope, come to be accepted by our students—convinced, as the old Dutchman put it, "by their own convincer":

> that emotions are subject to education, lest, without it they may well run amuck.
> that the discipline of precision, which is thought itself, has no task save that which comes from the play of imagination.
> that the function of thought is to "fix belief" on the ground of intelligence.
> that the business of being a thoughtful and perceptive human being is that of making judgments about better-or-worse, as well as about true-or-false.

If, perchance, such a conception of the purpose of the social studies would put us, its teachers, into conflict with our students, we would have reason to believe that some of their previous miseducation was being brought "to book."

Perhaps much of what I have tried to say is implicit in Socrates' warning to his friend Hippocrates. You may recall that Hippocrates was about to go to the house of Protagoras, the Sophist, to be taught by him.

It was this prospect which brought Socrates to speak as he did. After identifying knowledge as "the food of the soul," Socrates distinguished between buying knowledge and buying food. He spoke as follows:

> ... there is far greater peril in buying knowledge than in buying meat and drink; the one you purchase of the wholesale or retail dealer, and carry them away in other vessels, and before you receive them into the body as food, you may deposit them at home and call in an experienced friend who knows what is good to be eaten and drunken, and what not, and how much, and when. But you cannot buy the wares of knowledge and carry them away in another vessel; when you have paid for them you must receive them into the soul and go your way, either greatly harmed or greatly benefited. . . .[4]

It is worth knowing, is it not, the difference between shopping at the A & P chain store and going to school?

Notes

[1] See H. A. Hodges, *Wilhelm Dilthey, An Introduction.* New York: Oxford University Press, 1944.

[2] "Social Sciences Among the Humanities." *Measure* 1:63–4; Winter 1950.

[3] "Ideas: Man is not Primarily a Fact." *Saturday Review*, February 15, 1958.

[4] The *Protagoras.*

Moral Development and the New Social Studies

LAWRENCE KOHLBERG

The invitation to speak to this group came at the right time. During the past two years my colleagues and I have finally taken the plunge from doing research to piloting social studies curricula. Accordingly I hope this occasion will provide some chance to get some feedback and guidance from all of you with greater experience. This is particularly important to me because we are not interested so much in creating new curricula as in adapting already existing new social studies curricula and methods to what I conceive to be the fundamental aims of education, the stimulation of cognitive and moral development. In stating my goals in this fashion I wish to acknowledge my debt to the greatest modern educational psychologist and philosopher, John Dewey. In 1895, Dewey said:

> Only ethical and psychological principles can elevate the school to a vital institution in the *greatest of all constructions—the building of a free and powerful character*. Only knowledge of the *order and connection of the stages in psychological development can insure the maturing of the psychical powers*. Education is the work of *supplying the conditions* which will enable the psychological functions to mature in the freest and fullest manner.

The educational implications of Piaget's work in cognitive stage development and my work in moral stage development may be best understood as outgrowths of this statement of Dewey.

NOTE: This selection, an address delivered at the 52nd Annual Meeting of the NCSS, appeared in *Social Education*, May 1973, pp. 369–375. Reprinted by permission of Lawrence Kohlberg.

While Dewey clearly saw that education should be the supplying of the conditions of development through sequential cognitive and moral stages, seventy years of American educational psychology did nothing to aid Dewey's vision. Instead, it followed Thorndike's direction and viewed cognitive education as a matter of instruction and behavioral learning and moral education as a matter of transmitting culturally accepted values and behaviors. You are fortunate enough to have the world's most distinguished representative of this Thorndike tradition, B. F. Skinner, to speak to you later. For today, it is my job to present the major alternative vision of education, the cognitive-developmental tradition of Dewey. This tradition emigrated to Piaget's Switzerland where it was vastly enriched, and has now returned to this country and flourished this last ten years. My own work in moral development and moral education is part of it. The major theme of my talk, then, is the relation of this new-old cognitive-developmental psychology of moral and political development to that other trend of the sixties, the new social studies. Actually there is little intellectual effort needed to integrate these two trends because both trends stem directly from Dewey. I'm afraid I'm going to bore some of you by going over the Deweyite assumptions of the new social studies, but I get a bit alarmed when I see your workshop titles about being "with it." Dewey had an older conception of educational relevance that had nothing to do with being "with it," and it is this older conception which underlies the basic curriculum work of the sixties.

Before going into detail on the new social studies, I want to emphasize its larger Deweyite aim. This is the development of active thought about and concern for society. Such a development must necessarily center on a conception of social justice. Development of a sense of justice can, in turn, occur only in just schools.

While these Deweyite statements may sound like platitudes, they are entirely ignored by the dominant norms of education, which are still those of information-accumulation in the service of competitive academic achievement. With such norms, a hidden curriculum often develops, one which says that conformity to authority and competition for status are the values which count in the school.

It does no good to criticize the hidden curriculum, however, unless one can point to the mistakes in the explicit curriculum. Without changing the explicit curriculum, we can't change the hidden curriculum. A critique of the dominant curriculum need not be based on moral grounds alone. Recent research findings indicate that when I.Q. and social class are controlled for, grades and achievement tests based on acquisition of facts predict to almost nothing in later life except other school grades and achievement tests. It is not surprising to find that high school or college achievement do not predict to the deeper criteria of a worthwhile life, such as happiness, or moral contribution to a community. It is surprising and worth noting that achievement tests don't even predict to achievement in its gross American pragmatic meaning of mobility. High school students high on grades and achievement scores do no better economically than those low in achievement, college students high in achievement do no better than those low in achievement scores when social class background and I.Q. are controlled.

Most of you are not completely inspired by a vision of education's goals as upward mobility, but this is the only outside criterion which the rationale of academic achievement tests marked on a curve suggest. The ethical fallacy of education for upward mobility is that it can only mean elevation of some at the expense of others. In the form of compensatory education, however, education for mobility seemed nobler in purpose. As compensatory education was translated into practice its goal remained confounded by its pragmatic relativism; however, its goal was elevating the entire country above the 50th percentile on achievement tests. My colleague Sandy Jencks has completed an extensive study showing that compensatory education has failed to diminish economic inequality and proposes income redistribution instead of education to serve social justice. You can think the thing through without a computer, however. Obviously, the only way the schools can contribute to social justice is by developing a sense of justice in the young. And this can only be done by making the schools more just.

Having stated a Deweyite vision of the social role of the schools, let us go into curricular details. There are five basic postulates of the new social studies, all derived from John Dewey. The first is the replacement of rote-learned facts by an emphasis upon active thought and reasoning. The Deweyite emphasis upon active thought is reflected in such terms as inquiry-learning, as learning the application of scientific methods to social material, as critical or reflective thinking. This Deweyite root of the new social studies is especially explicit in the influential work of Hunt and Metcalf but is evident in most of the other curricula as well.

We have said that the first Deweyite element of the new social studies is the emphasis on active thought. Second, related to this emphasis on active thought is a recognition of the distinction between the content of thinking and the form or process of thinking. If there is a desirable process of thinking, then the development of such thought process can be stimulated regardless of content areas. The same basic patterns of inquiry and judgment are involved whether the material is American history, civics, or East Asian culture. The third postulate of the new social studies, then, is its necessarily interdisciplinary nature. The fourth related Deweyite postulate of the new social studies is the centrality of the problematic case, the use of relevant concrete cases representing social problems.

So far I have discussed four postulates of the new social studies which all refer to the cognitive, the scientific, the factual. Other postulates of the new social studies concern the role of value-judgment in social studies. Corresponding to the traditional emphasis upon social education as transmission of facts is the traditional emphasis upon transmission of the majority values of middle-class America. In the fifties there was great pressure on education not only to transmit the facts and technology needed to beat the Communists, but to transmit the traditional Americanism needed to ward off Communism. An example is the text, *Civics for Americans*, written by Clark, Edmonson and Dondineau in 1954. They say:

> *Civics for Americans* is a book designed to help young people develop the characteristics of good citizenship. Primarily these characteristics are devotion to the Constitutional government of the United States, respect for law and appreciation of the advantages of a free-enterprise economy, faith in God and man and in the tenets which distinguish our way of life. Willingness to assume the responsibilities of school citizenship is essential to developing these characteristics.

The so-called revolution of values of the sixties has, of course, made this rhetoric of Americanism archaic. As I shall point out, however, it is easy to relapse into more current-sounding rhetoric which rests on the same obsolete ethical and psychological foundation. The foundation of the old civic educator was the transmission of unquestioned truths of fact and of unquestioned consensual values to a passively receptive child. The polite word which the psychology of the fifties chose for value-indoctrination was "political socialization." This transmission of consensual values was usually defined in terms of what I call a bag of virtues, a set of desirable personality traits. "A Boy Scout is loyal, clean, reverent and brave." A good citizen shows respect for law, responsibility, etc.

As Clark, Edmonson and Dondineau say:

> Scientists have not as yet attempted to measure citizenship ability but we might find it interesting to try. We might find out whether a student would be placed in the stone, sponge, or spark group of citizens.
>
>   Do you: 1) know the rules of your school and try to obey them; carry out assignments promptly and to the best of your ability? 2) work on committees in the classroom and in other school activity if asked to do so? etc..."

As I say, while such rhetoric is dead, the view of social education as the transmission of consensual values through a bag of virtues is far from dead. If patriotism and the Red Menace is out, ecology and the ecological menace is in. Today the good ecological boy scout picks up litter in the environment as yesterday he helped the old lady across the street. Where yesterday he was loyal and reverent, today he is world-minded and aware. In saying this I am, of course, not criticizing an emphasis on ecological or world problems but only pointing to the limits of putting new content in old forms.

In contrast to the transmission of consensual values, the new social studies have been based on Dewey's conception of the valuing process. According to Dewey, factual scientific judgment and value judgments have important common characteristics and both represent aspects of a process of solution of problematic social situations. Just as there are rational, critical or reflective modes of reasoning about fact, there are rational, critical or reflective modes of valuing. Much of the new social studies effort to stimulate critical or reflective modes of valuing has gone under the banner of value clarification. In the work of Raths and Simon, this has an explicit derivation from Dewey.

The fifth postulate of the new social studies, then, was the need for clarification of values, for critical thinking about one's own value-assumptions in the context of situations of value-conflict. This, in turn, generates a sixth postulate of the new social studies, the need to focus upon situations and issues which are not only problematic but controversial. From this point of view, the new social studies generate objectives beyond analytic or reflective processes of reasoning and valuing. These objectives spring from a Deweyite recognition of social education as a process with forms of social interaction as its outcome. A Deweyite concern about action is not represented by a bag-of-virtues set of behavioral objectives. It is reflected in an active participation in the social process. This means that the classroom, itself, must be seen as an arena in which the social and political process takes place in microcosm. One form of this concern is reflected in the Oliver, Shaver and Newmann jurisprudential approach to the new social studies. This approach stresses the quality of discussion between students of controversial issues, discussion judged in terms of criteria of effective processes of conflict resolution in a democratic pluralistic society. Don Oliver has moved on from the discussion of controversial cases to a concern for processes of self-government and community in the school, an extension implicit in the Dewey canon.

While the new social studies of the sixties have worked out these Deweyite assumptions in a truly impressive way, they have neglected two central assumptions of the Deweyite canon. The first is the psychological assumption of cognitive and moral stages and the parallel assumption that education is supplying the conditions for development through the stages. The second is the philosophic recognition of ethical principles as defining the aims of social education. Just as there are non-arbitrary principles of scientific method and judgment, there are non-arbitrary ethical principles of value-judgment. In the social area, these principles are the principles of social justice elaborated by the liberal tradition from John Locke to Mill and Dewey, and most recently in John Rawls' major new book, *A Theory of Social Justice.*

It is these two themes of Dewey which have been elaborated in my work on moral stages and I believe these two themes correct certain basic gaps in the new social studies. Let me first turn to the easy part, the psychological part. Let me start with cognitive development. For the purposes of the new social studies, the most important findings in cognitive development are the verifications of Piaget's description of adolescence as the period of development of *abstract, reflective* thought. More exactly, adolescence is the period of transition from logical inference as a set of *concrete operations* to logical inference as a set of *formal operations* or "operations upon operations." "Operations upon operations" imply that the adolescent can classify classification, that he can combine combinations, that he can relate relationships. It implies that he can think about thought, and create thought systems or "hypothetico-deductive" theories. This involves the logical construction of all possibilities—that is, the awareness of the observed as only a subset of what may be logically possible. In related fashion, it implies the hypothetico-deductive attitude, the notion that a belief or proposition is not an immediate truth but a hypothesis whose truth value consists in the truth of the concrete propositions derivable from it.

An example of the shift from concrete to formal operations in social studies may be taken from the work of E. A. Peel. Peel asked children what they thought about the following event: "Only brave pilots are allowed to fly over high mountains. A fighter pilot flying over the Alps collided with an aerial cable-way, and cut a main cable causing some cars to fall to the glacier below. Several people were killed." A child at the concrete-operational level answered: "I think that the pilot was not very good at flying. He would have been better off if he went on fighting." A formal-operational child responded: "He was either not informed of the mountain railway on his route or he was flying too low. Also, his flying compass may have been affected by something before or after take-off setting him off course and causing collision with the cable."

The concrete-operational child assumes that if there was a collision the pilot was a bad pilot, the formal-operational child considers all the possibilities that might have caused the collision. The concrete-operational child adopts the hypothesis that seems most probable or likely to him. The formal-operational child constructs all possibilities and checks them out one by one.

Now what is striking about the development of formal operations is its closeness to the cognitive goals of the new social studies as reflective, hypothesis-testing and analytic thinking. When this is understood, certain difficulties and ambiguities in the new social studies become apparent. First, social inquiry or analytic thinking cannot be taught, although its development can be stimulated and extended. Our research findings indicate that only 53% of middle-class sixteen- to eighteen-year-olds are fully capable of formal operational thought. If sizable portions of adolescents are incapable of hypothetical inquiry, they are unlikely to find the new inquiry training appealing or stimulating. No matter how relevant and colorful one makes problems of a society, these problems are still too abstract to be problems for students who are not yet formal operational. Something similar is to be said with regard to notions of social science methods of generalization and proof involved in the new social studies. In these regards, Jerry Bruner's notions were misleading, his notion of the structure of the disciplines and his notion that any discipline could be taught at any cognitive level by appropriate techniques. Social science and legal disciplines, as patterns of thought, are extensions of a natural mode of thought, that of formal operations. They are not really relevant models of thought for children at an earlier stage of thought.

Moral Stages

Let me turn now from cognitive to moral stages which I think are of even greater significance to social studies education. These stages are defined in the table in your handout. They have been verified by an eighteen-year longitudinal study of fifty American males interviewed every three years from ages ten to twenty-eight. The study indicates that all go through the same sequence of stages. While the rate of development of the stages and the terminal point of adult development are different for different individuals, the nature and the order of the stages of moral thought are the same for all. The cultural universality of the stages and their order has been confirmed in a number of cross-cultural studies including a longitudinal study in a Turkish village. Some of the age trends for the stages are presented in the figures in the handout.

When one speaks of moral stages, one does not generally think of something directly related to social and civic education. One thinks, perhaps, of the development of conscience, of an internal motive or monitor for moral decision. Conscience, however, is only one of ten major issues or institutions used to define the stages. Other issues are more familiar to social studies, the issues of law, of civil liberties, of authority, of property, etc. Each of these institutions is understood and valued in a new way at each new stage. To illustrate, we will cite the conceptions of civil rights of Johnny, a bright middle-class boy. He is responding to the following dilemma:

Before the civil war, we had laws that allowed slavery. According to the law if a slave escaped, he had to be returned to his owner like a runaway horse. Some people who didn't believe in slavery disobeyed the law and hid the runaway slaves and helped them to escape. Were they doing right or wrong?

This dilemma involves the issues of conscience, of law, and of civil liberties. Johnny answers the question this way when he is ten.

They were doing wrong because the slave ran away himself, they're being just like slaves themselves trying to keep em away.

He is asked, "Is slavery right or wrong?" He answers:

> Some wrong, but servants aren't so bad because they don't do all that heavy work.

Johnny's response is Stage 1, *punishment and obedience orientation*. Breaking the law makes it wrong; indeed, the badness of being a slave washes off on his rescuer. He does not yet have concepts of rights.

At age thirteen he is asked the same question. His answer is mainly a Stage 2 *instrumental relativism of rights*. He says:

> They would help them escape because they were all against slavery. The South was for slavery because they had big plantations and the North was against it because they had big factories and they needed people to work and they'd pay. So the Northerners would think it was right but the Southerners wouldn't.

So early comes Marxist relativism of class interest. He goes on:

> If a person is against slavery and maybe likes the slave or maybe dislikes the owner, it's okay for him to break the law if he likes, provided he doesn't get caught.

Skipping to age nineteen, in college, Johnny is Stage 4, *orientation to maintaining a social order of rules and rights*. He says:

> They were right in my point of view. I hate the actual aspect of slavery, the imprisonment of one man ruling over another. They drive them too hard and they don't get anything in return. It's not right to disobey the law, no. Laws are made by the people. But you might do it because you feel it's wrong. If fifty thousand people break the law, can you put them all in jail? Can fifty thousand people be wrong?

Johnny here is oriented to the rightness and wrongness of slavery, itself, and of obedience to law. He doesn't see the wrongness of slavery in terms of equal human rights but in terms of an unfair economic relation, working hard and getting nothing in return. The same view of rights, in terms of getting what you worked for, leads Johnny to say about school integration:

> A lot of colored people are now just living off of civil rights. You only get education as far as you want to learn, as far as you work for it, not being placed with someone else, you don't get it from someone else.

Rightness for John is defined by "50,000,000 Frenchmen can't be wrong." Here in Massachusetts, at least, we can say, "Yes, they can be." John had not reached Stage 5 when last interviewed at age twenty-four. There is, however, hope; we have had some subjects move from Stage 4 to Stage 5 in their late twenties.

We do not know when Martin Luther King moved from Stage 5 to Stage 6 but he left us this Stage 6 statement concerning civil rights and civil disobedience:

One may well ask, "How can you advocate breaking some laws and obeying others?" The answer lies in the fact that there are two types of laws, just and unjust. One has not only a legal but a moral responsibility to obey just laws. One has a moral responsibility to disobey unjust laws. Any law that uplifts human personality is just, any law that degrades human personality is unjust. An unjust law is a code that a numerical or power majority group compels a minority group to obey but does not make binding on itself. This is difference made legal.

You can see how this Stage 6 view takes into account the Stage 5 claims of the social contract and constitutional law. As I have illustrated the stages, they represent an increasing awareness of justice and a disentangling of justice from the particular accepted rules of the culture. A concern about justice is, however, present at every stage of development. I like to cite, as an example, the earliest moral act of one of my sons. At the age of four my son joined the pacifist and vegetarian movement and refused to eat meat, because as he said: "It's bad to kill animals." In spite of lengthy Hawk argumentation by his parents about the difference between justified and unjustified killing, he remained a vegetarian for six months. Like most Doves, however, his principles recognized occasions of just or legitimate killing. One night I read to him a book on Eskimo life involving a seal-killing expedition. He got angry during the story and said: "You know, there is one kind of meat I would eat, Eskimo meat. It's bad to kill animals so it's all right to eat them."

This eye for an eye, tooth for a tooth concept of justice is Stage 1. You will recognize, however, that it is a very genuine though four-year-old sense of justice. Fundamental to the sense of justice are the concepts of reciprocity and equality. At each stage these concepts take on a new form.

In stressing justice as the core of moral development, I need to note that justice or fairness is only one of four decision-making orientations, each available at every stage. These orientations are the rules-orientation, the pragmatic or utilitarian consequences orientation, the justice orientation and the conscience or ideal-self orientation. Each stage has a different concept of rules, of utility, of fairness and of a good or ideal personality. But we have also been able to define substages at each stage: an A stage oriented to rules and pragmatic consequences and a B stage oriented to fairness. While individuals sometimes skip a B substage, most eventually end at a B or fairness substage of whatever highest stage they attain.

The examples I have used suggest that moral stages lie at the core of political or social value-decisions. To more systematically demonstrate this, Al Lockwood interviewed adolescents around two sets of dilemmas. The first were our standard set. The second were public policy dilemmas taken from Don Oliver's curriculum. Moral stage could easily be defined on both sets of dilemmas. There was a significant correlation of forty-two between moral maturity on the standard moral dilemmas and on the policy dilemmas, with mental age or cognitive maturity controlled.

What Do You Do About Moral Stages?

Given the existence of moral stages, what do you do about them? Certainly one wants to go beyond value-clarification. Value-clarification procedures have usually been based on the assumption that all values are relative. As summarized by Engel (1970) this position holds that:

> In the consideration of values, there is no single correct answer but value clarification is supremely important. One must contrast value clarification and value inculcation.
>
> This is not to suggest, however, that nothing is ever inculcated. As a matter of fact, in order to clarify values, at least one principle needs to be adopted by all concerned. That principle might be stated: in the consideration of values there is no single correct answer. More specifically it might be said that the adequate posture both for students and teachers in clarifying values is openness.

While we agree with Engel in stressing openness and avoidance of inculcation, we do not agree that all values are relative nor do we teach children value-relativity, which in its strong sense is an unsound doctrine, both philosophically and in terms of social science fact. There are culturally universal moral values differently conceived at each stage. The order of the stages also is universal and it is an order of moral adequacy, an increasing approximation to a rational philosophy, as conceived by moral and political philosophers. Rawls' *Theory of Social Justice* is a good statement of Stage 6.

If relativism is an incorrect philosophic view, then the educational objective of stimulation of moral stage development cannot be called indoctrinative. First, it is non-indoctrinative because it is not addressed to transmitting specific value-content but to stimulating a new way of thinking and judging. Second, it is non-indoctrinative because it is not imposing something alien on the student. Movement to the next stage is movement in a direction natural to him, it is movement in the only direction he can go. Finally, it is non-indoctrinative because the core of moral stages is a sense of rights and justice. Our whole objection to indoctrination presupposes a sense of rights, but such a sense of human rights can only occur through the process of moral development.

We have discussed developmental moral education as non-indoctrinative in its objectives. It is also non-indoctrinative in its methods which are not very different than methods of value-clarification. As first elaborated by Moshe Blatt, our classroom method stressed use of the kind of dilemmas and the kind of argument between students which evokes cognitive-conflict, a sense of disequilibrium about one's own position.

Second, it involved confrontation of students at adjacent stages. Laboratory studies by Turiel and Rest had demonstrated that adolescents comprehend all stages below their own and sometimes the next stage up, and that they prefer the highest stage they comprehend. When adolescents were exposed to all stages, the most change occurred to exposure to the next stage up.

Blatt could make use of these principles because most classrooms contain students at three stages. Blatt had students at the two lowest stages confront one another, then moved to a confrontation with the third stage. Blatt conducted these discussions with junior high and high school students in ghetto schools, in suburban schools, in working-class white schools. His results held across these variables. Each classroom showed significant upward movement in moral thought, compared to controls. Amount of change varied from class to class. In Blatt's best class two-thirds of the children moved to the next stage up. In his worst, only 15% moved a stage. All classrooms' change was to the next stage up. And all classrooms remained significantly above controls on one-year follow-up.

Blatt's work was a good beginning but we are still far from having optimal methods for a developmental social studies. Of even more importance, we need to expand Blatt's procedures to form a developmental approach to social studies actually usable in the schools. Two pilot projects supported by the Stone Foundation are attempting to do that. It did not take much persuasion by Bill Leary, Boston's superintendent, to get us to start a project which would integrate our moral development approach with an existing new social studies curriculum. This was Bill Gibson's law curriculum for inner-city adolescents, as elaborated by Phil Gibbons. Gibbons and Phil Moskoff are relating points of substantive law to a Blatt-type discussion of moral and legal dilemmas at Jamaica Plain High School. If, as we hope, there is substantial change through this program, we plan to extend it to other Boston schools. I may add that the marriage of moral discussion and law is natural. At lower stages there is great difficulty distinguishing the legal and the moral, and students often demand a knowledge of the law to approach a moral dilemma. Our law project is cooperating with a parallel history project of Ted Fenton's incorporating the moral discussion approach. A second elementary school project led by Bob Selman is the subject of a workshop tomorrow. This project involved developing verbal dilemmas and pretesting to see whether discussing the dilemmas was something that engaged first and second graders. Satisfied that it was, we consulted on filmstrip adaptations of these dilemmas. We are now pretesting and post-testing children involved in these filmstrip discussions led by four different teachers. Our hope is that these two projects will help communicate to teachers an understanding of the developmental approach which they can apply to any new social studies curricula.

You will wonder whether we are concerned about moral action as well as moral reasoning. When Blatt was working in a suburban school, the principal said, "What are you doing all this verbal moral discussion for when we need your help with moral behavior problems of pregnancy, drugs and theft." I told him we'd like to work on moral action but he had to understand that the core of moral action was a sense of justice. To develop moral action we would want the students to express their sense of justice as well as talk about it and make the school more just. If he indeed wanted to make his school more just, we would be glad to help him. That ended his interest in getting our help on moral behavior. We did find a prison that was interested, however. For the past two years we have aided the prison staff to develop a just community approach in one of the cottages based on a self-government community meeting, as well as moral discussion. While there have been many ups and downs, it has gone amazingly well and we think we can stimulate moral action as well as moral thought.

When we have translated this experience into creating a more just school, I'll want to come back and talk again.

MACOS: The Push for a Uniform National Curriculum

JOHN B. CONLAN

In recent months [1975] there has been considerable national discussion of Man: A Course of Study *(MACOS), a social studies program of the Education Development Center. In an effort to clarify some of the issues,* Social Education *is publishing the following two statements: one is a commentary by Peter B. Dow of EDC on the most frequently asked questions about MACOS; the other is a statement by Congressman John B. Conlan (R-Arizona), a member of the Committee on Science and Technology of the U.S. House of Representatives.*

The controversial fifth-grade social studies program "Man: A Course of Study," and the federal government's role in helping its small group of ardent promoters to spread its use throughout the nation, has placed teachers and school officials squarely in the middle of a political thicket.

Thousands of parents across America view MACOS as a dangerous assault on cherished values and attitudes concerning morals, social behavior, religion, and our unique American economic and political life-style.

As Peter Dow states elsewhere in this issue, MACOS "is designed to raise questions, not to answer them." The course allots half a year to study the social behavior and mating habits of birds, fish, and baboons, with the implicit view that man not only evolved from lower animals but also derived his social behavior from them.

Children are then exposed for a full semester to the alien Netsilik Eskimo subculture, in which the following practices are rationalized and approvingly examined in free-wheeling classroom discussions:

NOTE: This article appeared in *Social Education*, October 1975, pp. 388–392. Reprinted by permission of John B. Conlan.

- Killing the elderly and female infants
- Wife-swapping and trial marriage
- Communal living
- Witchcraft and the occult
- Cannibalism

Many educators, including an anthropoligist at Cornell University originally associated with the MACOS project, have condemned the course as imparting a dishonest view of man. They say it is a "brainwash," stifling academic freedom of teachers and the development of children. These educators view the federal government's role to promote MACOS and other curriculum programs as an ominous move toward a uniform federal standard in education.

Parents also consider the National Science Foundation's aggressive role to induct teachers and school decision-makers into the university-based MACOS promotion and marketing network—to spread the MACOS "gospel"—as an insidious attempt to take over education and the upbringing of their children.

In areas where school districts and universities are participating in these efforts to bring MACOS and similar federally-funded programs into local schools, an adversary relationship is building up between parents and their local school systems. Political leaders are being asked to help parents and local school officials regain local control, free from federal interference, that they consider rightfully theirs.

Dubious Justification for NSF's MACOS Role

Defenders of MACOS and other radical departures from traditional education made their pitch for federal funding and massive implementation efforts by claiming that the complex multimedia approach and controversial materials of this "innovative" approach to teaching were unacceptable to commercial publishers, thus justifying considerable government support to get their program off the ground and into schools.

While this begs the question of why any federal agency would spend $4.2 million developing an unmarketable program, they accurately state the problem. MACOS was rejected by 58 major publishers of school instructional materials. Only through some highly questionable arrangements between Education Development Center, the MACOS developer, and the National Science Foundation was it possible to put Curriculum Development Associates in the business of publishing MACOS commercially.

A special discount on royalties owed to the federal government was arranged to make MACOS commercially viable. Royalties are required so that federally-funded curriculum materials will not undercut competition from other publishers of school programs. In this case, to make MACOS fly, NSF cut the royalty rate owed by CDA by half so MACOS *could* undercut competition.

In addition, NSF spends between $200,000 and $250,000 or more each year to help promote and market MACOS. This money is used to hold promotion conferences for school decision-makers and officials, to lobby them to buy the program. Universities throughout the country apply for and receive substantial NSF grants to train teachers in the MACOS philosophy and pedagogy, and to enlist the support of other local educators and school officials for the program.

All these arrangements are currently being investigated by Congress, and the House of Representatives has ordered NSF not to subsidize promotion and marketing of elementary and secondary school materials next year. Congress said no federal funds should be used to promote school materials unless parents and educators have given widespread assurance that a real national need exists for such involvement.

MACOS is not the only program affected by this funds cut-off. NSF is currently promoting about 50 different school programs for nation-wide dissemination. Education Development Center is this month holding its initial educator promotion conference, with a $96,000 NSF grant, to launch its promotion and marketing educator network for "Exploring Human Nature," the tenth-grade sequel to MACOS. NSF will have to stop funding the marketing of all these programs.

Curriculum "Innovation" Has Become Big Business

Make no mistake about it: Curriculum "innovation" is Big Business for EDC. This multi-million dollar operation, which gets more than 87 percent of its funds from U.S. and foreign government agencies, is involved in a worldwide effort to push its particular brand of education. EDC receives almost 33 percent of its funds from NSF, which has pumped more than $33.6 million its way since 1963. EDC's social studies programs are developed by Jerome S. Bruner and like-minded behaviorists, whose philosophy has come under increasing fire in academic and professional circles.

Among the thousands of letters I have received from throughout the country since the MACOS issue came before Congress, one typically perceptive writer—a clinical psychologist from the East—recently wrote me this personal view about the type of operation EDC and NSF are involved in:

> Public schooling in the past 20 to 30 years has become Big Business in every unfortunate sense of the word. It has spawned an entirely new professional, the Educator. An administrator and authority on education

whose knowledge and experience are often sadly lacking as to teaching, children, or the classroom itself.

Schools have become the arena for the productions of social and behavioral scientists, to whom progress is all too synonymous with change and reform. Schools are the scene of all sorts of quasi-experimentation and, I am tempted to add, exploitation. At times it seems that the child and parent, whose interests should be primary, are in danger of becoming mere grist for the mill of the educational program and theory.

We have seen an incredible expansion of school programs to include almost every aspect of the child's life, his physical health, recreation, mental health, and now his social well-being. There has been an endless succession of revisions of educational practices, innovative procedures, or "enrichments." Hopes have been raised for the Open Classroom and Permissiveness. Children have been spared the indignity of grades.

Parents have struggled with New Math, tried to adapt to patterns of social and emotional guidance. Teachers have struggled with new methods of teaching, tried to tailor subject matter to the individual child and to be counselor and friend to both parent and child, not "just teacher."

The public has meekly, even proudly met the astronomical costs, approved new bond issues and paid the taxes. Yet today we are confronted with increasingly bitter evidence that our schools are failing in large degree to teach basic knowledge or skills, and their social efficacy is deteriorating rapidly and tragically.

Moral Relativism to Blame for Social Ills

Onalee McGraw, parent and housewife whose doctorate in government makes her a particularly effective coordinator and spokesman for the National Coalition for Children, recently spoke about deteriorating education and school standards in testimony before the Senate subcommittee that authorizes the NSF's budget.

She appeared to urge an end to MACOS funding and a drastic reform of NSF education grant management practices, saying that current NSF policies were responsible for supporting a growing monopoly over education by social engineers and experimental psychologists.

She cited courses like MACOS as the cause of frightening functional illiteracy, and social and moral confusion among today's high school students. The inability of young adults to communicate effectively—to speak or write in a way that will allow them to compete effectively in the competitive world of work—and their lack of hard factual knowledge or understanding of their own country and the world around them she laid at the feet of behavioral social studies and "hip" literature courses that have replaced other good courses in geography, history, economics, English, and hard sciences, especially in the early and middle grades.

"This adversely affects their decision-making ability, as well as their appreciation and understanding of other people and complex issues," Mrs. McGraw told the Senators.

She further declared that the education philosophy of MACOS that all questions, values, and moral issues are "open" and relative is to blame for the nation's most pressing social problems. Contemporary courses teaching children to question and discard their parents' views, moral standards, and religious beliefs, she said, are largely responsible for:

- The tremendous upsurge of teenage violence and vandalism, teen gang vigilantism, and disrespect for adult authority
- Uncivil behavior and disregard for sensitivities of others
- Disregard for property rights and the importance of private ownership in a free society
- Alcoholism and drug use among young people
- An epidemic venereal disease rate, unmarried living, and a high divorce rate among young married couples
- Disdain for the work ethic
- Callousness, cynicism, growing hedonism, and belief in the occult among young people

Many professional people blame Bruner and other educational theorists, whose courses are vehicles for moral relativism and behavior modification, for these social ills. And from another scholar who has worked intensively with children and parents for a number of years as a clinical psychologist comes this hard-hitting observation:

I have great awareness and respect for that fine line which exists between the legitimate use and dangerous abuse of psychological knowledge and practice. Educators and psychological "experts" may develop programs or advocate techniques with the best of intentions. But we are learning from experience that these scientific experts are not necessarily right and do not have all the answers. Many things they have proposed have not borne the expected fruit or have back-fired.

It is also fairly obvious that the climate of opinion today among most behavioral scientists and educators is that it is both justified and desirable to change or mold children's social attitudes, "free" them from traditional ways of thinking which are considered "prejudiced" or "stereotyped" and viewed, behavioristically, as the more or less superficial learned products of cultural patterns.

The impact of such thinking and attitudes on the part of our social scientists has had and is having increasingly far-reaching effects on our social and political life. These effects are subtle, hard to evaluate, much less to fully anticipate, especially when they are made a part of the educational process itself.

They undoubtedly affect those less obvious and less well understood aspects of children's emotional and intellectual development: Their security, identity, and their capacities for personal commitment and feelings about themselves in relation to others in ways which are unpredictable and may be undesirable.

"No Wonder Parents Are Up in Arms"

Hundreds of thousands of parents and teachers share this concern about the education theories of Bruner and Dow, which thanks to massive infusions of taxpayers' dollars are being experimented on thousands of children in MACOS classrooms. What should be done?

> [L]et us not impose or anticipate [moral relativity and cultural eclec-ticism] by spurious scientific meddling. Certainly not at the expense of the securities of tradition or of family solidarity, least of all in young children who desperately need for healthy development feelings that there *are* those who know, at least in part, what is right and good for them. With such security, they can grow toward a maturity which allows for a secure independence with capacities to make realistic and ap-propriate choices as to what is right and good for themselves.
>
> We see failure to achieve this kind of maturity in far too many of our young adults today: Those who have no clear sense of themselves, their own identity or others, unable to define their own values or chart their course, without landmarks in a shifting world. They are dissatisfied, un-happy, and unproductive.
>
> These are not the children of a rigid traditional Victorian background or narrow authoritarian schooling. Far from it. They are largely the product of our modern school system, our liberated homes and intellec-tualized society. We had better take a second look at where we are "at."

This is the view of thousands of parents who have written to Mem-bers of Congress, bitterly complaining about the National Science Foun-dation's support and promotion of MACOS and similar school programs.

Many of them had no idea that courses like MACOS were in their local schools until Johnny and Mary started coming home with some of the outrageous notions that so many children pick up in MACOS classrooms. Take, for example, this conclusion recorded in Richard M. Jones' *Fantasy and Feeling in Education*, following an actual classroom discussion between teacher and students about the Netsilik custom of killing unwanted female babies:

> *Teacher:* "This has been a very good discussion. Now I'd like to tell you something. When I first heard about this custom that the Netsilik have [of killing girl babies], I almost had a sick feeling much like you had: 'It's mean, it's cruel, it's stupid.' Then I found out something else that made a difference. The Netsilik don't really like to abandon babies, but they believe a baby has no soul until it has a name. So what might they do to help their feelings out?"
> *Student:* "Not name the baby if they're going to abandon it."
> *Teacher:* "Right."
> *Student:* "Then they're not murderers. . . ."

Another student, similarly set adrift morally after MACOS instruc-tion, was recently asked by a reporter for the *Montgomery County (Md.) Sentinel* to comment on the Netsilik practice of senilicide:

"I'm saying I would probably do this," mused one youngster on abandoning his mother-in-law. "I don't know if I really would if I really had to. I don't know what would be right."

Students throughout the country are facing the same moral and spiritual quandary as the result of MACOS teaching. Following criticisms about MACOS in Congress, Peter Dow sent letters to almost 1,000 key educators in his EDC promotion network throughout the country, urging their letter-writing campaign and other activities in support of MACOS.

I received several packets of letters from entire classes of students as a result of Dow's appeal, as well as copies of letters to editors from teachers. It was sad to see some children, obviously at the urging of teachers, rationalize Netsilik killing of the elderly by claiming it is no different or worse than life in American nursing homes.

Other children's letters rationalized Netsilik wife-swapping with the argument, "They have to if their own wives get sick." No wonder parents are up in arms.

Local Diversity or a National Curriculum?

This is where the political crunch I initially referred to comes in. Our system was not devised so that an elite corps of unelected professional academics and their government friends could run things regardless or in spite of public wants and needs. Local control of schools means local control by citizens and school officials to commission and choose particular course materials they want—not the nationwide promotion and lobbying for particular curriculum materials, using tax dollars, by EDC and NSF, with inducements for local educators to lobby local school districts to select them.

This is how the EDC-NSF relationship works, and this is what local citizens want Congress to stop. It's not a question of censoring materials or stopping local school districts from choosing whatever courses they want on their own. It's a question of stopping a dangerous trend toward a uniform national curriculum in social studies, in complete defiance of the need and popular demand for diversity in American education.

What's good for Phoenix schools might not be good for New York, and vice versa. What my Navajo Indian constituents want may not be what is needed in schools of Peoria, Illinois.

It is my view that the National Science Foundation should get out of the promotion and marketing business for *all* curriculum programs. This means that NSF must conduct a thorough "needs assessment" before it even develops such programs, to make sure there is a substantial national need, and then let programs sell on their own merits in the commercial marketplace, without federal subsidies, once they are available.

NSF should not give preferred royalty discounts to commercial publishers of federally-developed school materials. Federal funds should not absorb any part of the publisher's normal cost for teacher training to bring down a program's total cost, thus undercutting competition from other good or better programs.

NSF should not provide massive outlays of taxpayers' dollars to universities to "implement" particular courses, adding more leverage for the adoption of courses endorsed by "certain" academic circles and their bureaucratic friends.

Universities in the NSF-funded EDC promotion and marketing network should not be permitted to give graduate credit for higher salaries to local teachers who learn how to use EDC curriculum materials, as inducements for those teachers to become lobbyists for local adoption of EDC courses.

And NSF should not commit itself to fund future grant applicants lobbied by EDC to adopt or promote their curriculum programs at various national professional educator conventions. Such a scheme for about $1.2 million of future funding for the promotion and marketing of "Exploring Human Nature" was tentatively approved by NSF in its recent $96,000 initial grant for disseminating the course.

In the final analysis, this is a political issue that will be settled in Congress, unless NSF officials and responsible educators lance the boil within the education profession. Both parents *and* teachers have a vital stake in the outcome of this issue, because academic freedom of both hangs in the balance.

But most importantly, the American public's willingness to continue paying the very high price for all education rests on its continued faith in teachers and schools as perpetuators of the community's way of life, its basic beliefs, its moral standards, its religious convictions, and our nation's political and economic freedom.

That continued faith is the ultimate prize to be won or lost by the education community in this curriculum controversy.

MACOS Revisited:
A Commentary on the Most Frequently Asked
Questions About Man: A Course of Study

PETER B. DOW

In recent weeks something of a national discussion has been taking place regarding Education Development Center's elementary social studies program, *Man: A Course of Study*. This discussion has generated many questions, ranging from the goals and purposes of the program and its effect on children and teachers to the arrangements for distribution and marketing that resulted from EDC's publishing agreement with Curriculum Development Associates, Inc. In 1965 I joined EDC as deputy director of *Man: A Course of Study* and worked closely with Jerome Bruner until July of 1966, when I became director of the program. From 1966 to 1970 I supervised the development through two major revisions, collaborated in the design of the innovative dissemination system, and negotiated the final publishing contract with CDA. As director of EDC's Social Studies Program from 1967 to 1974, and now as a Senior Associate with EDC, I have followed the fortunes of *Man: A Course of Study* closely for the past ten years. The following is an effort to summarize the facts related to the questions most frequently raised.

1. What Is *Man: A Course of Study*?

Man: A Course of Study is a course for upper elementary school children in the study of human behavior that is organized around the question "What is human about human beings?" The goals of the program are

NOTE: This article appeared in *Social Education*, October 1975, pp. 388–389, 393–396. Reprinted by permission of Peter B. Dow.

threefold: to give students a set of models for thinking about the social world, to provide them with some intellectual tools for investigating human behavior, and to evoke in children an appreciation of the common humanity that all human beings share. To achieve these goals, the developers of the course devised a series of units drawn from several well-researched studies of animal behavior; constructed exercises and materials that permit children to gather data, formulate hypotheses, explore inferences, and compare information gathered from a variety of sources, including their own direct observations; and created an extensive case study of a culture very different from our own. These materials, units, and exercises draw upon a wide variety of media, including games, records, pictures, charts, a diversity of written materials, together with an extensive library of ethnographic film. These materials are specifically designed to accommodate a wide variety of skill levels and learning styles, and they have been organized to promote an open-ended exploration of the uniqueness of human beings as a species and the underlying similarities that unite all races, ethnic groups, and cultures. Recurring themes include the life cycle, learning, dependency, parental care, adaptation, dominance, affection and love, aggression, social organization, language, technology, beliefs, and values. These themes are explored from different perspectives throughout the course.

Man: A Course of Study begins by exploring the uniqueness of human beings by contrasting human behavior to a series of animal studies, which include salmon, herring gulls, and free-ranging baboons. In the salmon unit, children encounter a remarkable species. The young are born in the quiet tributaries of our western rivers, make their way early in life downstream and into the Pacific Ocean, grow to full maturity in five years, and then, playing out one of nature's most dramatic life stories, challenge those same rivers, fighting swift currents, leaping waterfalls, and enduring weeks without food to return to their birthplace, spawn, and die of hunger and exhaustion. Compared to human life, the salmon case offers some intriguing contrasts: here is a species that survives without parents, without formal learning, without any form of social organization to provide parental protection. The cost is high—only about two in five thousand survive to reproduce—and the contrast points up several important features of the human life cycle: the prolonged overlap between generations, the importance of learning, and the centrality of parents and other adults in ensuring the care, protection, and survival of the young.

The second case study, based on the pioneering work of Niko Tinbergen and Konrad Lorenz, explores the behavior of herring gulls. These materials focus on the pairbond between male and female and the role that parents play in the care of the young. Like us, herring gulls are choosy about their mates, and both male and female invest heavily in the care, feeding, and protection of the young. But unlike human beings, gulls are confined to territories, restricted in their social behavior to a limited repertoire of innate responses, and possess only the most rudimentary forms of communication. Against this contrasting "family group" found in nature, children can explore the meaning of parenting in human society, the relationships between parents and children, and the function of the family as the primary social group. Indeed, exploring the meaning of family as the principal building block in all human societies is a major concern of *Man: A Course of Study*.

From herring gulls, children turn to an exploration of the social organization and behavior of the most socially complex of all nonhuman primates, free-ranging baboons. This unit is based on the studies carried out by Sherwood Washburn and Irven DeVore in Kenya in the early 1960s. Baboon studies have been greatly expanded since that time, and they continue to raise provocative questions about human behavior. (See the May 1975 issue of *National Geographic Magazine*.) The baboon unit extends children's exploration of social behavior to a consideration of life in groups beyond the family where many individuals, occupying different roles, cooperate to ensure the survival of all the members. Baboons achieve this through a dominance hierarchy in which the three or four strongest and most socially adept males form a central clique that defends the group against predators, leads the troop to fresh sources of food, and provides for the care and protection of mothers and infants. Females, in turn, fill comparable roles, caring for the young, dominating the social life of the troop, and mediating the aggressive exchanges between adult males. The well-adapted but inflexible structure of the baboon troop, with its fixed roles and limited communication system of a few sounds and gestures, provides a productive contrast for considering the alternative social structures available to human beings who can alter the roles of males and females, experiment with both hierarchical and cooperative administrative systems, and continuously explore new dimensions of social interaction.

Against this backdrop of comparative animal studies, which help children to see that social behavior can be viewed in an orderly and systematic way, and that human beings have important social attributes not possessed by any other species—such as language, an immense learning capacity, and an ability to alter the social world in which we live—children then turn to an examination of a culture very different from our own, the Netsilik Eskimos. This study is based on the ethnographic work of the Danish explorer Knud Rasmussen, who spent several months with the Netsilik while crossing the Arctic in 1923, and on the later studies of anthropologist Asen Balikci, who served as a scholarly advisor in the preparation of the materials. The unit portrays traditional Eskimo life as Rasmussen saw it, beginning with the summer fishing camp, following the seasonal migration that includes caribou hunting in the fall, jigging for trout at the autumn river camp, and concluding with an extending study of life in the midwinter sealing camp where many Eskimo families come together to face the harshest season of the year. Here children can see an example of how one group of human beings has learned to cope with the most alien environment on earth with little to draw upon but the snow, the skin and bones of the animals they hunt, and the resourcefulness that has given mankind the edge over his circumstances during 2 million years of human history. Remarkably, these Eskimos reveal that it is man's unique social behavior, as well as his technological ingenuity, that makes survival possible under such severe conditions. Cooperation between male and female is crucial to the survival of both: men hunt and fashion tools; women care for children, make clothing, and feed their families. Men collaborate to hunt, forming lifelong partnerships as firm as our marriage bond, and food is shared in ritual patterns that link families together in a web of economic and social reciprocity that ensures the welfare of every member. Games, storytelling, and religious rituals provide humor and amusement, discharge aggression, help to dispel fear, and celebrate the symbolic cohesiveness of Netsilik life. Warfare is unknown, and interpersonal violence is so rare that there are no rules to govern it. Ostracism is the fate of those who would violate the social order.

Like ourselves, the Netsilik face moral dilemmas. Theirs include the problem of first-born female children in a culture that needs males to hunt, and the burden of caring for old people beyond their productive years. The warmth of Eskimo feeling toward the young and old is legendary, yet there are rare cases where men and women have had to make the agonizing choice of exposing a newborn infant or allowing an aging parent to stay behind on the ice in order to ensure the protection of other members of the social group. These dilemmas are presented to children not to promote cultural relativism but to expose them to the universal moral problem of who shall live and who shall die that all cultures face.

Man: A Course of Study closes with a look at Eskimo life today. In present-day Pelly Bay, the Netsilik live in heated houses, attend church, drive snowmobiles, have access to a medical clinic, hunt with rifles, attend school, own and operate a DC-4, and draw welfare checks. Under construction is a tourist lodge complete with an igloo bar. Most of these changes have taken place since the original *Man: A Course of Study* materials were completed. Therefore, to bring the course up to date, EDC now has under preparation a set of materials that will examine the impact of these more recent changes, the forces that brought them about, and the costs and benefits that Eskimos have experienced in this transition to life in the modern world.

2. What Happens to Children in This Course?

Man: A Course of Study is designed to raise questions, not to answer them. To achieve this, the materials have been designed to provide maximum opportunity for open-ended exploration. The basic "text" is natural sound and, for the most part, unnarrated film. The films are designed to simulate the experience of an observer in the field, and children are encouraged to derive their own questions and draw their own conclusions from watching them. Because this basic information is available to all children, regardless of reading ability, sharing of ideas and diversity of points of view is greatly facilitated. Teachers often remark that they cannot predict who will contribute most on a given day because the film-based approach invites all children to respond. This open-ended teaching strategy is supported by a collection of booklets that presents information in many different ways and accommodates a diversity of learning styles in contrast to the undifferentiated approach of a textbook. A data book, a set of field notes, an ethnography, a novel, a book of poems, a collection of myths, an "Observer's Handbook," a variety of concept books, and a collection of fact-filled "mini-texts" all foster this diverse approach. Thorough evaluation accompanied the development of these materials and learning strategies, and shaped the choices of the developers as the course evolved. In a nationwide evaluation in over 100 classrooms during 1967–1968 under the direction of the head of the Harvard Office of Tests, we learned that children, when asked what they learned about human behavior from the course, most often stressed the qualities of interdependence; responsibility for self, family, and society; persistence; ingenuity; initiative, and capacity for survival. In the area of learning skills, the strongest gains were in reading ability, attention span, perseverance, increased conceptual vocabulary, active listening, and critical thinking. On the critical question of attitude change, the major shift appears to have been in the direction of more positive feelings toward learning and toward the subject of social studies. For many students, social studies became their favorite subject while they were taking *Man: A Course of Study*. In a later study by David Martin that looked specifically at the issue of ethnocentrism, *Man: A Course of Study* students were shown to make significantly positive gains, when compared with control groups, in their willingness to accept other cultures while retaining strong, positive attitudes toward their own culture.

3. What Happens to Teachers?

One of the most impressive results of *Man: A Course of Study* has been its effect on teachers. Created prior to the open education movement, in the early years the course often entered classrooms where teachers had been accustomed to dominating the discussion. Because of its diversity of materials and emphasis on student data gathering and small-group instruction, teachers found it nearly impossible to conduct their classes in the traditional way. Consequently, visits to classrooms showed a dramatic shift early in the year toward student-centered instruction.

This was particularly pronounced in urban classrooms where traditional methods of instruction were more customary and where disciplinary problems may have been more severe. The engaging quality of the materials, particularly the films, freed teachers to explore new ways of supporting student learning. Pedagogical innovation became a central issue in many teacher seminars.

Another interesting finding was the power of the content of the course to engage teachers. The many new ways of looking at and thinking about social behavior imbedded in *Man: A Course of Study* often turned out to involve teachers equally with their students, and these fresh ideas became a stimulus for teachers to reconsider the power of new ideas as well as new teaching techniques in promoting learning. When teachers became excited about the course content itself, this seemed to affect the enthusiasm of students. As one student put it:

> We've gotten into half-hour long discussions on the entire opposite subject, yet just sprouting little by little, and it's really interesting and the teacher gets really wrapped up and she keeps going along and we learn a lot more than what we would have started out with and it isn't rigid.

In most cases, teachers found the training seminars extremely valuable. Here several teachers could come together to share their insights and problems with respect to issues of both content and pedagogy, and many found these sessions the most interesting part of teaching the course. Evaluation results revealed higher student performance and student interest in classes taught by teachers who attended these seminars and workshops than among students of teachers who did not, and these findings confirmed EDC's prediction regarding the need for a teacher education program to accompany the course.

4. What Do Parents Think of *Man: A Course of Study*?

Over the five years since *Man: A Course of Study* was published in 1970, there have been several instances of parent opposition to the course. In most cases, this opposition has come from parents who are unfamiliar with the program and very often from parents who have not had children in the course. From the earliest testing days, EDC has urged school systems not to impose the course on children of parents who opposed it, and to our knowledge, most school systems have made provision for children of such parents to take alternative courses of study. In the early days, few formal efforts were made to involve parents in curriculum decision-making, but in recent years, Curriculum Development Associates, Inc., has been vigorous in its efforts to include parents in the adoption process. Two years ago, in Jacksonville, Florida, two hundred parents participated in the final meeting where *Man: A Course of Study* was selected, and more recently, at St. Peter's School, a Catholic archdiocesan school in Mansfield, Ohio, not only did parents participate in the selection of the course but one hundred parents signed up to take an adult version of *Man: A Course of Study* offered by the school. Parents are currently involved in the selection process that is going on now in several major cities as well as in the social studies adoption proceedings currently underway in California.

5. Why Was It So Difficult to Find a Publisher?

Man: A Course of Study was a first. It was the first program to teach anthropology in the elementary school, the first program to provide a full set of multimedia materials, including film as an integral part of instruction, and it was the first program to make teacher training a prerequisite for use. For all these reasons, it presented a formidable challenge to a commercial publisher. In addition, the content of the course was regarded by some as controversial, and the cost of the program exceeded what schools normally pay for basic texts. From the outset EDC knew that special publishing arrangements would be needed, and the developers appealed to publishers to join with EDC in the invention of an alternative to commercial selling that would involve professional educators in the dissemination process. A dozen publishers expressed interest, but none were willing to incur the risk of this novel approach to distribution. We then approached the film distributors, several of whom were interested, but all felt unqualified to handle the training and logistical problems associated with such a complex package. Curiously, publishers continued to praise the program while backing away from the publishing challenge. In February 1969, the American Textbook Publishers Institute joined with the American Educational Research Association to honor Jerome Bruner for his contribution to education, calling *Man: A Course of Study* "one of the most important efforts of our time to relate research findings and theory in educational psychology to the development of new and better instructional materials" and "enormously suggestive of what we could and should be doing to equip the instructional process adequately."

Believing that an effective publishing, training, and dissemination system could be invented, EDC applied to NSF for funds to set up an interim distribution network in the spring of 1969. This network employed no salesmen but established six strategically placed regional centers on university campuses and drew upon the talents of university professors and classroom teachers to provide information and teacher training to local school districts. The system proved so successful that within six months EDC received strong interest from four publishers and firm publishing proposals from two, Westinghouse Learning Corporation and Curriculum Development Associates, Inc. Both offered to allocate to EDC an amount equivalent to 15 percent of gross sales to support professional services, evaluation, and future development of course materials. EDC selected CDA over Westinghouse on the basis of the firm's superior capacity to establish a dissemination network of educational professionals, and its offer to replace the NSF-funded training system with a dissemination network of its own design. EDC signed a contract with CDA in July 1970. By 1972 CDA had completed the development of an alternative to the NSF-funded regional center approach. Thus EDC and CDA maintained the integrity of the course design, preserved the training requirement, and turned *Man: A Course of Study* into a commercially feasible enterprise.

6. What About the Costs of the Program?

In the 13 years since the National Science Foundation funded the first filming project, NSF has spent approximately $6.5 million on the development and implementation of *Man: A Course of Study*. Approximately $4.3 million of this has financed the creation of materials, and the balance has gone for implementation activities. These figures compare favorably with curriculum programs of similar impact. The figure for development cost is misleading, however, for it includes funds that were used to develop an unsuccessful high school program, and several other elementary school projects that never became a part of *Man: A Course of Study*. In addition, the figure includes about $1 million for the Netsilik Eskimo film series, only a portion of which is used in *Man: A Course of Study*. The full series is in worldwide distribution, and these films have been used at every level from kindergarten to graduate school. Furthermore, they have been edited for extensive television showings in Canada, Great Britain, Germany, and Japan. In the spring of 1970, CBS ran a one-hour version in prime time entitled "Eskimo: Fight for Life," which played to one of the largest audiences on record for this kind of material. More than 25 million viewers have seen these films, and they are still in great demand. One American public broadcast station is currently considering running the entire ten-hour series next year.

While the television audience for the films alone would seem to justify the initial expenditure, the elementary school audience remains relatively small, estimated in 1973 at 1,700 schools and approximately 200,000 students in this country and abroad. There is some evidence that the course has had a much wider impact than the size of the classroom sales would indicate, however. It has increasingly found its way into preservice education programs, and while it would be hard to trace the cause to *Man: A Course of Study*, it is perhaps more than coincidental that many commercial publishers are now producing anthropologically-based materials for the elementary school, and multimedia formats are increasingly in demand. According to one reckoning, there are nearly 30 competing programs to *Man: A Course of Study* now in the educational marketplace. This is a substantial change from 1968, when publishers informed EDC that there was no call for such material in the schools.

7. What About Jerome Bruner? How Did He Become Involved with *Man: A Course of Study* and What Were His Motives?

While at Harvard, Jerome Bruner became interested in the curriculum movement in the late 1950s, chaired the famous Woods Hole Conference in 1959, and wrote the conference report entitled *The Process of Education*, which became the classic exposition of the child-centered philosophy of the educational reformers of the 1960s. The book has been translated into 20 languages and has sold more than 400,000 copies. The central argument of the book is that, as Bruner put it, "intellectual activity is anywhere the same, whether it is at the frontier of knowledge, or in the third grade classroom." This bold hypothesis, now sometimes questioned, had the effect of opening educators' minds to the possibility that through improved educational methods children could achieve new heights of intellectual awareness. Far from wishing to mold children's minds in any particular direction, Bruner sought to explore the limits of children's intellectual growth, and formed an instructional research group at EDC in 1964 to examine the impact of new curricula on children. When he assumed the directorship of *Man: A Course of Study* in 1964, his main interest was in learning more about how children form concepts about the social world and, as the course developed, he insisted upon continuous modifications of the materials and adjustments of grade level to respond to what the instructional research group discovered about the interests, learning styles, and ways of knowing of children in *Man: A Course of Study* classrooms. The spirit of Bruner's inquiry was well expressed by him in a recent letter:

> I have always had the conviction that the academic student of human development should take an active part in trying to improve the state of public education, much in the same spirit as the student of other aspects of human growth seeks to improve the practice of pediatrics. Unfortunately, the criteria for good health and for being well educated are not equally plain. I have tried to resolve the lack of clarity about what constitutes a well educated man by favoring diversity and openness, *not* trying to shape minds to one pattern, but to make it possible for a growing mind to develop according to its own interests and values and to make it possible for people to find their own ways of contributing to the society. That, it seems to me, is the essence of democratic education.

Conclusion

One of the curious dimensions of the current debate about *Man: A Course of Study* is that so few people have bothered to ask children what they think of the program. Often the unhappy consequence of this kind of controversy is that children themselves are the last to be heard. In hundreds of classrooms across the country children may lose this program, if this debate continues, with little chance to voice their views. Some, however, have spoken out, including a young boy from Middle Haddam, Connecticut, who wrote the following letter to the *Middletown Press* a few weeks ago:

> Editor:
>   Being a seventh grader who took the "Man, A Course of Study" (MACOS) last year, I feel compelled to reply to a recent letter against "MACOS." In response to the statements made by the Coalition for Children of Chevy Chase, Maryland, I say the course material in no way promotes infanticide, cannibalism, murder, killing old people, or any of the other things said.
>   As far as "wife-swapping," the Eskimoes need their wives to survive. It is in no way like American wife-swapping as is implied in the letter.
>   I can't say there aren't any scenes of Netsilik Eskimoes killing seals and eating them, but this is how they survive. To say the films used show Eskimoes "eating their eyeballs and other organs and drinking their blood" is a gross exaggeration. Their so-called "bestiality" isn't half as bad as American hunters who kill animals just for the sport of it. The Netsiliks use every single part of the animals they kill, and they even have certain rituals and taboos resulting in kindness to the animals.
>   It is also stated that "MACOS" is an invasion of privacy. Students are required to discuss and compare intimate personal attitudes and behavior of themselves and their families. I did not feel my privacy being invaded and I did not flunk the course.
>   Something rather interesting is that this year we are studying Social Science and right now we are learning about culture. One of our major concepts deals with the fact that wars occur partially because one culture doesn't understand another, and "MACOS" helped me understand another culture.
>   We have a poster in one of our classrooms which says "I cannot learn to decide . . . if you make my decisions. I cannot learn to be myself . . . if you tell me what to be. Let me choose what I must learn."
>   To me it was an interesting course and I feel I got a lot more out of it than a history course where I merely regurgitate dates and names.
>
> (Signed) Ben Kahn
> Main Street

How Do We Stand with the Pledge of Allegiance Today?

HYMAN KAVETT

I pledge allegiance to the flag of the United States of America and to the Republic for which it stands, one Nation, under God, indivisible, with liberty and justice for all.[1]

This is the latest version of the Pledge of Allegiance. It is used in daily ceremonies by students in schools throughout the country. The author of the Pledge could not foresee in 1892[2] that the recitation of these words would become the subject of many court battles involving the First and Fourteenth Amendments to the U.S. Constitution. That first version of the Pledge had appeared in a periodical called the *Youth's Companion.* Its patriotic message was soon perceived by a nation whose citizens had recently agonized through a civil war and its aftermath. With the twentieth century about to begin, the Pledge made possible an open expression of dedication and faith. By 1924, the Pledge had been changed somewhat so as to read as it does today,[3] with the exception of the words "under God" which were added in 1954.[4]

Expressing noble ideals of "liberty and justice for all," the Pledge may be traced back to the goals of the nation's Founding Fathers, the Declaration of Independence, and Lincoln's Gettysburg Address.[5] One sentence long, it remains a brief declaration of patriotism. But objections were voiced and legal cases continue to arise based on ethical, civic, or religious scruples. The widespread requirement of the daily Pledge ceremony in public schools has brought about responses from

NOTE: This article appeared in *Social Education*, March 1976, pp. 135–140. Reprinted by permission of Hyman Kavett.

teachers and students that are at times condemnatory and at times funny, and which seriously question the effectiveness of mandated patriotism.

In a series of teacher interviews, the following comments were offered recently by a sample of elementary and secondary teachers. A fair proportion reported that they carried out the daily requirement "religiously." Others described their point of view differently:

> There's a lack of meaning, no good sense, just plain silliness, in demanding a pledge to the flag on a daily basis. My students just won't do it!

> Students are too sophisticated for that ritual every single day. I get through the salute as fast as possible and I don't make any fuss if some students do not participate.

> It's the same in my homeroom. The ceremony is a farce. We were without a flag for three weeks; someone stole it and no replacement was available. We used to salute the corner of the room.

> I salute the flag only on Friday during Assembly because I am visible there. I don't want to rock the boat. I like my job too much.

> I just go through the motions.

> I just don't bother.

Some stated that the Pledge is broadcast over the school's intercom system and those students who want to pledge are told to stand; those who don't want to—with no questions asked—are told to sit quietly. It is over in a matter of seconds.

The teachers also related some of the students' feelings in the matter: certain religions prohibit rendering obeisance to any graven image, including a flag; some students are simply bored or disinterested in the daily ritual; others take serious exception to the words "with liberty and justice for all," maintaining that the whole Pledge is thereby rendered hypocritical and unrealistic. Teachers of the elementary grades are quick to substantiate their view that recitation of the Pledge is meaningless to children; the words are too long and the concepts beyond their understanding. The following quotations of elementary school students are evidence of the manner of recitation:

- I pledge the pigeons to the flag. . . .
- I took the pigeons to the flag. . . .
- . . . with liberty and just sticks for all.
- . . . and to the republic Richard Stands. . . .
- . . . one nation, invisible. . . .
- . . . and to the republic for witches stands. . . .
- . . . one nation, under guard. . . .

When Daniel Lang, a reporter for the *New Yorker* magazine, visited the Rush-Henrietta, New York, school district, scene of the non-participation in the Pledge ceremony by teacher Mrs. Susan Russo, he asked school officials if he could observe a daily Pledge ceremony. Lang describes it this way:

> Rittenhouse (an assistant principal) and I entered a homeroom a minute or two before its daily ritual got under way. The Pledge was over almost as soon as it began, the boys and girls facing a flag stationed in a corner of their room. I had no sense of being witness to a meditative occasion, as Breese saw it. A few students did not even say the words, and scarcely even for ideological reasons. One boy spent the time wrestling himself out of his sweater; another tossed a pencil into the air a few times; a boy and a girl gazed at each other.[6]

State laws on education mandate that the Pledge be recited daily. This means that a student and teacher have an opportunity to reaffirm each day a publicly stated patriotism whether they believe it or not. Constant repetition, while serving as reinforcement towards memorization, renders the spirit of the Pledge meaningless. Remember, also, that high school students have already had more than ten years of daily pledging.

There cannot be any patriotic spirit when meaningless parroting of words takes place. You cannot have the emotional outpouring which was evident, for example, when Susan Agnew led thousands of people in the Pledge at Fort McHenry, Baltimore, on Flag Day, June 14, 1973.[7] A totally different situation exists when students are expected to affirm, reaffirm, and daily declare allegiance from Monday through Friday, week in and week out. Even the most dedicated teachers and administrators admit that boredom, disinterest, lack of attention, and, finally, disrespect, are evident during these few seconds of the Pledge ceremony. And, as indicated earlier, many teachers admit that they pay no attention to their students' behavior during the ceremony: the words are something to mumble, hardly to think about during these few seconds, and besides the schedule for the day is pressing and the bell for change of periods is about to ring in a few seconds.

Obviously, more instruction is needed regarding the meaning of the Pledge.[8] There is also a need for a more rational approach to the whole ceremony. The Pledge of Allegiance is suffering from overexposure and it has been relegated to an insignificant part of a student's life. The daily ceremony has become meaningless and the Pledge as a historical declaration has received some shabby treatment. The Pledge should be reserved for *infrequent, important, ceremonial* occasions. Then, and only then, should the Pledge of Allegiance be recited. Prior to these occasions, a teacher should define and discuss the meaning of the Pledge; the words must be explained as well as the symbolism and historical background.

Legislative Requirements and Court Decisions

State legislatures, on the other hand, have mandated daily recitation. In New York State, the law reads in part:

> ...it shall be the duty of the Commissioner of Education to prepare, for the use of the public schools of the state, a program providing for a salute to the flag and a daily pledge of allegiance to the flag....[9]

This legislation has been amended several times: the Pledge of Allegiance was included in L. 1956; the word "daily" was inserted in L. 1963.[10]

In the State of New Jersey, a similar piece of legislation reads:

> [Every board of education shall] require the pupils in each school district on every school day to salute the United States flag and repeat the following pledge of allegiance to the flag: I pledge allegiance to the flag of the United States of America and to the republic for which it stands, one nation, under God, indivisible, with liberty and justice for all, which salute shall be rendered with the right hand over the heart....[11]

It may be almost impossible to effect any change in state legislatures even with careful explanation and documentation.[12] Legislators and their constituents consider it a patriotic duty to require a daily pledge ceremony; to do otherwise would be unpatriotic. Undoubtedly, there would also be resistance to change from veterans groups and civic organizations, and there will be threats—"if you vote down the Pledge, we vote down your budget...." So the laws will probably remain in unamended form: the daily pledge will be mandated, and the effect of the ceremony will continue to diminish and diminish until one day there will be a realization that a sense of patriotism cannot be developed through meaningless daily repetition. Perhaps, at that time, some reasonable change in the law will be considered and the Pledge will be removed from the commonplace, overexposed, overused, unrespected position it holds today.

What if the law is amended and students still refuse to participate on those *infrequent, important, ceremonial* occasions?[13] That is their right and they are protected by the First and Fourteenth Amendments; the Constitution does not stop at the schoolhouse door. It would be safe to predict that with greater knowledge and understanding will come greater participation. This does not mean "more frequent participation" because such frequency is unnecessary and redundant. It means, instead, "more meaningful participation." The warmth and spirit which accompany a sense of belonging in a patriotic sense can have a long-lasting effect on a young adult when he or she is well informed, understanding, tolerant, and has not been droned to insensitivity with needless repetition.

Consider next the student with moral scruples: he does not believe there is "liberty and justice for all," or he just refuses to salute and recite every day. The student believes the Pledge to be a statement of hypocrisy and he refuses to participate; he may even refuse to stand. Refusal on these grounds has confused and confounded school supervisors; objections on religious grounds had been the only acceptable reason for allowing non-participation.[14]

Recent objection to reciting has not been only based on religious conviction, and much evidence of confusion exists. After two students at Junior High School 217, Briarwood, Queens, New York, had been suspended for refusing to say the Pledge (10-7-69) and for refusing to stand or leave the room, they were back in the classroom two days later (10-9-69) on the ruling of a Federal court order.[18] The Federal District Court temporarily enjoined the New York City Board of Education from ordering students to leave the classroom, stating that the students had a constitutional right to remain seated during the Pledge until the school could prove that the students' action materially infringed on other students' rights or caused any disruption.[16] Soon afterwards, the New York City High School Principals Association urged that the Pledge ceremony be suspended when the new term began (1-25-70). Several court cases were pending and there was no definitive ruling on the legal status of the ceremony: New York State Education Law required the Pledge of all students, yet court decisions protected students' rights not to participate.[17]

An editorial appearing in the *New York Times* on January 29, 1970 took the High School Principals Association to task for urging members to omit the daily Pledge of Allegiance. The right of students to remain seated was also questioned.[18]

On January 30, 1970, one day after the *New York Times* editorial, Deputy Education Commissioner Johnson issued a letter instructing school administrators throughout New York State that the Pledge ceremony was to be continued. Student objectors and non-participants, he maintained, were the responsibility of the courts: the Pledge ceremony itself, however, was to be carried on for the greater population of participating students.[19] The High School Principals Association then reversed its earlier decision (2-1-70) and urged the New York City high schools to continue daily recitation of the Pledge "for the time being."[20] The Association, of course, was acting on Commissioner Johnson's recommendation. Clarification of the issue finally emerged in the *Goetz v. Ansell* decision 477 F. 2d. 636 (1973): any student may remain silently seated during the Pledge ceremony without threat of suspension, and without being asked to leave the room. The *Goetz v. Ansell* decision clarified matters a great deal. Prior to this decision, school administrators were acting on the decision by Commissioner Nyquist in *Matter of Bielenberg*

9 Ed. Dept. Rep. 196 (1970) in which the student was not required to say the Pledge but the student was required to stand or leave the room while others participated.[21]

Of course, there was much publicity accompanying non-compliance by students and teachers in the Pledge ceremony. There was widespread sensitivity and wariness on the part of legislators and school people alike. A few examples are:

Governor Mandel of Maryland signed a bill requiring teachers to lead their classes in the Pledge (5-30-70). Implementation of this bill was delayed by the Circuit Court until pending litigation could be decided.[22] A few days later in a totally separate action (6-6-70), Governor Sargent of Massachusetts vetoed a bill requiring daily recitation of the Pledge and certain parts of the Declaration of Independence.[23] When the principal of Exeter (New Hampshire) High School, Mr. B. G. MacArthur, suspended the daily Pledge ceremony, he was overruled by his local school board.[24] In Monroe, Connecticut, the superintendent of schools recognized the disrespect being displayed during the Pledge and decided to limit the frequency of the ceremony. It was his stated intention to use the Pledge as a stimulant to encourage thought and discussion (9-24-73). He, too, was overruled by his school board.[25] A short while later, the local chapter of the Veterans of Foreign Wars condemned the actions of school officials who encouraged "unpatriotic acts" (10-10-73).[26]

Several attempts have been made to modify the Pledge so that students will not object on moral grounds. In 1970, an Eastchester, New York high school principal, Dr. L. N. D'Ascoli, along with the senior class president, N. Gruberg, began what they described as a national campaign to change the wording of the last phrase of the Pledge. The proposed change involved substitution of the words "seeking liberty and justice for all" for the phrase "with liberty and justice for all." This high school effort inspired student letters to state legislators, members of Congress, and to hundreds of student council presidents in New York State high schools.[27]

At the 1970 White House Conference on Children, a proposal was made to modify the Pledge in the following manner:

I pledge allegiance to the flag of the United States of America and to the republic for which it stands, and dedicate myself to the task of making it one nation under God, indivisible, with liberty and justice for all.[28]

A letter to the editor of the New York Times suggested a simplified Pledge. This version read:

I pledge allegiance to the United States of America, one nation, in search of liberty and justice for all.[29]

An unusual suggestion to modify the Pledge ceremony has been made by Forrest L. McAllister, editor of the magazine The School Musician Director and Teacher. He recommended a

... simple musical rendition of the salute to the flag rather than a recitation of the words of the Pledge. He felt it would be more attractive to youth in musical form and that it would create a better understanding of what the Pledge really means.[30]

Any change in the Pledge of Allegiance must be made by Act of Congress with Presidential approval. None of the aforementioned proposals has been seriously considered; none is being considered now.

While the flag is a symbol representing the nation and its people, non-participation in declaring "liberty and justice for all" sometimes leads to denial of liberty. Prior to the *Barnette* decision in the U. S. Supreme Court 319 U.S. 624, 87 L.Ed. 1628 (1942) and the *Goetz* decision (477 F. 2d. 636, 1973) in New York State, resistance on the part of a student to the daily performance of the Pledge elicited expressions of hostility, coercive demands, and threats of reprisal.[31] When the student continued in his or her refusal, he or she was threatened with suspension or expulsion. If the student persisted in resisting coercion, the act of removal took place: the student was usually suspended from school. In the past, such action meant that the student was labelled "juvenile delinquent" as well. A great deal of courage, conviction, and stamina was needed to resist the pressures of school and community. A teacher, too, had to be exceptionally brave or foolhardy not to participate. Those teachers who did refuse to participate on moral grounds have been the target for ostracism, loss of job, long drawnout and expensive law suits, blacklisting, and hate-mail.[32]

School officials rely on state and local board of education regulations for justification in carrying out acts of reprisal against non-conforming students. Perhaps these officials are not entirely to blame; the pressures by local boards and by community groups are strong. School people, however, who continue to coerce students to comply are themselves breaking the law. The danger to the nation of imposing rigid concepts of loyalty was pointed out by Henry Steele Commager. He stated that such an effort was

> ... a confession of fear, a declaration of insolvency. Those who are sure of themselves do not need reassurance, and those who have confidence in the strength and virtue of America do not need to fear either criticism or competition. The effort is bound to miscarry.[33]

Additionally, Supreme Court Justice Jackson, in delivering the opinion in the *Barnette* case (*supra*), stated that:

> ... ultimate futility of such attempts to compel coherence is the lesson of every such effort from the Roman drive to stamp out Christianity as a disturber of its pagan unity, to the Inquisition, as a means to religious and dynastic unity, down to the fast-failing efforts of our present totalitarian enemies. Those who begin coercive elimination of dissent soon find themselves exterminating dissenters. Compulsory unification of opinion achieves only the unanimity of the graveyard.

Coercion[34] was evident in the action of the Board of Education of Central School District No. 1 of the Towns of Rush, Henrietta, Pittsford, and Brighton, Monroe County, New York, when they adopted a policy which stated:

> ... students who hold a sincere conviction giving rise to a conscientious objection to the Pledge of Allegiance shall establish this fact with a written statement indicating the reasons and rationale for such convictions. These written statements shall be signed by the student and his parents or those in parental relationship to him and shall be submitted to the principal of the school.[35]

Commissioner Nyquist of the New York State Board of Education ordered that the board of education in question

> ... rescind its regulation requiring a written statement signed by the parents of a pupil who wishes to refrain from reciting the pledge of allegiance (sic).[36]

The Commissioner also ordered that any statements already obtained were to be removed from the student's records. This ruling now appears in CRRNY—108.5 (1)—Decisions of the Commissioner, as part of the New York State Title 8—Education Regulations (161-Ed. 7-31-73).[37]

The Situation Today

What then is the situation today? There have been many legal disputes regarding the Pledge. Disposition of these cases has not been easy or simple, or quickly disposed of through administrative channels, legislative action, or lower court decisions. Cases dealing with the Pledge almost always move to higher courts. Currently, based on several legal decisions, a high school student in New York State may remain seated silently during the ceremony.[38] The student does not have to leave the room, nor may he be suspended or expelled because of non-participation.[39] The student is not required to stand or make any "gestures of acceptance or respect: a salute, a bowed or bare head, a bended knee."[40] The student does not have to affirm his loyalty by "word or act," the act of standing is itself considered part of the Pledge.[41] New York State Education Regulations require that students stand for the Pledge, but standing "is no less a gesture of acceptance and respect than is the salute and the utterance of the words of allegiance."[42] Any "deeply held convictions" possessed by the individual assume priority consideration: standing in silence can no more be required than the Pledge itself.[43]

The *Barnette* case is regarded as a landmark in questions concerning the Pledge of Allegiance: reference has been made to *Barnette* in current New York State cases and decisions made by the commissioner. The principle has been firmly established that a student in the public school need not be obliged to recite the Pledge.[44] Earlier Supreme Court litigation, *Minersville School District v. Gobitis* 310 U.S. 586 (1940), was effectively reversed. In that case, the requirement for participation by public school students was upheld. These two legal decisions make fascinating reading: they are part of the history of American constitutional law.[45] Their arguments serve as a basis for legislative action, as precedents for decision in current litigation, and as guides to state boards of education. Justices Black and Douglas, concurring in *Barnette*, stated that the principle of state legislatures having freedom of action in dealing with local school problems was sound (as in *Gobitis, supra*) but the application in the *Barnette* case was wrong. They were speaking of the action in West Virginia where the opinion of Justice Frankfurter in *Gobitis* was used to mandate a daily salute and pledge from all students. This action was declared unconstitutional in *Barnette*. A state legislature may mandate the performance of a daily pledge ceremony but it is unconstitutional for it to require participation by students and teachers. In this respect, the statement of Justice Jackson, again in *Barnette*, can serve as a guide to state legislatures:

> . . . if there is any fixed star in our constitutional constellation, it is that no official, high or petty, can prescribe what shall be orthodox in politics, nationalism, religion, or other matters of opinion or force citizens to confess by word or act their faith therein. If there are any circumstances which permit an exception, they do not now occur to us.[46]

Justices Black and Douglas further reinforced the right of the individual to remain silent and not participate during the Pledge ceremony when they stated:

> . . . words uttered under coercion are proof of loyalty to nothing but self-interest. Love of country must spring from willing hearts and free minds.[47]

To this statement can be added Judge Kaufman's statement in the Russo case:

> . . . patriotism that is forced is false patriotism, just as loyalty which is coerced is the very antithesis of loyalty.[48]

Conclusion

In conclusion, the opinion of this educator is that the Pledge is too important to be treated shabbily. Yet, because of daily usage, the ceremony is overdone and has been relegated to an unimportant role in daily school routine: words are uttered under coercion.

Legislators should recognize the current situation and amend the law: the Pledge should be reserved for *infrequent, important, ceremonial* occasions. *Instruction into the meaning and ideals expressed in the Pledge should be an ongoing practice.*

Refusal by students to participate in the ceremony may not be disallowed. Teachers, too, have the same rights; the rights and guarantees of the Constitution do not stop at the schoolhouse door.

Above all, a more rational approach is needed to the Pledge of Allegiance ceremony. There must be an awareness that patriotism cannot be forced and mere recitation cannot achieve allegiance. A *New York Times* editorial (11-19-72) states it quite succinctly:

> ... virtually no other country today asks its schools to engage in such daily ceremonial routines normally reserved for special occasions. While there is widespread agreement that love of country is usually based on a mixture of emotions and intellect, many educators feel that the schools' role is more naturally that of bolstering the intellectual foundations of patriotism by rational discussion and sound teaching.[49]

Notes

1. 36 U.S.C.A. #172, states that the following is designated as the pledge of allegiance to the flag: I pledge ... for all ... as stated in text.
2. *Encyclopaedia Britannica.* 1968. Vol. 18, p. 42.
3. The original version of the Pledge was: I pledge allegiance to my flag and the republic for which it stands; one nation, indivisible, with liberty and justice for all. *Ibid.*
4. *U.S. Code 1954, Cong. and Adm. News,* p. 2339.
5. *Ibid.*
6. *New Yorker,* July 30, 1973, p. 47.
7. *New York Times,* June 15, 1970, p. 23.
8. Teaching about the Pledge of Allegiance may be difficult. There is hardly a word about the Pledge in any elementary or secondary school social studies textbook. This writer examined about a dozen sets of books used in public schools today and did not find a single historical reference to the Pledge: nothing about its origins, what it says, what it means, why it is said, and why it has become law in the United States.
9. 52 N.Y. Jur. Schools #435.
10. *Ibid.*
11. N.J.S.A. 18A:36-3(c) 1968.
12. The Senate of the New York State Legislature, after a highly emotional debate about patriotism, passed a bill mandating daily recitation of the Pledge in all public schools. *New York Times,* April 27, 1973, p. 41.
13. Senator Eugene McCarthy states in *Dictionary of American Politics* (Baltimore, Maryland: Penguin Books, 1968, p. 119) that the Pledge of Allegiance is a "declaration of loyalty made by United States citizens. It is used on patriotic occasions such as national holidays and at events where the United States flag plays a central role."

[14] *West Virginia State Board of Education v. Barnette*, 319 U.S. 624, 87 L.Ed. 1628 (1942).

[15] *New York Times*, October 8, 1969, p. 35; October 10, 1969, p. 96.

[16] *New York Times*, December 11, 1969, p. 37.

[17] *New York Times*, January 26, 1970, p. 1.

[18] *New York Times*, January 26, 1970, p. 36.

[19] *New York Times*, January 31, 1970, p. 33.

[20] *New York Times*, February 2, 1970, p. 24.

[21] In *Matter of Bielenberg* 9 Ed. Dept. Rep. 196 (1970), Commissioner Nyquist upheld Central School District #1 of Highlands, New York (Orange County) in requiring compliance with the board's ruling. *Matter of Bielenberg* has been superseded by *Goetz v. Ansell, supra.*

[22] *New York Times*, May 31, 1970, p. 40; also refer to: *State v. Lundquist*, 278 A. 2d 263 (1971) Maryland, which involved a social science teacher who "claimed he would refuse to engage in a mandatory flag salute ceremony, not for religious reasons, but because he could not in good conscience force patriotism upon his classes." The Court of Appeals of Maryland concluded that the salute requirement and punishment provision of the Maryland law was "unconstitutional and void."

[23] *New York Times*, June 7, 1970, p. 31.

[24] *New York Times*, April 18, 1972, p. 35.

[25] *New York Times*, September 25, 1973, p. 35.

[26] *New York Times*, October 11, 1973, p. 8.

[27] *New York Times*, December 12, 1970, p. 49.

[28] *New York Times*, December 19, 1970, p. 1.

[29] *New York Times*, June 15, 1970, p. 23.

[30] M. S. Miller, "Music Will Bind a Nation Together," *The School Musician Director and Teacher*, 1971, p. 46.

[31] The Senate of the State of Tennessee passed a bill recently (*New York Times*, March 21, 1974, p. 83), approving punishment for those who refuse to stand for the pledge of allegiance to the flag (sic).

[32] Reference is made to the case of Mrs. Susan C. Russo, former art teacher in Sperry High School, Rush-Henrietta School District, near Rochester, New York. Mrs. Russo was dismissed in June 1970 for abstaining from the recitation of the Pledge. Mrs. Russo stood silently during broadcast of the Pledge over the public address system. Her contract for reappointment was not renewed in spite of excellent evaluation reports. Mrs. Russo brought suit charging that she was protected by the First and Fourteenth Amendments. The school district did not deny that; it contended that Mrs. Russo was dismissed for insubordination. *Russo v. Central School District No. 1. Towns of Rush, Etc.*, 469 F. 2d 623 (2nd Cir. 1972) was in the courts for several years and finally elicited a landmark Court of Appeals decision written by Judge Irving R. Kaufman. The United States Supreme Court refused to hear the appeal by the school district, thereby letting stand the Court of Appeals decision.

Mrs. Russo was to be reinstated, awarded damages, and given the right to abstain from recitation of the Pledge. She was not given a job in the district, however, until Federal District Judge John O. Henderson ordered the Rush-Henrietta administration to reinstate her. (August 30, 1973). Mrs. Russo is now employed as an art teacher at Roth Junior High School, a different school in the same district.

There are several other examples:

Mr. L. Church, a high school teacher in Cheboygan, Michigan (*New York Times*, November 7, 1971, p. 72), was dismissed for failing to stand during the Pledge and singing of the National Anthem.

Mr. L. Bates, a teacher at H. D. Perry School, Hollywood, Florida, was suspended by the Broward County School Board for refusing to recite the Pledge (*New York Times*, November 27, 1970, p. 41).

Mrs. C. Hanover of Roxbury, Connecticut, an English teacher, was suspended for refusing to say the Pledge with her class (*New York Times*, February 23, 1970, p. 24.).

33 Henry Steele Commager, "Who Is Loyal to America?," as reprinted in *Primer of Intellectual Freedom*. Howard Mumford Jones (ed.), Cambridge, Mass.: Harvard University Press, 1949, p. 31.

34 "Coercion" is defined in this instance as "an avoidable external process deliberately inflicted to restrict, tilt, or deform the victim's range of discretion so as to exclude some of his choices or to impose one's own. ..." "it is the process of excluding or imposing choices....", as quoted from: Ernest van den Haag, *Political Violence and Civil Disobedience*. New York: Harper and Row, 1972, p. 62.

35 Decision 8252. *Matter of Bustin*, 10 Ed. Dept. Rep. 168 (1971).

36 *Ibid.*

37 Commissioner Nyquist commented as follows in substantiating his decision:

It is well settled that a student has the right to refrain from reciting the pledge of allegiance (*West Virginia State Board of Education v. Barnette*, 319 U.S. 624, 87 L.Ed. 1628) (1942), as long as the student's actions in claiming free speech do not interfere with the rights of others (*Tinker v. Board of Education*, 393 U.S. 503, 21 L.Ed.2d. 731; *Matter of Bielenberg*, 9 Ed. Dept. Rep. 196) (1970).

Note: *Tinker v. Board of Education* upheld the right of students to wear black armbands to school, where such action did not cause interference with school processes. The Court held that First Amendment rights, applied in light of the special characteristics of the school environment, are available to students, and stated: "Accordingly, this case does not concern speech or action that intrudes upon the work of the school or the rights of their students." In *Matter of Bielenberg*, the student was not required to say the Pledge. The student was requested, however, to stand or leave the room while others participated. Commissioner Nyquist upheld the Central School District #1 of Highlands, New York (Orange County) in requiring compliance with the board's ruling. *Matter of Bielenberg* has since been superseded by *Goetz v. Ansell, supra.*

38 *Goetz v. Ansell* 477 F. 2d 636 (1973).

39 *Ibid.* J. Joseph Smith, Circuit Court Judge, filed the opinion enjoining school officials from disciplining students for remaining seated during the pledge ceremony. The regulation which required a student who refused to salute the flag to stand or leave the classroom was invalid. Judge Smith stated "... if the state cannot compel participation in the pledge, it cannot punish non-participation. And being required to leave the classroom during the pledge may reasonably be viewed by some as having that effect, however benign defendants' motives may be." See *Abington School District v. Schempp*, 374 U.S. 203, 292, 83 S. Ct. 1560, 1608, 10 L. Ed. 2d 844 (1963); Brennan, J.,

concurring. "The excluded pupil loses caste with his fellows, and is liable to be regarded with aversion, and subjected to reproach and insult."

40 *West Virginia State Board of Education v. Barnette*, 319 U.S. 624, 63 S.Ct. 1178, 87 L. Ed. 1628 (1943). Id. at 632, 63 S. Ct. at 1182. Id. at 642, 63 S. Ct. 1178.

41 CRRNY 108.5(b). The regulations of the Commissioner of Education specify that "in giving the Pledge to the flag, the procedure is to render the Pledge by standing with the right hand over the heart."

42 *Banks v. Board of Public Instruction*, 314 F. Supp. 285, 296 (S.D. Fla. 1970) (three judge court), aff'd mem., 450 F. 2d 1103 (5th Cir. 1971). The decision of the three judge court in Banks was appealed to the Supreme Court, which vacated and remanded "so that a fresh decree may be entered from which a timely appeal may be taken to the United States Court of Appeals...." 401 U.S. 988, 91 S. Ct. 1223, 28 L. Ed. 2d 526 (1971). The single judge then entered an order adopting the findings of fact and conclusions of law of the three judge court concerning the First Amendment issue. The order was then affirmed by the circuit court. (Cit. in *Goetz v. Ansell, supra.*)

43 *Goetz v. Ansell, supra.*

44 E. C. Balmeier, *Landmark Supreme Court Decisions on Public School Issues.* Charlottesville, Virginia: The Michie Co., 1973, pp. 51–52.

45 D. O. McGovney, and H. Pendleton, *Cases on Constitutional Law.* 3rd ed. Indianapolis, Indiana: Bobbs-Merrill Co., 1955, pp. 998–1006.

46 *West Virginia State Board of Education v. Barnette, supra.*

47 *West Virginia State Board of Education v. Barnette, supra.*

48 *Russo v. Central School District No. 1, Towns of Rush, Etc., supra.*

49 *New York Times*, November 19, 1972, editorial.

VII.

Sexism

As a number of linguists have pointed out, English is an ambiguous language—which is the reason why we tie a boat fast when we want to keep it in one place, and yet run fast when we want to move away quickly from that place; or why we cleave through a piece of meat to cut it apart, and yet cleave to each other to keep close together.

English is a difficult language, too, in which to treat the sexes equitably. Thus, in the past, one-sided words such as "he," "him," and "man" have been used to represent both men and women. Even when a conscientious effort is made to eliminate linguistic discrimination, word problems may remain. Jane Brown Maas, president of a prominent New York advertising firm, asks: "If it's true that we've come a long way, baby, then why are they still calling us baby?"

This section of the anthology presents analyses of several aspects of sexism, including the field of language. Although a distinction is made between words and actions, it is also recognized that a change in the approach to the English language is a necessary step toward the elimination of deeper problems of sexism.

The title of the first selection, "Psychology Constructs the Female; or The Fantasy Life of the Male Psychologist (with Some Attention to the Fantasies of His Friends, the Male Biologist and the Male Anthropologist)," by Naomi Weisstein, then associate professor of psychology at Loyola University of Chicago, has the distinction of being the longest title ever published in *Social Education*. Yet, on reading the article, one may have the impression that the title is only part of what the author might have written if she had been permitted additional space by the editor. Certainly, she does not hesitate to take on and attempt to demolish a variety of ideas held by researchers. Her conclusion is as direct as her analysis: "... the uselessness of present psychology (and biology) with regard to women is simply a special case of the general conclusion: one must understand the social conditions under which women live if one is going to attempt to explain the behavior of women. And to understand the social conditions under which women live, one must be cognizant of the social expectations about women."

> Women arrived in 1619.... They held the Seneca Falls Convention on Women's Rights in 1848. During the rest of the nineteenth century, they participated in reform movements, chiefly temperance, and were exploited in factories. In 1923 they were given the vote. They joined the armed forces for the first time during the second World War and thereafter have enjoyed the good life in America.

That, according to Janice Law Trecker, who taught English at L. P. Wilson Junior High School in Windsor, Connecticut, is how one might summarize the history and contributions of American women—at least, as far as commonly used high school textbooks are concerned. It is a pattern, she writes, that presents a stereotyped picture of the American woman, "passive, incapable of sustained organization or work, satisfied with her role in society, and well supplied with material blessings."

In "Women in U.S. History High School Textbooks," Trecker analyzes textbooks in detail to document the basis for her conclusions. The article proved to be a milestone in the history of *Social Education.* The response of readers was among the heaviest that the journal ever received.

What is objectionable about Thomas Paine declaring, "These are the times that try men's souls"? What is disturbing about Abraham Lincoln saying, "fourscore and seven years ago our fathers brought forth on this continent a new nation...."? Elizabeth Burr, Susan Dunn, and Norma Farquhar, who collaborated on an examination of "The Semantics of Sexism," answer these and related questions in the article "Women and the Language of Inequality." They focus primarily on the semantics of textbooks, where a key question is: "What's in a word?" More than we realize, stress the authors, as they demonstrate how certain words can eliminate the identities of women, and how masculine terms can even turn women into luggage!

In the years that followed the publication of these articles, publishers made conscientious efforts to eliminate sexism in textbooks. They provided written guidelines for authors, used consultants to check the validity of terms in books, and urged authors and editors to explore alternate ways of identifying individuals and of describing action. Words, economist Stuart Chase had written in *Power of Words,* are what hold society together. Concerted efforts were now being made to prevent words from also dividing society.

Psychology Constructs the Female; or the Fantasy Life of the Male Psychologist (with Some Attention to the Fantasies of His Friends, the Male Biologist and the Male Anthropologist)

Naomi Weisstein

It is an implicit assumption that the area of psychology which concerns itself with personality has the onerous but necessary task of describing the limits of human possibility. Thus when we are about to consider the liberation of women, we naturally look to psychology to tell us what "true" liberation would mean: what would give women the freedom to fulfill their own intrinsic natures. Psychologists have set about describing the true natures of women with a certainty and a sense of their own infallibility rarely found in the secular world. Bruno Bettelheim, of the University of Chicago, tells us (1965) that "We must start with the realization that, as much as women want to be good scientists or engineers, they want first and foremost to be womanly companions of men and to be mothers." Erik Erikson of Harvard University (1964), upon noting that young women often ask whether they can "have an identity before they know whom they will marry, and for whom they will make a

Note: This article is a revised and expanded version of "Kinder, Küche, Kirche as Scientific Law: Psychology Constructs the Female," published by the New England Free Press. It appeared in *Social Education*, April 1971, pp. 362–373. Reprinted by permission of Naomi Weisstein.

home," explains somewhat elegiacally that "Much of a young woman's identity is already defined in her kind of attractiveness and in the selectivity of her search for the man (or men) by whom she wishes to be sought. . . ." Mature womanly fulfillment, for Erikson, rests on the fact that a woman's ". . . somatic design harbors an 'inner space' destined to bear the offspring of chosen men, and with it, a biological, psychological, and ethical commitment to take care of human infancy." Some psychiatrists even see the acceptance of woman's role by women as a solution to societal problems. "Woman is nurturance. . . ," writes Joseph Rheingold (1964), a psychiatrist at Harvard Medical School," . . . anatomy decrees the life of a woman . . . when women grow up without dread of their biological functions and without subversion by feminist doctrine, and therefore enter upon motherhood with a sense of fulfillment and altruistic sentiment, we shall attain the goal of a good life and a secure world in which we live it." (p. 714)

These views from men who are assumed to be experts reflect, in a surprisingly transparent way, the cultural consensus. They not only assert that a woman is defined by her ability to attract men, they see no alternative definitions. They think that the definition of a woman in terms of a man is the way it should be; and they back it up with psychosexual incantation and biological ritual curses. A woman has an identity if she is attractive enough to obtain a man, and thus, a home; for this will allow her to set about her life's task of "joyful altruism and nurturance."

Business certainly does not disagree. If views such as Bettelheim's and Erikson's do indeed have something to do with real liberation for women, then seldom in human history has so much money and effort been spent on helping a group of people realize their true potential. Clothing, cosmetics, home furnishings, are multi-million dollar businesses: if you don't like investing in firms that make weaponry and flaming gasoline, then there's a lot of cash in "inner space." Sheet and pillowcase manufacturers are concerned to fill this inner space:

> Mother, for a while this morning, I thought I wasn't cut out for married life. Hank was late for work and forgot his apricot juice and walked out without kissing me, and when I was all alone I started crying. But then the postman came with the sheets and towels you sent, that look like big bandana handkerchiefs, and you know what I thought? That those big red and blue handkerchiefs are for girls like me to dry their tears on so they can get busy and do what a housewife has to do. Throw open the windows and start getting the house ready, and the dinner, maybe clean the silver and put new geraniums in the box. *Everything to be ready for him when he walks through that door.* (Fieldcrest 1966; emphasis added.)

Of course, it is not only the sheet and pillowcase manufacturers, the cosmetics industry, the home furnishings salesmen who profit from and make use of the cultural definitions of man and woman. The example above is blatantly and overtly pitched to a particular kind of sexist stereotype: the child nymph. But almost all aspects of the media are normative, that is, they have to do with the ways in which beautiful people, or just folks, or ordinary Americans, or extraordinary Americans should live their lives. They define the possible; and the possibilities are usually in terms of what is male and what is female. Men and women alike are waiting for Hank, the Silva Thins man, to walk back through that door.

It is interesting but limited exercise to show that psychologists and psychiatrists embrace these sexist norms of our culture, that they do not see beyond the most superficial and stultifying media conceptions of female nature, and that their ideas of female nature serve industry and commerce so well. Just because it's good for business doesn't mean it's wrong. What I will show is that it *is wrong*; that there isn't the tiniest shred of evidence that these fantasies of servitude and childish dependence have anything to do with women's true potential; that the idea of the nature of human possibility which rests on the accidents of individual development or genitalia, on what is possible today because of what happened yesterday, on the fundamentalist myth of sex organ causality, has strangled and deflected psychology so that it is relatively useless in describing, explaining or predicting humans and their behavior. It then goes without saying that present psychology is less than worthless in contributing to a vision which could truly liberate—men as well as women.

The central argument of my article, then, is this. Psychology has nothing to say about what women are really like, what they need and what they want, essentially because psychology does not know. I want to stress that this failure is not limited to women; rather, the kind of psychology which has addressed itself to how people act and who they are has failed to understand, in the first place, why people act the way they do, and certainly failed to understand what might make them act differently.

The kind of psychology which has addressed itself to these questions divides into two professional areas: academic personality research, and clinical psychology and psychiatry. The basic reason for failure is the same in both these areas: the central assumption for most psychologists of human personality has been that human behavior rests on an individual and inner dynamic, perhaps fixed in infancy, perhaps fixed by genitalia, perhaps simply arranged in a rather immovable cognitive network. But this assumption is rapidly losing ground as personality psychologists fail again and again to get consistency in the assumed personalities of their subjects (Block, 1968). Meanwhile, the evidence is collecting that what a person does, and who he believes himself to be, will in general be a function of what people around him expect him to be, and what the overall situation in which he is acting implies that he is. Compared to the influence of the social context within which a person lives, his or her history and "traits," as well as biological makeup, may simply be random variations, "noise" superimposed on the true signal which can predict behavior.

Some academic personality psychologists are at least looking at the counter evidence and questioning their theories; no such corrective is occurring in clinical psychology and psychiatry. Freudians and neo-Freudians, Adlerians and neo-Adlerians, classicists and swingers, clinicians and psychiatrists, simply refuse to look at the evidence against their theory and practice. And they support their theory and their practice with stuff so transparently biased as to have absolutely no standing as empirical evidence.

To summarize: the first reason for psychology's failure to understand what people are and how they act is that psychology has looked for inner traits when it should have been looking for social context; the second reason for psychology's failure is that the theoreticians of personality have generally been clinicians and psychiatrists, and they have never considered it necessary to have evidence in support of their theories.

Theory Without Evidence

Let us turn to this latter cause of failure first: the acceptance by psychiatrists and clinical psychologists of theory without evidence. If we inspect the literature of personality, it is immediately obvious that the bulk of it is written by clinicians and psychiatrists, and that the major support for their theories is "years of intensive clinical experience." This is a tradition started by Freud. His "insights" occurred during the course of his work with his patients. Now there is nothing wrong with such an approach to theory *formulation*; a person is free to make up theories with any inspiration which works: divine revelation, intensive clinical practice, a random numbers table. But he is not free to claim any validity for his theory until it has been tested and confirmed. But theories are treated in no such tentative way in ordinary clinical practice. Consider Freud. What he thought constituted evidence violated the most minimal conditions of scientific rigor. In *The Sexual Enlightenment of Children* (1963), the classic document which is supposed to demonstrate empirically the existence of a castration complex and its connection to a phobia, Freud based his analysis not on the little boy who had the phobia, but on the reports of the father of the little boy, himself in therapy, and a devotee of Freudian theory. I really don't have to comment further on the contamination in this kind of evidence. It is remarkable that only recently has Freud's classic theory on the sexuality of women—the notion of the double orgasm—been actually tested physiologically and found just plain wrong. Now those who claim that fifty years of psychoanalytic experience constitute evidence enough of the essential truths of Freud's theory should ponder the robust health of the double orgasm. Did women, until Masters and Johnson (1966), believe they were having two different kinds of orgasm? Did their psychiatrists intimidate them into reporting something that was not true? If so, were there other things they reported that were also not true? Did psychiatrists ever learn anything different than their theories had led them to believe? If clinical experience means anything at all, surely we should have been done with the double orgasm myth long before the Masters and Johnson studies.

But certainly, you may object, "years of intensive clinical experience" is the only reliable measure in a discipline which rests for its findings on insight, sensitivity, and intuition. The problem with insight, sensitivity, and intuition is that they can confirm for all time the biases that one started out with. People used to be absolutely convinced of their ability to tell which of their number were engaging in witchcraft. All it required was some sensitivity to the workings of the devil.

Years of intensive clinical experience is not the same thing as empirical evidence. The first thing an experimenter learns in any kind of experiment which involves humans is the concept of the "double blind." The term is taken from medical experiments, where one group is given a drug which is presumably supposed to change behavior in a certain way, and a control group is given a placebo. If the observers or the subjects know which group took which drug, the result invariably comes out on the positive side for the new drug. Only when it is not known which subject took which pill, is validity remotely approximated. In addition, with judgments of human behavior, it is so difficult to precisely tie down just what behavior is going on, let alone what behavior should be expected, that one must test again and again the reliability of judgments. How many judges, blind, will agree in their observations? Can they replicate their own judgments at some later time? When, in actual practice, these judgment criteria are tested for clinical judgments, then we find that the judges cannot judge reliably, nor can they judge consistently: they do no better than chance in identifying which of a certain set of stories were written by men and which by women; which of a whole battery of clinical test results are the products of homosexuals and which are the products of heterosexuals (Hooker, 1957); and which of a battery of clinical test results *and* interviews (where questions are asked such as "Do you have delusions?"—Little & Schneidman, 1959) are products of psychotics, neurotics, psychosomatics, or normals. Lest this summary escape your notice, let me stress the implications of these findings. The ability of judges, chosen for their clinical expertise, to distinguish male heterosexuals from male homosexuals on the basis of three widely used clinical projective tests—the Rorschach, the TAT, and the MAP—was *no better than chance*. The reason this is such devastating news, of course, is that sexuality is supposed to be of fundamental importance in the deep dynamic of personality; if what is considered gross sexual deviance cannot be caught, then what are psychologists talking about when they, for example, claim that at the basis of paranoid psychosis is "latent homosexual panic"? They can't even identify what homosexual anything is, let alone "latent homosexual panic."[1] More frightening, expert clinicians cannot be consistent on what diagnostic category to assign to a person, again on the basis of both tests and interviews; a number of normals in the Little & Schneidman study were described as psychotic, in such categories as "schizophrenic with homosexual tendencies" or "schizoid character with depressive trends." But most disheartening, when the judges were asked to rejudge the test protocols some weeks later, their diagnoses of the same subjects on the basis of the same protocol differed markedly from their initial judgments. It is obvious that even simple descriptive conventions in clinical psychology cannot be consistently applied; that these descriptive conventions have any explanatory significance is therefore, of course, out of the question.

As a graduate student at Harvard some years ago, I was a member of a seminar which was asked to identify which of two piles of a clinical test, the TAT, had been written by males and which by females. Only four students out of twenty identified the piles correctly, and this was after one and a half months of intensively studying the differences between men and women. Since this result is below chance—that is, this result would occur by chance about four out of a thousand times—we may conclude that there is finally a consistency here; students are judging knowledgeably within the context of psychological teaching about the differences between men and women; the teachings themselves are simply erroneous.

You may argue that the theory may be scientifically "unsound" but at least it cures people. There is no evidence that it does. In 1952, Eysenck reported the results of what is called an "outcome of therapy" study of neurotics which showed that, of the patients who received psychoanalysis the improvement rate was 44%; of the patients who received psychotherapy the improvement rate was 64%; and of the patients who received no treatment at all the improvement rate was 72%. These findings have never been refuted; subsequently, later studies have confirmed the negative results of the Eysenck study. (Barron & Leary, 1955; Bergin, 1963; Cartwright and Vogel, 1960; Truax, 1963; Powers and Witmer, 1951). How can clinicians and psychiatrists, then, in all good conscience, continue to practice? Largely by ignoring these results and being careful not to do outcome-of-therapy studies. The attitude is nicely summarized by Rotter (1960) (quoted in Astin, 1961): "Research studies in psychotherapy

ing upwards from 15 volts through 450 volts; for each of four consecutive voltages there are verbal descriptions such as "mild shock," "danger, severe shock," and, finally, for the 435 and 450 volt switches, a red XXX marked over the switches. Each time the stooge answers incorrectly the subject is supposed to increase the voltage. As the voltage increases, the stooge begins to cry in pain; he demands that the experiment stop; finally, he refuses to answer at all. When he stops responding, the experimenter instructs the subject to continue increasing the voltage; for each shock administered the stooge shrieks in agony. Under these conditions, about 62.5% of the subjects administered shock that they believed to be possibly lethal.

No tested individual differences between subjects predicted how many would continue to obey, and which would break off the experiment. When forty psychiatrists predicted how many of a group of 100 subjects would go on to give the lethal shock, their predictions were orders of magnitude below the actual percentages; most expected only one-tenth of one percent of the subjects to obey to the end.

But even though *psychiatrists* have no idea how people will behave in this situation, and even though individual differences do not predict which subjects will obey and which will not, it is easy to predict when subjects will be obedient and when they will be defiant. All the experimenter has to do is change the social situation. In a variant of the experiment, Milgram had two stooges present in addition to the "victim"; these worked along with the subject in administering electric shocks. When these two stooges refused to go on with the experiment, only ten percent of the subjects continued to the maximum voltage. This is critical for personality theory. It says that behavior is predicted from the social situation, not from the individual history.

Finally, an ingenious experiment by Schachter and Singer (1962) showed that subjects injected with adrenalin, which produces a state of physiological arousal in all but minor respects identical to that which occurs when subjects are extremely afraid, became euphoric when they were in a room with a stooge who was acting euphoric, and became extremely angry when they were placed in a room with a stooge who was acting extremely angry.

To summarize. If subjects under quite innocuous and non-coercive social conditions can be made to kill other subjects and under other types of social conditions will positively refuse to do so; if subjects can react to a state of physiological fear by becoming euphoric because there is somebody else around who is euphoric or angry because there is somebody else around who is angry; if students become intelligent because teachers expect them to be intelligent, and rats run mazes better because experimenters are told the rats are bright, then it is obvious that a study of human behavior requires, first and foremost, a study of the social contexts within which people move, the expectations as to how they will behave, and the authority which tells them who they are and what they are supposed to do.

Biologically Based Theories

Biologists also have at times assumed they could describe the limits of human potential from their observations of animal rather than human behavior. Here, as in psychology, there has been no end of theorizing about the sexes, again with a sense of absolute certainty. These theories fall into two major categories.

One biological theory of differences in nature argues that since females and males differ in their sex hormones, and sex hormones enter the brain (Hamburg & Lunde in Maccoby, 1966), there must be innate behavioral differences. But the only thing this argument tells us is that there are differences in physiological state. The problem is whether these differences are at all relevant to behavior.

Consider, for example, differences in testosterone levels. A man who calls himself Tiger[3] has recently argued (1970) that the greater quantities of testosterone found in human males as compared with human females (of a certain age group) determines innate differences in aggressiveness, competitiveness, dominance, ability to hunt, ability to hold public office, and so forth. But Tiger demonstrates in this argument the same manly and courageous refusal to be intimidated by evidence which we have already seen in our consideration of the clinical and psychiatric tradition. The evidence does not support his argument, and in some cases, directly contradicts it. Testosterone level co-varies neither with hunting ability, nor with dominance, nor with aggression, nor with competitiveness. As Storch has pointed out (1970), all normal male mammals in the reproductive age group produce much greater quantities of testosterone than females; yet many of these males are neither hunters nor are they aggressive. Among some hunting mammals, such as the large cats, it turns out that more hunting is done by the female than the male. And there exist primate species where the female is clearly more aggressive, competitive, and dominant than the male (Mitchell, 1969; and see below). Thus, for some species, being female, and therefore, having less testosterone than the male of that species means hunting more, or being more aggressive, or being more dominant. Nor does having *more* testosterone preclude behavior commonly thought of as "female": there exist primate species where females do not touch infants except to feed them; the males care for the infants (Mitchell, 1969; see fuller discussion below). So it is not clear what testosterone or any other sex-hormonal difference means for differences in nature of sex-role behavior.

In other words, one can observe identical sex-role behavior (e.g., "mothering") in males and females despite known differences in physiological state, i.e., sex hormones. What about the converse to this? That is, can one obtain differences in behavior given a single physiological state? The answer is overwhelmingly yes, not only as regards non-sex-specific hormones (as in the Schachter and Singer 1962 experiment cited above), but also as regards gender itself. Studies of hermaphrodites with the same diagnosis (the genetic, gonadal, hormonal sex, the internal reproductive organs, and the ambiguous appearances of the external genitalia were identical) have shown that one will consider oneself male or female depending simply on whether one was defined and raised as male or female (Money, 1970; Hampton & Hampton, 1961):

"There is no more convincing evidence of the power of social interaction on gender-identity differentiation than in the case of congenital hermaphrodites who are of the same diagnosis and similar degree of hermaphroditism but are differently assigned and with a different postnatal medical and life history." (Money, 1970, p. 432.)

Thus, for example, if out of two individuals diagnosed as having the adrenogenital syndrome of female hermaphroditism, one is raised as a girl and one as a boy, each will act and identify her/himself accordingly. The one raised as a girl will consider herself a girl; the one raised as a boy will consider himself a boy; and each will conduct her/himself successfully in accord with that self-definition.

So, identical behavior occurs given different physiological states; and different behavior occurs given an identical physiological starting point. So it is not clear that differences in sex hormones are at all relevant to behavior.

There is a second category of theory based on biology, a reductionist theory. It goes like this. Sex-role behavior in some primate species is described, and it is concluded that this is the "natural" behavior for humans. Putting aside the not insignificant problem of observer bias (for instance, Harlow, 1962, of the University of Wisconsin, after observing differences between male and female rhesus monkeys, quotes Lawrence Sterne to the effect that women are silly and trivial, and concludes that "men and women have differed in the past and they will differ in the future"), there are a number of problems with this approach.

The most general and serious problem is that there are no grounds to assume that anything primates do is necessary, natural, or desirable in humans, for the simple reason that humans are not non-humans. For instance, it is found that male chimpanzees placed alone with infants will not "mother" them. Jumping from hard data to ideological speculation researchers conclude from this information that *human* females are necessary for the safe growth of human infants. It would be as reasonable to conclude, following this logic, that it is quite useless to teach human infants to speak, since it has been tried with chimpanzees and it does not work.

One strategy that has been used is to extrapolate from primate behavior to "innate" human preference by noticing certain trends in primate behavior as one moves phylogenetically closer to humans. But there are great difficulties with this approach. When behaviors from lower primates are directly opposite to those of higher primates, or to those one expects of humans, they can be dismissed on evolutionary grounds—higher primates and/or humans grew out of that kid stuff. On the other hand, if the behavior of higher primates is counter to the behavior considered natural for humans, while the behavior of some lower primate is considered the natural one for humans, the higher primate behavior can be dismissed also, on the grounds that it has diverged from an older, prototypical pattern. So either way, one can select those behaviors one wants to prove as innate for humans. In addition, one does not know whether the sex-role behavior exhibited is dependent on the phylogenetic rank, or on the environmental conditions (both physical and social) under which different species live.

Is there then any value at all in primate observations as they relate to human females and males? There is a value but it is limited: its function can be no more than to show some extant examples of diverse sex-role behavior. It must be stressed, however, that this is an extremely limited function. The extant behavior does not begin to suggest all the possibilities, either for non-human primates or for humans. Bearing these caveats in mind, it is nonetheless interesting that if one inspects the limited set of existing non-human primate sex-role behaviors, one finds, in fact, a much larger range of sex-role behavior than is commonly believed to exist. "Biology" appears to limit very little; the fact that a female gives birth does not mean, even in non-humans, that she necessarily cares for the infant (in marmosets, for instance, the male carries the infant at all times except when the infant is feeding [Mitchell, 1969]); "natural" female and male behavior varies all the way from females who are much more aggressive and competitive than males (e.g., Tamarins, see Mitchell, 1969) and male "mothers" (e.g., Titi monkeys, night monkeys, and marmosets, see Mitchell, 1969)[4] to submissive and passive females and male antagonists (e.g., rhesus monkeys).

But even for the limited function that primate arguments serve, the evidence has been misused. Invariably, only those primates have been cited which exhibit exactly the kind of behavior that the proponents of the biological basis of human female behavior wish were true for humans. Thus, baboons and rhesus monkeys are generally cited: males in these groups exhibit some of the most irritable and aggressive behavior found in primates, and if one wishes to argue that females are naturally passive and submissive, these groups provide vivid examples. There are abundant counter examples, such as those mentioned above (Mitchell, 1969); in fact, in general, a counter example can be found for every sex-role behavior cited, including, as mentioned in the case of marmosets, male "mothers."

But the presence of counter examples has not stopped florid and overarching theories of the natural or biological basis of male privilege from proliferating. For instance, there have been a number of theories dealing with the innate incapacity in human males for monogamy. Here, as in most of this type of theorizing, baboons are a favorite example, probably because of their fantasy value: the family unit of the hamadryas baboon, for instance, consists of a highly constant pattern of one male and a number of females and their young. And again, the counter examples, such as the invariably monogamous gibbon, are ignored.

An extreme example of this maiming and selective truncation of the evidence in the service of a plea for the maintenance of male privilege is a recent book, *Men in Groups* (1969) by Tiger (see above and footnote 3). The central claim of this book is that females are incapable of honorable collective action because they are incapable of "bonding" as in "male bonding." What is "male bonding"? Its surface definition is simple: ". . . a particular relationship between two or more males such that they react differently to members of their bonding units as compared to individuals outside of it" (pp. 19–20). If one deletes the word male, the definition, on its face, would seem to include all organisms that have any kind of social organization. But this is not what Tiger means. For instance, Tiger asserts that females are incapable of bonding; and this alleged incapacity indicates to Tiger that females should be restricted from public life. Why is bonding an exclusively male behavior? Because, says Tiger, it is seen in male primates. All male primates? No, very few male primates. Tiger cites two examples where male bonding is seen: rhesus monkeys and baboons. Surprise, surprise. But not even all baboons: as mentioned above, the hamadryas social organization consists of one-male units; so does that of the Gelada baboon (Mitchell, 1969). And the great apes do not go in for male bonding much either. The "male bond" is hardly a serious contribution to scholarship; one reviewer for *Science* has observed that the book ". . . shows basically more resemblance to a partisan political tract than to a work of objective social science," with male bonding being ". . . some kind of behavioral phlogiston" (Fried, 1969, p. 884).

In short, primate arguments have generally misused the evidence; primate studies themselves have, in any case, only the very limited function of describing some possible sex-role behavior; and at present, primate observations have been sufficiently limited so that even the range of possible sex-role behavior for non-human primates is not known. This range is not known since there is only minimal observation of what happens to behavior if the physical or social environment is changed. In one study (Itani, 1963), different troops of Japanese macaques were observed. Here, there appeared to be cultural differences: males in 3 out of the 18 troops observed differed in their amount of aggressiveness and infant-caring behavior. There could be no possibility of differential evolution here; the differences seemed largely transmitted by infant socialization. Thus, the very limited evidence points to some plasticity in the sex-role behavior of non-human primates; if we can figure out experiments which massively change the social organization of primate groups, it is possible that we might observe great changes in behavior. At present, however, we must conclude that, since given a constant physical environment non-human primates do not seem to change their social conditions very much by themselves, the "innateness" and fixedness of their behavior is simply not known. Thus, even if there were some way, which there isn't, to settle on the behavior of a particular primate species as being the "natural" way for humans, we would not know whether or not this were simply some function of the present social organization of that species. And finally, once again it must be stressed that even if non-human primate behavior turned out to be relatively fixed, this would say little about our behavior. More immediate and relevant evidence, i.e., the evidence from social psychology, points to the enormous plasticity in human behavior, not only from one culture to the next, but from one experimental group to the next. One of the most salient features of human social organization is its variety; there are a number of cultures where there is at least a rough equality between men and women (Mead, 1949). In summary, primate arguments can tell us very little about our "innate" sex-role behavior; if they tell us anything at all, they tell us that there is no one biologically "natural" female or male behavior, and that sex-role behavior in non-human primates is much more varied than has previously been thought.

Conclusion

In brief, the uselessness of present psychology (and biology) with regard to women is simply a special case of the general conclusion: one must understand the social conditions under which women live if one is going to attempt to explain the behavior of women. And to understand the social conditions under which women live, one must be cognizant of the social expectations about women.

How are women characterized in our culture, and in psychology? They are inconsistent, emotionally unstable, lacking in a strong conscience or superego, weaker, "nurturant" rather than productive, "intuitive" rather than intelligent, and, if they are at all "normal," suited to the home and the family. In short, the list adds up to a typical minority group stereotype of inferiority (Hacker, 1951): if they know their place, which is in the home, they are really quite lovable, happy, childlike, loving creatures. In a review of the intellectual differences between little boys and little girls, Eleanor Maccoby (1966) has shown that there are no intellectual differences until about high school, or, if there are, girls are slightly ahead of boys. At high school, girls begin to do worse on a few intellectual tasks, such as arithmetic reasoning, and beyond high school, the achievement of women now measured in terms of productivity and accomplishment drops off even more rapidly. There are a number of other, non-intellectual tests which show sex differences; I chose the intellectual differences since it is seen clearly that women start becoming inferior. It is no use to talk about women being different but equal; all of the tests I can think of have a "good" outcome and a "bad" outcome. Women usually end up at the "bad" outcome. In light of social expectations about women, what is surprising is not that women end up where society expects they will; what is surprising is that little girls don't get the message that they are supposed to be stupid until high school; and what is even more remarkable is that some women resist this message even after high school, college, and graduate school.

My article began with remarks on the task of the discovery of the limits of human potential. Psychologists must realize that it is they who are limiting discovery of human potential. They refuse to accept evidence, if they are clinical psychologists, or, if they are rigorous, they assume that people move in a context-free ether, with only their innate dispositions and their individual traits determining what they will do. Until psychologists begin to respect evidence, and until they begin looking at the social contexts within which people move, psychology will have nothing of substance to offer in this task of discovery. I don't know what immutable differences exist between men and women apart from differences in their genitals; perhaps there are some other unchangeable differences; probably there are a number of irrelevant differences. But it is clear that until social expectations for men and women are equal, until we provide equal respect for both men and women, our answers to this question will simply reflect our prejudices.

Notes

[1] It should be noted that psychologists have been as quick to assert absolute truths about the nature of homosexuality as they have about the nature of women. The arguments presented in this article apply equally to the nature of homosexuality; psychologists know nothing about it; there is no more evidence for the "naturalness" of heterosexuality than for the "naturalness" of homosexuality. Psychology has functioned as a pseudo-scientific buttress for our cultural sex-role notions, that is, as a buttress for patriarchal ideology and patriarchal social organization: women's liberation and gay liberation fight against a common victimization.

[2] I am indebted to Jesse Lemisch for his valuable suggestions in the interpretation of these studies.

[3] Schwarz-Belkin (1914) claims that the name was originally *Mouse*, but this may be a reference to an earlier L. Tiger (putative).

[4] All these are lower-order primates, which makes their behavior with reference to humans unnatural, or more natural; take your choice.

References

ASTIN, A. W., "The Functional Autonomy of Psychotherapy." *American Psychologist,* 1961, *16,* 75–78.

BARRON, F. & LEARY, T., "Changes in Psychoneurotic Patients with and without Psychotherapy." *Journal of Consulting Psychology,* 1955, *19,* 239–245.

BERGIN, A. E., "The Effects of Psychotherapy: Negative Results Revisited." *Journal of Consulting Psychology,* 1963, *10,* 244–250.

BETTELHEIM, B., "The Commitment Required of a Woman Entering a Scientific Profession in Present-Day American Society." *Woman and the Scientific Professions,* the MIT Symposium on American Women in Science and Engineering, 1965.

BLOCK, J., "Some Reasons for the Apparent Inconsistency of Personality." *Psychological Bulletin,* 1968, *70,* 210–212.

CARTWRIGHT, R. D. & VOGEL, J. L., "A Comparison of Changes in Psychoneurotic Patients during Matched Periods of Therapy and No-therapy." *Journal of Consulting Psychology,* 1960, *24,* 121–127.

ERIKSON, E., "Inner and Outer Space: Reflections on Womanhood." *Daedalus,* 1964, *93,* 582–606.

EYSENCK, H. J., "The Effects of Psychotherapy: an Evaluation." *Journal of Consulting Psychology,* 1952, *16,* 319–324.

FIELDCREST—Advertisement in the *New Yorker,* 1965.

FRIED, M. H., "Mankind Excluding Woman," review of Tiger's *Men in Groups. Science, 165,* 1969, 883–884.

FREUD, S., *The Sexual Enlightenment of Children.* Collier Books Edition, 1963.

GOLDSTEIN, A. P. & DEAN, S. J., *The Investigation of Psychotherapy: Commentaries and Readings.* New York: John Wiley & Sons, 1966.

HAMBURG, D. A. & LUNDE, D. T., "Sex Hormones in the Development of Sex Differences in Human Behavior." In Maccoby (ed.), *The Development of Sex Differences.* Stanford University Press, 1966, 1–24.

HACKER, H. M., "Women as a Minority Group." *Social Forces,* 1951, *30,* 60–69.

HAMPTON, J. L. & HAMPTON, J. C., "The Ontogenesis of Sexual Behavior in Man." In W. C. Young (ed.), *Sex and Internal Secretions,* 1961, 1401–1432.

HARLOW, H. F., "The Heterosexual Affectional System in Monkeys." *The American Psychologist,* 1962, *17,* 1–9.

HOOKER, E., "Male Homosexuality in the Rorschach." *Journal of Projective Techniques,* 1957, *21,* 18–31.

ITANI, J., "Paternal Care in the Wild Japanese Monkeys, *Macaca Fuscata."* In C. H. Southwick (ed.), *Primate Social Behavior.* Princeton: Van Nostrand, 1963.

LITTLE, K. B. & SCHNEIDMAN, E. S., "Congruences among Interpretations of

Psychological and Anamnestic Data." *Psychological Monographs,* 1959, *73,* 1–42.

MACCOBY, ELEANOR E., "Sex Differences in Intellectual Functioning." In Maccoby (ed.). *The Development of Sex Differences.* Stanford University Press, 1966, 25–55.

MASTERS, W. H. & JOHNSON, V. E., *Human Sexual Response.* Boston: Little Brown, 1966.

MEAD, M., *Male and Female: A Study of the Sexes in a Changing World.* New York: William Morrow, 1949.

MILGRAM, S., "Some Conditions of Obedience and Disobedience to Authority." *Human Relations,* 1965a, *18,* 57–76.

MILGRAM, S., "Liberating Effects of Group Pressure." *Journal of Personality and Social Psychology,* 1965b, *I,* 127–134.

MITCHELL, G. D., "Paternalistic Behavior in Primates." *Psychological Bulletin,* 1969, *71,* 339–417.

MONEY, J., "Sexual Dimorphism and Homosexual Gender Identity." *Psychological Bulletin.* 1970, *74,* 6. 425–440.

POWERS, E. & WITMER, H., *An Experiment in the Prevention of Delinquency.* New York: Columbia University Press, 1951.

RHEINGOLD, J., *The Fear of Being a Woman.* New York: Grune & Stratton, 1964.

ROSENTHAL, R., "On the Social Psychology of the Psychological Experiment: The Experimenter's Hypothesis as Unintended Determinant of Experimental Results." *American Scientist,* 1963. *51,* 268–283.

ROSENTHAL, R., *Experimenter Effects in Behavioral Research.* New York: Appleton-Century-Crofts, 1966.

ROSENTHAL, R. & JACOBSON, L., *Pygmalion in the Classroom: Teacher Expectation and Pupil's Intellectual Development.* New York: Holt, Rinehart & Winston, 1968.

ROSENTHAL, R. & LAWSON, R., "A Longitudinal Study of the Effects of Experimenter Bias on the Operant Learning of Laboratory Rats." Unpublished Manuscript, Harvard University, 1961.

ROSENTHAL, R. & FODE, K. L., "The Effect of Experimenter Bias on the Performance of the Albino Rat." Unpublished Manuscript, Harvard University, 1960.

ROTTER, J. B., "Psychotherapy." *Annual Review of Psychology,* 1960, *11,* 381–414.

SCHACHTER, S. & SINGER, J. E., "Cognitive, Social and Physiological Determinants of Emotional State." *Psychological Review,* 1962, *69,* 379–399.

SCHWARZ-BELKIN, M., "Les Fleurs de Mal." In *Festschrift for Gordon Piltdown.* New York: Ponzi Press, 1914.

STORCH, M., "Reply to Tiger," 1970. Unpublished Manuscript.

TIGER, L., *Men in Groups.* New York: Random House, 1969.

TIGER, L., "Male Dominance? Yes. Alas. A Sexist Plot? No." *New York Times Magazine,* Section N, Oct. 25, 1970.

TRUAX, C. B., "Effective Ingredients in Psychotherapy: an Approach to Unraveling the Patient-therapist Interaction. *Journal of Counseling Psychology,* 1963, *10,* 256–263.

Women in U.S. History High School Textbooks

JANICE LAW TRECKER

Early in our history, enterprising groups of English gentlemen attempted to found all-male colonies. The attempts were failures, but the idea of a society without women appears to have held extraordinary appeal for the descendants of those early colonists. Throughout our history, groups of intrepid males have struck off into the wilderness to live in bachelor colonies free from civilization and domesticity.

The closing of the frontier and the presence, even from the earliest days, of equally intrepid females ended these dreams of masculine tranquility. Yet, the hopeful colonists may have had their revenge. If women have had their share in every stage of our history, exactly what they did and who they were remains obscure. Ask most high school students who Jane Addams, Ida Tarbell, or Susan B. Anthony were, and you may get an answer. Ask about Margaret Sanger, Abigail Duniway, or Margaret Brent, and you will probably get puzzled looks. Sojourner Truth, Frances Wright, Anna Howard Shaw, Emma Willard, Mary Bickerdyke, Maria Mitchell, Prudence Crandall, and scores of others sound like answers from some historian's version of Trivia.

Interest in the fate of obscure Americans may seem an esoteric pursuit, but this is not the case. History, despite its enviable reputation for presenting the important facts about our past, is influenced by considerations other than the simple love of truth. It is an instrument of the greatest social utility, and the story of our past is a potent means of

NOTE: This article appeared in *Social Education*, March 1971, pp. 249–260, 338. Reprinted by permission of Janice Law Trecker.

transmitting cultural images and stereotypes. One can scarcely doubt the impact of history upon the young in the face of recent minority groups' agitation for more of "their history."

Minority groups are perhaps not the only ones with a complaint against the historians and the schools, nor are they the only ones to show the effects of stereotypes. Consider the most recent reports of the President's Commission on the Status of Women. According to the 1968 report of the Commission, *American Women*, in the fall of 1968 only 40% of entering college freshmen were women. The lag in female participation in higher education is even more noticeable at the graduate level. Statistics from the Commission's 1968 report indicated that women earned only 1 in 3 of the B.A. degrees and M.A. degrees granted and only 1 in 10 of the doctorates. It is seldom noted that this represents a percentage decline from the 1930's when women received 2 in 5 B.A. degrees and M.A. degrees, and 1 in 7 Ph.D. degrees. The loss of potential talent this represents is clear from the Commission's information that among the top 10% of our high school seniors, there are twice as many girls as boys with no college plans.

Able girls are not entering science and mathematics in any great number, and, according to the *Conant Report*, they fail to take courses and programs commensurate with their abilities. There seems to be a clear need for an examination of the factors which permit the loss of considerable amounts of female talent.

The Education Committee of the President's Commission on the Status of Women was concerned about this loss, noting that:

> Low aspirations of girls are the result of complex and subtle forces. They are expressed in many ways—even high achievement—but accompanied by docility, passivity, or apathy. The high motivation found in the early school years often fades into a loss of commitment and interest, other than in the prospect of early marriage.

The Committee found some of the reasons for this loss of motivation are the stereotypes of women in our culture and in the lingering ideas of female inferiority.

Educators should be aware that the school is one of the means by which the stereotypes of women and their capacities are transmitted. As one of the main cultural forces in the society, the school shares a responsibility for the diminished aspirations of its female students. Looking at the position of women in our society, one would have to be very sanguine to say that the education of American girls needs no improvement. Something is wrong when women are concentrated in a relatively few, lower-paid positions; when there are few women represented in the upper levels of government and industry; and when the symptoms of discontent and frustration are all too clearly manifesting themselves among militant young women.

Something is indeed wrong, and educators should begin a rigorous investigation of their programs and practices in order to discover if they are reinforcing the cultural pressures which discourage talented girls.

Analysis of High School Textbooks

A reasonable place to start, considering the admitted obscurity of most women in American history, is the United States history text. Are the stereotypes which limit girls' aspirations present in high school history texts?

The answer is *yes*. Despite some promising attempts to supplement the scant amount of information devoted to women in American history texts, most works are marred by sins of omission and commission. Texts omit many women of importance, while simultaneously minimizing the legal, social, and cultural disabilities which they faced. The authors tend to depict women in a passive role and to stress that their lives are determined by economic and political trends. Women are rarely shown fighting for anything; their rights have been "given" to them.

Women are omitted both from topics discussed and by the topics chosen for discussion. For example, while only a few women could possibly be included in discussions of diplomacy or military tactics, the omission of dance, film, and theater in discussions of intellectual and cultural life assures the omission of many of America's most creative individuals.

Women's true position in society is shown in more subtle ways as well. While every text examined included some mention of the "high position" enjoyed by American women, this is little more than a disclaimer. Wherever possible, authors select male leaders, and quote from male spokesmen. Even in discussions of reform movements, abolition, labor—areas in which there were articulate and able women leaders—only men are ever quoted. Even such topics as the life of frontier women is told through the reminiscences of men. When they are included, profiles and capsule biographies of women are often introduced in separate sections, apart from the body of the text. While this may simply be a consequence of attempts to update the text without resetting the book, it tends to reinforce the idea that women of note are, after all, optional and supplementary. Interestingly enough, the increase in the amount of space devoted to Black history has not made room for the black woman. In these texts Black history follows the white pattern, and minimizes or omits the achievements of the black woman. Like the white woman, she is either omitted outright, or is minimized by the topics selected.

These assertions are based upon the examination of over a dozen of the most popular United States history textbooks. Most were first copyrighted in the sixties, although several hold copyrights as far back as the early fifties, and one text is copyrighted back to 1937. Included are the following:

Baldwin, Leland D. and Warring, Mary. **History of Our Republic.** Princeton, D. Van Nostrand Co., Inc., 1965.

Bragdon, Henry W. and McCutchen, Samuel P. **History of a Free People.** New York, The Macmillan Company, 1965.

Brown, Richard C.; Lang, William C.; and Wheeler, Mary A. **The American Achievement.** New Jersey, Silver Burdett Company, 1966.

Canfield, Leon H. and Wilder, Howard B. **The Making of Modern America.** Boston, Houghton Mifflin Company, 1964.

Frost, James A.; Brown, Ralph Adams; Ellis, David M.; and Fink, William B. **A History of the United States.** Chicago, Follett Educational Corporation, 1968.

Graff, Henry E. and Krout, John A. **The Adventure of the American People.** Chicago, Rand McNally, 1959.

Hofstadter, Richard; Miller, William; and Aaron, Daniel. **The United States—The History of a Republic.** Englewood Cliffs, Prentice-Hall, Inc., 1957.

Kownslar, Allan O. and Frizzle, Donald B. **Discovering American History.** 2 Vols., New York, Holt, Rinehart & Winston, 1964.

Noyes, H. M. and Harlow, Ralph Volney. **Story of America.** New York, Holt, Rinehart & Winston, 1964.

Todd, Lewis Paul and Curti, Merle. **Rise of the American Nation.** (1 Vol. & 2 Vol. editions) New York, Harcourt, Brace & World, 1966. 2 Vol. edition includes selected readings.

Williams, T. Harry and Wolf, Hazel C. **Our American Nation.** Ohio, Charles E. Merrill Books, Inc., 1966.

Collections of Documents

Hofstadter, Richard. **Great Issues in American History.** 2 Vols., New York, Vintage, 1958.

Meyers, Marvin; Kern, Alexander; and Carvelti, John G. **Sources of the American Republic.** 2 Vols., Chicago, Scott, Foresman & Company, 1961.

All entries indexed under "Women" were examined and various other sections and topics where information about women might reasonably be expected were examined. Particular attention was paid to women in colonial and revolutionary times, education, the women's rights movement and suffrage, reform movements, abolition, the Civil War, labor, frontier life, the World Wars, family patterns, the present position of women, and all sections on intellectual and cultural trends. The resulting picture is a depressing one.

Based on the information in these commonly used high school texts, one might summarize the history and contributions of the American woman as follows: Women arrived in 1619 (a curious choice if meant to be their first acquaintance with the New World). They held the Seneca Falls Convention on Women's Rights in 1848. During the rest of the nineteenth century, they participated in reform movements, chiefly temperance, and were exploited in factories. In 1923 they were given the vote. They joined the armed forces for the first time during the second World War and thereafter have enjoyed the good life in America. Add the names of the women who are invariably mentioned: Harriet Beecher Stowe, Jane Addams, Dorothea Dix, and Frances Perkins, with perhaps Susan B. Anthony, Elizabeth Cady Stanton and, almost as frequently, Carry Nation, and you have the basic "text." There are variations, of course, and most texts have adequate sections of information on one topic, perhaps two, but close examination of the information presented reveals a curious pattern of inclusions and neglects, a pattern which presents the stereotyped picture of the American woman—passive, incapable of sustained organization or work, satisfied with her role in society, and well supplied with material blessings.

1. REVOLUTIONARY AND EARLY FEDERAL PERIODS

There is little information available in most texts concerning the colonial woman, or on her daughters and granddaughters in the revolutionary and early federal periods. The amount of information ranges from one textbook's two paragraphs on women's legal and social position to another textbook's total absence of anything even remotely pertaining to women during the early years of American history. Most texts fall in between. Some attention is commonly paid to the legal disabilities inherited from English law, although one textbook limits itself to "tobacco brides" and a note about William Penn's wife. Usually, little is said about the consequences of the social, political, and legal disabilities of the colonial woman, although the sharp limitations of the nineteenth century and the exploitation of the working-class women in the early industrial age were a direct result of woman's lack of political influence and her gradual exclusion from "professional" and skilled jobs. The texts are especially sensitive to the problem of religious and clerical prejudices against women. The long opposition of most American religious groups to women's rights is almost never suggested.

The perfunctory notice taken of women's education in the early period is discussed below. It should be noted, however, that few texts take any note of sectional differences in women's education or in other aspects of the position of women.

Although a number of texts mention the high regard in which the colonial woman was held, few are named and only one gives much information about the amount of work done outside the home by colonial women. Women mentioned are Pocahontas and Anne Hutchinson. Sections on Pocahontas tend to favor discussion of such questions as "Did Pocahontas really save John Smith?," rather than on any information about her life or the lives of other Indian women. Anne Hutchinson is almost always subordinated to Roger Williams. In one book, for example, she is described as another exile from Massachusetts. In more generous texts, she may receive as much as a short paragraph.

In general, the treatment of the early periods in American history stresses the fact that the America of the colonies, and early republic, was a "man's world." The authors wax eloquent over the "new breed of men." Any doubt that this might be merely linguistic convention is soon removed. The colonial farmer is credited with producing his own food, flax, and wool, in addition to preparing lumber for his buildings and leather goods for himself and his family. What the colonial farmer's wife (or the female colonial farmer) was doing all this time is not revealed, although plenty of information exists. Such passages also convey the unmistakable impression that all the early planters, farmers, and proprietors were male.

Education is important in consideration of the position of women because, as Julia Cherry Spruill points out in *Women's Life and Work in the Southern Colonies*, lack of opportunities for education finally ended women's employment in a variety of areas as technology and science made true "professions" of such occupations as medicine. In the early days, women, despite stringent legal restrictions, participated in almost all activities save government, the ministry of most religions, and law (although the number who sued and brought court cases is notable).

Usually, if any notice at all is taken of the education of girls and women, it is limited to a bland note that ". . . girls were not admitted to college" or "Most Americans thought it unnecessary or even dangerous to educate women." These statements are presented without explanation. A mention of the existence of the dame schools completes the information on women and education.

After the colonial-revolutionary period, it is rare for more than one paragraph to be devoted to the entire development of education for women. Often, none of the early educators are mentioned by name. The facts that women literally fought their way into colleges and universities, that their admission followed agitation by determined would-be students, and that they were treated as subservient to male students even at such pioneering institutions as Oberlin, are always absent. The simple statement that they were admitted suffices.

2. SECTIONS ON RIGHTS AND REFORMS

The most information about women appears in two sections, those on women's rights and suffrage and general sections on reform. Yet a full page on suffrage and women's rights is a rarity and most texts give the whole movement approximately three paragraphs. The better texts include something on the legal disabilities which persisted into the nineteenth century. These sections are sometimes good, but always brief. Most of them end their consideration of the legal position of women with the granting of suffrage, and there is no discussion of the implications of the recent Civil Rights legislation which removed some of the inequities in employment, nor is there more than a hint that inequities remained even after the nineteenth amendment was passed.

Leaders most commonly noted are Susan B. Anthony, Elizabeth Cady Stanton, and Lucretia Mott. Aside from passage of the nineteenth amendment, the only event noted is the Seneca Falls Convention of 1848. Even less space is devoted to the later suffrage movement. Anna Howard Shaw is seldom mentioned and even Carrie Chapman Catt is not assured of a place. The western leaders like Abigail Duniway are usually absent as are the more radical and militant suffragettes, the members of the Woman's Party. Alice Paul, leader of the militants, is apparently anathema.

This is perhaps not too surprising, as the tendency in most texts is to concentrate on the handicaps women faced and to minimize their efforts in their own behalf. One textbook, which dutifully lists Seneca Falls, Stanton, Mott, Wright, Anthony, Stone, and Bloomer, tells very little about what they did, noting "the demand for the right to vote made little headway, but the states gradually began to grant them more legal rights." The text mentions that by 1900 most discriminatory legislation was off the books and describes the post-Civil War work of the movement in these terms: "the women's rights movement continued under the leadership of the same group as before the war and met with considerable success." Later two lines on suffrage and a picture of a group of suffragettes complete the story. Lest this be considered the most glaring example of neglect, another textbook devotes two lines, one in each volume, to suffrage, mentioning in volume one that women were denied the right to vote and returning to the topic in volume two with one line on the nineteenth amendment in the middle of a synopsis of the twenties. This book actually includes more information on the lengths of women's skirts than on all the agitation for civil and political rights for women.

Other texts show a similar lack of enthusiasm for the hundred years of work that went into the nineteenth amendment. One places woman suffrage fifth in a section on the effects of the progressive movement. Catt, Anthony, and Stanton are mentioned in a line or two, while whole columns of text are devoted to Henry Demarest Lloyd and Henry George.

At times there appears to be a very curious sense of priorities at work even in textbooks which give commendable amounts of information. One book uses up a whole column on the Gibson Girl, describing her as:

... completely feminine, and it was clear that she could not, or would not, defeat her male companion at golf or tennis. In the event of a motoring emergency, she would quickly call upon his superior knowledge . . . .

The passage goes on to point out that this "transitional figure" was politically uninformed and devoted to her traditional role. One would almost prefer to learn a little more about the lives of those other "transitional figures," the feminists, yet there is almost no mention of their lives, their work, or their writings.

Only one text quotes any of the women's rights workers. It includes a short paragraph from the declaration of the Seneca Falls Convention. The absence in other texts of quotes and of documentary material is all the more striking, since a number of the leaders were known as fine orators and propagandists. Books of source materials, and inquiry method texts, are no exception; none of those examined considers woman suffrage worthy of a single document. One book is exceptional in including one selection, by Margaret Fuller, on the topic of women's rights.

The reformers and abolitionists are slightly more fortunate than the feminists. Three women are almost certain of appearing in history texts, Harriet Beecher Stowe, Jane Addams, and Dorothea Dix. Addams and Stowe are among the few women quoted in either source books or regular texts and, along with the muckraking journalist Ida Tarbell, they are the only women whose writings are regularly excerpted. Addams and Dix are usually given at least one complete paragraph, perhaps more. These are sometimes admirably informative as in certain sections on Dix. Other reformers, including the women abolitionists, both white and black, are less fortunate. The pioneering Grimké sisters may rate a line or two, but just as often their only recognition comes because Angelina eventually became Mrs. Theodore Weld. None of the female abolitionists, despite their comtemporary reputations as speakers, is ever quoted. Interest in Black history has not made room for more than the briefest mention of Harriet Tubman, whose Civil War services are deleted. Sojourner Truth and the other black lecturers, educators, and abolitionists are completely absent. The texts make little comment about the nineteenth century's intense disapproval of women who spoke in public, or of the churches' opposition (excepting always the Quakers, from whose faith many of the early abolitionists came).

Women journalists are given even less notice than the early lecturers. The women who ran or contributed to newspapers, periodicals, or specialized journals and papers for abolition, women's rights, or general reform are rarely included.

The reform sections of these high school texts frequently show the same kind of capriciousness that in sections on the twenties assigns more space to the flapper than to the suffragette. In discussions on reform movements, they give more prominence to Carry Nation than to other more serious, not to say more stable, reformers. The treatment of temperance is further marred by a failure to put women's espousal of temperance in perspective. Little stress is placed on the consequences for the family of an alcoholic in the days when divorce was rare, when custody of children went to their father, and when working women were despised. Nor is there much mention of the seriousness of the problem of alcoholism, particularly in the post-Civil War period.

3. NEGLECTED AREAS

The most glaring omission, considering its impact on women and on society, is the absence of a single word on the development of birth control and the story of the fight for its acceptance by Margaret Sanger and a group of courageous physicians. The authors' almost Victorian delicacy in the face of the matter probably stems from the fact that birth control is still controversial. Yet fear of controversy does not seem a satisfactory excuse. The population explosion, poverty, illegitimacy—all are major problems today. Birth control is inextricably tied up with them as well as with disease, abortion, child abuse, and family problems of every kind. Considering the revolution in the lives of women which safe methods of contraception have caused, and the social, cultural, and political implications of that revolution, it appears that one important fact of the reform movement is being neglected.

A second, largely neglected area is the whole question of woman's work and her part in the early labor movement. Although the American woman and her children were the mainstays of many of the early industries, for a variety of social and political reasons she received low wages and status and was virtually cut off from any hopes of advancement. The educational limitations that gradually forced her out of a number of occupations which she had held in pre-industrial days combined with prejudice to keep her in the lowest paid work. Whether single, married, or widowed, whether she worked for "pin money" or to support six children, she received about half as much as a man doing the same or comparable work.

Obviously under these conditions, women had exceptional difficulties in organizing. Among them were the dual burden of household responsibilities and work, their lack of funds, and in some cases their lack of control over their own earnings, and the opposition of male workers and of most of the unions.

Despite these special circumstances, very little attention is paid to the plight of the woman worker or of her admittedly unstable labor organizations. Information on the early labor leaders is especially scanty; one textbook is unique with its biographical information on Rose Schneiderman. On the whole, the labor story is limited to the introduction of women workers into the textile mills in the 1840's. As a caption in one book so concisely puts it, "Women and children, more manageable, replaced men at the machines." Others note the extremely low pay of women and children, one text calling women "among the most exploited workers in America." Anything like a complete discussion of the factors which led to these conditions, or even a clear picture of what it meant to be "among the most exploited," is not found in the texts.

Several things about women and labor are included. Lowell mills receive a short, usually complimentary, description. The fact that the Knights of Labor admitted women is presented. There then follows a hiatus until minimum wage and maximum hour standards for women workers are discussed. The modern implications of this "protective legislation" is an area seldom explored.

Despite the fact that abundant source material exists, the sections on labor follow the familiar pattern: little space is devoted to women workers, few women are mentioned by name, and fewer still are quoted. Most texts content themselves with no more than three entries of a few lines each.

The absence of information on the lives of women on the frontier farms and settlements is less surprising. In the treatments of pioneer settlements from the colonial era on, most texts declare the frontier "a man's world." This is emphasized by the importance the authors place on descriptions and histories of such masculine tools as the Pennsylvania rifle and the ax, the six-shooter, and the prairie-breaker plow. One textbook is perhaps the most enthralled with these instruments, devoting five pages to the story of the six-shooter. Scarcely five lines are spent on the life of the frontier woman in this text, and most other works are also reticent about the pioneer woman.

Only "man's work" on the frontier is really considered worthy of description. This is particularly puzzling, since there was little distinction in employment, and marriage was a partnership with lots of hard work done by each of the partners. On pioneer farms, typical "woman's work" included, in addition to all the housework, the care of poultry; the dairy—including milking, feeding, tending to the cows, and making butter and cheese; the care of any other barnyard animals; the "kitchen" or vegetable garden; and such chores as sewing, mending, making candles and soap, feeding the hired hands, and working in the fields if necessary.

Considering these chores, it is hard to see why discussions of pioneer farming content themselves with descriptions of the farmer's struggles to plow, plant, and harvest. The treatments of the frontier period also omit mention of the women who homesteaded and claimed property without the help of a male partner. According to Robert W. Smuts in *Women and Work in America*, there were thousands of such women. Information about the women on the frontier tends either to short descriptions of the miseries of life on the great plains frequently quoted from Hamlin Garland or to unspecific encomiums on the virtues of the pioneer woman. One text states:

... [the women] turned the wilderness into homesteads, planted flowers and put curtains in the windows. It was usually the mothers and school teachers who transmitted to the next generation the heritage of the past.

The relationship between women's exertions on the frontier and their enlarged civil and political liberties in the Western states and territories is often noticed. Their agitation for these increased privileges is generally unmentioned.

With little said about women's life in general, it is not surprising that few are mentioned by name. Sacajawea, the Indian guide and interpreter of the Lewis and Clark expedition, shares with Dix, Stowe, and Addams, one of the few solid positions in United States history texts. Occasionally the early missionaries to Oregon territory, like Narcissa Whitman and Eliza Spaulding, are included, and one book even adds a "profile" of Narcissa Whitman. Most, however, only mention the male missionaries, or include the fact that they arrived with their wives.

4. CIVIL WAR PERIOD

Like the frontier experience, the Civil War forced women from all social strata into new tasks and occupations. In *Bonnet Brigades*, a volume in the *Impact of the Civil War Series*, Mary Elizabeth Massey quotes Clara Barton's remark that the war advanced the position of women by some fifty years. Great numbers of women dislocated by the war were forced into paid employment. The war saw the entry of women into government service, into nursing, and into the multitude of organizations designed to raise money and supplies for the armies, to make clothing, blankets, and bandages. The result of this activity was not only to force individual women outside of their accustomed roles, but to provide the experience in organization which was to prove valuable for later suffrage and reform movements. The war helped a number of women escape from the ideas of gentility which were robbing women in the East of much of their traditional social freedom, and brought women of all classes into the "man's world." In addition to the few women who served as soldiers, women appeared in the camps as nurses, cooks, laundresses, adventurers; they served in the field as spies, scouts, saboteurs, and guides; they worked in the capitals as the "government girls"—the first female clerks, bookkeepers, and secretaries. Women opened hospitals, set up canteens, and developed the first primitive forms of what we know as USO clubs and services. After the war, they served as pension claims agents, worked to rehabilitate soldiers, taught in the freedman's schools, entered refugee work, or tried to find missing soldiers and soldiers' graves.

Of all these activities, women's entry into nursing is the only one regularly noticed in the texts. The impact of the war upon women, and upon the family structure, is barely mentioned, although a few texts include a paragraph or two on the hardships which women faced during the conflict. The only women mentioned by name are Clara Barton and Dorothea Dix, who held the position of superintendent of women nurses. Other women, like Mary Bickerdyke, who was known both for her efforts during the war and for her work for needy veterans afterwards, are omitted. No other women, black or white, are named, nor is there any information on the variety of jobs they held. The special problems of black women in the post-war period rarely get more than a line, and the efforts by black women to set up schools and self-help agencies are omitted.

5. THE TWO WORLD WARS

While women in the Civil War era receive little attention, even less is given to them during the two World Wars. In both cases, their wartime service is glowingly praised, but few details are presented. At least half of the texts examined make no note at all of women's wartime activities during the first World War; in a number of others, the story of women's entry into what were formerly labeled "men's jobs" is dealt with in a captioned picture.

As far as social changes between the wars, a number of texts devote several paragraphs to the "liberation of women" and to their changing status. In one textbook there are four paragraphs devoted to these liberated ladies—the only two mentioned being Irene Castle and Alice Roosevelt. Like other texts, this one devotes a considerable amount of space to fashions and flappers and to the social alarm which they occasioned.

There is little about the later stages of the rights' movement, although two textbooks note the relationship between women's wartime service and the increasing willingness of the nation to grant rights and privileges to women. One limits itself to three sentences, noting women's work "in factories and fields" and their efforts behind the lines overseas. "Women's reward for war service was the Nineteenth Amendment which granted them the franchise on the eve of the 1920 election." Readers might wish for greater elaboration.

The period from the depression to the present day receives the same laconic treatment in the texts. The one woman sure of notice in this period is Frances Perkins, Roosevelt's Secretary of Labor. She receives at least a line in most texts and some devote special sections to her. Frances Perkins appears to be the "showcase" woman, for no other American woman is regularly mentioned—this includes Eleanor Roosevelt, who is omitted from a surprising number of texts and who is mentioned only as Roosevelt's wife in quite a few more.

The World War II era marked the beginning of the Women's Military Corps. This fact is invariably mentioned, usually with a captioned picture as an accompaniment. As in World War I, women entered factories, munitions plants, and "men's jobs" in great numbers. This development rarely gets more than a paragraph and the differences between the experience in World War I and the longer exposure to new jobs in World War II are seldom elucidated. The impact of the war on women and specific information about the variety of jobs they held is sketchy or nonexistent.

Information on women in the post-war era and in the present day is hardly more abundant. The history texts definitely give the impression that the passage of the nineteenth amendment solved all the problems created by the traditional social, legal, and political position of women. Contemporary information on discrimination is conspicuously absent. The texts are silent on current legal challenges to such practices as discriminatory hiring and promotion and companies' failures to comply with equal pay legislation. They do not take account of agitation to change laws and customs which weigh more heavily on women than on men. There is nothing about recent changes in jury selection, hitherto biased against women jurors, or reform of discriminatory practices in criminal sentences; there is no information on the complex problems of equitable divorce and guardianship, nor on the tangled problem of separate domicile for married women.

A number of texts do, however, provide good information on changes in the structure of the family, or provide helpful information on general social and political changes. The impression, insofar as these sections deal directly with American women, is a rosy picture of the affluence and opportunities enjoyed by women. Many books note the increasing numbers of women employed in the learned professions, but never the percentage decline in their numbers. While women undoubtedly enjoy more rights, opportunities, and freedoms than in many previous eras, the texts give an excessively complacent picture of a complex and rapidly changing set of social conditions.

6. INTELLECTUAL AND CULTURAL ACHIEVEMENTS

A final glimpse of the position of the American woman may be gained from sections dealing with intellectual and cultural trends and achievements. Since most texts extol the role of women in preserving culture and in supporting the arts, one might expect women to be well-represented in discussions of the arts in America. A number of factors, however, operate against the inclusion of creative women. The first, and one which deprives many creative men of notice as well, is the extreme superficiality of most of these discussions. Intellectual and cultural life in America is limited to the mention of a few novelists and poets, with an occasional musician or playwright. Only a few individuals in each category are ever mentioned, and the preference for male examples and spokesmen, noticeable in all other topics, is evident here as well. In individual texts, this leads to such glaring omissions as Emily Dickinson and Margaret Fuller. To be fair, the text guilty of ignoring Miss Dickinson appears to feel that John Greenleaf Whittier was one of our greatest poets, yet ignorance of American poetry is hardly an acceptable excuse.

Dickinson and Fuller, however, are among the small, fortunate circle including Harriet Beecher Stowe, Willa Cather, and Margaret Mitchell who are usually named. The principles governing their selection and decreeing the omission of other writers like Edith Wharton, Ellen Glasgow, Eudora Welty, and Pearl Buck are never explained. Apparently their presence or absence is determined by the same caprice which decrees Edna St. Vincent Millay the only modern female poet.

Only a handful of texts discuss painters and sculptors, but of those that do make some effort to include the visual arts, only one reproduces a painting by Mary Cassatt. Georgia O'Keeffe is also represented in this text. Other texts, even when including Cassatt's fellow expatriates, Sargent and Whistler, omit her—an exclusion inexplicable on grounds of quality, popularity, or representation in American collections. Contemporary art is totally ignored and everything after the Ashcan School is left in limbo. This omits many painters of quality and influence, including the many women who have entered the arts in the twentieth century.

More serious than the sketchy treatment given to the arts covered by the texts is the omission of arts in which women were dominant or in which they played a major part. Dance is never given as much as a line. This leaves out the American ballerinas, and, even more important, it neglects the development of modern dance—a development due to the talents of a handful of American women like Isadora Duncan, Martha Graham, and Ruth St. Denis.

There is a similar neglect of both stage and screen acting. If film or drama are to be mentioned at all, directors and writers will be noted. It hardly seems necessary to point out that acting is an area in which women have excelled.

Music sees a similar division with similar results. Composers and instrumentalists, chiefly men, are mentioned. Singers, men and women, are omitted. This particularly affects black women. Only one textbook mentions Marian Anderson and Leontyne Price. White classical singers are ignored as are the black women jazz singers.

If intellectual and cultural developments are limited to areas in which men were the dominant creative figures, it is obvious that American women will not receive credit for their contributions. It also seems clear that such superficial accounts of the arts are of questionable value.

Summing Up

Although it is tempting to imagine some historical autocrat sternly decreeing who's in and who's out—giving space to Harriet Beecher Stowe but not to Marianne Moore; to Dorothea Dix but not Mary Bickerdyke; to Pocahontas but not Margaret Brent; to Susan B. Anthony but not Abigail Duniway—the omission of many significant women is probably not a sign of intentional bias. The treatment of women simply reflects the attitudes and prejudices of society. Male activities in our society are considered the more important; therefore male activities are given primacy in the texts. There is a definite image of women in our society, and women in history who conform to this image are more apt to be included. History reflects societal attitudes in all topics, hence the omission of potentially controversial persons like Margaret Sanger or that militant pioneer in civil disobedience, Alice Paul. Sensitivity to social pressure probably accounts for the very gentle notes about religious disapproval of women's full participation in community life and for omission of contemporary controversies, especially on sexual matters, which would offend religious sensibilities.

Another factor which affects the picture of women presented in these texts is the linguistic habit of using the male pronouns to refer both to men and to men and women. While this may seem a trivial matter it frequently leads to misunderstanding. Discussing the early colonists, for example, solely in terms of "he" and "his" leads to the implication that all early proprietors, settlers, planters, and farmers were men. Given the cultural orientation of our society, students will assume activities were only carried on by men unless there is specific mention of women.

To these observations, authors of high school texts might reasonably respond that their space is limited, that they seek out only the most significant material and the most influential events and individuals; that if dance is omitted, it is because more people read novels, and if such topics as the role of female missionaries or colonial politicians are neglected, it is for lack of space. One is less inclined to accept this view when one notices some of the odd things which authors do manage to include. One feels like asking, "How important was Shays's Rebellion?". Should the Ku Klux Klan receive reams of documentary material and woman suffrage none? Do we want to read five pages on the six-shooter? Is two columns too much to give to Empress Carlotta of Mexico, who lived most of her life in insanity and obscurity? Is the aerialist who walked a tightrope across Niagara Falls a figure of even minor importance in American History? Is Henry Demarest Lloyd more important than Carrie Chapman Catt? Are the lengths of skirts significant enough to dwarf other information about women?

There are other questions as well: How accurate is the history text's view of women and what images of women does it present? The texts examined do very little more than reinforce the familiar stereotypes.

It should be clear, however, that changes in the construction of high-school-level history texts must go beyond the insertion of the names of prominent women and even beyond the "profiles" and "special sections" employed by the more liberal texts. Commendable and informative as these may be, they are only the beginning. Real change in the way history is presented will only come after those responsible for writing it, and for interpreting the finished product to students, develop an awareness of the bias against women in our culture, a bias so smooth, seamless, and pervasive, that it is hard to even begin to take hold of it and bring it into clear view. Until this awareness is developed, until the unquestioned dominance of male activities and the importance of male spokesmen and examples is realized, texts will continue to treat men's activities and goals as history, women's as "supplementary material."

One sees this quite clearly in the existence of sections dealing with women's rights, women's problems, and women's position, as if women's rights, problems, and position were not simply one half of the rights, problems, and position of humanity as a whole, and as if changes in women's position and work and attitudes were not complemented by changes in the position, work, and attitudes of men. A sense of the way the lives and duties and achievements of people of both sexes is intermeshed is needed in expositions of life in all periods of American history.

To do this it is clear that material hitherto omitted or minimized must be given more consideration. For example, information about mortality rates, family size, and economic conditions must be included, along with more information on the impact of technological change, on the mass media, and on moral and religious ideas. More information about how ordinary people lived and what they actually did must be included as well as information drawn from the ideas and theories of the educated classes.

This is not to deny that certain developments have had far more effect on women than on men, or that women's experience might be different from men's: for example, the early struggles to form unions. Nor is it to deny that more information on women leaders is needed and more space for their particular problems and achievements. More information on all aspects of women's life, work, and position—legal, social, religious, and political—is needed, but more information alone, no matter how necessary, will not really change histories. What is needed, besides more information, is a new attitude: one which breaks away from the bias of traditional views of women and their "place" and attempts to treat both women and men as partners in their society; one which does not automatically value activities by the sex performing them; and one which does not relate history from the viewpoint of only half of the human family.

Women and the Language of Inequality

ELIZABETH BURR,

SUSAN DUNN,

and NORMA FARQUHAR

A language is not merely a means of communication: it is also an expression of shared assumptions. Language thus transmits implicit values and behavioral models to all those people who use it. When basic assumptions change, the idioms which express them become obsolete. The pages that follow suggest certain changes in language designed to eliminate phraseology that reflects outdated assumptions concerning women.

Subsuming Terminology

For purposes of this article, subsuming terms are masculine terms which are commonly believed to include or refer to females as well as males. In fact, however, such terms operate to exclude females. When told that "*Men* by the thousands headed west," or that "The average citizen of the United States is proud of *his* heritage," the young reader simply does not form a mental image which includes females. It is of no avail for a parent or teacher to explain that *men* means *both men and women*, or that *he* means *both he and she*. Even an adult is unlikely to picture a

NOTE: This article appeared in *Social Education*, December 1972, pp. 841–845. Reprinted by permission of Norma Farquhar.

group of amicable females when reading about "men of good will."
Similarly, when taught that *man*-made improvements have raised
America's standard of living, or that a task requires a certain amount of
*man*power, a child cannot be expected to develop the concept that
females as well as males have participated in the developmental process.

Educational literature dealing with human origins provides striking
examples of how subsuming terminology can lead to distorted concepts.
In such literature illustrations of reconstructed skeletons and skulls are
generally identified as male and labeled Peking *Man*, Neanderthal *Man*,
Java *Man*, Cro-Magnon *Man*, and so on. Although common sense tells us
that many prehistoric individuals must have been women, nowhere are
females represented as *examples* of a type. Such treatment cannot fail
to suggest to young readers that females are a substandard or deviant
form of being—a rib, as it were, taken from *"Man."* In the same way,
constant reference to *"man*-made" implements has apparently inspired
illustrators to portray only males making stone tools, although we have
no way of knowing for certain the sex of the individual who made any
given prehistoric implement.

Usage of the words *man* (without a definite article) and *men* to
represent human beings in general or adults in general is also objectionable on the ground of ambiguity. Since both of these words are also
frequently used to denote males only, it often becomes a matter of
making an educated guess as to whether the author means males and
females both, or males only. It is also possible that such terms are
employed to conceal the author's lack of information concerning the
sexual composition of a group.

Authors and editors alike are so accustomed to the use of subsuming terminology that the greatest care needs to be taken to ensure its
elimination. Subsuming masculine terms must be replaced by clearly
inclusive or neutral words such as *citizens, inhabitants, women and
men, human beings, people, individuals*, and so on. Phrases such as
manpower and *man-made* may be replaced by *human energy, made by
men and women* or *manufactured;* the words *forefathers* and *fathers* (in
the sense of "forefathers") should be replaced by *precursors* or *ancestors;* and the word *brotherhood* should be replaced by *amity, unity,
community* or some other non-sex-related term.

The Hypothetical Person as Male

A frequently occurring example of the male orientation of textbooks is
the use of hypothetical males as examples. "If a *man* wanted to travel
from South Carolina to Massachusetts in 1750..." "The *man* of tomorrow may live in a totally prefabricated house." "A discontented *man*

could move west." In textbooks females seldom participate in hypothetical financial transactions. Thus we find explanations such as the following: "If a *man* sold a piece of land, *he* had to put a two-shilling stamp on the deed." "When a *man* went to the bank to borrow money . . ." "A *man's* taxes depended upon . . ."

Unless it has been verified that females never engaged in the activities mentioned, the word *man* should be replaced by the word *one* or *person*. Students should not be given the false impression that only males traveled, became discontented, needed money, paid taxes, etc.

In a similar vein, textbooks picture the "average" and the "typical" person as a male: "The average American does not *himself* manufacture most of the things *his* family needs." "The American was a new kind of *man*." Writers should keep in mind the fact that "the average *man*" is not the average "*person*," and that any discussion of national traits is one-sided if it refers to males only.

Male-Oriented Quoted Material

[Authors' italics.] (1) "*Men* since the beginning of time have sought peace . . ." (General Douglas MacArthur); (2) "The American is a new *man*, who acts upon new principles; *he* must therefore entertain new ideas, and form new opinions . . ." (J. Hector St. John de Crèvecoeur); (3) "These are the times that try *men's* souls." (Thomas Paine); (4) "The New Englander, whether *boy* or *man*, in a long struggle with a stingy or hostile universe, had learned also to love the pleasure of hating; *his* joys were few." (Henry Adams). The above and similar quotations which are to be found in textbooks reflect the opinion that females are of no consequence. Such quotations are permissible in textbooks only as examples of contemporary prejudiced attitudes toward women.

Some documentary material, however, will inevitably be regarded as necessary in a textbook in spite of the fact that it is couched in male-oriented language. A case in point is the Gettysburg Address: "Fourscore and seven years ago our *fathers* brought forth on this continent a new nation, conceived in liberty, and dedicated to the proposition that all *men* are created equal . . . and that government of the *people*, by the *people*, for the *people*, shall not perish from the earth." If this or similar male-oriented documents are quoted, the textbook should point out the male orientation of the language. Any textbook quoting the Gettysburg Address should, for instance, indicate that when President Lincoln spoke of *people* he had in mind *males*, because at the time of his famous speech females were not permitted to vote and were denied many other legal rights enjoyed by men.

Nobody Knows Her Name

Reflecting a time when females were in fact the possessions first of their fathers and then of their husbands, who were empowered by law to beat them, sell them, or otherwise dispose of them arbitrarily, girls and women are still referred to primarily in the obsolete terms of those who "own" them. In textbooks, females are typically referred to merely as *wives* (Mrs.), *daughters* (Miss), or *mothers of* males who are clearly identified by name and occupation. Such possessive terms of reference deliver the implicit message that in and of themselves females are of no particular interest or importance and reflect the assumption that marital status is *the* crucial fact of life for women.

Compare, for example, the following two sentences: (1) George Ferris married the daughter of the wealthy Boston banker, Edward Howell. (2) Alice Howell of Boston, heir to a banking fortune, married George Ferris. The second sentence recognizes Alice as a person in her own right; the first, in which she is *nameless*, suggests that whatever shadowy identity she may have possessed depended upon the identity first of her father and then of her husband. Similarly, phrases such as "the farmer's wife" clearly convey the idea that the female was merely a possession of the farmer and was not herself a farmer, when in fact the wives of most small farmers were themselves farmers *in every sense of the word.*

Textbook writers who wish to give equal linguistic treatment to the sexes should *cite females by their complete names and occupations* whenever possible, should eliminate "Miss" and "Mrs." from their writing vocabularies, and should refer to "men and women on farms" or "farming men and women," rather than to "farmers and their wives."

Differential Generic Terminology

Textbooks frequently use generic terms such as those (italicized) in the following sentences: "The *peasants* toiled in the fields." "The *pioneers* suffered many hardships." "*Beggars* slept in doorways." The preceding examples do not make it clear whether the italicized generic terms refer to both men and women or to men exclusively.

However, textbook writers also use language such as the following: "*Peasant women* were oppressed." "*Pioneer women* suffered many hardships." "*Beggar women* slept in doorways." But the same writers rarely use such language as: "Peasant *men* were oppressed." "Pioneer *men* suffered many hardships." "Beggar *men* slept in doorways."

From all of the above it must be concluded that authors tend to blur *men* with *people in general*; i.e., they are willing to let *men* stand for *people in general* and to let the deeds of *people in general* be attributed to *men*. At the same time, they are not willing to blur *women* with *people in general* or to permit *women* to represent *people in general.* One never sees a picture of *women* captioned simply "farmers" or "pioneers." Linguistic failure to permit women to be "people" mirrors a long tradition of male supremacy and a socially induced need to keep women in a separate and unequal category—to keep them "in their place."

The effects of differential generic terminology can be seen clearly in the following sentence: *"Muslims* resented seeing *their wives and daughters* go unveiled." In a female-oriented version of the language of inequality the sentence would read: *"The husbands of the Muslims* resented seeing *them* go unveiled." If the terminology for males and females were equal the sentence would read: *"Muslim men* resented seeing *Muslim women* go unveiled."

Writers must make explicit the sexual composition of a neutral generic term in such cases as the above. In other words, if a *group of women* cannot be referred to simply as "peasants" or "Muslims" neither should a *group of men* be so labeled. Similarly, all references to "men and their wives" should be revised to "men and women" or "husbands and wives."

Mother's Baby But Father's Heir

Because women in our society have traditionally been expected to assume the full burden of child care, textbooks tend to describe young children who still need care as the mother's but to describe male offspring who are seen as heirs and female offspring of marriageable age as the father's. (1) "Abraham Lincoln, *his* wife and *his* son . . ." (2) "Mothers could leave *their* young children at Hull House." (3) "Sacajawea carried *her* infant son . . ." (4) "Balboa married *the daughter of an Indian chief."* (5) "Anne Hutchinson had fifteen children . . .".

In (1) the wording should have been "Abraham and Mary Lincoln and *their* son . . ." In (2) unless it had been verified that fathers never left *their* children at Jane Addams' kindergarten at Hull House, the word "parents" should have been used instead of "mothers." In (3) Sacajawea's husband was also present on the expedition that made her famous, so any account should refer to *their* son. In (4) the Indian woman is viewed as her father's possession. In (5) it should have been stated that Anne Hutchinson *and her husband* were the *parents* of fifteen children. In short, textbooks should recognize, wherever possible, the relationship of both parents to their children.

Women as Luggage

Textbooks have a tendency to describe migrations of human populations in the following terms: (1) "The pioneer took his family west in a covered wagon." (2) "Men trekked over the mountains with their wives, children, and cattle." (3) "Some Forty-niners took their families with them." In each of the foregoing examples women are regarded more as luggage than as human beings. By such treatment women are deprived of their true status as pioneers, travellers, or seekers-after-gold in their own right.

Unless it has been determined that in such instances the females under discussion were moved *involuntarily*, authors should write: "Americans moved west...," "Families trekked over the mountains...," and so on, instead of speaking of *men* who *brought along* wives. Authors should also make their readers aware of the fact that single women and female heads of family participated in the westward movement and other migrations.

Male-Oriented Glossing of Terms

Textbooks frequently define or explain words which are applicable to either or both sexes as though they applied exclusively to males. For example, "militia" has been explained as "*men* who...."; "dictator" as "a *man* who...."; "Forty-niners" as "*men* who...."; "monarchy" as a "nation ruled by a *king*." Students may thus be led incorrectly to believe that women cannot join a militia or be dictators, that women were not also "Forty-niners," and that only males may be monarchs. Such gratuitous exclusion of females should be avoided.

Neutral Occupational Terminology

Occupational terms ending in "-man"—such as airman, fireman, cameraman, anchorman, statesman, workman, iceman, repairman, watchman and salesman—are objectionable because they suggest that certain fields of endeavor are closed to women. Pre-modern terms such as bondman or ploughman, used in a discussion of pre-modern times, may be permissible, but modern sex-affiliated terms should be eliminated. They not only give young people false impressions about their future vocational prospects; they also tend to perpetuate discriminatory practices that do indeed exist.

Authors who do not want to use or invent new terminology can evade the issue by recasting entire sentences. For example, "Mr. Jones sent for a TV repairman" can be revised to "Mr. Jones called a TV repair service." The ending "-man" is, however, increasingly being replaced by "-person" to form terms like "chairperson." The word "salesperson" is already accepted, and other neutral terms will gain acceptance as the decisive influence of language on the attitudes and lives of people becomes more widely understood.

Terms To Be Avoided

"Just a *housewife*" is a frequently heard expression, the pejorative nature of which is indisputable. It conveys the derogatory attitude of society toward the woman who works as a homemaker and the consequent self-contempt which she feels. The term *housewife*, moreover, clearly suggests that domestic chores are the exclusive burden of females. It gives female students the idea that they were born to keep house and teaches male students that they are automatically entitled to laundry, cooking, and housecleaning services from women in their families. The inculcation of such attitudes is inconsistent with the ideal of equal educational and vocational opportunities. The term *housewife* should therefore never be used.

Similarly, where men are referred to as *men* rather than *husbands*, but women are referred to as *wives* rather than *women*, the textbook is again treating men as *persons, not husbands*, and women as *wives, not persons*. The term *wife* should therefore be used only sparingly.

The following terms and expressions should be regarded as demeaning and should not be used: *lady* (as synonym for adult female), *girl* (as synonym for adult female), *the little woman, the weaker sex*, and *squaw*.

Such terms as *author, aviator, heir, laundry worker, sculptor, singer, poet, Jew*, and *Negro* are neuter terms which are *without exception* properly applicable to both females and males. The use of words ending in "feminine" suffixes, such as *authoress, aviatrix, heiress, laundress, sculptress, songstress, poetess, Jewess*, and *Negress* is unacceptable. Terms ending in "feminine" suffixes imply that females are a special and unequal form of the correct neuter expression. Thus, to speak of Edna St. Vincent Millay as a *poetess* is to exclude her from the legitimate circle of *poets*; to speak of Amelia Earhart as an *aviatrix* denies her full status as *aviator*; to speak of Golda Meir as a *Jewess* denies her full status as a *Jew*; and so on. In cases where it is necessary to indicate the sex of the individual, the expressions "female poet," "female aviator," "female Jew" and so on may be used. However, in modifying neuter terms the word "lady" (as in "lady lawyer," "lady doctor," "lady poet," and so on) is never acceptable.

In conclusion, authors and publishers who seek to provide a just portrayal of the sexes in textbooks must include material which accurately represents the role of women in history and society and use language which permits readers to perceive women as whole human beings.

VIII.

Diversity in Unity

"UNITED WE STAND, DIVIDED WE FALL" has become such a popular adage that it is sometimes forgotten that it is also very old. A credit line should be given to the person we identify as Aesop, who initially made that observation in the cautionary tale of The Four Oxen and the Lion. Indeed, every generation from ancient times to the present has had to wrestle with the problem of establishing viable relationships between the one and the many, the small group and the large, the minority and the majority.

British astronomer Sir Arthur Eddington wrote: "We often think that when we have completed our study of *one* we know all about *two*, because 'two' is 'one and one.' We forget that we still have to make a study of 'and.'" The point that he was illustrating—that the relationship is as important as the things it connects—is of particular importance in the articles that appear in this section, "Diversity in Unity."

On November 22, 1963, President John F. Kennedy was assassinated while riding in a motorcade down the streets of Dallas, Texas. Eight days later historian John Hope Franklin was called upon to deliver a major address at the 43rd Annual Meeting of the National Council for the Social Studies in Los Angeles. Franklin began by declaring that the tragic event of eight days ago would inevitably affect virtually everything that would follow it. Next, he reminded the audience that the deeply mourned president had been extremely sensitive to the problems involving the dignity of human beings and troubled by the outright defiance of laws against segregation and discrimination. Franklin then traced the history of attacks on human freedom and dignity in the United States. In his address, "The Dignity of Man: Perspectives for Tomorrow," he stressed that "We who are committed to the study of history and of the evolution of our social institutions must surely be sensitive to the importance of removing artificial and spurious restrictions on the human being if all men are to achieve the dignity and respect that are their birthright."

The use of the expression "Tell It Like It Is" was widespread in 1969, and its call for honesty, fairness, and completeness in the presentation of facts had considerable impact throughout the United States. Some historians thought of the expression as a popular version of nineteenth-century historian Leopold von Ranke's *wie es eigentlich gewesen ist* (to show the past "as it actually happened," or to show the past "how it really was") and considered it a desirable point of view.

It was not surprising, therefore, that Louis R. Harlan, professor of history at the University of Maryland, drew on the expression for the title of his article, "Tell It Like It Was: Suggestions on Black History." From Harlan's perspective, "The slogan *E pluribus unum*, one out of many, may have come upon hard times recently, but it is even so the framework in which black history and all other history must be placed, unless we are going to abandon Americans' noblest dream."

"A Talk with a Young Mexican American," a taped interview arranged by Dell Felder, then of the College of Education at the University of Houston, is filled with provocative comments: "I have something I want to read you: '. . . It sounded like [the teacher] said George Washington's my father. I'm reluctant to believe it. I suddenly raise my *mano*. If George Washington's my father, why wasn't he Chicano?'" "When you get into a history class, and you begin studying ancient civilizations, and maybe a paragraph is given to civilizations in South America, and you spend three weeks on Egypt and four weeks on Greece, there's something lacking." "I can remember in Student Council we gave the principal a nice rifle that cost a couple of hundred dollars. . . . If we had given somebody $300 as an incentive for winning some kind of scholarship for summer. . . , I think we could have done a lot more good." The logic of the young Mexican American is impressive in its directness.

The cover of the May 1972 issue of *Social Education* featured photographs of Comanche chief Quanah Parker and anthropologist Francis LaFlesche. The caption read: "How many students are aware of the achievements of these and other distinguished Indians?" It was a cover designed to call attention to the inattention given to the histories and cultures of Native Americans. Strong reader reactions indicated that many social studies educators shared the journal's concern.

Most of the rest of the May 1972 issue was devoted to articles on teaching about Native Americans. In her article, "Issues in Teaching About

American Indians," Hazel W. Hertzberg of Teachers College, Columbia University, discusses mental set, selecting materials, elements in a general history of Native Americans, and ethnic studies in the curriculum. Studying others, she concludes in the spirit of Alexander Pope, will lead to something equally important—studying ourselves.

The experiences of ethnic groups have been a fundamental part of American life and history. One thinks at once of Ole Edvart Rölvaag's *Giants in the Earth*, Jeanne Wakatsuki Houston and James D. Houston's *Farewell to Manzanar*, and Elia Kazan's *America! America!* Yet, it was only in the last two decades that ethnicity received widespread attention throughout the United States. One manifestation of this was the increased number of major articles concerning ethnic relations that appeared in *Social Education* and other journals.

Few scholars were as well qualified as James A. Banks, professor of education at the University of Washington, Seattle, to comment on ethnicity. In his article, "Teaching for Ethnic Literacy: A Comparative Approach," Banks stresses that "a vital ethnic studies program should enable students to derive valid generalizations about the characteristics of all of America's ethnic groups, and to learn how they are alike and different, in both their past and present experiences."

"I am what you would call a 'White Ethnic.' Not just an ordinary, garden-variety white ethnic, but, rather, a textbook example of one. My four grandparents were Czech. . . . My childhood friends and schoolmates had such surnames as Novak, Dvorak, Kostohryz, Staszak, Waszak, Woijcek, Bohac, Bilak, Fencil, Fojt, and Jelinek." Thus begins John Jarolimek's article, "Born Again Ethnics: Pluralism in Modern America." Jarolimek, who was then associate dean for undergraduate studies and teacher education in the College of Education at the University of Washington, Seattle, proceeds to examine the ideologies of ethnic relationships and to express his own point of view: "If, as a society, we adopt a social policy that stresses diversity instead of unity, and if we make ethnic pluralism a major cornerstone of the education of our young people, we should not be unmindful of the fact that we are sowing the seeds of widespread social conflict."

Over two centuries have passed since Pierre Eugène du Simitière, consultant to the first committee on a device for a Great Seal for the United States, suggested a design that featured the motto *E Pluribus Unum*. Recommended by Franklin, Adams, and Jefferson, that design and motto were adopted by the Congress of the Confederation (although it continued to be called the Continental Congress) in 1782. In the years that followed, numerous efforts were made to see if the idea of "one out of many" could be brought into reality. In the final article in this section, "Immigration in the Curriculum," John J. Patrick, director of the Social Studies Development Center at Indiana University, analyzes three approaches that were used: monolithic integration, ethnocentric pluralism, and pluralistic integration. Is there a paradox in the term "pluralistic integration"? If there is, the author still feels that it is a desirable one.

The Dignity of Man: Perspectives for Tomorrow

JOHN HOPE FRANKLIN

The tragic event of eight days ago will inevitably affect virtually everything that will follow it. It is inseparably connected not only with the way in which we shall evaluate the accumulation of hate and arrogance that deranges human beings and drives them to acts of violence; it is also related to the way in which the citizens of this country will proceed to eliminate the conditions in our life that breed hatred and bigotry. It is not too much to say, moreover, that this event will profoundly affect the way in which, in the future, we shall look at the sweep of history that preceded it. Perhaps we shall view the last years and decades as a period in which our efforts to learn to live together in peace and harmony were insufficient. Perhaps we shall learn the obvious lesson that the past is a great and wise teacher. Our great dereliction is that we have turned our eyes away from the pages of history and have not permitted it to teach us even the most obvious lessons.

The late and deeply mourned President was extremely sensitive to the problems with which this conference is concerned. Problems of education were high on his own agenda, and he was constantly calling upon Congress and the nation to join him in a vigorous attempt to solve them. He favored public aid to public education. He was opposed to racially segregated education, and he was deeply troubled by the snail's-pace compliance with court desegregation orders in some places and

NOTE: This selection, an address delivered at the 43rd Annual Meeting of the NCSS, appeared in *Social Education*, May 1964, pp. 257–260, 265. Reprinted by permission of John Hope Franklin.

outright defiance of the law in other places. He was particularly pained by the curse of disadvantage and poverty that persisted in our society of privilege and plenty; and he earnestly sought ways to curtail school drop-outs and to eliminate the causes of juvenile delinquency. By the passionate articulation of his own philosophy and by his vigorous prosecution of a program, he held up for all the world to see his deep commitment to education and to truth.

The historian should be immensely pleased with the theme of this conference. It reveals a real appreciation for the past, especially as it relates to planning for the future. It recognizes the fact that this organization is aware of its responsibility and its role in facing some of the major problems of our time. Every member of this conference can be happy with a theme that deals with a problem that is as old as man himself and that has been a principal concern of this country from its beginning. It was the search for a place in which they could live out their lives in dignity that led Europeans to come to this country in the seventeenth century. The Leyden Agreement of 1618, the Mayflower Compact of 1620, the Fundamental Orders of Connecticut of 1639 express in their own distinct ways this continuing search on the part of the early settlers. The risks they were willing to run and the dangers they were willing to face were a measure of their determination to forge a new society in which their own concepts of their own dignity could be translated into a reality.

By the time that the events occurred that brought in their wake the movement for independence, mutual respect and self-esteem had come to be regarded as central features in the New World society. The violation of one's essential self-esteem or the challenge to one's essential dignity was an offense against society and the individual; and redress of such a grievance was clearly a matter worth fighting for, worth dying for. On more than one occasion a Samuel Adams, a James Otis, or a Thomas Jefferson made it clear that life, liberty, and the pursuit of happiness were unalienable rights and that any attempt to violate them was indeed an attempt to subvert and insult the dignity of every human being. For, as Crèvecoeur said in his *Letters of an American Farmer*, a new man, the American, had emerged; and appreciating fully his own role and his own destiny in shaping the course of human freedom, he would not—he could not—yield to any force, however great, that compromised that freedom.

As the years went by, the refinement of the concept of human dignity continued. In 1829 the Workingmen's Association of Philadelphia condemned all artificial distinctions and inequalities that were countenanced or perpetuated by law. A few years later, Samuel Whitcomb, the son of a Massachusetts blacksmith, declared that "the highest possible attainments in all those acquisitions which adorn an individual and render glorious a nation, is to reward the industry of each, and ... to secure the highest possible degree of equality in the condition and advantages of every citizen...." In 1851 a Pennsylvania journalist, George Lippard, fearful that the cherished dignity of the American was being subverted, organized the Brotherhood of the Union. It would, he declared, "eschew bigots of all stripes—bigots called by name or title whatsoever—eschew, avoid, and turn away from them as from the smell of a plague-pit." It welcomed men, real men, he said. "It is glad to be helped by men who are in earnest, and who will work for the cause."

By the middle of the nineteenth century the cause of human freedom and dignity had become a great crusade. It had become a part of the American creed. The zeal with which the cause was advanced was unmatched in our history. Religious freedom, freedom of speech and press, freedom of movement, the right to seek a redress of grievances, and the right to participate in the determination of public policy were precious adornments of American society. For the preservation and, indeed, the enhancement of these adornments, many Americans worked with energy and dedication. These were the adornments whose advocacy helped to define a bit more precisely what in this country came to be regarded as the nature of the dignity of man.

The evolution of the concept of the dignity of man in the United States was not without its European connections, nor was it at any significant variance with Europe's best thought on the subject. John Locke's view of the relationship of man to government and of the restraints that should be placed on government to insure the integrity and dignity of man found a congenial climate and a warm reception in this country. "Where is the man that has incontestable evidence of the truth of all that he holds, or of the falsehood of all he condemns," John Locke asked in 1690. "There is reason to think that if men were better instructed themselves they would be less imposing on others," he concluded. He could well have been an American asking that question in the eighteenth or nineteenth century. Regardless of what the form of government, Rousseau declared, it cannot exceed the limits of public expedience and it cannot impose fetters that are useless to the community and it must allow the individual to do whatever "does not harm others."

But Rousseau had another observation that was as true of the United States in the nineteenth and twentieth centuries as it was when he said it on the opening page of *The Social Contract* in 1762. "Man is born free; and everywhere he is in chains," he asserted. Jefferson himself said a few years later that all men were created equal; and his eloquent advocacy of human dignity captured the imagination of peoples around the world and set the stage for a crusade for human freedom in a dozen Spanish and French colonies in the New World. But even as the author of the Declaration of Independence made his eloquent assertion, his own country had begun its systematic program to deny human freedom and to degrade human dignity. As the United States gained its political independence, its commitment to human slavery deepened. The Constitution, that secured "the blessings of liberty" to the founding fathers and to their posterity, also carefully protected the institution of human bondage. Human dignity in the United States became the dignity for the white man only. The stopping of the foreign slave trade could hardly have been labeled an act of civility, for simultaneously the domestic slave became big business. The new capital at Washington became the "very seat and center" of a most lively traffic in black men, women, and children. Slave pens, slave breeding, and the wanton disregard for simple human decency came to characterize the everyday practice of those white men who claimed that they came to the New World to enhance the dignity of man. One could see these practices over a vast region stretching from Baltimore to New Orleans. And even in the Middle States and New England, the wealth of merchant princes and bankers was channeled into the slave markets and back again into the coffers of those who vowed that their hands were neither soiled nor bloodied by the filth and barbarity of trading in human flesh. All over the New World, with very few exceptions, human slavery came to be regarded as an anachronistic barbarism. And the United States, the oldest republic in the New World, remained one of those precious exceptions.

These inconsistencies—these subversions of human dignity—were the beginning of the loss of moral leadership on the part of the United States. The British lost confidence in this country when they discovered that it made no serious effort to enforce the closing of the foreign slave trade and winked at the smuggling of thousands of slaves from Africa each year. The new republics of Latin America lost confidence in this country when they discovered that American Senators and Representatives did not want to participate in the first inter-American conference because delegates from this country might have to sit "cheek by jowl" with black statesmen from Haiti. The world lost confidence in this country when it discovered that much of the ingenuity and resourcefulness of the nation was expended in promulgating doctrines of racial superiority that sought to rationalize and justify slavery in the United States.

The outstanding failure of the United States during its first century of independence was its unwillingness to bestow upon every human being within its borders the fundamental elements of human dignity. Jefferson's words regarding the equality of all men were repudiated. In their place was substituted a set of doctrines that brought forth a variety of distinctions based on race and color. Even as the concept of democracy unfolded in the young republic, it was a concept of white democracy built on the sweat and toil and tears of millions of black human beings.

The outstanding failure of the United States during its second century of independence has been its persistent denial of complete freedom to those who a hundred years ago received emancipation in name only. Eight months after issuing the Emancipation Proclamation, Abraham Lincoln at Gettysburg called for a "new birth of freedom." It was a call to Americans—white Americans—to dedicate themselves to the principles of human dignity that their forebears had articulated but had not practiced. The great Civil War President was scarcely in his grave before it became clear that the "new birth of freedom" had been aborted. Only begrudgingly did the nation extend to the freedmen some of the rights to which all free men were entitled and without which they could not even maintain their freedom. Not one former Confederate state, in the two years following the Civil War when former Confederates were in power, gave the slightest attention to the matter of providing even the rudiments of an education for the former slaves. The former Confederates enacted elaborate legislation to keep the former slaves in "due subordination" and they did not exempt the slaves from taxation—to support the schools that were exclusively white. Only the policy of the federal government, which provided some education for Negroes through the Freedmen's Bureau, indicated any appreciation for the need of education on the part of Negroes. Nor was any thought given to the matter of enfranchising Negroes. In the period of Andrew Jackson, Americans had boasted that the exercise of the franchise was the great school of democracy. At that time Americans had urged universal white manhood suffrage without regard to education or property. Now these same Americans, or their descendants, insisted that suffrage for Negroes, regardless of how great their education or how extensive their property, was inimical to the interests of a free and civilized society.

As Lincoln's call for a new birth of freedom was being repudiated, the noble concept of the dignity of man began to crumble in the United States. For the first time in the nation's history Americans began to talk about the need of people to earn their rights and privileges as citizens. Rights that were once unalienable had now to be earned. Rights that whites enjoyed by virtue of being born were, indeed, withheld from Negroes; and they could scarcely be earned at all. White Klansmen, who had praised the extension of the franchise to ignorant whites, resorted to every conceivable act of duplicity and barbarity to save democratic institutions from pollution at the hands of Negroes who merely wanted to be treated as human beings. White supremacists, whose doctrines were broad enough to include in their claim of superiority every element of the white population, denounced every Negro, however educated or stable or accomplished, as a threat to the peace and good order of the community.

The degradation of human dignity continued in the years that followed; and it made even more remote the chances for building of a society based on the quality of the mind and heart rather than one based on race and color. On the one hand the nation built its great educational institutions into even greater and wealthier citadels dedicated to the pursuit of truth. But vast numbers of Americans continued to believe that the color of one's skin somehow had something to do with the assimilation of knowledge. Indeed, many of the great educational institutions themselves promoted the idea that there were inherent racial differences that made it impossible for Negroes to learn. Even where there was the grudging admission that perhaps Negroes could assimilate knowledge, educators, politicians, and even religious leaders advocated separate institutions. This was apparently in the effort to make certain that Negroes and whites could not discover the indisputable fact that they were not different in any important respects.

In the spirit of the inscription on the base of the Statue of Liberty this country welcomed the tired and the poor from many lands. It invited them to lose themselves in the gigantic melting pot which symbolized America's capacity to transcend national, cultural, and racial lines. This was the land of opportunity. Serb, Croat, Armenian, Italian, Greek, Russian, Jew, and Gentile made their way to the promised land. If some Americans expressed concern over the emergence of a multicultural society, the general attitude was one of making assimilation possible. The general assumption was that in time the numerous strains would blend into the whole, as America's vaunted melting pot worked its wonders. But Negroes who had been here long before the nineteenth century were not to be included in the magic process. While America accepted whites of whatever nation, culture, or religion, it rejected out of hand any suggestion of equality or dignity for Negroes. It cheered the publication of Charles Carroll's *The Negro A Beast*. It hailed Thomas Dixon's diatribe against the Negro people entitled *The Leopard's Spots*. It twisted the Darwinian theory to suit its own preconceived notions about the Negro's unfitness to survive. It placed a grotesque sign, "For Whites Only," on America's great melting pot. Even those in the places of moral leadership stood idly by when Negroes were lynched, burned at the stake, subjected to the terror of the race riot, and denied the basic protections guaranteed to citizens by the Constitution.

The century that has elapsed since Lincoln called for a new birth of freedom is a century filled with paradoxes and contradictions. It is a century filled with the struggles of the black man to move into the main stream of American life, and it is a century filled with the determination of a considerable segment of the white population to keep the black man out of that main stream. It is a century in which we have witnessed the tragic and wanton disregard of the democratic dogma and the dignity of man. In the century that followed the emancipation of the slaves, some Americans want to believe that the major theme of this country's history of freedom is the Negro's accomplishments—contributions, some like to call them. But this theme, however estimable, can hardly be the major theme in a country whose basic assumptions are supposed to be the right of the individual to enjoy respect for his person and the opportunity to exploit his talents. The major theme of this first century of freedom for Negroes is the continued rejection on the part of America of its own doctrines of freedom and equality and the persistent degradation of the human personality. The most remarkable development of the last century is not what the Frederick Douglasses, the W. E. B. Du Boises, the Booker Washingtons, the Charles Drews, the George W. Carvers, the Marian Andersons, and the James Baldwins have accomplished. The most remarkable development is the continued attack on the dignity of man and, indeed, the persistent rejection of the new birth of freedom on the part of the J. K. Vardamans, the Pitchfork Ben Tillmans, the "Tomtom" Heflins, the Woodrow Wilsons, the James O. Eastlands, the George Wallaces, the Ross Barnetts, and the Harry F. Byrds. The most remarkable development is the manner in which the Klansmen, the White Citizens Councils, the lily-white labor unions, and the industrial bigots, and the 101 members of Congress who denounced the Supreme Court in 1955, have succeeded in renewing and keeping alive the false and un-American principle that human dignity is "for whites only."

As we approach the end of our second century of political independence and as we begin the second century of the emancipation of the slaves, we should be in an excellent position to view the shortcomings of our fundamental social philosophy and the derelictions in our public and private policies. We should be in a position to gain some perspectives for the future and some lessons by which we should be guided. We who are committed to the study of history and of the evolution of our social institutions must surely be sensitive to the importance of removing artificial and spurious restrictions on the human being if all men are to achieve the dignity and respect that are their birthright. Our great and lamented President, John Fitzgerald Kennedy, reminded his fellow citizens that they had not yet become fully committed to the full and unqualified support of human dignity for all persons. In his message to Congress in June—the message in which he called for new civil rights legislation—he spoke eloquently of the dignity of man. "No one has been barred on account of his race from fighting or dying for America," the President declared. "There are no 'white' and 'colored' signs on the foxholes or graveyards of battle. Surely, in 1963," he continued, "one hundred years after emancipation, it should not be necessary for any American citizen to demonstrate in the streets for the opportunity to stop at a hotel, or to eat at a lunch counter in the very department store in which he is shopping, or to enter a motion picture house, on the same terms as any other customer.... Many Negro children entering segregated grade schools at the time of the Supreme Court decision in 1954 will enter segregated high schools this year, having suffered a loss which can never be regained. Indeed, discrimination in education is one basic cause of the other inequities and hardships inflicted upon our Negro citizens."

But the achievement of human dignity in the United States is not merely an achievement of human dignity for Negroes. The darker peoples of the United States are merely the vehicles by which the nation may test the extent of the commitment to its fundamental principles. It is axiomatic that when a nation or a people seeks to exclude a part of the nation or a part of the people from freedom or equality or dignity, it erects a society on a shaky foundation. In time, it may collapse or fail and destroy the arrogance and discrimination that it sought to perpetuate. "Slavery degrades not only the enslaved but the slave-holder," Thomas Jefferson said. In like fashion, human degradation and human indignity spread their venom alike on the perpetrator and the victim. The lessons of history make it clear what our view of tomorrow must be. The failure during the last two centuries to secure human dignity for all peoples is a grave indictment of the quality and validity of the society that we have forged. As we move toward a tomorrow, we can make it as bright or as dark as we want it to be. It will be dark if we continue to attempt to create artificial distinctions based on race and make a mockery of the dignity of man by cursing his color or condemning him for his station in life. It will be dark if we continue to think that we can teach our youth that they are better because their skin is white and that they must work to keep their darker peoples "in their place" of degradation and indignity. The morrow will be surely dark if our energies are expended on the thankless and hopeless task of exorcising the forces of truth and creating false notions of superiority based on race, color, religion, or national origins.

We can have a bright tomorrow. It will be bright if we concede to our fellows the same sense of self-esteem and self-respect that we want for ourselves. It will be bright if we teach our youth that in the past we have faltered because we stooped to human slavery and because we had not the wisdom or the prudence to give it up gracefully. It will be bright if we have the humility to surrender to the principles of true equality that have really never prompted our policies or our actions and if we concede that we have no claim to greatness as a people or as a nation if we cannot reach down and touch the most disadvantaged member of society and view him as a sacred, dignified human being.

We who teach must first be learners. We must learn the lessons of the past, even if they are painful lessons. We must also learn to apply those lessons to our view of tomorrow, even if they require readjustment in our thinking and courage in our actions. We who are committed to the pursuit of truth and the spread of truth can surely be as vigorous in our pursuits as President Lincoln was when he called for a new birth of freedom a century ago. We can surely be as committed toward the strengthening of our society as President Kennedy was when he called on this nation to redeem her promises of freedom and equality. We can look forward, like Lincoln and Kennedy, to the time when the nation will rise to the position where she can save herself from the ridicule of the world that mocks her hypocrisy. We can look forward to the time when the nation will spare herself of the scorn that she must surely heap upon herself so long as her commitments in the field of human relations remain unfulfilled. In this great, rich, privileged land of ours, the dignity of man has too long been trampled upon. If we would escape the calumny and the scorn of tomorrow's children and if we would prove equal to our role as the conservators and purveyors of truth, we must realize that the dignity of man is not yours or mine to give or to deny. It is ours merely to recognize.

Tell It Like It Was: Suggestions on Black History

LOUIS R. HARLAN

Anyone speaking today on the subject of Black or Negro History has to build a bridge not only between the professional historian and the high school teacher but also between both of these groups and the non-professional but intensely interested black militants who want to use history as an instrument to promote group solidarity, a more optimistic self-image, and in some cases as an instrument of racial revolution or nationalism. I assume that many of you are social studies teachers in secondary schools, however, and I will move on as quickly as possible to specific suggestions of ways in which Negro themes may be woven into the instruction in the classroom. The all-important contribution I can make on that line as a professional historian is in the details rather than the generalities.

First, however, as though to clear the decks for the main action, let us consider the limits of history as a social instrument. What can it do and what can it not do to reform and remake the world? While my remarks will be addressed to the young black militants who propose to remake Black History, in the storefront classrooms of the ghetto, I do not want by what I say to encourage complacency on the part of the social studies teacher. His failure and that of the professional historian to give justice to the black man in the court of history have helped to bring us to the present pass.

My mixed reaction to much of the propagandistic Black History of

NOTE: This selection, an address delivered at the 48th Annual Meeting of NCSS, appeared in *Social Education*, April 1969, pp. 390–395. Reprinted by permission of Louis R. Harlan.

the last few years stems as much from my social values as from my role as a professional historian. I belong to the "old-fashioned integrationist" group—the liberal and radical whites and Negroes over thirty who were engaged in the struggle for a racially integrated society in the 1950's and who still believe that the open society, to which all people have access, is a worthy and attainable goal. I realize that there is a contrary view held by those disillusioned not only by recent setbacks but also by a lifetime of being black in white America, who are saying that integration may be a noble dream, an iridescent dream, but still a dream. They say that integration is as much a romantic and escapist fantasy as the back-to-Africa and other escapist movements in the American black past which have taken the form of separatism. I am willing to concede the possibility that all this is so. But my integrationist views rest on a set of values, which we might consider as ideals which we approach as closely as we can. Black to me is beautiful, and I want American society to have this beautiful and saving element in its makeup. On the other hand, I hope that I am not a slot-machine integrationist. I would accept and even welcome such an assertion of Black Power and of pluralistic cultural power as would permit black people to march proudly rather than shuffle in to full participation in American society. I would urge whites to show self-restraint as Negroes experiment with their own style, even if this takes separatist forms which we can hope will be only temporary and tactical. In other words, I accept and welcome Black Power in most of its forms but fear the mystique, what I might call the theology, of black separatism and black cultural nationalism that often accompanies it. Black nationalism is no worse than any other nationalism, but historians who have seen the pathological effects of nationalism in the twentieth century are in no mood to encourage new cults of nationalism or separatism or "chosen people" cults anywhere in the world.

I would say to black revolutionaries who want to enlist all of black culture but particularly Black History in the cause of racial revolution, you may be right but I think you are wrong to get all hung-up on history. Most successful revolutions have defied history, have considered the past not a glorious heritage but a record of men's sins and follies. Revolutionaries don't need a past; they build their movement on a realistic view of the present and a glowing vision of the future. Marxism, of course, is an exception. It developed in the nineteenth century under the intellectual influence of Hegelian philosophy. Marx felt somehow that to give legitimacy to his conception he had to plunge it into the moving stream of history; he had to give it inevitability by a theory of historical determinism. As a result of this entanglement with history, Marxians have experienced real "hang-ups" when objective reality has failed to fit Marxian historical models and intuitions of historical forces, as in the example of Marxist revolutions succeeding not in the mature economies of western Europe but in the peasant societies of Russia and China.

History is more than a matter of re-creating the past in a mechanical, value-free way. The historical perspective is worth something, hard to measure but significant, for policy making, because history is actually an extension of human memory and experience. But if you try to make history jump through hoops it was not made to jump through, it may bite! Particularly if it is bad history to begin with. John Hope Franklin, the country's leading Negro historian, recently criticized black revolutionaries for their accusing and ill-formed understanding of the American Negro past. Rather than see all the black leaders of the past be given a verdict of guilty for race betrayal, says Franklin, "I would suppose that it would be best that our forebears remain obscure unobserved figures, at least at peace with the world and safe from their blaspheming progeny."

Equally deplorable to historians is the tendency of many popular black historians to change the tortured odyssey of the black man along Freedom Road into a succession of sugar-coated success stories, designed to give black children a more favorable and hopeful self-concept but dangerous because they are bad history. This is what August Meier calls "cherry-tree history," the black man's answer to the Fourth of July orator's or the Thanksgiving Day preacher's idea of our American national heritage. What good will it do to trade the old stereotypes and myths for new ones? Crispus Attucks may replace Molly Pitcher, but neither one plays a significant part in our history nor I hope in our classroom teaching about it. Did Booker T. Washington really chop down the cherry tree with his little hatchet? We couldn't care less. We don't need a lot of cotton candy about success heroes of the sports and entertainment worlds, but a realistic view of why so much of the talent and drive of black Americans has been forced into these channels. We need to get our students to face the realities of the scars of bondage and the nature of life as shaped by the institutions of Southern agriculture and the Northern urban ghetto.

Let me move on, then, from what I consider bad history because it does not afford a clear, rational view of the real world to what I would consider good history if it does afford that clear view. I'll first suggest five interpretive themes in Negro or Black History, and then turn to some specific examples.

Interpretive Themes

The first of these themes is the persistence of white racism. When W.E.B. Du Bois declared in 1903 that "The problem of the twentieth century is the problem of the Color Line," he was certainly prophetic, but if he had looked backward, he would have seen that it was a big problem of the nineteenth century as well. We need to take a more realistic, disillusioned look at the national record, the American way of life, in race matters. It is not a pretty picture. We do not have a liberal tradition in race relations. The white nine-tenths of the United States population, north as well as south, have since the earliest days of slavery pushed the black group to the bottom of society, a bottom shared—persistently shared—by all the other non-white minorities in our country, the Indians, Mexican-Americans, Chinese, Japanese, and Puerto Ricans, darker than most of us and at the bottom not because of individual or group difference in ability or potential but because they are dark and because the white nine-tenths wanted things that way. What has prevailed in American society, from the eighteenth century on, has not been the glittering generalities of the Declaration of Independence, that all men are created equal, or of the 14th Amendment, that there shall be no discrimination on account of color. What has prevailed, instead, has been the white-built and white-owned and white-serving institutions of repression and subordination. What we historians need to do is stop wasting our time looking for the glints and lights of hope in our national past. The National Advisory Commission on Civil Disorders set the right tone for this reinterpretation in its report last spring. It said: "Race prejudice has shaped our history decisively; it now threatens to affect our future." It said elsewhere: "What white Americans have never fully understood—but what the Negro can never forget—is that white society is deeply implicated in the ghetto. White institutions created it, white institutions maintain it, and white society condones it." And finally it warns in its basic conclusion: "Our nation is moving toward two societies, one black, one white—separate and unequal."

So we come to the second interpretive theme, which derives from the first. Black Americans, unlike white Americans, do not have a progressive history. Here lies the ultimate difficulty in the self-glorifying Black History that is all success story—that it encounters an unbridgeable credibility gap. There may have been a glorious age in Africa, but for the black man in America the glorious age is in the future. Instead of progress upward through striving, success, and victory in the classic American pattern—up from slavery—Negroes in fact have gone from one bad situation to another, from slavery to segregation, from plantation to ghetto, from cotton patch to rat-infested slum. People used to say that the mechanical cotton picker would do what Lincoln had failed to do, really free the Negro. But where did the displaced cotten-field Negro go? To Watts, or to some similar slum and social graveyard. I would urge you to consider both the ironic perspective and the interpretations of August Meier and Elliott Rudwick's survey of Negro history, *From Plantation to Ghetto* (1966). As for the present, the Riot Commission report underscores the fact that we celebrated the civil rights gains of the past decade too early. They are important steps toward a more egalitarian future, but they have been vitiated in the present by tokenism, gradualism, and persistent racialism of the white man on the street. So the hopes and rising expectations of the black man in the street turn to ashes. When Martin Luther King told us only yesterday that he had a dream, one America, freedom for all his people, this dream was simply the American dream in black guise, the dream of winning out and having the good life. But instead of coming true, it blew up in his face, killed by white racism in one way or another.

This brings us to a third interpretive theme, which follows from the first two: the theme of the recurrence of the same challenges and responses time and again in Negro history. In other words, the cyclical character of Negro history. Let me give you a couple of illustrations. What were the big issues involving Negro soldiers in the Civil War? First, there was the question whether they were for the war, as a white man's war, then whether they would be enlisted or drafted, then whether they should be in integrated or separate units, then whether there should be equal pay and equal opportunity to become officers, then whether they would fight bravely and the whole question of Negro morale in the face of the discrimination, then panic at the end of the war about what black men with guns, who had been taught how to use them, would do when they returned to civilian life. Now, the interesting thing about these issues of the Civil War is that when we read the history of the black soldier in the Revolution there were the same issues, and also in World Wars I and II, and even the Spanish-American War and to some extent Korea and Viet Nam. There is an amazing recurrence pattern, and it comes from the persistence of white racism and the consequent lack of basic progression in the life we have forced black men to live in white America. The more it changes, the more it is the same thing. Another illustration is the various forms of Negro response to their predicament in America. At the turn of the twentieth century, faced by the lynchings, race riots, segregation and discrimination of that day, there were three main forms of Negro response: strengthening black institutions within a segregated society, the black power way of Booker T. Washington; militant protest with a goal of integration and full participation, as symbolized by Du Bois and the Niagara Movement; and emigrationism and black nationalism, as symbolized by Bishop Henry M. Turner and later by Chief Sam and Marcus Garvey. All of these have parallels today: the black power approach of Stokely Carmichael and others, conceived of as a tactical method; the civil rights movement of the 1950's and 1960's; and separatist black nationalism of the Black Muslims and also of the faction of Black Power militants who are creating a mystique, a theology, and a mythological history to strengthen the lines of alienation from white America.

The three themes I have stressed so far, you will notice, are all in the framework of social history. So let me mention only briefly, without extended discussion, two other themes which suggest a more hopeful future for black men in America. One of these is Negro cultural history, used in both the sociologists' and anthropologists' sense of a set of patterns of behavior that have evolved and become customary among a group of people, and the other definition—the history of the artistic expression of a people. These things are so closely intertwined that they cannot be separated anyhow. But my point here is that, given the persistence of white racism, the improbability of full integration of lower-class Negroes into the larger American society in the near future, it behooves us to study more closely than we have the Negro institutions built up behind the segregation wall—the family, church, business, mutual-aid, and even the low-life institutions like the numbers racket and the "pushers." On the "brighter" side of the coin, we need to study and to include in our teaching about the Negro experience in America also his rich cultural contribution to America through the spirituals, jazz, the dance, and a rich Southern rural Negro folklore which has distinct African roots. The capacity of Negroes to survive and preserve a degree of sanity in this society is worth study. This brings together the static and progressive themes.

The fifth theme in a way contradicts what I said before about the static and cyclical character of Negro history. There is one big new element in the past half-century which has wrought great changes in the lives of black folk—urbanization. And the city promises great changes also for the future. For middle class Negroes, the city has often meant a limited liberation. They could gain status usually only by exploiting the ghetto poor, and even then they could not enjoy this status freely in the larger American society because they were black. For lower class Negroes, the city has too often meant a new slavery, the "dark ghetto," with its rat-infested stores and homes, its social pathology. The economics of job discrimination meant that in a typical family the father couldn't support the family and so drifted away, the mother had to work at a domestic or menial job and left the children to grow up on the streets—streets teeming with crime and corruption that a cynical white police force tolerated and exploited. But Americans tend to respond to crises, and just as the emergence of the Third World, hesitating between East and West, had more to do with the civil rights movement of the 1950's and 1960's than many of us would like to admit, so the crisis of our inner cities—not just "burn, baby, burn" but the whole stinking cancer at the heart of our urbanized lives—may in the 1970's force us into a creative response.

Suggestions for Teachers

Let us turn from these interpretive themes, which I hope will help to provide you with a clear-eyed perspective in which to view the American racial past. I come now to a few specific suggestions.

In the first place, I would urge you to begin by dealing with concepts, with what race is and isn't. There is a rich anthropological and sociological and psychological literature on this subject, but I would recommend as a clear and authoritative reference the UNESCO Statement on Race, published in book form with explanations for the layman by Ashley Montagu. There should be a well-thumbed copy in your school library.

In dealing with the West African background of the Afro-American, you should recognize right away that this is a subject about which there is deep, basic conflict among scholars, and also that it is one which has important implications politically, in relation to black separatism, among other things. The crux of the question is that of the thickness or thinness of African cultural survivals among New World Negroes, and by implication the larger question of the strength and health of the American Negro subculture that has evolved out of the differentness of the black man's experience in America. Everyone recognizes some Africanisms in Negro speech, song, dance, religion, but the question is, how much, and there is not agreement on whether Negro family structure, the basic social institutional unit, is influenced by the matrifocal family of West African societies or is chiefly the product of economic or social forces of either slavery or the ghetto. The best brief treatment of the scholarly controversy is in Meier and Rudwick, *From Plantation to Ghetto* (1966).

Slavery—I cannot imagine anyone teaching American history without talking about slavery. But in the past most of the writing was from the side of or through the eyes of the master. This was partly because it was the master who made the written record, but also because of conscious or unconscious white racism. Kenneth M. Stampp, *The Peculiar Institution* (1956), went a long way toward correcting this. It is concerned with the effect of slavery on the slave. But more recently there has been an inclination to say that his treatment of the psychological aspects was too unsophisticated, so a historian, Stanley Elkins, and a novelist, William Styron, have made what seem to me rather unsuccessful attempts to reinterpret the psychology of the slave. I am not recommending them to you. On the other hand, the comparative treatment of slavery in the United States with that of the West Indies and South America is a very active line of scholarship right now, and you could greatly enrich your teaching on the subject by using Frank Tannenbaum, *Slave and Citizen: The Negro in the Americas* (1946); Herbert S. Klein, *Slavery in the Americas: A Comparison of Cuba and Virginia* (1966); the recent articles comparing slave revolts in the New World, by Eugene Genovese; and such specialized works as Gilberto Freyre, *The Masters and the Slaves* (1946), on Brazilian slavery.

The experience of Negroes in the North in both pre-Civil War and post-Civil War should be presented in the illusionless way that would explain the vigorous Negro protest movement throughout the nineteenth century and also the despair that fostered emigration movements throughout the same period. I don't want this to deteriorate into a catalog of titles, but would suggest that food for such a realistic look at the Northern welcome to the Negro is available in such books as Leon Litwack, *North of Slavery* (1961); Rayford Logan, *The Negro in American Life and Thought, The Nadir, 1877–1901* (1954); and the documentary by James McPherson, *The Negro's Civil War* (1965).

Just to touch briefly on a few other specifics: Try to view Reconstruction less in the melodramatic, good-guys, bad-guys framework of the past, and more as a noble experiment which failed because white America mistakenly thought it could give the black man freedom without equality. When you come to segregation, don't try to pretend that it did not or does not exist, in the hope that maybe therefore it will go away, as some textbooks seem to. You should assume that your high school students are budding young adults who need to be brought face to face with the real world. Don't be so carried away with the Jackie Robinson story or the Negro success hero of the *Up from Slavery* type that you assume that they are typical and ignore the repressions of white America. Some textbooks seem to suggest that if any Negro doesn't fight his way out of the slums like a handful of sports or entertainment heroes have, then it is his own fault.

When comparing Negroes with other ethnic minorities we should take heed of Chapter 9 of the Riot Commission Report, "Comparing the Immigrant and Negro Experience." In answer to the question many white Americans ask, why the Negro has been unable to escape from poverty and the ghetto like the European immigrants, the Commission points out these facts. The maturing economy offered the Negro migrant little employment for his unskilled labor as compared with the demand for such labor when the European immigrants were coming into the country. Secondly, in white America, racial discrimination has put a burden on the backs of black men, keeping them out of the high-reward and high-status occupations. Thirdly, whereas political opportunities played an important part in enabling European immigrants to escape from poverty, this avenue has been almost completely closed to Negroes. In proportion to population, the Negro proportion of important political posts is extremely low—in Mayor Daley's Chicago as much as in Boss Tweed's New York. Fourthly, there were cultural factors at play, such as the strong patriarchal families of the immigrants and the fact that small businessmen had a ready-made market in the ethnic culture of the immigrants, with their language barrier, ethnic foods, and so on. Also, slavery had prevented the development of a small-business tradition among Negroes as compared with immigrants. Fifthly, many descendants of European immigrants ignore the time factor; they forget how long it took them to work out of poverty; whereas the Negroes have been concentrated in the cities for only two generations. And then there is the final, somewhat intangible but important factor, that the typical European immigrant possessed and was possessed by what we call "the American dream"—the promise that society offered that with hard work and perseverance a man and his family could achieve not only material well-being but status. In contrast to this open-ended society, the Negro in the urban ghetto today faces a dead-end. "New methods of escape," says the Riot Commission, "must be found for the majority of today's poor."

Finally, I urge you to acquaint your students with the beauty as well as the pathology of black life in America by assigning them reading matter in which Negroes speak directly. I have in mind the autobiographies of Douglass, Washington, Du Bois, and Malcolm X, the anthologies of Negro writing by James Weldon Johnson (*The Book of American Negro Poetry*), Sterling Brown, Arthur Davis, and Ulysses Lee (*The Negro Caravan*), and Alain Locke (*The New Negro*), and such classics of Negro writing as Du Bois, *Souls of Black Folk*, Richard Wright's *Black Boy*, and Ralph Ellison's *The Invisible Man*.

To summarize what I have tried to say, on the one hand I appeal to you to give a compensatory emphasis to the role that black people have played in the American past, but on the other hand to avoid the new distortions which would come from a propagandistic use of history to promote Negro cultural nationalism and separatism. This is not to deny that an oversimplified "cherry tree" history may serve to promote Negro pride or white compassion, but such uses of history are better left to the public outside of the classroom door. Both the historian and the teacher have an obligation to a broad and balanced search for truth about the past which transcends ethnic or ideological loyalties. To fulfill this function, to promote a humanistic understanding of our fellow humans, we need to take account of a black past that has villains as well as heroes, sufferings as well as successes, shades of grey as well as black and white. And, as Mary McLeod Bethune wisely pointed out, we need both the white and the black keys to play the piano. The black past, in the American context, must be presented in meaningful relation to the parallel and converging experiences of white Americans. The slogan *E pluribus unum*, one out of many, may have come upon hard times recently, but it is even so the framework in which Black History and all other history must be placed, unless we are going to abandon American's noblest dream.

A Talk with a Young
Mexican American

In relation to your educational experiences in [the city of L.], tell me about it. How many years since you were in school there?

It's been about six years since I was in the [L.] school. First of all, I think you should know a little bit about [this city]. In [L.] the Gringo is in the minority, instead of vice versa. People are bilingual on the street there. You go into the shops and everybody is speaking Spanish. Some shops have to call people who speak English to wait on you, and sometimes you won't get waited on. Not because you speak Spanish . . . but because you speak English. In [L.], things are kinda turned around and there is a difference. But it is not a great deal different in school, I don't feel. The top administrator for years—I don't know how bilingual he is, but I know he is not a Mexican American. The schools for a long while didn't have that many Mexican American teachers. There were plenty, but it wasn't in proportion to the population; and I can remember, for instance, my early years of schooling were in a Catholic school and the teachers, I don't think, were bilingual. English was spoken. But then no one ever heard of having a bilingual class.

All your instruction was in English?

All my instruction was in English.

Were you a native Spanish speaker?

This is the thing. From a very early age, I heard both languages, so I never had a problem. I heard good English and I heard Pocho and good Spanish as well. I didn't have any problems.

NOTE: The taping of this interview with a young Mexican American was arranged by Dell Felder. The interview appeared in *Social Education*, October 1970, pp. 643–647. Reprinted by permission of Dell Felder.

How about the other kids?

The other kids did, of course, and I kinda wondered what was going on. I especially began waking up in junior high school because they had what they called accelerated classes. This was kinda like the honor kids, you know, and all the kids that were in the majority—most of the Mexican kids at school—weren't in those classes. I was in those classes, and maybe two or three other people who had last names like . . . Gonzales, Gutiérrez, but the rest were not; and I just can't believe that in a school that size . . . that there were that few people qualified for those classes, or qualified for the honor society.

Who were Mexican American?

Who were Mexican American. That school had been going on for quite a while, it was predominantly Mexican American. I was the first Mexican American ever elected to their Student Council presidency. . . . It was kind of a shocking thing when I realized what had happened there—that I was elected more because my last name was [G.] than for me, I thought. Then I went back and looked at the past presidents of Student Councils and the representation in the Student Council, and saw it was mostly Anglo-dominated. I am *not* using this as a criticism, I'm just saying there is something wrong with the statistics here. Of course, statistics don't always pan out the way they are supposed to anyway. Educational opportunity—if you had money, you went to school, to college; if you didn't, you didn't go. It was as simple as that. Scholarships were available, but nobody made any effort to recruit anybody. The counseling was absolutely inadequate—it was inadequate for anybody; and the people that started complaining about the counseling were the WASP kids because their parents wanted them to go to good schools . . . see?

What is a WASP kid?

Well, I am referring to a WASP kid in this instance to mostly people from the air base who went to [this] junior high school; kids who were not Mexican American and whose parents were middle class or upper middle class. Those kids in the accelerated classes, the classes I was in during my last years, the parents would come and want to know how should I get this kid to have the number of credits he needs to get into an academic program to go on to college. The counselors there were even giving *them* inadequate information, so you can imagine what was going on for somebody who didn't have the grades. So the counseling was inadequate. From [there] I went on to another private Catholic school. It's the best one in [L.]. I think now they are even giving exams to even go there. We were told that if you don't intend to go on to college we don't want you here. This was not to shock you, it was just to let you know that you were going to get an academic program at the school.

So you didn't go to a public high school?

I didn't go to a public high school, no. In fact, any Mexican American in [L.] that was serious about going to college tried to avoid the public schools there because they do not prepare you for college. My sister is a teacher at one of those. In fact, she is a teacher at the oldest and biggest public high school there. So, I'm not speaking out against this because I have no stake there. My brothers went there.

To public school?

To public school—all the way through. I went for part of my elementary education and then junior high school education, but I had, of course, friends who went there and we had exchanges once in a while and I'd ask them how they were doing. I visited some of their classes when they had programs, etc.

What kind of experiences did your friends have in the public schools that you can recall?

Well, there were not instances of overt discrimination—you can't go to college! But, there are programs ... that seek to elevate and help college-aspiring Mexican Americans find colleges and, find money; and to the best of my knowledge, none of that information was available there at the school. They advertise scholarships like everybody else, but then the minute you had to take your CEEB or you had to take a competitive examination, you had *not* been prepared for those kinds of exams in the public school—you just weren't. The classes there—for instance, my sister-in-law is teaching English literature and so forth. She's not teaching people how to speak English, but she's teaching English, as it is called in the high school. I think she is teaching at the junior or sophomore level. Everytime I go home, she shows me the reports they're writing. She shows me some stuff they're doing and the English is just *pathetic*. Somehow these kids have *not* been prepared; and they have been promoted. Somebody is incompetent when you reach high school and you speak English that poorly or you write it. I'm not talking about talking with an accent, but using your grammar that poorly, or you can't write a decent paragraph, or write a decent sentence. There is something wrong in the high schools and I'm not saying we should toughen up and flunk everybody that can't speak English. I'm saying somehow in elementary and junior high school, those kids were not prepared. If they were sent on when they should have been, not because they should have been held back so to speak, but they shouldn't be sent on until they are *ready* for it. That's one criticism I have. I think the situation is especially bad in [L.] because [L.] has a very large migrant population. This is the home base for the migrants. You see, before they go up to Ohio, before they go to Michigan, before they go to California—when there is no picking to be done during the winter months—they come down to [L.] They live there, they send their kids to school, and then maybe in the middle of the year they'll have to pick up and leave to go pick crops. I know, for instance, in [one valley] their school year is ending this week because next week those kids have gotta go. Well, you can imagine what happens if the livelihood of your father depends on leaving next week; and you don't finish the last three weeks of school, you don't get your exams in, you don't get promoted—this creates all kinds of havoc. I can remember kids, even in junior high school, much older than I was, in the same class. And at that age you're more mature physically and psychologically, and you have all kinds of "hang ups" being in a class if you're, say, 17, and the kid next to you is 13. You feel funny there. You're bigger, you're different—you're a different person. You're different in important peer group ways that are important to the social dynamics of a classroom—you know more about that than I do. But, it makes for all kinds of barriers to learning, and that's important. You mentioned before something about the social studies, I have something I want to read you. "I'm sitting in my history class, the instructor commences rapping. I'm in my U. S. history class, and I'm on the very verge of napping. The Mayflower landed on Plymouth Rock, tell me more, tell me more. Thirteen colonies were settled—I've heard it all before. What did he say? Dare I ask him to reiterate—oh, why bother! It sounded like he said George Washington's my father. I'm reluctant to believe it. I suddenly raised my *mano.* If George Washington's my father, why wasn't he Chicano?" You know, if social studies, which in junior high or high school usually takes the form of history until it gets into political science, is a discipline that deals with giving perspective, I think this is the root cause for what goes on in classes with Mexican Americans that's *horrible!* There is no perspective that they have. The guy that wrote that poem . . . wants to know what his point of view is when he's being presented all of this. Where does he stand? Where does he stand in the perspective of human events? Where does he stand in all kinds of things? And he doesn't have a point of view to go on. When you get into a history class, and you begin studying ancient civilization, and maybe a paragraph is given to civilizations in South America, and you spend three weeks on Egypt and four weeks on Greece, there's something lacking. I liked history and I never had problems, but that was the worst class for most kids. Most Mexican Americans in my junior high school hated it; it was completely irrelevant to their experience. I like it, so I studied it anyway. I'd study it on my own and filled in the gaps, but they wouldn't. So what happened? They flunked. That was one of the worst subjects we had.

What do you think they need in terms of an education that they are not getting?

Let me read something here. MAYO in [H.] published this: "Education—We seek to control school districts or individual schools in order to make the institution adapt itself to the needs of the Chicano community rather than the present form of making the Chicanos student adapt to the school. We seek to change the curriculum, quality of instruction, attitudes of administrators and teachers, methods of financing the school and methods of instruction." That's pretty ambitious. But I think what they are talking about there is a total picture that involves all kinds of things, that [refers to the question] what does the Mexican American need in school. I don't know if my concepts of what school should be is realistic anymore. I don't know if it's to give you more options and make you a free man, or liberate you, or if it is to give you vocational preparation so you can get out and get a job. I'm torn between two things because I think both are necessary, but one takes precedence over the other. I think for a student who graduates from high school, there is little chance of going to college—and I have statistics that support that statement. You can get an idea from this—college deferments go to 60 percent of the Anglo population while only 2 percent or less of the Chicanos are able to get a college deferment. You have to get a college deferment to go to college, so that will give you an indication of what's behind that figure. My point was, I don't know if saying that we should prepare all Mexican Americans to go to college is a realistic and practical thing at this point. But I don't think Mexican Americans are being prepared vocationally; because when they get out of school, even the industries today want more than just vocational preparation. Suppose a boy has 34 credits in shop. If you've ever visited one of those shops, unless it is an excellent school—I saw a good program up in [D.]. It was good because industry had come in and [a major corporation] was sponsoring it and giving them the equipment and the instruction. It's time wasted on just practical things like nailing, hammering, using machines and tools. It's important that you have maybe a couple of credits in that, but not to get stuck in so to speak "vocational." Vocational classes in English are always the worst English classes—the standards expected are the lowest. I think if you demand good standards, not to flunk people out, but demand high standards and then help them until they reach those standards in English, and mastering some of the so-called reasoning tools that we have, so that they can sit down and take one of those exams and make a decent grade on it, that's good. I think that's a very important thing—even for people in vocational.

Opening options for them?

The things that these kids are competing against in the home are just fantastic! Yesterday, we went to four or five migrant homes. It wasn't new to me, but it was brought home again. I don't think any of those had indoor plumbing. One didn't even have water—they had to bring in a little pump and pump it from somebody else's pipe. It was outside of course. There were seven children in one family—two adults—and there were two rooms. That's not uncommon among migrant kids. I'm not saying all Mexican Americans in [L.] are migrants, that's not true. But the family usually comes to the country as a migrant and they maintain those standards for quite a while until they make a big break somehow and reach the lower middle class, what America might consider a low middle class, and from then you jump on up. Most of the kids are competing against those kinds of conditions where the father may make the total of $2,000 a year. College is out of the question. And in many cases high school is out of the question—you've got to get out and make a living. The young girls start working as maids. In [L.], when I was growing up, they were making 25 cents an hour in the businesses there. You can't afford books, you can't afford football games or clothes. Take the total picture—suppose the kid does make it into school, parents do send him to school, just take the financial handicap. If other people are dressing kinda nice and you want to be accepted so badly, and you want to be part of the group, it's only natural for any kid growing up. You don't have any money for any of the assemblies, much less football games, or for trips any place. Sometimes you don't have money for supplies. And sometimes they mercilessly collect money in schools for all kinds of campaigns—send our football team here, or get the principal a nice present. I can remember in Student Council, we gave the principal a nice rifle that cost a couple of hundred dollars. The sponsor of the Student Council suggested it and ramrodded it through. Well, at that age group, we just weren't aware of what was going on. But, if we had given somebody $300 as an incentive for winning some kind of scholarship or studying for the summer, or something, I think we could have done a lot more good. But, we didn't have *that kind* of money. We would collect thousands and thousands of dollars—one year two and another year three for the March of Dimes—where there were families there, in that school, whose kids could have had polio and couldn't afford operations. There is a discrepancy between the way money was used and what the needs are. So money is a very big thing in handicapping the students. Also, and it was just brought home to me, somebody said awhile ago, can you imagine an Anglo in a [L.] middle-class family who has a child that is 6 or 7 years old sending that child to a school where only Spanish is spoken? Can you imagine that! I couldn't conceive a parent doing that and accepting the grades the kid brought home, accepting the problems that would happen, accepting the social consequence of the kid being discriminated against because he is white and not brown. That brought home to me what these kids go through when they are placed in the elementary schools. I'm jumping from school to school to school because it's part of the total picture, it seems to me. I would just like for them to have the same kinds of tools to compete with when they get out of school. To compete for jobs, to compete to get into college, compete for scholarships that most other kids have. . . . It's not all a question of money, but a great deal of it is a question of money; and then what happens is that a Mexican American will get to college, get out, and when he has gone through—this is what's so horrible—the people who are interested in problems of migrants usually turn out like me—kids of middle-class or upper middle-class Mexican American backgrounds who haven't been fighting every step of the way. I can go into a migrant home and not feel threatened that I am going right back into that situation. But students who do get out and were in those situations, for most part are "sell outs." They accept most white middle-class values, which are not in themselves wrong, but do alienate them from the community that needs their help very much.

Is there any way they can accept both sets of values and be comfortable as human beings?

I haven't had to check myself into an institution yet. I feel very comfortable in our society; and I feel very comfortable when I'm around just Mexican Americans. I kept laughing at [D.] yesterday, because I felt in my element, and I knew she didn't. I was just smiling to myself because she'd come up and whisper, "How do you say 'supplies' in Spanish?", and, for the first time, I had people asking me things. I just smiled and [D.] said, "You're just making me pay for being a WASP." "I'm not making you pay," I said, "I'm just enjoying the difference here." And I was enjoying the difference in a funny kind of way. I felt completely at home, and I didn't feel as ill at ease here in the office as [D.] felt down there. So I think it is possible—probably [R.] has felt the same. You know what it is? I think you have to be exceptional to do that, you really do! You have to have so much on the ball that you can get into accelerated classes, and you can see the way they think, the way they do things, and you can see that it has some merit too. It doesn't have total merit.

Does the school cause a Mexican American kid to lose his identity?

You betcha it does. The school is what screws them up so much. When your teachers are mostly white, they don't share the sensitivity to the things that we think are petty. We think they're petty, but when you feel you are different because of those things—the kinds of expressions you use, the kinds of food you eat—and that difference is inferior, then there is something wrong. They don't get it in their homes. I'm sure their parents don't raise them to be superior. You go to a home and you see the kids running around, the way they talk to their parents; and then you see the same kid in the classroom. He'll stand like this and he'll look down—this is not just when you speak to him, nor is it just in the elementary schools. On this health thing, [B.] said, "What are you all doing on mental health?" I had it written down that I think it is an important aspect. I am not sure what my point of view is, or how I will attempt this. He said, "Have you ever noticed the way they stand?" I said, "I was just thinking of that, [B.]." Now, *he* had noticed it too. "They stand hunched over, they stand very subservient, cast their eyes down." . . . There is so much of an unreal status differential there that it's even exhibited in their posture. So I think the schools give the children a feeling of inferiority because, number one, it presents them with situations that cause them to fail—that don't help them to succeed. So they get into school, they start flunking out; and you begin to think you are not so good when you fail all the time. When the American dream, certainly at this point, is that everybody goes to college—which I think is absurd and ridiculous—and everything is geared toward that, and this is what the teachers are having you aspire for, you are competing. The extremes people go to get their kids in a good preschool program, my God! When society is geared up so much for that manifestation, you can imagine how the Mexican American fits into a society that accepts those competitive values for education. When his kid is flunking out, his kid doesn't speak English, *he* doesn't speak English, he can't possibly help his kid. He is working so hard and earning such little money that he doesn't have the time, even if he has the tools. So it seems our society offers people the option of either going to school and getting a good job or not going to school or, what is worse, going to school and flunking out. If you don't go to school you have an excuse, and if you go to school and flunk, you have no excuse. Then you do poorly when you get out. Most Mexican Americans fit into the latter category, the flunking out. The drop-out rate is 80 percent before you finish high school—among Mexican Americans. That's a staggering percentage when you look at the same percentage, not for WASPS, but the Blacks. The Blacks are ahead of us in education—educational achievement and educational advancement. Once a Mexican American does get out of school, his color is not as big a hindrance; maybe he's not as black as somebody else, or as dark as, and that's why once the Mexican American gets out of college, he usually does very well for himself professionally—much better than the Blacks. But it's getting in and getting out that's the problem college-wise. I think that's even kind of a very ambitious goal at this point. Thinking of getting people out of college—it's getting them out of high school and junior high school. It's getting them to reach a point successfully so that they can go to junior high school in Ohio or in California or in New

York or in the Midwest someplace, and be able to move into a junior high school there and compete well. It's across the board—it's not just competing for college.

What's going to do it?

Well, that's why I asked to work here. I think that if the schools are gonna do it, I think it's starting early enough and I think it should start in elementary schools, starting with bilingual programs. I'm not saying this is going to do it, but I think that it's a start—a starting point. I think if we can get the child to reach junior high school with the knowledge of English—not at the expense of his knowledge of Spanish—and with some kind of success behind him, that he'll take the incentive and the initiative on his own and he'll manage to wind his way through the morass of the school systems and get out and be able to compete in the society.

Do you think the major problems are the language handicaps he faces and the fact that the school doesn't respond to that and the self-identity problems, the alienation that is really imposed on him by the curriculum and by the type of instructional program?

I think that pretty well covers it. There's a lot that's supportive about your financial condition, perhaps. Maybe the way they are sent to school. Here in [A.], TEAM is fighting the so-called plan for integration which is gerrymandering the school districts after they received orders from Washington to desegregate—stop the *de facto*, if not the *de jure* segregation. They gerrymandered the districts and what they are doing is integrating Blacks and Browns now. The Whites—only two percent of the White student population here in [A.] has been affected. This to me is not integration. And, it's not the fact that Blacks and Browns don't want to get together, but it's common knowledge that the people who are teaching the Blacks, the people who are teaching Browns, come up against such tremendous handicaps endemic to each social category, each cultural category, rather, each cultural group, that mixing two peoples' problems is not going to solve anything. So, I mean, it's not just self-identity, the language handicap, it's also the way classes are mixed. It's the financial condition, it's the kind of tools they have made available to them, as far as counseling is concerned. Maybe they should start counseling much earlier than junior high school. Who knows? . . . What happens is that there reaches a point of no return and I think we haven't pushed that point of no return back far enough—as far as educational success is concerned.

Issues in Teaching About American Indians

HAZEL W. HERTZBERG

The present interest in including the study of American Indians in the social studies curriculum is clearly part of a much broader concern with ethnicity and race, with the nature of nationality, and with profound conflicts over the uses of the past. These concerns and conflicts are not confined to the United States but are worldwide in their manifestations. Without them, it is unlikely that teaching about American Indians would be commanding any serious interest at all. But the specific historical context in which this interest arises brings to it a number of unresolved problems and unexamined assumptions. I propose to discuss a few of these, not so much to offer solutions, but to open up questions which as teachers of social studies we, and our students, should consider.

The Problem of Mental Set

The first problem concerns the mental set which both teachers and students bring to the study of American Indians. We know much less about non-Indian attitudes toward Indians as they have developed through time than we know about attitudes toward other "minorities," but what is known should make us extremely cautious about assuming that attitudes which apply to them also apply to Indians. There has never been a body of literature or rationale defining the Indian as a

NOTE: This article appeared in *Social Education*, May 1972, pp. 481–485. Reprinted by permission of Hazel W. Hertzberg.

permanent enemy or outcast inferior, as in the case of blacks. Nor has there been a national consensus against intermarriage. In fact, many non-Indians boast of an Indian ancestor and marriages between Indians and non-Indians have always been fairly common. We have had one Indian Vice-President: Charles Curtis, a member of the Kaw tribe, was Herbert Hoover's Vice-President after having been successively a congressman and senator from Kansas. Prejudice against Indians has often been virulent, but it has tended to be local, directed against local Indians on local reservations, and not necessarily extended to other Indians.

The social studies teacher would do well to find out insofar as he can what attitudes his students have toward Indians before he decides on his selection of materials and emphases. Probably he will find some variation of three major images of the Indian which are very widespread, very persistent, and which have deep historic roots. These are the noble savage, the ignoble savage, and the victim.

The idea of the noble savage is certainly one of the most influential and hardy in American history, both invigorating and responding to a primitivistic strain in European thought. It has reappeared periodically in numerous guises and with varying degrees of sophistication. It pictures the Indian as living in a simple, happier state, in harmony with the world of nature. He is proud, silent, loyal, honorable, reverent, and magnanimous. Civilization in this view is usually seen as inherently corrupting but also as an irresistible force whose triumph is certain no matter what the cost to the noble savage. Thus many believers in the noble savage have been able to reconcile their admiration for Indian virtues with their acquiescence in the submergence or destruction of Indian societies. In fact, the idea of the noble savage has usually been held by people whose actual knowledge of Indian life was minimal. Today the idea of the Indian as noble savage is again popular, essentially as a manifestation of a deep distrust of civilization and many of its works and of a desire for a simple, healthy, incorrupt, uncomplicated, "natural" society existing in harmony with a beneficent nature. Much of the current popularity of books and films about Indians partakes of noble savagery while fashions in beads, fringes, headbands, buckskins, and other "Indian" paraphernalia express this longing in another way.

If through the noble savage we thus reveal our desires and discontents, through the ignoble savage we reveal our fears. The ignoble savage is merciless, cruel, dirty, lying, violent, implacable, vengeful, full of duplicity and guile. He demonstrates how fortunate men are to be civilized and to have freed themselves from dependence on "nature red in tooth and claw." Ignoble savagery was a convenient view of the Indian for those who wished to exploit, dispossess, or kill him. It is still sufficiently pervasive to make some people afraid of Indians.

In the third image, the Indian is seen as a victim. He is passive, dependent, inert, apathetic, helpless, powerless. A variant of this conception is the drunken Indian, an image about which real Indians are extremely sensitive. Sometimes Indians are thought of as having moved through the three images successively: beginning as noble savages they become ignoble savages in reaction to the white man's violence and arrogance and end up as victims.

All of these images can be supported by selected examples as can most stereotypes. There are plenty of available noble savages, ignoble savages, and victims, especially since a good deal of literature on Indians, including much contemporary comment, is cast in these terms. But none of these images is based on systematic knowledge of Indian society and all are ways of using the Indians as surrogates for something in non-Indian life. All are profoundly ahistorical and one-dimensional. And, unhappily, many textbooks reflect one or another or some combination of them.

When images of the persistence and power of the noble savage, the ignoble savage, and the victim are combined with the lack of historical knowledge most teachers have about Indians, the results can be countereducational. It is all too likely that many teachers and students will head straight for the materials which support their own images of the Indians, not out of malice but because they are not aware of their own biases. Better to let well enough alone than to strengthen dehumanizing stereotypes. For these ways of viewing Indians affect contemporary Indian people who struggle with them in defining their relationships with non-Indians, their views of themselves, and the effects of these images on governmental policies.

Selecting Materials

One criterion in selecting material for teaching about American Indians might therefore be its possible role in combatting stereotypes about Indians, favorable as well as unfavorable. In order to get beyond the stereotypes, students need a far more balanced and rounded picture of Indian historical development than they now get. They need to know more than a tale of broken treaties, or of war-bonneted Plainsmen, or of poverty-stricken reservations. They need to look at such a major American historical theme as the frontier, not just as a thin edge of a white settlement bordering the trackless wilderness but rather as a dividing line between different regions of human occupation involving differing uses and conceptions of the land and man's relationship to it, and they need to understand why people on both sides of the frontier perceived it as they did.

If students think of Indians only as bloodthirsty warriors or buffalo hunters, they might study the history of the Five Civilized Tribes in

Oklahoma where Indians built a prospering commonwealth in Indian Territory with a panoply of institutions such as schools, churches, legislatures, and towns in which Indian and non-Indian organizational forms as well as genes were blended. They might ponder the presence among Indians in Indian Territory of class distinctions, of divisions between town and back-country people, and of Indian ownership of black slaves.

A rounded and more complex view of Indian history and its development necessarily means that we must go beyond political history. Much American political history presents Indians in the role of fighters or treaty-signers after which they virtually disappear. In most textbooks, only at critical turning points in American governmental Indian policy may Indians even be mentioned, such as Removal in the 1830's, President Grant's peace policy, the Dawes Act of the 1880's, and the Indian New Deal. This is not surprising since scholarly monographs about a single administration often omit entirely a discussion of Indian policy. Where does one learn about the Indian administrations of Theodore Roosevelt or Woodrow Wilson in this century or those of Abraham Lincoln or Grover Cleveland in the last? So influential a book as Arthur Schlesinger's *Age of Jackson* omits entirely any discussion of the decisive role Jackson played in Indian affairs. Thus there are very few models for the integration of Indian affairs into political history and those that exist tend to be quite one-sided. In any case it is questionable how much political history students can grasp unless it is set in a larger cultural context.

Such a context may be provided through an anthropological approach which illuminates the way of life of a particular Indian society and explores the views of the world held by its members. Studying the normal patterns of a culture helps students get inside it so that they can have some conception of the society as a whole. Indians seen only in their moments of contact with non-Indians, as in treaty-making or war, are one-dimensional figures and it is difficult to understand their actions even in these limited roles if one does not know the context from which they arise. The basic social and cultural institutions with which anthropology deals, such as the family or religion, are also those with which the student has had deep and continuous experience in his own life, and through them he can establish points of contact between his everyday world and the everyday world of a very different culture. In this process he may develop new perspectives on himself as well as on the unfamiliar society he is studying. Through exploring an Indian culture, the student may thus explore his own.

He may learn also that the small societies in which most men in the past have lived are by no means as simple as he imagines. Most people think of tribal societies as "simple," which usually means having a small population and a relatively simple technology. This is quite accurate but may be misleading. Tribal societies are often very complex in other ways: in religion and language, for instance, in an individual's mastery of technical skills, and in relationships among people. Studying Indian cultures can help students avoid equating simplicity of technology with poverty of thought.

A wealth of information on specific American Indian cultures is available in the anthropological literature. In addition some materials are also explicitly designed for classroom use. The study of an Indian culture in depth can be useful in ways far beyond the knowledge acquired of that culture: for example, the student can develop conceptual tools for the analysis of tribal cultures in many parts of the world. But the focus on the patterns and regularities of a culture may also make it seem divorced from time, and, in fact, many anthropological studies are somewhat hazy as to time, being cast in what is sometimes referred to as the "ethnological present." If we are to achieve a sense of real Indian men and women living in real times and real places, we need to acquire some knowledge of the development of Indian societies over a long period of time.

Unfortunately there are only a few good general Indian histories—two of the best being William T. Hagan's *American Indians* and Ruth Underhill's *Red Man's America*—and only a few good tribal histories. This dearth of general Indian histories is not due simply to stubborn ethnocentrism as some might suspect, although this has played a role. Much more important is the great difficulty of the task which has discouraged historians and caused them to focus on specialized studies in Indian affairs.

Elements in a General History of American Indians

It is instructive to consider what would be encompassed in a general history of American Indians. Logically it would begin some thirty or forty thousand years ago and would deal with what is known of literally hundreds of societies as they changed through time. If this immense period is telescoped and we begin only with white contact, a general history should encompass the subsequent changes in the hundreds of aboriginal groups, speaking over two hundred distinct languages, who lived in what is now the continental United States some four hundred and fifty years ago. These societies were characterized by a wide range of economic activities, technological development, religious beliefs, kinship systems, conceptions of proper and improper behavior, and social and political roles. The relationships of these groups to each other over time, the widely varying ways in which people of such diverse cultures responded to the European invaders, the impact of Indian and non-Indian societies on each other, the evolving relationship of Indians to the American government and to non-Indian groups in the wider society, the traditional and persistent animosities and friendships among tribal groups, the process of evolution of the idea of "Indian" itself (a European rather than an aboriginal conception and one lacking the rich associations of band, tribe, and locality), the migration of Indians to the cities and the relationship between urbanized and rural Indians, the emergence of Pan-Indian movements which transcend local and tribal allegiances—all of these are basic to an understanding of Indian history.

Simply thus to enumerate some of the elements that would be included in a general Indian history seems staggering. But it is also useful in calling our attention to the historic and contemporary cultural diversity in Indian life, far greater than that of any other "minority," in reminding us that the Indian present is a product of a changing past, and in making us cautious in generalizing too quickly from a few examples. In choosing among the many materials and themes available in the voluminous literature on Indians, one criterion might therefore be that the materials show both cultural diversity and historical development.

On Ethnic Studies in the Curriculum

Because interest in including the American Indians in the curriculum has developed in the wake of ethnic studies, many of the same patterns may be repeated and some of the same mistakes made. Black studies, by far the most common form of ethnic studies, has all too often been introduced hastily, poorly integrated into the American history curriculum or isolated from it, and handled quite uncritically. In many cases the past is seen so selectively through the eyes of the present as to distort it seriously. Even black leaders as important as Booker T. Washington have often received short shrift. A balanced historical treatment has sometimes been sacrificed in the mistaken view that the development of both a positive self-image for black students and an understanding and sympathy for black life by nonblacks requires an entirely unblemished, virtuous black past, cast largely in terms of present concerns, and a pat division of history into good guys and bad guys. This kind of stance, so benumbingly familiar to generations of students who were similarly taught American history, simply reverses these roles while retaining a simplistic conception and is both poor social studies and poor image building. A fraudulent past is not in the long run a sustaining one and when disillusionment sets in, it is apt to be bitter. Many young people who study Dick-and-Jane social studies in elementary school develop a severe case of culture shock in American History I in college—and often in high school. A similar reaction has already been observed in both black and white students in many black studies programs. As interest wanes, black studies are being dropped in a number of schools. Although we are unlikely to return to the time when black history was almost entirely ignored, or taught in a highly unsympathetic or paternalistic manner, the current reaction against black studies programs might have been both anticipated and at least partially forestalled.

American Indian studies are unlikely to enter the curriculum in the same manner as black studies. Indians form a tiny minority of the population and, except in a few places, American Indian history will probably not attain a place in the curriculum directly through the efforts of local Indian groups. While an Indian organization like the American Indian Historical Society in California seems to have had a considerable impact on social studies instruction in the state, such efforts are not likely to be anywhere near as widespread as were those supporting black studies. Groups like the A.I.H.S. favor integration into American history courses, rather than the introduction of separate courses, a format more likely to insure permanent inclusion of American Indian history than would the separate courses which can more easily be dropped.

What may well carry over from black and other ethnic studies programs is a model of minority history which, if applied uncritically, would seriously distort Indian history. Despite some similarities in the relationship of other ethnic and racial groups to the American past, Indians have a unique place in American history and will continue to have a unique relationship to the American government and the American people by virtue of their prior possession of this continent and their permanent possession of tribally-owned lands. These relationships also help to give them a distinctive view of themselves, one which specifically denies that they are "culturally deprived." While many modifications will be worked out in the relationship between the tribes and the Federal Government, it is almost impossible to conceive of a situation in which the relationship will be ended, so disastrous have such attempts been in the past. Therefore, cultural differences among tribes will continue, sustained by the continuity of Indian communities on Indian lands.

An increasing number of Indians will move to the cities, pushed by reservation poverty and pulled by wider opportunities, a process that is likely to continue even though more employment is created on reservations. Although they may visit and even retire to the reservation, many college-educated Indians are unlikely to want to live permanently in rural isolation any more than do other college-educated people: the so-called brain drain seems to be a universal phenomenon. Therefore, in the future Indians will live in both rural and urban communities, probably linked in part by a Pan-Indian subculture which transcends, bypasses, or encompasses tribal identities and which produces Pan-Indian movements led by educated urban Indians. The interests of urban and rural Indians often coincide, especially when there is continued contact with the reservation, but sometimes they are antithetical and their styles will probably be quite different, as they are now. Since urban voices are more easily heard than rural ones and rural people are less likely than urban people to be wise in the ways of the media, equity will require that other Americans learn to assess what each is saying and for whom each speaks. While some patterns similar to the above exist in other racial and ethnic groups, only Indians have permanent land-based communities to which they must always define a relationship and which in turn helps to define their relationship to the larger society.

Impact on Our Views of the American Past

A final and basic issue in teaching about American Indians concerns its impact on our views of the American past and on our intellectual and spiritual equipment for entering the future. If we are to teach about American Indians in an honest, responsible, and humane way, we are going to see many aspects of American history from new and more complex perspectives. The frontier will be seen from both sides. The winning of the West will also be the losing of the West. The Civil War will also be a civil war among the tribes. One of the most important and resistent targets of civil service reform will be the Indian Service. As the frontier closes, the Ghost Dance will sweep the plains in a last desperate attempt to reclaim by supernatural means an aboriginal paradise from which the white man has disappeared. At the same time an Indian Congressman, later to become Vice-President of the United States, will be elected from Kansas. The Progressive movement will have its Indian wing. The great assault on the public lands in the Harding administration in the Twenties will encompass the attempt to steal Indian lands also. The Indian New Deal, with its treasuring of the Indian land base and the creation of tribal constitutions, will become one of the most significant aspects of the New Deal itself. The history of reform movements will no longer be complete without the history of Indian reform. Our definition of the American farmer will expand to include the Indian farmer, and in the urban population we will see the urban Indian. In these and many other ways, American Indians, in all their variety, will be seen as integral parts of the American past and as living people who share the uncertainties, and pain, and hope of the American present.

In looking at our history from this new perspective, the temptation will be great to portray the American past in relationship to Indians as an unrelieved record of villainy. This is all the more likely because it fits so well our current tendency to flagellate the past and because so much of the material on Indians now appearing in the media supports and reflects this mood. Moreover, the fact that most teachers know so little about Indian history outside of battles has its corollary in the fact that they also know little about the history of white relations with Indians outside of battles. In setting the record straight we may be tempted to stand it on its head. Surely we should be able to right a deep injustice without creating a new one. The American past is peopled not solely with treaty breakers and despoilers as some imagine, but also with men and women who fought for Indian rights, with individuals with a sense of fairness and justice who were unwilling to sit idly by and see Indians cheated, with intelligent and sensitive government officials and legislators as well as with venal ones, with people who had a deep respect for Indian cultures as well as people who had none. Indian policies have been widely debated from the beginning of our history and Indian programs supported and opposed by important sections of our population, including Indians. We should be wary of peopling the past with stereotypes of whites which have no more validity than the stereotypes of Indians we are trying to banish. We should come to terms with the past as it was, not as we may imagine it to be.

Conceptions of American nationality have historically been critical in defining the relationship of American Indians to the rest of the American people. We are, I believe, just beginning a search for a new definition of American nationality as we recoil from the prospect of accelerating intergroup hostilities and conflicts. In our attempt to formulate a new way of looking at ourselves which will allow us to live together peaceably, which will respect our differences but assert our commitment to common ideals beyond group parochialisms, American Indians can present us with the hard questions. For their tribal reservation base involves an indefinite perpetuation of group differences. At the same time their fate as tiny minorities depends on a just and viable social and political order. Individuals among them who wish to pursue a life different from or apart from the tribe should obviously have the right to do so. We can deny none of these claims without perpetuating terrible injustices. Thus the study of American Indians can help us to redefine, as we must, our own relationship to the past and to the society of which we are all a part.

Teaching for Ethnic Literacy:
A Comparative Approach

JAMES A. BANKS

Beyond the Melting Pot: Ethnicity in American Society

When *The Melting Pot*, a play written by the English Jewish author Israel Zangwill, was staged in New York City in 1908, it became an overwhelming success. The great ambition of the play's composer-protagonist, David Quixano, was to create an American symphony that would personify his deep conviction that his adopted land was a nation in which all ethnic differences would amalgamate and a novel man would emerge from this new ethnic synthesis. The play, considered an inferior one by drama critics, was eagerly embraced by Americans because it embodied an ideology that was pervasive in the United States at the turn of the century.

However, even when the play was first performed there were salient indications, even if Americans preferred to ignore them, that ethnic communities and cultures were deeply interwoven into the American social fabric, and that the theme portrayed in Zangwill's play did not accurately reflect the status of ethnicity in America. The protagonist completes his symphony by the play's end. "Individuals, in very considerable numbers to be sure, broke out of their mold, but the groups remained. The experience of Zangwill's hero and heroine was *not* general. The point about the melting pot is that it did not happen."[1] Despite the blatant inconsistencies between the play's theme and American social

NOTE: This article appeared in *Social Education*, December 1973, pp. 738–750. Reprinted by permission of James A. Banks.

reality, Americans held tenaciously to the idea that ethnic cultures would vanish in the United States.

However, as reality boldly confronted the melting pot ideology, many Americans began to embrace it less enthusiastically. "It was an idea close to the heart of the American self-image. But as a century passed, and the number of individuals and nations involved grew, the confidence that they could be fused waned, and also the conviction that it would be a good thing if they were to be."[2] It is significant that later in his life, Zangwill was very much the antithesis of the melting pot prototype. "He was a Zionist. He gave more and more of his energy to this cause as time passed, and retreated from his earlier position on racial and religious mixture."[3]

Despite the facts that the architect of the melting pot concept later reversed his earlier position, and that ethnic cultures are endemic in the American social order, today many Americans still believe that ethnic groups should and will eventually abandon their unique cultural components and acquire those of White Anglo-Saxon Protestants. Contemporary melting pot advocates, unlike David Quixano, rarely envision a true cultural synthesis, but rather a domination of Anglo-Saxon culture traits in America. A classical example in the 1960's were the educators who formulated compensatory education programs. One of the major goals of these programs was to acculturate Afro-Americans, Mexican-Americans, and other lower-class ethnic minority groups so that they would be colored Anglo-Saxons. That these programs were largely a failure is due in no small part to the lack of respect and recognition which their architects gave to the importance of ethnicity in their formulation of programs for minority groups.

Social science specialists in ethnic relations have abundantly documented the fact that ethnicity and ethnic cultures are integral parts of our social system, and that these aspects of American life are exceedingly resistant to change or eradication.[4] As Glazer and Moynihan have perceptively stated, "... [ethnicity] is fixed deep in American life generally; *the specific pattern of ethnic differentiation, however, in every generation is created by specific events.*"[5] (emphasis added)

In recent years, we witnessed a number of events which reinforced and intensified ethnic identification and allegiance. During the Ocean Hill-Brownsville controversy in the New York Public Schools in 1968, Blacks and Jews formed antagonistic coalitions. Most members of these two ethnic groups interpreted the event in ethnic terms because the majority of teachers in the city schools were Jewish, and most of the students involved in the controversy were Afro-American.

Ethnicity also strongly influences American politics. When John F. Kennedy was a presidential candidate in 1960, Catholics throughout America went to the polls and supported him overwhelmingly partly because he was Catholic. A large percentage of the public officials in

Chicago are Irish-Catholic because of the number of Irish-Catholics in that city who vote or sanction political appointments. Politicians take advantage of their ethnic names when they are campaigning for political office in predominantly ethnic neighborhoods. When Edmund S. Muskie made an aborted attempt to become the Democratic presidential candidate in 1972, he emphasized his feelings of ethnic kinship when soliciting support in Polish-American communities. The overwhelming Black vote was largely responsible for the election of Black mayors in Gary, Indiana; Cleveland, Ohio; and Newark, New Jersey in the 1960's.

Politics is only one significant area in American life in which ethnicity looms large. While many upwardly mobile members of other ethnic groups acquire Anglo-Saxon culture traits, they tend to confine their primary social relationships to their ethnic communities.[6] The reasons why this is the case are highly complex. *Institutional racism and discrimination have been major factors, especially in the cases of ethnic minorities.* However, some ethnic group members prefer to socialize with members of their own groups even when they have other options. Historically, this has been to some extent true of European immigrants. However, prejudice and discrimination often have also limited their social options. Nevertheless, especially in recent years with the emergence of ethnic pride among minorities, many of their most vocal spokesmen frequently express a desire to limit many of their primary social contacts to members of their ethnic groups. This is true for many of the more militant spokesmen among Afro-Americans, Chicanos, Asian-Americans, Puerto-Rican Americans, and Native Americans.

Participation in close social relationships and marriage are two areas in which ethnic divisions and cleavages are steep in American society. Jewish-Americans usually marry other Jews.[7] Blacks most often marry Blacks, and Catholics usually marry Catholics. To some extent a kind of pan-Catholicism has developed in America since the various ethnic groups which are predominantly Catholic, such as Italian-Americans, Polish-Americans, and Slovak-Americans, often intermarry. However, Spanish-speaking Americans, who are also predominantly Catholic, rarely intermarry or participate in the primary social groups with Catholics of European descent. Thus, Catholic society, too, has extreme ethnic divisions, despite the fact that some degree of pan-Catholicism has emerged.[8]

Since the Black Revolt of the 1960's, we have witnessed an intensified movement among ethnic minority groups to glorify their ancient pasts, and to develop ethnic pride within group members. Especially among the intellectuals and social activists within these groups, there has emerged a tremendous interest in ethnic foods, history, values, and other unique cultural components. A greater sense of what Gordon calls a *sense of peoplehood* has also developed within these groups.[9] The small Black middle class, pejoratively dubbed the "Black bourgeoisie" by the late sociologist E. Franklin Frazier, partly because he felt that they despised the Black lower classes,[10] has developed a great deal of interest in their more humble brothers in recent years. These groups are now undergoing a process which Sizemore has conceptualized as *Nationalism.*[11] Whenever an ethnic group intensifies its search for identity and tries to build group cohesion and solidarity, some degree of ethnocentrism and rejection of "out groups" emerges.

In a perceptive and seminal historical and sociological analysis, Sizemore documents how European ethnic groups also experienced this stage at various points in American history. This "stage is the *nationalist* stage, in which the excluded group intensifies its cohesion by building a religio-cultural community of beliefs around its creation, history and development. The history, religion, and philosophy of the nation from which the group comes dictate the rites, rituals and ceremonies utilized in the proselytization of the old nationalism. Because of rejection by White Anglo-Saxon Protestants and the ensuing exclusion from full participation in the social order, the excluded group embraces its former or future nation. For the Irish-Catholics, it becomes Ireland; for the Polish Catholics it is Poland; and for the Jews it is Zion-Israel. The intense nationalistic involvement increases separatism."[12] During this state, ethnic groups also reject "out-groups," and "projects its negative identities toward other groups."[13]

Ethnicity, then, is an integral and salient part of the American social order. A sophisticated understanding of our society cannot be grasped unless the separate ethnic communities (which exist regionally as well as socially) that constitute American society are seriously analyzed from the perspectives of the various social sciences and the humanities. To treat *ethnicity* in America like the "Invisible Man," or to contend that ethnic groups in the United States have "melted" into one, is both intellectually indefensible and will result in a gross misinterpretation of the nature of American life. *It is also insufficient to conceptualize ethnicity in America only in terms of ethnic minority groups.* While these groups, because of institutional racism and discrimination, are the most socially and regionally isolated, and physically identifiable groups in America, ethnic divisions also exist among Americans of European origin.

Irish-Catholics rarely marry Jewish-Americans, and many first generation Greek-Americans would find it difficult to accept their daughter's marriage to a White Anglo-Saxon Protestant. It is true, especially among later generation White ethnic groups, that intermarriage and social mixture often occur. However, Polish-Americans, Greek-Americans, Italian-Americans and White Anglo-Saxons culture groups still confine many of their intimate social relations to their own ethnic group, and have a strong sense of ethnic identification. The prophecy that these ethnic cleavages would disappear has been made throughout American history. However, ethnic enclaves continue to exist partly because events evoke them anew in each generation.

Because ethnicity is a salient part of our social system, it is essential that students master the facts, concepts, generalizations and theories which they need to understand and interpret events which are related to intergroup and intragroup interactions and tensions. We need to help students to become more *ethnically literate,* and consequently more tolerant of cultural differences.

Recent Trends in Ethnic Studies

In recent years, educators have begun to realize the importance of ethnicity in American society and the need to help students to develop more sophisticated understandings of the diverse ethnic groups which make up America, and a greater tolerance and acceptance of cultural differences. Responding largely to student demands and community pressure groups, educational institutions at all levels have made some attempts to put more information about ethnic groups into the social studies, language arts and humanities curricula.

The pressure to implement ethnic studies programs has come largely from America's oppressed ethnic minority groups, such as Afro-Americans, Mexican-Americans, Native Americans (Indians), and Puerto Rican-Americans. Because these groups have taken the lead in pushing for ethnic studies programs, (White ethnics are increasingly making similar demands), educators have created ethnic studies programs largely in response to their demands and needs as they perceived them. Consequently, *ethnic studies* has been conceptualized rather narrowly. *Most of the programs which have been devised and implemented are parochial in scope, fragmented, and were structured without careful planning and clear rationales.* Typically, school ethnic studies programs focus on one specific ethnic group, such as Afro-Americans, Native Americans, or Mexican-Americans. The ethnic group upon which the program focuses is either present or dominant in the local school population. A school district which has a large Puerto Rican population is likely to have a program in Puerto Rican Studies, but not one which teaches about the problems and sociological characteristics of other ethnic groups.

The results of these kinds of narrowly conceptualized programs, *even though the information which they teach students is essential,* is that they rarely help students to develop scientific generalizations and concepts about the characteristics which ethnic groups have in common, the unique status of each ethnic group, and to understand why ethnicity is an integral part of our social system. *Ethnic studies* must be conceptualized more broadly, and ethnic studies programs should include information about all of America's diverse ethnic groups to enable students to develop valid *comparative* generalizations and to fully grasp the complexity of ethnicity in American society.

An Expanded Definition of Ethnicity

The fragmentation in ethnic studies programs has resulted largely from the ways in which ethnicity and ethnic groups in America have been defined by curriculum specialists. Usually when a curriculum committee is formed to create an ethnic studies guide, the group does not deal with ethnicity in a broad sociological sense, but rather limits its conceptualization of an *ethnic group* to an *ethnic minority group*, and often to one specific group. We need to formulate a more meaningful and inclusive definition of an *ethnic group* in order to create more intellectually defensible ethnic studies programs.

What is an *ethnic group?* Individuals who constitute an ethnic group share a sense of group identification, a common set of values, behavior patterns, and other culture elements which differ from those of other groups within a society. Writes Rose, "Groups whose members share a unique social and cultural heritage passed on from one generation to the next are known as *ethnic groups*. Ethnic groups are frequently identified by distinctive patterns of family life, language, recreation, religion, and other customs which cause them to be differentiated from others. *Above all else, members of such groups feel a sense of identity and an 'interdependence of fate' with those who share the customs of the ethnic tradition.*"[14] [emphasis added] If we accept these definitions of an ethnic group, as do sociologists who specialize in ethnic relations, *then all Americans are members of an ethnic group*, since each of us belongs to a group which shares a sense of peoplehood, behavior patterns, and culture traits which differ from those of other groups.

Not only are Greek-Americans, Jewish-Americans, Italian-Americans and Polish-Americans members of ethnic groups, but those individuals who are descendants of the earliest European immigrants to America also belong to an ethnic group. Members of this group make up our largest ethnic group: *White Anglo-Saxon Protestants*. We often do not think of White Anglo-Saxon Protestants as members of an ethnic group because they constitute our largest ethnic group. However, because a group which shares a common culture and a sense of group identification is a majority within a society does not mean that it is not an ethnic group. Writes Anderson, "... white Protestants, like other Americans, are as much members of an ethnic group as anyone else, however privileged the majority of them might be."[15]

In my most recent work I conceptualize *ethnic studies* more generically than is often the case, and identify information, materials and strategies for teaching about White ethnic groups (such as White Anglo-Saxon Protestants and Jewish-Americans), as well as the experiences of ethnic minority groups, such as Mexican-Americans, Asian-Americans, and Native Americans. To conceptualize ethnic studies more narrowly will result in curricula programs which are too narrow in scope, and which will fail to help students to fully understand both the important similarities and differences in the experiences of the groups which constitute America. An ethnic studies program which omits treatment of the great migrations from Southern and Eastern Europe, that took place in the early 1800's, will not provide students with the perspective needed to grasp the complexity of the Chinese immigrations which began in the late 1800's. There were many similarities in the experiences of these two groups of immigrants, as well as significant differences. Both groups were uprooted, physically and psychologically, and were seeking opportunities in a nation which, in myth if not in fact, offered unlimited social mobility. Both groups experienced shock and alienation in their new country. However, while the Southern and Eastern European immigrants were often the victims of racist ideologies, these never reached the alarming proportions as on the West Coast with the coming of the Chinese sojourners. Also, the Europeans came to America intending to stay; the Chinese came hoping to earn their fortunes in the promised land and to return to China. The Europeans brought their wives and families, while the Chinese did not. This latter fact profoundly shaped the social development of the Chinese-American community.

A vital ethnic studies program should enable students to derive valid generalizations about the characteristics of all of America's ethnic groups, and to learn how they are alike and different, in both their past and present experiences.

Ethnic Minority Groups

While an ethnic group shares a common set of values, behavior patterns and culture traits, and a sense of peoplehood, an ethnic *minority* group can be distinguished from an ethnic group because it is characterized by several unique attributes. Although an ethnic minority group shares a common culture and a sense of peoplehood, it also has unique physical or cultural characteristics which enable persons who belong to dominant ethnic groups to easily identify its members and thus to treat them in a discriminatory way. This type of group is also a numerical minority and makes up only a small proportion of the population.[16]

As in most societies, ethnic minority groups in America are victims of racism, stereotypes, and are disproportionately represented in the lower socioeconomic classes and are heavily concentrated in the blighted sections of rural and urban areas. The *color* of most American ethnic minorities is one of their salient characteristics, and is a significant factor which has decisively shaped their experiences in the United States. *Any comparisons of European immigrants and America's non-white ethnic minorities which do not deal realistically and seriously with this exceedingly important variable are invidious and misleading.* These kinds of comparisons are often found in social science literature. While a Polish-American immigrant can Anglicize his surname, acquire Anglo-Saxon culture traits, and move into almost any white neighborhood without evoking much animosity, no matter how culturally assimilated an Afro-American becomes, his skin color remains a social stigma of immense importance to *all* white ethnic groups.

A special comment about *color* is warranted here. *Color* attains most of its significance from the perceptions which people have of it rather than from biological realities. Most Puerto Rican-Americans, for example, are Caucasians. However, since about ten percent of them have Negroid physical characteristics,[17] most White Americans consider *all* Puerto Ricans "non-White," and consequently treat them just as they treat other colored Americans, such as Chinese-Americans, Samoan-Americans, Filipino-Americans, and Korean-Americans. Thus, to be socially defined as *colored* does not necessarily mean that an individual's skin color is "non-White." An individual acquires his *color status* in the United States from his group identification, and not necessarily from the color of his skin (although some light-skinned ethnic minorities "pass" as White). Many Afro-Americans are genetically and in physical appearance quite Caucasoid. However, any person with any degree of *known* African descent, regardless of his physical appearance or genotype, is socially defined as *Black*.

Ethnic Studies and Ethnic Minorities: Recent Developments

In the 1950's, a vigorous protest movement, known as the "Black Revolt," emerged within Black communities and culminated in the late 1960's. Black Americans fought an unprecedented battle to achieve social and economic equality during this period. By using such tactics as sit-ins, freedom rides and boycotts, they succeeded in eliminating legal discrimination in interstate transportation, voting, and in public accommodation facilities. As the Black Revolt progressed, Black people tried to shape a new identity, and to shatter old and pervasive stereotypes about their culture and the contributions which Afro-Americans have made to American life.

Written history is an important factor which influences both how a group sees itself and how others view it. Keenly aware of this fact, Afro-Americans demanded that school history books be rewritten so that their role in shaping our nation's destiny would be more favorably and realistically portrayed. Civil rights groups, such as the National Urban League and the National Association for the Advancement of Colored People, pressured educators to ban schoolbooks which they considered racist and to buy books which accurately depicted the experience of African people in the United States. As the pressure on school districts mounted, they encouraged publishers to include more information about Afro-Americans in schoolbooks.

As the ruckus created by the demand for Afro-American studies intensified and spread, other ethnic minority groups initiated protest movements which had as one of their main goals the implementation of ethnic studies school programs which reflected their cultures. Mexican-Americans, Native Americans, Asian-Americans, and Puerto Rican-Americans argued that their histories had been written primarily from a White Anglo-Saxon Protestant point of view, which often described them insensitively, perpetuated stereotypes, or completely omitted discussion of them. A number of special publications, some of which were sponsored by civil rights organizations and others by state departments of education, documented the validity of the claims made by these groups.[18]

The response to the demands for new instructional materials and programs by ethnic minorities, other than Afro-Americans, has varied widely. Factors influencing the kinds of responses which school districts and publishers have made to their demands include their proportion within a local school population, the intensity with which the demands have been made, and the ethnic sensitivity of local educators. The responses by publishers have been determined primarily by economic factors, i.e., whether they felt that including more information about a particular minority group would increase book sales.

School districts and publishers have responded more to the demands for Black Studies programs and materials than to demands by other ethnic minority groups. This is primarily because Black demands have been more intensive and consistent, and Blacks constitute our largest ethnic minority. However, in some regions and school districts, such as in the Southwest and parts of the West, other ethnic minorities, such as Chicanos and Asian-Americans, exceed the number of Afro-Americans in the school population. In these districts educators have been more sensitive to the need for programs which deal with other minorities.

Criteria for Selecting Ethnic Minority Content

The dominant trend, however, is for educators to implement ethnic studies programs in schools and districts which have a high proportion of ethnic minority students, and for the ethnic studies programs within a school or district to focus only or primarily on the minority group which is either dominant or present within the school or district. Most ethnic studies programs have been formulated on the tenuous assumptions that ethnic content is needed *primarily* by ethnic minorities, and that a particular ethnic studies program should focus on the problems and contributions of the particular minority group found in the local school or district. *These assumptions, while widespread, are myopic and intellectually indefensible, and relegate ethnic minority studies to an inferior status in the school curriculum.*

When the author often asks educators in various regions of the nation about the kinds of ethnic studies programs which they have implemented, they often respond by saying that there are no Blacks in their schools and thus no need for an ethnic studies program. When other teachers are asked whether they include content about Puerto Rican-Americans or Asian-Americans in their ethnic studies programs, they often say, "No, because we have no Puerto Ricans or Asian students in our schools." However, they often hastily add that they have Black studies units in the fifth and eighth grades because there are a large number of Black students in their schools. *Perhaps unknowingly, educators who feel that ethnic minority content should only be studied by ethnic minorities, and that minorities only need to study content about their own cultures, have a condescending attitude toward ethnic minority studies and do not consider the ethnic minority experiences to be a significant part of American life.*

At several points in their schooling, all American students learn something about classical Rome and Greece, Medieval Europe, and the Italian Renaissance. Information about these cultures is included in the curriculum because most teachers believe that they have profoundly influenced Western man, and that a sophisticated understanding of them is necessary to interpret American society. The criterion used to determine whether these cultures should be taught is not whether there are students in the class who are descendants of ancient Rome and Greece, of Italy or Medieval Europe. Such a criterion would not be intellectually sound. For the same reasons, it should not be used to select content about other cultures, such as the minority cultures in America.

The criterion used to identify content for inclusion into the curriculum should be the same for all topics, cultures and groups, i.e., whether the content will enable students to develop valid generalizations and concepts about their social world and the skills and abilities to influence public policy. To use one criterion to select content about European cultures and another to select ethnic minority content is discriminatory and intellectually indefensible.

Who Needs Ethnic Studies?

Afro-American students, whether they live in New York City or in the Watts district of Los Angeles, as well as White students, regardless of their ethnicity or geographical region, need to seriously study *all* ethnic minority cultures because they are an integral part of American life. They should study about the Puerto Rican cultures found primarily in New York City, but also in Chicago and other regions of the United States. To fully understand American society, Jewish students in the suburbs of New York City should be exposed to information about Japanese-Americans and the dehumanizing and shocking experience which they endured in the so-called "relocation" camps during World War II, and about the 75,000 Mexicans who suddenly became a minority in the United States when this nation annexed a large chunk of Mexico's land in 1848 in the fateful *Treaty of Guadalupe Hidalgo.*

Indian students should study their history in this nation from a *Native American perspective.* However, if they learn that during the 1800's many White Southern and Eastern European immigrants in America also inhabited ghettos which contemporary social scientists said resulted from their *inferior genetic nature* (similar arguments are made about ethnic minorities today by such social scientists as Banfield, Jensen and Shockley),[19] they will understand that their present situation in America does bear *some* similarities to the histories of other American groups. This kind of knowledge will help students to gain needed perspective, and to better *understand,* but not necessarily accept, their own social situations.

By arguing that students need to study both their own and other cultures in order to fully comprehend American society, I am not suggesting that students who are members of specific minority groups should never study their cultures in specialized courses, or that such specialized knowledge is not vitally important, especially for oppressed minority students who have been denied the opportunity to learn about the problems and contributions of their peoples. I am not suggesting, for example, that Indian children, who often know little about their cultures, except myths invented and perpetuated by White social scientists, should not gain knowledge about their groups *prior* to studying other peoples and cultures. However, I am strongly arguing that knowledge only about one's own ethnic group is insufficient to help students to attain a *liberating* education and to fully grasp the complexity of the experience of their own ethnic group, or the total human experience. A Chinese-American student who only studies the sociology of the American-Chinese ghetto may conclude that the urban ghetto is a Chinese-American invention. However, he will be better able to make valid generalizations about the formation of ghettos if he studies White immigrants in the 1800's, and the contemporary urban experiences of Afro-Americans, Puerto Rican-Americans, Indians, and lower-class Whites, many of whom still live their entire lives within ethnic enclaves in cities such as New York and Chicago.

The Value of Ethnic Content

Ethnic content is needed by *all* students to help them to understand themselves and the social world in which they live. When studied from an interdisciplinary and comparative perspective, it can help students to broaden their understanding and concept of what it means to be *human* and enable them to better understand their own cultures and life-styles. Students should be helped to discover that while man is born with the physical capacities to become human, an individual becomes human only by learning the culture of his specific ethnic group. During their study of ethnic cultures, students can learn that while human beings have many of the same basic needs, such as love, protection, and security, different cultures within our society have devised a great variety of means to satisfy them. The religious ceremonies of the Orthodox Jew, Black soul food and spirituals, and Mexican-American literature can illustrate the wide range of culture elements within our society. When students study ethnic content, they will be more likely to consider ethnic minority persons *humans* and develop a more sophisticated understanding of their own lifestyles. As Kluckhohn, the perceptive anthropologist, wrote, "Studying [other cultures] enables us to see ourselves better. Ordinarily we are unaware of the specialized lens through which we look at life ... *Anthropology holds up a great mirror to man and lets him look at himself in his infinite variety.*"[20]

To help students develop what I call *ethnic literacy*, and to grasp the significance of ethnicity within American life, ethnic studies must focus on higher level concepts and generalizations, and not on discrete facts about isolated heroes and contributions. While facts are necessary to help students to acquire higher levels of knowledge, their mastery should not be the ultimate goal of instruction. Rather, facts should be used only as a *means* to teach major concepts and generalizations.

Planning Instruction

When planning ethnic studies curricula and units which have a comparative approach and focus, the teacher or curriculum committee should start by identifying key concepts within the social science disciplines which are related to ethnic content. These concepts should be higher-level ones which can encompass numerous facts and lower-level concepts and generalizations. They should have the power to organize a great deal of information and the potential to explain significant aspects of the ethnic experience. Each social science discipline contains concepts with these characteristics. Figure 1 contains a list of these types of concepts and their related disciplines which a teacher or curriculum committee can use to organize ethnic studies units or to incorporate ethnic content into the regular social studies program. In studying this list of concepts, the reader will note that some of them, such as *separatism* and *forced acculturation*, are clearly *interdisciplinary* concepts since the perspectives of several disciplines are needed to fully understand them.

I have categorized the concepts according to which discipline has

FIGURE 1. Organizing Concepts for Ethnic Studies Curricula

Discipline	Key Concepts	Discipline	Key Concepts
		History*	immigration
			migration
			change
		Political Science	power
Anthropology	culture		powerless
	culture diversity		separatism
	acculturation		oppression
	forced acculturation		social protest
	cultural assimilation		interest group
	race		legitimacy
	racial mixture		authority
	sub-culture		power elite
	syncretism		colony
	melting pot		colonized
	cultural genocide		rebellion
	ethnocentrism		
		Psychology	identity
Economic	scarcity		aggression
	poverty		repression
	production		displacement
	consumption		
	capitalism	Sociology	discrimination
	economic exploitation		ethnic group
			ethnic minority group
Geography	ethnic enclave		prejudice
	region		racism
	ghetto		socialization
	inner-city		status
	location		values

*Identifying organizing historical concepts is especially difficult because history does not possess unique concepts but uses concepts from *all* social science disciplines to study human behavior in the *past*. For a further discussion of this point see James A. Banks. "Teaching Black History with a Focus on Decision-Making," *Social Education*, Vol. 35 (November 1971), pp. 740-745, ff. 820-821.

made maximum use of them. While the concept of *separatism* is sociological as well as political, political scientists have contributed most to our understanding of this major idea. However, all social scientists use concepts from other disciplines. Rather than being a disadvantage to the teacher, the fact that many concepts which will help students to understand ethnic studies are *interdisciplinary* is a plus factor because the teacher should always try to help students to view human events from the perspectives of several disciplines.

After a teacher or a curriculum committee has selected key concepts from each of the disciplines, at least one *organizing generalization* related to *each* of the concepts chosen should be identified. Each organizing generalization should be a high-order statement which can help to explain human behavior in all cultures, times and places. It should not contain references to any particular culture or group, and should be a universal-type statement which is capable of empirical verification. A curriculum committee might select *immigration-migration* as an organizing or key concept (these two concepts are combined here because they are highly related), and choose this statement as the related key generalization:

> In all cultures individuals and groups have moved to different regions and within various regions in order to seek better economic, political and social opportunities. Movement of individuals and groups has been both voluntary and forced. [Universal Type Generalization]

After a universal-type generalization is identified, an intermediate-level generalization which relates to the higher-order statement should be formulated. In our example, this statement might be:

> Most individuals and groups who have immigrated to the United States and who have migrated within it were seeking better economic, political and social opportunities. Movement of individuals and groups to and within the United States has been both voluntary and forced. [Intermediate-Level Generalization]

When intermediate-level generalizations have been identified for each major concept, a lower-level generalization related to each of America's major ethnic groups should be stated. Identifying a lower-level generalization for each major ethnic group will assure that all groups will be included in the teaching units which will later be structured. These ethnic groups should be included in comparative ethnic studies units:

Native Americans (Indians)
Mexican-Americans (Chicanos)
White Ethnic Groups (including White Anglo-Saxon Protestants)
Afro-Americans
Asian-Americans (including Chinese-Americans, Japanese-Americans, Filipino-Americans, Korean-Americans, and Samoan-Americans)
Puerto-Rican Americans

Below are lower-level generalizations related to the key concept in our example for each of the major ethnic groups:

Native Americans: Most movement of Native Americans within the United States was caused by forced migration and genocide.
Mexican-Americans: Mexicans who immigrated to the United States came primarily to improve their economic condition by working as migrant laborers in the West and Southwest.

White Ethnic Groups: Southern and Eastern Europeans who immigrated to the United States came to avoid religious and political repression, and to improve their economic conditions.

Afro-Americans: Blacks migrated to Northern and Western cities in the early 1900's to escape lynchings and economic and political oppression in the South.

Asian-Americans: Many Asian-Americans who came to the United States expected to improve their economic conditions and to return to Asia. During World War II, Japanese-Americans were forced to move to federal concentration camps.

Puerto Rican-Americans: Puerto Ricans usually come to the United States Mainland seeking better jobs; they often return to the Island of Puerto Rico because of American racism and personal disillusionment experienced in the Mainland.

Teaching Strategies and Materials

When lower-level generalizations are identified for each ethnic group, the curriculum planner has solved the major *conceptual* problems in structuring an interdisciplinary program in comparative ethnic studies. However, several important steps remain. Teaching strategies and materials must be identified to teach *each* of the lower-level generalizations. A wide variety of teaching strategies, content and materials can be used to teach the experiences of America's ethnic groups. The generalization above about Native Americans can be effectively taught by using content related to the forced westward migration of the Cherokee which occurred during the Presidency of Andrew Jackson. This poignant migration is often called "The Trail of Tears." When teaching about Puerto Rican migrants, the only group currently migrating to the United States in significant numbers, the teacher can use such excellent books as Elena Padilla's *Up From Puerto Rico*, and Juan Angel Silen's *We, the Puerto Rican People.* Oscar Handlin's compassionate and sensitive book, *The Uprooted*, will give students a useful overview of the frustrations and problems encountered by the Southern and Eastern European immigrants to the United States. It is beyond the scope of this article to delineate strategies and materials for teaching comparative ethnic studies units. I have presented my ideas regarding these aspects of a conceptual social studies curriculum elsewhere.[21] The short bibliography at the end of this article will help the teacher to identify the necessary content for teaching ethnic studies using the approach set forth in this paper.

The Challenge

It is imperative that we take decisive steps to help students to develop ethnic literacy and a better understanding of ethnicity within America in these racially troubled times. Intergroup conflict poses a serious threat to our nation and the ideals of American democracy. Blatant racism, which was harshly condemned by influential commission reports in the sixties, raised its ugly head unabashedly in the seventies and became a powerful political weapon that was used advantageously by both political demagogues and America's most esteemed political leaders. Implementing sound, comparative ethnic studies programs will be an exceedingly difficult task. Such programs will be vehemently resisted by diverse pressure groups which are staunch enemies of those who advocate a culturally pluralistic curriculum and society. These types of groups are vigorously escalating their activities and attacks on teachers throughout the nation. Their growth has been greatly facilitated by the ominous political climate which now pervades the United States. However, these groups must be adamantly resisted by teachers with vision, courage and commitment.

The challenge is herculean. The odds are against us. The hour is late. However, what is at stake is priceless: the liberation of the hearts and minds of all American youth. Thus, we must, like Don Quixote, dream the impossible dream, reach for the unreachable star, and act decisively to right the unrightable wrong.

Notes

1. Nathan Glazer and Daniel P. Moynihan, *Beyond The Melting Pot: The Negroes, Puerto Ricans, Jews, Italians and Irish of New York City* (Cambridge: M.I.T. Press, 1970), p. 290.

2. *Ibid.,* pp. 288–289.

3. *Ibid.,* p. 290.

4. This proposition is thoroughly documented in Milton M. Gordon, *Assimilation in American Life: The Role of Race, Religion, and National Origins* (New York: Oxford University Press, 1964), and in Glazer and Moynihan, *op. cit.*

5. Glazer and Moynihan, *op. cit.,* p. 291.

6. Gordon, *op. cit.,* pp. 51–59.

7. The recent National Jewish Population Study conducted by the Council of Jewish Federation and Welfare Funds indicates that 69% of the Jews who married between 1966 and 1971 married other Jews. Thirty-one percent married gentiles. These figures show that while Jews now marry out of their ethnic group more often than in the past, the majority still marry other Jews. See Dorothy Rabinowitz, "The Trouble with Jewish-Gentile Marriages," *New York,* Vol. 6, No. 34 (August 20, 1973), p. 26.

8. *Ibid.,* pp. 201–202.

9. *Ibid.,* pp. 28–29.

10. E. Franklin Frazier, *Black Bourgeoisie* (Glencoe, Illinois: The Free Press, 1957).

11. Barbara A. Sizemore, "Is There a Case for Separate Schools?" *Phi Delta Kappan,* vol. 53 (January, 1972), p. 282.

12. *Ibid.,* p. 282.

13. *Ibid.*

14. Peter I. Rose, *They and We: Racial and Ethnic Relations in the United States* (New York: Random House, 1964), p. 11.
15. Charles H. Anderson, *White Protestant Americans: From National Origins to Religious Group* (Englewood Cliffs, N.J.: Prentice-Hall, 1970), p. xiii.
16. Out of a total of 204 million people in the United States in 1970, there were approximately 22 million Blacks, 5 million Mexican-Americans, 1.5 million Asian-Americans, 900,000 Puerto Rican-Americans, and 792,000 American Indians. *The Official Associated Press Almanac 1973* (Chicago: Quadrangle Books, Inc., 1972), pp. 142–143.
17. Glazer and Moynihan, *op. cit.*, p. xxv.
18. Examples are Michael B. Kane, *Minorities in Textbooks: A Study of Their Treatment in Social Studies Textbooks* (Chicago: Quadrangle Books, 1970); L. P. Carpenter and Dinah Rank, *The Treatment of Minorities: A Survey of Textbooks Used in Missouri High Schools* (Jefferson City: Missouri Commission on Human Rights, 1968); Task Force To Reëvaluate Social Science Textbooks Grades Five Through Eight, *Report and Recommendations* (Sacramento: California State Department of Education, 1971).
19. Edward C. Banfield, *The Unheavenly City* (Boston: Little, Brown, 1970); Arthur R. Jensen, "How Much Can We Boost IQ and Scholastic Achievement," *Harvard Educational Review*, vol. 39 (Winter, 1969), pp. 1–123; William Shockley, "Dysgenics, Geneticity, Raceology: Challenges to the Intellectual Responsibility of Educators," *Phi Delta Kappan*, vol. 53 (January, 1972), pp. 297–307.
20. Clyde Kluckhohn, *Mirror for Man* (Greenwich, Connecticut: Fawcett Publications, Inc., 1965), p. 19.
21. See James A. Banks, *Teaching the Black Experience: Methods and Materials* (Belmont, Calif.: Fearon Publishers, 1970); James A. Banks (with Ambrose A. Clegg, Jr.), *Teaching Strategies for the Social Studies: Inquiry, Valuing and Decision-Making* (Reading, Mass.: Addison-Wesley, 1973); and the author's book on which this article is based, noted earlier.

Recommended Readings

Afro-Americans
JAMES A. BANKS, *March Toward Freedom: A History of Black Americans* (Belmont, Calif.: Fearon Publishers, 1970).
JOHN HOPE FRANKLIN, *From Slavery to Freedom: A History of Negro Americans* (New York: Vintage Books, 1969).
AUGUST MEIER and ELLIOT M. RUDWICK, *From Plantation to Ghetto: An Interpretive History of American Negroes* (New York: Hill and Wang, 1966).
BENJAMIN QUARLES, *The Negro in the Making of America* (New York: Collier Books, 1964).

Asian-Americans
HARRY H. L. KITANO, *Japanese-Americans: The Evolution of a Subculture* (Englewood Cliffs, N.J.: Prentice-Hall, 1969).
BRUNO LASKER, *Filipino Immigration to Continental United States and Hawaii* (Chicago: University of Chicago Press, 1931).
H. BRETT MELENDY, *The Oriental Americans* (New York: Hippocrene Books, 1972).

WILLIAM PETERSEN, *Japanese Americans* (New York: Random House, 1971).

BETTY L. SUNG, *The Story of the Chinese in America* (New York: Collier Books, 1967).

Chicanos (Mexican-Americans)

RUDY ACUÑA, *Occupied America: The Chicano's Struggle Toward Liberation* (San Francisco: Canfield Press, 1972).

RUDY ACUÑA, *A Mexican-American Chronicle* (New York: American Book Company, 1967).

CAREY MCWILLIAMS, *North from Mexico: The Spanish-Speaking People of the United States* (New York: Greenwood Press, 1968).

MATT S. MEIER and FELICIANO RIVERA, *The Chicanos: A History of Mexican Americans* (New York: Hill and Wang, 1972).

JOAN W. MOORE (with ALFREDO CUELLAR), *Mexican-Americans* (Englewood Cliffs: Prentice-Hall, 1970).

Native Americans (Indians)

JACK D. FORBES (ed.), *The Indian in America's Past* (Englewood Cliffs: Prentice-Hall, 1964).

WILBUR R. JACOBS, *Dispossessing the American Indian* (New York: Charles Scribner's Sons, 1972).

STAN STEINER, *The New Indians* (New York: Delta, 1968).

OLIVIA VLAHOS, *New World Beginnings: Indian Cultures in the Americas* (New York: Fawcett, 1970).

Puerto Rican-Americans

JOSEPH P. FITZPATRICK, *Puerto Rican Americans: The Meaning of Migration to the Mainland* (Englewood Cliffs, N.J.: Prentice-Hall, 1971).

C. WRIGHT MILLS, CLARENCE SENIOR, and ROSE GOLDSEN, *Puerto Rican Journey* (New York: Harper and Row, 1950).

ELENA PADILLA, *Up from Puerto Rico* (New York: Columbia University Press, 1958).

JUAN ANGEL SILEN, *We, the Puerto Rican People* (New York: Monthly Review Press, 1971).

White Ethnic Groups

CHARLES H. ANDERSON, *White Protestant Americans* (Englewood Cliffs: Prentice-Hall, 1970).

MURRAY FRIEDMAN (ed.), *Overcoming Middle Class Rage* (New York: Westminster Press, 1962).

SIDNEY GOLDSTEIN and CALVIN GOLDSCHEIDER, *Jewish Americans: Three Generations in a Jewish Community* (Englewood Cliffs: Prentice-Hall, 1969).

JOHN HIGHAM, *Strangers in the Land: Patterns of American Nativism 1860–1925* (New Brunswick, N.J.: Rutgers University Press, 1955).

MICHAEL NOVAK, *The Rise of the Unmeltable Ethnics* (New York: Macmillan, 1972).

Born Again Ethnics: Pluralism in Modern America

JOHN JAROLIMEK

I am what you would call a "White Ethnic." Not just an ordinary, garden-variety white ethnic, but, rather, a textbook example of one. My four grandparents were Czech peasant people from South Bohemia who came to this country around 1890. Although my own parents were born in this country, they lived among immigrants or first-generation Americans whose backgrounds were much like their own. The ethnic folkways of Czech peasant people prevailed, including the use of the Czech language. Consequently, the language I learned as a child was Czech; English came later, fortunately before I entered school. My childhood friends and schoolmates had such surnames as Novak, Dvorak, Kostohryz, Staszak, Waszak, Woijcek, Bohac, Bilak, Fencil, Fojt, and Jelinek. Within the past decade, I have visited the birthplaces of my grandparents, and I maintain a correspondence with relatives in Czechoslovakia.

I provide this brief personal history so that you will understand that my interest in pluralism, ethnicity, bilingualism, and multicultural and ethnic heritage studies came about not only because these were movements and concepts important to me as a social studies educator, but because of personal reasons as well. Thus, for the past several years, I have devoted a substantial amount of my professional and personal time to this subject matter, including a year of sabbatical study during 1975–1976. In this presentation, I should like to share with you some of my observations, impressions, and conclusions.

NOTE: This article appeared in *Social Education*, March 1979, pp. 204–209. Reprinted by permission of John Jarolimek.

The "Melting Pot" Ideology

Let us begin with a few comments about the much maligned "melting pot" ideology. As everyone here knows, in the past decade there has been a great deal of criticism of the melting pot concept. But the criticism is to some extent contradictory. On the one hand, it is alleged that the melting pot did not really exist. Thus, some authors have referred to it as "the myth of the melting pot."[1] Other authors, especially those representing the white ethnic groups, declare that the melting pot idea stripped them of their ethnicity; that is, the melting pot so Americanized them, was so successful in facilitating assimilation, that they lost their ethnic identity—presumably this being something of great value to them, at least in a nostalgic, romantic way. But the critics cannot have it both ways—either the melting pot was a myth and did not really exist, or it was a powerful system of indoctrination imposed on aliens.[2] It could not have been both at the same time. Critics of the melting pot will need to resolve this contradiction.

A fair amount of published material dealing with white ethnics and the problems they encountered in becoming Americans, and the loss of their ethnicity, strikes me as rhetoric that is addressing a hidden agenda. Some of the advocates of ethnic heritage studies have attempted to equate the experiences of the white ethnics with those of the visible minorities. The more activist-oriented authors have taken the first letters of Polish-Italian-Greeks-Slavs and coined the acronym PIGS. (Never mind the redundancy of Poles being Slavic people.) Much is made of the fact that white ethnic groups have experienced ethnic slurs by being called polacks, bohunks, krauts, rooskies, wops, dagoes, and so on. It is as if their advocates are saying, "Hey, look, fellas, we've been called bad names, too, and nobody's given us any special breaks!"

I interpret the rise of the so-called unmeltable ethnics[3] as white backlash to the social, economic, and political gains made by visible minorities in recent years. However, the fact is that there is no way that the American experience of the white ethnic can be equated with that of the visible minority, because color has been, and to a great extent remains, the overwhelmingly handicapping characteristic when it comes to equality of opportunity, simply because it is visible. This is not to say that white ethnic people were not victims of discrimination and ridicule. Of course, they were taken advantage of when they were not able to speak and understand the language. They were sold unproductive farmland. Naturally, they were employed in the least desirable jobs.

Imagine a scene at a Chicago meat-packing plant at the turn of the century. A crowd of eager men and boys wait in the yard, hoping to be hired.

> Now and then a foreman came out and ran them over with his eye and picked out those that he wanted. "He looks for the round-toed shoes,"

someone said to me; "he wants those fresh from the old country, not Americanized enough to wear factory-made footwear. When they are squeezed dry he can get other fresh comers."[4]

Many white immigrants had no bed of roses as newcomers to this land, and I do not want to imply otherwise. All I am saying is that whatever white ethnics experienced along those lines was many times worse for the person of color. The white ethnic always has had, and continues to have, more options available and fewer obstacles to overcome than did the visible minorities.

But let us return to our discussion of the melting pot. Perhaps we would not be quite so harsh in our criticism of the melting pot if we put ourselves in the position of those Americans who were managing the affairs of this country at the time the immigrants were coming in such large numbers. A few years ago many American communities became alarmed when they were receiving a few immigrants from Southeast Asia. Altogether, 144,072 Vietnamese came to the United States following the war, a miniscule figure when compared with the number of immigrants who came to this country in the century preceding the passage of the restrictive immigration laws; i.e. 1824 to 1924. Some estimates indicate that 36,000,000 people came to this country during that century. In 1907, the United States received a record number of immigrants—1,285,349—a figure equal to the combined population of Dallas, Austin, and Corpus Christi. Imagine that number of people in one year! But the report of the Commissioner General of Immigration for 1907 indicated that the number should be reduced by 22 per cent to take into account alien departures. (We can, therefore, drop Corpus Christi from the total!) These were the so-called "Birds of Passage" who went back and forth across the Atlantic, some of them several times. How many of those 22 per cent returned to the States a second time and were counted again is impossible to know.

We do know that this migration of people from one part of the world to another—largely from Eastern and Southern Europe and in smaller numbers from Africa and Asia to the Western Hemisphere and especially to the United States—was the largest movement of human beings in the history of the world.

Where did these people come from? We have already said that most of them came from Europe—87.6 per cent, to be exact.[5] During the heavy migration between 1896 to 1915, 60 per cent of the arrivals were from three countries: Austria, Italy, and Russia. Those from Austria might have been German, Czech, Slavs, Poles, Croats, Slovenes, Serbs, Austrians, Swiss, Hungarians, or a variety of other national groups residing within the boundaries of the Dual Monarchy of Austria-Hungary. Prior to 1899, records on nationality were not kept by United States Immigration.

In 1870, *half* the people living in Chicago were foreign born, and 75 to 80 per cent of the city's population were of foreign stock, meaning that they were immigrants or children of immigrant parents. By as late as 1920, 40 per cent of the people living in this country were of foreign stock![6]

This influx of people from abroad, who were mainly uneducated peasant people who did not speak a familiar language and had unpronounceable names, precipitated very strong feelings against the immigrants. You will be interested in excerpts from documents published during this period we are talking about, excerpts that say something about the feeling toward the newcomers:

> Within the last decade new swarms of European immigrants have invaded America, drawn from their homes in the eastern part of Central Europe. There seems to be a danger that if they continue to come in large numbers they may retain their low standards of decency and comfort, and menace the continuance among the working class generally of that far higher standard which has hitherto prevailed in all but a few spots in the country.[7]

And this one from the July 24, 1910, Butte, Montana, *Evening News,* a full front-page story titled, "The Story of the Butte Bohunk." (To this day that issue of the *News* holds the record for a single day's sales.) Notice that the group referred to is considered non-white.

> ... This story tells of the bohunks, three thousand strong, who are driving the white man slowly but surely out of the camp. Many never saw a bohunk; they only know that the bread-winner is out of a job and some mysterious form of foreigner has taken his job. ...
>
> There are 3,000 bohunk miners in Butte today. Of these, 2,175 are working and the balance are being supported by their brothers and are ready to slip into every job where a white man is laid off. ...

Now if you were an educated, middle-class, white American living at the turn of the century, what would *your* attitude have been toward these immigrant people? What would *your* solution have been to the problem of dealing with them as residents of this great land of promise? Would *you* have supported the idea that they maintain their "ethnic purity" in their ghetto neighborhoods? Would *you* have supported a *Lau* decision, requiring bilingual instruction in those schools where the children's language was something other than English? Would *you* have been a champion of multiethnic education and multicultural education? If you had been a resident of Chicago in 1870, would *you* have been worried about the fact that half the city's population was foreign born?

You bet you would have been worried, as well you should have been. The situation had all the explosive ingredients that could have led to a national social disaster. But it is to the everlasting credit of this nation that it did what it should have with the immigrants—put them to work, sent their children to school, encouraged them to settle the lands of the frontier, and taught them the values of individualism, freedom, democracy, civic responsibility, independence, and respect for others. They were encouraged to break out of the ethnic enclaves and become a part of the mainstream of America.

Did this process of cultural assimilation or acculturation succeed?

The black scholar Thomas Sowell thinks so. In his article "Ethnicity in a Changing America" he indicates that attitude surveys since World War II show major reversals of public opinion on race and ethnicity, and rising rates of intermarriage further substantiate these changes. He then goes on to say, "... More than 40 per cent of all Japanese-American men now marry women who are not Japanese-American, and more than half of all Irish-American, German-American, and Polish-American married men are married to women outside their own respective ethnic groups. Ironically, the once popular concept of America as a 'melting pot' is now sweepingly dismissed by intellectuals at a time when it is closer to reality than before."[8]

Another very interesting example of cultural assimilation can be found in the social history of Hawaii. Around 1920, a group of mainland educators, committed to progressive pedagogy, took positions in Hawaii. Chief among these was a man whom some of you may have known, Miles Cary, who, as principal of the McKinley High School in Honolulu, developed its curriculum along the lines of progressive educational ideology. Many mainland educators, including John Dewey and William Heard Kilpatrick, saw McKinley High School as a symbol of progressive educational theory in practice. Lawrence Fuchs, in his social history of Hawaii, *Hawaii Pono*, calls the teachers of the 1920's and 1930's period in Hawaii "the godparents of modern Hawaii," and he refers to the public schools as "crucibles of democracy." Let me share with you this deeply moving account of Fuchs about the 1924 class of McKinley High School:

> In 1959, the year of statehood, more than half the classmates, many relatives and friends, and some faculty members of McKinley's class of 1924 met at the Hawaiian Village Hotel Long House for their thirty-fifth reunion. Among these sons and daughters of plantation laborers were medical doctors, dentists, lawyers, professors, and brilliantly successful businessmen. From Berkeley, California, came Dr. Rebecca Lee Proctor, who, thirty years before, had been a small Korean girl determined to go into medicine. Also present was Masaji Marumoto, then associate justice of the territorial Supreme Court and soon to be appointed associate justice of the Supreme Court of the fiftieth state. There, too, were Hung Wai Ching, son of an illiterate cook, now president of several corporations and member of the Board of Regents of the University of Hawaii; Chinn Ho, multimillionaire entrepreneur; Modesto Salve, a former plantation laborer and the first Filipino to graduate from a high school in Hawaii, now a successful businessman and civic leader; the former Kimiko Pearl Kawasaki, wife of Hawaii's most distinguished agricultural exten-

sion specialist, Baron Goto; and Stephen Kanda, one of the first nisei to be appointed principal of an Island high school. Perhaps the most illustrious of the 233 graduates of the class of 1924 was Hiram Fong, president of Finance Factors, former speaker of the House in the territorial legislature, and, within a year, to be elected to the U.S. Senate. A message of *aloha* was sent from the class of 1924 to Miles Cary, at the University of Virginia. Cary was to live only a few more months, just long enough to know that Hawaii had been accepted as a state by the U.S. Congress and, more importantly, that his boys and girls had learned their lessons well.[9]

The Shift to Pluralism

These examples and thousands more like them may not really be the melting pot in operation, but they have to represent something close to it. Whatever label you choose to attach to this process of cultural assimilation, it seems to have worked remarkably well. This being the case, one has to ask the questions, "Why did the emphasis shift somewhere in the mid-1960's to pluralism? What merit is there in encouraging and maintaining ethnic identity and cultural pluralism? Are there some special benefits in pluralism that accrue to (a) the individual; (b) the ethnic group; and (c) the larger society?"

There seems to be little doubt that the ethnic heritage revival, along with the emphasis on pluralism, has improved the lives of millions of people of this nation. Ironically, this has come about by bringing them *into* the mainstream of social and economic life of this nation. Most of the incentive programs of the past decade that were aimed at ethnic target groups dealt with ways of getting more individual blacks, Latinos, Asians, Native Americans, and others to participate *more fully* in the social, economic, and political benefits this society had to offer. This took the forms of legislative action dealing with anti-discrimination in employment, housing, and public accommodations; judicial review and court decisions; and, most importantly, education. There have been a great number of programs available to ethnic and racial minorities designed to encourage individuals to gain better educations for themselves and thereby prepare themselves for better paying and more prestigious occupations than they presently occupy.

Has the movement also benefited specific ethnic groups as groups? This is a more difficult question than the first one, because we can be less sure what a "benefit" to an ethnic group really is. If we mean that there is a greater awareness of the existence of these groups, it seems to me that the answer to our question is "yes." Is there greater social acceptance of ethnic groups today than there was two decades ago? I think the answer is definitely "yes." Do these groups have more social and political power than they had two decades ago? I think the answer is also "yes."

What about the larger society? Has it been enhanced as a result of the rise of pluralism and ethnic awareness? To the extent that these movements have made it possible for people representing a broader range of ethnic backgrounds to participate in social life, to be a part of the cultural and material affluence of this nation, the answer would have to be "yes." To the extent that these movements have been able to provide us with more accurate pictures of ourselves as a people, they have had an enriching and wholesome effect on the larger society. No country on earth can trace its roots to so many of the world culture hearths. This has been, and can continue to be, the source of strength and richness for us as a people.

It seems to me, therefore, that the rise of pluralism and increased ethnic awareness has had many desirable outcomes for the individual, for specific ethnic groups, and for society. The question now is, "Where do we go from here?"

Where Do We Go from Here?

My view on this is that we have done about as much as we ought to do in promoting ethnic identity and building ethnic awareness. To promote the notion of pluralism and ethnic diversity of this society much beyond what is being done today is likely to be counter-productive for the individual, the ethnic groups, and, most particularly, for the larger society. I believe it is not proper to deliberately instill in children and youth an exaggerated sense of ethnic pride. It is not morally right to encourage affective attachments to one's ethnic group to the extent that it encourages hostility toward other groups and society. It is detrimental to teach myths about one's ethnic origins as if they were factual accounts, because such teaching violates standards of sound scholarship.

These thrusts—i.e. those that overemphasize the relevance of ethnic identity—are contrary to the human values and social policies that have evolved in this country over the past two centuries. One of the values most strongly embraced by Americans is that an individual is to be judged as an individual and not as a member of this or some other group; i.e., to do otherwise would lead to a violation of one's civil rights. Undue emphasis on pluralism and ethnic identity leads toward separation and segregation, rather than toward integration of society. If played out to its ultimate conclusion, an emphasis on pluralism will result in further disadvantage to the ethnic minority groups simply because they are minorities and, therefore, hold less social power. These movements, when carried to the extreme, encourage ethnocentrism, racism, and demagoguery. We must not allow pluralism to flourish to the extent that it will shatter any sense of common identity that is essential to the political and social health of the nation. If this happens, it will lead to civil strife and conflict, as it has in every place in the world where pluralism, rather than unity, has been emphasized—Ireland, the Netherlands, Belgium, Cyprus, Central and South Africa, Canada, the Lebanese-Israeli-Palestinian complex, Southeast Asia, and so on. Pluralism has not had a good track record in enhancing benevolent feelings and peaceful relationships between and among people.

When we make too much of the ethnic variable, we should not be surprised to hear such statements as those Mayor Frank Rizzo of Philadelphia made prior to the recent election, to the effect that if black leaders "stand up and say, 'Vote black, vote black, vote black,' I'm going to say to the people of this city, 'Vote white.'" Also, he said to Jan Gorham, a black reporter with radio station WIP, "You know, I must see some more Italo-American reporters, or some Polish reporters; you know, some of the ethnics that represent our side. We can't get it with you."

In my state, Licensing Director Rossalind Y. Woodhouse, Washington's only black woman cabinet officer, made the statement that the first responsibility of black political leaders is to black groups, to which State Representative Otto Amen said, this "indicates to me she does not believe she is serving all the state's taxpayers, but instead only the position of the constituency she chooses to serve."[10]

And using personal correspondence from Hawaii, let me share this with you:

"John, I am not a rigid ethnic-oriented person. I am first of all an American-Hawaiian of Asian ancestry. I believe in our American heritage, although I may not agree with everything involved in this heritage. So it bothers me to see this ethnic boom, especially when it is centered on showing off how superior one is in contrast to another.... Of course, 'ethnic purity' is being overdone now, as though one can return to ancient times. What disturbs me greatly is the silence on this point from cultural anthropologists, sociologists, and psychologists. They need to help bring reason and common sense to this problem."

One might say, "Well, those are isolated examples and you really don't prove anything by citing an example or two from here and there." Perhaps not. Except that many persons can think of examples of ethnic group conflict from their own immediate experience back home. If, as a society, we adopt a social policy that stresses diversity instead of unity, and if we make ethnic pluralism a major cornerstone of the education of our young people, we should not be unmindful of the fact that we are sowing the seeds of widespread social conflict.

Recommendations

I should like to close this presentation with a series of recommendations:

(1) It seems to me that there would be much value in a reinterpretation of American history as taught in elementary and secondary schools

that would focus on immigration history. The late President John F. Kennedy, in his book *A Nation of Immigrants*, wrote, "All told more than 42 million immigrants came to our shores since the beginning of our history as a nation. Why they came here and what they did after they arrived make up the story of America."[11] I think that is essentially correct.

Also, the statement by Lydio Tomasi is relevant here:

"The United States got a good deal more out of immigration than just people. It acquired an 'immigrant culture' brought over by the 'huddled masses' no matter how tired and poor they were."[12]

The ethnic pluralism concept has the most credibility in the context of our cultural roots, because it is an objective reality that we are a pluralistic society in the sense of the diversity of our cultural origins. This can be dealt with by applying the procedures that characterize sound historical scholarship. We need to expose our young people more thoroughly to the idea that this country represents a *confluence* of world cultures. The term, "confluence of world cultures," is a good substitute for the melting pot because it implies what actually happened in America over the past 400 years. Here is where the world cultures came together like a giant river system, with its many tributaries flowing into one. These world cultures were transplanted in the soil of the New World, and, in the process, *they* were transformed. The ethnicities of Americans are variants of their parent cultures. They are closely related, but they are not the same. In the most literal sense, all people of the world are our brothers and sisters. No other nation is so well represented with people from the world's many cultures. You name it, we have it!

(2) My second recommendation is that we need to educate teachers more thoroughly about ethnicity as a social and psychological phenomenon, and to provide them with more information about many ethnic groups. Each ethnic group has had its own unique history, problems, and concerns. Teachers need to know what these are for the various ethnic groups: Native Americans, blacks, Chicanos or Latinos, Asians, Jews, European whites, and even subgroups of these larger categories. Koreans, for example, are often discriminated against by other Asians.

(3) Teaching an attachment to one's own ethnic identity should be kept within reasonable limits. To celebrate the "wearin' of the green" and attend or participate in a St. Patrick's Day parade seems to me not only acceptable but commendable; but to send money to the IRA to aid in the conflict in Northern Ireland seems to me to be excessive. It is one thing for American Jews to be sentimentally attached to Israel; it is another for them to intimidate Congressmen and Senators to the extent that they are reluctant to speak out on Middle East issues. Ditto for the Arabic-Americans, Greek-Americans, Turkish-Americans, and others who would like to, and who do, mix ethnicity with foreign policy formation. I

believe it is not in accordance with the political and social ideals of this nation to have political alliances formed solely on the basis of ethnicity. Not in 1979. On November 1, 1978 the *Seattle Times* carried the news story on "A New Ethnic Alliance Is Forming" whose purpose is "to organize millions of American citizens of Eastern European descent, long coveted by politicians of every stripe, into a unified political force." "... East Europeans comprise 15 per cent of the American people ... [but] they have participated far less in public affairs than either Hispanics or blacks," the article says, quoting *Battle Line,* a publication of the American Conservative Union. "A working paper outlining the plan listed the ethnic minorities at whom the appeal is to be aimed, in order of size: Poles, Czechs, Slovaks, Carpatho-Rusnaks, Ukrainians, Lithuanians, Hungarians, Russians, Latvians, Byelorussians, Estonians, Serbs, Croats, Romanians, Bulgarians, Slovenes, Armenians, Georgians, Albanians, and Cossacks."

It is not likely that anything but self-serving goals can be achieved through efforts of this kind. I see no reason why schools should encourage them by promoting unreasonable ethnic attachments. I am convinced that the affective aspects of ethnic identity should be soft-pedalled, that we should discourage the politicizing of the ethnic issue, that it should not be used as a weapon for social power.

It seems to me to be significant that the Declaration of Independence, the Constitution, and the Bill of Rights make no mention of the rights of ethnic groups.

- These documents do not say anything about pluralism.
- They do not say anything about multiculturalism.
- They do not even mention racial groups, except in one instance (the phrase "excluding Indians not taxed" appears in section 2 of the 14th Amendment).

But these documents have a great deal to say about the rights of individuals.

- "no person shall ..."
- "all persons shall ..."
- "the rights of citizens ..."
- "nor deny any person ..."

These expressions are used throughout these documents time after time, telling all who will listen that in this society it is the individual who is important, not the group from which he or she originated. Indeed, it expressly forbids discrimination on the basis of such identity.

What we need to do, it seems to me, is to stress over and over again those common core values—mainly freedom, equality, and human dignity—that lie at the very heart of the belief system of this society. Each generation of schoolchildren has to be taught what democracy is all about and must dedicate itself to its principles if freedom, equality, and human dignity are to survive.

(4) We should be doing more with the specific learning problems that children from particular ethnic environments are likely to have. It seems to me that we no longer have to lay the ethnic pluralism thing on teachers and communities in the heavy way that might have been needed a couple of decades ago. The bellicose confrontation strategies are or should be behind us. We have engaged in enough *mea culpa* breast-beating. Now let us get on with the business of defining the next several steps that are needed in order to help children and youth of all ethnic identities succeed in school and in life as American citizens. What does a child's ethnic background really have to do with how he or she learns, adapts to school, and makes life choices? This, it seems to me, is the relevant *educational* question that relates to ethnic identity.

(5) Finally, I would recommend that, as social studies teachers, we become better students of society. We need to have a better grasp of what things a society needs to do in order to thrive and grow, and, indeed, to survive. This is especially critical in a country such as ours that is highly heterogeneous. We should know that examples of disunity stemming from social diversity are nothing new; they can be found in antiquity. What to do with the person or group that is different from the rest—that does not seem to belong—has presented humankind with its most perplexing problems from the dawn of human history. As a matter of fact, in the Old Testament Book of Exodus, we find buried in that monologue a statement of great significance to those of us who live in America, where everyone is now or once was an alien. God says to Moses and therefore to the Jews and therefore to anyone who will listen, "You shall not molest or oppress an alien, for you were once aliens yourself in the land of Egypt."

Let me run that past one more time . . .

You shall not molest or oppress an alien, for you were once aliens yourself in the land of Egypt.

Notes

1. The notion that the melting pot was or is a myth appears frequently in the writings of advocates of pluralism. For example, see the works of Michael Novak, Andrew Greeley, Peter Schrag, Geno Baroni, Irving M. Levine, Richard Kolm, and others.

2. For a more detailed discussion of this idea, see Orlando Patterson, *Ethnic Chauvinism: The Reactionary Impulse.* Briarcliff Manor, New York: Stein and Day Publishers, 1977.

3. This term comes from the book by Michael Novak, *The Rise of the Unmeltable Ethnics: Politics and Culture in the Seventies.* New York: Macmillan Publishing Co., Inc., 1972.

4. Emily Greene Balch, *Our Slavic Fellow Citizens*. New York: Arno Press and *The New York Times*, 1969, p. 300.

5. Gerald Rosenblum, *Immigrant Workers: Their Impact on American Labor Radicalism*. New York: Basic Books, 1973.

6. David Danzig, "The Social Framework of Ethnic Conflict in America." New York: National Consultation on Ethnic America, Fordham University, 1968. Also published in *Overcoming Middle Class Rage*, M. Friedman, editor. Philadelphia: The Westminster Press, 1971.

7. James Bryce, *The American Commonwealth*, 1888.

8. Thomas Sowell, "Ethnicity in a Changing America," *Daedalus*, Winter 1978, p. 213.

9. Lawrence H. Fuchs, *Hawaii Pono: A Social History*. New York: Harcourt, Brace & World, Inc., 1961, pp. 297–298.

10. This account and the one cited in the foregoing paragraph were carried as news stories by the *Seattle Times* in the fall of 1978.

11. John F. Kennedy, *A Nation of Immigrants*, revised and enlarged edition. New York: Harper and Row, 1964, p. 84.

12. Lydio F. Tomasi, "The Ethnic Factor in the Future of Inequality." Staten Island, New York: Center for Migration Studies, 1973, p. 3.

Immigration in the Curriculum

JOHN J. PATRICK

Immigration is indisputably a central feature of the American experience. Historian Maldwyn Allen Jones claims that immigration has been "America's *raison d'être*" and "the most persistent and the most pervasive influence in her development." Furthermore, Jones says that "no other land has had for immigrants the attraction of the United States."[1] Callous statistics and stirring stories about the latest immigrants in popular books and magazines contribute strongly to our image as a symbol of hope, freedom and opportunity for a better life.[2] The United States has accepted more immigrants than any other nation. Most newcomers came from northern and western Europe until the 1880s. Since then, the ethnic mixture has become increasingly varied—a trend that continues today.[3]

Generally, school curriculum materials in the United States have reflected the conventional views of the larger society about the importance of immigration. However, educators, particularly social studies educators, have disagreed about how to treat immigration and ethnicity in the curriculum. The continuing debate can be catalogued and clarified by reference to three "ideal-type" conceptions: monolithic integration, ethnocentric pluralism and pluralistic integration.[4]

This article is a brief and general discussion of (1) the main themes of these three alternative conceptions, (2) the extent to which each conception has been reflected in the curricula of schools in the 20th century,[5] (3) the congruence of each conception with the reality of the immigrant experience in the United States, and (4) the compatibility of the three conceptions with education for citizenship in a democracy.[6]

NOTE: This article appeared in *Social Education*, March 1986, pp. 172–176. Reprinted by permission of John J. Patrick.

Monolithic integration is one-sided socialization, or assimilation, to an Anglo-Saxon ideal that is (or was) presumed to be *the* American heritage. Cultural uniformity through exclusion, one-way integration into a standarized society and Americanization as Anglo-Saxon homogenization are different phrases that describe a single view of how to treat various ethnic strains in U.S. education and society.

Monolithic integration was proposed fervently at the beginning of the 20th century in response to new waves of immigration from the "wrong sides" of Europe—the south and the east. American educational leaders feared the "strange ways" of these newcomers and called upon schools to assimilate them into a national character, which was presumed to be fully formed and fixed. Those unwilling or unable to assimilate would be unwelcome and unqualified for first-class citizenship.

Ellwood Cubberley was one of the more notable enunciators of monolithic integration or one-sided Americanization as the best way to deal with immigrants in the schools and to treat immigration as a topic in the curriculum. Cubberley presented his position on Americanization in a popular teacher education textbook:

> These Southern and Eastern Europeans were of a very different type from the North and West Europeans who preceded them. Largely illiterate, docile, often lacking in initiative, and almost wholly without the Anglo-Saxon conceptions of righteousness, liberty, law, order, public decency, and government, their coming has served to dilute tremendously our national stock and to weaken and corrupt our political life.... The problem which has faced and still faces the United States is that of assimilating these thousands of foreigners into our national life and citizenship. We must do this or lose our national character.[7]

Cubberley's view of Americanization dominated curriculum materials of the first half of the 20th century. Frances FitzGerald reports that after 1900 "the texts began to emphasize the English ancestry of Americans" and to distinguish "oldstock" Americans from the immigrants.[8] Leading textbooks highlighted the "critical need" to assimilate immigrants to a traditional and fixed ideal of the American heritage.[9]

An earlier study by Bessie Pierce (of textbooks published between (1915–1930) reported findings similar to those of FitzGerald. Pierce noted the strong nationalistic and patriotic tone of textbooks and pervasive moralizing about the urgent necessity to assimilate immigrants.[10] Current textbooks, by contrast, *tend to* reject monolithic integrationist viewpoints, which most contemporary educators in the social studies regard as outmoded or unacceptable.

At best, monolithic integration has represented partial truth. The Anglo-Saxon component of colonial America was only slightly more than half of the total population.[11] By 1850, Anglo-Saxon and various other ethnic elements were significantly blended into the emerging, multi-faceted American ways of life. By 1900, the mainstream culture that confronted immigrants was hardly an undiluted Anglo-Saxon civilization, but a spicy mixture derived from various sources.[12] Louis Adamic, an immigrant writer of the 1940s, perceived his new American heritage as an ongoing, unfinished blending of various heritages:

> The pattern of America is all of a piece; it is a blend of cultures from many lands, woven of threads from many corners of the world. Diversity itself is the pattern, is the stuff and the color of the fabric. Or to put it another way: The United States is a new civilization, owing a great deal to the Anglo-Saxon strain, owing a great deal to the other elements in its heritage and growth, owing much to the unique qualities and strong impetuses which stem from this continent. . . .[13]

Like Adamic, many ethnic group leaders have accentuated cultural diversity in the United States; some of them, however, have taken extreme positions. Their celebration of ethnic particularism and separatism is a radical response to the extremism of monolithic integrationists. Thus, their brand of pluralism is appropriately labeled ethnocentric in its primary or extensive concern with minority group interests.

The "new communalism" is sociologist Morris Janowitz's term for expressions of extreme pluralism during the period from 1950 to 1980. He writes: "Under the new communalism, emphasis on ethnic and racial nationalism momentarily outweighed concern with national citizenship."[14] This extreme pluralist position assumes a rigid persistence of ethnic group identity and denounces assimilation with fervent claims about "unmeltable ethnics."[15] Ethnocentric pluralism also assumes that the "melting pot" ideal is antithetical to American democracy, which is supposed to require ethnic pluralism for its fulfillment.[16]

Extreme emphasis on cultural diversity and ethnic pluralism in the curriculum was a popular position among social studies curriculum reformers of the 1960s and 1970s. This view was advocated as an educational antidote to bigotry and social injustice.[17] Most textbook publishers responded, at least partially, to the pressures of cultural pluralists. For example, FitzGerald reports that the history textbooks of the 1960s and 1970s began to deviate from integrationist viewpoints of an earlier period. She writes that they "cease to talk about 'the immigrants' as distinct from 'us Americans.'"[18]

FitzGerald notes that current textbooks represent the United States as a multiethnic and multi-racial society "to the extent that they include some material on all the large racial and ethnic groups, and that their photographs show people of all colors."[19] Furthermore, a few textbooks go so far as to follow the ethnocentric pluralist line in their claims that the distinct cultures of various ethnic groups have not been "melted away" and that neither the immigrants nor most of their descendents have been assimilated.[20] Janowitz claims that textbooks in history and civics have reflected the influence of "new communalists" by overemphasizing minority group rights and neglecting civic obligations and core values.[21]

To what extent does ethnocentric or extreme pluralism represent the way American society has been or is? Though this view of immigration is accurate for a portion of the society, ethnocentric pluralism is not generally true. For example, in 1972 the U.S. Bureau of the Census conducted a national survey of ethnic origins. About 40 percent of the white respondents would not identify with a particular ethnic group. The reason was that their ancestry was too mixed and/or remote from "old world" antecedents to sustain any sense of ethnic or national identity other than identification with the United States.[22] If pressed to find their "roots" millions of Americans would discover *three or more* ethnic strains in their ancestry. Such mixtures add up to identification only as an "American." Krug has estimated that there are "over 150 million people in America who have no particular ethnic affiliation."[23]

According to Thomas Sowell, intermarriages of people from different ethnic groups have been contributing significantly to the blurring of distinctions. He reports: "More than half of all marriages among Americans of German, Irish, British, or Polish ancestry are with people of different ethnicity, and Italian and Japanese Americans are not far behind."[24] Janowitz points out that the overwhelming majority of American immigrants "came as settlers" to start a new life in a new culture; they did not come as colonizers to perpetuate "old world cultures" in the U.S.[25]

However, there have been exceptions to this dominant pattern in the immigrant experience, which account for cases of persistent pluralism, like Mexican Americans of the southwest region. Their distinctiveness stems from the more than 200 years of colonization and settlement of the southwest by Spanish-speaking people prior to the region's conquest and annexation by the United States in 1848.

From the 1860s until today, thousands of Mexicans have crossed annually into the United States as immigrants or temporary residents. The proximity of Mexico and the deeply rooted Hispanic or Mexican culture of the "American/Mexican" borderlands has encouraged maintenance of a distinctive ethnic identity and has discouraged assimilation and acculturation of many Mexican immigrants into the mainstream social milieu. Janowitz believes that "the Mexicans are unique as an immigrant group in the persistent strengths of their communal bonds."[26]

The clashing claims of extreme integrationists and pluralists seem to pose a dilemma: Should American society be either culturally uniform or diverse? The monolithic integrationist wants to submerge ethnic group boundaries, and the extreme pluralist wants to accentuate them. However, one might distill the best elements of the two polar positions to form a paradoxical alternative, *pluralistic integration*.[27] This paradox assumes both the fundamental compatibilities and continuing tensions of national unity with social diversity.

Pluralistic integration assumes consensus about core civic values, which include toleration of and respect for the rights of individuals and ethnic minority groups. Pluralistic integration also denotes both support for majority rule and assumption of civic duties and responsibilities for the commonwealth, which include concern for the well being of various minority groups of the society.

John Higham brilliantly summarizes key terms of the paradoxical conception of pluralistic integration:

> In contrast to the integrationist model, it will not eliminate ethnic boundaries. But neither will it maintain them intact. It will uphold the validity of a common culture to which all individuals have access, while sustaining the efforts of minorities to preserve and enhance their own integrity.... Both integration and ethnic cohesion are recognized as worthy goals, which different individuals will accept in different degrees.[28]

R. Freeman Butts, a leading civic educator and historian, exemplifies current advocacy of pluralistic integration among curriculum reformers. In *The Revival of Civic Learning*, Butts says: "There is a continuing tension, sometimes overt conflict, between the values of *Unum* and the values of *Pluribus*, but I believe that civic educators must, just as American democracy must, honor and promote both."[29] Butts agrees with Higham, Janowitz and numerous contemporary curriculum reformers—such as Ernest Boyer, Theodore Sizer and Mortimer Adler—about the importance of emphasizing central civic values and knowledge of the American heritage in the core curriculum of schools.[30] Butts and Janowitz contend that a great need in curriculum development is reemphasis on civic unity and responsibilities, so as to redress a balance that has tilted excessively toward social diversity and group rights.[31]

Unlike the dominant curriculum materials of earlier eras, current textbooks *tend to be* compatible with the pluralistic integration position; most depict the rich ethnic and social diversity of the American people in combination with core civic values in the American heritage.[32] The norm for textbooks in the mid-1980s is to show a racially/ethnically mixed society.[33] Some analysts, however, claim that textbook treatments of core values have suffered during the past 20 years from an overemphasis on minority rights and a neglect of civic obligations.[34]

Educational critics and reformers are likely to continue the argument about the proper emphasis on unity and diversity in the curriculum of schools. Those who conduct the debate in terms of the pluralistic integration position eschew inflexible, either-or responses. They recognize that the key question is not whether one side or the other—pluralism or integration—should prevail, but what the balance between them should be, and to what end, and in light of what circumstances. To accept the challenge of this question is to direct the debate about immigration and ethnicity in the curriculum away from polemicism and dogmatism and toward pragmatism and realism.

Among the strengths of pluralistic integration is that it fits contemporary social reality better than the alternative conceptions.[35] Furthermore, it is compatible with the pragmatic American tradition of seeking the middle way in response to the complexities, ambiguities and polarities of social or political dilemmas.[36]

Conclusion

Of the three alternative conceptions of immigration in the curriculum, neither monolithic integration nor ethnocentric pluralism is as congruent with social reality as is pluralistic integration. There has been too much multifaceted or reciprocal "melting of the ethnics" to give much credibility to either one-sided Americanization or to extreme pluralism. Although the northern and western European components of the U.S. heritage (especially the Anglo-Saxon strain) have been very significant, the United States neither was, nor is, an exclusively Anglo-Saxon civilization, as the first conception assumes. If U.S. society is not homogeneous, it also neither was, nor is, an epitome of ethnic pluralism—as Austria-Hungary was and the Soviet Union is.

The third conception, pluralistic integration, recognizes the social complexity of a society in which ethnicity may vary significantly from one group to another and from one person to another, and in which the majority is sufficiently mixed in ancestry as to blur or dilute "old world" national identities and "new world" attachments to minority ethnic groups. Only a relatively few citizens of the United States have an intense and abiding loyalty to a minority ethnic group.

Of the three conceptions, pluralistic integration is more compatible with education for citizenship in the U.S. democracy. The first conception is elitist and unjustly discriminatory in its exclusion of certain minority groups from full enjoyment of civil rights and opportunities, unless they divest themselves of particularities through merger with the majority. The extreme pluralist view, though claiming affinity with democracy, is antithetical to majoritarianism in its excessive celebration of minority group rights and interests. Pluralism is primarily an argument for minority group rights and extreme or ethnocentric pluralism is practically a denial of the majority will.[37]

Pluralistic integration embodies majority rule with minority rights and thereby is most compatible with western theories of political democracy—derived from the Enlightenment—and with the American civic tradition, which Thomas Jefferson expressed eloquently in his first inaugural address: "All, too, will bear in mind this sacred principle, that though the will of the majority is in all cases to prevail, that will to be rightful must be reasonable; that the minority possess their equal rights, which equal law must protect, and to violate would be oppression."[38]

Pluralistic integration has a justifiable claim on the curriculum, because—in contrast to the alternative positions—it is more congruent with social reality and more compatible with the U.S. civic tradition. Thus, the paradoxical conception of pluralistic integration is an appropriate guide to decisions about how to treat immigration in the curriculum.

Notes

1. Maldwyn Allen Jones, *American Immigration* (Chicago: The University of Chicago Press, 1960). 1. See also Oscar Handlin, *The Uprooted* (New York, Grosset & Dunlap, 1951), 3.
2. Joan Morrison and Charlotte Fox Zabusky, *American Mosaic: The Immigrant Experience in the Words of Those Who Lived It* (New York: New American Library, 1980). In addition see the "Special Immigrants Issue" of *Time*, July 8, 1985.
3. *World Almanac & Book of Facts* (New York: Newspaper Enterprise Association, 1985), 254.
4. These "ideal-types" are rough and unqualified conceptions, which are useful points of reference for comparative analyses and judgments of phenomena. Viewpoints of various groups or individuals might be gauged as more or less congruent with these conceptions or traditions.
5. Statements of leading educators and evidence about the content of popular textbooks are used as rough indicators of the extent to which the three conceptions have been reflected in the curriculum.
6. The traditional overall goal of education for citizenship in a democracy is used as a criterion by which to make judgments about the three conceptions.
7. Ellwood P. Cubberley, *Public Education in the United States* (Boston: Houghton Mifflin, 1934), 485–486.
8. Frances FitzGerald, *America Revised: History Schoolbooks in the Twentieth Century* (New York: Random House, Vintage Books, 1980), 76–80.
9. Ibid., 38–40.
10. Bessie Louise Pierce, *Civic Attitudes in American School Textbooks* (Chicago: University of Chicago Press, 1930), 254–256.
11. Arthur M. Schlesinger, *The Birth of the Nation: A Portrait of the American People on the Eve of Independence* (Boston: Houghton Mifflin, 1968), 10–11.
12. Mark M. Krug, *The Melting of the Ethnics: Education of the Immigrants, 1880–1914* (Bloomington, IN: Phi Delta Kappa Educational Foundation, 1976), 95–104.
13. Louis Adamic, *A Nation of Nations* (New York: Harper & Bro., 1944), 6.
14. Morris Janowitz. *The Reconstruction of Patriotism: Education for Civic Consciousness* (Chicago: University of Chicago Press, 1983), 20.
15. Michael Novak, *The Rise of the Unmeltable Ethnics* (New York: Macmillan,

1971): W. H. Auden, "America is NOT a Melting Pot," *New York Times*, (March 18, 1972), 31.

16. Horace M. Kallen, "Democracy Versus the Melting Pot," *The Nation C* (February 18–25, 1915): 217–220.

17. James A. Banks, editor, *Teaching Ethnic Studies: Concepts and Strategies* (Washington, DC: National Council for the Social Studies, 43rd Yearbook, 1973); see Chapter 1. "Teaching Cultural Pluralism," by Mildred Dickeman, and Chapter 4, "Shattering the Melting Pot Myth," by Barbara A. Sizemore.

18. FitzGerald, 82–100.

19. Ibid., 98.

20. Ibid., 38–39; 104–105.

21. Janowitz, 145–149.

22. U.S. Bureau of the Census, "Characteristics of the Population by Ethnic Origin: March 1972," *Current Population Reports* P-20, No. 249, (Washington, DC: U.S. Government Printing Office, 1973), 11.

23. Krug, 103.

24. Thomas Sowell, *Ethnic America* (New York: Basic Books, 1981), 286–287.

25. Janowitz, 130–131.

26. Ibid., 129.

27. John Higham, *Send These to Me: Immigrants in Urban America*, rev. ed. (Baltimore: The Johns Hopkins University Press, 1984), 233–248.

28. Ibid., 244.

29. R. Freeman Butts, *The Revival of Civic Learning: A Rationale for Citizenship Education in American Schools* (Bloomington, IN: Phi Delta Kappa Educational Foundation, 1980), 127.

30. John Higham, 248; R. Freeman Butts, 141; Ernest Boyer, *High School* (New York: Harper & Row, 1983), 94–104; Theodore Sizer, *Horace's Compromise* (Boston: Houghton Mifflin, 1984), 84–88.

31. R. Freeman Butts, 126–133; Morris Janowitz, 1–25; 192–203.

32. John J. Patrick and Sharryl Hawke, "Social Studies Curriculum Materials," *The Current State of Social Studies: A Report of Project SPAN* (Boulder, Colorado: Social Science Education Consortium, 1982), 128–129.

33. Ibid., 128.

34. Morris Janowitz, 145–169.

35. John Higham, 244–245.

36. Michael Kammen, *People of Paradox: An Inquiry Concerning the Origins of American Civilizations* (New York: Oxford University Press, 1972).

37. Morris Janowitz, 106–144; John Higham, 200–201.

38. Thomas Jefferson, "First Inaugural Address," *The Annals of America*, Volume 4 (Chicago: Encyclopaedia Britannica, Inc., 1968).

References

ADAMIC, LOUIS. *Two-way Passage.* New York: Harper & Bros., 1941.

ADAMIC, LOUIS. *A Nation of Nations.* New York: Harper & Bros., 1945.

ADLER, MORTIMER J. *The Paideia Proposal: An Educational Manifesto.* New York: Macmillan, 1982.

AUDEN, W. H. "America is NOT a Melting Pot," *New York Times*, March 18, 1972, p. 31.

BANKS, JAMES A., editor. *Teaching Ethnic Studies: Concepts and Strategies.* Washington, DC: National Council for the Social Studies, 1973.

BOYER, ERNEST L. *High School: A Report on Secondary Education in America.* New York: Harper & Row, 1983.

BUTTS, R. FREEMAN. *The Revival of Civic Learning: A Rationale For Citizenship Education in American Schools.* Bloomington, IN: Phi Delta Kappa, 1980.

CREMIN, LAWRENCE A. *The Transformation of the School: Progressivism in American Education, 1876–1957.* New York: Random House, Vintage Books, 1962.

CUBBERLEY, ELLWOOD P. *Public Education in the United States.* Boston: Houghton Mifflin, 1934.

DICKEMAN, MILDRED. "Teaching Cultural Pluralism." In *Teaching Ethnic Studies,* edited by James A. Banks. Washington, DC: National Council for the Social Studies, 1973, 4–23.

DINNERSTEIN, LEONARD, ROGER NICOLS and DAVID REIMERS. *Natives and Strangers: Ethnic Groups in the Building of America.* New York: Oxford University Press, 1979.

FITZGERALD, FRANCES. *America Revised: History Schoolbooks in the Twentieth Century.* New York: Random House, Vintage Books, 1980.

GARCIA, JESUS. "The American Indian: No Longer a Forgotten American in U.S. History Texts Published in the 1970s," *Social Education* 44 (February 1980): 148–152.

HANDLIN, OSCAR. *The Uprooted.* New York: Grosset & Dunlap, 1951.

HANDLIN, OSCAR. *Children of the Uprooted.* New York: Grosset & Dunlap, 1968.

HIGHAM, JOHN. *Send These to Me: Immigrants in Urban America,* rev. ed. Baltimore: Johns Hopkins University Press, 1984.

JANOWITZ, MORRIS. *The Reconstruction of Patriotism: Education For Civic Consciousness.* Chicago: University of Chicago Press, 1983.

JEFFERSON, THOMAS. "First Inaugural Address." In *The Annals of America,* vol. 4. Chicago: Encyclopedia Britannica, 1968.

JONES, MALDWYN ALLEN. *American Immigration.* Chicago: University of Chicago Press, 1960.

KALLEN, HORACE M. "Democracy Versus the Melting Pot," *The Nation* C (February 18–25, 1915): 217–220.

KALLEN, HORACE M. *Cultural Pluralism and the American Idea.* Philadelphia: University of Pennsylvania Press, 1956.

KAMMEN, MICHAEL. *People of Paradox: An Inquiry Concerning the Origins of American Civilization,* New York: Oxford University Press, 1972.

KRUG, MARK M. "Teaching the Experience of White Ethnic Groups." In *Teaching Ethnic Studies,* edited by James A. Banks. Washington, DC: National Council for the Social Studies, 1973, pp. 256–277.

KRUG, MARK M. *The Melting of the Ethnics.* Bloomington, IN: Phi Delta Kappa, 1976.

LIEBERSON, STANLEY. *A Piece of the Pie: Black and White Immigrant Groups Since 1880.* Berkeley: University of California Press, 1980.

MERRIAM, CHARLES E. *The Making of Citizens.* Chicago: The University of Chicago Press, 1931.

MORRISON, JOAN and CHARLOTTE FOX ZABUSKY. *American Mosaic.* New York: New American Library, 1980.

NOVAK, MICHAEL. *The Rise of the Unmeltable Ethnics.* New York: Macmillan, 1971.

PATRICK, JOHN J. and SHARRYL HAWKE. "Social Studies Curriculum Materials." *The Current State of Social Studies: A Report of Project SPAN.* Boulder, CO: Social Science Education Consortium, 1982, pp. 104–158.

PIERCE, BESSIE LOUISE. *Civic Attitudes in American School Textbooks.* Chicago: University of Chicago Press, 1930.

SCHLESINGER, ARTHUR M. *The Birth of the Nation: A Portrait of the American People on the Eve of Independence.* Boston: Houghton Mifflin, 1968.

SIZEMORE, BARBARA A. "Shattering the Melting Pot Myth." In *Teaching Ethnic Studies,* edited by James A. Banks. Washington, DC: National Council For the Social Studies, 1973, pp. 72–103.

SIZER, THEODORE R. *Horace's Compromise: The Dilemma of The American High School.* Boston: Houghton Mifflin, 1984.

SOWELL, THOMAS. *Ethnic America.* New York: Basic Books, 1981.

Time, "Special Immigrants Issue," July 8, 1985.

U.S. BUREAU OF THE CENSUS. "Characteristics of the Population by Ethnic Origin: March 1972," *Current Population Reports,* P-20, No. 249. Washington, DC: U.S. Government Printing Office, 1973.

World Almanac & Book of Facts. New York: Newspaper Enterprises Association, 1985.

IX.

The Future

A HUNDRED YEARS AGO it was still possible to describe the future in metaphoric terms of a shining horizon, a cornucopia of wonders, a golden age. As recently as 1972, Edward S. Cornish, president of the World Future Society, could write: "I believe that man will indeed create [a] utopia, because I believe that his good sense will eventually triumph; he will dispel the currently fashionable pessimism, and he thus will have the heart to work at the problems that he faces."

Today other people feel that the complicated and dangerous problems of the world mandate a more realistic view. Thus, Czechoslovakian-born author Milan Kundera writes in one of his novels: "People are always shouting they want to create a better future. It's not true. The future is an apathetic void of no interest to anyone. The past is full of life, eager to irritate us, provoke and insult us, tempt us to destroy or repaint it. The only reason people want to be masters of the future is to change the past. They are fighting for access to the laboratories where photographs are retouched and biographies and histories are rewritten."

Who is correct? Should one be optimistic or pessimistic about the future? Regardless of the different responses to this question—and perhaps because of them—the future has continued to fascinate most of us. This fact is reflected in the following three selections from *Social Education*.

The first is an article by Lewis Paul Todd, who served as editor of the journal for twenty-one years. His "View from the Country" warns against a death-oriented society and stresses that the crisis confronting humankind is one not of intelligence but of morals. Todd protests against what curriculum designer Noel F. McInnis called "thinking the world to pieces," and he urges that the separate pieces be brought together into "the whole of life" necessary for a viable future.

The interview with author Alvin Toffler makes clear that he, too, recognizes the necessity for synthesis. Toffler says: "At the time I wrote *Future Shock* there was no book on that subject; indeed, very little on the future in general. So I set out in a new direction. I moved away from the mob. If everybody's being a specialist, it's time for somebody to be a synthesist. . . ." Toffler, who also wrote the provocative *The Third Wave*, observes further that most of the discussion of the future is couched in extremely pessimistic language, "as though there were no options left to us, as though there is no way out of our cul-de-sac." He states with conviction that, in his judgment, such a view is false and a dangerous result of linear thinking.

"Four Futures for Social Studies" are explored by Irving Morrissett, a professor of economics who for many years served as executive director of the Social Science Education Consortium in Boulder, Colorado.

Which of the following four views that Morrissett outlines will prove to be the correct one: The inertia of the past will prevail; Education will move, slowly but surely—and maybe not so slowly—toward agreed-upon ideal states; The New Social Studies is not dead, but only sleeping; or A revolution requires a strong catalyst, computers may be it?

Or is there another alternative? Is there already in existence a new view that will move the teaching of social studies into a different and exciting direction?

The section—and the book—concludes with brief comments by Christa McAuliffe, the dedicated social studies teacher selected for the flight of the ill-fated *Challenger*. Her life was an affirmation of her words: "The future is for everyone!"

View from the Country

LEWIS PAUL TODD

The National Council for the Social Studies enters the second half century of its existence at a time when the world is confronted with a challenge unparalleled in the long course of human history. Man himself is threatened with extinction, or, more precisely, man threatens to extinguish himself and all other forms of life. It is in order, therefore, to ask how well the Council is prepared to exercise the leadership the social studies profession needs in these desperate times. Since my own response to that question includes certain reservations in regard to direction and purpose, and (more to the point) since for many years I have not been directly involved in classroom activities, it seems only fair to put into the record at the beginning of this discussion a brief description of the way of life that, for better or worse, has shaped and continues to shape my point of view.

For the past twenty-one years my home base has been a small New England village on the outer reaches of an arm of land that extends fifty-some miles out to sea. At this point the Cape is only about two miles wide. The ocean is on one side, the bay on the other, and the great dome of the heavens arches overhead from horizon to horizon. The older houses, those that were built when our nation was in its infancy, nestle in the shelter of the dunes where they have been protected through the years from the storms that sweep across this narrow land. Two churches and the town hall, symbols of God and of man's guardianship of the world around him, stand boldly on the crest of a hill where in an age long since vanished they served as beacons for sailors homeward

NOTE: This article appeared in *Social Education*, November 1970, pp. 755–759. Reprinted by permission of Lewis Paul Todd.

bound from the sea. Those of us who live here measure time not so much by the clock and the calendar as by the ebb and flow of the tide and the eternal rhythm of the seasons. Ours is a relatively quiet and peaceful way of life, one far removed from the turmoil of the city and the restlessness of the contemporary campus.

This, then, is the stage from which for more than two decades we have observed the changing world. We cannot say, as Thoreau did at Walden Pond, that "nature is sufficient." But the world of living things and the wild creatures that surround us more often than not seem more real than the news that reaches us through the mass media, most of which is a sorry commentary on the follies of the human species. And, granted its limitations, there is much to be said for a detached view. Here small events as often as not reveal larger meaning for anyone who has the time to observe and to reflect. Take, for instance, two incidents in which we were involved last fall and winter, in the one as an observer, in the other as a participant.

The winter was one of the coldest in the memory of even the Old Timers in these parts. In December the tidal marsh in front of our house began to freeze over, and within a week or two it was a solid mass of salt ice. Only the river that winds through the marsh remained open, and by January it, too, began to freeze. Now the average rise and fall of the tide at this point on the coast is nine and a half feet, and as the water flowed in and out under the ice it thrust the frozen surface up in huge, jumbled cakes until for the entire length of the valley down to the bay the scene was one of icy desolation. It was a hauntingly beautiful reminder of the long winter of the Ice Age, and an even more relevant reminder of the fate that awaits our planet if men do not mend their reckless ways.

As soon as the ice formed we began to put feed out for the flock of wild ducks, a mixture of blacks and mallards, that was wintering in the marsh. Now ducks must have open water to survive, for their feet and legs are vulnerable to freezing, and by January the flock was forced up the valley to the one stretch of the river that remained open. We could never get near the ducks, for as soon as we appeared they retreated around a bend out of sight, where they remained until we were gone. But one bitter afternoon as we started out on the ice two little heads appeared above the bank several hundred feet distant. We stopped, pail of cracked corn in hand, and watched the pair of ducks struggle up the icy bank and waddle toward us. It was rough going, for a brisk breeze was blowing and now and then the ducks would lose their balance and go tumbling across the frozen surface. But they always recovered and kept on coming. What went on in their tiny brains? Instincts of millions of years ruled against such behavior. But hunger proved more compelling than fear, and we like to think that somehow they realized we were not the enemy, but a friend. We remained motionless until they were within about five feet of us, and then, unwilling to see them go through any more of what must have been a terrifying experience, we scattered the corn on the ice and slowly, very slowly, withdrew.

Walking back to the house through the snow we recalled another incident we had witnessed a couple of months earlier. One November afternoon while walking across the dunes we came over a rise and looked down on a party of hunters near a house that had been closed for the winter. Four of the men, shotguns at the ready, had surrounded a small thicket. A fifth man, gun aimed to fire, stood on the porch of the house looking down into the brush. Five men armed with lethal weapons seeking the life of a tiny quail! And this in the name of "sport"!

Two small incidents, not really worth recording, some would say. Perhaps. But in one of the incidents the accent was on life, in the other on death. Affirmation or denial? Isn't this the central issue of our time? And where does the Council stand?

A Death-Oriented Society

Warnings that ours is a death-oriented society have been reaching us with growing frequency and ever greater insistence during the past three decades, but for the most part we have refused to listen, let alone act. One of the warning voices was that of John Collier, who in 1948 opened his book, *Indians of the Americas,* with a statement that has rung in our mind ever since we first read it.

"They [the Indians] had what the world has lost," Collier wrote. "They have it now. What the world has lost, the world must have again, lest it die. Not many years are left to have or have not, to recapture the lost ingredient.

"This is not merely a passing reference to World War III or the atom bomb—although the reference includes these ways of death, too. These deaths will mean the end if they come—racial death, self-inflicted because we have lost the way, and the power to live is dead.

"What, in our human world, is this power to live? It is the ancient, lost reverence and passion for human personality, joined with the ancient, lost reverence and passion for the earth and its web of life."[1]

How many of us back in 1948 understood what Collier was saying? How many of us even tried to understand? How many of us today really understand?

And yet our refusal to listen has brought us in 1970 to the brink of catastrophe. Responsible spokesmen warn us that unless current trends are arrested and reversed the human species has at best another two or three decades before it vanishes from the earth. Some responsible scientists warn that it may already be too late, that the biosphere itself is already poisoned beyond redemption, that the land and water and air are becoming so toxic that *all* life is doomed and in the not too distant future our planet will be as desolate as the moon.

No need to detail the horrors. In recent years the mass media has held them before our eyes so that even the most indifferent among us can no longer plead ignorance. And yet the recklessness continues. One after another of the species that were inhabiting the earth long before man appeared on the scene have become extinct. Today it is the human species that is endangered. We who arrogantly asserted dominion over all other living things and assumed the earth and its resources were ours to do with as we pleased have come to the end of our rope. An era has ended.

"What can an individual do?" Paul R. Ehrlich was asked. Ehrlich's reply: "Preach to the unconverted. Only a few million people realize that killing off the brown pelican is fundamentally killing us off, too; that we depend absolutely on the stability of complex ecological systems of which all these other things are part; that we're destabilizing them by killing other organisms. I'm afraid if you offered the vast majority of Americans tickets at $5 apiece to wring the neck of the last California condor, you'd have millions of takers."

There is a good chance that our five "hunters" who were seeking the life of a single tiny quail would be in line for a ticket. For some reason, men like to kill. Konrad Lorenz and those who share his conclusions make a persuasive case when they maintain that *Homo sapiens* has inherited the killer instinct from his remote ancestors.[2]

It is sobering to reflect on the fact that among all the species man alone wars upon his own kind. It is equally sobering to reflect on man's wanton extermination of the wild life that shares the planet with him. But most terrifying of all is our reckless abuse of the biosphere.

At the Paris Exposition in 1900, Henry Adams stood in awe before the dynamo. He saw it as a symbol of "ultimate energy." But with all due respect to Adams, the dynamo, a product of science and technology, is not a convincing symbol. The true source of energy is the delicate leaf on the tree and the microscopic phytoplankton that by the countless billions live in the seas. These are the agents that by the process of photosynthesis replenish the supply of oxygen in the atmosphere and convert the energy of the sun into the food upon which all life depends. Yet despite our awareness of this most fundamental of truths, man, the killer, heedlessly fills the marshes, the most fertile of all nature's food-producing organisms; ravages the land with his bulldozers; replaces the living carpet of greenery with lifeless ribbons of asphalt and concrete; and pollutes the soil and water and air with lethal poisons.

The fact that much of the depredation is committed unwittingly and in the name of progress in no way lessens the damage and relieves us of the responsibility. We know better. Or we *should* know better. And the social studies must share at least part of the blame for the ignorance and willfulness that continue to prevail. The social studies profession has failed to put first things first. A reordering of priorities is long overdue.

Intellectual Competence and the Crisis of Morals

Before we open *that* Pandora's box, let the record show that in recent years, especially during the decade just past, the social studies have made notable advances. At the turn of the century Henry Adams, to whom we referred a moment ago, observed that "nothing in education is so astonishing as the amount of ignorance it accumulates in the form of inert facts." Until recently the social studies courses have been among the most flagrant offenders in this regard, and it remains unhappily true that in far too many classrooms across the land the situation hasn't improved very much. But during the 1960's the advocates of "the new social studies" made a significant contribution by shifting the emphasis from the accumulation of inert facts to the development of intellectual competence. "Inquiry" and "discovery" and "significant concepts from the social sciences" have become widely circulated coins throughout the profession, with the result that many of the social studies classrooms have been transformed into increasingly vital centers of learning.

So far, so good. One can no more quarrel with the development of intellectual competence than one can with motherhood. But we have learned to our sorrow that the latter can be overdone, and we suspect that excessive concentration on the former may be equally disastrous in the long run.

The human mind is the most powerful instrumentality on the face of the earth. It enabled men to make the long climb out of bestial savagery into the light of civilization. It is responsible for all that men have and are. But as we know only too well, it serves the evil as effectively as it serves the good. Intelligent men developed Hitler's gas chambers. Intelligent men have developed the bacteriological, chemical, nuclear, and other weapons of mass destruction that today fill the world's arsenals.

Intellectual competence in itself is not enough. The crisis confronting mankind today is not a crisis of intelligence; it is a crisis of morals. In John Collier's words, "we have lost the way." The desperate need of our time is a sense of direction, of purpose, of meaning. And to the extent that "the new social studies" in their proper concern for process have slighted the equally essential matter of goals, to that extent they have failed and are failing the individuals and the society they were designed to serve.

There is another unfortunate by-product of undue emphasis on "inquiry." When we analyze, we take things apart. The purpose of this process is to see how the separate pieces are related one to another and in the end to reach an understanding of how the object we are examining works. Using refined methods of analysis and increasingly sensitive and delicate instruments, specialists have accumulated the knowledge that has given modern man his enormous power to manipulate the material world. But as Alfred North Whitehead warned nearly half a century ago, the specialist can be "a public danger." The problem is that "specialization produces minds in a groove. Each profession makes progress in its own groove.... But there is no groove of abstractions which is adequate for the comprehension of human life.... The directive force of reason is weakened. The leading intellects lack balance.... In short, the specialized functions of the community are performed better and more progressively, but the generalized direction lacks vision...."

In a later passage, Whitehead declared: "My own criticism of our traditional educational methods is that they are far too much occupied with intellectual analysis, and with the acquirement of formularised information...."[3]

Whitehead's reservations come to us over a time span of nearly 50 years, but they are even more relevant today than they were back in 1925. It seems that many of us in the social studies profession are slow learners. Some of us continue to expect our students to accumulate "inert facts" and "formularised information." Others, having agreed that rote learning is a waste of everyone's time, are emphasizing "intellectual analysis" on the grounds that it develops the mind and therefore equips the students for life in a rapidly changing world. A few, as evidenced by some of the experimental social studies projects, are using the techniques of the inquiry process to come to grips with the urgent problems of our times. May *their* number increase.

The Whole of Life

As matters now stand, man faces a decidedly precarious future. The course down which we are so recklessly plunging leads only to increasing misery and ultimate disaster. But the human mind has undreamed of potentials. Intelligence harnessed to the cause of human betterment can open up to men everywhere lives of as yet undreamed of richness and dignity.

"We live in a new cosmic world which man was not made for," Nobel prize-winning biologist Albert Szent-Gyorgyi recently reminded us. "His survival now depends on how well and how fast he can adapt himself to it, rebuilding all his ideas, all his social and economic and political structures. His existence depends on the question of whether he can adapt himself faster than the hostile forces can destroy him. At present, he is clearly losing out."[4]

Perhaps it is the peaceful setting of our New England village that allows me the luxury of the conclusion that the rebuilding of our ideas need not be a formidable undertaking. We must begin, I think, by placing the human species in the stream of evolution. An awareness of how man has evolved, of what he is and who he is, and what he has the capacity to become, is certainly one of the essentials of education, and never more so than today. It should be self-evident, but apparently is not to many people, that man is as much a part of nature as the leaves on the trees and the wild life that shares the earth with him. Only when we accept this, and accept it emotionally as well as intellectually, as among the most fundamental of all truths, and among the most pregnant, will we begin to develop a vital educational program.

In my view, the social studies as they now stand are not really "social." They have unwittingly reflected the prevailing arrogance that the earth is man's to do with as he wills and that all other manifestations of life can be brushed aside or ruthlessly exterminated on the ground that man is sufficient. Well, he isn't sufficient, as we are now learning to our dismay. The plants and animals can get along on this planet quite well without us, but we can't get along without them. The social studies will be worthy of the name only when they deal with the human species in relation to the whole of life.

The whole of life. The unity of all things. This is the conceptual rock upon which we must begin to rebuild our educational program.

Notes

1 John Collier. *Indians of the Americas: The Long Hope.* A Mentor Book (slightly abridged). New York: The New American Library, 1948, p. 7.

2 See Konrad Lorenz. *On Aggression.* New York: Harcourt, Brace and World, 1966.

3 Alfred North Whitehead. *Science and the Modern World.* Available as a Mentor Book. New York: The New American Library, 1959, pp. 175–177.

4 Albert Szent-Gyorgyi. *The Crazy Ape.* New York: Philosophical Library, 1970, p. 17.

Education and the Future:
An Interview with Alvin Toffler

Alvin Toffler, *author of* Future Shock *and* The Third Wave *and one of the most stimulating writers of our times, granted* Social Education *an exclusive interview in which he discussed matters of importance to social studies educators. He was interviewed by* Andrew Smith, *formerly Director of the Center for Teaching International Relations at the University of Denver and currently Executive Director of Global Perspectives in Education, New York.*

SMITH: *Your books* Future Shock *and* The Third Wave *seem to me to take on the incredibly difficult task of trying to synthesize a wide range of personal, as well as objective, data. Why did you start such a Herculean task?*

TOFFLER: *First of all, let me emphasize that my work is not just my own work; it also is the work of my wife, Heidi.*

I am the writer. I originate and conceptualize the books, but she is a very strong influence and intellectual force in helping me to shape the work. . . . shaping and getting my hands around the massive topic is partly a result of her encouragement and her pressure, because I am continually crying out at the difficulty of doing it, weeping and moaning. She keeps saying, "Synthesize, synthesize," and so it is she who really has encouraged the big-picture approach.

Individually, I've always placed a high value on originality and imagination, the artistic virtues, and I try to tackle projects that, by and large, others have not done. My first book was on the economics and sociology of the arts in the United States, which I wrote because there was no such book. Future Shock, *I believe, is an original conception, an*

NOTE: This interview appeared in *Social Education*, October 1981, pp. 422–426. Reprinted by permission of Curtis Brown, Ltd. and Alvin Toffler. Copyright © 1981 by Alvin Toffler.

original work. (I remember being encouraged at the time to write a book about, say, poverty, or to write a book about race, or a book about any of a number of issues that concern me deeply; but there are shelves filled with books on those subjects.) At the time I wrote Future Shock, *there was no book on that subject; indeed, very little on the future in general. So I set out in a new direction. I moved away from the mob. If everybody's being a specialist, it's time for somebody to be a synthesist....*

SMITH: *One of the really important points brought out in* The Third Wave, *as well as in* Future Shock, *was that we have been very atomistic in our thinking. We quite often are unable to communicate with people who have specialized in a different area. What you are trying to do is bridge those gaps?*

TOFFLER: *In a way I regard myself as an ambassador between these groups ... between scientists and humanists, for example. I try to create a model. In* The Third Wave *I created a model that I think any social studies teacher can quickly grasp and also manipulate usefully.... It's not mathematical, nor is it a "scientific" model. But it's a way of grappling with and organizing a vast array of materials.*

I also believe that too many social scientists insist that data must be impersonal—that data are only data if they are quantified or previously printed. Certainly, I want to know what is in the journals, though a journal article may very well be obsolete by the time it is published. But I also use my ears and nose and other senses in my attempt to understand the world. I interview. I nose around. I talk to working people, businessmen, not just scholars. So far as method is concerned, what I'm doing, or trying to do, is what I sometimes call "enriched journalism"—a combination of scholarship and journalism. It is what a journalist would do if he or she had lots of money and the time to travel, as well as the ability to go where the story is. I try to fuse observation with analysis and synthesis. And I try very hard to communicate clearly. I use books to influence people.

SMITH: *Books which can be read by the general public ...*

TOFFLER: *Books which can be read by the general public ...*

SMITH: *As well as new conceptualizations.*

TOFFLER: *Certainly. This is what I hope we're doing: creating a fresh synthesis.*

The Industrial Revolution universalized Cartesian thinking and the atomization and specialization of information. The newspaper, for example, is a perfect purveyor of Cartesian thinking. When you look at page one of any newspaper, you see ten stories that have no overt connection with one another. They're little modules—unconnected modules of data. Our newspapers and television split reality into discrete pieces. They have no synthesizing apparatus available to them.

In that sense, they are guaranteed to confuse readers and to create a chaotic image of reality. There are very powerful patterns in the changes taking place around us, but you could never detect them from your daily newspaper or evening news report. It seems to me there's a special urgency for people in the social studies to take on the task of synthesizing. We need to teach students to search for the connection between Page One and the Business Page, to see the connection between anthropological changes and pollution, [and between] energy and family life ... to find all those hidden connections. That is what all my work tries to do.

SMITH: *In your books* Future Shock *and* The Third Wave, *you offer a great deal of criticism of the schools as they currently exist. Can you elaborate on your criticism of the Second Wave school?*

TOFFLER: *Yes. It is easy to characterize the Second Wave school. Looking back over the past hundred years or more, it is clear that Second Wave society, classical industrial society, required a certain kind of work force. For the system to work, it needed workers who would show up at the factory on time, who would take orders, who would do repetitive work, and so on. Unconsciously, a school system took form that, on the surface, varied from one industrial country to the next, yet which, under the surface, had certain basic similarities. Thus there is, in every school system, an* overt *curriculum and a* covert *curriculum.*

At the overt level, there are differences from place to place. We teach American history. The Japanese teach Japanese history. But underneath, all of these systems teach three basic courses. The first is a course in punctuality. Kids must show up on time or be punished. The second is a course in obedience. (Even in schools that pride themselves on teaching kids to think and ask questions, the smartest kids quickly discover which questions not *to ask.) The third is a course in rote work. The school has the task of breaking the child into a life of routine and repetitive toil.*

In this sense, the schools of the industrial age were a highly efficient anticipation of what life would hold later on. They offered an advanced simulation of adult life. And that was, perhaps, a sensible thing for schools to do.

The problem is that the system still teaches the same covert curriculum, even though the world the child will enter no longer requires the same virtues. That's not the kind of work force that we're going to need in the future. Therefore, I think the time has come for fundamental changes in the nature of this kind of education.

Today's schools simulate the past, not the future.

Seen in perspective, American schools—as harshly critical of them as I am—are far and away better than the schools of most other Second Wave countries. But they are still busy mis-preparing kids, crippling them, in fact.

SMITH: *What will life be like in the Third Wave?*

TOFFLER: *There is no shorthand answer to that. In* The Third Wave, *I try to provide a systematic, though tentative, answer. Tentative, of course,* *because life will be what we make it. The decisions we make today will determine what our life will be like. The argument presented in* The Third Wave, *however, is that we should not despair, that we should not allow ourselves to be paralyzed by fashionable pessimism. There are constructive personal and social options available to us. Most of our discussion of the future today—whether in the business pages, with their descriptions of the out-of-control world economy, inflation of currency, interests rates, and so on; or in government reports on the environmental problem, or the food problem, or what have you—most of the discussion of the future is couched in extremely pessimistic, almost despairing, language, as though there were no options left to us, as though there is no way out of our cul-de-sac.*

I believe that's false. I believe it's a dangerous result of linear thinking.

SMITH: *Do you think there will still be a role for formal education?*

TOFFLER: *Yes, we moved toward "action learning"—for example, by sending teams of students and faculty and community people out to work in a community as part of their educational experience. There's still need for a place for them to come back together, to evaluate their experience collectively, to extend the learning that they have been doing in the outside world.*

SMITH: *The Third Wave school might have more community participation?*

TOFFLER: *Certainly more involvement with the community. A lot of the education could and should take place outside the classroom. One model might be for a group of students and a faculty member to identify a community problem, to recruit some community people, and then together, as a group, to go to work on that problem. Such problems might have to do with pollution, care of the elderly, traffic, noise, sanitation, crisis counselling, etc. In working to cure local community problems, there are immediate academic questions to be faced.*

If I'm working on the care of the elderly, I immediately have to know something about the health facilities in the community, which takes me back to general science and biology. I need to know something about the economics of local government, which takes me into government and civics. I need to know something about mathematics to be able to interpret the relevant social statistics.

Starting with any concrete problem, one can ramify out to the academic subjects that need to be learned. Linking learning to community service does several things at the same time. First, we motivate students so they don't say, "But, why do we have to learn this?" The answer is obvious. The community has a problem it cannot solve without your help; and to help, you need certain knowledge. Students, therefore, have to learn not because I say so, but because there's a real social purpose.

Second, we begin to help solve some of the social problems of the students themselves, who, by and large, are a lonely crowd. We create a team with close-knit ties that may continue for years. That's important in a world of very transient, noncommitted people.

Third, we begin to cross age-segregation lines. We bring old folks into the process from the community, along with the faculty and the students, so that students no longer are brought up in an age-segregated environment.

Fourth, we give students the feeling that they are productive members of society. Action learning, however, is only one of a multiplicity of possible alternative models of Third Wave education.

SMITH: *How do you see this differing from John Dewey?*

TOFFLER: *Dewey was saying, "Study the past for the sake of the present." I would add to that, "Study the future for the sake of the present." It isn't just history that we need to know. It is a fabulously valuable experience for students to start thinking about their own and the society's alternative futures. Dewey was marvelous. But he worked in a different period, when the creation of mass education was seen as a step toward democracy. Today we need to demassify education.*

SMITH: *What are some of the other elements you envision about education changing? You mentioned "action learning." What else is there?*

TOFFLER: *There is still a more significant development coming, which I think is going to happen whether school professionals are prepared for it or not: a significant amount of learning is going to shift back into the home. As more and more work is transferred from big centralized offices into homes equipped with video, computers, and word processors, parents will take on a greater educational role. This has enormous implications.*

But these developments—action learning and home learning—add a practical dimension to education that is sorely lacking today. And both can convey to the student a sense of participation and productivity.

SMITH: *What about the intellectual content?*

TOFFLER: *We need a fundamental shift of perspective as well. First, we need to introduce a transcultural dimension into what we teach—the realization that humans have different ways of living and solving their problems.*

Above all, we need to introduce a futures perspective and at least a modicum of optimism—some image of a possible and plausible and hopeful future.

Today we either send children through the schooling process and they come out ignorant—without a thought in their heads about the complex problems that we all face, from crises in food supply and energy to international relations, and so on—or else they are given so extremely pessimistic an image of our present dilemmas that they are paralyzed.

Both of those approaches produce people who are inadequate and incapable of coping. And both of them paralyze our social capacity to deal with our problems.

The object of The Third Wave *is not to present a Pollyannaish view of* the world, but to define systematically some of the positive options open to us, and to point out that, in fact, many of today's seemingly unrelated changes . . . form an interrelated pattern. Moreover, the pattern is at least potentially hopeful. What is springing up today is not just an extension of traditional industrial society, nor is it anarchy or chaos; instead, we are seeing the emergence of an alternative social system which is in fact workable, which has its own social institutions, values, and relationships. It is this hidden pattern that needs to be grasped.

To say that there is a coherent, alternative, decent, and potentially democratic future is to make an extremely radical statement nowadays. Yet schools that fail to give kids a vision of a workable future are crippling those kids, and are doing something extremely dangerous to democracy.

SMITH: *What would you do if you were a social studies teacher in a classroom today? What would you do differently?*

TOFFLER: *Well, knowing the reality, knowing that I am locked into that classroom, knowing that I cannot teach at home, that I cannot take my kids, easily anyway, into the community, that I am trapped within the bureaucratic frame of Second Wave education, I would, to the degree that I could, work against those constraints. . . . I would point out that the kinds of fundamental changes required are not money changes necessarily. They are changes in the way we structure information, the way we organize the process of learning. Those are structural changes that I would like to see made.*

Within the classroom, I would ask my students to look for uncommon relationships. I would reward students who see connections between events not otherwise normally seen in relationship to one another. I would emphasize and reward inference. I would try to make use, in whatever way I can, of what the community provides in the way of resources.

If I were teaching history, I might turn history upside down; I might start with the future and work backwards, and ask, "Here is a scenario of what the future might be like: What are the elements in today's society that could produce that future?" Then I would move backwards from today into the past and say, "What kinds of changes produced today?" If I were teaching history, I would ask the kids to question history, not just the factual basis of history but also the very function of history. I would encourage them, as much as I could, to get outside their cultural skins.

I would try to identify the social and political problems of the decades ahead and focus on some of them. American kids who know nothing about Central America may be in for an unpleasant surprise, when and if things blow up and draft notices start arriving in the morning mail. Kids who are unaware of our relationships with many other countries are going to be caught totally off guard by events in the next 10, 15, or 20 years. . . .

I would also try to introduce them to synthesizing models. It seems to me what kids have not got out of social science and history and government courses is synthesis. They are bombarded with facts, names, dates, places, and given very little in the way of manipulable models. To come out of a social studies course without some way of classifying and manipulating data is to have wasted one's time. It is not the individual facts that should be toted up in these tests at the end, but the student's ability to recognize a model, manipulate a model, construct a model, and particularly the ability to use multiple models to analyze the same information. That's what social studies teaching really ought to be about, as far as I'm concerned.

SMITH: We have focused a lot on the past, on the last books you wrote. What are you writing now?

TOFFLER: I'm really not writing. I'm reading. It'll be some months before I have the tranquility to write. What I'm working on is precisely what we are talking about. I am thinking about writing about the meaning of history, the nature of social causation, and the relationship of these to images of the future—a more theoretical and epistemological work. I am not yet committed to write that—I'm still thinking about it. But it fascinates me.

Four Futures for Social Studies

Irving Morrissett

In the absence of a reliable crystal ball, the best preparation for developing sensitivity to emerging trends for making likely projections of the future is an intimate acquaintance with the past and with the current status of one's field of expertise. The first publication of Project SPAN was a 200-page history of social studies reform from 1880 to 1980—a story of growth, committees and commissions, creativity, conservatism, hope, frustration, and numerous reinventions of the wheel. This history contributes much to an understanding of *The Current State of Social Studies*, SPAN's 300-page account of rationales, curriculum materials, instructional practices, and the status of social studies teachers.[1]

Among the findings reported in the SPAN work are the following:

- There is much confusion in the field about what a rationale is. The construction of a full and useful rationale for social studies is a very difficult task that has been seldom attempted.
- Currently, social studies/social science educators are greatly concerned about developing a definition of the social studies. Many of the definitions that have been put forth are statements of desirable goals or recommended procedures, rather than strict definitions.
- Three approaches to the teaching of social studies can be identified. "Conservative Cultural Continuity" is the dominant approach, with the "Process of Thinking Reflectively," "Intellectual Aspects of History and/or the Social Sciences," and variants of these as alter-

NOTE: This article appeared in *Social Education*, November/December 1984, pp. 511–512, 514, 516. Reprinted by permission of Irving Morrissett.

natives to the dominant approach.[2] In practice, combinations of the various approaches are used.

- Citizenship education is the most common single goal for social studies; the most common goal set is knowledge, skills, attitudes or values, and social participation.[3]

- The dominant pattern of social studies programs from kindergarten through grade 12—despite numerous variations that have occurred—is one that was established more than 60 years ago. The typical K–6 pattern is built on the "expanding environments" theme, while the curriculum in grades 7–12 consists of a pattern of United States history, world history, civics, and government. This dominant pattern has persisted due to the strength of tradition, the reinforcement of the pattern by textbook content, and the lack of a compelling alternative. There is little articulation or coordination of social studies programs between grade levels, particularly between the elementary and secondary grades.

- Students, teachers, administrators, and the public accept and rely on curriculum materials as essential aids to teaching, learning, and classroom management. Foremost among curriculum materials are textbooks, which are used in the great majority of classrooms. Compared to textbooks, supplementary materials including films, filmstrips, workbooks, and teacher-developed materials (other than tests) have slight use.

- Most competing texts for particular subjects and grade levels are very much alike in format, style, and content. The texts typically stress the transmission of information and avoid sensitive subjects. Some notable changes have occurred in textbooks in the past 20 years, particularly in the treatment of women and minorities and in the use of color and graphics. Changes in the amount of attention given to controversial topics and to variety in learning activities have been less extensive.

- The individual teacher is generally said to be the "key" in the learning process, but little is known about why this is true or how this proposition can be used to improve social studies/social science education.

- Teachers of elementary and secondary social studies, unlike their college-level counterparts, spend little time contemplating the goals of their activities; they are too preoccupied with problems of administration and management. Where common goals can be found, they are transmission of textbook knowledge to students and socialization, in the sense of instilling acceptable classroom and social behavior, getting acceptance of the norms and values of society, and, to a lesser extent, preparing students for successful participation in mainstream society.

- Teachers' most commonly perceived problems are students' poor reading ability and their apathy toward school. Other problems that concern teachers are lack of time to teach their subject, lack of materials and equipment, and lack of good sources of information about new methods and materials.
- Teachers teach the same subject in diverse ways, even when using the same textbooks in the same school system. Unfortunately, less information is available on the varieties of teaching methods than on central tendencies in teaching methods.
- Most instruction in elementary and secondary schools takes place in large groups. Much teacher time is spent on administrative duties and the maintenance of discipline. Preparation time is generally considered to be inadequate, and the students' time on task in the classroom is substantially less than 100 percent. Most of the time students and teachers spend in the classroom is focused on the use of curriculum materials. Lecturing or teacher talk is the most common mode of instruction, increasing in importance from the lower to higher grades.

These insights into the current state of social studies certainly give no definitive direction for predictions of the future, but should provide useful background information for assessing both the prospects and the desirability of various possible futures.

There are four views that one might take of the future of social studies/social science education. They are presented here as alternatives, but the hopeful futurist must be sensitive to all four.

View #1: The Inertia of the Past Will Prevail

The educational literature, including that of the social studies, is replete with accounts of reforms that failed. Most educational changes, however exciting and productive, depend upon the charisma and enthusiasm of one or a few individuals, who eventually get tired, move away, retire or die. A support system to nurture the innovative individual and then to extend the innovation is necessary but seldom exists. Support systems—at the school, district, board, state or national level—exist to preserve the system, not to change it. Professional jealousies inhibit the adoption of someone else's innovation; a teacher is too proud to borrow from the room next door; new directors of federal agencies must invent new thrusts to distinguish themselves from their predecessors. The energies of innovation, in toto weak at best, cancel each other.

In social studies, one reform movement after another has rediscovered the good ideas of previous movements, added a little on its own, had limited success in influencing the system, and faded into obscurity. The greatest effort of all, the "new social studies," which flourished from the early 1960s into the early 1970s, receiving unprecedented financing from public and private sources, has now had its epitaph written and rewritten many times.

The one notable success of an educational reform effort in the social studies tends to support the thesis that inertia will prevail, rather than that reform is possible. The National Education Association's Commission on the Social Studies produced a report in 1916 which recommended a pattern of subjects and courses for grades 7–12, and a K–6 sequence compatible with the 7–12 recommendation.[4] While the magnitude of the break with the past represented by these reports has sometimes been exaggerated, it is true that they had a substantial impact on the growing educational establishment, such that these recommendations were substantially in place throughout the country by the mid-20s. Voila! Change is possible! But is it? This pattern has remained in place, with minor deviations, to the present time, despite the great changes that have occurred in social knowledge and the needs of students and society.

As with many areas of great inertia and/or ignorance and/or uncertainty, a good case can be made that the best prediction of where education will be next year, five years from now, and possibly 10, 20, or 50 years from now, is that it will be pretty close to where it is now.

View #2: Education Will Move, Slowly But Surely—and Maybe Not So Slowly—Toward Agreed-Upon Ideal States

Educators have a great deal of knowledge about education that is not now being used, and there is substantial agreement on much of this knowledge including the following generalization. Students should be more actively involved in their education—doing more, listening less. Students of the same age have very different levels of ability and readiness, more individualization could make learning more efficient and more effective. Students have very different learning styles, with respect to pacing and timing, and different sensory perceptions; again, individualization and variety in teaching methods are the known route to more effective learning. A decrease in rote learning and an increase in problem-solving facility will better prepare students for their future. Smaller schools contribute to a sense of mutual support between and among student, teacher and administrators. The traditional content of textbooks, more in social studies than in others, needs to be brought up to current levels of knowledge in the social sciences. Goals and objectives need to be elaborated, clarified, and more generally agreed upon—particularly in social studies. Teachers need more moral and logistic support, more preparation time, less paperwork, more and better staff development opportunities. These and other recommendations for moving toward a desired state for social studies are elaborated in the SPAN report on *The Future of Social Studies.*[5]

While many educators agree on the desirability of many such changes, many also think of them as pie in the sky. There is too much inertia in the system; there is too much disagreement on how to achieve such goals, if not on the goals themselves; and the clincher is, it all costs far more money than will be available in any foreseeable future.

But the course of human development, since humans discovered the idea of progress a few centuries ago, has been remarkable. Whereas Socrates met death for his radical ideas, Copernicus was merely disgraced for disputing Ptolemy, and Einstein was honored for upsetting Newton. While the Agricultural and Industrial Revolutions were not nearly as rapid as political events from which they borrowed the concept of revolution, they were profound. In education, America moved in less than a century from education through high school for less than 10 percent of its citizens to about 90 percent. In only a few decades, the proportion of students experiencing post-secondary education moved from less than 20 percent to over 50 percent. In still less time, substantial progress has been made toward racial and sexual equity within our educational system.

Change is possible. It often occurs in directions that many welcome as progress. It can also happen in education.

View #3: The New Social Studies Is Not Dead, But Only Sleeping

The "new social studies" was part of a much wider movement of attempted social reform in the 1960s and 1970s. With respect to the organization and methods of education, many innovations were developed and tried: modular scheduling, open classrooms, team teaching, management by objectives, behavioral objectives, cross-age learning, games and simulations, activity packets, problem solving and computer-assisted instruction.

Drawing upon these and other organizational and methodological innovations, many social studies educators and social scientists embarked upon a great number of programs to revise the curriculum, disseminate new methods and materials, and educate or re-educate teachers. Many new materials were developed in anthropology, sociology, economics, political science, psychology, geography and history. The concepts and structures of the social science disciplines were drawn upon and in many cases were the principal fare. Other materials were interdisciplinary, emphasizing concepts and problems that cut across the established social science disciplines.

A few of the new materials were widely used in elementary and secondary schools, most received limited use, and some died in the pilot stage or in publishers' offices. Well before widespread dissemination could be expected or accomplished, national economic conditions, tightening school budgets, diminishing publishers' profits, and lack of apparent and immediate success blunted and then stopped the thrust of the new social studies—as was also the case with "the new math" and the "new science." As of 1982, little is heard of innovations of the 1960s and 1970s.

An important and neglected aspect of the decline of the new social studies is the decrease in concern for many social aspects of education. An important part of the educational reform movement of the 1960s and 1970s was an increased concern for portraying greater realism about nature and society. Value-laden issues—war, sex, economics, environment, and race—were introduced into many of the new curriculum materials, mostly in social studies. They reflected much of the concern with social problems of the broader society. With the exception of continuing and moderately effective concern for racial and sexual equity with respect to education and employment, most of these social concerns have been put on the back burner along with the new social studies.

While many may feel that the innovations of the new social studies are safely, permanently—and possibly deservedly—buried, another view holds that a tremendous legacy of new ideas for teaching methods and learning materials was accumulated and stored away in the 1960s and 1970s. This legacy may be a tremendous storehouse of knowledge, awaiting more favorable circumstances to be rediscovered, recalled, revised and put into practice to help bring about a basic restructuring of an antiquated system that many feel falls far short of the results that should be obtained, given the tremendous amount of financial and human resources devoted to our educational system.

View #4: A Revolution Requires a Strong Catalyst; Computers May Be It

Except for the 1916 report of the National Education Association, the success of which may be attributable to special circumstances, none of the many efforts for change have had much impact on social studies in the schools. The potent "Beard Commission" of the 1930s, depression and war, the virulent attacks of the 1950s, the humanistic stories of educational tragedies of the 1960s, and the new social studies—all had relatively little impact. Perhaps it takes a very strong catalyst—perhaps a major earthquake—to shake education out of its rut.

Computers may be such a catalyst. The first reaction to such a proposition may be that computers are just another fad, perhaps with some very legitimate promise for educational improvement, but no more so than many of the other innovations which took on the characteristics of fads and died. Computer-assisted instruction was seen as a great innovation, but it died along with the other innovations of the 1960s and 1970s.

Maybe so. But it may be that computers offer solutions to so many educational problems that basic and dramatic changes may occur through the use of computers. Individualized instruction, interactive learning, manipulative learning, visual learning, reduced paper work for teachers and administrators, and access to tremendous banks of data and programs offer prospects for unprecedented changes in teaching and learning methods and the organization of educational institutions. Among these dramatic prospects, not the least is the phenomenal decline in the cost of access to computer capabilities. Cost has been the reason—sometimes the excuse—for not adopting many other innovations. The bottom of the computer cost curve is not yet in sight.

Like most views of the future, my own view is a combination of cold prognostication and warm desire. The prospects that I see for the near and immediate future for social studies, with deliberately unspecified proportions of prediction and desire, are these:

1. A renewal of interest in a variety of social studies methods and materials—a reversal of the recent trend toward hardback, traditional texts;

2. A renewal of interest in broader social concerns, within and outside the educational system, related to a more realistic and more humane view of society and the world; and

3. A revolution in the content, methodology and organization of our educational enterprise, based on the computer.

Any one of these three movements could occur by itself and independently of the others. Another possibility is that all three would go forward together, mutually supportive. That could be very exciting.

Notes

1. Hazel Whitman Hertzberg. *Social Studies Reform, 1880–1980: A Project SPAN Report.* Boulder, CO: Social Science Education Consortium, 1981; Irving Morrissett, ed. *The Current State of the Social Studies: A Project SPAN Report.* Boulder, CO: Social Science Education Consortium, 1982.

2. Robert D. Barr; James L. Barth; and S. Samuel Shermis. *Defining the Social Studies.* Arlington, VA: National Council for the Social Studies, 1977.

[3] "Revision of the NCSS Social Studies Curriculum Guidelines." *Social Education* 43 (April 1979).

[4] National Education Association. *The Social Studies in Secondary Education.* Bulletin 28, 1916.

[5] *The Future of the Social Studies: A Report and Summary of Project SPAN.* Boulder, CO: Social Science Education Consortium, 1982.

Christa McAuliffe Comments on Launching Social Studies into Space

Christa McAuliffe, a social studies teacher and member of the National Council for the Social Studies for about ten years, was selected from 11,416 applicants to become the first teacher to orbit the earth. She made these comments in an interview with Managing Editor Kirk Stone of Social Education *about two months before the disastrous flight of the space shuttle* Challenger.

On Her Responsibilities in Space:

"I am a space observer
rather than an astronaut."

*On the Importance of Remaining
Approachable by Her Students:*

"If I don't, I won't be
able to get my helmet on."

On Teaching:

"I truly miss the kids.
I know that teaching is
what I want to do."

On the Future:

"When the rockets ignite,
I know that the adrenaline
will flow—but from
excitement, not fright.
. . . The future is for
everyone!"

NOTE: These comments were made in an article appearing in *Social Education*, January 1986, pp. 37–38. Reprinted by permission of Kirk Stone.

Index

Index

N